The Regulation of
Insider Dealing
in Britain

The Regulation of
Insider Dealing
in Britain

Jacqueline A.C. Suter BA, LLM,
Doctor of the European University Institute in Law
Administrator, Research and Documentation Division,
Court of Justice of the European Communities, Luxembourg

Butterworths
London & Edinburgh
1989

United Kingdom	Butterworth & Co (Publishers) Ltd , 88 Kingsway , LONDON WC2B 6AB and 4 Hill Street , EDINBURGH EH2 3JZ
Australia	Butterworths Pty Ltd , SYDNEY , MELBOURNE , BRISBANE , ADELAIDE , PERTH , CANBERRA and HOBART
Canada	Butterworths Canada Ltd , TORONTO and VANCOUVER
Ireland	Butterworth (Ireland) Ltd , DUBLIN
New Zealand	Butterworths of New Zealand Ltd , WELLINGTON and AUCKLAND
Puerto Rico	Equity de Puerto Rico , Inc , HATO REY
Singapore	Malayan Law Journal pte Ltd , SINGAPORE
USA	Butterworth Legal Publishers , AUSTIN , Texas ; BOSTON , Massachusetts ; CLEARWATER , Florida (D & S Publishers) ; ORFORD , New Hampshire (Equity Publishing) ; ST PAUL , Minnesota ; and SEATTLE , Washington

A CIP Catalogue record for this book is available from the British Library.

ISBN 0 406 70069 9

Typeset by Just Words Limited, Mill Road, Portslade, Brighton.
Printed and bound in Great Britain by Mackays of Chatham PLC, Chatham, Kent.

Preface

The growth of interest in insider dealing regulation has been rapid in recent years. It has also coincided with a major reappraisal of securities regulation, culminating in the Financial Services Act 1986.

The focus of this book is on the development of insider dealing regulation in Britain. Its starting-point is an empirical assessment of the extent of insider dealing and a discussion of the theoretical issues involved. The main body of the book is then devoted to an evaluation of regulation, by reference to both the substantive provisions and their enforcement, particular attention being paid to institutional arrangements.

This book is a revised, up-dated version of part of a wider comparative study entitled 'The Regulation of Insider Dealing in Britain and France', which formed a doctoral thesis at the European University Institute, Florence, Italy.

My thanks go first to Professor Dr. K.J. Hopt and Professor T.C. Dainbith, who were my thesis supervisors, for their further advice on publication. I am also very grateful to Dr. D.D. Prentice and Professor R.R. Pennington for their encouragement.

In addition, I am very pleased to thank Mrs J.M. Richards, who so cheerfully typed the drafts and am particularly grateful to the staff at Butterworths for their assistance.

Finally my thanks go to my parents and my brother, Mark, for all their support.

The law is stated as at 15 January 1989, though it has been possible to incorporate some later developments in the text and the Appendix.

Jacqueline Suter
Luxembourg
August 1989

Contents

Table of statutes

References in this Table to *Statutes* are to Halsbury's Statutes of England (Fourth Edition showing the volume and page at which the annotated text of the Act will be found.

Table of cases

L

M

N

O

P

Chapter 1

Introduction

I. INTRODUCTORY

Of all the issues that have confronted regulators of the securities markets, the regulation of insider dealing has proved among the most intractable. Experience of such regulation, which has attracted the unflattering label of 'the unwinnable war'[1], prompts reconsideration of the issue.

Attempts to define insider dealing raise the objection that the definition includes activities which are desirable. But subject to this proviso[2], a working definition of the term can be stated as follows:

> 'Insider dealing occurs where an individual or organisation buys or sells a security when knowingly in possession of some piece of confidential information which is not generally available and which is "price-sensitive", ie likely, if generally available, materially to affect the price of the security.'[3]

As attitudes towards such dealings changed from toleration to condemnation, the regulation of insider dealing became an important issue in securities regulation.

Whereas insider dealing regulation dates from the 1930s in the US, general legislation imposing a prohibition on insider dealing was passed in Britain in 1980. This measure, enforceable by criminal penalties, followed earlier attempts to raise insiders' standards of conduct by disclosure of their dealings, supplemented by common law obligations, the administrative measures of self-regulatory agencies and a legislative prohibition on various dealings by directors in options, enforceable by criminal penalties.

Essentially, the regulation of insider dealing raises three questions, two of which flow from a positive answer to the first, namely, should insider dealing be regulated? Secondly, why does insider dealing regulation take its present form? Thirdly, how should insider dealing be regulated?

This book considers these questions. After an empirical assessment of the extent of insider dealing and the theoretical considerations raised by the first question, this involves an evaluation of the regulation both as regards the substantive provisions and enforcement, with particular reference to institutional arrangements.

---

1. A.M. Louis, *'The Unwinnable War on Insider Trading,' Fortune*, 13th July, 1981.
2. See post, III. Theoretical considerations.
3. Council for the Securities Industry, Statement on Insider Dealing, CSI No.5 (1981), pp3-4.

II. EMPIRICAL ASSESSMENT

The extent to which insider dealing occurs is difficult to assess in the absence of an effective procedure for identifying such transactions. The difficulty is increased by the likelihood of many deals being conducted through a nominee or by a relative or friend and by insiders' reticence to talk about their activities. As a result, the number of abnormal price movements, cases and investigations are poor guides.

A. Abnormal price movements

Erratic price fluctuations may be caused by numerous factors, including sectoral influences or bid rumours. As insider dealing is merely one such factor, reliance on abnormal price movements would exaggerate its occurrence around specific events. This discrepancy was underlined in the year to 31st March, 1984[4], when the Stock Exchange examined 14,130 price movements followed, where there was no apparent reason for the price movements, by further investigations through the companies' brokers in 506 cases to check whether the company needed to make an announcement clarifying the situation. Fifty-nine preliminary enquiries into share dealings were authorised with information arising from twenty enquiries passed to the Department of Trade and Industry for further investigation. In the year to 31st March, 1988[5], the Stock Exchange examined 17,306 price movements of which 923 were the subject of further investigation through the companies' brokers.

B. Cases

Conversely, a simple measurement of the number of cases under-estimates its extent. Three prosecutions under the Companies Act (CA) 1980, involving four individuals, resulted in convictions in 1981 and 1982[6]. Two other prosecutions were not proceeded with in 1982[7]. There were no prosecutions in 1983[8] and in a 1984 prosecution, charges against two individuals were dismissed[9]. There were again no prosecutions in 1985[10] and in the fifteen months ending 31st March, 1987, two further prosecutions resulted in convictions[11]. Since then, five prosecutions, involving four convictions[12] and one acquittal[13], have been reported. However, investigations indicate that the problem is more widespread.

---

4. The Stock Exchange Quotations Department, Review of the Year to 31st March, 1984, pp6-7. Reasons for price movements were mainly obtained from TOPIC (the Stock Exchange's computer based information system), press and market reports.
5. The International Stock Exchange Primary Markets Division, Review of the Year to 31st March, 1988, p14.
6. See post, Chapter 3. Criminal Liability.
7. The Department of Trade and Industry, Companies in 1982 (1983), p15, Table 11.
8. Ibid, Companies in 1983 (1984), p15, Table 11.
9. Ibid, Companies in 1984 (1985), p16, Table 11.
10. Ibid, Companies in 1985 (1986), p17, Table 11.
11. Ibid, Companies in 1986-87 (1987), p21, Table 11.
12. *The Times*, 29th April, 1987; *The Financial Times*, 2nd July, 1987; 18th July and 26th November, 1988.
13. *The Independent*, 15th April, 1988; *The Financial Times*, 13th April, 1988.

C. Investigations

Prior to the CA 1980, the inability of the Panel on Take-overs and Mergers to detect other than a small proportion of cases was generally accepted.[14] In 1972, its chairman remarked 'I cannot help feeling . . . we sometimes catch the smaller fry whilst the big fish get away'.[15] In the four years prior to the implementation of the insider dealing provisions of Part V of the CA 1980[16], the Panel issued eight statements, involving nine individuals, on the results of investigations in which it had found breaches of the Code prohibition on insider dealing.[17] In the same period, only one statement issued by the Stock Exchange on its investigations into dealings disclosed a clear finding of impropriety.[18]

The existence of the 'big fish' was confirmed in the reports of inspectors appointed by the Department of Trade and Industry. These reports set out examples of insider dealing and related unethical conduct, some of which would now appear to fall within the statutory prohibition.[19]

Following implementation of Part V of the CA 1980, the Stock Exchange had referred eighty-four investigations into dealings to the Department of Trade and Industry as at 31st March, 1985.[20] By early 1988, the number of referrals had reached approximately 150.[1]

Further investigations have concerned financial journalists, whose recommendations often have an impact on share prices. In Britain, the dealings of a financial journalist during 1963-65 were strongly criticised[2]. Previously, a city editor is reported to have been called before the Stock Exchange Council for making money out of his column[3]. In 1973, another city editor resigned after a report that he had dealt in shares recommended in his newspaper[4]. Following a 1983 investigation, the Stock Exchange criticised the personal dealings undertaken by an editorial assistant employed by publishers of an investment newsletter[5]. In 1984, the rules for the control of the dealings of a journalist on a well-known investment magazine were condemned by the Stock Exchange.[6] In 1987, two employees of a publishing group were dismissed following allegations that they had dealt on the basis of their advance knowledge of the contents of a financial magazine published by the group.[7]

These isolated instances confirm the existence, but do not establish the extent of insider dealing. Indications of its prevalence are limited to the estimates of regulatory agencies, statistical surveys and empirical studies. Their accuracy has also been the subject of comment.

14. See eg The Panel on Take-overs and Mergers, Report on the Year ended 31st March, 1973, p9, and Report on the Year ended 31st March, 1981, p6; Committee to Review the Functioning of Financial Institutions, Report (Chairman: Sir Harold Wilson) Cmnd. 7937 (1980), para 1 144.
15. Statement by Lord Shawcross, Chairman of the City Panel on Take-overs and Mergers, 26th October, 1972.
16. Part V of the CA 1980 was implemented on 23rd June, 1980, by the Companies Act 1980 (Commencement) Order 1980, S.I.1980 No.745.
17. See post, Chapter 6. Administrative Regulation.
18. Statement by the Special Committee of the Stock Exchange on Scottish and Universal Investments Ltd., 30th November, 1976.
19. See post, Chapter 7. Investigation, I. The Department of Trade and Industry.
20. The Stock Exchange Quotations Department, Review of the Year to 31st March, 1985, p9.
1. *The Observer*, 17th January, 1988.
2. C. Raw, *Slater Walker* (1977), p84.
3. Ibid.
4. Ibid.
5. The Stock Exchange, News Release, 4th November, 1983.
6. *Sunday Times*, 12th February, 1984.
7. *The Observer*, 13th September, 1987.

D. Regulatory agencies

The initial response of the British authorities to calls for regulation was to play down the issue. In 1971, the Panel stated that cases of insider dealing were 'highly exceptional' and advantage was 'very rarely' taken of the 'possibility' for insiders 'to deal secretly in securities to their great personal profit'.[8] A senior Stock Exchange official asserted:

> 'The use of privileged information in share dealings in this country, when seen in relation to the number of companies whose shares are quoted and to the volume of business transacted, may be regarded as a rare occurrence. If improper dealings are suspected then the Stock Exchange Council may be requested, usually by Member Firms or by the Chairman of the Company concerned, to carry out an investigation. Such requests are normally accompanied by reasons or evidence of increased market activity and if acceded to, then the investigation is carried out by a Committee appointed by the Council. I cannot say whether the press carry out any enquiries, but certainly as far as any investigation by the Council is concerned the matter is strictly confidential until such time as the Council may decide to issue a Notice.'[9]

After examining the problems with the Stock Exchange in 1972, the Panel commented 'although some insider dealing clearly does take place . . . the incidence . . . has been much exaggerated'[10]. In 1973, an article in the Stock Exchange Journal entitled 'Insider trading – most charges are unfounded' stated that in the previous year investigations involving 850 bargains revealed that in only three cases could a charge have been laid under proposed legislation.[11] In 1975, the head of its Quotations Department said the Stock Exchange had conducted over 100 investigations in the previous five years, but uncovered only four cases.[12]

However, these assessments conflicted with others. In 1966, reference was made in the House of Commons to 'any number of examples in the last year or two' of insider dealing.[13] A 1967 survey[14] of eighty-two bids for companies quoted on the Stock Exchange found that, though depressed by some companies whose share prices fell, bid announcements were preceded by an average price rise of 15% in the previous month at a time when average Stock Exchange price rises did not exceed 5% in a month. The survey did not distinguish between insider and tippee dealing. In 1972, a well-known investment magazine recorded its impression that insider dealing had been a feature of the bull

---

8. Statement by the City Panel on Stock Exchange Dealings in the course of a take-over situation, 2nd April, 1971 (Norbury).
9. M.A. Weinberg '*Take-overs and Mergers*' (3rd ed.1971), p334. The official quoted was the Secretary to the Commissions and Dealings Committee Membership Department.
10. The Panel on Take-overs and Mergers, Report on the Year ended 31st March, 1973, p.9.
11. (1973) 12 Stock Exchange Journal, p12.
12. Chapter 17, Discussion, p.229 at p.259 (Mr. Knight) in Loss (ed.), *Multinational Approaches – Corporate Insiders* (1976). The standard used was a 'demonstration of connection', namely, a person 'who was shown to be connected with the company', p273.
13. H.C. Deb, Vol. 725, ser.5, col.116 (21st February, 1966).
14. *The Economist*, 13th May, 1967, pp701-702.

market which began in March 1971.[15] In 1973, concern about the extent of insider dealing was reiterated in the following terms:

'Far more "insider" dealing goes on than is realised',[16] and 'We have long believed that the volume of insider dealing, and its type was a scandal',[17] and
'Unrestricted "insider trading" has long been one of the more glaring abuses of the existing corporate system.'[18]

Subsequently, the Panel and the Stock Exchange conceded that the problem was more widespread, though emphasised the prevalence of tippee rather than insider dealing. In a 1977 Joint Statement,[19] they stated:

'When negotiations are in progress or arrangements are being discussed concerning price-sensitive matters, it has recently all too frequently been the case that the eventual announcement has been preceded by rumours and by an abnormal level of speculative activity in the shares concerned with a corresponding effect on the market price. This has happened most noticeably in the case of merger and take-over announcements. The Stock Exchange and, where appropriate, the Panel have conducted exhaustive investigations into dealings in many cases when a substantial market price movement has been observed in the course of the Stock Exchange's normal monitoring procedures and this movement has assumed a special significance in the light of the subsequent announcement. In almost every instance it has been found that where dealings have taken place they have been carried out by persons who are not insiders but who have acted on what turns out to be a wellfounded tip or rumour. Only very rarely does it appear that insiders have dealt directly or indirectly.'

This emphasis on the prevalence of tippee rather than insider dealing was endorsed by a journalist on the investment magazine in which the views expressed in 1972-73 have already been noted:

'Proven insider dealing by directors is very rare anyway – though perhaps partly because it is such a difficult thing to prove. The largest part of the problem is the misuse, deliberately or in error of privileged information by those in close contact with the market itself.'[20]

The emphasis on tippee dealing was reiterated by the Panel in 1978:

'Instances of genuine insider trading are extremely infrequent ... The real problem has been to identify and deal with cases where insiders may have passed on tips ... The tip may have been given for any number of reasons

15. *Investors' Chronicle and Stock Exchange Gazette*, 24th November, 1972, p767.
16. Ibid, 26th January, 1973, p309.
17. Ibid, 9th February, 1973, p521.
18. Ibid, 27th July, 1973, p392.
19. Joint Statment issued by the Stock Exchange and the Panel on Take-overs and Mergers on 14th April, 1977 'Announcement of Price-Sensitive Matters'. This is published as an Appendix to the Panel's Report on the Year ended 31st March, 1977, p13.
20. *Investors' Chronicle*, 28th October, 1977, p287.

ranging from sheer carelessness through to deliberate collusion.'[1]

The Panel re-echoed this view in 1981 when it reported:

> 'Although there have been such cases, it is not to be expected that a
> director of a company wanting to make a profit through insider trading
> will trade in his own name; much more likely is it that he will use a nominee
> or some apparently unconnected person. An even more likely offence is
> that a director will, either deliberately or carelessly, simply pass the price-
> sensitive information to such an unconnected person.'[2]

However, the regulatory agencies have since been reticent about the extent of
insider dealing following implementation of Part V of the CA 1980. But leading
financial journalists have been more forthcoming. After an unusual price
movement prior to a bid announcement in May 1983, one commented:

> 'What makes the instance particularly disturbing is that up to now the fact
> that insider dealing had been made a criminal offence seemed to have
> dampened the ardour of people wanting to take a quick turn. Or at the
> very least it has encouraged them to do so on a scale that would not result
> in any obvious share price movement. As it is, this one looks a stinker.'[3]

In January 1984, another stated:

> 'As all those closely connected with the stock market know, insider dealing
> goes on and on a large scale. It is certainly greater than the minnows
> sacrificed so far.'[4]

In May, another considered:

> 'Despite the fact that the practice is in some cases illegal, it seems to be on
> the increase ... Sadly the law on insider dealing seems so far to have proved
> largely toothless.'[5]

In August 1988, a further view was that:

> 'Insider trading is alive and well and continuing to flourish on both sides
> of the Atlantic and it would be dangerous to think otherwise. Of course,
> it is always possible to explain away the recent reports of wrongdoing in
> some of the biggest investment banks in London and New York as welcome
> evidence that the authorities are simply much better at catching people
> these days. There is an element of truth in this. But given the recurrence
> of these sorts of incidents, there must also be a suspicion that standards of
> acceptable behaviour are dropping.'[6]

---

1. Committee to Review the Functioning of Financial Institutions, Second Stage Evidence, Vol.1,
The Panel on Take-overs and Mergers (1979), paras 104-105.
2. The Panel on Take-overs and Mergers, Report on the Year ended 31st March, 1981, p7.
3. *The Guardian*, 8th May, 1983.
4. *The Times*, 7th January, 1984.
5. *The Financial Times*, 26th May, 1984.
6. Ibid, 16th August, 1988.

Further controversy surrounds the specific issue of the use of confidential information by merchant banks and others faced with a conflict of interests arising from information about a company obtained as corporate adviser or through board membership when they also act as investment advisers to other clients. After a wide-ranging enquiry, the Panel seemed generally satisfied in 1970 with measures taken to reduce the risk of misuse of information:

> 'In no case was it suggested that the use of inside information of this kind in such a manner would be other than wholly improper; in every case measures of one kind or another had been taken to guard against the possibility . . . in the whole course of the enquiry only one case came to notice in which any merchant banker at the level of partner or director appeared to be under suspicion of having misused inside information.'[7]

In contrast, a leading financial journalist expressed the view that insider dealing:

> 'is the stuff of which many merchant banks and city operators generate their share-dealing profits and in it is the life blood of the short-term trading that makes brokerage business profitable. Far from being an occasional wickedness, it is an integral part of city life . . . Merchant banks who sincerely claim that they keep the investment and company finance and advice sections of their business rigidly separated . . . are rarely the banks whose importance is increasing or whose fortunes were created by the current generation.'[8]

It is difficult to judge which assertion is correct. In 1975, it seemed that most people who had contact with such banks considered that the Chinese Wall, which separated corporate finance and investment client departments, was maintained.[9] But in 1984 the view that it was unknown for a Chinese Wall not to have a grapevine trailed over it, was openly expressed in investment circles.[10] Moreover, in August 1988, a leading financial column considered:

> 'it is clear that the new financial conglomerates are having difficulty adjusting to the potentially serious conflicts of interest which arise when you throw market makers, analysts, fund managers and corporate financiers into the same firm.'[11]

A recent concern has become that of large-scale professional insider dealing rings.[12] A well-constructed ring is thought to include merchant banks, solicitors, stockbrokers and accountants. It operates through nominee or front companies set up in offshore tax havens and secret bank accounts abroad. A ring member who came into contact with inside information would neither deal himself nor pass on the inside information to another ring member. Rather he would suggest to a ring member, through a pre-arranged system, that he should

7. The Use of Confidential Price-Sensitive Information. This is published as an appendix to the Panel's Report on the Year ended 31st March, 1970, p10.
8. G. Serjeant, 'Hands up a Man who isn't an Insider Trader', *Sunday Times Business News*, 5th November, 1972.
9. K.W. Wedderburn, Chapter 2, UK, p23 at p32 in *Loss*, op cit n12, p4, supra.
10. *The Times*, 15th May, 1984.
11. *The Financial Times*, 16th August, 1988.
12. *The Independent*, 16th November, 1988.

buy or sell shares in the companies involved. The tip would than quickly pass through the rest of the ring. To avoid alerting regulators, transactions would be made through several broking firms, usually on the instructions of offshore nominees. If questioned by investigators, the nominees would refuse to name clients, even if they knew. The profits would later be shared out. In 1988, a leading financial journalist commented that it is 'wellknown in the City that such rings . . . exist and . . . are big business'.[13]

E. Statistical surveys

However, doubts about the emphasis on tippee rather than insider dealing have been raised by statistical surveys. These focused on the questions of *(a)* what people would do and *(b)* what they would expect others to do if, as a member of the board of a large company, they learnt at a board meeting of an impending merger with a smaller company which had had an unprofitable year and whose shares were then selling at a price so low that they were certain it would rise when news of the merger became public knowledge.

In the US, these questions were put to 1,700 corporate executives.[14] Even after nearly thirty years of insider dealing regulation, the replies indicated that 42% would buy shares for themselves, 14% would tell a friend, 2% would tell a broker and 56% would do nothing. Their opinion of the average executive was lower as they considered 61% would buy for themselves, 46% would tell a friend, 11% would tell a broker, but only 29% would do nothing. On the basis that people prefer to portray themselves favourably, the latter set of replies were regarded as corresponding more closely to actual business practice.

When the same questions were put to 830 British company executives in 1971,[15] 6.4% replied they would buy for themselves, 1.3% would tell a friend, 1.1% would inform their broker, 89.4% would do nothing and 1.8% did not know. As regards the conduct of company directors, 12.5% thought they would purchase and 11.5% that they would tell a friend. They also considered improprieties were more likely to occur in small companies than in large ones.

These statistical surveys thus suggest both insider and tippee dealing occur on a significant scale. Yet though of interest, the findings should be treated with caution as a precise estimate since the samples are probably too small to draw valid conclusions.

F. Empirical studies

The conflicting estimates as to the extent of insider dealing are not resolved by empirical research on whether security prices fully reflect particular subsets of information.[16] In Britain, initial research has found inefficiencies with a potential for insider dealing, but these have not been further investigated. In the US, empirical tests have confirmed the occurrence and profitability of insider dealing, though they do not indicate the overall extent as the samples are

13. Ibid.
14. R.C. Baumhart, 'How ethical are businessmen?' (1961) 39 *Harv. Bus. Rev.*5.
15. S. Webley, *British Businessmen's Behaviour* (1971), pp8-9.
16. The background to this research, its wider findings and implications are considered post, III. THEORETICAL CONSIDERATIONS.

limited to trading over a short period of time, often just a particular event, or by reference to reporting insiders only. But by underlining the scope for insider dealing and because of the greater inefficiencies in Britain, the US findings may have wider significance.

Such empirical studies are mainly based on information disclosed under insider reporting requirements.[17] Evidence about transactions by non-reporting insiders is more limited.

1. *Reporting insiders*

(a) FORECASTS OF PRICE CHANGES

An early study of insider forecasting ability examined[18] insider transactions in fifty shares during 1957/61 to see whether insiders' average selling prices exceeded their average buying prices. Each month was classified as either a net buying or selling month for each share and transactions were assumed to be made at the month's average price. On this basis, insiders' average purchase and sale prices were estimated at $36.7 and $53.8 respectively, with a profit of $17.1 per share. By examining the proportion of net purchases at below-average prices and of net sales at above-average prices, the hypothesis that such profits were the result of random insider dealing was rejected.

To see whether insider transactions merely reflected the general market trend, insider market transactions for October-December 1959 were tested against subsequent share prices at intervals of six months, one year and two years. The study concluded:

> 'there is very little evidence that a definite relationship exists between insider transactions and subsequent price movements in relation to the general market trend . . . from these cross-section data, there is no sufficient evidence to prove that insiders in these 50 companies as a group had out-performed the market.'[19]

But these findings were criticised on methodological grounds.[20]

17. The Securities Exchange Act 1934 requires a director or officer of an issuer of a registered equity security or a beneficial owner of more than 10% of such a security to report to the SEC their beneficial ownership of the issuer's equity securities. Changes in ownership must be reported within ten days of the end of the month of transaction. The information is open to public inspection.
18. H.K. Wu, 'Corporate Insider Trading Profits and the Ability to Forecast Stock Prices', in (ed.) H.K. Wu and A.J. Zakon, *Elements of Investments: Selected Readings* (1965), p442.
19. Wu, op cit supra, p448.
20. First, differences in prices may indicate a tendency for insiders to sell after price rises rather than prescience. Secondly, due to transactions in high- and low-priced securities being lumped together, the difference between average buying and selling prices may merely reflect a predominance in buying lower-priced issues. Thirdly, the number of insiders who trade may be a better guide to insider expectations than the volume of shares traded. Whilst criticising complete disregard of the magnitude of the transaction, Lorie and Niederhoffer (J.H. Lorie and V. Niederhoffer, 'Predictive and Statistical Properties of Insider Trading' (1968) 11 *J. Law and Economics* 35 at 39-43) point out that substantial shareholders usually deal in larger amounts than other reporting insiders. Hence, a single transaction may dominate monthly activity irrespective of whether it is better informed. R.A. Brealey, *Security Prices in a Competitive Market* (1971), p120.

Other studies have examined insiders' ability to forecast price changes by buying before the announcement of good news and selling before bad news. A study of mergers, dividend and earnings announcements by Lorie and Nieder-hoffer[1] did not find systematic exploitation of confidential information by insiders, thereby corroborating two earlier investigations.[2] Finding prices often increased before and after the announcement of a dividend reduction and earnings decrease, they argued that analysis of insider trading around such events in isolation from a company's price movements would not disclose whether insiders profited from their information. The better approach was to analyse insider transactions before large share price changes (8% or more). This showed insiders were superior forecasters of large changes.

However, a more recent study[3] provides evidence that insiders time their trades in relation to announcements of their companies' earnings prospects. As annual earnings forecasts convey information affecting prices, there is scope for insiders to earn abnormal returns by trading prior to these announcements. The evidence indicates insiders earn abnormal returns to their information.

(b) INTENSIVE ACTIVITY AND PRICE MOVEMENTS

The proposition that the number of different insider purchasers or sellers in a month is a measure of the extent of insider interest in a security was also tested by Lorie and Niederhoffer.[4] For this, they referred to earlier unpublished studies[5] and tested the data against previous findings.

Rogoff had examined 45 companies in 1958 in which, within a month, three or more insiders purchased their company's shares, no insiders sold and at least two purchasers increased their holdings by over 10%. In the next six months, these shares out-performed the market by 9.5%. He also examined the number of occasions that companies with an excess of two or more buyers or sellers out-performed the market. This indicated that in the next six months, the odds in favour of an advance relative to the market were about 2.1 times as great in months in which there were two or more net buyers as when there were two or more sellers. Such differences would occur by chance less than 1 in 10,000 occasions.

Using different definitions and techniques, Glass had calculated for fourteen selected two-month periods the relative performance of companies for which there was intensive insider buying in 1961-65. His sample consisted of the eight companies with the greatest excess of buyers over sellers. In the next seven months, the selected companies were found to out-perform the market by an average of 10%.

1. Lorie and Niederhoffer, op cit supra, at 46-47.
2. M.C. Fischer, *The Relationship between Insiders Transactions, the Price of the Common Stock of their Respective Companies, the Standard and Poor's Stock Price Index and Price Stability.* (Unpublished Ph D. dissertation in American University Library 1975) 212-213; T.D. Driscoll, *Some aspects of Corporate Insider Stock Holdings and Trading under Section 16(a) of the Securities Exchange Act 1934,* ch.6. (Unpublished MBA thesis in University of Pennsylvania Library 1956). Both are referred to by Lorie and Niederhoffer, op cit n20, p9, supra, at 46.
3. S.H. Penman, 'Insider Trading and the Dissemination of Firms' Forecast Information' (1982) 55 *J.Bus.* 479.
4. Lorie and Niederhoffer, op cit supra, at 48-51.
5. D.L. Rogoff, *The Forecasting Properties of Insiders' Transactions.* (Unpublished DBA dissertation in Michigan State University Library 1964); G.A. Glass, *Extensive Insider Accumulation as an Indicator of Near-Term Stock Price Performance.* (Unpublished Ph.D. dissertation in Ohio State University Library 1966).

Lorie and Niederhoffer considered these earlier results 'suggestive but not decisive'.[6] The selected studies might have been particularly volatile and this could have accounted for their superior performance in a rising market.

To test the importance of the relationship between intensive insider dealing and subsequent price movements, they selected at random thirty securities from the second study. During 1961-1964 (mid), calculations of their month-end prices and the market average were made for the 315 occasions when two or more insiders bought or sold. As measured by Rogoff's procedure, these were not found to be useful predictors of performance in the next six months.

For more information on the possibility of using insider dealing data, they studied a sample of securities for a period when the exact dates of transaction were known. For each transaction the prices on the exact date of transaction and six trading days into the next month were determined. Percentage changes in price were computed over the next six months for comparison against the market average.

The results indicated both a strong relationship between insider dealing and price movements and an opportunity for investors to profit from knowledge of trading by insiders. Moreover, companies with intensive insider dealing were not significantly more volatile than other listed companies and the higher rates of return for the selected companies did not seem attributable to their volatility. Accordingly, they recommended faster and more complete dissemination of insider dealing data.

In assessing the value of insider dealing data and the speed of incorporation into the market price, Pratt and de Vere[7] investigated a larger sample of 52,000 insider transactions in about 800 shares during 1960-66. On average, shares bought predominantly by insiders rose by 9.6%. Moreover, analysis of price performance at the end of the following month showed insiders had lost little of their advantage. Even two months after the end of the month of intensive insider activity, there was still a substantial difference in returns, despite the Official Summary's availability for over a fortnight.

A random sample of five trading months covering 200 companies during 1962-68, was examined by Jaffe.[8] The results indicated that insiders possessed special information, though after adjustment for transaction costs only intensive trading samples with eight-month holding periods earned statistically large returns. Much information contained in the transactions remained undiscounted by publication date in the Official Summary, but transaction costs eliminated profits for outsiders except in intensive trading samples. The cause of the market's gradual adjustment was earmarked for further research. Apart from evidence of widespread breaches of regulations, these findings were

---

6. Lorie and Niederhoffer, op cit n20, p9, supra, at 51.
7. S.P. Pratt and C.W. De Vere, 'Relationship between Insider Trading and Rates of Return for NYSE Common Stocks 1960-66' in (ed.) J. Lorie and R. Brealey, *Modern Developments in Investment Management* (1972), p268.
Insiders were regarded as optimistic when three or more bought and none sold and as pessimistic when three or more sold and none bought. As intensive dealing had been found likely to persist for several months, repeated indications of unusual activity might be less significant than its first occurrence and so were excluded. This left 211 instances of insider optimism and 272 of pessimism for analysis.
8. J.F. Jaffe, 'Special Information and Insider Trading' (1974) 47 *J. Bus.* 410. By using a larger sample and making allowance for transaction costs, the relative rise of different securities and general market conditions, he sought to improve on previous techniques. As well as the initial sample, other samples of large transactions and of months of intensive trading were also examined.

regarded as highlighting the need for enforcement to concentrate on breaches when intensive trading occurred.

(c) GENERAL ACTIVITY AND PRICE MOVEMENTS

The last two studies were developed by Finnerty,[9] who argued that samples based on intensive trading criteria were biased towards insiders whose performance was likely to be superior. To test the 'average' insider's performance, he examined all registered insider transactions during 1969-71 by constructing an insider buy portfolio and an insider sell portfolio for each month and comparing the rates of return of insider portfolios with those for the market.

The results showed that insiders could out-perform the market in the short run, thereby corroborating previous studies. For the buy portfolio, most above-average returns were realised in the first six months. The large proportion realised in the first month suggests that the inside information rapidly became public knowledge and was discounted by the market or that knowledge of insider purchases prompts other investors to buy. Conversely, in the sell portfolio most below-average performances occurred uniformly throughout subsequent months. This may indicate that initially as insiders sell, either their inside information is not immediately released or information about insider sales is not immediately discounted by the market.

(d) SECONDARY DISTRIBUTIONS

Insider possession of special information was also confirmed by an analysis of secondary distributions[10] which found that to some extent the value of the information contained in such a distribution depended on the vendor. On the day of distribution, the vendor's identity was not generally known, but the greatest abnormal returns occurred when the vendor was an insider. By the time insiders had reported transactions, the market had fully adjusted to the information contained in the distribution. Though indicating prices adjusted efficiently to public information, these findings were also evidence that insiders often possessed important information about their company which was not generally known.

(e) CONSISTENCY OF PROFITABILITY AMONG COMPANIES

As investors could profit from ability to identify companies whose insiders consistently out-performed the market, insider performance in thirty companies during 1957-60 was compared with 1961-64.[11] But there was no evidence that insiders in particular companies traded with superior success during consecutive time periods.

9. J.E. Finnerty, 'Insiders and Market Efficiency' (1976) 31 *J.Fin.* 1141.
10. M.S. Scholes, 'The Market for Securities: Substitution versus Price. Pressure and the Effects of Information in Share Prices' (1972) 45 *J. Bus.* 179.
11. Lorie and Niederhoffer, op cit n20, p9, supra, at 51-52.

(f) CONTINUITY

An interesting statistical feature was continuity.[12] Successive insider transactions tended to be either purchases or sales and long runs of consecutive insider purchases or sales in a company often occurred. In a sample of 3,973 purchases and 3,277 sales, the odds in favour of a purchase followed by a purchase were three times as great as a purchase followed by a sale and the odds in favour of a sale after a sale were twice as great as after a purchase.

The significance of this finding is that one purchase indicates others are likely to follow, with the first purchase being more informative than subsequent ones. A change in direction from selling to buying indicates future purchases are to be expected, whereas a sale followed by a sale confirms preceding expectations as to the direction of insider activites. Hence, a change in direction of activity is probably important in deducing insider expectations.

(g) EFFECT OF REGULATION CHANGES

However, empirical evidence raises doubts about the effectiveness of recent regulation on reporting insiders. Jaffe[13] examined changes in the volume and profitability of insider dealing after each of three important decisions.[14] He concluded:

> 'There appeared to be few changes in the characteristics of trading attributable to the three cases. Only the Texas Gulf Sulphur decision seems to have had even a slight effect on the profitability of insider trading, and there is no evidence of any cumulative effect of the three events on profitability. Furthermore, the data do not suggest that the regulatory changes affected the volume of insider trading'[15].

He attributed these results to the relative smallness of the excess rate of return to insiders, the SEC's emphasis on the most obvious breaches and the apparently inadequate deterrent effect of the punishments used.

In testing efficiency, he found that whilst insiders could predict price movements in the short run better than in the long run, the information available to them still affected prices eight months later. Such inefficiency enabled insiders to earn significant profits.

2. Non-reporting insiders

Although empirical evidence on non-reporting insiders does not indicate the volume of insider dealing, it can examine the impact of trading on inside information in specific areas. As insider leakage was considered prevalent during unannounced merger plans, one study[16] examined the impact of trading on inside information before merger announcements by focusing on the daily

12. Ibid, at 45.
13. J.F. Jaffe, 'The effect of regulation changes on insider trading' (1974) 5 *Bell J.Econ. and Management Sci.*93.
14. Namely: (a) the *Cady Roberts* decision (8th November, 1961); (b) the *Texas Gulf Sulphur Co.* indictment (19th April, 1965), and (c) the *Texas Gulf Sulphur Co.* decision (19th August, 1966).
15. Jaffe, op cit n13, supra, at 114.
16. A.J. Keown and J.M. Pinkerton, 'Merger Announcements and Insider Trading Activity: An Empirical Investigation' (1981) 36 *J.Fin.* 855.

price movements of 194 acquired companies during 1975-78. The results suggested substantial trading on inside information, starting about one month before the public announcement with uncontrolled abuse in the five to eleven trading days prior to the announcement. Since the dramatic increase in trading volume was not due to registered insiders, this suggests many transactions were effected through third parties to avoid detection.

Further doubts about the effectiveness of regulation were raised by a comparison between the 101 listed and 93 unlisted companies in the sample, made to determine whether stock exchange regulation acted as a deterrent. This found only minor differences which were not statistically significant.

Another study[17] was indirectly concerned with the usefulness to investors of a particular subset of information. Segment earnings information for 1967-69 was first made public by many companies under 1970 SEC disclosure requirements. Tests of market efficiency were constructed to determine whether such information which, though not formally reported was usually contained in internal accounting records, was incorporated into share prices during 1968-70. For companies which did not publicly report either segment revenue or profit data before 1970, the market was found inefficient as regards such data in 1968 and 1969, but not 1970. Yet where companies had published reported segment revenue, though not segment profits information before 1970, abnormal returns conditional on a segment based trading rule strategy were relatively small. These results suggested investors could use non-public segment earnings information to anticipate to a large extent changes in earnings which would have been unexpected had they relied totally on consolidated data.

The findings of studies on non-reporting insiders are thus consistent with those on reporting insiders. Like other contributions to an empirical assessment of insider dealing, however, these empirical studies do not measure its extent.

Such uncertainty increases the difficulties in determining the regulation required and assessing its effectiveness. Hence, evaluation of insider dealing regulation is hampered by lack of knowledge about the extent of insider dealing which may, moreover, be incapable of ascertainment by empirical and statistical research.

III. THEORETICAL CONSIDERATIONS

The initial question of whether insider dealing should be regulated has given rise to considerable debate. The orthodox view in support of regulation has been fiercely criticised, particularly by Manne. In subjecting the issue to critical scrutiny, his controversial work[18] and the ensuing debate[19], together with

17. D.W. Collins, 'SEC Product – Line Reporting and Market Efficiency' (1975) 2 *J. Financial Economics* 125.
18. H.G. Manne, *Insider Trading and the Stock Market* (1966) (hereinafter cited as Manne).
19. Publication of Manne's book provoked considerable controversy: R.A. Schotland, 'Unsafe at any Price: A Reply to Manne, Insider Trading and the Stock Market' (1967) 53 *Va.L.Rev.*1425: J.A.C. Hetherington, 'Insider Trading and the Logic of Law' (1967) *Wis.L.Rev.*720 and M. Mendelson, 'The Economics of Insider Trading Reconsidered' (1969) 117 *U.Pa.L.Rev.*470.
Shorter book reviews included: (1967) *Duke L.J.*456 (D.J. Baum); (1968) 43 *Notre Dame Law.*465 (R. Garrett, Jr.); (1967) 55 *Calif.L.Rev.*1229 (R.W. Jennings); (1967) 42 *N.Y.U.L.Rev.*212 (H. Kripke); (1968) *66 Mich. L.Rev.*1317 (H. Marsh, Jr.); (1967) 53 *Va.L.Rev.*753 (N.S. Poser); (1968) 10.*S.Tex.L.J.*179 (B.H. Tunks); (1967) 16 *Buffalo L.Rev.*520 (A.H. Vogt); (1967) 21.*Sw.L.J.*405 (P.L. Wright) and (1966) 35 *Geo.Wash.L.Rev.*140 (J.F. Weston) and 146 (W.H. Painter).
A reply to his critics was contained in H.G. Manne, 'Insider Trading and the Law Professors' (1970)

subsequent empirical research, have helped clarify the nature of the problem.

As with other economic issues, insider dealing considerations fall into two main categories.[20] First, issues of efficiency are concerned with pareto-optimal resource allocation. Movement towards a more efficient solution could in principle result in each person being in a more preferred position with none in a less preferred position. Pareto-optimality is attained when no reallocation would make one person better off without making another worse off.

A market is allocationally efficient when scarce resources are channelled to their most productive uses.[1] Under conditions of perfect competition[2], prices will continuously reflect all available information and so provide reliable signals for resource allocation. Perfect competition is sufficient, but not necessary, for the efficient allocation of resources since transaction costs and taxes do not make allocational efficiency impossible.

Hence, an allocationally efficient capital market is one that efficiently transfers funds between lenders and producers by generating prices that continuously equate marginal rates of return (adjusted for risk) for all lenders and borrowers. Security prices establish a market-based rate of return. When prices reflect all available information, the market rate of return provides the most efficient allocation of capital. Furthermore, no group of individual investors is at a disadvantage in such a market.

Secondly, issues of equity deal with the choice among efficient solutions when each solution leaves some people better off, but others worse off. An example is the distribution of wealth among individuals in the economy. Security prices and price changes affect the distribution of wealth. Inequality of access to information, however, may enable informed investors to increase their wealth at the expense of the less informed.

---

23 *Vand.L.Rev.*547. This article led to an exchange of views with the SEC's solicitor: D. Ferber, 'The Case Against Insider Trading: A Response to Professor Manne' (1970) 23 *Vand.L.Rev.*621 and H.G. Manne, 'A Rejoinder to Mr. Ferber' (1970) 23 *Vand.L.Rev.*627.

More recent discussion includes: 'Note, A Framework for the Allocation of Prevention Resources with a Specific Application to Insider Trading' (1976) 74 *Mich.L.Rev.*975; 'Note, Economic Analysis of Section 16(b) of the Securities Exchange Act of 1934' (1976) 18 *Wm. and Mary L.Rev.*989; 'Note, The Efficient Capital Market Hypothesis, Economic Theory and the Regulation of the Securities Industry' (1977) 29 *Stan.L.Rev.*1031; W.H. Painter, *The Federal Securities Code and Corporate Disclosure* (1979), pp233-50; H. Kripke, *The SEC and Corporate Disclosure, Regulation in Search of a Purpose* (1979), pp292-297; V. Brudney, 'Insiders, Outsiders and Informational Advantages under the Federal Securities Laws' (1979) 93 *Harv.L.Rev.*322; K.E. Scott, 'Insider Trading, Rule 10b-5, Disclosure and Corporate Privacy' (1980) 9 *J.Legal Stud.*801; J.F. Barry III, 'The Economics of Outside Information and Rule 10b-5' (1981) 129 *U.Pa.L.Rev.*1307 and H. Heller, '*Chiarella*, SEC Rule 143-3 and *Dirks:* "Fairness" 'versus Economic Theory' (1982) 37 *Bus.Law.*517.

20. W.H. Beaver, *Financial Reporting: An Accounting Revolution* (1979), p188.

1. Barry, op cit n19, supra, at 1316-1319; M. Mendelson, 'Economics and the Assessment of Disclosure Requirements' (1978)1 *JCCLSR* 49 at 50-51; M.Firth, *The Valuation of Shares and the Efficient Markets Theory* (1977), pp1-3.

2. Perfect competition is defined by Barry, op cit n19, p14, supra, at 1316, to mean 'rivalry among large numbers of buyers and sellers when the following conditions are satisfied: (1) no market actor possesses monopoly power . . .; (2) each actor receives simultaneusly with every other actor complete and costless information about existing prices and technology; (3) markets are frictionless (ie there are no transaction costs or taxes, all assets are perfectly divisible and marketable, and there are no constraining regulations); (4) all investors can borrow or lend unlimited amounts of capital at a common and exogenously determined riskless rate, there are no restrictions on short sales and there are no barriers to arbitrage; (5) all investors and potential investors share the same time horizons and homogenous expectations about the means, variances and co-variances of returns among all assets, (ie about the implications of any given piece of information for security prices) and (6) all investors are risk-averse, single-period, expected-utility of terminal wealth maximisers who trade on the basis of the mean and variance of the distribution of returns'.

A. Efficiency issues

The efficiency issues raised by insider dealing have focused on two main problems. The first involves the economics of information, particularly whether there is a flaw in the market for information. The second concerns whether insider dealing should be a form of entrepreneurial compensation.

1. Market failure

The market failure problem has centred on information as a public good and the effects of insider dealing. These are supplemented by empirical tests which attempt to measure the efficiency of the market.

(a) INFORMATION AS A PUBLIC GOOD

Securities regulation provides two main methods whereby the flow of information to investors is affected. First, anti-fraud provisions may make it unlawful to make a false or misleading statement or to omit a material fact in certain transactions. Secondly, financial disclosure may be expressly mandated by legislative or other regulatory authority.

Their underlying rationale is based on the externality or public good aspect of market failure.[3] An externality exists when the actions of one party have effects on other parties who are not charged or compensated via the price mechanism. In consequence, the efficiency properties of a competitive market may not be achieved.

Positive externalities[4] occur where a party conveys uncompensated benefits to others with the result that there is under-production and under-consumption. Parties who benefit from this inefficiency are often termed 'free riders'. Where the positive externalities are such that the extra costs of providing benefits to another are zero and it is frequently difficult to exclude extra beneficiaries from an activity, the term 'public good' is used since private initiative may fail to provide the activity at all or may provide it in socially inappropriate amounts.[5]

The view that information is a public good is supported by Mendelson[6] on the basis that:

> 'if A is provided with or sold information, the amount available for B is undiminished even though the value may be diminished. It is practically impossible to provide A with the exclusive use of the information'.[7]

As it is not practical to confine information to shareholders, they cannot capture the entire value of the information. Information users will attempt to get as much of a free ride as possible and conceal its value to them. But private producers of information will lack the incentive to match the demand. He

---

3. Beaver, opcit n20, p15, supra, p189; L.J. White, *Reforming Regulation: Processes and Problems* (1981), pp28-29.
4. Conversely, negative externalities arise when a party imposes uncompensated costs on others through its actions, resulting in too low a price and excessive production or consumption. An example is pollution.
5. Eg national defence.
6. Mendelson, op cit n1, p15, supra.
7. Ibid, at 53-54.

concludes that as the market mechanism is not generally effective to produce public goods, regulation is necessary.

However, he acknowledges there is redundancy. Certain items of information may thus add little which is not already known; but rather than being wasteful, he emphasises redundancy may play a confirmatory role.[8]

Nevertheless, substantial redundancy implies that 'progress' in accounting disclosure may have had only a modest effect on the information content of reports. Whilst this does not mean accounting information cannot be improved, it suggests that many such efforts are subject to diminishing marginal returns.[9]

The externalities-based argument is also considered by Beaver[10], who cites examples of externalities in financial reporting. Where information about one company's productive opportunities conveys information about those of others, there will be a lack of incentive for full disclosure since, even though other companies benefit, the disclosing company is not compensated for the costs of disclosure. Similarly, when prospective shareholders neither participate nor share in bearing the costs of disclosure, less information is disclosed for the purposes of portfolio selection than under a collective agreement including them. Likewise, in a securities market where information is reflected in prices, the demand and incentives to pay for it may be zero.

He adopts a cautious approach, however, in advancing such an argument. This is mainly due to the lack of empirical evidence about the importance of potential externalities. By providing signals to investors on the quality of securities and reducing some of the risk, he accepts increased disclosure may result in higher share prices which redistribute disclosure costs. However, he contends it is 'cavalier'[11] to suggest such a market-price mechanism compensates for this problem and management incentives are aligned perfectly with market value maximisation. Hence, he considers it is unclear whether market failures are sufficiently material to justify regulation.

He also stresses market failure is an insufficient condition for disclosure regulation because it is 'naive to assume that regulation is costless or that the incentives and information of regulators is sufficient to ensure a socially desired result'[12].

Private sector collective agreements are referred to as an alternative method of dealing with these externalities, though he acknowledges the problem of compliance.

The challenge to disclosure regulation is based on confidence in the pricing mechanism of the unregulated market to provide an optimal amount of investment information. Applying the marginal cost pricing theory to the

8. Ibid, at 55. This view is supported by B. Lev, 'On the Adequacy of Publicly Available Financial Information for Security Analysis', p.123 at p.132 and H. Bierman, Jr., 'A Synthesis and Discussion', p.162 both in (ed) A.Rashad Abdel-Khalik and T.F. Keller, *Financial Information Requirements for Security Analysis* (Duke Second Accounting Symposium 1976).
9. Lev, op cit n8, supra, p132. This view is shared by M. Mendelson 'The Adequacy of Publicly Available Financial Information for Security Analysis, Comment', p150 at p152, in Abdel-Khalik and Keller, op cit n8, supra.
10. Beaver, op cit n20, p15, supra, pp189-190.
11. W.H. Beaver, 'The Implications of Security Price Research for Disclosure Policy and the Analyst Community', p65 at p66 in Abdel-Khalik and Keller, op cit n11, supra.
12. Ibid, at pp66-67.

processes generating information about market price, Stigler[13] argued price dispersion was a manifestation of ignorance in the market. He attempted to show buyers and sellers would incur costs canvassing for the best price until the expected benefit from further searching equalled its cost.

Recognising the value of information disclosed in financial statements may exceed its cost, Benston[14] contends that management, acting in shareholders' best interests, will provide the information to them and other investors according to their best estimates of how marginal costs and benefits accrue. Even if management does not, investors are free to purchase information in the market place.

In support of Benston's analysis, Gonedes[15] considered an unregulated market would provide an optimal amount of investment information. Private collectors would not only meet market demand, but would do so more efficiently than regulation.

However, this libertarian approach is open to criticism[16]. In the market for information, it is not clear that the pricing system is as efficient as supposed. To the extent that monopolistic exploitation of material information provides better returns than a free market sale, there is insufficient incentive for dissemination and so insiders may prefer to trade for their own account rather than sell their information[17]. Nor does Benston specify how management knows the value of disclosure in order to balance the marginal value of financial statements to shareholders against its marginal cost to the company. This approach also fails to take account of companies' resistance to accountancy reforms and their use of accounting devices[18] making evaluation more difficult. Even the underlying assumption that management's aim is to maximise profits is not necessarily accepted[19].

Placing a different interpretation on the market forces generating information, Lev[20] also argues there are strong incentives for the supply and demand of financial information. On the demand side, investors will bid for information on which to base their decisions on assessments of future distributions of securities returns. On the supply side, in competing to attract investor capital, companies will adjust the structure of their information systems to investor preferences.

13. G.J. Stigler, 'The Economics of Information' (1961) 69 *J.Pol.Econ.*213. See also J.K. Johansson and A. Boldman, 'Income, Search and the Economics of Information Theory: An Empirical Analysis (1979) 11 *Applied Econ.*435; McCall, 'The Economics of Information and Optimal Shopping Rules' (1965) 38 *J.Bus.*300; M.L. Weitzman, 'Optimal Search for the Best Alternative' (1979) 47 *Econometrica* 641.

14. G.J. Benston, 'The Value of the SEC's Accounting Disclosure Requirements' (1969) 44 *Accounting Rev.*515 at 516.

15. N.J. Gonedes, N. Dupuch and S.H. Penman, 'Disclosure Rules, Information – Production and Capital Market Equilibrium: The Case of Forecast Disclosure Rules' (1976) 14 *J. Accounting Research* 89 at 98-106. Gonedes does not consider all material would be disclosed gratuitously without the SEC: ibid, at 101.

16. Mendelson, op cit n1, p15, supra, at pp53-54.

17. Barry, op cit n19, p14, supra, at p1323.

18. Examples cited by Mendelson, op cit n1, p15, supra, at p54, are 'leasing to hide debt, the use of pooling of interest in an acquisition transaction to achieve a desired profile of earnings, and reporting the entire markup on instalment sales as current profit even though the instalments may stretch over years and the sale may abort before all payments are made'.

19. Other perceived goals are: (a) long-run survival, K.W. Rothschild, 'Price Theory and Oligopoly' (1947) 57 *Econ.J.*299; (b) making merely satisfactory profits, Margolis, 'The Analysis of the Firm: Rationalism, Conventionalism and Behaviourism' (1958) 31 *J.Bus.*187 and (c) maximising sales without necessarily maximising profits, W.Baumol, 'Business Behaviour, Value and Growth' (1959) 20. Lev, op cit n8, p17,, supra.

Though this argument identifies motivation, the diversity of investor groups raises difficulties in identifying investor preferences. Indeed, the incompatibility of a wide group of investors and an optimal information system is acknowledged by Lev: 'it will be impossible to design optimal information systems which will satisfy the preferences of wide, diverse groups of investors'[1]. Moreover, management would encounter considerable difficulty in identifying the information system preferences of investors.

Even when companies voluntarily disclose information, there are misgivings about its quality. In particular, voluntary disclosure may emphasise positive rather than negative information about a company.

Whilst Kripke[2] dismisses the academic arguments as irrelevant because they are abstracted from the economics of the capital markets[3], he also contends that an unregulated market will provide optimal disclosure. Potential buyers, such as private placees and underwriters, would use their bargaining power to negotiate the disclosure of material information. Similarly, on the trading market companies would supply sufficient information to attract investor interest and satisfy the needs of recommending brokers and analysts. However, this argument also overlooks inefficiencies in the market for investment information.

In the debate about the underlying rationale of disclosure regulation, supporters of an unregulated market for disclosure have failed to show that the free market processes would provide optimal investment information. But the controversy has served to focus attention on the public good status of investment information and the implications for regulation[4].

Investment information exhibits the characteristics of a public good. Once the information has been published, its use does not diminish the total supply and individual users cannot exclude others from using it.

However, the theory of public good does not fully describe the market for investment information. The information disclosed by regulation forms only part of the total information reflected in prices and is supplemented by information based on the activities of competing information intermediaries. The early use of private investment information enables an intermediary to enjoy part of its value, though the extent is related to the efficiency of the market.

The private good aspect of investment information emphasises the importance of information searches and processing that contribute to market efficiency. It raises questions, however, of regulation involving the process whereby information is disseminated from companies to information intermediaries, particularly the circumstances in which the latter can receive and act on information that is not generally available. For just as the activities of information intermediaries can contribute to market efficiency, the manner of disseminating information that is generally available can hinder market efficiency.

Yet this private good aspect does not undermine the market failure rationale of regulation. An issuer has large cost advantages over information intermediaries in producing many kinds of information about itself. Instead of reducing

1. Ibid, p125.
2. Kripke, op cit n19, p14, supra, pp117-125.
3. Ibid, p118: 'The whole academic argument is irrelevant because it deals with information produced in some kind of empty state of the world, instead of negotiated securities disclosure, where the recipient has some bargaining chips and uses them. Thus, economics of this kind of information cannot be abstracted from the economics of the capital markets'.
4. Barry, op cit n19, p14, supra, p1323; Lev, op cit n8, p17, supra, p134; Bernstein, op cit n8, p17, supra, p159; E.E. Comiskey, 'The Adequacy of Publicly Available Financial Information for Security Analysis: A Comment', p144 at p147 in Abdel-Khalik and I. Keller, op cit n8, p17, supra.

their numbers, disclosure regulation subsidises information intermediaries and increases the flow of information to the market. Moreover, in contributing to the broader information reflected in prices, the activities of information intermediaries may partly be a public good.

(b) EFFECTS OF INSIDER DEALING

In his analysis of the effects of insider dealing, Manne also treats information as a commodity. The stock market is described as in many respects an exchange for information with the market placing a value on information[5].

For the purposes of the insider dealing issue, two broad categories of information are distinguished. Termed 'second category information'[6], inside information is defined as knowledge of specific events or probability of future events that would substantially affect the price of a company's shares and which is 'capable of physical exploitation in the market by some individuals before the matter becomes public knowledge'[7]. The other is termed first category information[8], which is generally available from trade journals, the financial press and published data on companies, even though some may be understood only by the financially sophisticated. As second category information is released to the public, the share price will increase according to the value of the information. The information then becomes first category information and as such ceases to be useful for insider dealing.

These distinctions are regarded as essential to understanding the development of two different techniques for marketing information. Under the first, inside information is exploited by buying or selling shares before the information becomes public and the share price responds. The second technique is the exchange of inside information. At an informal level, exchanges may occur in the social circles in which company executives move, such as golf clubs. More elaborate exchanges are operated by investment banks and brokerage houses, the main devices being membership of company boards and the operation of 'clearing houses'[9]. By enabling a person to capitalise on information available to directors, board membership may be intended as a reward for benefits received or expected. Clearing houses act as intermediaries of exchange where persons have accounts in which they may 'deposit' information and 'draw out' information deposited[10].

Whilst it is doubtful whether exchange techniques operate as systematically as suggested and the clearing houses are an admitted metaphor, this overall picture of business reality has been described as probably 'fairly accurate, though cynical'[11]. Accordingly, this raises the question of whether such marketing should be discouraged by legal measures or encouraged as performing a valid function.

5. Manne, p47.
6. Ibid, p54.
7. Ibid, p55.
8. Ibid, p48.
9. Ibid, p66.
10. Difficulties are recognised in evaluating deposits determining who ought to be entitled to participate and in avoiding leakages of information to non-participants. Nevertheless, he argues that investment banks and brokerage houses can overcome these difficulties through the use of priority lists of persons entitled to be 'told particular bits of information or advised to buy certain shares' (p71) and the operation of discretionary accounts with which transactions can be made for someone without any leakage of information.
11. Painter, op cit n19, p14, supra, p235.

Instead of being preceded by an attempt to evaluate insider dealing on its merits, Manne argues that the development of the law has been strongly influenced by lawyers' assumption that insider dealing is wrongful. This assumption is attributed to their tendency to think in terms of the relationship between buyer and seller and their 'equity approach with its overtones of fairness and morality'[12], so that their acceptance or rejection of a practice will reflect their notion of the mutual fairness of a transaction between parties. In contrast, he asserted that the economists' approach is characterised by its concern with social planning for the whole. Economists regard individuals as 'a fungible commodity, each substitutable for another'[13] and fairness concerns 'the propriety of allocation of resources or income among large distinguishable bodies or groups of individuals'[14].

His assertion that 'the insider's gain is not made at the expense of anyone'[15] is based on his theoretical analysis of the market effects of different trading rules. He tries to establish that a rule of free insider trading will result in gradual price changes as an increasing number of people receive and rely upon the information. Conversely, a no insider trading rule generates steeper price changes: no discernible price movement occurs until information is published whereupon a flood of orders results in a sharp price change.

As a result, Manne argues a free trading rule operates to the advantage of all investors except speculative traders[16]. The long-term investor is unlikely to be harmed by insider dealing. He is not interested in the timing of disclosure because the value of his investment will increase as the market price reflects insider dealing and the leakage of inside information. Hence, he has no interest in preventing insider dealing because 'by holding on to his shares, the investor will ultimately realise the value of any good news developed for his company'[17].

Rather, it will be the 'price function' or speculative trader who benefits from a full disclosure rule. Here 'to the extent that gambling psychology motivates his participation in the stock market, the speculator will favour a rule generating sharp fluctuations in stock prices over a rule allowing only gradual changes'[18]. His interests are thus protected by good news and injured by bad. But since he must act quickly before the inside information is reflected in price, the benefits will be limited. His real interest would usually be to receive the information in advance of disclosure[19].

However, according to Manne, the long-term investor derives the full benefit of insider dealing only by retaining his shares. When he sells, the question remains whether insider dealing harms those long-term investors who trade prior to the disclosure of good news. In dealing at a price which is lower than it would be on disclosure of the inside information, such sellers lose the difference between the market price received and that which they would have

12. Manne, p3.
13. Ibid.
14. Ibid.
15. Manne, p61.
16. Speculative traders are termed 'price function' traders on the basis that their trades are motivated by price changes. They are contrasted with 'time function' traders whose transactions occur because of external events unrelated to the price of stock. Such events include changes in investment needs and government policies and economic events that affect the entire equity capital market (Manne, p95) and are 'first-category information'.
17. Manne, p106.
18. Ibid, p108.
19. Thus, the effect of the sales is to substitute one group of shareholders for another: a group of shareholders who might have sold anyway, were not entitled to the inside information and were mainly speculative traders, are replaced by another group which ultimately receives the benefit.

received upon disclosure. As this loss is reduced by the extent to which the price has risen at the time they sold, Manne argues that long-term investors still benefit because they would have realised even less if the insiders were not trading[20].

He thus supports the general arguments of a former SEC Commissioner that, if anything, insider dealing benefits the seller[1]. As the effect of insider dealing on the basis of good news is to raise the price, both the purchaser's costs and seller's gains are increased.

Arguments as to the seller's gain will be of little comfort to a seller who argues that had he known what the insider knew, he would not have sold. In deciding to sell, he sells at a lower price than if the information had been disclosed. He is also deprived of information relevant to his investment decision. The fact that the seller's loss is contingent does not mean that the insider's gain is not made at the expense of anyone.

Moreover, Manne does not consider the position when insiders sell on the basis of bad news. In these circumstances other investors purchase at a higher price than if the information had been disclosed and again their investment decision is made in ignorance of relevant information.

Accordingly, whether insiders sell on good news or bad news, their gain or avoidance of a loss is made at the expense of other investors, who cannot make such a profit or avoid such a loss. Far from making insiders better off without making other investors worse off, these transactions hinder the attainment of a more efficient solution. Since the information on which insiders trade is not reflected in prices, optimal resource allocation is impaired.

(c) MARKET EFFICIENCY

Recent research on the relationship between information and the behaviour of security prices originated in response to claims in investment circles that market inefficiencies existed, but security analysis could find mispriced securities. However, its significance extends to the stock market's primary role of optimal resource allocation[2].

20. This view was echoed in 'Insider Trading' (*Justice* 1972), para2: 'when a director buys on the market in the knowledge of a forthcoming bid for the company, the seller of the shares would probably have put his share up for sale anyway and the price he gets may, in fact, have been slightly raised by the fact that the director is in the market as a buyer'.
1. J.M. Whitney, II, 'Section 10b-5: From Cady, Roberts to Texas Gulf: Matters of Disclosure' (1965) 21 *Bus.Law* 193. Whitney argued that when the insider does not induce the sale, his purchases do not harm the seller. In addition, the probability that the seller would not have sold had disclosure been made to him cannot harm him when the company has valid reasons for non-disclosure. Hence, if neither causes harm, he argues that purchasing and failing to disclose cannot cause harm.
2. As the market where investment funds are raised, the optimal allocation of resources chiefly concerns the primary market. But the primary market is smaller than the secondary market and most of the efficiency tested relates to efficiency in the secondary market.
However, efficiency in the secondary market is relevant to the allocation of resources in the primary market, the chief link being the pricing function of the secondary market. The price of a company's securities on the secondary market reflects investors' expectations as to earnings and dividends and the rate of return. The expected rate of return depends on the risk of uncertainty perceived and constitutes the cost of equity capital to a company. Though not directly observable, this rate can be deduced approximately from the quoted price. The cost of equity capital is important because it acts as a criterion for a company's investment decisions and this serves as a device to allocate investment on the primary market. For such investment should only be made where the promised return exceeds the cost of funds invested, the cost being deduced from security prices in the secondary market. Hence, where they reflect all available information about a company's prospects, security prices on the secondary market serve as a guide to a company's cost of capital and result in optimal

This empirical research has led to the development of the efficient markets theory. Though the evidence is conflicting and incomplete and the theory is not fully developed, the growing body of evidence relating to its validity means the theory, the empirical evidence and the implications for disclosure and insider dealing regulation should be reviewed[3].

In general terms, a securities market is efficient[4] when security prices fully reflect the information available[5]. This definition implies that security prices will adjust instantaneously and in an unbiased manner to any new information released to the market.

The sufficient conditions for market efficiency are no transaction costs in trading securities, all information is costlessly available to all market participants and all investors agree on the implications of current information for the current price and distributions of future prices of each security[6]. Under such market conditions, it was proved that prices would fluctuate randomly[7].

The sufficient conditions do not describe markets in practice. But it was argued that existing capital markets may nevertheless be efficient since the necessary conditions are less stringent:

resource allocation on the primary market.

Apart from the pricing mechanism, there is a further link between secondary and primary markets. 'Fair' prices in the sense of fully reflecting publicly available information and cheap transactions in the secondary market should inspire confidence and so make it easier for investors to invest, change and realise investments. In tending to reduce the cost of capital for all companies, they should encourage investment on the primary market.

3. This review is based on: (a) E.F. Fama, 'Efficient Capital Markets: A Review of Theory and Empirical Work' (1970) 25 *J. Fin.* 383; (b) J.H. Lorie and M.T. Hamilton, *The Stock Market: Theories and Evidence* (1973); (c) B. Lev, *Financial Statement Analysis: A New Approach* (1974); (d) T. Dyckman, D. Downes and R. Magee, *Efficient Capital Markets and Accounting* (1975); (e) Firth, op cit n1, p15, supra; (f) Barry, op cit n19, p14, supra and (g) Beaver, op cit n20, p15, supra.

4. The term efficiency may be used in three senses; allocational, external and internal. An allocationally efficient market is one which allocates capital to users in such a way that those who can make the best use of capital are taken care of first, while those who make the poorest use of capital are the last to receive.

In an externally efficient market, prices fully reflect available information.

Internal efficiency is concerned with whether transaction costs are so high as to discourage dealing by outsiders who keep the market externally efficient and whether those not required to bear transaction costs make excessive returns. Though necessary to allocational efficiency, external efficiency is not synonymous with it since allocational efficiency also requires internal efficiency. The distinction between external and internal efficiency is more fully considered in R.R. West, 'Two Kinds of Market Efficiency' (1975) 31 *Fin.Analysis J.*, p.30 (Nov.-Dec.).

5. Lorie and Hamilton, op cit n3, p23, supra, p270.

6. Fama, op cit n3, p23, supra, at 387.

7. P.A. Samuelson, 'Proof that Properly Anticipated Prices Fluctuate Randomly' (1965) 6 *Industrial Management Review* 41; B. Mandelbrot, 'Forecasts of Future Prices, Unbiased Markets and Martingale Models' (1966) 39 *J.Bus.* Special Supp242.

In general terms, this proof was based upon competition and agreement among investors. Strong competition among investors is assured by costless information and trading. These competitive forces and agreement among investors about the implications of new information cause prices to adjust instantaneously and in an unbiased manner to new information.

This is more apparent in an inefficient market when these conditions are absent. When information is costly to obtain and then does not flow freely, the first investors to obtain the information will capitalise on it. In the case of favourable information, their purchases will cause an initial price increase followed by further increases as more investors become aware of the information. In the adjustment period, prices do not fully reflect the information and there will be dependencies in stock price changes due to the series of successive increases. But if investors could obtain the information costlessly and agree on its implications, they could take prompt action and their transactions would result in an instantaneous price change and an unbiased reflection of the information in the share price.

'As long as transactors take account of all available information, even large transaction costs that inhibit the flow of transactions do not in themselves imply that when transactions do take place, prices will not "fully reflect" available information. Similarly (and speaking . . . somewhat loosely), the market may be efficient if "sufficient numbers" of investors have ready access to available information. And disagreement among investors about the implications of given information does not in itself imply market inefficiency unless there are investors who can consistently make better evaluations of available information than are implicit in market prices'[8].

Empirical research[9] has been concerned with whether prices fully reflect particular subsets of information. Whilst not independent[10], three categories of market efficiency have been distinguished.

First, the weak form states that prices fully reflect the information implied by the historical sequence of prices. Hence, chartists and others cannot consistently out-perform the market by predicting future price movements from studying past security prices. Prices would respond only to new information or occurrences.

Secondly, the semi-strong form asserts that prices fully reflect all publicly available information. Doubts about the traditional rationale of securities regulation are raised by the conclusion that trading strategies based on published information will not lead to abnormal returns because prices reflect new information before investors can trade on it. In particular, it suggests the regulatory authorities and disclosure requirements waste resources by requiring companies and investors to incur costs in providing information already reflected in prices and by attempting to obtain compliance.

Thirdly, the strong form purports to show that prices fully reflect all information, including unpublished information. In these circumstances, insiders cannot consistently out-perform the market because prices already reflect

8. Fama, op cit n3, p23, supra, at 387-388.
9. For empirical purposes, the general definition of an efficient market has been interpreted in terms of a fair game model. When security prices fully reflect all publicly available information, by implication price behaviour will be such that investment based on the information impounded in historical prices will be fair game. An investor's expected profit will be zero and above average gains cannot be expected by trading in an efficient market unless access is available to information which the market would react to if it were available.
The fair game model is a direct implication of the efficient markets theory. Where investment proves not to be fair game so that an investor's expected profit is positive, security prices have not reflected all publicly available information, especially that information enabling the investor to obtain above-average returns.
Moreover, the fair game model provides testable hypotheses of the efficient markets theory. Where price behaviour is such that investment based on publicly available information is fair game, this excludes success for trading systems based on previous price data.
Empirical testing of the efficient markets theory requires specification of the process of security price formation. An important category of these processes is the expected return theories according to which, conditional on some relevant information set, the equilibrium expected return on a security is a function of its risk. In particular, the capital asset pricing model states that in equilibrium the expected return on a security will equal the pure interest rate plus a premium which is a function of the security's systematic risk.
As there are potentially an infinite number of investors and investment strategies, the theory is not directly provable. But empirical studies can test whether security price and portfolio behaviour under specific test conditions are consistent with the theory.
10. When the market is efficient in the semi-strong form, it is also efficient in the weak form, because if price changes exhibit dependence by implication the price has reacted slowly to published information. Similarly, a market efficient in the strong form would also be efficient in the weak and semi-strong forms because the price would not otherwise capture all relevant information.

inside information. This assertion obviates the need to regulate insider dealing since if prices fully reflect all available information, non-insiders who deal at the market price will enjoy the equivalent of complete knowledge which includes the unpublished information known to the insider.

According to strong form efficiency, inside information confers an advantage only when the insider knows that no-one else has the information. But it is doubtful whether an insider can be sure that prices do not already fully reflect the information known to him[11]. When another person trades ahead of him, the market price will begin to impound the inside information.

On this analysis, when the market price fully reflects all available information, but an insider believes it does not, the insider's performance will be inferior to that of unsophisticated investors who trade on the assumption of strong form efficiency. His purchases will increase the price beyond that justified by the information and the insider will pay more than the security is worth. Except for his mistaken buying pressure, the price will fall to that dictated by the information. His loss will be increased by transaction costs.

Similarly, the performance of an investor who trades in reliance on a particular method of analysis will be inferior to that of the market insofar as the method is not as novel as he believes. More specifically:

'Any prediction model or method of financial analysis that becomes publicly known will quickly lose its usefulness because the value of the derived information (eg predictions) will already be reflected in security prices. Analytical tools are therefore self-destructive in efficient markets unless kept secret, and even then their useful life is relatively short. Therefore, ingenuity, originality and secrecy are necessary conditions for successful financial analysis. Efforts should be continually made to design new models and tools and to obtain access to new information sources. In short, the objective is to transform publicly available information to inside information by the application of original tools and techniques'[12].

Hence, strong-form efficiency suggests insider dealing should be encouraged. Rather than placing other investors at a disadvantage, insider dealing contributes to market efficiency and benefits non-insiders by increasing the flow of valuable information to the market.

In comparison with the US, research on other stock markets is limited. Differing structures and institutions mean US findings should not necessarily be imputed elsewhere. Whilst British tests have confirmed those findings in certain areas, any implications derived solely from US studies[13] in other untested areas are subjective opinions.

(i) The weak form.   Most weak form research has tested the extent of dependence of successive price changes. Relying on common statistical tools, such as serial correlation and runs analyses, US studies found only negligible departures from randomness.

---

11. Barry, op cit n19, p14, supra, p1334.
12. Lev, op cit n3, p23, supra, p242.
13. A.B. Moore, 'Some Characteristics of Changes in Common Stocks', in (ed.) P. Cootner, *The Random Character of Stock Market Prices* (1967) p139; E.F. Fama, 'The Behaviour of Stock Market Prices' (1965) 38 *J.Bus.*34.

In Britain, an early investigation[14] into commodity prices, including share prices, had found evidence that security prices followed a random walk. Subsequent serial correlation tests[15] of dependence revealed little or no serial correlation. Some data was also analysed by runs tests, though again provided no significant evidence of dependence[16]. But as a later study[17] found evidence of non-randomness in the share prices of small lightly-traded companies, this suggests there may be inefficiencies because small companies are less well researched.

Other weak form tests have concentrated on the profitability of trading rules. US studies[18] indicated that the returns were insufficient to meet transaction costs. Likewise, in Britain, it was found[19] that filter strategies[20] did not achieve above average returns.

(ii) The semi-strong form.   To examine whether prices fully reflect all publicly available information, semi-strong tests have focused on the speed of price adjustment to a specific kind of event. US research into the impact of new information on share prices has included announcements of capitalisation issues[1], the purchase or sale of large shareholdings[2], secondary market issues[3], discount rate changes[4], annual[5] and quarterly earnings announcements[6], accounting procedure changes[7] and earnings estimates by company officials[8].

14. M.G. Kendall, 'The Analysis of Economic Time Series Part I: Prices' (1953) 96 *J. Royal Statistical Society* 11.

15. R.A. Brealey, 'The Distribution and Independence of Successive Rates of Return from the British Equity Market' (1970) 2 *J.Bus.Fin.*No.2, p.29; S.W. Cunningham, 'The Predictability of British Stock Market Prices' (1973) 22 *Applied Statistics* 315; M.M. Dryden, 'A Statistical Study of U.K. Share Prices' (1970) 17 *Scottish Journal of Political Economy* 369.

16. Brealey and Dryden, op cit n15, supra.

17. D.H. Girmes and A.E. Benjamin, 'Random Walk Hypothesis for 543 Stocks and Shares Registered on the London Stock Exchange' (1975) 2 *J.Bus.Fin. and Accounting* 135.

18. S.S. Alexander, 'Price Movements in Speculative Markets; Trends or Random Walks', in Cootner, op cit n13, p25, supra, p119 and 'Price Movements in Speculative Markets; Trends or Random Walks No.2' in Cootner, op cit n13, p25, supra, p338; E.E. Fama and M. Blume, 'Filter Rules and Stock Market Trading Profits' (1966) 39 *J.Bus.* Special Supp 226; J.L. Evans, 'An Analysis of Portfolio Maintenance Strategies' (1970) 25 *J. Fin.* 561; P. Cootner, 'Stock Prices: Random vs. Systematic Changes', in Cootner, op cit n13, p25, supra, p231.

19. M.M. Dryden, 'Filter Tests of U.K. Share Prices' (1970) 1 *Applied Economics* 261.

20. These provide signals to buy and sell when share prices have moved a certain percentage away from a high or low point.

1. E.F. Fama, L. Fisher, M. Jensen and R. Roll,' The Adjustment of Stock Prices to New Information' (1969) 10 *Int'l.Econ.Rev.* 1 (Feb.); K.B. Johnson, 'Stock Splits and Price Change' (1966) 21 *J.Fin.*675

2. A. Krauss and H. Stoll, 'Price Impacts of Block Trading in the New York Stock Exchange' (1972) 27 *J.Fin.*569

3. M.S. Scholes, 'The Market for Securities: Substitution versus Price, Pressure and the Effects of Information in Share Prices' (1972) 45 *J.Bus.*179.

4. R. Waud, 'Public Interpretation of Federal Reserve Discount Rate Changes: Evidence on the Announcement Effect' (1970) 38 *Econometrica* 231.

5. R. Ball and P. Brown, 'An Empirical Evaluation of Accounting Income Number' (1968) 6 *J. Accounting Research* 159; W.H. Beaver, 'The Information Content of Annual Earnings Announcements' (1968) 6 *J. Accounting Research,* Supplement 67.

6. P. Brown and J.W. Kennelly, 'The Informational Content of Quarterly Earnings: An Extension and some Further Evidence' (1972) 45 *J.Bus.*403; R.G. May, 'The Influence of Quarterly Earnings Announcements on Investor Decisions as Reflected in Common Stock Price Changes' (1971) 9 *J. Accounting Research,* Supplement 119.

7. R.S. Kaplan and R. Roll, 'Investor Evaluation of Accounting Information; Some Empirical Evidence' (1972) 45 *J.Bus.*225; R. Ball, 'Changes in Accounting Techniques and Stock Prices' (1972) 10 *J.Accounting Research,* Supplement 1; T.R. Archibald, 'Stock Market Reaction to the Depreciation Switch-Back' (1972) 47 *Accounting Review* 22.

8. G. Foster, 'Stock Market Reaction to Estimates of Earnings per share by Company Officials' (1973) 11 *J. Accounting Research* 25.

These studies have concluded that publicly available information is either already anticipated in the share price[9] or the share price responds so quickly that investors cannot out-perform the market from their knowledge of the information. Though some discrepancies were found, they were considered sufficiently small not to violate the semi-strong form. The issue of whether prices react 'properly' to information is difficult to assess since experts may disagree on the propriety of the response, though early research focused on events where consensus among experts was most likely.

These conclusions, however, are subject to two limitations. First, there is contradictory evidence[10]. This includes studies that show apparently abnormal returns regarding low price earnings ratios[11] and the announcement of favourable earnings[12]. Yet many of the contradictory studies fail to allow for risk, information costs or transaction costs so it is unclear whether inefficiencies would remain after allowance for these factors[13]. Other anecdotal evidence[14] and sudden company failures are consistent with inefficiencies.

The second limitation concerns the simplifying assumptions made by the market model designed for empirical tests[15]. Though many assumptions have contributed to a better understanding of the market without undermining the operational validity of the setting they purport to describe, some require further consideration. In particular, the assumption of homogeneous expectations is recognised as a poor description of reality, but its impact on empirical tests has not been adequately examined.

Research in Britain has also provided support for the semi-strong form. Investigations into the effect of capitalisation issues[16] found they had no impact on share prices. Another analysis[17] revealed that inflation-adjusted earnings of companies had been discounted by the market. Results of tests[18] on the impact of a company's earnings announcements on the share prices of companies in similar industries showed that nearly all abnormal price adjustment occurred on announcement day, thereby confirming the efficient and rapid incorporation of new information into share prices. In addition, a study of investment

9. Eg, Ball and Brown, op cit n5, p26, supra; Brown and Kennelly, op cit n6, p26, supra. The anticipatory effect may be due to the availability of other information that enables investors to revise expectations about earnings. Though consistent with investors attempting to predict earnings, this effect is also consistent with earnings merely being correlated with those events that investors perceive to convey information. Beaver, op cit n20, p15, supra, p151.

10. Dyckman, Downes and Magee, op cit n3, p23, supra, Chapter 3.

11. S. Basu, 'The Investment Performance of Common Stocks in relation to their Price-Earnings Ratios: A Test of the Efficient Market Hypothesis' (1977) 32 *J.Fin.*663.

12. O. Joy, R. Litzenberger and R. McEnally, 'The Adjustment of Stock Prices to Announcements of Unanticipated Changes in Quarterly Earnings' (1977) 15 *J. Accounting Research* 207.

13. Dyckman, Downes and Magee, op cit n3, p23, supra, p81.

14. L. Bernstein, 'In Defence of Fundamental Analysis' (1975) 31 *Financial Analysts J.*57 (Jan/Feb)

15. Dyckman, Downes and Magee, op cit n3, p23, supra, pp81-82.

16. M.A. Firth, 'An Empirical Examination of the Applicability of Adopting the AICPA and NYSE Regulations on Free Share Distributions in the U.K.' (1973) 11 *J. Accounting Research* 16; Firth, 'The Incidence and Impact of Capitalisation Issues', Occasional Paper No.3 (1974); Firth, 'An Empirical Investigation of the Impact of the Announcement of Capitalisation Issues on Share Prices' (1977) 4 *J.Bus.Fin and Accounting* 47.

17. R.C. Morris, 'Evidence of the impact of inflation accounting on share prices' (1975) 5 *Accounting and Business Research* 82.

18. M.A. Firth, 'The impact of earnings announcements on the share price behaviour of similar type firms' (1976) 86 *Economic Journal* 296.

analysts[19] in leading newspapers found that, though they often provided a source of new information to the market[20], by the next trading day share prices had been marked up to a level which fully discounted the information so investors following such recommendations could not profit from the advice.

Further results[1] consistent with the semi-strong form were provided by the finding that after the release of financial results for 120 randomly selected listed companies in 1976-78, abnormal price movements and an above average level of shares traded and deals transacted were confined to the week of release. Though preliminary announcements were largely anticipated by the market, their release resulted in the provision of substantial additional information and had the greatest impact. Similarly, whilst some items had been disclosed in the preliminary announcement, the annual report and accounts provided further important information. In contrast, AGMs, usually held three to four weeks after release of the annual report and accounts, did not appear to provide an above average level of information. The interim report also seemed to give substantial information. A greater impact amongst smaller companies[2] was attributed to reduced analyst attention.

Similarly, analysis of declarations of large investment holdings in 1973[3] showed that the market discounted the bulk of new information quickly. Despite a long adjustment period, the market could be regarded as efficient since profitable trading rules could not be devised. But in the thirty days preceding the declaration, abnormal share price behaviour was observed. This was attributed to either an information leak or strong pre-announcement buying of investors building up their stakes, though the influence of either factor was not determined.

A similar pattern of price behaviour was revealed in two studies of take-overs and mergers. First, a study of brewery and distillery mergers during 1955-72[4] found that the market began to anticipate a merger at least three months before its announcement. During that period, abnormal share price returns averaged 27%, but as the sample contained only mergers later known to be successful no profitable trading rules could be devised and so these abnormal gains did not necessarily imply inefficiency. After the announcement, opportunities for abnormal returns were limited and any apparent gains would be wiped out by transaction expenses.

A second investigation into take-overs in 1973-74[5] found that after the announcement of a bid, the information was quickly and accurately incorpo-

19. M.A. Firth, 'The performance of share recommendations made by investment analysts and the effects on market efficiency' (1972) 4 *J.Bus.Fin.*58.

20. Often gained by interviews with company officials, op cit n19, supra, p65.

1. M.A. Firth, 'The Relative Information Content of the Release of Financial Results Data by Firms' (1981) 19 *J. Accounting Research* 521.

2. Similarly, in the US it was argued small companies might witness higher amounts of abnormal information from accounting reports than larger companies, C.E. Verrechia, 'On the Theory of Market Information Efficiency' (1979) 1 *J. Accounting and Economics* 77. Some empirical support was provided by E.B. Grant, 'Market Implications of Differential Amounts of Interim Information' (1980) 18 *J. Accounting Research* 255.

3. M.A. Firth, 'The Information Content of Large Investment Holdings' (1975) 30 *J.Fin.*1265. Under the C.A. 1967, ss 33-34 the disclosure threshold was then 10% and the notification period fourteen days. Following his findings, Firth advocated a lowering of the disclosure threshold and a reduction in the notification period. The 1967 requirements were amended by C.A. 1976, ss.26-27 to 5% and five days respectively.

4. J.R. Franks, J.E. Broyles and M.J. Hecht, 'An Industry Study of the Profitability of Mergers in the United Kingdom' (1977) 32 *J.Fin.*1513.

5. M.A. Firth, *Share Prices and Mergers* (1976).

rated in share prices, but abnormal price increases in offeree shares occurred before announcements. This pre-announcement behaviour might imply information leaks which, if confined to a small number of investors, would constitute a major inefficiency. But the investigation was unable to distinguish this source of inefficiency from possible heavy pre-announcement buying by the offeror[6]. These findings support the semi-strong form, subject to inefficiencies prior to announcements.

Though research in Britain is less extensive, there is nevertheless considerable evidence consistent with the semi-strong form. But there is evidence of inefficiencies for small companies and specific information. Futher research is required to determine their nature and who profits from them. The results are also subject to the same methodological limitations as US studies.

(iii) The strong form.   Tests of the strong form to see whether prices fully reflect all available information have centred on groups that might be expected to have superior information enabling them to out-perform the market. The groups chosen are investment advisers and managers, specialists and insiders.

INVESTMENT PORTFOLIOS.   US studies[7] have tried to determine whether fund managers generally have access to special information enabling them to generate 'abnormal' expected returns and whether some funds were better at uncovering such special information than others[8]. The results showed mutual funds did not out-perform randomly selected portfolios of similar risk and no consistently successful mutual funds were identified. Whilst possibly indicating fund managers do not use special information for the benefit of fund shareholders, the results have been interpreted as probably meaning that mutual fund managers compete in an efficient market with other portfolio managers of approximately equal competence.

Similar British studies found unit trusts did not out-perform the market and many had significantly inferior performance[9]. Surveys of pension funds[10] have also been regarded as evidence of a high level of efficiency since most showed no significant differences in performance. But as a few funds demonstrated above average performance, the possibility of superior performance was admitted. Likewise, a study of stockbrokers' recommendations[11] found no advantage could be derived from them, though if in unusual cases recommendations were

6. In the US, this problem was studied by A.J. Keown and J.M. Pinkerton, 'Merger Announcements and Insider Trading Activity: an Empirical Investigation' (1981) 36 *J.Fin.*855, see supra II. EMPIRICAL ASSESSMENT, **F. Empirical Studies.**
7. M. Jensen, 'The Performance of Mutual Funds in the period 1945-64' (1968) 23 *J.Fin.*389; W.F. Sharpe, 'Mutual Fund Performance' (1966) 39 *J.Bus.*Special Suppl.119; J.L. Treynor, 'How to Rate Management of Investment Funds' (1965) 43 *Harv.Bus.Rev.*63.
8. As no attempt was made to determine responsibility for high returns, the special information leading to high performance could be either keener insight into the implications of publicly available information than is implicit in market prices or monopolistic access to specific information. Hence, these tests are not strictly strong form tests.
9. C. Ward and A. Saunders, 'U.K. Unit Trust Performance 1964-74' (1976) 3 *J.Bus.Fin. and Accounting* No.4, p83; M.A. Firth, 'The investment performance of unit trusts in the period 1965-75' (1977) 9 *J. Money Credit and Banking* 597.
10. J.P. Holbrook, 'Investment performance of pension funds' (1977) 104 *J. Institute of Actuaries* No.425; P.H. Richards, 'Sharp performance among pension funds', *(1978) Investment Analyst No.51, p.9.*
11. M.D. Fitzgerald, 'A proposed characterisation of the UK brokerage firms and their effects on market prices and returns', *European Finance Association 1974 Proceedings* (1975).

not made public, bias could be introduced according to the availability and timing of recommendations. By highlighting the difficulty of beating the market, these studies challenged professionals' claims to superior selection.

SPECIALISTS.   Evidence of strong form inefficiency was provided by an analysis of market making on the New York Stock Exchange[12], which concerned floor traders' monopolistic access to information. In particular, the list of unexecuted orders[13] in a specialist's book was found to be important information about likely future price behaviour. This information is not available to the general public and the evidence indicates that specialists apparently use the information to generate monopoly profits. However, for non-specialists, such profits would be wiped out by transaction costs.

There is no comparable British research, but the above results were interpreted[14] as suggesting that jobbers on the Stock Exchange could also benefit from their special knowledge of trading levels in particular shares.

INSIDERS.   Whereas US studies have found inefficiencies as regards insider dealing[15], there is little comparable evidence for Britain. Semi-strong tests revealed inefficiencies with a potential for insider dealing, but apart from the study of investment analysts[16] which did not find evidence of insider dealing, further research is required to ascertain whether the potential for profit contained in other inefficiencies is exploited by or on behalf of insiders or their tippees.

Pending such research, it can be noted that as the semi-strong and strong forms are not independent, evidence of inefficiencies in the semi-strong form means that the market will not be efficient in the strong form. More widespread semi-strong inefficiencies in Britain thus point to probable inefficiencies exploited by insiders, though this assumption is unsupported by empirical evidence.

(iv) Implications.   Perfect efficiency creates a presumption against regulation since perfect efficiency is more likely than regulation to provide pareto-optimality. Conversely, when there are inefficiencies, regulation may be justified if it offsets those inefficiencies.

The empirical evidence of inefficiencies does not support the argument that disclosure requirements are superfluous. All available information does not reach the market prior to its required disclosure. Trading on insider reports has also enabled investors to out-perform the market.

Even when the market is efficient in the semi-strong form, disclosure may improve efficiency by inducing and providing confirmation of other disclosures. The knowledge that accurate information must be given under disclosure provisions reduces the incentive to delay disclosure of material information or to disclose misleading information[17]. Nevertheless, semi-strong efficiency sug-

12. V. Niederhoffer and M.F.M. Osborne, 'Market Making and Reversal on the Stock Exchange' (1966) 61 *J.Am.Statistical* A.897.
13. These may be either buy limit orders (to buy at a specified price or lower) or sell limit orders (to sell at a specified price or higher). These are distinguished from orders to buy or sell at market, which are at the lowest selling or highest buying price of another investor.
14. R.J. Briston, *Introduction to Accounting and Finance* (1981), p428.
15. See supra, II. EMPIRICAL ASSESSMENT, **F. Empirical Studies.**
16. Firth, opcit n19, p28, supra.
17. Barry, op cit n19, p14, supra, p1351.

gests that disclosure by listed companies should be directed primarily towards sophisticated investors.

However, any attempt to regulate insider dealing must take account of the distinction between corporate and market information in relation to a company's affairs[18], both of which may be material to investment decisions. The former emanates from within the company and directly relates to expected earnings or assets. Corporate information includes knowledge of a significant discovery, cancelled orders, a dividend increase or potential merger. In contrast, market information is external to the company and concerns information that will have an impact on the market price of a company's securities independently of any expected changes in the company's earnings or assets. Examples are government or administrative decisions and knowledge of such matters as a forthcoming take-over offer, broker's recommendation, sale of a large holding or a significant discovery by a competitor.

Although efficiency considerations support the regulation of insider dealing, these vary for corporate insiders, such as directors, officers and employees, and for others who, in the course of their occupation or profession or otherwise, acquire inside information. In the latter case, many are employed to generate market information and this gives rise to different efficiency considerations.

Through their control of the company, corporate insiders create an impression of the company's affairs which, when it becomes incorrect, it is the function of disclosure provisions to remedy. Having the information required for the correction, insiders can provide the relevant information as between themselves and outsiders at least cost, especially in a market where outsiders have little opportunity to deal directly with and make enquiries of insiders[19]. The cost of prohibiting insiders from dealing on inside information is the inhibition on their seeking personal profits from dealing. Unless insider dealing is an effective compensation device[20], such a cost is tolerable.

Whilst insiders' decisions to buy or sell provide information about a company's prospects and facilitate accurate revaluation of its securities, this advantage must be weighed against the loss of efficiency due to the incentives created for insiders to conceal information about the company whilst they engage in trading[1]. To the extent that insiders can control the release of information, a prohibition on dealing on inside information removes an impediment to its prompt disclosure and so increases market efficiency in pricing[2]. A rule allowing insiders to trade on inside information creates considerable temptation to disserve the company and its shareholders either immediately, as with a decision to delay or accelerate the release of information to serve their own trading or borrowing needs, or remotely, as by decisions on the conduct of company affairs and financial reporting.

18. A. Fleischer, Jr., R.H. Mundheim and J.C. Murphy, Jr., 'An Initial Inquiry into the Responsibility to Disclose Market Information' (1973) 121 *U.Pa.L.Rev.*798-802; Brudney, op cit n19, p14, supra, at 329-330 and Heller, op cit n19, p14, supra, at 522-523.
In take-overs and mergers, the distinction between market and corporate information was analysed by Fleischer, Mundheim and Murphy (at p810) as operating in the following manner; whilst knowledge of a bid is market information, knowledge of the potential shift in control of the offeree company is important to an evaluation of the offeree's investment worth and so can be characterised as corporate information; when the offeree's assets or earnings are material relative to the offeror, information concerning the contemplated bid is material corporate information about the offeror.
19. Brudney, op cit n19, p14, supra, at 345.
20. See infra, *2. Entrepreneurial compensation*.
1. R.A. Posner, *Economic Analysis of Law* (2nd ed., 1977), p308.
2. Brudney, op cit n19, p14, supra, at 334.

Apart from corporate insiders, when a person in the course of his occupation or profession or otherwise, acquires unpublished price-sensitive information which he is not lawfully permitted to disclose or which public traders cannot lawfully acquire, use of that information by him to his own advantage and the latter's disadvantage is likely to be counterproductive in economic effect[3]. A rational trader in a market who knows that the other party has an informational advantage will refrain from dealing or demand a risk premium. Where a market is believed to contain a large number of such persons, some investors will refrain from dealing and others will incur costs to avoid dealing with such persons or to overcome informational advantages corruptly. All such responses raise the cost of capital for a company and so impede optimal measure allocation.

Nevertheless, the retention of informational advantages in securities transactions for some traders is supported by the consideration that exploration for relevant corporate and market information is a service of value in the functioning of the market[4]. The sooner information relating to a company's assets or prospects is found, the more accurately it is appraised. In turn, the more immediately this results in a purchase or sale, the more precisely will a share price reflect the company's value. Hence, the market will function efficiently in terms of resource allocation and the opportunities for insider dealing will be reduced.

A return must be offered, however, to meet the costs incurred by outsiders in terms of expenditure of effort, time and money in research and of talent and training in analysis. This could be the opportunity to profit from being the first to discover the information. Thus, market efficiency will be enhanced by encouraging the pursuit and analysis of such information, particularly as the search is not merely for bargains, but also for developable values in companies and, in some instances, outsiders may have their own ideas about how to develop such latent values as alterations in production processes or marketing techniques.

2. Entrepreneurial compensation

Further economic arguments over insider dealing have focused on its use as a compensation device. The importance attached to Manne's central proposition that insider dealing is the appropriate form of compensation for entrepreneurs[5] can be gauged from his assertion that 'a rule allowing insiders to trade freely may be fundamental to the survival of our corporate system'[6]. This assertion assumes practical significance from indications that insider dealing has been used as such compensation[7].

The concept of the entrepreneur is borrowed from economic theorists[8] who viewed the entrepreneur as the 'organiser of uncertainties'[9] with the function of making new combinations of productive factors[10]. His particular task is to arrange these factors into combinations which produce new and hitherto

3. Ibid, at 356.
4. Ibid, at 341-343.
5. Manne, pp111-169.
6. Ibid, p110.
7. J. Slater, *Return to Go* (1977); C. Raw, *Slater Walker* (1977).
8. Mainly F.H. Knight, *Risk Uncertainty and Profit* (1921) and J.A. Schumpeter, *The Theory of Economic Development* (1934). Both are referred to in Manne, pp111-129.
9. Manne, p118.
10. Ibid, p116.

unpredictable results. Not confined to inventions, entrepreneurial activity comprises innovation in a broad sense and includes an imaginative merger or sales campaign or a method of financing.

The entrepreneurial role is distinguished both from the capitalist who risks his financial resources in contributing the goods required by the enterprise and from the manager whose skill is 'primarily a learnable mechanical activity'[11], since his task is to perform the predictable. While the same person may perform more than one of these roles, in theory there remains a 'profound distinction'[12] between them.

This distinction is reflected in the form of compensation considered appropriate for each role. Whereas the capitalist is compensated by interest payments or dividends, the manager receives a salary, prestige and fringe benefits, such as profit-sharing, bonuses, stock options and pension plans. But these are inappropriate rewards for the entrepreneur because they fail to provide an adequate incentive for further innovational activity. Rather, Manne's solution is to allow the entrepreneur to trade on his inside knowledge. As the process of innovation results in inside information, his reward is directly linked to the value of his contribution.

However, the validity of Manne's argument is questionable. First, as regards the concept of the entrepreneur, critics[13] have pointed to the difficulty of isolating and evaluating entrepreneurial activity. Whilst there may be conceptual differences between entrepreneurial and managerial functions, in practice they are usually 'inextricably intermingled'[14]. Other than in situations of conspicuous achievement, it is difficult to distinguish either innovators from managers or between creative and managerial activities. The difficulty is increased by the institutionalisation of innovational activity so that invention is often a matter for organised teams of employees and exploration for new resources has become part of the role expected of management. The entrepreneurial contribution in other business activities may be even more obscure: whilst advance knowledge of events, such as possible mergers, enables insiders to profit from the anticipated price movements occasioned by such developments, it is difficult to identify the entrepreneurial element in such transactions.

Secondly, the appropriateness of insider dealing as compensation for entrepreneurial activity is debatable. As a compensation device, it operates in an arbitrary manner with the amount received by the entrepreneur bearing no relation to services rendered. In particular, it enables insiders to avoid a loss through their knowledge of bad news and so rewards failure.

Rather than leaving the entrepreneur free to evaluate his own contribution, a preferable approach is for the company to evaluate people. In so doing, it will have regard to past performance and expected future performance. The availability of salary increases and promotion to other employees does not disqualify them from being adequate compensation for innovation and an incentive for continued innovation. When a company fails to reward the entrepreneurial contribution adequately, it risks losing the entrepreneur to a competitor.

A third objection lies in the difficulty of confining the rewards of insider dealing to entrepreneurs. As an innovation becomes institutionalised within a company, the information will be known to insiders generally and opportunities

11. Ibid, p115.
12. Ibid.
13. Eg. Painter, op cit n19, p14, supra, pp238-240; Hetherington, op cit n19, p14, supra, at 725-730; Mendelson, op cit n19, p14, supra, at 486-490.
14. Painter, op cit n19, p14, supra, p239.

for insider dealing become available to those without entrepreneurial functions. Manne's reply that it is 'extremely difficult to identify individuals performing the entrepreneurial functions or to know the precise moment at which an individual performs an entrepreneurial act'[15] would seem to confirm the elusiveness of the concept of the entrepreneur and in so doing, undermines the validity of his general thesis.

In an attempt to overcome this objection, he argues there is in effect a policing of inside information as a result of the interplay of the enlightened self-interest of individuals within the organisation. More specifically:

> 'Information is not a free good, and we should not assume, without more information than we now possess, that its distribution is generally capricious, arbitrary, random or uncontrolled. Rational, self-serving individuals will not blithely and willingly allow information of tremendous value to pass freely to individuals who have no valid claim upon it. The safe assumption is that individuals with power to control the flow of valuable information do so rationally and allocate it in a market-like system of exchange . . . The insider entrepreneur has more incentive than anyone else to prevent arbitrary pay-offs for he will lose more than anyone else'[16].

Yet his proposed policing devices raise doubts about both the practical implementation and desirability of his assertion. To maintain the secrecy of valuable information, he argues:

> 'It is possible to isolate bookkeepers and others who have access to valuable information until that information has been effectively exploited by others. When the first successful drill core was identified by the geologist of Texas Gulf Sulphur at Timmins, Ontario, he ordered all workers to remain in the camp while word of the find was sent back to the home office . . . If the employee objects to these seeming indignities there is no great social problem. He is free to seek another job where conditions are more to his taste'[17].

On the basis that insiders have the most to lose from indiscriminate disclosure, Manne considers they have an incentive to design appropriate policing devices. Furthermore:

> 'These devices may become so institutionalised that few overt actions to make information secure will be necessary. Strong moral strictures addressed to subordinate employees may have this effect. So may sound-proof walls and doors with locks'[18].

Defending these devices by reliance on strong moral strictures is unlikely to cut any ice with many employees who consider insider dealing morally indefensible. The argument that enlightened collective self-interest will ensure internal self-policing presupposes the existence of an elite committed to distributing inside information 'rewards' in a fair and orderly manner and fails to take account of the influence of power and prestige on behaviour. Moreover,

15. Manne, p156.
16. Ibid, p158.
17. Ibid, p168.
18. Ibid, p169.

reliance on doors with locks is as reprehensible as the 'police state tactics'[19] regarded as necessary for government policing of prohibited insider transactions which he asserts would require 'spying on social meetings, computerised friendships, total disclosure of all financial affairs and decisions, the necessity to explain every profit'[20].

Manne's response to these objections was to argue:

> 'It really does not make any difference who gets the unexploited information or whether we can pin the tag 'entrepreneur' on him. To reach the general conclusion of my thesis, it will be sufficient merely to posit that the flow of information to individuals without legal constraint is not random. About this there should be no argument, for if the flow is random, everyone has equal chance to benefit from it, and there would be no significant "insider" problem. Thus, presumably everyone agrees that in an unregulated or partially regulated information market, the flow of new information will to some extent be directed'[1].

He then proceeds to argue that when the flow of information is directed, the recipients will have the incentive to produce more information by furthering those developments which are the source.

However, he does not support his assertion with any evidence that entrepreneurs receive inside information. As distinct from being entrepreneurs, the recipients may rather have chanced to be in the right place at the right time.

Moreover, the ability to use inside information for personal trading is not necessary as a stimulus to produce the information[2]. Rather than being acquired for use in personal trading, information about the value of securities which is obtained in circumstances that preclude the recipient from disclosing it or suggest that the source will not disclose it to others, is generally sought and made available in the course of fulfilling other purposes, such as providing services or selling goods to the source of information or others. It will thus be produced without the stimulus of personal gains from trading and be useful for the purposes for which it was generated.

Permission to trade for their own benefit on the basis of such information also encourages insiders to disserve the company and its shareholders by mishandling company affairs or obscuring information. The likelihood of manipulation is increased since such permission gives an insider a personal interest in the impact of disclosure on the price of his company's shares. When insiders have control over the timing of disclosure, insider dealing invites timing to obtain maximum market response. Even without control over timing, insiders' advance knowledge of the timing and content of disclosure may encourage them to time their buying so as to affect price.

Accordingly, Manne's proposition that insider dealing provides appropriate compensation for entrepreneurs is incorrect. Rather, inefficiencies in the pricing mechanism are compounded by the inefficiency of insider dealing as a device for compensating entrepreneurs. The inappropriateness of insider dealing as entrepreneurial compensation is further underlined by equity considerations.

19. Ibid, p165.
20. Ibid.
1. Manne, op cit, n19, p14, supra at 582.
2. Brudney, op cit n19, p14, supra, at 356.

B. Equity issues

The main impetus for insider dealing regulation has stemmed from considerations of equity. Prominent among these have been a concern about ethical standards and the perceived relationship between insider dealing and public confidence in the securities markets. Against this background there have been various formulations of the fairness considerations that support insider dealing regulation. As alternative forms of regulation have different implications for the distribution of wealth between insiders and other investors, the insights provided by the theories of economic regulation will be considered prior to analysis of the choice of insider dealing regulation.

1. Ethical standards

The pressure to regulate insider dealing owed much to public disquiet about standards of conduct in business activities. In well-publicised take-over bids, attention was drawn to incidents involving unlawful loans to directors, asset stripping and insider dealing.

The concern with ethical standards was expressly recognised by both the Council for the Securities Industry[3] and the Justice Report[4] when they argued 'it is contrary to good business ethics that a man holding a position of trust in a company should use confidential information for his personal benefit'. On this basis, the CSI termed insider dealing a 'reprehensible' practice[5]. This view was echoed in descriptions of insiders by the Panel as 'dishonourable men'[6] and by its former Chairman as having 'betrayed ethical principles which forbid "insider" dealings'[7].

In turn, this concern was reflected in the courts where as regards liability for negligence, a more rigorous duty of care was imposed on professional persons, such as accountants and solicitors. Whilst similar standards of care are not required of company directors, the courts have nevertheless more readily acknowledged the problems of minority shareholders.[8]

This development has also been paralleled by a movement towards professionalisation[9]. Traditionally, the professions were limited to the Church, armed services, law and medicine. More recently there has been a trend for people in other occupations to aspire to professional status and to attempt to turn the occupation into a profession and themselves into professional people. Though the extent of professionalisation varies widely, members of professional groups tend to become attached to their professional association and codes of conduct.

3. Council for the Securities Industry, 'Statement on Insider Dealing' (June, 1981), para4, published as an appendix to its Report on the Year to 31st March, 1981.
4. Justice, 'Insider Trading' (1972), para3.
5. CSI, 'Department of Trade Inspections and Prosecutions' (1979), para40.
6. Statement by the City Panel on Stock Exchange Dealings in the course of a take-over situation, 2nd April, 1971 (Norbury).
7. Statement by Lord Shawcross, Chairman of the City Panel on Take-overs and Mergers, 26th October, 1972.
8. *Wallersteiner v Moir (No2)* [1975] 2 WLR 389; *Clemens v Clemens Bros Ltd* [1976] 2 All.ER.268; *Daniels v Daniels* [1978] 2 All ER 89.
9. (ed) H.M. Vollmer and D.L. Mills, *Professionalisation* (1966); A.M. Carr-Saunders and P.A. Wilson, *The Professions* (1933).

In turn, these have important consequences for aspects of business activity. For participants in the securities markets, many codes of conduct now contain insider dealing provisions[10].

2. Public confidence

Public confidence in the securities markets is generally regarded as an essential condition for the fulfilment of their role in the economy. More specifically, people will more readily invest in securities when the market operates fairly and efficiently[11]. In this context, it is argued that insider dealing regulation enhances public confidence and results in increased investor participation[12].

In the US, the view that investor confidence had been undermined to the extent of requiring the introduction of extensive disclosure requirements and insider dealing restrictions has been challenged[13]. Nevertheless, Congress believed such requirements were a prerequisite to the restoration of public confidence after the market disasters of 1929 and 1930 and revelations in subsequent investigations[14]. Apart from the prejudice to investors, it was informed that the suspicion created by the existence of fraud and insider dealing discouraged the entry of investors into the market and so raised the cost of capital.

In Britain, the regulatory agencies have emphasised the importance of fairness to public confidence. Apart from protecting investors, the Stock Exchange considers its rules 'above all, maintain public confidence in the ethical and financial integrity of the stock market'[15]. In addition, the Panel has stated:

> 'One of the principal objectives of any regulatory authority must be to maintain a securities market in which shareholders and potential shareholders have confidence that when they deal with their investments they will receive fair treatment. If this confidence is not maintained people will cease to invest through the market. Fair dealing and equal treatment as between shareholders must exist and be seen to exist and it must be possible to carry out transactions with speed and certainty'[16].

10. The professional associations having codes of conduct with insider dealing provisions are outlined in Chapter 2, The Regulatory Framework, and the contents of such codes considered in Chapter 6, Administrative Regulation.
11. *Consumer and Corporate Affairs Canada, Proposals for a Securities Market Law for Canada, Vol 2 Commentary* (1979), p59.
12. R.A. Schotland, 'Unsafe at Any Price: A Reply to Manne, Insider Trading and the Stock Market' (1976) 53 *Va.L.Rev.*1425 at 1440-1442; W.H. Painter, *The Federal Securities Code and Corporate Disclosure* (1979), pp249-250; L. Loss, 'The Fiduciary Concept as Applied to Trading by Corporate "Insiders" in the US' (1970) 33 *MLR* 34 at 36.
13. G. Benston, *Corporate Financial Disclosure in the U.K. and U.S.A.* (1976), p19; G. Benston, 'Required Disclosure and the Stock Market, An Evaluation of the Securities Exchange Act of 1934' (1973) 63 *Am.Econ.Rev.*132; G. Stigler, *The Citizen and the State, Essays on Regulation* (1975), p.114.
14. A.G. Anderson, 'The Disclosure Process in Federal Securities Regulation; A Brief Review' (1974) 25 *Hastings L.J.* 311; J.M. Landis, 'The Legislative History of the Securities Act of 1933' (1959) 28 *Geo. Wash. L.Rev.*29; H.R. Rep.No.85 73d Cong., 1st. Sess.2-4 (1933); H.R. Rep.No.1383, 73d Cong., 2d Sess. 4-5; S. Rep.No.1455, 73d Cong., 2d Sess.153 (1934); S. Rep.No.792, 73d Cong., 2d Sess.12-13 (1934).
15. N. Goodison (Chairman of the Stock Exchange), 'The Regulatory Role of the Stock Exchange' (1981 Stockton Lecture), p4.
16. The Panel on Take-overs and Mergers, *Supervision of the Securities Market* (1975), p1.

British regulators have also accepted the relationship between public confidence and insider dealing. Discussing insider dealing proposals, the Department of Trade stated: 'the successful operation of the system demands a high degree of confidence in fair dealing on the Stock Exchange and, indeed, securities generally, whether or not publicly quoted'[17]. The CSI also considered insider dealing 'damages public and indeed international confidence in the securities market'[18]. Similarly, whilst regarding much of the disquiet about the alleged extent of insider dealing as 'emotive and unjustified', the Panel commented: 'its very existence is damaging to the confidence upon which a securities market must be founded'[19].

Moreover, in an early prosecution under the Companies Act 1980, the judge endorsed the view that insider dealing regulation was justified by the need to maintain investor confidence. He considered:

> 'the mischief of offences of this type tends, quite wrongly, to put the integrity of the entire City at risk. People begin to wonder if they can really trust the institutions in the City'[20].

A lack of empirical studies as to why investors participate and others refrain from investing in the securities markets makes it difficult to determine the factors affecting investor participation. Relevant factors probably include economic, business and market conditions, companies' earnings trends and other matters pertinent to securities evaluation[1].

Empirical evidence suggests many investors trade on inside information and expect others to do so[2]. Indeed, the growth in institutional investment may be assisted by small investors' awareness of their informational disadvantages. There is also no evidence that insider regulation has introduced to the market any investors who may previously have been discouraged by insider dealing. The relationship between insider dealing and public confidence may thus be more tenuous than supposed[3].

3. Fairness

Both the concern with ethical standards and the perceived relationship between insider dealing and public confidence form the background to the development of various formulations of underlying fairness considerations. As implementation of broad anti-fraud requirements in the US has given rise to more critical examination of fairness considerations, reference will largely be

17. Department of Trade, 'Company Law Reform', Cmnd.5391 (1973), para15.
18. Council for the Securities Industry, 'Statement on Insider Dealing' (June, 1981), para4, published as an appendix to the Report on the Year to 31st March, 1981.
19. The Panel on Take-overs and Mergers, Report on the Year ended 31st March, 1973, p9.
20. Judge Alistair Troup, cited by B.A.K. Rider, 'The first case of secondary insider dealing' (1982) 4 *Co. Law* 117.
1. H. Heller, '*Chiarella,* SEC Rule 14e-3 and *Dirks:* Fairness versus Economic Theory' (1982) 37 *Bus.Law 517* at 555-556.
2. SECTION II, EMPIRICAL ASSESSMENT.
3. E.S. Herman, 'Equity Funding, Inside Information and the Regulator' (1973) 21 *UCLA Rev.*1 at 17; D.D. Prentice, 'Insider Trading' (1975) *CLP* 83 at 100-101; Wedderburn in (ed.) L. Loss, *Multinational Approaches – Corporate Insiders,* p70; J.F. Barry, III. 'The Economics of Outside Information and Rule 10b-5' (1981) 129 *U.Pa.L.Rev.*1307 at 1352-1353; Heller, op cit n1, supra, at 555-556; H. Demetz, 'Perfect Competition, Regulation and the Stock Market', p16 in (ed.) H.G. Manne, *Economic Policy and the Regulation of Corporate Securities* (1969).

made to that debate.

In an early contribution in Britain, prior to the expansion of administrative requirements and recent developments in civil liability, the Jenkins Committee recommended enactment of a statement of the general fiduciary duty of a director[4]. Its purpose was to:

> 'protect a person – whether or not a member of the company or companies concerned – who suffers loss because a director has taken unfair advantage at his expense of a particular piece of confidential information about the company or any other company'[5].

A wider view was taken by the Department of Trade when it endorsed 'the general desirability of ensuring equality of information to all potential or actual investors' and 'the need to ensure so far as practically possible that the market operates freely on the basis of equality between buyer and seller'[6]. Though extending beyond directors, legislation has fallen short of achieving this objective.

In the US, the range of persons covered by anti-fraud requirements clearly includes corporate insiders, such as directors, officers and employees. Their disclosure obligations stem from fiduciary principles. The rationale of such application of anti-fraud requirements was analysed by the SEC in the Cady Roberts case[7] as resting on two main elements:

> 'First the existence of a relationship giving access, directly or indirectly, to information intended to be available only for a corporate purpose and not for the personal benefit of anyone, and second, the inherent unfairness involved where a party takes advantage of such information knowing it is unavailable to those with whom he is dealing'[8].

According to this analysis, insiders have acquired the information at the company's expense and in order to conduct its business for the benefit of all shareholders, irrespective of personal rewards from dealing. As well as efficiency considerations[9], this analysis has been interpreted by Brudney as based on both the narrow premise of fidelity and the broader concept of equity[10].

As regards fidelity considerations, insiders are not entitled to an informational advantage in dealing with shareholders because the insiders acquired the information as agents or fiduciaries of the shareholders whilst pursuing the latters' business. Shareholders are equally entitled to the information or at least not to be disadvantaged by the lack of such information when dealing with their agents. In these circumstances, an insider purchase is made at the expense of selling shareholders to whom the information belongs. The case of a sale should not alter an insider's legal obligations as to the use of corporate information in the transaction. An insider is no more justified in resorting to concealment to induce a person to become, than to cease to be, his beneficiary.

---

4. Report of the Company Law Committee (Chairman: Lord Justice Jenkins), Cmnd.1749 (1962), paras99(a) and (b).
5. Ibid, para89.
6. The Department of Trade, 'Company Law Reform', Cmnd.5391 (1973), para15.
7. *In re Cady, Roberts & Co.*, 40 SEC 907 (1961).
8. Ibid, at 912.
9. See supra **A. Efficiency issues,** 1. *Market failure,* (c.) MARKET EFfiCIENCY, (iv.) *Implications.*
10. Brudney, op cit n19, p14, supra, at 344-346.

The broader equity considerations relate to the inability of other investors to erode insiders' informational advantages lawfully. Other investors cannot lawfully obtain material corporate information from the company except with the company's consent (which the insider knows will not be given). In such circumstances, insider dealing is considered 'unfair' because the insider has a lawful monopoly on access to the information:

> 'The unfairness is not a function merely of possessing more information – outsiders may possess more information than other outsiders by reason of their diligence or zeal – but of the fact that it is an advantage which cannot be competed away since it depends upon a lawful privilege to which an outsider cannot acquire access'[11].

These considerations apply both when the information is market or other information and irrespective of whether the information is acquired through being an insider:

> 'The duty not to deal with their beneficiaries in trust assets on the basis of informational advantages about the trust does not rest on how they obtained the informational advantage. In part the stricture derives from dependence and expectation. And in part it prophylactically avoids the necessity for policing the evanescent line which separates information obtained as an insider and information not so obtained'[12].

But implementation of the fiduciary principle in dealings between fiduciaries and their beneficiaries extends the range of persons subject to anti-fraud requirements beyond such corporate insiders. These others will be considered in turn[13].

The fiduciary principle also applies to companies. Hence, when a company sells its securities, neither management nor existing shareholders are permitted to benefit from non-disclosure of material information to purchasers. Likewise, when it buys its own securities, it has no right to overreach some shareholders so that others benefit from non-disclosure. The fiduciary duty is based on the principle that all shareholders are entitled to equal access to information from the company when it deals with them.

A further application of the fiduciary principle concerns certain tippees. Like insiders, such persons as accountants, lawyers and financial advisers are given corporate information for corporate purposes and are remunerated other than by expected personal rewards from dealing. By analogy, any person to whom inside information is either sold or given is also included. In the former case, a purchaser has the same informational advantage as an insider. In the latter case, it may be assumed that the information is given for value, whether in the form of cash, reciprocal information, prestige or status. Whether the information is sold or given, it is the selective disclosure which is regarded as objectionable. But this objection does not apply to persons such as analysts when it is apparent from the manner of disclosure that a corporate insider does not treat the information as being for his own personal benefit and inaccessible to public investors.

In addition, the fiduciary principle extends to market professionals who deal

11. Ibid, at 346.
12. Ibid.
13. Ibid, at 346-349.

with their clients. In these circumstances, fiduciary responsibilties are derived not only from the formers' privileged access to information, but it is also based on a felt need to protect those who rely on professional advice.

However, wider formulations have also received support in the US. Apart from the SEC chairman's emphasis on the concept of 'inherent unfairness' in the *Cady Roberts* case[14], in another case the court endorsed the SEC assertion that Rule 10b-5[15] is 'based in policy on the justifiable expectation of the securities market place that all investors trading on impersonal exchanges have relatively equal access to material information'[16].

Yet it was also recognised that if intended to eliminate all informational advantages, the equal access approach would inhibit the research and analysis required for market efficiency[17]. This recognition resulted in attempts to reformulate the underlying fairness considerations.

An early article[18] concerned with the concept of a duty to the market and the extension of Rule 10b-5 to persons not covered by traditional fiduciary concepts, suggested a modified fairness approach that would require balancing efficiency values against equality values involved by a specific market activity. As to the fairness of trading on superior knowledge, this approach would require 'in each instance a careful examination of the role of the party whose actions are complained of, the nature of the alleged wrongdoing and the expectation of the aggrieved parties'[19]. As this approach would substitute vagueness for clear

14. 40 SEC 907 at 912 (1961).
15. Though it does not expressly refer to insider trading, the main control of insider trading in the US has been Rule 10b-5 promulgated under s10(b) of the Securities Exchange Act 1934. These provide:
(10) It shall be unlawful for any person, directly or indirectly, by the use of any means or instrumentality of interstate commerce or of the mails, or of any facility of any national securities exchange . . .
(b) To use or employ, in connection with the purchase or sale of any security not so registered, any manipulative or deceptive device or contrivance in contravention of such rules and regulations as the Commission may prescribe as necessary or appropriate in the public interest for the protection of investors . . .
(5) It shall be unlawful for any person, directly or indirectly, by the use of any means or instrumentality of interstate commerce, or of the mails, or of any facility of any national securities exchange,
(a) to employ any device, scheme or artifice to defraud,
(b) to make any untrue statement of a material fact or to omit to state a material fact necessary in order to make the statements made, in the light of the circumstances under which they were made, not misleading, or
(c) to engage in any act, practice, or course of business which operates or would operate as a fraud or deceit upon any person, in connection with the purchase or sale of any security.
In regulating purchases of securities, Rule 10b-5 supplemented s17 of the Securities Act 1933 which only applied to sales. Rule 10b-5 may be invoked both by the SEC in criminal, equitable or administrative proceedings and by private parties either personally, as a class or derivatively against those in breach. There is now an extensive body of case law under Rule 10b-5.
16. *SEC v Texas Gulf Sulphur Co.*, 401 F.2d833, 848 (2d.Cir.1968), cert.denied, 394 US 976 (1969).
17. Uncertainties remain as to the mechanism by which relevant information is reflected in security prices and the extent to which denial of trading rewards for discovering new information will curtail its pursuit. In theory, a system of mandated disclosure, combined with a requirement to equalise relevant information among traders, may produce information that makes security prices reflect underlying values as much as a system rewarding discovery values. Though required sharing will eliminate the reward for discovering new information, the information will be provided by the mandated disclosure system and accompanying anti-fraud provisions. But lack of empirical evidence makes it difficult to assess the cost benefits of the respective systems. Brudney, op cit n19, p14, supra, at 342.
18. A. Fleischer, Jr., R.H. Mundheim and J.C. Murphy, Jr., 'An Initial Inquiry into the Responsibility to Disclose Market Information' (1973) 121 *U.Pa.L.Rev.*798.
19. Ibid at 822.

standards, it was argued the application of the fairness approach should require disclosure only when imposed by specific legislation or a 'special relationship' between the parties.

Subsequently, Brudney[20] has urged a general rule which forbids the exploitation of unerodable informational advantages that one trader has over another. Although anti-fraud requirements are designed to implement the fiduciary principle in dealings between fiduciaries and their beneficiaries whether involving insiders and shareholders or persons having a 'special relationship', he asserts that they are not so confined but, being based on a broader premise, extend to armslength relationships:

> 'Another – indeed the essential – element which makes an informational advantage unusable by those who possess it in dealing with those who do not is the inability of the latter to overcome it lawfully, no matter how great their diligence or large their resources'[1].

When formulated in terms of equal access to material information, this does not require equality or sharing of information, but the denial of an informational advantage to those either precluded by law from public disclosure or who, though not so precluded, obtain it from a source that will not make it public so that the public cannot lawfully obtain it. Its rationale is based on the Cady Roberts concept of the 'inherent unfairness' of using such informational advantages. This formulation also recognises that the need to encourage the private pursuit of information imposes limits on the persons and information subject to regulation[2].

This formulation was consistent with an exception for a trader's own intentions[3] and hence at variance with SEC proposals whose effect would be to extend take-over disclosure requirements, which imposed a disclosure obligation on a potential offeror only when he had acquired 5% of securities in the intended offeree, to a potential offeror's initial acquisitions. The SEC argued that before the bid announcement, leaks and disparities between 'insiders' (designees of the potential offeror) and the public could cause market disruption, as a result of artificial demand for offeree securities, and the stampede effect that take-over requirements were designed to prevent. As he considered the SEC was motivated by the apparent inconsistency of applying traditional anti-fraud requirements to agents, such as printers, yet permitting the principal to exploit his informational advantages over the same sellers who are protected against the agent, Brudney criticised the SEC's reliance on the special demands of the take-over procedure to justify such extension.

Like other anti-fraud measures, take-over requirements seek to protect public investors from use of informational advantages by bidders, agents or allies for their own trading benefits during the same period. But such protection did not require early disclosure of the bidder's intentions. Whilst disclosure of initial acquisitions minimises opportunities for cheating by agents, any saving to the bidder is marginal. Moreover, without the rule the potential offeror has an interest both in keeping market prices low and in an orderly market before the bid announcement. In these circumstances, denial of the informational

20. Brudney, op cit n19, p14, 7 supra.
1. Ibid at 354.
2. See supra, **A. Efficiency Issues,** *1. Market failure,* (c.) MARKET EFFICIENCY, *iv. Implications* and *2. Entrepreneurial compensation.*
3. Brudney, op cit n19, p14, supra, at 371-376.

advantage to the potential offeror in respect of his own intentions is 'a material interference with the legitimate enhancement of market efficiency in pricing securities'[4].

However, the Supreme Court rejected the analysis based on the unerodable informational advantage and adopted a more restrictive interpretation in *US v Chiarella*[5]. This was a criminal prosecution for wilful breach of Rule 10b-5 by a printer's employee who, having acquired inside information about a prospective bid and offer price in the preparation of take-over documents, purchased shares in the offeree before the bid announcement. Reversing the Second Circuit's judgment, the Supreme Court declined to hold there was 'a general duty between all participants in market transactions to forgo actions based on material non-public information'[6]. In the absence of specific legislation or the existence of a fiduciary relationship, there was no duty to disclose. Whilst such a duty may exist between insiders and the company's shareholders, it did not arise between complete strangers dealing through impersonal markets.

The Supreme Court was not unanimous. One dissenting opinion argued that the theft of non-public information was in itself sufficient to trigger an 'absolute duty'[7] to disclose. Another considered that a duty of disclosure was imposed whenever 'structural disparity in access to material information' provided investors with a trading advantage that could not be duplicated by others through legal means.[8]

The American Law Institute's Federal Securities Code makes it unlawful to trade on the basis of any non-public information in the securities of an issuer as to which the trader is an insider or tippee of an insider, whether the information be inside information emanating from the issuer or outside information obtained from other sources[9].

In his commentary, Loss states:

'It is hard to find justification today for imposing a fiduciary's duty of affirmative disclosure on an outsider who is not a 'tippee' ... Section 1603 reflects no universally applicable theory of market egalitarianism'[10].

Though he advocated a new category of quasi-insiders to cover persons with special access to non-corporate information, he felt its development should await judicial decisions.

Some development occurred in the Second Circuit's judgment in *Chiarella* with the development of the market insider concept: 'a financial printer ... is as inside the market itself as one could be'[11]. The court emphasised that 'betting on a "sure thing" is anathema to the ideal of "fair and honest markets" established as the foundation' of securities regulation[12]. But this approach was rejected by the Supreme Court.

In response to the Supreme Court decision in *Chiarella*, the SEC exercised its rule-making authority under section 14(e) of the Williams Act to promulgate a

4. Ibid at 375.
5. 588 F.2d.1358 (2d.Cir.1978), revsd 445 US 222 (1980).
6. 445 US 222, at 233.
7. Ibid at 240.
8. Ibid at 251.
9. S1603.
10. Ibid, Comment 2(j).
11. 588 F.2d.1358 (2d.Cir.1978), at 1364.
12. Ibid at 1362.

disclose-or-abstain rule concerning take-overs[13]. Subject to certain exceptions, Rule 14e-3 applies a disclose-or-abstain provision to the possession of material information relating to a take-over where the person knows or has reason to know that the information is non-public and was received directly or indirectly from the offeror, the offeree, any affiliates or any person acting on behalf of either company.

The narrower approach of the Supreme Court, as compared to the SEC, was also apparent in the *Dirks* case[14] which underlined the tension between the concern for fairness in the distribution and availability of inside information and the concern for market efficiency. Initially, the SEC censured Dirks, who was an investment adviser, for breach of Rule 10b-5 when he took advantage of inside information obtained from a former employee of Equity Funding Corporation, investigated the company, tried to inform the SEC and told his clients who sold. The inside information related to a fraud against insurance companies through the sale of false insurance policies to reinsurers, whose effect was to inflate falsely the published earnings and assets of Equity Funding. After heavy sales of Equity Funding securities and a sharp drop in their price, trading was suspended and the company subsequently filed a petition for reorganisation.

Reversing the SEC and a court of appeal's decision upholding the SEC, the Supreme Court decided that the SEC had been wrong to censure Dirks. It also added that the SEC's rigid view on insider dealing regulation threatened to impair private initiative in uncovering violations. Market analysts often acquired information from corporate officers and passed this on to clients. It was in the nature of this type of information and of the markets that such information could not be made available simultaneously. Imposition of insider dealing liability solely because a person knowingly received material private information from an insider and dealt on it could have an inhibiting influence on the role of market analysts which the SEC had acknowledged to be necessary to the preservation of a healthy market.

However, the controversy over the precise formulation of underlying fairness considerations is due to the wider implications of insider dealing. Through its impact on security prices and price changes, insider dealing reallocates resources and so has effects on the redistribution of wealth between insiders and other investors.

C. Theories of economic regulation

As these effects have a different impact on the various interest groups, the selection of a particular form of insider dealing regulation is a social choice. The choice among alternative forms of regulation involves bargaining between interest groups and also within interest groups, such as sophisticated and unsophisticated investors who may prefer different types of regulation. In the debate on regulation, they voice their opinions through political and economic channels.

In this context, economists have advanced two main theories to explain that the existence of economic regulation. Initially, the public interest theory asserted that regulation was introduced for the protection and benefit of the

13. H. Heller, '*Chiarella,* SEC Rule 14e – 3 and *Dirks:* Fairness versus Economic Theory' (1982) 37 *Bus.Law* 517 at 541; J.E. Siegel, 'US Insider Trading Prohibition in Conflict with Swiss Bank Secrecy' (1983) *4 JCCLSR* 353 at 355.
14. Heller, op cit n13, supra, at 546; *The Times*, 7th July, 1983.

public or large subsections thereof. But disillusion with regulatory systems led to development of the capture theory, which views regulation as an attempt by competing interest groups to acquire economic privileges: 'as a rule, regulation is acquired by the industry and is designed and operated primarily for its benefit'[15].

1. The public interest theory

Based on economics, the public interest theory[16] asserts that regulation is supplied in response to public demand for the correction of inefficient or inequitable market practices. Such market failures arise when the free market produces excessive or insufficient amounts of a product or services and at prices which are either too high or too low.

Examples of market failure are natural monopoly, pollution and safety. In the financial markets, the free market is regarded as being readily susceptible to fraud, manipulation and deception.

The theory is based on two assumptions. First, economic markets are fragile and prone to operate inefficiently. Secondly, regulation is assumed to operate without cost. On the basis of such assumptions, it was argued that regulation was a response to public demand to remedy inefficiencies and inequities in the operation of the free market. The existence of a market imperfection in itself provided the justification for regulatory provisions which were assumed to operate effectively and costlessly.

However, empirical research has not found any positive correlation between regulation and the existence of external costs or benefits or monopolistic market structure. The assumption that regulation is an effective and costless investment to alter market behaviour has also been rejected. Empirical evidence indicates that specific regulatory programmes cannot be explained on the basis that they contribute towards efficiency or equity.

The inadequacy of the public interest theory to describe the operation of regulation in practice has resulted in two viewpoints. One rejects the correction of market imperfections as the goal of regulation[17]. Instead, regulation is regarded as part of a political-economic process in which competing groups seek to promote their own interests and reallocate wealth amongst themselves. As regulatory agencies thus perform the same role as legislators with power to tax and confer benefits, the agencies are as subject to political pressures.

The other considers regulatory failures are attributable to legal and procedural problems which can be remedied by reforms. Though instituted for bona fide public purposes, this view accepts:

> 'nearly all regulation authorities, however structured and wherever lodged, are subject to generally similar criticisms; that their procedures are cumbersome, that they do not make their policies sufficiently clear and that they tend to be overly responsive to the interests of the industries they regulate'[18].

15. G.J. Stigler, 'The Theory of Economic Regulation' (1971) 2 *Bell J. Econ. and Management Sci*.316.
16. The public interest theory is discussed more fully by: R.A. Posner, 'Theories of Economic Regulation' (1974) 5 *Bell J. Econ. and Management Sci*.335; S.M. Phillips and J.R. Zecher, *The SEC and the Public Interest* (1981).
17. See *infra 2. The capture theory.*
18. R. Noll, *Reforming Regulation* (1971), p.viii.

In particular, disclosure requirements have been criticised for still lacking a clear goal, thereby raising difficulties in assessing their effectiveness and the desirability of changes[19]. Moreover, the latitude conferred on regulators makes them vulnerable to political and economic pressures from the legislature and other interest groups, especially in the regulated industry.

The proposed reforms are based on improving performance by a clearer definition of regulatory goals. More specific aims than protection of the public interest would facilitate both assessment of performance and accountability and also ease the pressures from interest groups.

Yet even as reformulated[20], the market failure theory overlooks evidence that socially undesirable results of regulation may be sought by interest groups in the industry. In particular, regulation may be sought where unregulated competition is considered 'excessive'. There is also little evidence of mismanagement by regulatory agencies or any satisfactory explanation why they might be expected to be less effective than other organisations.

When viewed as an honest but unsuccessful attempt to promote the public interest, the public interest theory is more plausible in the light of two other factors. First, many of the tasks assigned to regulatory agencies are intractable problems. Hence, the agencies' failure and the resulting inefficiencies are not surprising. Yet this fails to explain why such tasks are assigned to agencies. Secondly, the cost of effective legislative supervision increases with output[1]. As the costs of bargaining implicit in legislation rise rapidly with the number of bargainers, the legislature cannot respond efficiently to a heavier workload by an increased membership. This leads to greater delegation to agencies and less supervision of their activities. It also suggests the 'life cycle' theory whereby an agency is created when there is a strong legislative interest in the problem, but in time the need to deal with other problems means the legislature is less able to monitor the agency. But the life cycle theory approximates to versions of the capture theory.

Nevertheless, even allowing for these factors, the public interest theory provides no indication of how perception of the public interest is given legislative expression, particularly when in conflict with private interests. As a result, the absence of regulatory systems which deal with real market failures cost-effectively has led to further reformulations with emphasis on the effect of regulation on resource allocation and the process of choice of regulatory systems.

2. The capture theory

Drawing on a wide range of disciplines, the capture theory takes several forms. Marxist and radical versions argue that since big business controls social institutions, it controls regulatory agencies. Yet this fails to explain why much economic regulation is sponsored by liberal groups and opposed by industry.

A version supported by political scientists[2] stresses the importance of interest groups and argues that in time regulatory agencies become dominated by the regulated industries. But it does not suggest why producers rather than consum-

19. H. Kripke, *The SEC and Corporate Disclosure: Regulation in Search of a Purpose* (1979); L. Sealy, 'The "Disclosure" Philosophy and Company Law Reform' (1981) 2 *Co. Law* 51.
20. Posner, op cit n16, p45, supra, at 337-341.
1. I. Ehrlich and R.A. Posner, 'An Economic Analysis of Legal Rule Making' (1974) 3 *J. of Legal Studies* 257.
2. Posner, op cit n16, p45, supra, at 341-343.

ers achieve this influence and so under-estimates the extent to which the interests of consumer groups may be promoted by regulatory agencies. Moreover, it does not provide an explanation for when one agency regulates separate industries with conflicting interests.

Known as the economic theory of regulation, the economic version of the capture theory outlined by Stigler[3] relies on an extended notion of market behaviour as expressed through the political system. As the reallocation of resources by regulation enables certain groups to benefit at the expense of others, those concerned will express their preferences through political and economic channels and their reaction will depend primarily on how regulation affects their wealth. The basis of this theory is that:

'the essential commodity being transacted in the political market is a transfer of wealth with constituents on the demand side and their political representatives on the supply side. Viewed in this way, the market here, as elsewhere, will distribute more of the good to those whose effective demand is highest'[4].

It thus focuses on the response of regulators to interest groups and the way in which regulation is introduced and evolves[5].

Whereas those with a slight interest will have little incentive to organise a response to regulatory proposals, those with a more substantial interest will need to organise an effective response to bid for or against regulation. This is the crucial stage since the cost of organising groups varies with their size. The resulting dominance of small groups is explained in terms of the relationship between group size and the costs of using the political process.

In a political system characterised by infrequent voting on a variety of issues, the dominant group size is restricted initially in that voting in politics will be less precise than the expression of market place preferences. On a specific issue, a voter's expenditure on information about the merits of an issue and politicians' views will be determined by prospective costs and gains. Since a voter with a small stake will not incur this cost, a policy which furthers the interests of a minority may be accepted.

The dominant group size is also limited by the costs of organisation. Groups with a large stake in regulation must approach the politician willing to implement it. Apart from providing votes, this involves contributions to resources in the form of campaign expenses or employment of party workers. But these costs will rise with the size of the group. As larger groups will arouse stronger opposition from those substantially affected, so the costs of organisation will increase.

Since the cost per member of organising a group increases with the size of the group, this will result in the regulatory system being dominated by a small group with a large stake in regulation. Because consumers are usually a large group with diffused interests, the small group dominance will usually be by those representing the producer protection interest. The capture theory thus rejects the consumer protection emphasis of the public interest theory.

The rationale of legislators voting against economic policies harmful to

3. Stigler, op cit n15, p45, supra.
4. S. Peltzman, 'Toward a More General Theory of Regulation' (1976) 19 *J. Law and Econ.* 211.
5. This outline draws on: Stigler, op cit n15, p45, supra; Posner, op cit n16, p45, supra; Phillips and Zecher, op cit n16, p45, supra; J. Hirschleiffer, op cit n16, p45, supra; Phillips and Zecher, op cit n16, p45, supra; J. Hirschleiffer, 'Comment' (1976) 19 *J. Law and Econ.*241; G. Becker, 'Comment' (1976) 19 *J. Law and Econ.* 245.

society is attributed to the need to seek a coalition of voter interests more durable than those opposed to the industry's policy proposals. Hence, the capture theory is ultimately one of the optimum size of effective political coalitions in the framework of a general model of the political process.

The capture theory also provides a contrast to the public interest theory in that the public interest as defined in the latter may not be an important feature of regulation. Since a regulatory programme seeks to balance the interests of well-organised groups, regulation will be established and modified in response to changes in the balance between these competing interest groups. As this process will tend to favour small groups, regulatory programmes would also serve the public interest only coincidentally.

In these circumstances, regulators would not be inclined to discuss well-defined and measurable goals, to measure the size and direction of wealth transfer or to favour low cost choices in expanding regulations. Rather, there will be a tendency to make regulation obscure and complicated and to impose high costs on potential challengers of regulatory decisions.

The pattern of small well-organised groups with a large stake in regulation being favoured at the expense of large but less organised groups with a diminished interest has been regarded[6] as applicable to the SEC's disclosure programme which requires about 10,000 companies to furnish information periodically and when new capital is raised. Apart from the SEC, its main support is derived from accountants and lawyers responsible for preparing the documents and others who obtain benefits at little cost, such as financial analysts, portfolio managers and other market professionals. Yet the costs fall on companies to be passed on to shareholders, employees and others who deal with the company. Disclosure requirements would also be in the public interest in fulfilling their goals of providing information to improve price appraisal and thereby reduce price manipulation, fraud and deceit. But it is argued there is little evidence that the requirements have succeeded in achieving these goals.

The capture theory also suggests that regulation does not serve one economic interest exclusively. In balancing the interests of different groups, a regulatory system may tax or confer benefits on various groups at different rates, including exemptions or zero-ratings. In terms of corporate disclosure requirements, regulatory taxation is borne by smaller firms at a higher rate in relation to assets than larger firms.

Whilst a significant advance over other theories, the capture theory still contains significant weaknesses[7]. As it does not specify the number of members of a coalition that maximises the likelihood of regulation, it does not provide a basis for predicting which industries will be regulated. Rather, it is limited to providing a list of criteria for use in predicting whether an industry will obtain favourable legislation.

In addition, it neglects the role of regulators who are themselves an interest group. As they too should be aiming at wealth maximisation, they should likewise benefit at the expense of consumers and regulated firms. If wealth is the ultimate goal, majority maximisation will not be the only aim since politicians should accept some risk of defeat in return for an adequate monetary payment, whether direct or indirect. By implication, when majority maximisation is only a partial aim, there will be diminishing returns to the size of majority for politicians.

6. Phillips and Zecher, op cit n16, p45, supra, pp22-23.
7. Posner, op cit n16, p45, supra, at 347; Hirschleiffer, op cit n5, p47, supra.

It is also an over-simplification to identify the regulator with an elected politician as this overlooks substantial differences in regulators' behaviour. A civil servant with permanent tenure may be regarded as having a motivation to increase the scope and detail of regulation since he usually stands to gain from an expansion in his agency's size and activity. In contrast, it is assumed that an independent commissioner, appointed for a limited period and often having other business interests, is less likely to be so motivated. The regulatory system is also determined by the motivations, authorities and constraints imposed by others involved in the political process, such as judges and legislators.

Moreover, while allowing for competition among candidates for regulatory power and interest groups in bidding for favourable regulation, the capture theory does not allow for competition between regulatory agencies. That availability of choice among regulatory jurisdictions for those regulated may contribute to lax regulation is exemplified by the choice of Delaware as the legal domicile of most major US companies.

As with the public interest theory, empirical evidence[8] is insufficient to support the economic version of the capture theory. In part, this stems from the lack of testable hypotheses formulated by the theory, but the case studies themselves contain significant weaknesses, and rather than being systematic, they focus on isolated cases. Much of the evidence accords with any version of the interest group theory as distinct from the economic theory; but some findings are difficult to reconcile with the economic theory. The effects of economic regulation are also difficult to trace. Moreover, the evidence is largely dependent on a rejection of the public interest rationale in which regulation is cloaked, yet such rejection may be questionable.

In addition, the public interest rhetoric of regulatory discussion and policy remains unexplained. Use of language that, according to the economic theory, is uninformative and misleading imposes costs which are presumably incurred only because of off-setting benefits. Such benefits may be related to increasing the costs to the public of obtaining accurate information about the impact of regulation on their welfare.

Nevertheless, the public interest and capture theories are important in any analysis of regulation. Though both are open to criticism, they provide useful insights for analysis.

Accordingly, whilst theoretical considerations point towards insider dealing regulation, they also highlight the tension between efficiency and equity considerations. The balance desired between such considerations is a policy decision.

However, the existence of inefficiencies in the market for information only raises the possibility that regulation could remedy those inefficiencies. Inefficiencies in the market could be compounded by imperfections in regulation that impede the redistribution of wealth sought by regulation.

8. This is summarised by Posner, op cit n16, p45, supra, at 350-356.

Chapter 2

The Regulatory Framework

The effects of insider dealing regulation on the distribution of wealth, coupled with these theories of regulation, underline the importance of competing claims on any scheme of insider dealing regulation. As a background to the analysis of substantive provisions, consideration will first be given to these interest groups and the channels through which they voice their preferences in the regulatory system.

Such outline is facilitated by the recent reform of investor protection legislation by the Financial Services Act 1986, which was preceded by public debate of the regulatory structure. Focal points for debate were provided by: a 1974-76 Department of Trade review which invited the views of interested parties on whether the system of regulation needed reform; a Committee of Inquiry appointed by the Prime Minister to conduct a broader review of the functioning of financial institutions, whose report[1] (known as the 'Wilson Report') was published in 1980; and the Review of Investor Protection by Professor Gower, which was commissioned by the Secretary of State for Trade in 1981 following the failures of certain firms (who were not members of the Stock Exchange) involved in investment management with a loss of clients' funds and malpractice in the London commodities markets.

The overall effect of the 1974-76 Department of Trade review[2] and the 1980 Wilson Report[3] was to extend statutory regulation to insider dealing, though otherwise to seek to enhance the role of self-regulation, notably by the establishment of the Council for the Securities Industry[4]. But both these reviews cited the other's proximity as a reason to restrict its own proposals.

Following a 1982 Discussion Document[5], the final recommendations of the Review of Investor Protection were published in 1984 in a report[6] which is usually referred to as the 'Gower Report'. These recommendations also took account of such developments as the urgent need for legislation to implement the EEC Directives on listed securities[7] and the settlement of the reference to the Restrictive Practices Court of the Stock Exchange's Rule Book[8]. The key proposals of the Gower Report were that the Prevention of Fraud (Investments) Act 1958 should be replaced by an Investor Protection Act. Subject to certain exceptions, the Act would make it a criminal offence to carry on any type of investment business unless registered with the Governmental agency responsible for administration of the Act or through membership of a recognised self-

---

1. *Committee to Review the Functioning of Financial Institutions Report,* Chairman: The Rt. Hon. Sir Harold Wilson, Cmnd.7937 (1980); also referred to as the 'Wilson Report'.
2. *The Times,* 22nd October, 1976.
3. Wilson Report, Cmnd. 7937 (1980), Chapters 21-22 and 25.
4. Bank of England Press Notice, 30th March, 1978.
5. *Review of Investor Protection,* a Discussion Document by Professor L.C.B. Gower (1982).
6. *Review of Investor Protection, Report: Part I* by L.C.B. Gower, Cmnd. 9125 (1984).
7. See post IX. Recognised investment exchanges and clearing houses.
8. Ibid.

regulatory agency. The Act would establish a framework in which responsibility for policy issues, overall surveillance and residual regulation of investment business would be conferred on a Governmental agency. Such agency could be either the Department of Trade and Industry or a new self-standing Commission answerable to the Secretary of State. But day-to-day regulation would so far as possible be undertaken by self-regulatory agencies, initially based on existing professional bodies and organisations, recognised by the Governmental agency. Whilst legislation on public issues, take-overs and insider dealing should be transferred from the Companies Acts to the Investor Protection Act, the substantive changes proposed were limited to extending insider dealing provisions to cover market dealings in any securities or options or futures relating to securities (whether of a company or not) and all public servants, whether central or local. The provisions in the Companies Acts relating to compensation to directors for loss of office should also be strengthened.

After the Secretary of State had invited responses to these proposals, the Government announced its intention to introduce legislation in the 1985-86 Parliamentary session. Postponing details to a White Paper in 1985[9], it indicated that its preferred approach was self-regulation in a statutory framework, involving the establishment of two regulatory bodies. This approach followed advice from the Governor of the Bank of England who, in the light of the unco-ordinated responses of City[10] interest groups to the Gower Report, had set up a group to advise him on the structure and operation of self-regulatory groupings[11]. The problems of reform were further complicated by the changing structure of City financial institutions to offer banking, broking, unit trust and insurance services.

The new regulatory framework was introduced by the FSA 1986. Its basic principle is that no person may carry on investment business unless he is either an authorised person or exempt. Whilst powers to regulate investment business were initially conferred on the Secretary of State for Trade and Industry, most have been transferred to the 'designated agency', namely the Securities and Investment Board (SIB). Out of line with the Gower recommendations, the SIB is not a Governmental agency, but a private company fulfilling public functions. Whilst authorisation to carry on investment business can be obtained directly from the SIB, provision is made for authorisation by virtue of membership of a recognised self-regulating organisation (SRO). Firms may also be authorised by holding certificates issued by a recognised professional body (RPB). Apart from the Bank of England, exemptions from authorisation include recognised investment exchanges (RIES), notably the Stock Exchange, in their capacity as such. The Take-over Panel remains a non-statutory body, though is linked to the regulatory framework established by statute.

I. THE DEPARTMENT OF TRADE AND INDUSTRY

The Department of Trade and Industry (the 'Department') is the Government Department concerned with the regulation of trade and commerce. As such, it

---

9. The Department of Trade and Industry, *Financial Services in the UK: A New Framework for Investor Protection*, Cmnd.9432 (1985).
10. The term is used to describe the major financial institutions, which are mainly situate in the City of London.
11. See, post, V. The Bank of England.

is responsible for the Government's objective:

> 'to enable commercial transactions to take place in a publicly known and equitable legal framework which is conducive to the efficient use of national resources.'[12]

Duties relating to the regulation of companies and investment business are conferred primarily[13] on the Secretary of State for Trade and Industry, who is a corporation sole with a corporate seal[14] and acts through officials in the Department[15]. He is also President of the Board of Trade from which position his functions are derived historically[16].

Although certain powers can be exercised without Parliamentary authority under the royal prerogative[17], the Department's duties are almost all defined by Parliament which alone can provide it with the supply of money necessary for its operations. These can be legislative, administrative or judicial functions. Indeed, the nature of certain functions exercised by the Department is sometimes unclear[18].

However, the Department cannot resort to a constitutional regulatory power. As statutory authority is indispensable, any rules and regulations not duly made under Act of Parliament are legally ineffective. Moreover, the limited law-making powers conferred on the Department[19] are subject to abrogation or alteration by Act of Parliament and unlike legislation by Act of Parliament, delegated legislation may be held by a court to be ultra vires[20].

Although the general law and various statutes govern the conduct of companies and securities transactions by providing criminal and civil liability[1], the main statutes conferring functions on the Department are the CA 1985, the IDA 1985 and the FSA 1986. Whereas the IDA 1985 is restricted to that specific problem, the CA 1985 and the FSA 1986 constitute the legal framework for the regulation of companies and the securities markets.

The CA 1985 provides for the formation, management and winding-up of companies and confers three main areas of responsibility on the Department. First, it checks compliance with the Act's provisions, especially accounting matters, submission of annual returns and formalities of management. Secondly, it investigates the affairs of 'live' companies to protect shareholder and creditor interests from mismanagement and fraud. Thirdly, it investigates the

12. J.P. Miller and D.E. Luke, 'Law Enforcement of Public Officials and Special Police Forces' London, p.137 (Home Office 1977 unpublished), cited in *Royal Commission on Criminal Procedure, Research Study No.10, Prosecutions by Private Individuals and Non-Police Agencies,* by K.W. Lidstone, R. Hogg and F. Sutcliffe (1980).
13. As under the Companies Act 1985, the Companies (Insider Dealing) Act 1985 and the Financial Services Act 1986. But under the Banking Act 1987, the Bank of England is the responsible authority.
14. The Secretary of State (New Departments) Order 1974 (S.I.1974 No.692)
15. Ministers of the Crown Act 1974, s.4(2), Sch2, para2.
16. See J.A.C. Suter, 'The Regulation of Insider Dealing in Britain and France' (Doctoral thesis, E.U.I., Florence 1985), pp.2.4. and 2.121-122.
17. Ibid, pp.2.4 and 2.122-123.
18. Eg, the Department's power to appoint an inspector to investigate a company's affairs under CA 1985, s432(2); see, post, Chapter 7. Investigation.
19. Eg, CA 1985 and FSA 1986.
20. De Smith, *Constitutional and Administrative Law,* Fifth edition by H. Street and R. Brazier (1985), p.345.
1. Eg. at common law, conspiracy to cheat or defraud or under the Theft Act 1968, obtaining credit by fraud, fraudulent conversion by directors, false statements to members or creditors and false accounting.

affairs of wound-up companies through the Official Receiver.

Whereas specific provision is made by the FSA 1986 for the Department to appoint inspectors to investigate suspected insider dealing[2], its responsibility for insider dealing prosecutions is defined by the IDA 1985. This provides that proceedings for an offence may only be instituted by the Secretary of State or by or with the consent of the DPP[3].

Replacing the PFIA 1958, the FSA 1986 establishes a new scheme for the regulation of investment business. In particular, it regulates the carrying on of investment business, makes related provisions for insurance companies and for friendly societies, introduces provisions in regard to the official listing of securities, offers of unlisted securities, take-over offers and insider dealing, contains provisions as to disclosure of information obtained under fair trading, banking, company and insurance legislation and provides for securing reciprocity with other countries for the provision of financial services.

Under the FSA 1986, the powers for regulating investment business were initially conferred on the Secretary of State, with most functions being transferable, by delegation order, to a 'designated agency' (the SIB) subject to certain criteria being satisfied[4]. Most of the functions capable of transfer to the SIB, which are, in general, those relating to the regulation of investment business conferred on the Secretary of State by Part I (ss.3-113)[5], FSA 1986, have been so transferred[6]. Any function may be transferred wholly or in part[7]. Some functions may be transferred subject to a reservation that they are exerciseable concurrently with the SIB[8]. However, the FSA 1986[9] specifically precludes the transfer to the SIB of the Secretary of State's functions relating to: certifying equivalence of investor protection in other Member States; the extension or restriction of exemptions from the prohibition of carrying on investment business; the restriction or extension of the kinds of investment to which the provisions precluding conduct being regarded as market manipulation apply and their restriction to apply only to certain offers of existing investment; the exemption from the statutory restrictions on the issue of investment advertisements; the authorisation of unit trusts and other collective investment schemes based in an EEC Member State or other designated countries; the Financial Services Tribunal and the duty of auditors of authorised persons to report to the supervisory authorities. Certain functions relating to the recognition of overseas investment exchanges and overseas clearing houses are also not transferable[10].

Moreover, following the transfer of functions, the Secretary of State retains important powers of intervention over the SIB[11]. These concern the composition of its governing body, the resumption of transferred functions, the alteration of SIB rules and other regulations and directions to the SIB in regard to Community or other international obligations.

In addition, in the special competition regime applicable to investment services, it is the Secretary of State, not the Restrictive Practices Court, on whom important powers of decision are conferred. Following the transfer to the SIB

2. FSA 1986, ss177-178.
3. IDA 1985, s8(2).
4. FSA 1986, s114(1), (2) and (3).
5. Ibid, s114(4); see, post, VI. The Securities and Investments Board.
6. Financial Services Act 1986 (Delegation) Order 1987, S.I.1987 No.942.
7. FSA 1986, s114(7).
8. Ibid, s114(8); see, post, VI. The Securities and Investments Board.
9. Ibid, s114(5).
10. Ibid, s114(6).
11. See, post, VI. The Securities and Investments Board.

of the function of recognising SROs, investment exchanges and clearing houses, the SIB may not recognise such a body unless the Secretary of State has granted leave[12]. Such leave may only be granted after consulting the Director General of Fair Trading and upon being satisfied that either the rules and regulations do not have, and are not intended to have or likely to have, to any significant extent the effect of restricting, distorting or preventing competition or, if they do, the effect is not greater than necessary for the protection of investors. With a view to preventing restrictive practices being developed, the SIB must also forward to the Secretary of State copies of notices received under notification requirements[13] of any amendment, revocation or addition to the rules or guidance of a recognised organisation or investment exchange and, in the case of an investment exchange, of the making, termination or variation of any clearing arrangements[14]. In turn, if it appears to the Secretary of State that, apart from the delegation order, he could himself have revoked the recognition order or directed the body to take specified steps to meet the competition requirements or make alterations to the rules for that purpose, then the Secretary of State can, notwithstanding the delegation order, revoke the recognition order or direct the SIB either to direct that specified steps be taken or itself make appropriate alterations to the rules[15]. As the designated agency, the same competition regime applies to the SIB[16]. In addition, separate provisions place the rules and practices of recognised professional bodies, to the extent that they relate to investment business, on broadly the same footing as those of an SRO, while leaving unchanged the existing provisions of competition law as they apply to most of the body's activities[17].

For the performance of its statutory functions, the Department has a Financial Services Division, a Companies Division and an Insolvency Service[18]. Responsibility for insider dealing lies with the Financial Services Division.

However, the Department is beset by the problem of scarce resources. Accentuated by the complexity of conduct such as fraud and insider dealing, this limits the scope for enforcement.

In the performance of its duties, the Department is subject to supervision by the House of Commons Select Committee on Trade and Industry. It can also be the subject of ad hoc enquiries, such as the Committee to Review the Functioning of Financial Institutions (the 'Wilson Committee') which reported in 1980.

Within the legal framework for the regulation of companies and financial services, the Department's role in insider dealing regulation mainly involves the investigation[19] and prosecution[20] of alleged offences. Following the enactment of the criminal prohibition in 1980 and of a specific investigative power in 1986, company investigations are less significant in this role.

12. FSA 1986, s120(1) and (2).
13. Ie, under FSA 1986, ss14(6) and 41(5).
14. FSA 1986, s120(3). In the case of a clearing house, notification is required of a change in the persons for whom it provides clearing services.
15. FSA 1986, s120(4).
16. Ibid, s121.
17. Ibid, s127.
18. Civil Service Yearbook (1988), cols.582-586.
19. See, post, Chapter 7. Investigation.
20. See, post, Chapter 3. Criminal Liability.

II. THE DIRECTOR OF PUBLIC PROSECUTIONS (THE 'DPP')

DPP[1] involvement stems from the provision whereby proceedings in England and Wales for breach of the IDA 1985 may only be instituted by the Secretary of State or by or with leave of the DPP[2]. This provision is intended to ensure that there is some control of prosecutions, including preventing frivolous prosecutions brought privately, and consistency in prosecution decisions. Whilst prosecutions are normally brought by the Department, the DPP has on occasion been involved.

The DPP's general duties are discharged under the superintendence of the Attorney General[3]. These are: to take over the conduct of all criminal proceedings, other than specified proceedings, instituted on behalf of a police force; to institute and have the conduct of criminal proceedings in any case where it appears to him appropriate because of the importance, difficulty or otherwise of the case; to take over the conduct of all binding over proceedings instituted on behalf of a police force and to discharge such other functions as may from time to time be assigned to him by the Attorney General[4]. The DPP also has duties relating to the provision of advice and assistance to the police and the conduct of appeals and other proceedings. In addition, the DPP heads the Crown Prosecution Service[5]. Under certain companies legislation, the consent of the DPP is required to commence a prosecution[6].

In regard to its role in the investigation and prosecution of fraud, a significant development was the establishment, in 1985, of the Fraud Investigation Group (FIG) within the DPP[7]. This superseded the practice of setting up ad hoc task forces of lawyers and police to deal with individual cases. Whilst police and non-police investigations continued to change from case to case, the designation of DPP staff to deal with fraud marked a new departure. In 1986, there were three divisions of lawyers, with a support staff of accountants.

The establishment of the FIG coincided with an increased workload, the number of fraud cases reported to the DPP increasing from 304 in 1983 to 593 in 1985[8]. Whilst some cases or serious or complex fraud now fall within the remit of the Serious Fraud Office, the latter supplements, but does not replace the FIG[9].

III. THE SERIOUS FRAUD OFFICE

Established by the Criminal Justice Act 1987, the Serious Fraud Office is headed by its Director[10]. Appointed by the Attorney General, the Director of the Serious

1. The Prosecution of Offences Act 1985, s2(1) and (2) provides that the DPP shall be appointed by the Attorney General and must be a barrister or solicitor of not less than ten years' standing.
2. IDA 1985, s8(2). In Scotland, proceedings are under the control of the Lord Advocate.
3. Prosecution of Offences Act 1985, s3(1).
4. Ibid, s3(2).
5. Ibid, s1(1).
6. CA 1985, s732. In regard to the DPP, this section refers to CA 1985, ss210, 324 and 329.
7. *Fraud Trials Committee Report* (Chairman: The Right Honourable The Lord Roskill, P.C.) (1986), paras2.23-2.31; M. Levi, *Regulating Fraud* (1987) p.177.
8. Levi, op cit. supra, p.177.
9. Ibid, p.285.
10. CJA 1987, s1(1). The Serious Fraud Office is constituted for England and Wales and Northern Ireland.

Fraud Office discharges his functions under the superintendence of the Attorney General[11].

As to his functions, the Director may investigate any suspected offence which appears to him on reasonable grounds to involve serious or complex fraud[12]. He may also, if he thinks fit, conduct any such investigation in conjunction either with the police or with any other person who is, in the Director's opinion, a proper person to be concerned in it[13]. In regard to prosecutions, the Director may institute and have the conduct of any criminal proceedings which appear to him to relate to serious or complex fraud and may take over the conduct of any such proceedings at any stage[14]. In addition, the Director is required to discharge such other functions in relation to fraud as may from time to time be assigned to him by the Attorney General[15].

The Serious Fraud Office has a staff of more than 80, including 26 lawyers and 19 accountants[16]. Contrary to the Roskill recommendations relating to the possible establishment of such a body[17], police officers are not members of its staff, answerable to the Director. Instead, officers are seconded to the Serious Fraud Office to work on particular cases; in particular, the Serious Fraud Office works in close co-operation with the City of London fraud squad, of which 15 – 20 officers work with the Serious Fraud Office staff in the same building. However, police officers continue to work under the command of their own senior officers. Such division is criticised as running the risk of inefficiency and as unlikely to contribute to the training of specialist fraud squad officers[18].

IV. THE POLICE

Although certain matters are enforced by Government departments and the police role in prosecutions diminished with the introduction of the Crown Prosecution Service, the limited resources of the DTI, the DPP and the Serious Fraud Office, together with the Crown Prosecution Service's reliance on police investigation, continue to give the police an important role in enforcement in regard to offences relating to companies and securities transactions. In an insider dealing prosecution involving a civil servant with the Office of Fair Trading, the case was transferred to the City of London Police because the civil servant was a DTI employee[19].

As most serious cases occur in London, the task of investigation falls mainly to the Company Fraud department within both the Metropolitan and City of London police forces. This joint squad was established in 1946 to investigate commercial frauds and related matters[20]. Many of its investigations contain a

11. CJA 1987, s1(2). Provisions relating to the Director's remuneration, power to appoint staff and duty to report to the Attorney General on the discharge of his functions are contained in CJA 1987, Sch1, paras 1-3.
12. CJA 1987, s1(2). As to the powers exerciseable for the purposes of such an investigation, see, post, Chapter 7. Investigation.
13. CJA 1987, s1(4).
14. Ibid, s1(5).
15. Ibid, s1(6).
16. (1988) Business Law Review 105.
17. *Report of the Fraud Trials Committee* (Chairman: The Right Honourable the Lord Roskill, P.C.) (1986), para2.48 and Recommendation No.2.
18. (1988) Business Law Review 105.
19. *The Independent*, 23rd April, 1988.
20. L.H. Leigh, *The Control of Commercial Fraud* (1982), pp.246-255; M. Levi, *Regulating Fraud* (1987), pp.120 and 138.

foreign element. Other fraud squads exist on a regional basis, though their size and expertise vary considerably.

In terms of efficiency, present arrangements have disadvantages[1]. Officers do not have specialist training in accountancy or commercial law. Short practical courses provide an introduction, but most knowledge is acquired through experience. Promotion prospects within fraud squads are limited.

V. THE BANK OF ENGLAND

Although not immediately apparent from its formal legal status and authority, the functions of the Bank of England and its consequent relations with both the Government and the City have given the Bank a key role in the regulation of the securities markets.

Created in 1694 by Act of Parliament and a Royal Charter under letters patent authorised thereby, the Bank of England was made a public corporation by the Bank of England Act 1946. This Act formalised the Bank's role as a public institution since the Bank had long ceased to operate in any way other than as a central bank subject to ultimate government authority. Although the stock of the Bank was brought into public ownership by transfer to the Treasury[2], in itself the change of ownership appears to have made relatively little difference.

Probably of greater constitutional significance was the enactment of the principle of public control. This was effected by providing a statutory basis of regulation which conferred a power on the Treasury[3] from time to time to give such directions to the Bank as, after consultation with the Governor, it was thought necessary in the public interest. In the event, this provision has in general been declaratory rather than served to define the Treasury-Bank relationship.

Subject to such directions, the affairs of the Bank were to be managed by its governing body, the Court of Directors[4], in accordance with any charter of the Bank in force and bye-laws thereunder. The 1946 Act also specified the structure of the Court of Directors[5]. However, the statutory provisions only partially reflect the Bank's structure and organisation, with the Court's main work being carried out through standing committees which meet regularly. Moreover, in practice, the power of the Governor has far exceeded that apparent from statute.

Though not defined by the 1946 Act, many of the Bank's functions are central to the conduct of economic policy. Apart from advising the Government on economic policy, it is responsible for the execution of monetary policy, management of the national debt, control of bank credit, administration of the exchange equalisation account and note circulation. Until their removal, it was responsible for the administration of exchange controls. As central bank, it acts as banker to the Government, the main commercial banks and foreign central banks. It is also responsible for supervision of the banking sector and has a more general responsibility for the good order of the financial system as a whole, including oversight of the securities markets.

1. Leigh, op cit. n20, p56, supra, pp.225-233; Levi, op cit. n20, p56, supra, pp.150-151.
2. Bank of England Act 1946, s1; the Bank of England (Transfer of Stock) Order 1946 (S.R. & O. 1946 No.238).
3. Bank of England Act 1946, s4(1).
4. Ibid, s4(2).
5. Ibid, s2(2).

A. The regulation of banking

Although its role as banking supervisor was placed on a statutory basis only in 1979, the Bank has long supervised part of the banking sector. Traditionally based on 'suasion'[6], the Bank's supervision covered those institutions regulated for monetary policy purposes and was exercised with their consent which was given in return for certain privileges[7]. This method involved gentlemen's agreements restricting the type of business undertaken and observance of the Bank's advice and suggestions.

Following increased interbank competition and the 1973-74 secondary banking crisis involving a support operation[8], the Bank's supervision was extended by administrative action in 1974. More frequent and detailed information was requested periodically from a wider range of institutions and organisational changes within the Bank acknowledged the increased importance of prudential regulation.

In turn, these arrangements were placed on a statutory basis[9] as a response partly to the extension of prudential regulation to the secondary banking sector which rendered reliance on 'suasion' inadequate and partly to the EEC banking harmonisation programme[10]. As well as establishing a legal definition of a bank, the Banking Act 1979 conferred powers of authorisation and supervision on the Bank and provided for insurance against depositor loss. But it sought to preserve the flexibility of previous requirements for prudential regulation.

However, after the Johnson Matthey Bankers affair[11] revealed important weaknesses in the Bank's supervision of the banking system[12], the Bank's powers were more clearly defined by the Banking Act 1987. This Act now provides the framework for regulating 600 banks in the City, of which 400 are foreign, and 'where a flicker of the Governor's eyebrows no longer obtains instant results – or is even understood by many of the players'[13].

Under the 1987 Act, the Bank is given general supervisory and specific regulatory functions. A Board of Banking Supervision was established for the purpose of advising the Bank on the exercise of its functions under the Act.

A system of authorisation by the Bank of all deposit-taking institutions replaces the previous system, which was based on a distinction between recognised banks and licensed deposit-takers. An authorisation may be revoked or restricted by the Bank by notice or surrendered by the authorised institution. The Bank is required to publish a statement of principles in accordance with which it acts or proposes to act in carrying out its duties and functions under the Act. It also has power to give directions to an institution if desirable in the

---

6. E.P.M. Gardener, 'Legal Rules versus "Vicarious Participation" in Bank Prudential Regulation', p.34 in (ed.) J. Revell, *Competition and Regulation of Banks* (1978).
7. Eg, under the Exchange Control Act 1947 and the Income and Corporation Taxes Act 1970.
8. The Select Committee on Nationalised Industries, Sub-Committee C: Minutes of Evidence: Bank of England Report and Accounts for the year ended 28th February, 1977 (1977-78) H.C. 166-i and 166-ii; 'The secondary banking crises and the Bank of England's support operations' (1978) 18 B. of E. Q.B. 230.
9. *The Licensing and Supervision of Deposit-Taking Institutions,* Cmnd.6584 (1976); J. Revell, 'Reforming U.K. bank supervision' (1976) 126 The Banker 1021; T.M. Ashe, 'Supervising the Banks' (1979) 29 N.L.J.1160.
10. First Council Directive 77/780/EEC of December 12, 1977, on the coordination of laws, regulations and administrative provisions relating to the taking up and pursuit of the business of credit institutions (O.J.1977, L/322/30).
11. M. Reid, *All-Change in the City* (1988), pp.224-233.
12. *Banking Supervision,* Cmnd.9695 (1985).
13. *The Financial Times,* 29th January, 1988.

interests of depositors and potential depositors. In addition, the Bank has power to serve a notice of objection on a prospective or existing controller of an authorised institution. An appeals procedure is established. Extensive powers of investigation are conferred on the Bank.

As to other features of the 1987 Act, the Deposit Protection Scheme under the 1979 Act is continued. New provision is made for the control (involving the Bank) of the use of banking names and descriptions and of overseas institutions with representative offices in the U.K. In addition, restrictions are imposed on the disclosure of information.

B. Oversight of the securities markets

As part of its responsibilities for the financial system as a whole, the Bank has a general interest in the efficient and fair operation of securities markets[14]. As trading centres, such markets establish guides to the value of securities and provide a mechanism to enhance the liquidity of government and corporate securities. In meeting the various liquidity preferences of savers, the securities markets facilitate the transfer of funds from lenders of money to governments and companies seeking capital for investment in productive assets[15]. They thus function as a financial intermediary in the overall capital market with the distinguishing feature of permitting direct ownership of securities on such conditions that investors bear directly the risk of loss.

Although they allocate a relatively small amount of the total capital market savings, the securities markets are important because the value of their turnover is still substantial[16] and they have an extended influence on resource allocation. Apart from indicating the cost of raising capital by further issues of securities, a company's share price often determines the availability and cost of capital from other sources because the company's business prospects and management have been assessed by underwriters, investment advisers and investors. The securities markets' significance is further enhanced by wider public benefits, such as encouraging investment in productive assets and enabling investors to participate in the ownership and control of companies.

Apart from a general interest in the securities markets, the Bank has a particular interest based on its own operations in government securities, which are important in the execution of monetary policy and management of the national debt. As regards companies, these operations have been complemented by statutory provisions[17] limiting companies' ability to release new issues.

However, compared to the money markets and the banking system, the Bank has a 'less central'[18] interest in the securities markets. As a result, its supervision

14. Committee to Review the Functioning of Financial Institutions, Second Stage Evidence, Vol.4 *The Bank of England* (1979), p.107: *Supervision of the Securities Markets: Non-statutory Aspects* (1978).
15. The role of the securities market is more fully considered by: (a) M. Firth, *The Valuation of Shares and the Efficient Markets Theory* (1977), Chapter 1; (b) N. Goodison (Chairman of the Stock Exchange), 'The Regulatory Role of the Stock Exchange' (1981 Stockton Lecture); (c) I. Friend, 'The Economic Consequences of the Stock Market' (1972) 62 *Amer.Econ.Rev.*212 and (d) J.L. Howard, 'Securities Regulation: Structure and Process', p.1611 at pp.1630- 47 in *Consumer and Corporate Affairs Canada, Proposals for a Securities Market Law for Canada,* Vol.3 Background papers (1979).
16. Wilson Report, Cmnd.7937 (1980), Appendix 3.325-326.
17. The Borrowing (Control and Guarantees) Act 1946, ss 1 and 3(4).
18. Wilson Report, Cmnd.7939 (1980), Appendix 3.316.

has been 'more in the nature of general surveillance'[19] with an overall concern for their efficient and fair operation, but with detailed regulation left to others.

Effected by its contacts with the main organisations involved, the Bank has played a leading role in developments in securities regulation, especially in regard to self-regulation[20]. Its involvement dates from 1959 when, after well-publicised take-over bids had raised questions about City practice, the Governor requested representatives of those involved to form a working party to consider what guidance could be given. The outcome was the publication of Notes on Amalgamations of British Businesses. To improve the handling of issues of public policy affecting the City in 1973-74, the Governor also took the initiative in establishing specialist committees with consultative functions; these included the City Liaison Committee, the City Capital Markets Committee and the City Company Law Committee. Further Bank initiatives led to the establishment of agencies responsible for regulation, notably the Panel on Take-overs and Mergers in 1968 and the Council for the Securities Industry in 1978, and for the co-ordination of regulation, namely, the Joint Review Body in 1977. The Bank also encouraged the formation in 1980 of the Association of Licensed Dealers in Securities, the forerunner of the self-regulating organisation, FIMBRA

In the 1980's, the Bank's influence on regulatory developments continued with particular emphasis on modernisation. In this connection, the Bank proved to be an important influence on the decision in July 1983 by the Secretary of State for Trade and Industry to settle the proceedings brought by the Office of Fair Trading against the Stock Exchange under the Restrictive Trade Practices Act 1976[1]. Under the terms of the settlement, the Stock Exchange agreed to amend certain restrictive rules in return for exemption from the restrictive practices legislation. In conjunction with the Treasury, the Bank persuaded the Secretary of State that proceedings before the Restrictive Practices Court were an unsuitable method of examining the Stock Exchange Rule Book. The Bank's initiative was prompted by its concern at the lack of competitiveness of the Stock Exchange in international securities trading. Compared to large and well capitalised international broking houses, Stock Exchange firms were small and lacked the capital to cope with more than domestic business. In consequence, their share of the total volume of securities trading in London was rapidly declining and they lacked the resources to expand overseas to any significant extent.

Moreover, under the terms of settlement, an important role was conferred on the Bank. On reaching his decision, the Secretary of State announced that arrangements would be made for the Department of Trade and Industry and the Bank to monitor implementation of the measures agreed and the evolution of the Stock Exchange as an efficient, competitive and suitably regulated central market which afforded proper protection to investors. Because of its greater knowledge of the financial markets, the Bank thus became the main guiding force over fundamental changes in securities trading in London[2].

The Bank's influential role in developments in securities regulation was underlined in relation to the reform proposals which culminated in the FSA 1986. In an attempt to achieve a workable consensus on developments following

19. Committee to Review the Functioning of Financial Institutions, Second Stage Evidence, Vol.4, *The Bank of England* (1979), para16.
20. These developments are considered in more detail in J.A.C. Suter, 'The Regulation of Insider Dealing in Britain and France' (Doctoral thesis, E.U.I., Florence, 1985), pp.2.25-2.28.
1. *The Guardian,* 21st July, 1983; *The Sunday Telegraph,* 31st July, 1983.
2. See, post, Chapter 6. Administrative Regulation, II. Conflicts of Interest.

the Gower Report, the Bank announced in 1984 the appointment of a group of 10 City figures to advise the Governor on the structure and operation of the self-regulatory groupings for the securities industry[3]. In subsequent developments leading to the passage of legislation, the Bank continued to play an influential role.

In the current regulatory framework, the Governor of the Bank of England has powers under both statutory and non-statutory regulation, as well as enjoying informal influence. Under the FSA 1986, the Governor has power, jointly with the Secretary of State, to appoint and remove the chairman and other members of the SIB governing body[4]. In addition, the Governor appoints the Chairman, Deputy Chairmen and a further non-representative member of the Panel on Take-overs and Mergers[5]. Whilst formal regulation and internationalisation have rendered the Bank's informal contacts less important, its influence in the City was illustrated in 1987 when, under pressure from the Government and the Bank, the chief executive and the corporate finance head (a former Director of the Panel) of a leading merchant bank resigned following disclosures in the Guinness affair[6].

C. Accountability

As neither a ministry in its own right nor subsumed within a Government department nor dependent on Parliament for funds, the Bank's special institutional position resulted in less Parliamentary supervision[7]. Indeed, traditionally, it did not even disclose sufficient information for its performance to be evaluated, with proper accounts being published only in the 1970s. In 1969, the Bank was included in a new Order for reference for the Select Committee on Nationalised Industries, though many of its activities were excluded. For the functions performed as the Government's agent, the Bank was accountable to the Treasury and through it to Parliament; yet until 1979, only Treasury ministers and officials, not the Governor or Bank staff, appeared before Parliamentary committees dealing with monetary policy.

However, Parliamentary control was extended in 1979 with the introduction of a departmental Select Committee structure. The Bank was brought within the terms of reference of the Treasury and Civil Service Department. Like Treasury ministers and officials, the Governor and Bank officials can now be required to answer questions on the full range of their activities. In addition, the Bank's annual report has become more detailed and includes a report on the exercise of the Bank's powers under banking legislation.

3. *The Times*, 24th May, 1984; *The Guardian*, 24th May, 1984 and *The Sunday Times*, 27th May, 1984.
4. FSA 1986, Sch7, para1(2). Under the FSA 1986, the Bank itself is an exempted person for the purpose of authorisation under that Act: s35; by virtue of s43, money market institutions listed by the Bank of England are also exempted.
5. The City Code on Take-overs and Mergers, Introduction, para2(a).
6. M. Levi, *Regulating Fraud* (1987), p.327.
7. The issue of accountability is considered more fully in Suter, op cit. n20, p60, supra, pp.2.30-2.33. In regard to the problems of accountability as illustrated by the Johnson Matthey affair, see A.C. Page, 'Self-Regulation: The Constitutional Dimension' (1986) 49 M.L.R. 141 at 162-163.

VI. THE SECURITIES AND INVESTMENTS BOARD (THE 'SIB')

Established in 1985, the SIB was formed with a view to becoming the designated agency responsible for administering the system of regulating investment business created by the FSA 1986[8]. Though the exercise of statutory powers by the agency was thus envisaged, the SIB is a private company limited by guarantee; as such, it differs from most quangos in the UK and other Securities Commissions in the common law world[9].

In turn, important features of the SIB's constitution derive from the FSA 1986, thereby distinguishing it from other limited companies. Specifically, Sch7, para1 requires the appointment of a chairman and a governing body consisting of the chairman and other members. Responsibility for their appointment lies with the Secretary of State and the Governor of the Bank of England acting jointly; provision is also made for their removal from office by this method[10]. As to qualifications, members of the governing body must include not only persons experienced in investment business, but also other persons, who are regular or professional users of the services of investment businesses[11]. In addition, the composition of the governing body must be such as to secure a proper balance between the interests of persons carrying on investment business and of the public[12]. In 1987 the governing body comprised eighteen members, of which the Chairman and Chief Executive were full-time members[13]. The other directors were part-time non-executive members, six being 'lay' or non-practitioner representatives of the public. However, it has been suggested that movement in the direction of the SEC model of five full-time Commissioners, all experienced in investment business but who sever their connections with it during their tenure of office is essential if the governing body is to govern effectively[14].

Most of the Secretary of State's functions capable of transfer[15] to the SIB were transferred in 1987[16]. The powers transferred include: the recognition of SROs, revocation of recognition, the seeking of compliance orders and the alteration of rules of an SRO; the recognition or withdrawal of recognition from a professional body; the grant, refusal, suspension or withdrawal of direct authorisation to an investment business; the withdrawal of recognition from a person authorised in another EEC Member State; the grant or refusal of recognition for an investment exchange or for a clearing house (except for an overseas investment exchange or clearing house); the making of rules regulating the conduct of business, compensation funds and the segregation of clients' money and the investigation of persons carrying on investment business and the prosecution of certain offences. The functions of issuing injunctions and restitution orders against authorised businesses and petitioning for winding-up orders can be transferred subject to a reservation that the function is to be exerciseable by the Secretary of State concurrently with the SIB[17]. A transfer of

8. FSA 1986, s114(1) and (2).
9. L.C.B. Gower, '"Big Bang" and City Regulation' (1988) 51 M.L.R. 1 at 12.
10. FSA 1986, Sch7, para2.
11. Ibid, para3.
12. Ibid.
13. The Securities and Investments Board, Chairman's Statement, (June 1987)
14. Gower, op cit. n9, supra, at 13.
15. FSA 1986, s114(4).
16. Financial Services Act 1986 (Delegation) Order 1987, S.I.1987, No.942. References to the Secretary of State in the context of the FSA 1986 should therefore be read accordingly.
17. FSA 1986, s114(8).

functions relating to the investigation of collective investment schemes or persons carrying on investment business is required to be subject to such a reservation[18].

However, some of the Secretary of State's functions relating to the regulation of investment business are expressly excluded from the power of transfer[19], as are certain functions relating to the recognition of overseas investment exchanges and overseas clearing houses[20]. In addition, the FSA 1986 did not provide for the transfer to the SIB of functions relating to the public issue of securities and the disqualification or restriction of a foreign firm from carrying on investment, insurance or banking business in the UK on grounds of reciprocity[1]. As they are conferred under the IDA 1985, the powers to prosecute insider dealing are also not capable of transfer to the SIB. Moreover, the SIB was not given, and did not seek, powers to prosecute offences likely to involve serious or complex fraud, such as those created by s.47, FSA 1986 relating to misleading statements and practices. This reflected the significant additional expertise and resources this would require and the need to avoid confusion in jurisdiction with the Serious Fraud Office[2].

Following the transfer of functions, the Secretary of State retains important powers over the SIB. First, acting jointly with the Governor of the Bank of England, he may remove members of the governing body[3]. Secondly, he may resume any or all of the functions transferred if it appears that the SIB no longer meets the qualifications of Sch7, FSA 1986, is unable or unwilling to discharge any or all of the transferred functions or, in the case of a power to make rules or regulations, that the SIB's rules and regulations do not afford a sufficient level of investor protection[4]. Thirdly, the Secretary of State may direct the SIB to alter its rules, regulations, guidance or practices if these are considered to be uncompetitive[5]. Fourthly, he may also direct the SIB to take, or not to take, action incompatible with the UK's Community or other international obligations[6].

In turn, the SIB is required to prepare an annual report on the discharge of its functions; it is required to report to the Secretary of State who must lay a copy before Parliament[7]. The SIB thus reports to Parliament through the Secretary of State. The Secretary of State is also authorised to give the SIB directions about its accounts and their audit[8].

In regard to its status and immunities, it is made clear that the SIB shall not be regarded as acting on behalf of the Crown nor shall its members, officers and servants be regarded as Crown servants[9]. However, statutory immunity from liability in damages is granted to the SIB and any of its members, officers and servants in respect of anything done, or omitted to be done, in discharging its functions unless the act or omission is shown to have been in bad faith[10]. The

18. Ibid.
19. Ibid, s114(5); see, ante, I. The Department of Trade and Industry.
20. Ibid, s114(6).
1. Ibid, s114(4).
2. Butterworths, *Financial Services Law and Practice* (1987), A. [22].
3. FSA 1986, Sch7, para1(2).
4. Ibid, s115. The power is exercisable by draft order subject to affirmative resolution of each House of Parliament.
5. FSA 1986, s121(3).
6. Ibid, s192(1).
7. Ibid, s117(1) and (2).
8. Ibid, s117(3).
9. Ibid, Sch9, para1.
10. Ibid, s187(3).

immunity is confined to liability in damages; hence, judicial review is not excluded.

In the build-up to operational status, the number of SIB staff increased sharply. In May 1987, the staff numbered 78, with further increases anticipated[11].

The SIB is funded by application and periodical fees paid by those subject to its regulation[12]. In setting such fees, the SIB may take into account its initial costs[13]. Non-payment of periodical fees can lead to revocation of authorisation[14].

VII. THE RECOGNISED SELF-REGULATING ORGANISATIONS (THE 'SROs')

Most investment businesses are authorised to carry on business through membership of a recognised SRO. In this connection, the SIB is authorised, under powers transferred from the Secretary of State, to 'recognise' SROs which satisfy statutory criteria designed to ensure that they are credible self-regulatory bodies with rules at least as equivalent as those of the SIB[15]. The significance of such recognition is that membership of a recognised SRO confers authorised person status[16].

A. The Individual Self-Regulating Organisations

Under the present arrangements, there are five recognised SROs[17]. Due to the scope of their activities, the large financial conglomerates belong to more than one SRO.

1. The Securities Association (The 'TSA')

A company limited by guarantee, the TSA was formed in 1986, following the merger of the Stock Exchange and the International Securities Regulatory Organisation (ISRO). Its function is to regulate: dealing and arranging deals in securities, futures and options; advising corporate finance customers and arranging deals with them; investment management, mainly for private clients, where this is not the main activity; advising on and arranging transactions in other investments, notably life insurance and unit trusts, where these are incidental to the firm's main business.

11. The Securities and Investments Board, Chairman's Statement (June 1987)
12. FSA 1986, ss112-113.
13. Ibid, Sch9, para11.
14. Ibid, s113(5) and (7).
15. FSA 1986, ss8-11.
16. Ibid, s7(1).
17. E.Z. Lomnicka and J.L. Powell (eds.), *Encyclopaedia of Financial Services Law* (1987), Chapter 8, and The College of Law, *The Financial Services Act 1986* (1988).

2. The Financial Intermediaries, Managers and Brokers Regulatory Association (FIMBRA)

Formed in 1986 as the successor to NASDIM[18], FIMBRA was a recognised association under the PFIA 1958. A company limited by guarantee, it is mainly concerned with regulating the provision of financial services by independent investment intermediaries to retail customers. More specifically, its regulatory scope is: advising on and arranging deals in life assurance and unit trusts; the provision of investment advice and management services to retail customers and advising on and arranging deals in securities provided they are incidental to these activities.

3. The Association of Futures Brokers and Dealers Limited (AFBD)

Incorporated in 1984, the AFBD was established to provide an SRO for the financial and commodity futures and options sector. Its function is to regulate all brokers, dealers, advisers and managers in futures contracts, contracts for differences and related options and their dealings in securities where these are ancillary to such transactions.

4. The Investment Management Regulatory Organisation (IMRO)

Incorporated in 1986, IMRO was formed on the initiative of leading merchant banks to cover their fund management activities, though now also comprises unit trust managers and trustees and in-house pension managers. Its function is to regulate investment management where this constitutes the sole or main activity of a member or where the member is a major investment manager in his own right, and advising on and arranging deals in investments which are incidental to main investment management.

5. The Life Assurance and Unit Trust Regulatory Organisation (LAUTRO)

Formed in 1986, LAUTRO's membership comprises life assurance companies, friendly societies and operators of regulated collective investment schemes. Its regulatory scope is retail marketing of life assurance and unit trusts and the carrying on of investment business by its life assurance members.

B. Self-Regulating Organisations

The term 'self-regulating organisation' is defined in terms of the statutory functions to be performed. Specifically, an SRO 'is a body (whether a body corporate or an unincorporated association) which regulates the carrying on of investment business of any kind by enforcing rules which are binding on persons carrying on business of that kind either because they are members of that body or because they are otherwise subject to its control'[19].

As to the recognition process, an application must be made to the SIB in the

---

18. The National Association of Securities Dealers and Investment Managers, which, in turn, was the successor to the ALDS, formed with Bank of England encouragement: see, ante, V. The Bank of England.
19. FSA 1986, s8(1).

prescribed manner and be accompanied by such information as it may reasonably require[20]. The main standard to be applied by the SIB in deciding whether to make a recognition order is whether the SRO has rules and procedures governing its authorisation at least as equivalent to those laid down by the SIB for those seeking direct authorisation[1]. In addition, an SRO must have a 'scope' rule precluding members from carrying on, without separate authorisation or exemption, the kinds of investment business not regulated by the SRO[2]. As to other requirements relating to rules and procedures, the rules and practices of the SRO must be such as to secure that its members are fit and proper persons to carry on investment business of the kind it regulates[3]. The SRO must have fair and reasonable rules and practices for admission, expulsion and discipline, including adequate provision for appeal[4]. It must also have adequate arrangements and resources for effective monitoring and enforcement of its rules[5]. The composition of the governing body must ensure a proper balance between the interests of the different members of the organisation and between the interests of the organisation or its members and the interests of the public[6]. The SRO must have effective arrangements for the investigation of complaints[7] and must also be able and willing to promote and maintain high standards[8].

Recognition may be refused on the grounds of failure to satisfy a specified requirement, the existence of another SRO regulating the same kind of investment business or that its rules[9], guidance or clearing arrangements would infringe the provisions relating to the prevention of restrictive practices[10].

In the event of an SRO failing to fulfil its statutory functions, the SIB is authorised to revoke recognition. This power is exerciseable on the grounds that: the SRO's rules and procedures do not satisfy the statutory requirements for recognition; the SRO has failed to comply with its obligations under the FSA 1986 or the SRO's continued recognition is rendered undesirable by the emergence of another SRO[11]. This last ground could enable the SIB to strengthen the regulatory framework by forcing out weaker SROs[12]. In addition, the Secretary of State may revoke recognition of an SRO if its rules, guidance or practices or any practices of its members have, or are intended or likely to have, to a significant extent the effect of restricting, distorting or preventing competition and that effect is greater than necessary for the protection of investors[13]. An effect of revocation is that the SRO's members are no longer authorised to carry on investment business by virtue of the SRO.

As an alternative to the drastic measure of revocation, two other measures are provided in the event of an SRO failing to fulfil its statutory functions. First, when the SIB considers that the statutory requirements for recognition have not been satisfied or that the organisation has failed to comply with a continuing

20. Ibid, s9(1) and (2).
1. Ibid, s10(2) and Sch2, para3(1).
2. Ibid, s10(3).
3. Ibid, Sch2, para 1(1).
4. Ibid, para2.
5. Ibid, para4.
6. Ibid, para5.
7. Ibid, para6.
8. Ibid, para7.
9. Ibid, s10(4) and (5).
10. Ibid, ss119-128.
11. Ibid, s119(1).
12. A.J. Wedgewood, G.A. Pell, L.H. Leigh, C.L. Ryan, *A Guide to the Financial Services Act 1986* (1986), p.23.
13. FSA 1986, ss119(3) and 120(4).

obligation, it may apply to the court for a compliance order[14]. The court may then order the organisation to take such steps as the court directs for securing that the requirement is satisfied or the obligation is complied with[15].

Secondly, where the rules of the organisation do not provide investors with adequate protection and after consulting the organisation, the SIB may direct the organisation to alter, or itself alter, the organisation's rules in such manner as it considers necessary for securing that the rules satisfy those requirements[16]. Any such direction is enforceable by mandamus[17]. This method has the advantage of enabling the SIB to move quickly to change an organisation's rules when investor protection so requires[18]. To balance the power conferred on the SIB, the SRO's are empowered to apply to the court. If the court is satisfied that the rules without the alteration satisfied the requirements or other alterations proposed by the organisation would have the same result, the court may set aside the alterations or direction and authorise the organisation to make the alterations proposed by it. However, the setting aside of an alteration shall not affect its previous operation[19]. In addition, if the SIB considers that the rules or practices of an organisation do not satisfy the requirements for recognition in respect of any one of the different kinds of investment business which it regulates, the SIB may, instead of revoking the revocation order or applying for a compliance order, direct the organisation to alter, or itself alter, the organisation's rules so that they preclude a member from carrying on investment business of that kind unless he is authorised for that purpose otherwise than by virtue of membership of the organisation or he is an exempted person in respect of that business[20]. The alteration of rules by, or pursuant to a direction of the SIB or a court order, does not preclude their subsequent alteration or revocation by that organisation[1]. Abuse of this provision by an SRO would form grounds for revocation of recognition or an application for a compliance order.

Statutory immunity from liability for damages is granted to a recognised SRO and any of its officers, servants or members of its governing body in respect of anything done, or omitted to be done, in discharging its functions unless the act or omission is shown to have been in bad faith[2]. However, the public function of SROs makes their acts and decisions amenable to judicial review[3].

VIII. THE RECOGNISED PROFESSIONAL BODIES (THE 'RPBs')

In recognition of the role of professionals as an important source of investment advice and services, the FSA 1986 contains a specific method for authorisation for professions when the practice of the profession is not, wholly or mainly, the carrying on of investment business. The method centres on the recognition of professional bodies.

Reflecting a preponderance of solicitors and accountants, the recognised professional bodies are: the Law Society of England and Wales; the Law Society

14. Ibid, s12(1).
15. Ibid, s12(2).
16. Ibid, s13(1) and (4).
17. Ibid, s13(3).
18. Wedgwood, Pell, Leigh and Ryan, op cit. n12, p66, supra, p.26.
19. FSA 1986, s13(5).
20. Ibid, s13(2).
1. Ibid, s13(8).
2. Ibid, s187(1). The functions to which this provision applies are set out in s187(2) and (5).
3. *Bank of Scotland, Petitioner,* Scots Law Report, (1988) Times, 21 November.

of Scotland; the Law Society of Northern Ireland; the Institute of Chartered Accountants in England and Wales; the Institute of Chartered Accountants of Scotland, the Institute of Chartered Accountants in Ireland; the Institute of Actuaries and the Insurance Brokers Registration Council.

Under the recognition system, a professional body recognised by the SIB may issue a certificate[4] to its members, enabling them to carry on investment business of the kind regulated by the body[5]. In this connection, a professional body is a body which regulates the practice of a profession which is not, wholly or mainly, the carrying on of investment business[6].

The recognition process is similar to that for SROs. Thus, an application for recognition must be made to the SIB in the prescribed manner and include such information as it may reasonably require[7]. The SIB must be satisfied that the professional body has rules which impose acceptable limits on the kinds of investment business which may be carried on by persons certified by it[8] and that it meets certain criteria[9]. In particular, the professional body must regulate the practice of a profession in the exercise of statutory powers or for a statutory purpose[10], have certain rules, practices and arrangements in regard to certification[11] and have rules which provide equivalent investor protection to that provided by the SIB conduct of business rules for those seeking direct authorisation[12]. The professional body must also have adequate arrangements and resources for effective monitoring and enforcement of compliance with its rules[13], including provision for the withdrawal or suspension of certification. In this connection, the arrangements for enforcement must provide a proper balance between the interests of the persons certified by the body and the interests of the public; in particular, those responsible for enforcement must include a sufficient number of independent persons. In addition, the professional body must have effective arrangements for the investigation of com-

4. By s15(2), FSA 1986, such a certificate may be issued by a recognised professional body to an individual, a body corporate, a partnership or an unincorporated association. A certificate issued to a partnership must be issued in the partnership name and authorises the carrying on of investment business in that name by the partnership to which the certificate is issued, by any partnership which succeeds to that business having previously carried it on in partnership: s.15(3).
5. FSA 1986, s15(1).
6. Ibid, s16(1). By s16(2), the expression 'members of a professional body' means individuals who, whether or not members of the body, are entitled to practise the profession in question and, in practising it, are subject to the rules of that body. The expression 'rules of a professional body' means the rules (whether or not laid down by the body itself) which the body has power to enforce in relation to the practice of the profession in question and the carrying on of investment business by persons practising that profession or which relate to the grant, suspension or withdrawal of authorisation certificates, the admission and expulsion of members or otherwise to the constitution of the body.
7. FSA 1986, s17(1) and, by virtue of s17(2), s9(2)-(6).
8. Ibid, s18(3).
9. Ibid, s18(2) and Sch3.
10. Ibid, Sch3, para1.
11. Ibid, Sch3, para2 which provides that the professional body must have rules, practices and arrangements for securing that no person can be certified as authorised to carry on investment business unless the certified person is either an individual who is a member of the body or a person managed and controlled by one or more individuals, each of whom is a member of a recognised professional body and at least one of whom is a member of the certifying body; where the certified person is an individual his main business must be the practice of the profession regulated by the certifying body and he must be practising that profession otherwise than in partnership; where the certified person is not an individual that person's main business must be the practice of the profession or professions regulated by the recognised professional body or bodies of which the individual or individuals mentioned above are members.
12. FSA 1986, Sch3, para3.
13. Ibid, para4.

plaints[14] and be willing and able to promote and maintain high standards[15].

The SIB's power of recognition is discretionary. It may refuse to recognise a professional body, even where it meets the specified criteria[16]. When the SIB refuses an application, it must notify the applicant in writing, stating the reasons for refusal[17].

In regard to revocation of recognition, the SIB may revoke a recognition order at any time on the ground that the requirements for recognition are not satisfied or that the body has failed to comply with its obligations under the FSA 1986[18]. As a less drastic alternative, the SIB may apply to the High Court for an order (a 'compliance order') directing the body to take steps to ensure that the requirement is satisfied or that the obligation is complied with[19]. However, in contrast to the rules of SROs, the SIB has no power to change the rules of RPBs.

Unlike the SROs, the RPBs do not enjoy statutory immunity from liability for damages. They may, nevertheless, make it a condition of the issue of an investment business certificate that neither the body nor its officers, servants or members of its governing body is to be liable for damages for anything done, or omitted to be done, in discharging its functions unless the act or omission is shown to have been in bad faith[20].

IX. RECOGNISED INVESTMENT EXCHANGES AND CLEARING HOUSES

Both the running of an investment exchange, with the function of providing an organised market for the transaction of investment business, and the running of a clearing house, with the function of providing clearing services relating to transactions on an investment exchange, normally constitute the carrying on of investment business for the purpose of the FSA 1986[1]. Whilst a requirement of authorisation thus prima facie applies, exemption provisions obviate this requirement in the case of investment exchanges and clearing houses recognised by the SIB[2]. Such bodies are exempt in respect of anything done in their capacity as such; membership of such a body is not an alternative method of obtaining authorisation as an investment business. Separate provision is made for the recognition, and exemption, of overseas investment exchanges and clearing houses recognised by the Secretary of State[3].

A. Recognised investment exchanges (The 'RIEs')

The status of RIE has been conferred on several exchanges, including the London International Financial Futures Exchange Ltd. (LIFFE), LIFFE Options Plc and the International Stock Exchange of the United Kingdom and the Republic of Ireland Ltd[4]. Due to its significance for insider dealing regulation,

14. Ibid, para5.
15. Ibid, para6.
16. Ibid, s18(1).
17. Ibid, s18(4).
18. Ibid, s19(1).
19. Ibid, s20(1) and (3).
20. Ibid, s187(6). As to the relevant functions, see s187(7).
1. FSA 1986, s1 and Sch1.
2. Ibid, ss36-39.
3. Ibid, s40.
4. Other RIEs are: the Baltic Futures Exchange; the International Petroleum Exchange of London Ltd.; the London Commodity Exchange (1986) Ltd. and the London Metal Exchange Ltd.

this last will be considered in more detail.

1. The International Stock Exchange

Incorporated as a private limited company in November 1986 following the decision of the Stock Exchange and the International Securities Regulatory Organisation to come together[5], the International Stock Exchange derives its importance from its regulatory powers over the market with the largest number of securities transactions. However, it has no legal monopoly and alternative markets exist.

The Exchange's regulatory role was significantly modified as a result of the FSA 1986. Whereas the Stock Exchange formerly combined the roles now performed by a recognised SRO and an RIE, a separation of functions was imposed by this legislation. Consistent with this separation and in conjunction with the formation of the International Stock Exchange, the Securities Association was created as a separate body to become the SRO through which most members of the former Stock Exchange would seek authorisation under the FSA 1986. Both new bodies have a degree of cross-membership at Council and Committee level and employ the services of the Exchange's administration, thereby drawing on its previous regulatory experience[6].

Moreover, the degree of freedom enjoyed by the Exchange from governmental or statutory control[7] was considerably circumscribed by the FSA 1986. Apart from having had to meet the statutory requirements for recognition, its continuing role as an RIE is dependent upon compliance with its statutory obligations, with non-compliance running the risk of triggering the SIB's powers to revoke recognition or, less drastically, to seek a compliance order[8]. The Exchange is also subject to the special competition regime applicable to the financial services sector[9].

The Exchange's modified regulatory role coincided with important market changes, which culminated in 'Big Bang' in October, 1986[10]. Initially, in an agreement with Government in 1983, the Stock Exchange agreed to abandon certain restrictive rules in return for exemption from the restrictive practices legislation. New rules, which came into effect in October 1986, abolished fixed minimum commissions and permitted outside firms to enter the market. With the abolition, in March 1986, of the rule limiting outside ownership to a 29.9% interest in member firms, institutions with large capital resources merged with jobbers or brokers with market expertise.

The view that the single capacity system, with its separation of functions between brokers and jobbers, would not survive the abolition of fixed commissions proved well-founded. The single capacity system was replaced by the competing market maker system, whereby member firms were permitted to act as jobber and broker and become registered market makers. As such, they are

---

5. *The International Stock Exchange of the UK and the Republic of Ireland Ltd.*, Annual Report 1987, p.3.
6. Ibid
7. *Review of Investor Protection*, A Discussion Document by Professor L.C.B. Gower (1982), para3.22.
8. FSA 1986, s37; see, post, 2. Investment exchanges.
9. Ibid, ss119-128; see, ante, I. The Department of Trade and Industry.
10. A brief outline of these events is contained in *Halsbury's Laws of England* (4th edition) Supplement 1988, Vol.45 Stock Exchange, p.1 and A. Tunc, *Le droit anglais des sociétés anonymes (1987), para55.*

required to maintain two-way prices, though enjoy the tax advantages previously conferred on jobbers and have access to money brokers in the event of needing to borrow stock. The new system prompted mergers between bankers, jobbers and brokers; it also had the result of a wider spread of stock being dealt in and of opening up the market to more members, including overseas firms.

At the basis of the new system, new technology in the form of the Stock Exchange Automated Quotation System (SEAQ) came into operation in October 1986 and provides computerised information to dealers and the public. Irrespective of their location, SEAQ places all Stock Exchange members on an equal footing, with access to information about all market makers' quotations. A consequence is that deals are done by telephone, rather than on the market floor.

In organisational terms, control of the Exchange's affairs lies with the Council as directors. Apart from two ex officio members (the Chief Executive and the Government Broker) and three lay members, its thirty-five members are drawn from the Exchange's members[11]. The Council is headed by a Chairman, who is assisted by two Deputy Chairmen.

On most issues, the Council delegates responsibility to the Chairman and his deputies or to one of the committees responsible for various aspects of market administration and regulation. It employs a Chief Executive and, in the UK, about 2,000 staff[12].

The Exchange has three main areas of regulatory activities. These concern its members, companies whose securities are traded on the Exchange and other market users.

(a) THE REGULATION OF MEMBERS

The Exchange's regulation of members is based on its Rules and Regulations. These provide for the organisation of the market, including the competing market maker system and the terms on which members may deal with each other and with clients. Rules concerning membership and member firms' solvency and financial position receive special attention. The creation of a false market is forbidden[13].

In regard to disciplinary matters, the Exchange investigates alleged misconduct. In addition to breach of the Rules or Regulations or good practice[14], this includes insider dealing[15], an adverse finding by another regulatory body and breach of the City Code[16]. Members and their employees are required to attend and give evidence[17]. Following initial assessment by the Professional Standards Panel, a matter may be referred to the Disciplinary Committee, which hears a charge and may impose a penalty, subject to appeal to the Disciplinary Appeals Committee and notification by the Council[18]. The penalties are reprimand by the Chairman or Council, censure, suspension either from trading or of the

11. *International Stock Exchange,* op cit n5, p70, supra, pp.2 and 19.
12. Ibid, p.20.
13. Rule 301.2-301.4.
14. Rule 23.1a.
15. Insider dealing would infringe both Rule 23.1d: 'conduct the manner of which is detrimental to the interests of the Stock Exchange' and Rule 23.1e: 'conduct the manner of which is dishonourable or disgraceful or improper or unbecoming the character of a Member'; City Capital Markets Committee, Supervision of the Securities Market (1974), paras23-24.
16. Rule 23.1g.
17. Rule 20.1-20.4.
18. Rule 24.1-24.3.

right to enter any trading floor or use any system, and expulsion; alternatively or additionally a fine may be imposed[19].

(b) THE REGULATION OF COMPANIES

To comply with EEC Directives[20], the official listing of securities now has a statutory framework. Regulation is based on a prohibition of the inclusion of investments in the Official List, unless the provisions of Part IV, FSA 1986[1] are complied with.

In this framework, the Council of the Stock Exchange is the 'competent authority' to issue listing rules[2]. These provide for the admission of securities to listing, the contents of listing particulars and the continuing obligations of listed companies.

In the performance of their functions, the Council is subject to governmental control. In regard to its status as competent authority, the Secretary of State has power to transfer the powers of the Council as competent authority to another body, not only at the request of the Council, but also if he believes that the Council is exercising its powers in a manner which is unnecessary for the protection of investors or that it is necessary to transfer the functions for the protection of investors[3]. In addition, the Secretary of State has a reserve power to direct the Council to comply with Community and international obligations[4].

In regard to admissions to listing, no securities can be admitted except on an application to the Council in accordance with the procedure in the listing rules[5] and unless the Council is satisfied that both the listing rules and any other requirements imposed by it in relation to that application are complied with[6]. Provision is made both for the Council to discontinue listing where special circumstances preclude normal regular dealing in the securities and for suspension of listing[7].

Whilst the detailed disclosure requirements are specified in the listing rules, a general duty of disclosure is imposed by statute. The listing particulars must contain all such information as investors and their professional advisers would reasonably require, and reasonably expect to find there, for the purpose of making an informed assessment of the assets and liabilities, financial position, profits and losses and prospects of the issuer of the securities and the rights attaching to those securities[8]. In the event of a significant development between the preparation of listing particulars and the commencement of dealings relating to a matter to be disclosed in the listing particulars, supplementary

---

19. Rule 24.4.
20. Directive 79/279 on the conditions for the admission of securities to official Stock Exchange listing, O.J. 1979 L66/21; Directive 80/390 on listing particulars, O.J. 1980 L100/1 and Directive 82/121 on information to be published on a regular basis by companies whose shares are listed, O.J. 1982 L48/26.
1. Ss142-157; these replaced the Stock Exchange (Listing) Regulations 1984, S.I. 1984 No. 716, implementing these three Directives.
2. FSA 1986, s142(6).
3. Ibid, s157.
4. Ibid, s192.
5. Ibid, s143. This provision also requires the consent of the issuer to listing and prevents the listing of securities of a private company.
6. FSA 1986, s144(1).
7. Ibid, s145.
8. Ibid, s146(1).

listing particulars must be submitted[9]. Non-disclosure of information may be authorised on the grounds that disclosure would be contrary to the public interest, would be seriously detrimental to the issuer of the securities or, in the case of certain securities[10], is unnecessary for the potential buyers and dealers in such securities[11]. Provision is made for civil liability in respect of misrepresentations or omissions in listing particulars or supplementary listing particulars[12].

Once securities are admitted to Official Listing, a continuing obligation to provide the market with regular information is imposed[13]. In the context of insider dealing regulation, the most relevant disclosure requirements are those involving timely disclosure and insider reporting, including those laid down by the City Code[14].

Other continuing obligations transcend disclosure. In particular, companies whose securities are admitted to Official Listing must adopt rules governing dealings by directors in terms no less exacting than those of the Model Code[15].

In 1980, the Unlisted Securities Market (USM) was established by the Stock Exchange in response to a sharp increase in transactions in securities of unlisted companies and Government policy of encouraging small companies unable to comply with the requirements for Official Listing or afford the expense. Set out in the 'Green Book'[16], the requirements for admission to the USM are less stringent than for the Official List. But analogous continuous disclosure requirements are contained in a General Undertaking, which similarly refers to the City Code and the Model Code.

The establishment of the Third Market in 1987 marked a similar development. This market was established for companies for which neither a Listing nor inclusion in the USM is appropriate[17].

(c) THE REGULATION OF OTHER MARKET USERS

In regard to other market users, the Exchange's prime concern is with improper dealings. In this connection, its two main initiatives are the Model Code for securities transactions by directors of listed companies and the monitoring of unusual price movements and conducting preliminary investigations.

As to the former, reference has been made to the requirement for companies admitted to official listing and to the USM to adopt rules governing dealings by directors in terms no less exacting than those of the Model Code[18]. However, the binding nature of the Model Code, or substitute provisions, on individuals arises through incorporation of those provisions in their contracts of service or employment or individuals' acceptance of their employer's right to make rules governing their conduct. Enforcement of the Model Code thus lies with the company.

Concerning unusual price movements, the responsibility for initial monitoring lies with the Quotations Department. In the event of apparent untoward

9. Ibid, s147(1).
10. Namely, those which fall within FSA 1986, Sch1, para2 as modified by s142(3)(b).
11. FSA 1986, s148(1).
12. Ibid, ss150-152.
13. Admission of Securities to Listing, Section 5, Chapter 2.
14. See, post, Chapter 5. Disclosure.
15. Admission of Securities to Listing, Section 5, Chapter 2, para45; see, post, Chapter 6. Administrative Regulation.
16. The Stock Exchange, Unlisted Securities Market.
17. Ibid, The 3rd Market.
18. See, ante, 2. Regulation of companies.

activity the matter is referred to the Surveillance Division for further investigation[19]. Prior to the CA 1980, this could lead to a full investigation, though the inability to compel non-members to attend reduced its effectiveness[20]. Where take-overs were involved, the matter was referred to the Panel. When instances of insider dealing were found, the Stock Exchange published the result of its investigations, thereby using disclosure as a sanction against conduct condemned as unethical. In the 1970s, the adoption of more stringent self-regulatory provisions opened a wider range of enforcement, either by a professional association for breach of its own code or by a listed company when the Model Code applies. Since the CA 1980, Stock Exchange practice has been to refer, after preliminary investigation, suspected cases of insider dealing to the Department of Trade and Industry for further investigation and a decision on prosecution. Any further action by professional bodies or by listed or USM companies is now ancillary to the Department's role as the main authority for enforcing the criminal prohibition on insider dealing.

2. Investment exchanges

Application may be made to the SIB by any body corporate or an unincorporated association for an order declaring it to be an RIE[1]. The procedure, adopted by reference, is the same as for recognition as an SRO[2].

As a prerequisite to recognition, the investment exchange must comply with certain specified criteria[3]. In this connection, the exchange must have sufficient financial resources for the proper performance of its functions[4] and its rules and practices must ensure that business is conducted in an orderly manner and so as to afford proper protection to investors[5]. In particular, it must limit dealings on it to investments in which there is a proper market and, where relevant, impose information requirements on issuers of investments so that persons dealing in the investments have proper information for determining their current value[6]. Moreover, the exchange must have arrangements for ensuring the performance (either directly or through a recognised clearing house) of transactions effected on it[7] and must either have, or secure the provision of, satisfactory arrangements for recording such transactions[8]. It must also have adequate arrangements and resources for the effective monitoring and enforcement of compliance with its rules and any clearing arrangements made by it[9]. In addition, it must have effective arrangements for the investigation of complaints[10] and be willing and able to promote high standards and to co-operate with the regulatory authorities[11].

The SIB's power of recognition is discretionary. It may refuse to recognise an

19. See, post, Chapter 7. Investigation, VI. The Stock Exchange.
20. J.A.C. Suter, *The Regulation of Insider Dealing in Britain and France* (1985), pp.7.72-7.90.
1. FSA 1986, s37(1).
2. Ibid, s37(2).
3. Ibid, s37(4) and Sch4.
4. Ibid, Sch4, para1.
5. Ibid, para2(1).
6. Ibid, para2(2).
7. Ibid, para2(4).
8. Ibid, para2(5).
9. Ibid, para3.
10. Ibid, para4.
11. Ibid, para5.

investment exchange, even where it meets the specified criteria[12]. When the SIB refuses an application, it must notify the applicant in writing, stating the reasons for refusal[13].

As to revocation of recognition, the SIB may revoke a recognition order if the specified criteria are not satisfied or the exchange has failed to comply with its obligations under the FSA 1986[14]. Less drastically, the SIB may seek a compliance order[15].

B. Recognised clearing houses (The 'RCHs')

The status of RCH has been conferred on two bodies. These are the International Commodities Clearing House Ltd. and GAFTA Clearing House Company Ltd.

Application may be made to the SIB by any body corporate or an incorporated association for an order declaring it to be an RCH[16]. The procedure adapted by reference, is the same as for recognition as an SRO[17].

As a prerequisite to recognition, the clearing house must comply with certain specified criteria[18]. These are that: it has sufficient financial resources for the proper performance of its functions; it has adequate arrangements and resources to ensure the effective monitoring and enforcement of compliance with its rules; it provides clearing services of a standard that would enable an investment exchange to satisfy the requirements of Schedule 4 and it is willing and able to promote high standards and to co-operate with the regulatory authorities.

The SIB's power of recognition is discretionary. It may refuse to recognise a clearing house, even where it meets the specified criteria[19]. When the SIB refuses an application, it must notify the applicant in writing, stating the reasons for refusal[20].

In regard to revocation, the SIB may revoke a recognition order if the specified criteria are not satisfied or the clearing house has failed to comply with its obligations under the FSA 1986[1]. A less drastic course is for the SIB to seek a compliance order[2].

C. Overseas investment exchanges and clearing houses

An investment exchange or clearing house based overseas may be granted recognition, and thus exemption, by the Secretary of State, provided it satisfies certain criteria[3]. These are that: it is subject to supervision, in the country in which its head office is situated, which provides protection to investors equivalent to that provided in the UK; it is able and willing to co-operate with UK

12. Ibid, s37(3).
13. Ibid, s37(5).
14. Ibid, s37(7).
15. Ibid, s37(8).
16. Ibid, s39(1).
17. Ibid, s39(2).
18. Ibid, s39(4).
19. Ibid, s39(3).
20. Ibid, s39(5).
1. Ibid, s39(7).
2. Ibid, s39(8).
3. Ibid, s40(2).

supervisory and regulatory bodies by sharing information and otherwise, and adequate arrangements exist for such co-operation between supervisory bodies in the head office country and UK authorities. In determining whether to make a recognition order, the Secretary of State may have regard to any restrictions imposed on UK persons in regard to the financial markets of the head office country[4]. The Secretary of State also has powers to revoke recognition orders and to seek compliance orders[5].

Two recognised overseas exchanges are the National Association of Securities Dealers Automated Quotations System and Sydney Futures Exchange Ltd.

X. THE PANEL ON TAKE-OVERS AND MERGERS

The Panel was established in 1968 on the initiative of the Governor of the Bank of England to supervise implementation of the City Code on Take-overs and Mergers. Though formerly an arm of the CSI, it is not an arm of the SIB.

The Panel is a non-statutory body primarily composed of representatives of organisations whose members are actively engaged in the securities markets and are responsible for substantial shareholdings in, and providing finance for, British industry[6]. In addition, the Chairman, Deputy Chairman and a further non-representative member are appointed by the Governor of the Bank of England[7].

Although non-statutory, the Panel is linked to the regulatory framework established by statute. The SIB and relevant SROs require investment businesses to co-operate with the Panel in enquiries and investigations. By statutory instrument, the Panel is designated under the CA 1985, the FSA 1986 and the Banking Act 1987 to receive information obtained by other regulatory authorities, the disclosure of which is restricted by statute[8]. By way of sanction, failure by a person authorised by the SIB or an SRO to comply with the Code or a ruling of the Panel may lead to withdrawal of authorisation under the FSA 1986[9]. Moreover, some of the bodies represented on the Panel are recognised in accordance with the FSA 1986.

However, in contrast to the Securities Association and other self-regulatory organisations where the relationship between the organisation and members is contractual in nature, the Panel is a self-regulatory body set up by the self-regulatory organisations and other professional bodies with authority over their members. Its introduction attempts to extend the Code to individuals not directly affiliated to bodies represented on the Panel:

4. Ibid, s40(3).
5. Ibid, s40(4).
6. The bodies represented on the Panel are: the Association of British Insurers, the Association of Investment Trust Companies, the British Merchant Banking and Securities Houses Association (with separate representation for its Corporate Finance Committee), the Committee of London and Scottish Bankers, the Confederation of British Industry, the Financial Intermediaries, Managers and Brokers Regulatory Association, the Institute of Chartered Accountants in England and Wales, the International Stock Exchange of the UK and the Republic of Ireland Limited ('The Stock Exchange'), the Investment Management Regulatory Organisation, the National Association of Pension Funds, the Securities Association and the Unit Trust Association: The Code, Introduction, para2(a).
7. The City Code on Take-overs and Mergers (the 'City Code'), Introduction, para2(a).
8. Ibid, para2(c). Eg, the Financial Services (Disclosure of Information) (Designated Authorities) (No.2) Order 1987, S.1.1987 No.859.
9. City Code, Introduction, para1(c).

'The responsibilities described in the Code apply most directly to those who are actively engaged in the securities markets. They are also regarded by the Panel as applying to directors of companies which are subject to the Code and to persons or groups of persons who seek to gain or consolidate effective control of such companies. They also apply to all professional advisers, insofar as they advise on the transactions in question. These responsibilities apply irrespective of whether those involved are directly affiliated to any of the bodies whose representatives are members of the Panel. The Panel also expects any other persons who issue circulars to shareholders in connection with take-overs to observe the highest standards of care'.

But without the consent of the individuals concerned, any corresponding extension of the Panel's authority is ineffective. Like any other individual or body, the Panel may express its views on a party's conduct and it is thought that the Panel enjoys the further protection of qualified privilege against liability for defamation[10]. Beyond that, agreement to accept the Panel's jurisdiction is required[11]. With professional people, agreement can be given by their professional body.

Day-to-day work is delegated to the Panel executive which consists of a Director General, two Deputy Directors General, three Secretaries, nine Assistant Secretaries and small supporting staff[12]. The aim is a balance of merchant banking, stockbroking, legal and accounting backgrounds[13]. To provide continuity, the two Deputy Directors General are permanent employees, but most staff serve on secondment from the private sector, the Bank of England and the Department of Trade and Industry.

The Panel executive is responsible for the general administration of the Code[14]. This includes, either on its own initiative or at the instigation of third parties, the conduct of investigations and the monitoring of relevant dealings, in connection with the Code. The executive is available both for consultation and to give rulings on points of interpretation before or during take-over or merger transactions. In the event of any doubt as to whether a proposed course of conduct is in accordance with the General Principles or Rules, the importance of consulting the executive is emphasised[15].

However, the smallness of the Panel executive militates against extensive involvement. Advance approval of bids is not required. Though take-over documents must be filed on publication, preclearance is not necessary and the executive relies on the Quotations Department to alert it to non-compliance by listed, USM and Third Market companies. It operates mainly by advance consultation by a party or adviser about a problem or subsequent complaint by another party or adviser that the Code has been broken. Occasionally, it has initiated investigations, particularly into suspected insider dealing before the CA 1980, though it relied on the Stock Exchange to monitor price movements.

In regard to co-operation with other authorities[16], the Panel co-operates with other regulatory authorities, such as the Department of Trade and Industry, the

10. J.A.C. Suter, *The Regulation of Insider Dealing in Britain and France* (1985), p.7.97.
11. *Abbott v Sullivan* [1952] 1 KB 189.
12. *The Panel on Take-overs and Mergers*, Report on the Year ended 31st March, 1988, p.2.
13. *Committee to Review the Functioning of Financial Institutions*, Second Stage Evidence, Vol.1. The Panel on Take-overs and Mergers (1979), para68
14. City Code, Introduction, para2(b).
15. Ibid, para3(b).
16. Ibid, para2(c).

SIB, the SROs, the Stock Exchange and the Bank of England. This co-operation extends to the mutual exchange of information and, where appropriate, reporting breaches of the Code to the relevant authority. The Panel works closely with the Stock Exchange in monitoring dealings. As mentioned, the SIB and relevant SROs require investment businesses to co-operate in Panel enquiries and investigations and the Panel is designated under companies, financial services and banking legislation to receive regulatory information, whose disclosure is restricted by statute.

The full Panel is a supervisory body which meets regularly to receive progress reports and consider questions of policy. It also deals with disciplinary cases, exceptionally difficult or important cases and contested executive rulings, usually at ad hoc meetings[17]. Proceedings[18] are informal and private; there are no rules of evidence. Individuals are normally expected to conduct their own cases, though they may be accompanied by their advisers.

A right of appeal lies to the Appeal Committee[19] in three circumstances: where the Panel both finds a breach of the Code and proposes to take disciplinary action; where it is alleged that the Panel has acted outside its jurisdiction; or in respect of any refusal by the Panel to recognise, or any decision of the Panel to cease to recognise, a market-maker or fund manager as an exempt market-maker or exempt fund manager as the case may be. With leave of the Panel, an appeal may lie in other cases; but the Panel does not normally grant leave to appeal against a finding of fact or a decision on the interpretation of the Code. The Chairman of the Appeal Committee, who normally has held high judicial office, sits with two Panel members not previously involved with the decision under appeal. It does not normally hear new evidence.

The Code consists of ten General Principles, thirty-eight Rules (with accompanying Notes) and four Appendices (comprising three Guidance Notes and a Code of Practice), the detailed content of the Code having grown in response to the requests for advice by parties and their advisers. The Introduction states that the General Principles are 'essentially a codification of good standards of commercial behaviour and they should have an obvious and universal application'. As for the Rules, some 'are no more than examples of the application of the General Principles . . . Others are rules of procedure designed to govern specific types of take-over'.

The difficulty of devising detailed rules to cover all circumstances was met by a general provision[20] that the spirit as well as the precise wording of the General Principles and the ensuing Rules must be observed and that the General Principles and the spirit of the Code apply in areas or circumstances not explicitly covered by any Rule. This has the advantage of making the Code effective in a wider range of circumstances than could be covered by a statutory code[1] when different rules of interpretation apply and loopholes may be legitimately found[2]. The Panel has also emphasised too great a reliance on detailed rules would result in the Code lagging behind current practices[3] and

17. Ibid, para3(c) and (d).
18. Ibid, para3(e).
19. Ibid, para3(f).
20. General Principles, Introduction.
1. *Weinberg and Blank on Take-overs and Mergers,* (Fourth edition) by M.A. Weinberg, M.V. Blank and A.L. Greystoke (1979), para1205 ('Weinberg and Blank').
2. *The Panel on Take-overs and Mergers,* Report on the Years ended 31st March, 1975 and 1976, Foreword by Lord Shawcross, p.4.
3. *The Panel on Take-overs and Mergers,* op cit. n13, p77, supra, para42.

that advice about the Code's application to a proposed transaction can be obtained by consulting the Panel at the outset[4].

Nevertheless, this approach raises other difficulties. When parties and their advisers have to act quickly and effectively, a clear set of rules provides a better reference point than principles of indeterminate scope. Other than not seeking technical ways around the rules, the meaning of the requirement to observe the spirit of the Code is uncertain[5]. This requirement was criticised before Department of Trade inspectors by Counsel for a company chairman:

> 'The Code by its very definition is either a Code or it is nothing . . . it is wholly undesirable practice if the Panel lend their support to it of trying to extend their already voluntary judisdiction by nebulous and general pronouncements which leave people not knowing what they may do'[6].

Two main themes can be distinguished among Code provisions[7]. First, it is for offeree shareholders to decide the outcome of an offer. For this purpose, it requires provision of adequate information and time to decide, an offeror must obtain voting control before declaring its offer unconditional, tactics designed to frustrate the bid are prohibited, during an offer disclosure of dealings is imposed and information given to one prospective offeror must be given to other prospective offerors. Secondly, there must be equitable treatment as between offeree shareholders. To this end, the highest price paid over a reasonable period before the offer must be offered to all shareholders, the acquisition of control is regulated with any premium shared among all shareholders, insider dealing is prohibited, partial bids and sales of controlling interests are regulated and an offeree board must seek outside advice.

Reflecting the Code's concern with the protection of offeree shareholders, its scope of application is determined by reference to the nature of the company which is the offeree or potential offeree, or in which control[8] may change or be consolidated[9]. The Code applies primarily to offers for all listed and unlisted public companies (and, where appropriate, statutory and chartered companies) considered by the Panel to be resident in the UK, the Channel Islands or the Isle of Man[10]. However, on the basis that private companies also use the facilities of the securities market, the Code also applies to offers for private companies considered to be so resident, but only when: (i) their equity share capital has been listed on the Stock Exchange at any time during the ten years prior to the relevant date; or (ii) dealings in their equity share capital have been advertised in a newspaper on a regular basis for a continuous period of at least six months in the ten years prior to the relevant date; or their equity share capital has been subject to a marketing arrangement as described in s163(2)(b), CA

---

4. The Panel on Take-overs and Mergers, Supervision of the Securities Market (1975), p.8.

5. P.L. Davies, *The Regulation of Take-overs and Mergers* (1976), p.40.

6. *Ferguson and General Investments Ltd. (formerly known as Dowgate and General Investments Ltd.); CST Investments Ltd.*, Report by J. Jackson, Q.C. and K.L. Young, T.D., F.C.A., (1979), p.9.

7. Weinberg and Blank, para 1206.

8. 'Control' means a holding or aggregate holdings, of shares carrying 30% or more of the voting rights of a company, irrespective of whether the holding or holdings gives or give, de facto control; and except for the purpose of Rule 11 (nature of consideration to be offered) 'voting rights' means all the voting rights attributable to the share capital of a company which are currently exerciseable at a general meeting.

9. City Code, Introduction, para4(a).

10. Under this provision, the Code also applies to all offers for companies considered by the Panel to be resident in the Irish Republic if their shares are listed on The Stock Exchange or dealt in on the Unlisted Securities Market, on the Third Market or under Stock Exchange Rule 535.3.

1985 at any time during the ten years prior to the relevant date (eg their shares have been dealt in on the Unlisted Securities Market); or (iii) they have filed a prospectus for the issue of equity share capital at the Companies' Registry at any time during the ten years prior to the relevant date. But recognising that Code provisions may not be appropriate to all statutory and chartered companies or to all such private companies, the Panel has indicated that it will apply the Code with a degree of flexibility in suitable cases.

In regard to the transactions to which it applies[11], the Code is concerned with take-over and merger transactions, however effected, of all relevant companies. These include partial offers, offers by a parent company for shares in its subsidiary and certain other transactions where control of a company is to be obtained or consolidated. References in the Code to 'take-overs' and 'offers' include, where appropriate, all such transactions. However, the Code does not apply to offers for non-voting, non-equity share capital.

Early fears of a conflict between the law and the Code proved unfounded, with Panel cases rarely also coming before the courts. Rather, the courts tended to regard the Code as a statement of enlightened commercial and financial practice. In an early case[12], parts of the Code were quoted and used as a guide to good commercial practice. Lord Denning said 'although the Code does not have the force of law, nevertheless it does denote good business practice and good business standards'. In a later case[13], the court recognised that 'the provisions of the City Code set out a code of conduct which has been laid down by responsible and experienced persons in the City as being fair and reasonable'[14] and the courts may have regard to any flouting of the Code or Panel directions.

However, consistent with the judicial tendency to look at the nature rather than the source of a power, the Panel's decisions have recently been held[15] to be subject to judicial review. Whilst upholding the Panel's decision in the case, the Court of Appeal held that having regard to the wide-ranging nature and importance of the matters covered by the Code and to the public consequences of non-compliance with the Code, the Panel was performing a public duty when prescribing and administering the Code and its rules, and was subject to public law remedies; an application for judicial review would lie in an appropriate case. Nevertheless, since leave to apply was required, the court could, by refusing to entertain an unmeritorious application made merely as a tactic in a take-over battle, ensure that its jurisdiction was not used to frustrate the purpose for which the Panel existed. The court could meet the need for speed and finality by restricting the grant of certiorari and mandamus to cases where there had been a breach of natural justice, and by allowing the Panel's contemporary decisions to take their course in all other cases and considering the complaint and intervening, if at all, later and in retrospect by means of declaratory orders. These would enable the Panel not to repeat any error and would relieve the individuals of the disciplinary consequences of any erroneous finding of breach of the Code.

11. City Code, Introduction, para4(b).
12. *Dunford and Elliott v Johnson and Firth Brown Ltd.* [1977] 1 Lloyds Rep.505, C.A.
13. *Re St. Piran Ltd.* [1981] 3 All E.R.270.
14. Ibid at 277.
15. *R v Panel on Take-overs and Mergers, ex parte Datafin plc.* [1987] 1 All E.R.564. The test would be whether something had gone wrong of a nature and degree which required the intervention of the court: *R v Panel on Take-overs and Mergers, ex p Guinness plc.* [1988] NLJR 244.

Several provisions of the Code and aspects of the Panel's work impinge on insider dealing[16]. Apart from restrictions on insider dealing, the Code requires secrecy before an announcement and early announcements[17]. The Panel also deals with conflicts of interest[18] and its investigations[19] and sanctions[20] have not only underlined the limitations of self-regulation, but pointed to other problems of insider dealing regulation.

In the debate on insider dealing regulation, the need to review the problem was publicly accepted by the Chairman of the Panel in 1972. In response to press comments, he set out the Panel's approach to insider dealing in the context of take-overs and mergers and summarised his personal view in the following terms:

> 'As for "insider" dealings not within our take-over jurisdiction, the matter is, I think, one for consideration in connection with changes in the Company Law to be introduced next year. I would point out, however, that the fact that the City Panel and, for that matter, the Stock Exchange lack legal powers of interrogation or of requiring the production of documents by no means necessitates the establishment of a great structure like the Securities and Exchange Commission in the US. Investigations into "insider" dealings form only one small facet of the many sided functions of the Panel and the Stock Exchange. It would be a misfortune and it would be totally unnecessary to impose a slow moving statutory control over these numerous activities which are so well discharged at present. The more I see of it, the more I think the voluntary machinery best. All that is required is some limited statutory power of enquiry, possibly vested in the Companies Section of the Department of Trade and Industry, thus slightly extending their already wide powers of investigation. These are matters for further discussion with the authorities. Meanwhile, the Panel will continue to act as strongly as it can when dealing with abuses of this or any other kind within its jurisdiction'[1].

Subsequently, in relation to the Secretary of State's review of possible amendments to company law, the Panel publicly announced in 1973 that it and the Stock Exchange had concluded the mere enactment of a criminal prohibition would be a very powerful deterrent[2]. Civil remedies were regarded as likely to be expensive, time consuming and in themselves an insufficient deterrent. With regard to enforcement, the Panel added:

> 'It might no doubt be possible to establish a special division of the Department of Trade and Industry with power to enquire and prosecute as in the case of the Inland Revenue, but on general grounds it is thought preferable that this matter, like other company offences, should be left to the normal law enforcement authority, namely, the Police'[3].

16. See, post, Chapter 6. Administrative Regulation.
17. See, post, Chapter 5. Disclosure.
18. See, post, Chapter 6. Administrative Regulation.
19. See, post, Chapter 7. Investigation; investigation problems prior to the CA 1980 are considered in Suter, op cit. n10, p77, supra, Chapter 7.
20. See, post, Chapter 6. Administrative Regulation.
1. Statement by Lord Shawcross, Chairman of the City Panel on Take-overs and Mergers, 26th October, 1972.
2. The Panel on Take-overs and Mergers, Statement on Insider Dealing, 2nd February, 1973.
3. Ibid.

The Panel's view that insider dealing should be made a criminal offence, with enforcement in accordance with normal Companies Act practices, was reiterated in its response to the 1974 Inquiry of the Department of Trade on the supervision of the Securities Market[4], in its evidence to the Wilson Committee[5] and in its Annual Reports[6].

The foregoing provides an outline of the regulatory agencies involved in insider dealing regulation. The substantive aspects of such regulation will now be considered from the angle of criminal liability, civil liability, disclosure, administrative regulation and investigation.

4. The Panel on Take-overs and Mergers, op cit. n4, p79, supra, p.5.
5. The Panel on Take-overs and Mergers, op cit. n13, p77, supra, para104.
6. *The Panel on Take-overs and Mergers,* Report on the Year ended 31st March, 1973, p.9, and Report on the Year ended 31st March 1977, p.7.

Chapter 3

Criminal Liability

I. INTRODUCTORY

The imposition of criminal liability raises two important issues. One is the question of why the criminal sanction was chosen. Another concerns the effectiveness of the criminal sanction as a measure of control.

A. Choice of criminal liability

Consideration of the choice of criminal liability is hindered by the lack of a single comprehensive definition of crime. Attempts to formulate a definition of crime by reference to something that threatens or is generally believed to threaten serious harm to the community, something committed with evil intent or something forbidden in the interests of the most powerful sections of society have not withstood the objection that some crimes elude each definition and some forms of behaviour under each definition are not recognised as crimes[1]. There is thus no satisfactory definition which includes the many acts and omissions which are criminal yet excludes those which are not. An act may be made criminal simply because the criminal, rather than civil, process is regarded as the more effective means of control.

Despite the objection that it is circular, the argument that a crime is anything forbidden or punishable under the criminal law provides a starting point for considering the choice of the criminal sanction. Yet such circularity also means that the reasons for making something unlawful generally lie in policy considerations which may be expressed in other measures. In relation to insider dealing, both instruments used to pursue the objectives of regulation, namely, a prohibition on dealing by insiders on the basis of inside information and mandated disclosure of information by companies and individuals, may be enforced by criminal, civil or administrative penalties.

Nevertheless, the significance of the distinction between instruments is subordinate to their common purpose and effect. In each case, the aim is to change the behaviour of individuals and companies by altering the relative costs of their behaviour according to whether or not it conforms to policy considerations[2]. Whilst financial costs are the most obvious, relative costs do not exclude other costs, such as moral ones.

As applied to the introduction of criminal liability for insider dealing, this analysis views the function of the measure as being to impose costs on those who breach the prohibitions in question. Faced with these prohibitions, insiders will calculate the costs and benefits of proposed transactions in the light of criminal liability.

1. L. Radzinowicz and J. King, *The Growth of Crime* (1977), p.117.
2. T.C. Daintith, European University Institute Seminar paper (1981), p.9a.

1. The economic model of criminal behaviour

Such analysis draws heavily on the economic model of criminal behaviour[3]. This model is derived from the Benthamite utilitarian view that as people are rational maximisers of satisfaction, they will avoid committing an act which yields them more pain than pleasure. Transposed in economic terms, people engage in acts which yield them the most value net of cost and so can be deterred from criminal activity by a punishment system that makes the cost of criminal activity greater than value. Hence, to an economist, a criminal is a person who has chosen to engage in criminal activity because the expected utility of such behaviour to him, after deduction of costs, exceeds that of any legitimate alternative activity.

Whilst the expected costs and benefits of alternative activities will vary from person to person, the calculation of advantages can thus be altered by changing any of the various factors which determine such choice. The immediate costs are those of a person's own time or incurred in obtaining resources or services. Other potential costs are the amount of the penalty, whether in the form of a fine or imprisonment, together with the financial, psychological and social costs of investigation and prosecution. But these other costs must be discounted by the risk of detection and prosecution. A further cost is the 'moral cost' of committing a crime in the sense of the impact on a person's self-respect. All such costs must be weighed against the expected benefits as measured in financial, psychological and social terms. In turn, these benefits are related to the amount of wealth available for distribution and the ability of potential victims to protect themselves against victimisation.

However, the economic model of criminal behaviour raises two main objections[4]. First, it may be regarded as artificial and simplistic to consider the sole objective of all legal measures as being to alter the relative costs and benefits of a person's behaviour. As regards the use of the criminal sanction, it is further argued that this economic model distorts the distinctive moral character that precedes rather than follows from its use and imposes evaluation in qualitative terms. It thus fails to distinguish the criminal sanction from other measures, such as taxes, and subsidies which do not proclaim such moral imperatives and are to be evaluated in quantitative terms.

This objection has provoked two responses. One supported by purists counters that, irrespective of whether criminal measures proclaim moral imperatives, their use and impact is assisted by reference to economic criteria, such as relative costs. But even accepting that a rational calculation is often made of the relative costs and benefits of criminal activity and legitimate alternative activity, the validity of any rational calculation in respect of some acts, such as those committed in a rage or when drunk, is doubtful. Thus, a preferable response is that the significance of any specific moral implications attaching to criminal prohibitions is limited to their impact on the choice and application of legal measures. Whereas the moral implications associated with a criminal sanction may sometimes render inappropriate the creation or application of a criminal measure, in other cases use of the criminal sanctions may enhance such measure's effectiveness by increasing the moral costs of detection and conviction. Rather than imposing separate treatment for the criminal sanction, such

---

3. This has been developed and discussed by: G.S. Becker, 'Crime and Punishment: An Economic Approach' (1968) 76 J.Pol.Econ.169; G.J. Stigler, 'The Optimum Enforcement of Laws' (1970) 78 J.Pol.Econ.526; I. Ehrlich, 'The Deterrent Effect of Criminal Law Enforcement' (1972) 1 J. Legal Studies 259 and R.A. Posner, *Economic Analysis of Law* (2nd ed.1977), Chapter 7.
4. Daintith, op cit. supra, pp.11-14.

distinguishing characteristics are seen as reinforcing the need for a common concept to which the distinguishing characteristics of all types of legal measures may be related.

A second objection follows from the subjective nature of the calculations that influence a person's behaviour. On the basis that government cannot know the value placed by a person on the relevant costs and benefits, it is argued that government cannot influence behaviour by altering the variables of the calculus. But this objection loses its force where governmental concern relates to aggregate decisions with its resulting emphasis on the number of persons who change their decisions rather than which persons do so. In such circumstances, directing a measure at each person is merely a means of pursuing aggregate ends.

2. Modern penal theory

Apart from drawing heavily on the economic model of criminal behaviour, the deterrent aim of the criminal law is also supported by modern penal theory. The latter adopts a broad analysis of the impact of criminal sanctions:

> 'The idea is that punishment as a concrete expression of society's disapproval of an act helps to form and strengthen the public's moral code and thereby creates conscious and unconscious inhibitions against committing crime'[5].

According to this analysis, the threat and imposition of punishment may have a motivating influence apart from the creation of fear, through an expression of social condemnation of the forbidden act. The criminal law is 'not only a price tariff, but rather also is an expression of society's disapproval of a particular act – a disapproval which may work in subtle ways to influence behaviour'[6]. Emphasis is thus placed on the long-term ability of criminal sanctions to strengthen moral inhibitions and to stimulate habitual law-abiding conduct. In terms of the economic model, such ability may also be viewed as increasing the moral costs of the activity in question. Yet the very subtlety of the operation of deterrence makes its impact difficult to assess.

3. Difficulties relating to the choice of criminal liability

Although the general deterrent effect of the criminal law supported by modern penal theory militates against exclusive reliance on other measures, the criminal sanction is not the sole means of deterrence[7] and various factors point to caution in its use. With the expansion of the criminal sanction to a wider range of activities, the risk of people breaching the criminal law increases. In turn, the stigma attached to conviction is reduced, particularly for offences of strict

5. J. Andenaes, 'General Prevention – Illusion or Reality?' (1952) 43 J. Crim.L.C. & P.B.176 at 179
6. J. Andenaes, 'General Prevention Revisited: Research and Policy Implications' (1975) 66 J.Crim.L.338 at 341.
7. Radzinowicz and King, op cit. n1, p83, supra, Chapters 5 and 6; L.H. Leigh, *Policy and Punitive Measures in respect of Economic Offences*, p.115 in The Council of Europe, Twelfth Conference of Directors of Criminological Research Institutes (1977) and L.H. Leigh, 'Securities Regulation: Problems in relation to sanctions', p.513 at pp.514-531 in *Consumer and Corporate Affairs Canada, Proposals for a Securities Market Law for Canada*, Vol.3 Background papers (1979).

liability. As the number of offences exceeds the enforcement capacity of investigators and the courts, enforcement becomes selective and sometimes inconsistent and so calculations of the risk of prosecution are altered accordingly. On occasion, the criminal sanction may also be insufficiently flexible and its impact may be further weakened by delays in enforcement.

In addition, there are specific enforcement difficulties associated with particular fields, such as securities regulation[8]. The transactions in question may be arranged by sophisticated groups of professionals who deal through nominees. Investigations must then analyse orders, trace bank accounts and financing arrangements. Their complexity may impose selective prosecution. Subsequent proceedings may also be lengthy and costly, particularly when transactions are part of a wider fraudulent scheme.

In the light of these factors, the availability of other measures to influence conduct has fuelled controversy over the choice of measures in deterring specific activities. In particular, the progressive extension of governmental regulation has focused attention on the use of administrative sanctions. Key issues[9] are the erosion of traditional mens rea concepts to uphold enforcement efficiency and the impact on the overall effectiveness of the criminal law of extending the criminal sanction to prohibit and condemn conduct which is regarded as morally neutral rather than fundamentally and inherently wrong.

Whilst facilititating the expansion of criminal law to the broad range of activities that government seeks to regulate, the circular definition of crime also hinders it in providing criteria that assist in determining the choice of the criminal measure as against other measures. There is thus a danger that the criminal sanction will be resorted to in response to pressure to regulate a particular activity without considering certain aspects, such as enforceability. This danger is particularly acute when regulators entertain doubts about a particular course of action.

A further difficulty associated with the use of a particular measure, such as the criminal sanction, stems from an inability to determine whether the measure produces the effects hoped for. The development of methods to separate the influence of a particular measure from other social conditions and influences is still in its infancy. One form of analysis has been the Interrupted Time Series[10] which is a quasi-experimental design used as a substitute for the unfeasible true experiment. Whilst this design has contributed to analysis of the impact of increased penalties for speeding and the introduction of the breathalyser, the extent to which the Interrupted Time Series design can be applied to measures introduced to deal with other criminal activities is unclear.

Although difficult to evaluate the choice of the criminal sanction by reference to a comprehensive set of criteria, its choice in relation to prohibitions on insider dealing, provided that problems of proof are surmountable, is more readily acceptable than for certain other activities since the equity considerations that support insider dealing regulation operate against regarding such

8. R.W. Ogren, 'The Ineffectiveness of the Criminal Sanction on Fraud and Corruption Cases: Losing the Battle against White-Collar Crime' (1973) 11 Am.Crim.L.Rev.959.

9. These are discussed by: S.H. Kadish, 'Some Observations on the Use of Criminal Sanctions in Enforcing Economic Regulations' (1963) 30 U.Chi.L.Rev.423; H.V. Ball and L.M. Friedman, 'The Use of Criminal Sanctions in the Enforcement of Economic Legislation: A Sociological View' (1965) 17 Stan.L.Rev.195.

10. D.T. Campbell and H.L. Ross, 'The Connecticut Crackdown on Speeding: Time Series Data in Quasi-Experimental Analysis' (1968) 3 Law and Society Rev.33; H.L. Ross, D.T. Campbell and G.V. Glass, 'Determining the Social Effects of a Legal Reform: The British 'Breathalyser' Crackdown of 1967' (1970) American Behaviourial Scientist 493.

conduct as morally neutral. But this consideration is tempered by the empirical assessment which points to an ambivalent attitude, particularly with regard to tipping and tippee dealings and in turn suggests that many insiders and their tippees do not regard themselves as members of a criminal class. Hence, the insider dealing issue is not one that lends itself to a simple reaction.

B. Effectiveness of criminal liability

Having decided to introduce a criminal prohibition, the second issue concerns its effectiveness. This requires consideration of questions such as whether the legislative prohibition deals adequately with insider transactions and whether it is being adequately enforced, both from the point of view of the initiation of proceedings and sanctions imposed on those convicted. These questions will be considered by reference to the substantive provisions.

II. STATUTORY PROVISIONS

The first general legislation enacted for the purpose of imposing criminal liability on insiders in relation to their dealings was Part V, CA 1980, now contained in the IDA 1985 as amended by the FSA 1986. Previously, criminal liability was restricted to directors' dealings in options under provisions imposed by the CA 1967[11] and now reproduced in the CA 1985.

Reflecting disapproval of speculation by directors, it is an offence under the CA 1985 for a director of a company to buy (for money or any other consideration) an option to call for delivery or to make delivery at a specified price and within a specified time of a specified number or amount of relevant shares or debentures[12]. Relevant shares or debentures are those listed on a stock exchange in Great Britain or elsewhere and issued by the company of which he is a director or by any of its subsidiaries, its holding company or by any subsidiary of its holding company[13]. It is also an offence for a director to buy 'put and call' options whereby a director may either call for or make delivery at a specified price and within a specified time of a specified number or amount of such securities[14].

The prohibition on the purchase of such options applies to a shadow director as to a director[15]. In the CA 1985, 'director' is defined to include any person occupying the position of director, by whatever name called[16]. A 'shadow director' means a person in accordance with whose directions or instructions the directors of the company are accustomed to act[17]. However, a person is not deemed a shadow director by reason only that the directors act on advice given by him in a professional capacity[18].

The prohibition extends to the spouse or infant child of a director[19]. However, it is a defence for the spouse or child to prove that he or she had no

---

11. CA 1967, s25 as amended by CA 1981, Sch3, para28.
12. CA 1985, s323(1).
13. Ibid, s323(3).
14. Ibid, s323(1).
15. Ibid, s323(4).
16. Ibid, s741(1).
17. Ibid, s741(2).
18. Ibid.
19. Ibid, s327.

reason to believe that his or her spouse or parent was a director of the company in question.

Breach of these provisions renders a person liable to a fine or imprisonment or both[20]. However, prohibited dealings are not stated to be invalid[1]. Where he suspects a breach, the Secretary of State can appoint an inspector to investigate and report[2].

Since directors have inside information and can influence the future market value of securities, such transactions involve a conflict between directors' own interests and their duties to the company. Hence, the Jenkins Committee[3] recommended a prohibition on such option dealings, stating:

> 'A director who speculates in this way with special information is clearly acting improperly, and we do not believe that any reputable director would deal in such options in any circumstances'[4].

The prohibitions in the CA 1985 cover a limited category of option dealings in listed securities, the Jenkins Committee recommendation having been only partially implemented by the CA 1967. In particular the CA 1985 does not extend to the acquisition of such options in securities in private companies or in the securities of a public company that have not been granted a stock exchange listing. As regards listed securities, it does not include the purchase of either (a) a right to subscribe for shares or debentures or (b) debentures that confer a right to subscribe for or to be converted into shares of the company in question[5].

The novelty of the scope of the CA 1980 was questioned by those who considered s13, Prevention of Fraud (Investments) Act 1958 capable of applying to insider dealing[6]. Though the 1958 Act was repealed by the FSA 1986[7], a similar provision was re-enacted in the FSA 1986. In particular, s.47(1) provides that any person who makes a statement, promise or forecast which he knows to be misleading, false or deceptive or dishonestly conceals any material facts or recklessly makes (dishonestly or otherwise) a statement, promise or forecast which is misleading, false or deceptive, is guilty of an offence if he does so for the purpose of inducing (or is reckless as to whether it may induce) another person either to enter or offer to enter into an investment agreement (or to refrain from doing so), or to exercise (or refrain from exercising) any rights conferred by an investment. It is immaterial whether the person being induced is the person to whom the statement, promise or forecast is made or from whom the facts are concealed[8].

20. Ibid, s323(2).
1. It is submitted that, unless the third party from whom the option was bought did not act in good faith, prohibited option dealings are not invalid: *Palmer's Company Law*, Twenty-fourth edition under the general editorship of C.M. Schmitthoff with specialist editors, Vol.1 The Treatise (1987), para29-17.
2. CA 1985, s446.
3. *Report of the Company Law Committee* (Chairman: Lord Justice Jenkins), Cmnd.1749 (1962), paras90 and 99(c).
4. Ibid, para90.
5. CA 1985, s323(5).
6. B.A.K. Rider, 'The Crime of Insider Trading' [1978], J.B.L.19; A. Yoran *Insider Trading in Israel and England* (1972), p.64; D. Sugarman, *The Regulation of Insider Dealing*, p.51 at p.56 in (ed.) B.A.K. Rider, *The Regulation of the British Securities Industry* (1979); L.H. Leigh, *The Control of Commercial Fraud* (1982), p.120.
7. FSA 1986, Sch17, Part I.
8. Ibid, s47(1). By virtue of s47(4), s47(1) applies where one or more of the following territorial conditions are satisfied: (1) the statement, promise or forecast is made in or from, or the facts are

In most cases the issue of liability would turn on whether an insider's failure to disclose that he was in possession of unpublished price sensitive information, constituted dishonest concealment of a material fact. In the case of false statements, it appears that the section would extend to the omission of a fact that makes the statements made misleading[9]. In view of the scope of the IDA 1985 and the uncertainty as to the interpretation of s.47(1), it seems that resort to this provision would be contemplated only in circumstances when the insider dealing was not within the scope of the IDA 1985.

Rather, reliance is placed on the IDA 1985 as amended. As distinct from a broad anti-fraud measure, this legislation contains tightly-drawn detailed requirements whose key provision states:

'1. – (1) Subject to section 3, an individual who is, or at any time in the preceding 6 months has been, knowingly connected with a company shall not deal on a recognised stock exchange in securities of that company if he has information which –

(a) he holds by virtue of being connected with the company,

(b) it would be reasonable to expect a person so connected, and in the position by virtue of which he is so connected, not to disclose except for the proper performance of the functions attaching to that position, and

(c) he knows is unpublished price sensitive information in relation to those securities'.

The operation of the IDA 1985 raises four main issues: the definition of insider; the meaning of inside information; the restrictions to be placed on insiders and penalties[10]. In considering these issues, reference will be made to the insider dealing proposals contained in the 1973[11] and 1978[12] Companies Bills, both of which were lost in Parliamentary dissolutions.

---

concealed in or from, the UK; (b) the person on whom the inducement is intended to or may have effect is in the UK or (c) the agreement is or would be entered into or the rights are or would be exercised in the UK.

9. *R v Kylsant* [1932] 1 K.B.442.

10. Commentaries on Part V CA 1980 include: V. Joffe, *The Companies Act 1980* (1980), Chapter 11; D.D. Prentice, *The Companies Act 1980* (1980), Chapter 16; D. Sugarman, 'Insider Dealing: An Introduction' (1981) 2 Co.Law 13; T.M. Ashe, 'Insider Dealing: Some Practical Guidelines' (1981) 2 Co.Law 20; Leigh, op cit. n6, p89, supra, p.113; D.M. Branson, 'Insider Trading' [1982] J.B.L.342, 413 and 536 and *Gower's Principles of Modern Company Law*, Supplement to the Fourth Edition by L.C.B. Gower (1981) (hereinafter referred to as the 'Gower Supplement').

11. Commentaries on the 1978 Bill are provided by: Sugarman, op cit. n6, p88, supra; Council for the Securities Industry, Insider Dealing Clauses in Draft Companies Bill (1st November, 1978); Insider Trading: Clauses 57-63 of the Draft Companies Bill, Report by a Working Party established jointly by the Law Society's Standing Committee on Company Law and the Company Law Sub-Committee of the City of London Solicitors Company (October, 1978); Gower's *Principles of Modern Company Law*, Fourth Edition by L.C.B. Gower, J.B. Cronin, A.J. Easson and Lord Wedderburn of Charlton (1979), p.157 and B.A.K. Rider, 'Companies Bill 1978: Insider Trading' (1978) 128 N.L.J.1236.

12. The provisions of the 1973 Companies Bill are discussed by: The Law Society's Standing Committee on Company Law, Memorandum on Clauses 1 to 19 of the Companies Bill (1974); D.D. Prentice, 'Insider Trading', 1973 C.L.P.83 and City Company Law Committee, Insider Dealing (1976).

A. The definition of insider

There are several approaches to the problem of defining an insider[13]. One attempts to identify specific persons for the purposes of liability, such as directors, officers and employees. Whilst responsive to a theory of accountability for corporate office, such designation represents a compromise with a view to certainty. Rather than covering all who have access to or who may act on inside information, liability is restricted to specific persons who may misappropriate information.

Switching from a person's identity to the broader context of the nature and source of his information, a functional approach to the definition of insider is based on access to inside information. The access test is based on the Cady, Roberts[14] concepts of a 'relationship giving access' to information intended for a corporate purpose only, not another's personal benefit, and of the 'inherent unfairness' of knowingly exploiting informational advantages unavailable to others. As well as those within the company, irrespective of seniority of position, it includes persons outside but retained by the company, such as accountants, legal advisers, engineers and consultants. Yet insofar as the access test emphasises the relationship with the company as distinct from the qualitative nature of the information, it excludes investment advisers, journalists and others who may have 'access' to information without having any formal relationship such as agent or employee.

To close this gap, a possession test defines an insider as anyone in possession of inside information. But it is doubtful whether liability should extend to someone who has by chance overheard an item which turns out to be inside information. Leaving aside the practical issue of whether inside information is thereby published, such a definition could inhibit dealings that contribute to market efficiency and to the extent that fairness is equated with equal access[15], do not raise objections of unfairness. The position is different when a person knows the information is confidential and comes from an insider source, though the person then has more than mere possession.

1. Individuals connected with a company

Adopting the access approach, the IDA 1985 primarily defines an insider as, subject to certain provisos[16], 'an individual . . . connected with a company'[17]. But the concept of a listed insider has not been completely abandoned since an individual is treated as connected with a company when he is a director of the company[18] or a related company[19]. As the latter is defined[20] as any body

13. This discussion also draws on leading US and Canadian works: A. Bromberg and L. Lowenfels, *Securities Fraud and Commodities Fraud* (1979) (hereinafter referred to as 'Bromberg'), Chapter 7; V. Brudney, 'Insiders, Outsiders and Informational Advantages under the Federal Securities Laws' (1979) 93 Harv.L.Rev.322; W.H. Painter, *The Federal Securities Code and Corporate Disclosure* (1979), Chapter 5; American Law Institute, Federal Securities Code, Proposed Official Draft (1978) and M. Yontef, *Insider Trading*, p.629 in Consumer and Corporate Affairs Canada, Proposals for a Securities Market Law for Canada, Vol.3 Background Papers (1979).
14. *In re Cady Roberts & Co.*, 40 S.E.C.907 (1961). See, ante, Chapter 1. Introduction.
15. See, ante, Chapter 1. Introduction.
16. The individual must be 'knowingly' connected with a company and this relationship may either be current or have existed within the previous six months, as to both of which see infra.
17. IDA 1985, s1(1) and (2).
18. By IDA 1985, s11(a) 'company' means any company, whether or not a company within the meaning of CA 1985.
19. IDA 1985, s9(a).
20. Ibid, s11(b).

corporate which is a company's subsidiary, holding company or fellow subsidiary, directors within a group of companies are included. Yet unlike the 1978 Bill, other officers, employees or substantial shareholders of the company or group are not listed insiders[1].

In all other cases, an access test alone is used to determine whether an individual is connected with a company. This connection is established when he occupies a position (a) as an officer[2] (other than director) or employee of the company in question or a related company or (b) involving a professional or business relationship between himself (or his employer or a company of which he is a director) and the company in question or a related company which in either case may reasonably be expected to give him access to unpublished price sensitive information about the securities of either company and which he would not be reasonably expected to disclose, except for the proper performance of his functions[3]. The test is thus objective. On the assumption that their positions may reasonably be expected to give access to unpublished price sensitive information about the securities, this definition is wide enough to cover a company's secretary, solicitors, accountants, auditors, bankers, important customers, printers[4] and messengers.

However, this objective test narrows the range of individuals within the definition of insider. It excludes individuals such as employees or other individuals in the specified professional or business relationship, who occupy positions that quite unexpectedly give them access to unpublished price sensitive information. Hence, an individual's formal position prevails over the qualitative nature of the information. Whereas both efficiency and equity considerations support the inclusion of such individuals as insiders, the IDA 1985 imposes liability only when they fall within its definition of tippee.

For both types of connected individual, the definition is further restricted in that an individual must be 'knowingly' connected with a company[5]. Knowledge is not specifically defined. But it would seem that, unlike certain other insider dealing provisions which apply where an individual 'knows or has reasonable cause to believe'[6] that a particular state of affairs exists, knowledge is limited to actual knowledge or recklessness[7] and constructive knowledge is not imputed. Thus, an individual unaware of his connection due to complex group holdings will not be covered. Yet this additional proviso increases the problems of proof. In particular, with an individual other than a director, it may be difficult to prove that he knew his position might reasonably be expected to give him access to unpublished price sensitive information. If so, liability again arises only when an individual is within the definition of tippee contained in the IDA 1985, even though an individual who knows he has unpublished price sensitive information is more properly an insider.

However, attempts to avoid liability by resignation in anticipation of a transaction are forestalled. Liability extends to individuals connected with a company within the previous six months[8].

1. Companies Bill 1978, cl63 (1)(a) and (b).
2. By CA 1985, s744 'officer' in relation to a body corporate, includes a director, manager or secretary.
3. IDA 1985, s1(1) and (2).
4. Cf. *Chiarella v US*, 445 U.S.222 (1980). See, ante, Chapter 1. Introduction.
5. IDA 1985, s1(1) and (2).
6. Ibid, ss1(3)(a) and 2(1)(a).
7. Joffe, op cit. n10, p89, supra, para11.104.
8. IDA 1985, s1(1) and (2).

Another important restriction concerns the definition of insider by reference to individuals with the result that companies are not included[9], even though they deal in securities and hold and obtain information corporately. This restriction acknowledges that multi-divisional companies would encounter difficulties in the event of knowledge acquired by one division being imputed to another. Traditionally, in the case of a merchant bank, such difficulties would arise when, after a director in its corporate finance department had acquired inside information through his board membership or a proposed underwriting, its investment client department dealt in the securities of the company in question, even though its decision was not influenced by the inside information known only to its director. As liability under the IDA 1985 largely depends on the insider's knowledge that he is dealing on inside information, an extension of insider liability to companies would involve provision for a Chinese Wall defence where barriers to internal communication had been erected.

Instead, the IDA 1985 attempts to counter the use of a company for insider transactions by imposing liability on individuals acting for it. It is also an offence for an individual to counsel or procure any other 'person' to deal in securities on the basis of inside information[10] or to communicate inside information to any other 'person'[11]. 'Person' includes a body corporate. Hence, individuals acting for a company will be liable when the company deals on inside information in a manner prohibited for an individual.

Nevertheless, loopholes remain. An example is cited[12] as arising where Company A, which is a shareholder but not a holding company of Company B, knows of a possible take-over bid for Company B, the information having been obtained by virtue of Company A sitting on the board of Company B as a corporate representative. As a company, Company A is not an individual connected with a company. Hence, when inside information is obtained from Company A and used to deal in securities, it would appear no offence has been committed because the information is not obtained from an 'individual connected' with Company B and the provisions relating to tippee liability do not seem to apply.

The exclusion of companies from the definition of insider now contained in the IDA 1985 and in the 1978 Bill contrasts with the approach of the 1973 Bill. The latter provided[13] that a company did not commit an offence by reason of, or having obtained, any information in the possession of a director or employee of that company if:

'(a) the decision to enter into the transaction was taken on its behalf by a person other than the director or employee; and
 (b) arrangements were then in existence for securing that the information was not communicated to that person and that no advice with

---

9. In contrast, the CA 1985, s98(1) and (2) imposes criminal liability on a relevant company with regard to transactions or arrangements for a director of the company or its holding company in breach of CA 1985, s85. But a company can presumably be liable for procuring or abetting an insider dealer offence.
10. IDA 1985, s1(7).
11. Ibid, s1(8).
12. A. Blake, 'The Proposed Crime of Insider Dealing' (1978) 1 Preston Law Rev.39 at 42 cited by Sugarman, op cit. n10, p89, supra at 15.
13. Companies Bill 1973, cl14(3).

respect to the transaction was given to him by a person in possession of the information; and

(c) the information was not in fact so communicated and advice was not in fact so given'.

Preferable to the approach initially contained in Part V, CA 1980, this provision would have endorsed use of the Chinese Wall though in such a way as to exclude liability only when the Wall existed and had not been breached. Arguments for omitting sub-paragraph (b) have been advanced on the ground that it is immaterial whether this provision has been observed when the requirements of sub-paragraphs (a) and (c) have been met[14]. But this underestimates the importance of such arrangements in ensuring compliance since companies wishing to rely on the defence must show that they have adopted the requisite safeguards[15].

Moreover, the scope for abuse of inside information by companies was widened by the power subsequently introduced by the CA 1981[16] and re-enacted in the CA 1985[17] authorising companies to purchase their own shares, thereby reversing a well established rule to the contrary[18]. The suggestion[19] that as the statutory provisions imposed liability on individuals, it would be desirable to clarify those liable in respect of corporate repurchases was not taken up. At present, it seems the individuals acting for a company would be liable under the prohibition on counselling or procuring another person to deal on the basis of inside information[20] unless, when its market purchases[1] were likely to affect the price of its shares, the company had disclosed its intended re-purchases.

The access test contained in the IDA 1985 means that the definition of insider is limited to individuals having the requisite connection with the company. Though motivated by the desire to encourage individuals to search for corporate and market information, such a definition excludes all individuals having access to unpublished price sensitive information but not connected with the company, irrespective of whether their activities contribute to market efficiency. For those not so connected, the IDA 1985 supplements its access test by extending liability to individuals contemplating a take-over offer, public servants and tippees.

2. Individuals contemplating a take-over offer

The prohibition on dealing applies to certain transactions in the prospective offeree by individuals contemplating a take-over offer, but who are not con-

14. Law Society, op cit. n12, p89, supra, p.9; City Company Law Committee, op cit. n12, p89, supra, para12.
15. Prentice, op cit. n12, p89, supra, p.105.
16. CA 1981, ss46-52.
17. CA 1985, ss162-172.
18. *Trevor v Whitworth* (1887) 12 AppCas409, H.L.
19. *The Department of Trade, The Purchase by a Company of its Own Shares,* Cmnd.7944 (1980), para59 at footnote 25. The footnote also refers to Canadian legislation which, when this power was enacted, expressly provided that the company was then an insider.
20. IDA 1985, s1(7).
1. IDA 1985 does not apply to private deals, see post. The desirability of protection for private companies was also discussed in the *Department of Trade,* op cit. n19, supra, para46.

nected with the company[2]. Thus, an individual who was or is (whether with or without another person) contemplating a take-over offer[3] for a company 'in a particular capacity' may not deal in that company's securities 'in another capacity' if he knows that the information that the offer is contemplated or is no longer contemplated is unpublished price sensitive information in relation to those securities[4].

However, this provision raises difficulties of interpretation. The point at which a take-over offer is 'contemplated' may be difficult to determine. A certain fixity of purpose will presumably be required even though completion of all arrangements prior to the making of a formal offer will not be necessary[5].

In addition, the meaning of 'capacity' is unclear in significant respects[6]. Whilst breach of this prohibition involves an individual acting in different capacities, the prospective offeror is usually[7] a company acting on its board's decision. It is uncertain whether an offeror director who deals on the inside information obtained through his directorship, is in breach of this prohibition since prima facie it is the company and not the director which is contemplating the take-over offer. But if the contemplation of a take-over offer 'in a particular capacity' is construed to include in the capacity of agent, a director who deals on the inside information will be in breach of this prohibition.

It is also unclear whether a merchant banker (or other professional adviser) who makes market purchases of securities for a client as a preliminary to a take-over offer for a company, may deal in those securities on behalf of another client. Assuming the merchant banker knows that the information that the take-over offer is contemplated is unpublished price sensitive information, it is unclear (a) whether the first client is 'contemplating' the take-over offer; or (b) if so, whether the merchant banker (whether or not apprised of the first client's intentions is 'contemplating' such an offer; or (c) whether the merchant banker (assuming that he is in contemplation of a take-over offer and acts solely as agent for both clients) is contemplating the offer in one capacity and dealing in the securities in question in another capacity.

3. Public servants

Initially confined in the public service context to Crown servants[8], the definition of insider in the IDA 1985 was extended by the FSA 1986[9] to cover all public servants – central or local. In consequence, the statutory provisions[10] also apply to a public servant or a former public servant who, by virtue of his position, holds

2. As to the basis of regulating such transactions, see, ante, Chapter 1. Introduction. For earlier regulation of insider dealing during take-overs and mergers, see, post, Chapter 6, Administrative Regulation. Where an individual is connected with the company, he will be prohibited from dealing under IDA 1985, s1(2).
3. By IDA 1985, s14, the term 'take-over offer for a company' is defined as an offer made to all the holders (or all the holders other than the person making the offer and his nominees) of the shares in the company to acquire those shares or a specified proportion of them or to all the holders (or all the holders other than the person making the offer and his nominees) of a particular class of those shares to acquire the shares of that class or a specified proportion of them.
4. IDA 1985, s1(5).
5. Prentice, op cit. n10, p89, supra, para313.
6. Joffe, op cit. n10, p89, supra, para11.112.
7. An exception is a bid by trustees of a pension fund.
8. CA 1980, s69. This section was re-enacted in IDA 1985, s2.
9. FSA 1986, s173.
10. IDA 1985, s2.

information which he knows is unpublished price sensitive information in relation to securities of a particular company. Unlike an individual who must be knowingly connected with a company or have been so connected within the previous six months, there is no requirement that an individual knew he was a public servant nor limitation in time to six months.

The term 'public servant' is defined[11] to mean (a) a Crown servant, (b) a member, officer or servant of a designated agency, competent authority, or transferee body (within the meaning of the FSA 1986), (c) an officer or servant of a recognised self-regulating organisation, recognised investment exchange or recognised clearing house or (d) any person declared by order to be a public servant. Power to make such an order, exerciseable by statutory instrument[12], is vested in the Secretary of State[13]. Where it appears to him that the members, officers or employees of or persons otherwise connected with anybody appearing to him to exercise public functions may have access to unpublished price sensitive information relating to securities, he may by order declare that those persons are to be public servants for the purposes of the IDA 1985.

Notwithstanding the wider definition of public servant, the IDA 1985 applies only to a limited range of non-corporate insiders. Other individuals with access to inside information yet not connected with the company are covered by these statutory provisions only when they fall within the definition of tippee.

4. Tippees

The considerations applicable to the various tests for defining insiders are also relevant to the issue of tippee liability, whether the tippee receives a tip from an insider or another tippee. In the US, the usual approach is to consider the tippee's actual or constructive knowledge of the source of the information, the degree of specificity of the information involved, the extent of 'diffusion' among several persons or between levels of tippees and any other factors relevant to the information's accuracy[14]. The same standards should thus be imposed on second and third level tippees, though as the chain lengthens, so the likelihood of the information's reliability decreases. When the information becomes rumour, those acting on it should fall outside the scope of insider restrictions since they assume the risk of the information being untrustworthy.

Use of the access test results in the inclusion of a tippee when he acquires confidential information either from an insider in an access relationship to the company or from the tippee of such a person, provided the tippee knows the person from whom he obtains the information is such an access insider or tippee. But it excludes other tippees who, on the basis of a possession approach alone, are insiders.

Based on the definition of insider, tippee status is determined primarily by reference to the access test. In this respect, both the CA 1980 and 1978 Bill[15] departed from the approach of the 1973 Bill[16] which listed those treated as a

11. Ibid.
12. Ibid.
13. Ibid.
14. Bromberg, 7.5(6).
15. Companies Bill 1978, cl57(5).
16. By the Companies Bill 1973, cl16(3) a person's associates were defined as:
(a) that person's spouse and any relative of that person or that person's spouse;
(b) any trustee of any trust in relation to which that person is a settlor or under which that person or any associate of his within paragraph (a) above benefits or is capable of benefiting;
(c) any company,   *n16 continues overleaf*

person's associates. Under the provisions now contained in the IDA 1985, a tippee is an individual who has information which he knowingly obtained (directly or indirectly) from an individual connected with a particular company or at any time within the previous six months so connected, in circumstances where the tippee either knows or has reasonable cause to believe that (a) the other individual held the information by virtue of being so connected and (b) because of the latter's position it would be reasonable to expect him not to disclose the information except for the proper performance of the functions attaching to that position[17]. This definition can thus cover an individual's spouse, relatives, friends, partners and employees. Provided 'indirectly' is held to refer to the connected individual from whom the information is obtained rather than the form in which the information is obtained, sub-tippees will be included. But the extent to which the recipient must be aware of particulars about his source restricts the scope of tippee status.

A further difficulty relating to tippees, which threatened to render the IDA 1985 ineffective in regard to a wide range of tippee dealings, arose over the interpretation of the word 'obtained' in a case considered by the House of Lords.[18] A businessman held himself out as a potential purchaser of a publicly quoted company. Whilst his approach was being discussed with the merchant bank, a take-over by another company was agreed. The bank's employee informed the businessman of the agreement and that an announcement would be made shortly. She also told the businessman that the information was sensitive and confidential and his receipt of it made him an insider. Ten minutes later, the businessman bought 6,000 shares in the offeree company and five weeks after the announcement of the take-over, sold the shares at a profit of £3,514. In the Southwark Crown Court, he pleaded not guilty to two offences under the IDA 1985. The prosecution conceded that he had taken no step directly or indirectly to secure, procure or acquire the information given to him. His counsel submitted that there was no evidence that he had obtained the information from the 'connected' individual (the employee), that he had merely received it and that the prohibition on dealing in s1(4) did not operate against him since the proper construction of 'obtained' in s1(3) connoted active conduct on his part. The trial judge upheld the defence submissions and directed an acquittal. Without affecting the acquittal, the Attorney General then referred two points of law to the Court of Appeal, under s36 of the Criminal Justice Act 1972, as to (a) whether the word 'obtained' in s1(3) had the restricted meaning of 'acquired by purpose and effort', or had a wider meaning, and (b) whether an individual who had, from another, information within the scope of the IDA 1985 and was otherwise within the scope of the prohibitions contained in ss1(4), (6) and 2 might be an individual who had 'obtained' within

(i) in the case of which that person or any associate of his within paragraphs (a) or (b) above, either alone or with all or any of the others, is entitled to exercise, or control the exercise of, one-third or more of the voting power at any general meeting, or

(ii) which is, or the directors of which are, accustomed to act in accordance with the directions or instructions of that person or of any associate of his within paragraph (a) above;

(d) any partner, employee or employer of that person;

(e) any director or employee of:

(i) any company of which that person is a director or employee; or

(ii) any related company of that company;

(f) any employee of a person (other than a company) of whom that person is an employee.

17. IDA 1985, s1(3).

18. *Attorney General's Reference (No. 1 of 1988) The Times*, 14th April, 1989; Law Reports, *Financial Times*, 18th April, 1989; *Financial Times*, 17th April, 1989.

the terms of ss1(3), (6) and 2.

The Court of Appeal (Criminal Division)[19] gave their opinion on those points of law by saying that (a) the word 'obtained' in s1(3) had a wider meaning than 'acquired by purpose and effort' and (b) an individual who had, from another, information within the scope of the IDA 1985 and was otherwise within the scope of the prohibitions contained in ss1(4), (6) and 2 might be an individual who had 'obtained' within the terms of those sections. He therefore committed an offence if he dealt in the securities to which the information related. Giving the judgment of the court, Lord Lane C.J. considered that the dictionary definitions of 'obtain' were capable of supporting the contention of either party, namely, the Attorney General's contention that it meant to 'acquire in any way' and the respondent's contention that it meant to 'procure as the result of purpose or effort'. However, the conclusive factor was that Parliament intended to penalise the recipient of inside information who dealt in the relevant securities, whether he procured the information from the primary insider by purpose and effort, or came by it without any positive action on his part. He added that that conclusion would have the advantage of avoiding the fine distinctions which would otherwise have to be drawn between what was and what was not a sufficient purpose or effort to satisfy the narrow meaning of 'obtain'. Moreover, they would have been 'distinctions so fine as to be almost imperceptible, and would have done nothing to enhance the reputation of the business world for honesty or of the criminal law for clarity'.[20] Pursuant to the dealer's application, the Court of Appeal referred the points of law to the House of Lords.

Giving a satisfactory finality to the issue[1], the House of Lords held that it would answer the questions posed by the reference in the same way as the Court of Appeal. On the basis that the object of the IDA 1985 was to prevent insider dealing, Lord Templeman stated that Parliament could not have intended that a man who asked for information which he then misused should be convicted of an offence while a man who, without asking, learnt the same information which he also misused should be acquitted. Referring to the dealer's reliance on the principle that any ambiguity in a penal statute should be resolved in favour of the defence[2], Lord Lowry considered this submission had to be qualified by Lord Reid's observation in *DPP v Ottewell* that the principle 'only applies where, after full inquiry and consideration, one is left in real doubt'.[3] He then proceeded to examine whether Parliament must have intended the word 'obtained' to have a restricted meaning or a wider one. Five points assisted the Crown. First, the offence was dealing on a stock exchange in securities of a company in defined circumstances; whether the secondary insider solicited the information or merely received it did not increase or diminish the undesirability of his making use of it. Secondly, the 1977 White Paper[4] tended to show that the mischief consisted of dealing in securities while in possession of confidential information. Thirdly, he contrasted the position of the primary and secondary dealer. A primary insider was forbidden to use any information of the specified description. One might properly ask why a secondary insider should be

19. [1989] 2 WLR 195.
20. Ibid at 206.
1. Following this ruling it is anticipated that other prosecutions, adjourned pending the outcome of the House of Lords judgment, will now proceed: *The Times*, 14th April, 1989.
2. *Tuck & Sons v Priester* (1887) 19 QBD 629 at 638.
3. [1970] A.C. 642 at 649.
4. Department of Trade, *The Conduct of Company Directors*, Cmnd. 7037 (1977), para22.

prohibited only from using part of the information which might come into his hands, namely, that procured by his own efforts: the procurement was not the guilty act. Fourthly, the object of the legislation must be partially defeated if the narrow meaning of 'obtained' was adopted. Fifthly, that meaning would create a need to make fine distinctions which would not arise if the wider meaning prevailed. Having weighed these points and others advanced by the dealer, and not forgetting that the IDA 1985 was a penal statute, Lord Lowry was satisfied that the wider meaning was the meaning which Parliament must have intended the word 'obtained' to have in the Act and that accordingly there was no room for the kind of ambiguity on which the dealer had attempted to rely.

The outcome of this case also has important implications for the tippees of individuals contemplating a take-over offer or of public servants. For, in the absence of the requisite connection with a company, the definition of tippee is similarly extended to individuals who knowingly obtain inside information from such individuals. Tippee status is thus conferred on an individual who knowingly obtains from an individual contemplating a take-over[5], information that a take-over offer is contemplated or is no longer contemplated[6]. Tippee prohibitions also apply to an individual who knowingly obtains unpublished price sensitive information in relation to the securities of a particular company (directly or indirectly) from a public servant or former public servant who that individual knows or has reasonable cause to believe held the information by virtue of his position or former position as a public servant[7]. Hence, subject to these conditions, lay members of government boards are covered. But unlike a tippee of an individual connected with a company, there is no provision analogous to the requirement[8] that the tippee must also know or have reasonable cause to believe that because of the other individual's position, it would be reasonable to expect him not to disclose it except for the proper performance of his duties.

Prosecutions have covered a variety of insiders. One was the managing director of a company[9] and another the director of a related company[10]. Others were insiders by virtue of a professional or business relationship, namely, a partner in an investment management firm[11] and the secretary to a director in a merchant bank[12]. Another case involved the private secretary to the group chairman[13]. The most publicised conviction was that in 1987 of the joint managing director of the securities arm in a merchant banking group in the City[14]. Until then, the most prominent person convicted was the director of a well-known company which had begun researching another company with a view to a take-over bid[15]. As to professionals, three practising accountants have been charged[16]. In regard to the category of public servants, one civil servant has

5. As defined in IDA 1985, s1(5).
6. IDA 1985, s1(6).
7. Ibid, s2(1)(c) and s1(2).
8. Ibid, s1(3)(b).
9. *The Financial Times*, 26th November, 1988.
10. B.A.K. Rider, 'Determined efforts being made to enforce law on insider dealing' (1982) 3 Co.Law 185.
11. B.A.K. Rider, 'Insider dealing: where now after a prosecution and absolute discharge?' (1981) 2 Co.Law 278.
12. B.A.K. Rider, 'Prosecution pending over insider dealing allegations' (1982) 3 Co.Law 133; The Financial Times, 25th January, 1983.
13. *The Financial Times*, 18th July, 1988.
14. Ibid, 2nd July, 1987.
15. *The Times*, 29th April, 1987.
16. *The Financial Times*, 16th April, 1988.

also been charged[17]. An important category of persons charged (though not of those convicted) has been that of tippees. These include the husband of the secretary to a director in a merchant bank[18], two close relatives of the chairman of a financial services group[19], the brother of the civil servant charged[20], a businessman to whom information was passed by a merchant bank (which, in turn, warned him that he thereby became an insider)[1] and two employees of a stockbroking firm who obtained inside information from a client connected with the company[2].

Liability under the IDA 1985 arises when an insider deals on the basis of inside information.[3] Hence, the meaning of inside information is central to the operation of the IDA 1985. As with the definition of insider, the concept of unpublished price sensitive information is a key element in this definition.

B. The meaning of inside information

Subject to one improbable exception[4], individuals connected with a company, public servants and their tippees are not liable unless the information used was originally inside information in that (1) it was held by a connected individual or public servant by virtue of his connection or position and (2) it would be reasonable to expect him not to disclose it except for the proper performance of his functions[5]. As with individuals contemplating a take-over offer and their tippees[6], these other insiders must also (3) know that the information used is unpublished price sensitive information[7].

The first limb contains the requirement that the information has been held by a connected individual or public servant by virtue of his connection or position. Yet this conflicts with the principle that 'the duty of [insiders] not to deal with their beneficiaries in trust assets on the basis of informational advantages about the trust does not rest on how they obtained the informational advantage'[8] and with the City Company Law Committee's view that it would not be 'realistic' to leave a person free to deal in such circumstances[9].

The second requirement is that the information must be of such a nature that it would be reasonable to expect a connected individual or public servant not to disclose it except for the proper performance of his duties. Its purpose is probably to make insiders liable only for the improper use of what would be considered confidential information[10]. In contrast to other parts of the definition of inside information which are subjective, the test is objective: whether it would be reasonable to expect insiders not to disclose the information.

Thirdly, the insider must know that the information is unpublished price

17. *The Independent*, 23rd April, 1988.
18. Rider, op cit. n12, p98, supra.
19. *The Times*, 6th May, 1988.
20. *The Independent*, 26th March, 1988.
1. Ibid, 15th April, 1988.
2. (1985) 6 Co.Law 97.
3. IDA 1985, ss.1(3), (4), (5), (6), (7) and (8) and 2.
4. Where a tippee has reasonable cause to believe (wrongly) that the information was inside information in this sense, he would then theoretically be liable provided the information was unpublished price sensitive information: *Gower Supplement*, op cit, n10, p89, supra, pp636-638, footnote 84.
5. IDA 1985, ss1(1), (2) and (3) and 2(1) and (2).
6. Ibid, s1(5) and (6).
7. Ibid, s1(1), (2) and (3) and 2(1) and (2).
8. Brudney, op cit. n13, p90, supra at 346. See, ante, Chapter 1. Introduction.
9. City Company Law Committee, op cit. n12, p98, supra, para13.
10. Prentice, op cit. n10, p89, supra, para301.

sensitive information in relation to the securities of a company with which an individual is connected or in the case of a public servant, in relation to the securities of a particular company[11]. 'Unpublished price sensitive information' is defined[12] as information which:

> '(a) relates to specific matters relating or of concern (directly or indirectly) to that company, that is to say, is not of a general nature relating or of concern to that company; and
> (b) is not generally known to those persons who are accustomed or would be likely to deal in those securities but which would if it were generally known to them be likely materially to affect the price of those securities'.

In certain circumstances, liability extends beyond unpublished price sensitive information in relation to the securities of a company with which an individual is connected[13]. When the information relates to any transaction (actual or contemplated) involving two companies or one company and the securities of another or to the fact that such transaction is no longer contemplated, it will include that information, provided the insider knows the information is unpublished price sensitive information, even though it relates to the securities of that other company. Such information can include information concerning a take-over, joint venture or the placing of a large order. But the restriction of an insider's liability to information relating to a particular transaction is more selective than the application of fiduciary principles[14]. Though not limited to legally enforceable agreements, the scope of a transaction 'involving' one company and another is unclear[15].

Other anomalies arise from the wording of this extension, even though it apparently applies when the other company is 'free standing' and where it is a subsidiary[16] of a third company[17]. Whilst an individual is prohibited from dealing in securities of a subsidiary in relation to which he holds unpublished price sensitive information[18], which he knows relates to that subsidiary and which relates to a transaction (actual or contemplated) involving both the company with which he is connected and the subsidiary, or involving one of them and the securities of the other, or to the fact that any such transaction is no longer contemplated, this provision does not prohibit him from dealing in the securities of the holding company of that subsidiary, as it will not be possible to prove that the unpublished price sensitive information relates to a transaction involving the holding company and the company with which the individual is connected, or involving one of those companies and the securities of the other, or to the fact that such a transaction is no longer contemplated. Likewise, an individual connected with a company who is prohibited from dealing in the securities of another company will not[19] be prohibited from dealing in the

11. IDA 1985, s1(1) and (3) and 2.
12. Ibid, s10.
13. Ibid, s1(2) and (3).
14. See n9, p99, supra.
15. Prentice, op cit. n10, p89, supra, para307.
16. Except for a wholly owned subsidiary when dealing in its securities is impossible.
17. Joffe, op cit. n10, p89, supra, para11.108.
18. Provided it would be reasonable not to expect the information to be disclosed except in the proper performance of the functions attaching to his position.
19. Even when he holds the information by virtue of his connection and it would be reasonable to expect him not to disclose that information except for the proper performance of the functions

securities of a subsidiary of that other company, unless he knows the unpublished price sensitive information relates to a transaction involving the subsidiary and the company with which he is connected, or involving one of those companies and the securities of the other, or to the fact that such a transaction is no longer contemplated.

In the case of individuals contemplating a take-over offer and their tippees, inside information is separately defined. Individuals contemplating a take-over offer must know that the information that the offer is contemplated or is no longer contemplated is unpublished price sensitive information in relation to the securities of the intended offeree[20]. Similarly, their tippees must know that such information is unpublished price sensitive information[1].

The term 'unpublished price sensitive information' is narrower than the 1978 Bill's definition of inside information as information which:

'(a) is not generally available; and
(b) would, if it were so available, be likely materially to affect the price of those securities'[2].

The narrower meaning now contained in the IDA 1985 followed criticism of the broad definition in the 1978 Bill.

These criticisms centred on the consequences of including a wide range of information which was neither generally available nor necessarily confidential. Particular concern was expressed[3] that the concept of 'information not generally available' would inhibit useful activities. Market professionals, such as investment analysts and investment managers of insurance companies, pension funds and investment trusts, may obtain information which is not confidential and would be available to others. Because of the imprecision of the concept, it was feared their activities would be restricted. There were also fears that directors and employees could be precluded from dealing in their companies' shares and so discouraged from holding such shares since, because of their position, these individuals would always have information about their companies' affairs within the definition of inside information in the 1978 Bill.

Other proposals were made to meet these criticisms. The CSI suggested that references to 'information not generally available' be amended to 'specific information not available on request'[4]. The Law Society recommended substituting 'confidential to the company' for 'not generally available'[5].

Also responsive to these criticisms, the distinction in the IDA 1985 between general and specific information excludes much of the information known to market professionals, directors and employees. In addition, the informational advantages enjoyed by jobbers and certain other market professionals were preserved by specific exceptions from the operation of the legislation[6].

However, the IDA 1985 does not provide a test for determining whether

attaching to his position.
20. IDA 1985, s1(5).
1. Ibid, s1(6).
2. Companies Bill 1978, clause 57(1).
3. T. Renton, M.P. Member of the House of Commons Standing Committee on the Bill, cited by Sugarman, op cit. n11, p89, supra, p.65.
4. C.S.I. Press statement, 1st November, 1978.
5. Report by a Working Party established jointly by the Law Society's Standing Committee on Company Law and the Company Law Sub-Committee of the City of London Solicitors Company, op cit. n11, p89 supra, para6.
6. See post.

information relates to 'specific matters' relating or of concern to the company or is of a 'general nature' relating or of concern to the company. In response to comments about the difficulty of distinguishing specific from general information, the government merely stated that the distinction corresponded to the difference between 'day-to-day knowledge' and 'knowledge of important factors which, when revealed to the market, will shift the price of the shares'[7].

The issue of whether an item of information constitutes unpublished price sensitive information is thus a question of fact for the court in each individual case. But it would seem that information relating to the state of the company's financial affairs would be information relating to 'specific matters' for this purpose[8]. It would also appear that unpublished price sensitive information is not confined to information of a confidential nature, but is broader in scope, comprising both corporate information and market information, such as information about dealings by third parties in the company's shares or advance knowledge of a stockbroker's report.

Yet as regards tippees, it seems that an individual who receives an unexplained indication (directly or indirectly) from an individual connected with a company that it would be in his interests to deal in the securities of that company, is not subject to the prohibition on tippee dealing since he has not received 'information' relating to those securities. As the tippee must know the information is unpublished price sensitive information, the prohibition on tippee dealing applies only when the tip involves matters of specific, not general, concern to the company. Hence, an underwriter will breach the tippee prohibition when he deals in the securities of a client company upon receipt of specific unpublished price sensitive information from a director of a client company about that company (but not when he has been informed that it would be to his advantage to deal)[9].

Further uncertainty attaches to the definition of 'unpublished' as 'not generally known to those accustomed or likely to deal' in the securities. But this suggests that insiders can deal only when the information is generally known to these persons and fully reflected in the price of the securities. Whilst it may be argued that insiders are placed at a disadvantage when required to wait until the price rise since the rise results from the information becoming generally known to those accustomed or likely to deal, the argument conflicts with this definition[10].

In practice, it was suggested that of the elements of the definition of unpublished price sensitive information, the materiality test would govern[11]. When unpublished information has a material impact on the price of securities, it must have been specific since this is the basis of the distinction between general and specific matters. Moreover, when such information has an impact on the price of securities, then according to the efficient markets theory it cannot have been generally known. Thus, information 'likely materially to affect the price of securities' implies that it is both non-public and specific.

The cases before the courts provide examples, but the small number of prosecutions, coupled with the effect of a high proportion of guilty pleas, have meant that the courts have not been required to interpret the definition of 'unpublished price sensitive information'. In the first prosecution, the information was knowledge that the structure of a trust was to be altered so that it could

7. Parliamentary Debates, Standing Committee A, Eleventh Sitting, 6th December, 1974, at col.561
8. Joffe, op cit. n10, p89, supra, para11.002.
9. Ibid, para11.110.
10. Ashe, op cit. n10, p89, supra, p.21.
11. Prentice, op cit. n10, p89, supra, para305.

become a specialised energy trust, information which resulted in a 40p increase in the price of each share[12]. A subsequent case concerned information about a take-over of the company with which the insider was connected[13]. In another case, the insider passed on, and the tippee dealt on, information relating to a likely offer for the shares of a company with which the insider was connected[14]. In other prosecutions, one defendant was aware of the impending announcement of a new share offer[15] and another knew that there was going to be a senior management shake-up[16]. In a further prosecution, the information was a director's knowledge that the company had begun researching another, with a view to making a take-over bid[17]. In a case involving two charges, one related to knowledge that a stake was being built up for a client and the other involved knowledge that a bid was due to be announced[18].

Hence, many aspects of the definition of unpublished price sensitive information still remain unclear, there having been no judicial interpretation of such phrases as 'specific matters', 'directly or indirectly' and 'not generally known'. Similar uncertainty surrounds the phrase 'likely materially to affect the price', especially whether the test is objective or subjective[19]. The issue of when a matter of a general nature relating or of concern to a company becomes a specific matter in this respect may also be difficult to determine, particularly as an item of information may be 'general' for some individuals but, due to their knowledge, 'specific' for others. As well as the examples contained in the Stock Exchange's Model Code[20], reference may be made to the US experience.

Although the materiality concept in the US[1] is formulated in various ways, its purpose is usually to permit a distinction between significant matters and those which are so unimportant as not to affect substantially an investment decision. In open-market transactions, the test is an objective one of investment judgment or significant market effect. In direct personal cases, the test is essentially objective but in view of a party being better placed to appreciate the other's position an element of subjectivity has been introduced by taking account of the relations between the parties and by partly tailoring ideas of materiality to the plaintiff or defendant; as a result, a more flexible approach prevails.

In the *Cady, Roberts* case[2], the SEC emphasised that, like the courts, it had

12. Rider, op cit. n11, p98, supra.
13. Rider, op cit. n10, p98, supra.
14. Rider, op cit. n12, p98, supra; *The Financial Times*, 25th January, 1983.
15. *The Financial Times*, 26th November, 1988.
16. Ibid, 18th July, 1988.
17. *The Times*, 29th April, 1987.
18. *The Financial Times*, 2nd July, 1987.
19. The City Company Law Committee, op cit. n12, p89, supra, para17, argued that 'the answer to the question whether the release of information not previously "generally available", would materially affect the price of the relevant securities is necessarily a subjective one. In most cases, the expectations that are formed in the market about a company will govern the effect on the price of its securities when information is released. The market tends to be sensitive to developments in companies and, except for sudden and unexpected recurrences, will often, to a degree, successfully guess at and anticipate the progress that a company is making. Information about profits, favourable or unfavourable contracts, etc, which on the face of it might be expected to move the price of a company's securities may, when announced, not do so, or if market expectations are too high may even lead to perverse moves in an opposite direction'.
This issue is also discussed in EEC Commission, Directorate-General Financial Institutions and Taxation (XV/220/74-EN; XV/A/3), Minutes of the Working Party on Transactions in transferable securities (Insider Trading) held in Brussels on 4th and 10th July, 1979, pp.8-12
20. See, post, Chapter 6, Administrative Regulation.
1. Painter, op cit. n13, p99, supra, p.168; Bromberg, 7.4 and 8.3.
2. *In re Cady, Roberts & Co.*, 40 SEC 907 (1961). See, ante, Chapter 1. Introduction.

'consistently held that insiders must disclose material facts which are known to them by virtue of their position, but which are not known to persons with whom they deal and which, if known, would affect their investment judgment'[3]. To the objection that this test would create uncertainty and confusion as regards the need for disclosure, the SEC countered:

> 'There should be no quandary on the facts here presented. While there may be a question as to the materiality and significance of some corporate facts and as to the necessity of their disclosure under particular circumstances, that is not this case. Corporate dividend action of the kind involved here is clearly recognisable as having a direct effect on the market value of securities and the judgment of investors'[4].

Various formulations of materiality were laid down in the *Texas Gulf Sulphur* case in which the information in question related to a mineral discovery. The lower court applied the test of what with reasonable certainty 'would have had a substantial impact on the market price of the stock'[5]. But this was qualified by other parts of the opinion that expressed materiality in terms of information which 'in reasonable and objective contemplation might affect the value', 'would clearly affect investment judgment' or 'directly bears on the intrinsic value'[6].

On appeal, this approach was rejected by the Second Circuit as too conservative. A low threshold of materiality was set: 'not only information disclosing the earnings and distributions of a company, but also those facts which affect the desire of investors to buy, sell or hold'[7]. Speculators were included among the reasonable investors used to measure materiality[8]. Moreover, trading by insiders and their tippees provided evidence of materiality[9]. Though there was some support for the view that the 'once-in-a-lifetime' nature[10] of the discovery suggested the low threshold of materiality ought to be restricted to the particular circumstances of the case[11], extensive reference has since been made to the *Texas Gulf Sulphur* judgment in setting standards for determining materiality.

Thus, in the light of the *Texas Gulf Sulphur* case, the materiality concept was analysed as being determined by four overlapping tests[12]. These were:

'(1)   Facts which, if disclosed, would be reasonably likely to have a substantial market effect;

(2)   Facts which would be important to a reasonable, (including speculative) investor;

(3)   Facts which are "material" upon a balancing of both the indicated probability that the event will occur and the anticipated magnitude of the event in the light of the totality of the company activity; and

---

3. Ibid at 911.
4. Ibid at 915.
5. *SEC v Texas Gulf Sulphur Co.* 258 F.Supp.262 (S.D.N.Y.1966).
6. Ibid at 280.
7. *SEC v Texas Gulf Sulphur Co.* 401 F.2d.833 at 844 (S.D.N.Y.1966).
8. Ibid at 849 and 850.
9. Ibid at 851. This argument had been rejected by the lower court, 258 F.supp.262 at 283.
10. 401 F.2d 833 at 869 per Judge Friendly.
11. Bromberg, 7(4)(3)(c).
12. Painter, op cit. n13, p90, supra, p.172.

(4) The importance attached to the facts by those who knew of them, as reflected by the manner in which they traded securities'.

Of these tests, the substantial market impact test and the reasonable investor test are the most important and best regarded as alternatives to each other, whilst the significance of the others varies with the facts[13]. The reasonable investor test emphasises the individual[14]. It is also related to the Second Circuit's statement of the statutory purpose as being to remove informational inequities of the market so that all investors have equal access to rewards in securities transactions[15]. It is linked to the substantial market impact test in that individual investors in the aggregate constitute the market. Apart from taking account of this collective effect, the substantial market impact test requires that such effect be significant and is thus more restrictive and realistic as the decisions of different investors to buy, sell or hold may cancel each other out, with minimal impact on the market price. As the market determines the value of information, it thus provides a better model for determining materiality. In the third test, the probability element reflects much investor judgment, but does not specify the odds and may readily be distorted by hindsight.

In direct personal cases, the test of materiality is normally an abstract one, namely, would a reasonable man think it significant. But with open market transactions, independent evidence of materiality may be available in the form of price reaction, thereby affording a more realistic test in terms of the market's actual reaction as distinct from what a reasonable market would do[16]. In line with the view that there may be no such thing as a reasonable market, a test based on the market's actual reaction provides a better guide to losses from quantifiable market reactions. Two main objections have been raised to this test. First, anticipatory trading may mean that at the time of disclosure there is no price movement because this has already occurred. But as the market is usually reacting to various other factors, it is difficult to isolate any individual factor. Secondly, it relies on hindsight and thus appears unfair. Whilst a reasonable market standard avoids some of these difficulties, it also involves at least as much guesswork. In the event of any demonstrable market reaction, this would doubtless be relevant in applying the reasonable market standard.

Applied to insider dealing, the Federal Securities Code expresses the 'materiality' concept in terms of alternative tests of a significant effect on market price or importance to a reasonable person in the light of certain factors. Thus, an insider is required to disclose a 'fact of special significance' if it is not 'generally available'[17]. More precisely:

> 'a fact is "of special significance" if (1) in addition to being material it would be likely on being made generally available to affect the market price of a security to a significant extent, or (2) a reasonable person would consider it especially important under the circumstances in determining his course of action in the light of such factors as the degree of its specificity, the extent of its difference from information generally available previously and its nature and reliability'[18].

13. Bromberg, 7(4)(3).
14. But not from a subjective point of view.
15. 401 F.2d 833 at 851-852.
16. Bromberg, 8.3.
17. Section 1603.
18. Section 257. These are similar to the criteria for determining tippee liability.

Although the formulation of criteria assists in determining materiality, their application to particular facts is difficult. Both the small number of British prosecutions and extensive examples provided by US cases suggest that the matter can be satisfactorily resolved only on a case-by-case basis.

C. Restrictions placed on insiders

The operation of the IDA 1985 is based on a prohibition on dealings, supplemented by prohibitions against the counselling or procuring of dealing and the communication of information. But the scope of these prohibitions is circumscribed by defences and exclusions.

1. Prohibited transactions

Applicable to dealings on certain types of securities exchange, the statutory provisions are primarily directed at dealings in securities (including contracts for differences by reference to securities) on a recognised stock exchange. For this purpose, a 'recognised stock exchange' is extended to include dealing through an 'investment exchange'. But the prohibition on dealings on a recognised stock exchange is further extended to dealings in advertised securities through or by an off market dealer who is making a market in the securities. In addition, the prohibitions on (a) the counselling or procuring of dealings and (b) the communication of information, apply to dealings outside Great Britain on any stock exchange other than a recognised stock exchange. However, private dealings, including dealings through an intermediary, otherwise than on the types of securities exchange covered by the statutory provisions, fall outside its scope.

(a) DEALINGS ON A RECOGNISED STOCK EXCHANGE

(i) Prohibition on dealing by individuals connected with a company.   An individual who is, or at any time in the preceding six months has been, knowingly connected with a company is subject to two prohibitions on dealing on a recognised stock exchange. First, he may not deal in securities of that company if he has information which (a) he holds by virtue of being connected with the company, (b) it would be reasonable to expect a person so connected and in the position by virtue of which he is so connected not to disclose except for the proper performance of the functions attaching to that position and (c) he knows is unpublished price sensitive information in relation to those securities[19]. Secondly, an individual so connected may not deal in the securities of any other company if he has information which (a) he holds by virtue of being connected with the first company, (b) condition (c) above is satisfied, (c) he knows is unpublished price sensitive information in relation to those securities of that other company and (d) relates to any transaction (actual or contemplated) involving both the first company and that other company or involving

19. IDA 1985, s1(1).

one of them and securities of the other or to the fact that such transaction is no longer contemplated[20].

DEALING.   A positive act of buying or selling is imposed by the definition of dealing which provides that:

> 'a person deals in securities if (whether as principal or agent) he buys or sells or agrees to buy or sell any securities'[1].

As a result, the use of inside information to buy or sell securities breaches the IDA 1985, whereas its use to prevent a purchase or sale does not. Likewise, it seems that an individual prohibited from dealing will not breach the prohibitions against counselling or procuring dealing or against communicating information, either by expressly advising against dealing or by giving advice of a nature that deters dealing[2].

SECURITIES.   The definition of securities is not restricted to listed securities which, in turn, mean 'any securities of the company listed on a recognised stock exchange'. But in the case of a company within the meaning of the CA 1985 or a company registered under Chapter II of Part XXII of the CA 1985 or an unregistered company, 'securities' also include (even if they are not listed securities) any shares, any debentures or any right to subscribe for, call for or make delivery of a share or debenture[3]. Both the terms 'share' and 'debenture' have the same meaning in relation to companies which were not incorporated under the CA 1985 as in relation to companies which were so incorporated[4].

CONTRACTS FOR DIFFERENCE.   Initially limited to dealing in company securities, the scope of the statutory provisions was extended as a result of an amendment by the FSA 1986[5] to cover dealings in contracts for difference. In particular, a person who (whether as principal or agent) buys or sells or agrees to buy or sell investments within para9, Sch1 of that Act, where the purpose or pretended purpose mentioned in that paragraph is to secure a profit or avoid a loss wholly or partly by reference to fluctuations in the value or price of securities, is treated as if he were dealing in those securities[6]. Contracts for difference by reference to securities are defined as rights under a contract for difference or under any other contract the purpose or pretended purpose of which is to secure a profit or avoid a loss by reference to fluctuations in the value or price of property of any description or in an index or other factor designated for that purpose in the contracts[7].

RECOGNISED STOCK EXCHANGE.   The term 'recognised stock exchange' is extended to mean The Stock Exchange and any other investment exchange which

20. Ibid, s1(2).
1. Ibid, s13(1).
2. Prentice, op cit. n10, p89, supra, para315.
3. IDA 1985, s12(a).
4. Ibid, s16(1).
5. FSA 1986, s176.
6. IDA 1985, s13 (1A).
7. FSA 1986, Sch1, para9.

is declared by an order of the Secretary of State to be a recognised stock exchange for the purposes of the IDA 1985[8]. In turn, an 'investment exchange' means:

> 'an organisation maintaining a system whereby an offer to deal in securities made by a subscriber to the organisation is communicated, without his identity being revealed, to other subscribers to the organisation, and whereby any acceptance of that offer by any of those other subscribers is recorded and confirmed'[9].

Apart from covering Ariel, this extension was designed to prevent avoidance of insider dealing legislation by an expansion of dealings outside the Stock Exchange through the establishment of other organisations maintaining a system for dealing in securities.

(ii) Prohibition on dealing by individuals contemplating a take-over offer.   An individual who is contemplating, or has contemplated, making (with or without another person) a take-over offer for a company in a particular capacity, may not deal on a recognised stock exchange in securities of that company in another capacity if he knows that information that the offer is contemplated, or is no longer contemplated, is unpublished price sensitive information in relation to those securities[10].

(iii) Prohibition on dealing by public servants.   A public servant or former public servant may not deal on a recognised stock exchange in the securities of a particular company (relevant securities) on the basis of information which (a) is held by him by virtue of his position or former position as public servant, (b) it would be reasonable to expect him not to disclose except for the proper performance of the functions attaching to that position and (c) he knows is unpublished price sensitive information in relation to the relevant securities[11].

(iv) Prohibition on dealing by tippees.   Prohibited dealing by connected individuals is paralleled by similar prohibitions for their tippees[12]. An individual who has information which (a) he knowingly obtained (directly or indirectly) from another individual who is connected with a particular company or was at any time in the six months preceding the obtaining of the information so connected, (b) he knows or has reasonable cause to believe it would be reasonable for the connected individual, by virtue of his connection and position, not to disclose except for the proper performance of the functions attaching to that position, may not deal on a recognised stock exchange in the securities of that company if he knows that the information is unpublished price sensitive information in relation to those securities. He is also prohibited from so dealing in the securities of another company if he knows that the information is unpublished price sensitive information in relation to those securities and it relates to any transaction (actual or contemplated) involving the first company

8. IDA 1985, s16(1). This provision was amended by FSA 1986 Sch12, para5.
9. Ibid, s13(2).
10. Ibid, s1(5).
11. Ibid, s2.
12. Ibid, s1 (3) and (4).

and the other company or involving one of them and securities of the other or to the fact that any such transaction is no longer contemplated.

These prohibitions are supplemented by others paralleling those imposed on individuals contemplating a take-over offer and public servants. An individual who has knowingly obtained (directly or indirectly), from an individual contemplating a take-over offer, information that the offer is being contemplated or is no longer contemplated, may not deal on a recognised stock exchange in securities of that company in another capacity if he knows that information that the offer is contemplated, or is no longer contemplated, is unpublished price sensitive information in relation to those securities[13]. In addition, an individual who knowingly obtains information (directly or indirectly) from a public servant who that individual knows or has reasonable cause to believe has held the information by virtue of his position or former position as a public servant may not deal on a recognised stock exchange in the securities of a particular company in relation to which the individual knows the information is unpublished price sensitive information[14].

(v) Counselling or procuring dealing.   With the aim of countering avoidance of prohibited dealing by an insider advising or persuading third parties to deal in securities either for their own account or as his nominees, an individual who is prohibited from dealing in any securities on a recognised stock exchange is also prohibited from counselling or procuring any other person (including a body corporate) to deal in those securities, knowing or having reasonable cause to believe that that person would deal in them on a recognised stock exchange. This prohibition thus applies to connected individuals and their tippees, individuals contemplating a take-over offer and their tippees[15] and public servants and their tippees[16].

In contrast to the prohibition on dealing by tippees[17], an individual otherwise subject to the prohibition on counselling or procuring dealing is in breach of this prohibition merely by counselling or procuring a third party to deal in the securities of a company even without divulging unpublished price sensitive information to that third party. In these circumstances, a director prohibited from dealing as a connected individual will breach the prohibition on counselling or procuring dealing merely by advising a third party to deal in the company's securities even without giving reasons for such advice. But in dealing, it seems the third party will not breach the prohibition on tippee dealing[18].

(vi) Communicating information.   In an attempt to reduce further the scope for tippee dealing, another prohibition relates to the communication of information. Thus, an individual who is prohibited from dealing by reason of his having any information, may not communicate that information to any other person (including a body corporate) if he knows or has reasonable cause to believe that that or some other person will make use of the information for the purpose of dealing or of counselling or procuring another person to deal in those securities on a recognised stock exchange[19].

13. Ibid, s1(6).
14. Ibid, s2.
15. Ibid, s1(7) and s4.
16. Ibid, ss2 and 4.
17. Ibid, s1 (3) and (4).
18. See ante.
19. IDA 1985, s1(8).

The need for supplementary prohibitions to counter avoidance of the main prohibition on dealing by insiders was underlined in early prosecutions. Whilst two individuals were in breach of the prohibition on dealing in the securities of the company with which they were connected[20], another individual was charged with counselling or procuring another to deal in the securities of the company with which she was connected[1] and, in turn, the tippee was charged both with dealing in those securities in breach of the prohibition on tippee dealing and with counselling or procuring another to deal in the securities in question[2].

(b) DEALINGS OTHERWISE THAN ON A RECOGNISED STOCK EXCHANGE

(i) Off-market deals.   Individuals prohibited from dealing in securities on a recognised stock exchange are also prohibited from engaging in off-market dealing, subject to an exception for international bond issues[3]. Off-market dealing consists of dealing other than on a recognised stock exchange in the advertised securities of any company either (a) through an off-market dealer, who is making a market in those securities in the knowledge that (i) he is an off-market dealer, (ii) he is making a market in those securities and (iii) the securities are advertised securities or (b) as an off-market dealer who is making a market in those securities or as an officer, employee or agent of such a dealer acting in the course of the dealer's business[4]. The prohibition on off-market dealing also extends to (a) counselling or procuring a person to deal in advertised securities in the knowledge or with reasonable cause to believe that he would deal with them in the manner prohibited and (b) communicating any information in the knowledge or with reasonable cause to believe that it would be used for such dealing or for such counselling or procuring[5].

The meaning of 'advertised securities' and 'off-market dealer' are thus central to the operation of these prohibitions. The term 'advertised securities' means listed securities or securities in respect of which, not more than six months before the dealing occurs, information indicating the prices at which persons have dealt or were willing to deal in those securities has been published for the purpose of facilitating deals in those securities[6]. Hence, securities which once had a published price and were dealt in within a more general market are excluded if they have not been dealt in within in a six-month period before the relevant dealing. An 'off-market dealer' is an authorised person within the meaning of the FSA 1986[7].

For the purpose of the prohibition on off-market deals, an individual is taken to deal in advertised securities as an off-market dealer if he deals in such securities or acts as an intermediary in connection with deals made by other persons in such securities[8]. Thus, an individual prohibited from dealing in securities on a recognised stock exchange is also prohibited from dealing in

20. Rider, op cit. n10, p98, n11, p98, supra.
1. Rider, op cit. n12, p98, supra; *The Financial Times*, 25th January, 1983.
2. Ibid.
3. See post.
4. IDA 1985, s4.
5. Ibid.
6. Ibid, s12(c).
7. Ibid, s13(3). This provision was amended by FSA 1986, s174(4).
8. Ibid, s13(4)(a), which further provides that references to such a dealer's officer, employee or agent dealing in such securities shall be construed accordingly.

such securities either (a) as principal or acting as intermediary in connection with deals made by other persons in such securities, or (b) as an officer, employee or agent of an off-market dealer.

Conversely, an individual is taken to be dealing through an off-market dealer if the off-market dealer is (a) a party to the transaction, (b) an agent for either party to the transaction or (c) acting as an intermediary in connection with the transaction[9]. But the circumstances in which an off-market dealer is regarded as an intermediary are unclear; whereas he would seem to act as an intermediary if, in the course of his business, he introduced parties to a prospective transaction, it is uncertain whether he will be so acting if he introduces such parties at a social gathering, particularly if the introduction is not effected with a view to making a gain for himself.

For the purpose of the insider dealing legislation, an off-market dealer is taken to make a market in any securities if in the course of his business as an off-market dealer he holds himself out both to prospective buyers and to prospective sellers of those securities (other than particular buyers or sellers) as willing to deal in them otherwise than on a recognised stock exchange[10]. Hence, this would not include an off-market dealer who indicated to individual clients to arrange a transaction, whereby one of those clients sold securities to another.

(ii) Dealings on a foreign stock exchange. On the basis that an individual who leaks information should not escape liability merely because his tippee intends to take advantage of the information in one way rather than another, an individual who by reason of his having information, is prohibited from dealing on a recognised stock exchange is subject to two further prohibitions[11]. First, he may not counsel or procure any other person to deal in those securities in the knowledge or with reasonable cause to believe that the other person would deal in the securities outside Britain on any stock exchange (other than a recognised stock exchange). Secondly, he is forbidden to communicate that information to any other person in the knowledge or with reasonable cause to believe that the other person or some third party will make use of the information for the purpose of dealing or of counselling or procuring any other person to deal in the securities outside Britain on any stock exchange (other than a recognised stock exchange). But dealing on a stock exchange outside Britain (other than a recognised stock exchange) is not forbidden by the IDA 1985.

These two further prohibitions will often concern the securities of foreign companies. As the terms 'share' and 'debenture' have the same meaning in relation to companies not incorporated under the CA 1985 as they have in relation to companies so incorporated, the prohibitions relating to dealings on a foreign stock exchange include any share in the share capital of a foreign company or any debentures, debenture stock, bonds or securities of such a company whether consituting a charge on the assets of the company or not[12].

It seems inconsistent to restrict a tipper's liability to cases where he has reasonable cause to believe that the tippee proposes to deal on a stock exchange rather than privately. But this restriction accords with the object of the IDA 1985

9. IDA 1985, s13(5).
10. Ibid, s13(4)(b)..
11. Ibid, s5.
12. By virtue of IDA 1985, s16.

as being to protect markets[13] and its application to dealings on certain types of securities exchange, but not private dealings.

(iii) Private dealings.   However, the omission of private dealings overestimates the ability of people to protect themselves against insiders. Even when the City Company Law Committee supported the exclusion of private dealings from criminal liability, it recommended the strengthening of civil remedies against insiders.

In this respect, the IDA 1985 differs from the proposed requirement for disclosure of insider status in the 1978 Bill. Regardless of whether the insider held inside information, the 1978 Bill contained a provision[14] that:

> 'An individual who is, or at any time in the preceding six months, has been knowingly connected with a company shall not deal privately[15] (a) in any securities of that company, or (b) where he knows that that company or its securities are involved in a transaction (actual or contemplated) with another company or that that company is involved in such a transaction with the securities of another company, in the securities of the other company, unless he first discloses to the person with whom he proposes to deal the fact that he is a person to whom this subsection applies'.

Defences were available to an insider who proved either (a) he knew that that fact was already known to the person to whom he would otherwise have disclosed it or (b) he took all reasonable steps to ensure that that fact was disclosed[16]. In addition to criminal liability, express provision was made for civil remedies in the form of rescission of the transaction[17] or compensation for loss sustained due to non-disclosure[18]. These remedies were also stated not to deprive a person of a remedy for misrepresentation or breach of contract otherwise available to him[19].

But this provision was unsatisfactory. It meant that even when not in possession of inside information, an individual who failed to disclose his insider status in a transaction outside a recognised stock exchange was subject to the same penalties as an insider who dealt on a recognised stock exchange on the basis of inside information. Moreover, where the insider held inside information, it did not act as an incentive for public disclosure of the information in question. But the legislation, now contained in the IDA 1985, did not explore alternative solutions.

As a result, its failure to cover private dealings facilitates the avoidance of criminal liability by encouraging insiders to deal otherwise than on a securities exchange to which the prohibitions apply.

2. Defences and exclusions

However, the prohibitions on dealing are not absolute in that insiders who deal

13. Gower Supplement, op cit, n10, p89, supra, pp636-638, footnote 84.
14. Companies Bill 1978, cl 59(1).
15. By the Companies Bill 1978, cl 59(3), the term 'deal privately' meant deal otherwise than on a recognised stock exchange.
16. Companies Bill 1978, cl 59(2).
17. Ibid, cl 61(1).
18. Ibid, cl 61(2).
19. Ibid, cl 61(3).

whilst in possession of inside information are not necessarily liable. With a view to permitting dealings where insiders do not deal to exploit inside information, the IDA 1985 provides for general defences. Other dealings are also excluded mainly to enable market professionals to carry on certain activities.

(a) DEALING OTHER THAN TO MAKE A PROFIT OR AVOID A LOSS

This controversial defence provides that an individual is not liable by reason of having any information from:

> 'doing any particular thing otherwise than with a view to the making of a profit or the avoidance of a loss (whether for himself or another person) by the use of that information'[20].

This provision was introduced to counter any deterrent effect of insider dealing legislation on directors and employees holding shares in their companies[1].

But defences based on an insider's personal needs have been objected to in principle on the ground that the mere fact of circumstances necessitating a profitable dealing does not mean an insider should retain the profits[2]. In relation to civil liability, this defence is not available to a fiduciary called to account.

In terms of formulation, the difficulty with the defence contained in the IDA 1985 is that the making of a profit or avoidance of a loss is a motive in most dealings. When a similar defence was introduced in the 1978 Bill[3], the CSI recommended[4] that the defence be redrafted on the lines of the one contained in the 1973 Bill[5] so that it applied when making a profit or avoiding a loss was not a primary motive. But the 1973 Bill's distinction between primary and subsidiary motives attracted the criticism that it would facilitate avoidance of liability on a scale that undermined the operation of the proposed legislation[6]. In this context, a preferable approach was proposed by the Law Society in its comments on the 1978 Bill. As the legislative objective was to prohibit an insider exploiting inside information irrespective of whether this occurred with a view to making a profit or loss for himself or another, it supported a provision in terms that:

> 'it shall be a defence to show that the accused did not deal for the purpose of exploiting the inside information in his possession'[7].

Judicial interpretation of this statutory defence remains unclear. But the failure to distinguish primary from subsidiary motives points to a narrow interpretation in which case an insider will be unable to rely on the defence when he has alternative assets.

The onus of proof is not expressly stated. But once the prosecution have

20. IDA 1985, ss3(1)(a), 7(1) and 5(2).
1. H.C. Deb. Vol.980, ser.5, col.147 (3rd March, 1980).
2. Eg, R. White, 'Towards a Policy Basis for the Regulation of Insider Dealing' (1974) 90 L.Q.R. 494 at 501.
3. Companies Bill, 1978, cl 57(6)(a).
4. CSI, *Insider dealing clauses in draft Companies Bill* (1st November, 1978, Appendix).
5. Companies Bill 1973, cl 14(1).
6. White, op cit. n12, p89, supra, p.501.
7. Law Society, op cit. n12, p89, supra, para12.

established that the insider dealt when in possession of inside information, the onus is on the defendant. This onus will also limit the scope of the defence.

(b) LIQUIDATOR, RECEIVER OR TRUSTEE IN BANKRUPTCY

A second defence also raises problems of interpretation. This provides that an individual is not liable by reason of having any information from:

'Entering into a transaction in the course of the exercise in good faith of his functions as liquidator, receiver or trustee in bankruptcy'[8].

But it is unclear how a liquidator, receiver or trustee in bankruptcy can be regarded as acting in 'good faith' except when his dealings are in accordance with his duties as such.

(c) JOBBERS AND MARKET MAKERS

In performing their duties, jobbers would occasionally have unpublished price-sensitive information within the meaning of inside information in the IDA 1985[9]. But because of the importance attached to their role in providing a continuous market, jobbers were afforded wide protection and an individual is not liable if (a) the information was obtained in the course of a business as a jobber and (b) was of a description which it would be reasonable to expect him to obtain in good faith in the course of that business[10]. A jobber thus falls outside this defence when the information was not obtained in the course of his business or was not of a description which he could reasonably be expected to obtain in the ordinary course of that business. For this purpose, 'jobber' means an individual, partnership or company dealing in securities on a recognised stock exchange and recognised by the Stock Exchange as carrying on the business of a jobber[11].

A corresponding defence for market makers was introduced by the FSA 1986[12]. Thus, an individual is not liable if (a) the information was obtained in the course of a business as a market maker and was of a description which it would be reasonable to expect him to obtain in the ordinary course of such a business and (b) he acts in good faith in the course of that business[13]. For that purpose, 'market maker' means a person (whether an individual, partnership or company) who holds himself out at all times in compliance with the rules of a recognised stock exchange as willing to buy and sell securities at a price specified by him and is recognised as doing so by that recognised stock exchange[14].

8. IDA 1985, ss3(1)(b) and 5(2).
9. Unpublished price sensitive information held by jobbers would not usually be obtained from the company or an individual connected with it and so would fall outside the meaning of inside information. But when so obtained, jobbers (unlike brokers) would be likely to obtain information on specific rather than just general matters so that they would not be protected by the emphasis on specific as distinct from general matters in the definition of unpublished price sensitive information.
10. IDA 1985, s3(1)(c).
11. Ibid.
12. FSA 1986, s174(1).
13. IDA 1985, s3(1)(d).
14. Ibid.

(d) COMPLETION OF TRANSACTIONS

A fourth defence is limited to insiders and their tippees prohibited from dealing in the securities of a company by virtue of having information about a transaction between that company and the company with which an insider is connected. When these individuals must carry out or complete such a transaction knowledge of which constitutes inside information, anything done 'to facilitate the completion or carrying out of the transaction' provides a defence[15].

(e) TRUSTEES AND PERSONAL REPRESENTATIVES

Limited protection is also provided to trustees and personal representatives, including individuals acting on behalf of a trustee or personal representative which is a body corporate, when they have unpublished price-sensitive information and are faced with a conflict of duties. In these circumstances, a trustee or personal representative who would otherwise be prevented from dealing in securities or from counselling or procuring any other person to deal in securities is, if he deals in those securities or counsels or procures any other person to deal in them, presumed to have acted otherwise than with a view to the making of a profit or the avoidance of a loss, provided that he acts on the advice of a person who (a) appears to him to be an appropriate person from whom to seek such advice and (b) did not appear to him to be prohibited from dealing in those securities[16]. But again the phrase 'otherwise than with a view to the making of a profit or avoidance of a loss' raises difficulties of interpretation[17].

As to the person whose advice is acted on, it is the appearance which determines whether reliance can be placed on this defence. Thus, it cannot be invoked when suspicious circumstances make it apparent to the trustee or personal representative that the adviser was not an appropriate person from whom to seek advice or was prohibited from dealing. As the state of mind of the trustee or personal representative is crucial, it is irrelevant that a reasonable trustee or personal representative would be put on enquiry in the circumstances.

However, the IDA 1985 provides no guidance to other individuals acting in a fiduciary capacity, but with conflicting duties, such as merchant bankers and stockbrokers. In this respect, the legislation did not adopt a Law Society proposal[18] relating to the 1978 Bill which was endorsed by the CSI[19] and recommended inclusion of a provision on the lines:

> 'A trustee of other persons acting in a fiduciary capacity (including a director of a company acting in his capacity as such) shall not be guilty of an offence under this part of this Act merely because, being in possession of such information as aforesaid, he deals or concurs in any dealing in such securities as aforesaid in his fiduciary capacity on the recommendation or advice of any person who is not, so far as he is aware, in possession of such information and notwithstanding any rule of law to the contrary, no such

15. Ibid, s3(2).
16. Ibid, s7.
17. See ante.
18. Law Society, op cit. n11, p89, supra, para15.
19. CSI, *Insider Dealing clauses in draft Companies Bill,* 1st November, 1978, Appendix.

person shall be accountable for breach of trust or breach of fiduciary duty by reason of his failure or refusal to make use of or impart such information to a co-trustee or to any other person'.

Hence, the position of individuals acting in a fiduciary capacity though with conflicting duties is uncertain and this is an area in which more detailed rules need to be devised. But the controversial view that a fiduciary has a duty to beneficiaries to exploit any information in his possession seems untenable in the light of the offences now contained in the IDA 1985. Moreover, both a multi-divisional financial institution and, when instructed by a client to sell a security, an investment adviser, who, on the basis of inside information, knows the sale is inopportune, appear to have a defence to an action for breach of fiduciary duty for non-disclosure of inside information on the ground that disclosure would be an offence since they would have 'reasonable cause to believe' the information would be used for dealing[20]. But in the case of the investment adviser, the problem is complicated in that the disclosure of inside information to deter dealings is apparently outside the IDA 1985.

(f) INTERNATIONAL BOND ISSUES

Introduced with the Eurobond market in mind, a further relaxation applies to individuals who deal in international bonds. A market for professional investors, participants in the Eurobond market were not regarded as needing the same protection as investors on the domestic securities markets. Without this exclusion, it was also feared that the Eurobond market would move to a centre with less stringent insider dealing requirements.

Individuals who deal in international bonds are excluded from the operation of the provisions relating to off-market deals in advertised securities and restricting the promotion of off-market deals abroad provided that such off-market dealing is done (a) by or on behalf of a person who is an authorised person in respect of that dealing (within the meaning of the FSA 1986) and (b) in conformity with rules made under that Act[1] as to the circumstances and manner in which action may be taken, before or during a specified period following the issue of international securities of any specified description for the purpose of stabilising their price[2].

D. Penalties

Breach of the insider dealing prohibitions of the IDA 1985 renders an individual liable to criminal sanctions. The maximum penalty is (a) on conviction on indictment, imprisonment for a term not exceeding seven years or a fine or both, and (b) on summary conviction, imprisonment for a term not exceeding six months or a fine not exceeding the statutory maximum, or both[3].

With a view to preventing frivolous private prosecution and ensuring consistency in prosecution decisions, proceedings may only be instituted in England

---

20. Prentice, op cit. n10, p89, supra, para326.
1. FSA 1986, s48.
2. IDA 1985, s6. This provision was substituted by the FSA 1986, s175 and replaces the former IDA 1985, s6 which re-enacted CA 1980, s71 as amended by CA 1981, s112.
3. IDA 1985, s8(1).

and Wales by the Secretary of State or Director of Public Prosecutions[4]. Reversing the approach of the CA 1980, special powers of investigation have now been conferred on the Department[5].

However, the IDA 1985 does not create any civil remedies. Indeed, as to the civil consequences of an offence, the legislation expressly states that no transaction is void or voidable by reason only that it was entered into in breach of the insider dealing prohibitions[6]. This provision acknowledges the difficulties of tracing shares in the hands of new owners and the prejudice that would otherwise be caused to bona fide purchasers.

Nevertheless, disgorgement of profit is not excluded. In accordance with general equitable principles, fiduciaries may be required to account to the company and in exceptional circumstances to individual shareholders[7]. Any fine imposed may also take account of an insider's profits. Moreover, under the Powers of the Criminal Courts Act 1973[8], a court which convicts an individual may make a discretionary award of compensation to any person who has suffered loss by reason of the offence or in the case of a Crown Court, may make a criminal bankruptcy order. But neither type of order can be made in circumstances where those who have suffered loss as a result of the offence cannot be identified and a magistrates' court has no power to make a compensation order exceeding £1,000.

In addition, a confiscation order may be made under Part VI, Criminal Justice Act 1988. This enables the Crown Court, in addition to dealing with the offender in any other way, to make an order requiring him to pay such sum as the court thinks fit[9]. The Crown Court may make such an order where (a) the offender is guilty of any offence to which Part VI applies and (b) it is satisfied that he has benefited from that offence[10] and that his benefit is at least £10,000[11]. For this purpose, a person benefits from an offence if he obtains property as a result of or in connection with its commission; his benefit is the value of the property so obtained[12]. Where a person derives a pecuniary advantage as a result of or in connection with the commission of an offence, he is to be treated as if he thereby obtained a sum of money equal to the pecuniary advantage[13]. Whilst the amount of a confiscation order must be at least £10,000, it must also not exceed either (a) the benefit in respect of which it is made or (b) the amount appearing to the court as that which might be realised at the time the order is made, whichever is less[14]. The making of a confiscation order is subject to a requirement of prior written notice by the prosecution[15]. Further provisions deal with statements relevant to making confiscation orders, definition of terms and enforcement[16].

4. Ibid, s8(2).
5. FSA 1986, ss177-178; see, post, Chapter 7. Investigation.
6. IDA 1985, s8(3).
7. See, post, Chapter 4. Civil Liability.
8. Ss35 and 39.
9. Criminal Justice Act 1988, s71(1).
10. Or from that offence taken together with some other offence of which he is convicted in the same proceedings, or which the court takes into consideration in determining his sentence, and which is not a drug trafficking offence.
11. Criminal Justice Act 1988, s71(2) and (7). Under s.71(3) a magistrates' court also has power to make a confiscation order. However, this power does not extend to insider dealing offences.
12. Criminal Justice Act 1988, s71(4).
13. Ibid, s71(5).
14. Ibid, s71(6) and (7).
15. Ibid, s72(1).
16. Ibid, ss73-75.

A further consequence of conviction of an insider dealing offence is that certain provisions of the Rehabilitation of Offenders Act 1974 do not apply to various matters under the FSA 1986[17]. This mainly concerns those in senior positions in business applying for authorisation to carry on investment business.

The sentencing practice of the courts has varied widely. The most surprising sentence was an absolute discharge in the first prosecution[18]. A partner in a firm of investment managers pleaded guilty to a breach of the main prohibition on insider dealing, having placed an order for 3,900 shares in a trust knowing that his firm was the manager of the trust and that on the following day, an announcement would be made stating that the structure of the trust would be amended to enable it to become a specialised energy trust. After the announcement, the price of each share rose by 40p. In imposing this sentence, the Edinburgh Sheriff Court appears to have been influenced by the defendant's decision to deposit £1,400 with his solicitor and undertaking to pay this sum to the jobber as compensation for the amount of loss suffered on executing the transaction. In mitigation, it was also asserted that the defendant was unaware of the insider dealing legislation and did not stand to gain personally as he had entered the transaction on behalf of a member of his family. Whilst the court's reluctance to impose a financial penalty may be explicable in terms of the restitution of profits and the defendant's loss of his job, the reasons for its choice of an absolute discharge as an alternative sentence are unclear from the reported facts.

However, the question of restitution of profits did not arise in a subsequent prosecution, when a magistrates' court imposed a sentence of six months imprisonment suspended for two years, together with an order for costs of £100[19]. The circumstances of this case underline the need to provide for criminal liability, even when the difficulties of making effective civil remedies available can be readily overcome. Using his solicitors as nominees, the managing director of a subsidiary of a company involved in take-over discussions took out an option contract on 50,000 shares of the company for £2,415 whilst in possession of inside information. Following these discussions, the company's lift division was taken over by another company and if the option had been exercised, the director would have made a profit of £10,835. But the option contract was unusual as the market price of the relevant shares had been static and on learning of the contract, the offeree chairman instructed the company's merchant banker to make enquiries. The Stock Exchange suspended dealings in the company's shares and the preliminary enquiry was conducted before the exercise of the option. The defendant pleaded guilty to breach of the main prohibition on insider dealing, though in mitigation it was said that the information in his possession was not concrete. It was further stated that the transaction was undertaken due to a desperate need for money to resolve a marital and financial dilemma. Apart from the option fee, the director lost his job and prospective directorship in the new company. Following his plea of guilty to the insider dealing offence, the Department offered no evidence on two other charges alleging failure to disclose and report his interests in the shares in accordance with statutory requirements for the disclosure of directors' interests in shares and debentures[20].

In another case involving a suspended prison sentence, heavy financial pen-

17. FSA 1986, s189 and Schedule 14.
18. Rider, op cit. n11, p98, supra.
19. Rider, op cit. n10, p98, supra.
20. See, post, Chapter 5. Disclosure, III. Insider Reporting.

alties were also imposed[1]. A, the former joint managing director of the securities arm in B, a City merchant banking group, pleaded guilty to two charges. In August 1986, A was asked by a US predator R, which was interested in taking over S, to built up a 4.9% holding in Y. After B started buying there was press speculation about a possible bid and buying was temporarily stopped. During the lull, A telephoned a former colleague in the US and asked him to buy £30,000 of S shares for him. The former colleague ordered call option contracts for himself and A, the transaction being carried out in the name of a Cayman Islands company. This was controlled by A and recognisable as his. The shares, in which they had invested over £45,000, were sold at a loss of £15,000 when the price fell. Subsequently, in November 1986, X had been interested in making an agreed bid for Y. Together with his fellow joint managing director, A attended a meeting on X's premises, at which the bid was discussed. By the time he left, A knew that a bid for Y would almost certainly be announced early the next day and that, if it was announced, B would be instructed by X to buy shares in Y at up to 260p per share before the announcement. A stayed the night at the home of his fellow joint managing director and at 6 a.m. the latter was telephoned and told a bid was to be announced. At about 6.15 a.m., A telephoned his former colleague in the US and told him to buy shares in Y as soon as possible. The latter placed an order for 60,000 Y shares at a price up to 239p, with London stockbrokers on behalf of the firm for which he worked. The transaction was booked in his employer's records in the name of the Cayman Island company. At 8.30 a.m., the agreed bid was announced. The price of Y shares rose sharply and the former business associate sold for £159,000, making a gross profit of £15,000. However, the purchase minutes before the announcement and the sale minutes afterwards attracted attention. A resigned from his job and later co-operated with inspectors from the Department.

At the Old Bailey in 1987, A was sentenced to twelve months imprisonment, suspended for two years, and fined £25,000. He was also ordered to pay £7,000 towards prosecution costs. The judge said that although the case had attracted much press attention, A's crime could not be compared with widely publicised offences in the US. However, he warned that future insider dealers, including those of good character, were unlikely to get away with suspended sentences.

In other cases, the emphasis has been on financial penalties. In an early prosecution[2], the charges related to (a) tippee dealing and (b) by both a connected individual and a tippee, counselling or procuring dealing. In this case, it was alleged that a secretary to a director of a merchant bank passed unpublished price sensitive information about a likely offer for the securities of a company with which she was connected through a business relationship, to her husband who worked in another merchant bank, knowing that he would use that information for dealing. Her husband was charged with dealing as a tippee and with counselling or procuring another to deal. Before the announcement of the offer at 155p a share, the market price of the shares was 102p. The couple were fined £4,000 each at a Crown Court and order to pay £1,000 costs.

In a subsequent case, the fine was considerably lower than the insider's gain[3]. A director, who worked for a well-known company, X, for thirty-eight years and resigned from the main board on 31st May 1984 on grounds of ill-health, bought 1,500 shares in another company, Y, early that year for 152p each. At the time,

---

1. *The Financial Times*, 2nd July, 1987.
2. Rider, op cit. n12, p98, supra; *The Financial Times*, 25th January, 1983.
3. *The Times*, 29th April, 1987.

X had begun researching Y with a view to making a take-over bid, which emerged in early May. X pulled out when Z made a rival bid. The director sold his shares to Z, making a profit of nearly £3,000. Following a plea of guilty, the director was fined £800 and ordered to pay £100 prosecution costs. Subsequently, the chairman of X commented that the former director was at worst guilty of a technical offence: 'it was a pure oversight, involving a tiny amount. Technically, he was guilty'. He added that there was no connection between the director's resignation and the purchase of shares in Y.

However, heavier fines have been imposed on two further occasions. In the first case[4], the private secretary to the group chairman purchased 7,500 shares in the company, knowing that there was going to be a senior management shake-up. One week later, he sold them at a profit of £4,000. The following month, he had used information given to him in confidence to try to buy 2,500 shares in another company. Had that transaction not been cancelled, his gain would have been £1,500. The defendant, who pleaded guilty, was fined £10,000 and ordered to pay £2,000 prosecution costs. The Recorder said that the defendant had never before been in any sort of trouble and a prison sentence would not be appropriate as he was in his 50's and had very little chance of obtaining a similar job. He also noted that at the time the defendant had financial and family worries.

In the second case[5], a managing director, before resigning, had exercised an option and bought 25,000 shares in the company at the preferential rate of 50p per share. He sold them for 128p each just before the public announcement of a new share offer, after which the share price dropped from 132p to 108p. The managing director denied the charge. He stated that he had sold the shares only because he had been wrongly told that he must sell within thirty days or lose the option. Following his conviction by a majority verdict, the defendant was fined £7,000. In fixing this sum, the judge stated that he was taking into account the heavy legal costs incurred by the defendant and the prejudice to his employment prospects.

Notwithstanding the increase, in 1988, from two to seven years in the maximum sentence of imprisonment, there has been little sign of the courts resorting to such heavy sentences. In the two cases where prison sentences have been imposed, they have been suspended. Despite the judicial warning in 1987 that future insiders were unlikely to get away with suspended sentences, it is unclear how an immediate term of imprisonment can be imposed on lesser offenders. Apart from that 1987 case, the fines have been moderate, with the gains accruing to insiders also having been small. A striking feature is the frequency with which insiders have also lost their job.

Although providing a technique for the enforcement of insider dealing legislation, the criminal law is limited both in its incidence and in its deterrent effect. By definition, criminal penalties can be imposed only after detection and proof of the offence. The deterrent effect of criminal penalties, particularly for an offence such as insider dealing where the cost-benefits of breaking the law are more likely to be evaluated rationally, are reduced by the prospects of the breach not being detected. This factor is influenced by the resources of the regulatory authorities and by the fact that even when detected, a heavy burden

4. *The Financial Times*, 18th July, 1988.
5. Ibid, 26th November, 1988.

of proof is placed on the prosecution. Hence, the limitations associated with the enforcement by the criminal law underline the need to consider provision for other enforcement techniques, such as civil actions.

Chapter 4

Civil Liability

The issue of whether provision should be made for civil remedies is one of the most controversial aspects of insider dealing regulation. Controversy surrounds both the principles on which liability may be based and the formulation of remedies themselves.

In striking contrast to the US, civil remedies have not been regarded as a necessary means of regulating insider dealing in Britain. When criminal liability for insider dealing was imposed, the legislation made no provision for civil remedies as an aid to enforcement.

In the passage through Parliament of the Bill which became the CA 1980, the Government resisted attempts to introduce clauses imposing civil liabilities on insiders. Its stance was at variance with the Companies Bills of 1973 and of 1978. Both Bills contained limited proposals for civil liability, though these fell short of providing a civil remedy to non-insiders in open-market transactions.

The Government's opposition to statutory civil remedies stemmed from the consideration that the then prevailing jobbing system and market structure generally made it impracticable to identify an investor who had made the loss represented by the insider's gain. In face-to-face transactions, it was of opinion that parties could make their own enquiries and include provisions relating to disclosure in the contract. In the Government's view, it was also established that under existing equitable rules fiduciaries had to account to the company for profits made by reason of information belonging to the company in their possession.

As a result, the civil liabilities of insiders are limited to common law obligations. These are founded on fiduciary concepts, though alternative remedies may also be sought in an action for breach of confidence and an action for breach of statutory duty.

In this chapter, consideration will be given to the extent to which fiduciary obligations compel insiders to account to their company and to shareholders and others. Other remedies, namely, an action for breach of confidence and an action for breach of statutory duty, will also be canvassed. In addition, reference will be made to insiders faced with conflicts of interest.

I. LIABILITY TO THE COMPANY

There is no reported decision in Britain on a claim by a company to recover insider dealing profits from an insider. Hence, the issue of whether insiders are accountable to their companies for such profits is unresolved.

However, a fruitful source of guidance is available in the law relating to fiduciaries. In this context, it is proposed to discuss fiduciary duties insofar as they impinge on this issue, the definition of insider in equity and the enforcement difficulties associated with accountability to the company.

A. Fiduciary duties

Whilst there are various formulations[1], it is a fundamental principle that fiduciaries must not place themselves in a position where their interest and duty conflict[2]. The objectives of the conflict of duty and interest principle are twofold. Emphasising the idea of conflict of duty or undertaking and interest, the first objective is to prevent a person who has undertaken to act for or on behalf of another in some matter from allowing any undisclosed personal interest to sway him from the proper performance of that undertaking. Reflecting distaste for profit from a position of trust, the second is to prevent a person from actually misusing the position his undertaking gives him to further his own interests. A difficulty is that in marginal cases stress on one objective rather than the other produces differing results.

The reason for the rule lies in a 'somewhat cynical'[3] view of human nature. In *Bray v Ford*[4], Lord Herschell commented:

'It does not appear to me that this rule is, as has been said, founded upon principles of morality. I regard it rather as based upon the consideration that, human nature being what it is, there is a danger of the person holding a fiduciary position being swayed by interest rather than duty, and thus prejudicing those whom he was bound to protect. It has, therefore, been expedient to lay down this positive rule'[5].

These observations reflect the influence of the decision *Keech v Sandford*[6]. In that 1726 case, a lessor refused to renew a lease to the trust, but allowed the trustee to renew it for his personal benefit. It was held that the trustee must hold the renewal on trust for his beneficiary because if a trustee, on the refusal to renew, might have a lease to himself, few trust estates would be renewed for the benefit of beneficiaries.

Consequent upon the no-conflict rule, fiduciaries are in breach of their duty if, without the consent of the company, they profit from a use of corporate assets, information or opportunities. Though little turns on the point, the 'secret profits' rule is viewed alternatively as an application of the no-conflict rule or after originating in the no-conflict rule, as having probably attained the status of a separate rule[7].

For the purpose of the no-conflict rule, a fiduciary is, in general terms,

1. The best-known statement is that of Lord Herschell in *Bray v Ford* [1896] A.C.44 at 51:
'it is an inflexible rule of a Court of Equity that a person in a fiduciary position . . . is not, unless otherwise expressly provided, entitled to make a profit; he is not allowed to put himself in a position where his interest and duty conflict'.
In *New Zealand Netherlands Society v Kuys* [1973] 1 W.L.R.1126 at 1129 P.C., Lord Wilberforce referred to an obligation:
'not to profit from a position of trust, or, as it is sometimes relevant to put it, not to allow a conflict to arise between duty and interest'.
Another authoritative statement is that of Lord Upjohn who, in *Boardman v Phipps* [1967] 2 A.C.46 at 123 H.L., described the rule in terms that:
'a person in a fiduciary capacity must not make a profit out of his trust which is part of the wider rule that a trustee must not place himself in a position where his duty and interest may conflict'.
2. P.D. Finn, *Fiduciary Obligations* (1977), para.464.
3. Ibid, para.465.
4. [1896] A.C.44.
5. Ibid at 51-52.
6. [1558-1774] All E.R. Rep.230.
7. *Palmer's Company Law,* Twenty-fourth edition under the general editorship of C.M. Schmitthoff with specialist editors, Vol.1 The Treatise (1987), para.63-23 (hereinafter referred to as '*Palmer*').

someone who has undertaken to act for or on behalf of another in some matter[8]. The existence of a fiduciary relationship is a question of fact in each case. In the company law context, the most frequent example of a fiduciary is the company director. But, as a matter of convenience, further discussion of the definition of an insider by reference to the term 'fiduciary' and the range of persons who have in practice assumed fiduciary duties is postponed to a subsequent section[9].

However, the term fiduciary has been confused with the concept of a trustee, especially with regard to directors. The true position of directors is that of agents for the company[10]. But directors are also regarded as trustees of the company's money or property in their hands or under their control[11]. Yet they are not in the same position as trustees of a will or settlement[12]. In particular, the duties of care and skill of directors normally differ from those of trustees[13].

These distinctions have been important because in the event of inside information being considered corporate property, insider dealings by directors would constitute an abuse of corporate property with the result that, under the rule in *Foss v Harbottle*[14], a derivative action by shareholders on behalf of the company would be permitted and the proprietary remedies attendant upon a constructive trust could be sought. In contrast, a finding that insider dealing is merely a breach of fiduciary duties has as its consequence that the action is in personam so that directors are merely under a personal duty to account and no such action by a minority is permitted. However, when the conduct constitutes unfairly prejudicial treatment under the CA 1985[15], the significance of these distinctions is eroded by the court's statutory discretion to authorise civil proceedings to be brought in the name and on behalf of the company by such person or persons and on such terms as the court may direct.

The significance of these distinctions was illustrated by the Privy Council decision in *Cook v Deeks*[16]. For a number of years, Company T had successfully obtained contracts to construct railways for CPR. In the course of one contract, two managers of T, who were also directors, negotiated for another contract. There were disagreements with another director, A, who had a 25% holding. When the contract was offered by CPR, three of T's four directors proposed that the contract be diverted to a new company which they formed and CPR agreed. In a purported ratification of their conduct by T, they subsequently exercised their votes as holders of 75% of the issued shares to pass a resolution at a general meeting of shareholders declaring that T had no interest in the contract. An action was brought by the plaintiff shareholder A, suing on behalf of himself and all other shareholders of T, for a declaration that the respondents namely, the other three directors of T and the new company, were trustees of the benefit of the contract made between the individual respondents and CPR, and for ancillary relief. The action was dismissed at first instance and this decision was

---

8. Finn, op cit supra, paras.467–468.
9. See, post, B. The definition of insider in equity.
10. *Re Faure Electric Accumulator Co.* (1888) 40 ChD141.
11. *Re Sharpe, Bennett, Masonic and General Life Assurance Co. v Sharpe* [1892] 1 Ch154 C.A.
12. *Re Bank of Syria, Owen and Ashworth's Claim, Whitworth's Claim* [1901] 1 Ch115, C.A.
13. *Re City Equitable Fire Insurance Co. Ltd.* [1925] Ch407, C.A. However, in *Bartlett and Others v Barclays Trust Co. Ltd. (Nos. 1 and 2)* [1980] 1 Ch515, it was held, inter alia, that where a trustee such as a corporation holds itself out as having the skill and expertise to carry on the specialised business of trust management, the duty of care of such a trustee is higher than the standard of care of the ordinary prudent man of business as demanded of a trustee without specialised knowledge.
14. See, post, C. Enforcement difficulties.
15. CA 1985, s.459; see, post, C. Enforcement difficulties.
16. [1916] 1 A.C.554, P.C.

affirmed by the Appellate Division of the Supreme Court of Ontario. Reversing these judgments, the Judicial Committee held that the benefit of the contract belonged in equity to the company T, and that the directors could not validly use their voting power to vest it in themselves.

The stringency of a fiduciary's duty to account to the company for unauthorised profits was underlined in the leading case of *Regal (Hastings) Ltd. v Gulliver*[17]. The company 'Regal', which owned a cinema, wished to acquire two other cinemas in Hastings with a view to selling the businesses of all three cinemas as a single concern. For this purpose, the directors formed a subsidiary with a capital of £5,000 in £1 shares to lease the two other cinemas. But the landlord insisted on a personal guarantee of the rent by the directors unless the subsidiary's paid-up capital was at least £5,000. The directors decided that the company could not provide more than £2,000 and were unwilling to give personal guarantees. Under a new plan, the company was to take up 2,000 shares at par. The further £3,000 was to be raised by four directors and the company's solicitor agreeing to subscribe for 500 £1 shares each whilst the chairman, who took no shares personally, persuaded two companies and an individual to subscribe between them for the remaining 500 shares. Ultimately, instead of selling the undertaking, the shares of the company and the subsidiary were sold to common purchasers at a profit of £2. 16s. 1d. on each of the shares of the subsidiary. The new controllers caused the company to bring an action for recovery of the profit made[18].

The action was dismissed by the court of first instance and a unanimous Court of Appeal. The latter reasoned that the 3,000 shares in the subsidiary had never belonged to Regal which, on the facts as found, could not have taken the opportunity to acquire them.

Although fraud had been alleged in the lower courts, the House of Lords found as a fact that all the transactions were bona fide[19]. Following well-known cases on trustees[20], the House of Lords reversed the decision of the Court of Appeal and unanimously held that in the circumstances the directors, other than the chairman, were in a fiduciary relationship to Regal and so liable to repay to it the profit they had made on the sale of the shares. A fiduciary's liability did not depend on fraud or absence of bona fides or on whether the profit would or should otherwise have gone to the plaintiff, or on whether he acted as he did for the benefit of the plaintiff or on whether the plaintiff had been damaged or benefited by his action. However, the degree of connection required between the action taken in the fiduciary position and the profit gained was unclear. Lord Macmillan expressed the principle on which his decision was based in terms that the directors were liable to account if:

'(i) what the directors did was so related to the affairs of the company that it can properly be said to have been done in the course of their management and in utilisation of their opportunities and special knowledge as directors, and (ii) what they did resulted in a profit for themselves'[1].

17. [1967] 2 A.C. 134n. [1942] 1 All E.R.378, H.L.
18. The plaintiffs did not claim that the profits belonged in equity to the company, eg *Cook v Deeks* [1916] 1 A.C.554, P.C. ante.
19. Other litigation casts doubt on this finding; *Cooper v Luxor (Eastbourne) Ltd.* [1939] 4 All E.R.411 at 416 per Scott L.J.
20. In particular, *Keech v Sandford* [1558-1774] All E.R. Rep.230
1. [1942] 1 All E.R.378 at 391-392.

According to Lord Russell of Killowen, the liability of the directors stemmed from the fact that the shares were acquired by the directors 'by reason, and only by reason of the fact that they were directors of Regal, and in the course of their execution of that office'[2]. Whilst the acquisition of information and opportunities by reason of their office may be a sufficient basis of liability, subsequent cases[3] suggest that the liability of fiduciaries is not so restricted.

In contrast, the House of Lords held that the chairman and solicitor[4] were not liable. Since he did not take the shares beneficially, the chairman was found not liable to repay the profit made by those who took the shares from him, as the latter were not in a fiduciary relationship to the company[5]. Likewise, the solicitor was not required to account for his profit because he had taken his shares not merely with the consent, but at the request of the board.

The company's claim was 'wholly unmeritorious'[6]. But the only reference to accountability as having the effect of reducing the purchase price was by Lord Porter who acknowledged that the purchasers of Regal would receive an 'unexpected windfall'[7] in that they would 'receive in one hand part of the sum which has been paid by the other'[8]. Nevertheless, he considered 'the principle that a person occupying a fiduciary relationship shall not make a profit by reason thereof is of such vital importance that the possible consequence in the present case is in fact as in law an immaterial consideration'[9].

However, the House of Lords' readiness to assume the 'vital importance' of the principle was unfortunate. In circumstances where a company wanted but was financially unable to acquire shares, it may be preferable to impose a pro-phylactic rule requiring directors even when acting in good faith, to account for profits from the sale of the shares[10]. Otherwise, directors may be tempted not to exert themselves fully on the company's behalf. But an alternative approach is to provide a range of defences so that directors are not held liable in specific circumstances, such as when they act in good faith or the opportunity was rejected by the company or the particular transaction was ultra vires or illegal for the company. In the Court of Appeal Lord Greene emphasised the business pressures:

> 'As a matter of business . . . there was only one way left of raising the money, and that was putting it up themselves . . . That being so, the only way in which these directors could secure that benefit for the company was by putting up the money themselves. Once that decision is held to be a bona

---

2. Ibid at 387. Similarly, Viscount Sankey (at 382) stressed that:
'At all material times they were directors and in a fiduciary position, and they used and acted upon their exclusive knowledge acquired as such directors. They framed resolutions by which they made a profit for themselves. They sought no authority from the company to do so, and, by reason of their position and actions, they made large profits for which, in my view, they are liable to account to the company'.
3. Eg. *Industrial Development Consultants Ltd. v Cooley* [1972] 1 W.L.R.443; *Canadian Aero Services Ltd. v O'Malley* (1973) 40 D.L.R.(3d) 371 (Can.S.C.)
4. Cf. *Boardman v Phipps* [1967] 2 A.C.46.
5. As to the liability of third parties, see post B. The definition of insider in equity.
6. *Gower's Principles of Modern Company Law*, Fourth Edition by L.C.B. Gower, J.S. Cronin, A.J. Easson and Lord Wedderburn of Charlton (1979), p.573 (hereinafter referred to as '*Gower*').
7. [1942] 1 All E.R.378 at 394.
8. Ibid.
9. Ibid.
10. G. Jones, 'Unjust enrichment and the fiduciary's duty of loyalty' (1968) 84 L.Q.R.472 at 497; W. Bishop and D.D. Prentice, 'Some Legal and Economic Aspects of Fiduciary Remuneration' (1983) 46 M.L.R.289.

fide one and fraud drops out of the case, it seems to me there is only one
conclusion, namely, that the [company's] appeal must be dismissed with
costs'[11].

The House of Lords' uncritical application of the principle enunciated in
Keech v Sandford[12] that a trustee could not renew a trust lease for his own benefit
thus meant that the policy considerations[13] relevant to directors were glossed
over.

The consequential problem of benefits recovered by the company accruing
to a purchaser of shares as the new owner of the share capital arose in a US case.
In *Pearlman v Feldmann*[14] an order was made to prevent those who had participated or acquiesced in the wrong from obtaining any benefit. The dominant
shareholder, F, who was also chairman and president, sold his holding in a sheet
steel manufacturing company, A, to company B, whose shares were owned by
various end users of steel sheets. As the purpose was to ensure users' supplies
during a period of steel shortage, the price paid to F included a premium. But
a consequence was that some of A's goodwill was sacrificed. Minority shareholders in A brought a derivative action to recover the premium paid for the shares.
It was held that F owed a fiduciary duty to and was accountable for the premium
to minority shareholders who were entitled to the extent of their respective
interests to recover in their own right, instead of the right of the company, since
neither company B nor its successors in interest should share in the account.

Whilst F had a triple role, the court was unwilling to accept that a lesser
obligation attached to any one role. But it emphasised the unusual nature of the
profit. In the case of insider dealing profits, an order in this form instead of one
for corporate recovery would have enabled F to retain his proportion of the
benefit in his personal capacity rather than the benefit ultimately reverting to
him in his capacity as shareholder. It is also of no benefit to the company's
creditors.

As in the *Regal* case where the action was brought by the company, corporate
recovery in *Pearlman* would have resulted in the benefits accruing to the
purchasers in the form of an unmerited reduction in the purchase price. A
power in the court to order payment to present or former shareholders could
overcome inequities associated with corporate recovery. But the remedy of
corporate recovery of insider profits would lose some of its deterrent effect to
the extent that the incentives of the company to bring an action would be
diminished by the risk of benefits being ordered to be paid direct to present or
former shareholders[15].

11. Unreported, but cited by Viscount Sankey in *Regal (Hastings) Ltd. v Gulliver* [1942] 1 All E.R.378
at 381.
12. [1558-1774] All E.R. Rep.230.
13. These are discussed later in this section.
14. 219 F.2d 173 (2d Cir.), cert. denied, 349 U.S.952 (1955); Note 'Pro-Rata Recovery in Stockhold-
ers Derivative Suits' (1956) 69 Harv.L.R.1314.
15. Legislative intervention has now countered the unjust consequences of corporate recovery in
one specific area (CA 1985, ss314-315). When it is a term of a take-over offer to be effected by a
purchase of shares that payment is to be made to a director of the company as compensation for
loss of office or in connection with his retirement from office, it is the duty of that director to take
all reasonable steps to secure that particulars regarding the proposed payment are disclosed in any
notice of the offer to any shareholders. Unless reasonable steps are taken, and, before the transfer
of any shares pursuant to the offer, the payment is also approved by a special meeting of
shareholders for whose shares the offer has been made and of shareholders of the class for whose
shares no offer has been made, the director is deemed to hold any sums received by him on account

Moreover, the *Regal* decision was anomalous in that the chairman and solicitor were not liable though they were the two most responsible for the plan. It appeared that the chairman was the dominant member of the board. In addition, the board had acted throughout on the solicitor's advice. Yet liability to account was restricted to the four directors who acquiesced in the plan. Even then, Lord Russell of Killowen considered that those four directors 'could, had they wished, have protected themselves by a resolution (either antecedent or subsequent) of the Regal shareholders in general meeting'[16].

However, it has been suggested[17] that the anomaly of the chairman and solicitor escaping liability would not have arisen if the company (instead of merely arguing their claim as one for profits owed to the company) had argued and the court had held that, by analogy with *Cook v Deeks*[18], the business opportunity exploited 'belonged' in equity to the company. In that event, the suggestion is that all six defendants could have been held jointly and severally liable as constructive trustees for the value of the 'property' improperly paid away and shareholders could not have ratified[19].

The distinction between the two decisions is regarded as difficult (and perhaps impossible) to draw[20] and hindered in that no reference was made to *Cook v Deeks* or the constructive trust remedy in the *Regal* judgment. One suggested distinction is that between misappropriation of corporate property and the making of an incidental profit. The latter is not regarded as corporate property unless it flows from use of the company's property[1]. In *Cook v Deeks*, the directors were regarded as misappropriating corporate property because it was their duty to acquire the contracts for the company. Hence, the shareholders in general meeting could not ratify[2] their conduct when the resolution is passed because of the directors' votes:

of the payment in trust for the shareholders who sold their shares as a result of the offer. The expenses of distribution are to be borne by the director and not retained out of the sum. But this provision is an exception to the general rule that directors owe their fiduciary duties to the company, not its individual members. In such circumstances, the directors become trustees for members, though only for selling shareholders and not for all members.

16. [1942] 1 All E.R.378 at 389.

17. L.S. Sealy, (a) 'The Director as Trustee' [1967] C.L.J.83 at 98, n.85 and (b) *Cases and Materials in Company Law* (2nd ed.1978), p.253.

18. [1916] 1 A.C.554, P.C.; see ante.

19. The question of ratification is discussed in the following paragraph. It is unclear whether, in *Regal*, Lord Russell envisaged ratification by an independent majority of shareholders or by the directors' own votes as shareholders. Sealy, op cit n17(b), supra at 253 refers to the latter so that it may be possible to reconcile his view with that of *Gower* cited in the following paragraph.

20. *Gower*, pp617-619; Sealy, op cit n17(b), supra, p.253; Palmer, para.64-25; K.W. Wedderburn, 'Shareholders' Rights and the Rule in *Foss v Harbottle*' (1843) 2 Hare 461.

1. R. Goff and G. Jones, *Law of Restitution* (2nd ed.1978), pp509-510.

2. In E.E. Palmer, D.D. Prentice and B. Welling, *Canadian Company Law* (2nd ed.1978) at 6-129, ratification is discussed in the following terms:

'The concept of "ratification" has been bandied about in the cases. Its precise import has been much misunderstood. "Ratification consists in adopting something which has been done or assumed to have been done". *Ashbury v Watson* (1885), 30 ChD.376 at 381 (C.A.) per Lord Esher M.R. . . .

The question whether a particular breach of fiduciary duty can be ratified cannot be answered without analyzing to whom the duty was owed. It is elementary law that the person to whom the duty was owed, may choose to refrain from pursuing a remedy for any breach of that duty. Ratification is nothing but a positive expression of an intent to exercise this choice.

Where a duty, fiduciary or otherwise, is owed to a corporation, it should follow from the elementary principle that the corporation may choose to ratify a breach of the duty. However, it is far from easy to determine who should be allowed to speak the notional will of the corporation.'

'Even supposing it be not ultra vires of a company to make a present to its directors, it appears quite certain that directors holding a majority of votes would not be permitted to make a present to themselves'[3].

Though it seems that making presents is not ultra vires[4], the onus is probably on directors to show that the presents were made and the resolution was passed bona fide for the benefit of the company as a whole. It is unlikely that this onus can be discharged when the directors' votes are decisive in securing the passage of the resolution[5]. Conversely, the *Regal* directors were seen as merely making an incidental profit so that the general meeting could ratify the directors' conduct and relieve them of liability. The difficulty is that they used information acquired as directors of Regal and in the event of the information being regarded as corporate property[6], the shares would belong in equity to the company. But it is suggested[7] that the present of the shares would not necessarily have been improper; when a company is financially unable to acquire the shares, there could be a bona fide decision by members that it was in the company's interests to allow directors to retain the shares and resulting profits, particularly when the votes of an independent majority of members cause the resolution to be passed. Another suggested distinction is that in *Cook v Deeks*, unlike *Regal*, the directors were in breach of their duty to act bona fide in the interests of the company. A fraudulent breach of this sort cannot be ratified[8].

As to the question of whether full disclosure to and approval by the board relieves a director of any duty to account for a profit made[9], the general principle is that the company is entitled to the unbiased advice of every director and so disclosure to and approval by the board is ineffective even if the director involved does not vote and is not counted in the quorum. But full disclosure to and approval by the board is effective in the case of an agent of the company other than director. Hence, the conclusion in *Regal* that the solicitor was not liable because 'he took the shares with the full knowledge and consent of *Regal*'[10]. Unless the articles authorise an independent quorum to act in the matter, the question of whether anything less than ratification by the company in general meeting will relieve a director of liability is unclear. But it has been argued[11] that where the company, acting through an organ authorised to act in the matter, has decided not in any circumstances to avail itself of the information or opportunity, then unless a director's use of it would enable him to compete with the company, it is difficult to see how that use could lead to a conflict of duty and interest, even though the director has not been expressly permitted to use it.

This last proposition is supported by the Privy Council decision in *Queensland Mines Ltd. v Hudson*[12]. H was chairman and managing director of AOE Ltd., which lacked the finance to take up an option over an area in Queensland,

3. *Cook v Deeks* [1916] 1 A.C.554 at 564, P.C. per Lord Buckmaster.
4. *Gower*, p.170.
5. Ibid, p.618.
6. See post.
7. *Gower*, p.618.
8. See, post, C. Enforcement difficulties, (b) Action by a shareholder, (i) Exceptions to the rule in *Foss v Harbottle*, Fraud on the minority where the wrongdoers have control.
9. Palmer, para.63-25; *Gower*, p.598.
10. [1942] 1 All E.R.376 per Viscount Sankey.
11. *Gower*, p.598 and Supplement.
12. (1978) 52 A.L.J.R.399, P.C. This case is noted by G.R. Sullivan, 'Going It Alone – *Queensland Mines v Hudson*' (1979) 42 M.L.R.711.

which was known to contain uranium. To exploit the option, H and K agreed to form Queensland Mines Ltd., which was incorporated in 1959 with two shareholders: AOE, which had the expertise, had a 49% interest and Factors Ltd., which provided the finance and was controlled by S Ltd., (the principal holding company of K and his family), held the remaining 51%. H was managing director of Queensland Mines until 1961 and then continued as a director until 1971. In 1960, H and K negotiated with the Tasmanian Government for other mining licences. Whilst H and K intended to form a new company to exploit any licence, they found it convenient to use Queensland Mines and H used its resources and good name to secure two licences. Shortly after these were issued to H in his own name in 1961, K told H that there was no possibility of his proceeding with the licences as he lacked the capital resources to do so. In response to a situation in which, having given large personal guarantees, he had immense personal obligations under the licences and no resources, H resigned as managing director of Queensland Mines and formed his own company. At a meeting of the Queensland Mines board in 1962, H gave a detailed report on the negotiations with the Tasmanian Government and in the light of the explanations and large amount of cash required to finance the project, the board decided not to pursue the matter any further. After a period of considerable difficulty and risk, H succeeded in interesting an American company and from 1966 received considerable royalties on the ore mined.

In 1971, Queensland Mines brought an action against H and his company, in which it claimed that H had abused his position as its managing director to make a profit for himself and sought relief by way of an account of past and future profits from certain mining operations in which H had allegedly been able to engage because of his position as managing director. H denied that he was acting in a fiduciary capacity at the relevant times when by his own substantial efforts he succeeded in establishing the existence of valuable mineral deposits in an area covered by a licence, admittedly issued to him at a time when he was managing director of Queensland Mines. In the Supreme Court of New South Wales, Wooten J found in favour of Queensland Mines on the issue of alleged breach of fiduciary duty, holding that H had acted in a way in which there was a conflict of interest between him and Queensland Mines and that he did not act with the latter's informed consent. But the trial judge dismissed the action as statute barred.

Reversing this decision on the substantive issue, the Privy Council held that whilst H could be regarded in the initial stages as to some extent acting through Queensland Mines regarding the mining venture, the undisputed events following K's withdrawal and culminating in the 1962 board meeting were open only to one construction, namely, that the board, with knowledge of the facts, had decided to renounce Queensland Mines' interest, whatever it was, in the mining venture and had assented to H doing what he could with the licences at his own risk and for his own benefit. The trial judge's finding that Queensland Mines was not informed of the existence of its interest could not stand. As from the 1972 board meeting, it could be said that (a) the venture was outside the scope of the trust and outside the scope of the agency created by the relationship of director and company, between H and Queensland Mines; or (b) the latter had given its fully informed consent to the matter not being pursued further, leaving H to do what he wished or could with the relevant licences in his own name relating to the venture. After the board meeting, there was thus no real sensible possibility of a conflict of interest between H and Queensland Mines, and as the latter had been fully informed of the facts and assented to H's exploitation of the venture in his own name, for his own gain and at his own risk and expense, there had been no breach of fiduciary duty as found by the trial judge and H was not liable to account as claimed. Hence, it was unnecessary to consider whether the action was statute barred.

It is difficult to object to the decision: the action was brought following years of expense and risk, when the venture was clearly profitable and both shareholders knew of H's conduct. On the aspect of informed consent, it is significant that though the decision was not taken by a wholly independent board or by the shareholders in general meeting, both shareholders of Queensland Mines were represented on the board and were aware of the facts. It has been suggested[13] that where the directors decide that the company should not or could not take the opportunity and some or all directors then take it, the courts will be slow to accept that the decision was bona fide.

However, in *Peso Silver Mines Ltd. v Cropper*[14], in which it adopted a lenient approach towards a director's accountability, the Canadian Supreme Court accepted that a rejection of a corporate opportunity by the board of directors was bona fide. In 1962, the appellant company, Peso, was offered three groups of mining claims, (the Dickson claims), one of which was contiguous to claims it already owned. The respondent, Cropper, was managing director of Peso. Its board of directors rejected the offer. It was common ground and the trial judge had found that the decision was made 'in the best of faith and solely in the interest of the appellant, and not from any personal or ulterior motive on the part of any director, including the respondent'[15]. Within a few weeks, Cropper and the two other directors of Peso, together with its consulting geologist, formed a private company (Crossbow) to take up the Dicksons claims. In 1963, Charter Oil Co. Ltd. acquired control of Peso. Friction developed between Charter's president and Cropper, who had been retained as executive vice-president. When requested to hand over his interests in Crossbow, Cropper refused and was dismissed. The Supreme Court of Canada unanimously upheld the judgment of the British Columbia Court of Appeal[16] which, by a majority, had dismissed the appellant's action for a declaration of constructive trust in relation to the Crossbow shares arising out of a breach of fiduciary obligation.

In his dissenting opinion in the Court of Appeal, Norris J.A. relied on *Regal* to conclude that Cropper should be required to account because he had obtained the information about the claims in the course of the execution of his office. The onus on the company was to prove that he could have acquired the information as a result of his office, not that he could only have done so. In that event, the question of bad faith, loss or the company's inability to take up the claim was irrelevant.

In contrast, speaking for the majority, Bull J.A. interpreted *Regal* as meaning that before a director was held accountable, the company had to establish that the particular transaction was entered into 'by reason of the fact, and only by reason of the fact, that they were directors and in the course of execution of that office'[17]. Without expressly considering the problem of the onus of proof, the

13. *Gower*, p.598.
14. (1966) 58 D.L.R.(2d) 1 (Can.S.C.). This case is noted by D.D. Prentice, '*Regal (Hastings) Ltd. v Gulliver* – The Canadian Experience' (1967) 30 M.L.R. 450 and S.M. Beck, 'The Saga of Peso Silver Mines: Corporate Opportunity Reconsidered' (1971) 49 Can.Bar.Rev.80.
15. (1966) 56 D.L.R.(2d) 117 at 150 per Bull J.A. and cited (1966) 58 D.L.R.(2d) 1 at 3 per Cartwright J.
16. (1966) 56 D.L.R.(2d) 117 (B.C.C.A.).
17. Ibid at 156.

Supreme Court seemed implicitly to adopt the standard imposed by the Court of Appeal:

> 'There is no suggestion in the evidence that the offer to the appellant was accompanied by any confidential information unavailable to any prospective purchaser or that the respondent as director had access to any such information by reason of his office'[18].

Apart from introducing the difficulty of designating the capacity in which an individual receives information, this onus of proof could place an impossible burden on the company where the same individual holds several directorships.

Both the Supreme Court and the majority in the Court of Appeal were strongly influenced by the bona fide rejection of the claims. In support, reference[19] was made to the dicta of Lord Russell of Killowen in *Regal*:

> 'In his judgment [in the Court of Appeal], Lord Greene, M.R., stated that a decision adverse to the directors in the present case involved the proposition that, if directors bona fide decide not to invest their company's funds in some proposed investment, a director who thereafter embarks his own money therein is accountable for profits which he may derive therefrom. As to this I can only say that to my mind the facts of this hypothetical case bear but little resemblance to the story with which we have had to deal'[20].

It is thought[1] that the Court of Appeal analysed the rejection of the claims as removing the conflict of interest problem rather than being tantamount to authorising the transaction. It considered that a 'bona fide rejection would be the best evidence that it would not be against its interest'[2]. However, it is doubtful whether rejection of the opportunity eliminated the conflict of interest problem because the decision to reject not only deprived the company of the benefit of the opportunity, but also facilitated its subsequent exploitation by the directors, who rejected it on the company's behalf.

At the root of the different conclusion reached by Norris J.A. and the majority in the Court of Appeal was a policy disagreement about the application of the traditional rules of Equity to the conduct of directors in modern companies. For the majority, Bull J.A. considered that in a time when 'substantially all business . . . [is] carried on through the corporate vehicle with the attendant complexities involved by interlocking, subsidiary and associated corporations', it would not be:

> 'enlighted to extend the application of these principles [in *Keech v Sandford*] beyond their present limits. That the principles, and the strict rules applicable to trustees upon which they are based, are salutary cannot be disputed, but care should be taken to interpret them in the light of modern practice and way of life'[3].

18. (1966) 58 D.L.R.(2d) 1 at 8.
19. (1966) 56 D.L.R.(2d) 117 at 158 per Bull J.A.; (1966) 58 D.L.R.(2d) 1 at 9 per Cartwright J.
20. [1942] 1 All E.R.378 at 391.
1. Prentice, op cit n14, p131, supra, at 453-454.
2. (1966) 56 D.L.R.(2d) 117 at 156.
3. Ibid at 154-155.

Conversely, Norris J.A. was of opinion that:

> 'the complexities of modern business are a very good reason why the rule should be enforced strictly in order that such complexities may not be used as a smoke screen or shield behind which fraud may be perpetrated'[4].

In delivering the judgment of the Supreme Court, Cartwright J. made reference to this policy disagreement.

However, in *Canadian Aero Service Ltd. v O'Malley*[5], the Canadian Supreme Court subsequently supported the strict application of equitable principles to directors and senior management. The plaintiff company, 'Canaero', was interested in carrying out the topographical mapping of Guyana. In 1961, its president, M, and an executive vice-president, Z, conducted preparatory work and negotiations for the company. The Canadian government extended its foreign aid programme in 1966 to finance such a project. Dissatisfied with limitations imposed on their authority within Canaero by its parent company and fearful of losing their positions if Canaero failed to get contracts, M and Z incorporated their own topographical mapping company, T Ltd., and became its president and executive vice-president respectively. They then resigned from Canaero. Both Canaero and T Ltd. were among companies that submitted tenders for the Guyana project. The contract was awarded to T Ltd., partly on the ground that its proposal 'covered the operation in much greater detail than might normally be expected'.

In an action against M and Z, Canaero alleged that they had breached their fiduciary duty by depriving it of 'the corporate opportunity which it had been developing'[6]. The action failed both at first instance and in the Ontario Court of Appeal. But delivering the judgment of the Supreme Court of Canada, Laskin J. held in Canaero's favour. As distinct from an account of profits, the relief granted took the form of an award of damages.

The decision was expressly based on misuse of a corporate opportunity. Having found that the relationship of M and Z to Canaero was fiduciary in character[7], which 'in its generality betokens loyalty, good faith and avoidance of a conflict of duty and self-interest'[8], Laskin J. stated:

> 'An examination of the case law . . . shows the pervasiveness of a strict ethic in this area of the law. In my opinion, this ethic disqualifies a director or senior officer from usurping for himself or diverting to another person or company with whom or with which he is associated a maturing business opportunity which his company is actively pursuing; he is also precluded from so acting even after his resignation where the resignation may fairly

4. Ibid at 139.
5. (1974) 40 D.L.R.(3d) 371 (Can.S.C.) This case is noted by: D.D. Prentice, 'The Corporate Opportunity Doctrine' (1974) 37 M.L.R.464 and S.M. Beck, 'The Quickening of Fiduciary Obligations: *Canadian Aero Service v O'Malley*' (1975) 53 Can.Bar.Rev.771.
6. (1974) 40 D.L.R.(3d) 371 at 373.
7. See post B. The definition of insider in equity.
8. (1974) 40 D.L.R.(3d) 371 at 382. Relevant factors in testing the conduct of directors against these standards were mentioned (at 391) as including:
'position or office held, the nature of the corporate opportunity, its ripeness, its specificness and the director's or managerial officer's relation to it, the amount of knowledge possessed, the circumstances in which it was obtained and whether it was special or, indeed, even private, the factor of time in the continuation of fiduciary duty where the alleged breach occurs after termination of the relationship with the company, and the circumstances under which the relationship was terminated, that is whether by retirement or resignation or discharge.'

be said to be prompted or influenced by a wish to acquire for himself the opportunity sought by the company, or where it was his position with the company rather than a fresh initiative which led him to the opportunity which he later acquired'[9].

The Supreme Court's decision in *Peso* was distinguished on the grounds that there was a finding of good faith in the rejection of the claims by the directors because of the company's strained finances, that rejection was held to terminate the company's interest in the claims, the company received many offers of mining properties and the claims were not essential to its success. Laskin J. added that evidence might have been overlooked which would have led to the result reached in *Regal*. He was also of opinion that it would be mistaken:

'to seek to encase the principle stated and applied in *Peso*, by adoption from *Regal (Hastings) Ltd. v Gulliver*, in the straight-jacket of special knowledge acquired while acting as directors or senior officers, let alone limiting it to benefits acquired by reason of and during the holding of those offices. As in other cases in this developing branch of the law, the particular facts may determine the shape of the principle of decision without setting fixed limits to it'[10].

A further contrast to *Peso* is found in the English decision of *Industrial Development Consultants Ltd. v Cooley*[11]. C, a distinguished architect, had worked in the gas industry for seventeen years and had been chief architect for West Midlands Gas Board. He was appointed managing director of IDC which was anxious to enter the public sector. No service agreement was signed. C then embarked on negotiations to obtain contracts for the company with the Eastern Gas Board, but without success because the Board disliked IDC's corporate set-up. Subsequently, the Board approached C, but indicated that they were only interested in employing him privately and did not want any trouble from his employers. To get this work, C falsely represented that he wanted to resign as managing director on grounds of ill-health. Within a few days of his release, C was engaged by the Board to carry on work which was in substance the same as that which IDC had unsuccessfully attempted to obtain. IDC sought an account for breach of fiduciary duty.

Roskill J. held that while C was managing director, a fiduciary relationship existed between C and IDC. Accordingly, C had a duty to disclose to IDC information obtained while managing director and of concern to IDC, including all information received in the course of his dealings with the Board. Instead, he had embarked on a deliberate course of conduct which had put his personal interests as a potential contracting party with the Board in direct conflict with his pre-existing and continuing duty as managing director to IDC. Hence, he was in breach of his fiduciary duty to IDC in failing to pass on the

9. (1974) 40 D.L.R.(3d) 371 at 382.
10. Ibid at 390.
11. [1972] 2 All E.R.162; [1972] 1 W.L.R.443. This case is noted by D.D. Prentice, 'Directors' Fiduciary Duties - The Corporate Opportunity Doctrine' (1970) 50 Can.Bar.Rev.623; H. Rajak, 'Fiduciary Duty of a Managing Director' (1972) 35 M.L.R.655 and J.G. Collier, 'Directors' duties – Conflict of duty and personal interests – Secret profits – Right of company to an account' [1972] C.L.J.222.

relevant information and in guarding it for his own personal purposes and profit. Consistent with earlier authorities[12], it was also held that because of his breach of duty, C was liable to account to IDC for all the benefit received or to be received under the contract with the Board. It was irrelevant whether IDC would have obtained the benefit of the contract but for C's breach of fiduciary duty, so that as a result of the order IDC would receive a benefit which it could not otherwise have received.

The decision illustrated the strictness of a director's duty to account. It reiterated that liability did not depend on whether the profit could have gone to the company. The defence that C was not in a fiduciary relationship with IDC because the information exploited was received in a private capacity, was rejected as mistaken on the ground that at the time C carried on business only as IDC's managing director. The decision also made it clear that resignation did not operate to terminate the fiduciary duty so that the fact of the profit having been made after C's resignation was irrelevant. The finding that C was under a duty to pass the information about the contract to the company notwithstanding that the offer was made to C privately is supported by the consideration that C was appointed to obtain for the company the sort of opportunity which he subsequently exploited himself. But it does not go so far as to establish a general duty to transmit information of commercial value to a company, with a consequent inhibition on multiple directorships in companies in the same line of business.

The controversy surrounding the rigorous application of the no-conflict rule was highlighted by the House of Lords in *Boardman v Phipps*[13]. The testator by his will established a trust. The trustees were the testator's widow, (who became senile and died), his daughter and an accountant (Mr. Fox). The trust owned 8,000 £1 shares in a private company. Dissatisfied with the company's accounts, the trustees' solicitor, Boardman, and a beneficiary, Tom Phipps, attended the AGM in an attempt to get Tom Phipps appointed a director. When this failed, they decided to make a 'take-over' bid personally for the outstanding 22,000 £1 shares in the company. The accountant agreed with the decision which was communicated to the testator's daughter.

In the negotiations, Boardman and Tom Phipps referred to their representative capacity and used information received at the AGM as the trustees' representatives. On the basis of their representation of the trust's holding, they obtained important information about the company, including that the company had various undervalued assets which could be liquidated. Boardman then wrote to the beneficiaries, including the testator's daughter and John Phipps, with an outline of the negotiations and sought their permission as to his assuming a personal interest given that initial inquiry was on the trust's behalf. At a subsequent meeting, Boardman gave explanations to John Phipps who, according to Boardman, was fully satisfied, but who the trial judge found had not been fully informed. The purchases of the outstanding shares, mostly at £4.10s. each, by Boardman and Tom Phipps with their own funds were highly profitable to the trust as well as themselves. The company made a capital distribution of £5.17s.6d. a share after which the shares were still worth more than £2 each. John Phipps brought an action against Boardman and Tom Phipps for an account of the profits attributable to his share in the trust fund.

12. *Regal (Hastings) Ltd. v Gulliver* [1942] 1 All E.R.378; *Boardman v Phipps* [1967] 2 A.C.46, [1966] 3 All E.R.721.
13. *Boardman v Phipps* [1967] 2 A.C.46.

At first instance, Wilberforce J.[14] held that Boardman and Tom Phipps were liable to account for the profit attributable to the plaintiff's share in the trust fund, less their expenditure incurred to enable it to be realised and making a liberal allowance for their skill and work in producing it. The Court of Appeal[15] unanimously affirmed the order of Wilberforce J.

By a majority of three to two, the House of Lords dismissed the appeal by Boardman and Tom Phipps and held them accountable. They had placed themselves in a special position, which was of a fiduciary character in relation to the negotiations with the directors of the company relating to the trust shares. Out of this special position and in the course of such negotiations, they obtained the opportunity to make a profit out of the shares and knowledge that the profit was there to be made. A profit was made and they were accountable accordingly. The House of Lords also held that the appellants had acted openly but mistakenly, in a manner which was highly beneficial to the trust and accordingly were entitled in the circumstances to payment on a liberal scale for their work and skill.

For the majority, Lords Hodson and Guest both considered that Boardman obtained the confidential information while acting as solicitor for the trustees and the information acquired could properly be regarded as property of the trust. Though they thus suggested that the profit was derived from misuse of trust property, they appeared to base their decisions on the judgments of Lord Russell of Killowen and Lord Wright in the *Regal* case. Lord Hodson concluded 'the appellants obtained knowledge by reason of their fiduciary position, and they cannot escape liability by saying that they were acting for themselves and not as agents of the trustees'[16]. Similarly, Lord Guest's reason for imposing liability was that the appellants had 'placed themselves in a special position which was of a fiduciary character in relation to the negotiations with the directors . . . Out of such special position and in the course of such negotiations they obtained the opportunity to make a profit out of the shares and knowledge that the profit was there to be made'[17].

Whilst accepting that 'information is, of course, not property in the strict sense of that word'[18], Lord Cohen expressly based his decision on the *Regal* case:

> 'Much of the information came the appellants' way when Mr. Boardman was acting on behalf of the trustees on the instructions of Mr. Fox, and the opportunity of bidding for the shares came because he purported for all purposes except for making the bid to be acting on behalf of the owners of the eight thousand shares in the company. In these circumstances, it seems to me that the principle of the *Regal* case . . . applies'[19].

But he emphasised that the use of any information or opportunity acquired by a trustee or agent in his capacity as such did not necessarily make him liable to account and liability must depend on the facts of the case. In this case, 'had the company been a public company and had the appellants bought shares on the market, they would not I think have been accountable'[20].

14. *Phipps v Boardman* [1964] 1 W.L.R.993. This case is noted by W.R. Cornish, 'The Profits of Self-Appointed Agents' (1965) 28 M.L.R.587.
15. *Phipps v Boardman* [1965] Ch992.
16. *Boardman v Phipps* [1967] 2 A.C.46 at 111.
17. Ibid at 118.
18. Ibid at 102.
19. Ibid at 103.
20. Ibid at 101-102.

In the *Regal* decision, the speeches of Lords Russell and Wright emphasised the actual misuse of a fiduciary position sub-rule of the no-conflict rule rather than the actual conflict of duty and interest sub-rule. However, Lord Cohen and Lord Hodson both found a conflict of duty and interest in Boardman as a solicitor in that the trustees might have asked him for his advice on an application to the court by the trustees for power to purchase the shares. Lord Cohen observed:

> 'Mr. Boardman was the solicitor whom the trustees were in the habit of consulting if they wanted legal advice. Granted that he would not be bound to advise on any point unless he were consulted, he would still be the person they would consult if they wanted advice ... but, in my opinion, Mr. Boardman would not have been able to give unprejudiced advice if he had been consulted by the trustees and was at the same time negotiating for the purchase of the shares on behalf of himself and Mr. Tom Phipps. In other words, there was, in my opinion, at the crucial date ... a possibility of a conflict between his interest and his duty'[1].

Likewise, Lord Hodson commented:

> 'No doubt it was but a remote possibility that Mr. Boardman would ever be asked by the trustees to advise on the desirability of an application to the court in order that the trustees might avail themselves of the information obtained. Nevertheless, whenever the possibility of conflict is present between personal interest and the fiduciary position, the rule of equity must be applied'[2].

In the Court of Appeal, Lord Denning had also pointed to the conflict of duty and interest in Boardman as a solicitor, but considered Boardman had an immediate duty to advise; he had

> 'placed himself in a position where there was a conflict between his duty to advise an application to the court and his interest to acquire the shares himself'[3].

The minority approach was that Regal was distinguishable. Viscount Dilhorne found that, though the appellants were in a fiduciary relationship to the trust as a result of their being employed as agents of the trust, the acquisition of the shares was outside the scope of the trust and the agency. Having emphasised that the appellants would have been liable to account for their profits if they had entered into engagements in which they had or could have had a personal interest conflicting with the interests of those they were bound to protect, he stated:

> 'On the facts of this case there was not, in my opinion, any conflict or possibility of a conflict between the personal interests of the appellants and those of the trust. There was no possibility so long as Mr. Fox was

1. Ibid at 103-104.
2. Ibid at 111.
3. *Phipps v Boardman* [1965] Ch992 at 1020.

opposed to the trust buying any of the shares of any conflict of interest through the purchase of the shares by the appellants'[4].

After examining the scope and ambit of Boardman's duty to the trustees, Lord Upjohn also concluded that there was no conflict of duty and interest on the facts proved:

'The phrase 'possibly may conflict' requires consideration. In my view it means that the reasonable man looking at the relevant facts and circumstances of the particular case would think that there was a real sensible possibility of conflict, not that you could imagine some situation arising which might, in some conceivable possibility in events not contemplated as real sensible possibilities by any reasonable person, result in a conflict'[5].

On the issue of whether there was a duty to advise on the lines suggested by Lord Denning, Lord Upjohn indicated that had it been raised in the action it might have been a 'very difficult matter'[6]. But he declined to 'condemn the appellants unheard'[7] on the point as it had neither been pleaded nor suggested in argument or cross-examination.

He also criticised as 'untenable'[8] the proposition of Russell L.J. in the Court of Appeal that:

'The substantial trust shareholding was an asset of which one aspect was its potential use as a means of acquiring knowledge of the company's affairs, or of negotiating allocations of the company's assets, or of inducing other shareholders to part with their shares'[9].

Rejecting the view that information could generally be regarded as property, Lord Upjohn commented 'in the end the real truth is that it is not property in any normal sense, but equity will restrain its transmission to another if in breach of some confidential relationship'[10]. In an attempt to pre-empt the formulation of a general rule that 'information learnt by a trustee during the course of his duties is property of the trust and cannot be used by him'[11], he pointed out that corporate trustees and others may have much information which though initially acquired in connection with a particular trust, can without prejudice to that trust be readily made available to other trusts with great advantage thereto. Rather, he asserted:

'The real rule is . . . that knowledge learnt by a trustee in the course of his duties as such is not in the least property of the trust and in general may be used by him for his own benefit or for the benefit of other trusts unless it is confidential information which is given to him (i) in circumstances which, regardless of his position as a trustee, would make it a breach of confidence for him to communicate to anyone, for it has been given to him expressly or impliedly as confidential; or (ii) in a fiduciary capacity

4. *Boardman v Phipps* [1967] 2 A.C.46 at 88.
5. Ibid at 124.
6. Ibid at 131.
7. Ibid at 132.
8. Ibid at 127.
9. *Phipps v Boardman* [1965] Ch992 at 1031.
10. *Boardman v Phipps* [1967] 2 A.C.46 at 128.
11. Ibid.

and its use would place him in a position where his duty and his interest might possibly conflict'[12].

As an example[13], he considered that where a trustee of two trusts X and Y, holding shares in the same small company, learnt encouraging facts about the company in his capacity as trustee of X, then in the absence of special circumstances, (eg X wanting to buy more shares), there was nothing improper in him communicating the information to his co-trustees of Y who were inclined to sell. But where the information made the trustees of X want to sell, he could not communicate it to his co-trustees of Y until the holdings of X had been sold since there would be a conflict, reflected in the prices that might be obtained. The test was whether the knowledge acquired was capable of being used for his own benefit to injure the trust. But that test could have no application in this case because there was no possibility of the information being used to injure the trust. The information was used not in connection with trust property but to enhance the value of trust property by the purchase of other property in which the trustees were not interested.

The issue of whether information should be classified as property[14] was left in doubt by the judgments. Such classification would have the effect of imposing a constructive trust in almost every case in which there has been a breach of fiduciary duty. In a case like *Regal*, a consequence would be to enable the company to recover not merely the profits made, but the shares themselves. The courts have been willing to regard commercially valuable information, particularly industrial information, as being the subject of proprietary interests. In one case[15], knowledge of sources of finance was held to be a corporate asset. This is consistent with some types of information, such as trade secrets, having certain of the attributes of property. In particular, information can be intrinsically valuable, the subject matter of a trust[16], communicated for a consideration and included in 'property' which passes to a trustee in bankruptcy[17]. Hence, Lord Upjohn apparently understates the proprietary characteristics of information. However, the fact that there can be a proprietary interest in information does not mean the information itself is property. Whereas information is a physical (or mental) concept, property is a legal concept: 'a legal institution the essence of which is the creation and protection of certain private rights in wealth of any kind'[18]. The constructive trust remedy is used as a device, of which a proprietary interest is a necessary part, to forge a particular remedy in particular circumstances. It is not available whenever there has been a breach of fiduciary duty[19]. A pre-existing proprietary interest must be identified before the trust remedy can be used.

However, the more controversial issue raised by the decision is the strictness with which traditional equitable principles should be applied to incidental profits made while conducting a trust or acting in some other fiduciary

---

12. Ibid at 128-129.
13. Ibid at 129.
14. This issue is discussed by: *Gower*, pp608-610; Finn, op cit n2, p123, supra, paras.293-296; Palmer, Prentice and Welling, op cit n2, p128, supra at 6-48-49; Jones, op cit n10, p126, supra, at 484-485 and G. Jons, 'Restitution of benefits obtained in breach of another's confidence' (1970) 86 L.Q.R.463 at 464-465.
15. *Bell Houses Ltd. v City Wall Properties Ltd.* [1966] 2 Q.B.656 C.A.
16. *Green v Folgham* (1823) 1 Sim. & St.398; 57 E.R.159.
17. *In Re Keene* [1922] 2 Ch475.
18. C.A. Reich, 'The New Property' (1963-1964) 73 Yale L.J.732.
19. *In Lister & Co. v Stubbs* (1890) 45 ChD.1 C.A. a claim to investments made by an agent out of secret commission was rejected.

capacity[20]. The problem was reflected in the form of order made. The House of Lords affirmed the letter of the strict law against incidental profits by requiring Boardman and Tom Phipps to account. But it betrayed the spirit of that law by ordering that they be paid on a liberal scale for their work and skill in obtaining the shares and profits thereon.

Subsequently, in *O'Sullivan and Another v Management Agency & Music*[1], the Court of Appeal rejected a submission that the exception in *Boardman v Phipps* crediting trustees with a profit element should not become the rule. The first plaintiff, a young and unknown pop musician (O), entered into an exclusive management agreement with M, a well-known manager. M operated through, and was a substantial shareholder in, a parent company, the first defendants (MAM Ltd.), who were music agents and two subsidiary companies, the second and fifth defendants, who were publishing and record companies respectively. M was also chairman of the board of the record company. Relying on M, O entered into agreements, inter alia, with the publishing and record companies and into a contract of employment with E Ltd., the fourth defendants, an associated company incorporated to receive artistes' foreign earnings. Due to O's success and to reduce his tax liability, the second plaintiff company, wholly owned by O, was incorporated to receive his UK earnings. There were further recording agreements between the plaintiff company and the record company and between the record company and E Ltd. The five agreements were prepared by S, the managing director of three of the companies and a co-director of E Ltd. O, who was wholly inexperienced in business matters and had become closely acquainted with M, signed them in reliance on M and without obtaining or being advised by either M or S to seek independent advice. The plaintiffs sought declarations that the agreements were and always had been void and unenforceable on the grounds that they were in unreasonable restraint of trade and had been obtained by undue influence. By the date of the trial, all the agreements had been performed and had lapsed.

At first instance, the judge accepted that the agreements were in restraint of trade. He found that M and, through M, the four associated companies, were in a fiduciary relationship with O and held that the agreements were accordingly to be presumed to have been obtained by undue influence. The judge granted declarations that the agreements were and always had been void and unenforceable and ordered, inter alia, that the agreements be set aside and that accounts be taken of the profits earned by the companies under the agreements. On appeal, inter alia, against the findings of undue influence against the companies and the orders of the court, the Court of Appeal allowed the appeal in part. It was held that the agreements were properly to be presumed to have been obtained by undue influence, but that since agreements in restraint of trade or those obtained by undue influence were voidable, the judge erred in law in holding that the agreements were void. On the account of profits, the Court of Appeal held that, though the parties could not be restored to their original position, the court had jurisdiction where a contract had been obtained by undue influence, to make such orders as were practically just between the parties; in the circumstances, it was just to order the agreements between O and the defendants to be set aside and to order the defendants to account for their profits, but credit should be given to them for their skill and labour in promoting O and making a significant contribution to his success; and,

20. This is discussed by: Bishop and Prentice, op cit. n10, p126, supra; Jones, op cit n10, p126, supra, at 486-497 and Beck, op cit n14, p131, supra, at 112-114.
1. [1985] QB428.

accordingly, the defendants were entitled to a reasonable remuneration, including a small profit element, but one that was considerably less than they would have received had O obtained independent advice before entering into agreements with them.

As to the profit-sharing element in the remuneration allowed, this order was less generous than that in *Boardman v Phipps*. This was explained by Fox L.J. in terms that:

> 'it would be one thing to permit a substantial sharing of profits in a case such as *Phipps v Boardman* . . . where the conduct of the fiduciaries could not be criticised and quite another to permit in a case such as the present where, though fraud was not alleged, there was an abuse of personal trust and confidence'.[2]

But he acknowledged that the business reality might be that the profits could never have been earned at all, as between fully independent persons, except on a profit-sharing basis. To achieve substantial justice between the parties, he considered that M and the MAM companies should receive an allowance for their skill and labour in contributing to O's success, such allowance to include a profit element. The form of order thus fuels the controversy over whether fiduciaries should be credited with a profit element.

However, when the issue was raised in *Guinness Plc. v Saunders*[3], the decisions in *Boardman v Phipps* and in the *O'Sullivan* case were distinguished. The two directors and another director of the company, as a sub-committee of the board of directors, agreed to pay the director £5.2 million for services in connection with the company's take-over bid. The company claimed recovery of the money on the ground that the second defendant received the payment in breach of his fiduciary duty as a director by not disclosing his interest in the agreement to the company's directors, as required by s317 (1), CA 1985. On finding that the second defendant had not disclosed his interest to a meeting of the board of directors, the Vice-Chancellor ordered him to repay the money to the company.

Dismissing the second defendant's appeal, the Court of Appeal held that a director's interest in a contract made with his company must be disclosed to a duly convened meeting of the board, not merely to a sub-committee of the board; the second defendant, having failed to disclose his interest as so required, had received the money as constructive trustee for the company, which was entitled to a repayment. In addition, it was held that any cross-claim to which the second defendant might be entitled for a quantum meruit at law or an allowance in equity for his services could not impeach or determine the company's title to receive the money, since the respective claims of the parties did not arise out of the same transaction. Both *Phipps v Boardman* and the *O'Sullivan* case were distinguished: they differed from the present case in that they were not concerned with claims for the recovery of property belonging to the company and wrongly retained by the second defendant. In *Phipps v Boardman*, the defendants had misused for their own benefit an opportunity (which belonged to the trust) to make a profit; they had not received trust property. In the *O'Sullivan* case, the action was for an account of profits made by the defendant in the course of managing O, the singer. Except for some

2. Ibid at 475.
3. [1988] 1 W.L.R.863.

copyrights which were ordered to be returned, there was no receipt of his property.

Although difficult to distinguish from the normal run of trust profit making opportunities, incidental profits are regarded[4] as possessing special characteristics in that: (a) the uncertainty is much higher than for other profit making opportunities; (b) their exploitation and probably their discovery is largely determined by the trustees' efforts, and (c) a trustee's failure to exploit the information would not constitute a breach of trust. The profits made by Boardman and Tom Phipps can be so categorised because the sort of opportunity would not occur with any regularity or predictability, its discovery and exploitation depended on the fiduciaries' exceptional efforts and a failure to exploit the opportunity would not have constituted a breach of trust. These characteristics are also shared by the profits in the *O'Sullivan* case in that: whilst highly profitable for a few composers and performers, the pop business is also a high risk one and even fewer achieve lasting success; that their discovery and exploitation was largely determined by the defendants is supported by O's lack of success both before and after his association with M and a failure to exploit the opportunity would not have constituted a breach of trust.

In such circumstances, the way in which the law allocates entitlement to such profits will have an important impact on the conduct of a trustee or fiduciary. A prohibition on trustee profit-making removes the incentive for trustees to seek out and exploit profit-making opportunities and trusts thereby suffer. Conversely, if a trustee can retain incidental profits, there is a risk of his using his position to seek out incidental profit-making opportunities which, from the point of the trust, would be imprudent.

A rule requiring a trustee to disgorge all incidental profits to the beneficiary has the advantage of minimising the costs of monitoring the trustee's performance. Just as the trustee has no incentive to manage a trust in ways which generate such opportunities and may be inimical to the trust, the beneficiary has no reason to fear that the trustee has an ulterior advantage in view. However, a disgorgement rule leads to productive inefficiency in the sense that innocent and lucrative opportunities will not be realised. Yet it is desirable to allow such information to be used and opportunities to be realised as, other things being equal, resources are allocated more efficiently when such freely available information is exploited. Hence, the effect of permitting the use of such information is to increase monitoring costs to all trusts, but also increase the expected joint revenues of trustee and beneficiary. When expected joint revenue discounted for any increased risk, exceeds increased monitoring costs, there is scope for a mutually beneficial deal between trustee and beneficiary. As the costs of negotiating such a bargain are often infinitely high, it is suggested[5] that the deal which should be specified by a 'standard form contract' embodied in the law is the deal the parties would have made for themselves if they could have foreseen the possibility of the particular event occurring and at no cost negotiated provision for it when they made their trusteeship contract. The terms of that contract would have depended on relative risk attitudes, incentives to efficient production and monitoring cost.

Derived from general considerations of the antecedent interests of the parties[6], two incidental profits principles are regarded as appropriate[7]. First, a

4. Bishop and Prentice, op cit n10, p126, supra, at 295.
5. Ibid at 296.
6. Ibid at 297-301.
7. Ibid at 301.

disgorgement rule should apply to incidental profits made by a fiduciary when earned on any project which might reasonably be thought properly trust business. Secondly, rules of distribution should apply when the fiduciary earns an incidental profit in consequence of knowledge acquired from his office as trustee, but when that profit was one which the trust either could not or would not realise. Such rules: (a) enable the fiduciary to keep a sum equal to a reasonable fee for his time, expertise and any risk borne; (b) provide for division of any remainder between fiduciary and trust in such proportion as the court thinks reasonable and knowledgeable men in the shoes of the parties would have agreed if they had considered the matter when the trusteeship contract was made, and (c) in default of other evidence, provide that any residue be shared equally between fiduciary and beneficiary.

A difficulty in *Boardman v Phipps* is Boardman's position as solicitor to the trust. To find a conflict of duty and interest in a solicitor on the ground that he might possibly be asked to advise overlooks that a solicitor might either decline to advise or declare an interest. Yet the view that Boardman should wait to be asked for advice takes a passive view of his duty as solicitor to the trust. An alternative view is that because of his interest, Boardman should have advised the trustees to seek independent legal advice. But the issue of whether he had an obligation to advise was not relied on in the pleadings or put in cross-examination. Hence, it is difficult to assess the extent to which the professional trustee was aware of particulars of the negotiations and whether he considered making an application to the court.

A consequence was that it was unclear whether the opportunity was one that the trust could or would not realise. Subject to it being such an opportunity, the ex post facto risk sharing contract implicitly imposed was consistent with the antecedent interests of the parties.

However, in the case of directors or others in a fiduciary relationship with companies, there is good reason to support a strict prophylactic rule rather than one which relieves them from liability in specified circumstances[8]. The monitoring of a director's conduct by colleagues is fraught with difficulties. When a director is in a dominant position in a company, there can be complex problems of proof in determining whether he has used this position to further his own interests. Moreover, in view of directors' power and influence over the company, the law should reinforce their responsibilities to bring business opportunities to the company's attention. Like insider dealing as compensation for entrepreneurial activity[9], a rule allowing directors to retain incidental profits would operate in an arbitrary manner and bear no relation to services rendered. Incentives mutually beneficial to director and company can be provided by contracts which contain provisions for remuneration related to corporate performance, such as payment by results.

The question of the constituency to whom directors owe their duties arose in *Heron International Ltd. v Lord Grade and Associated Communications Corpn plc*[10]. ACC carried on business in many branches of the entertainment industry and through a subsidiary, obtained a licence from the IBA to operate a television franchise. ACC was in financial difficulties and H, who was a director of ACC and held 51% of ACC non-voting shares through a company that he controlled (TVW), agreed to provide ACC with assistance on condition that he acquired control of ACC. One of his Australian companies, B, made a take-over bid for

8. n10, p126, supra.
9. See, ante, Chapter 1. Introduction.
10. [1983] B.C.L.C.244, C.A.

the ACC shares. The bid was virtually guaranteed of success in that the ACC directors, who controlled 53% of the company's voting shares, agreed to sell their shares to B and register the transfer. As a foreign company, B was disqualified from holding a television franchise and an agreement was reached with the IBA whereby it was agreed that the bid could go through and the subsidiary's licence would not be terminated provided steps were taken to ensure that ACC did not control or influence the subsidiary. H Ltd. also made a bid for the ACC shares and its bid placed a greater value on ACC than the B bid. But given the directors' acceptance of B's bid, H's offer could not succeed. Even if the ACC directors had refused to sell their shares to B, H's bid would have failed as it was conditional on acceptance by TVW for its non-voting shares which TVW was unwilling to sell. After H's offer was made, B made an offer matching that of H which, in turn, made a second offer increasing its terms. Suing as representatives of ACC shareholders, the plaintiffs (H and others) sought an interlocutory injunction to prevent the transfer of ACC shares to B. This was refused at first instance. With the approval of the Court of Appeal the parties decided to treat the appeal as the trial of the action.

Allowing the appeal, the Court of Appeal held, inter alia, that the directors, when exercising their power under the articles to register a proposed transfer, were under a fiduciary obligation to exercise the power in the interests of both the company and the shareholders, irrespective of the fact that as individuals they held a majority of the voting shares. Furthermore, the ACC directors could not advise the shareholders to refuse B's offer and at the same time, as directors, allow their own voting shares to be transferred to B. Where directors in the exercise of their powers had to consider rival bidders, the interests of the company were the interests of the current shareholders.

Although there is no reported decision in Britain on corporate recovery of insider profits, it is clear from the reasoning in the cases discussed that when a director or other person in a fiduciary relationship with the company has made use for his own purpose of price sensitive information acquired while a director or other fiduciary, he will be in breach of his fiduciary duty in the company and accountable to the company for any profits made[11]. It seems that corporate recovery would extend to profits made from dealing in shares not only of the company to which the fiduciary duty is owed, but also of another company[12]. As loss to a beneficiary is not a prerequisite to fiduciary accountability, corporate recovery is not precluded by the consideration that the company has not normally suffered any direct loss[13].

On the basis of similar equitable principles, such liability was explicitly recognised in the US case of *Diamond v Oreamuno*[14]. Two directors sold their shares on the basis of confidential information that there would be a sharp fall in the company's earnings. A shareholder brought a derivative action to require the directors to account for their 'profits' on the transaction, namely, the losses avoided by selling their shares in advance of the drop in the market value of the shares on publication of the information. The directors were held accountable

---

11. *Gower*, p.631; Palmer, para.29-14; D.D. Prentice, 'Insider Trading' [1975] C.L.P.83 at 85-86 and *City Company Law Committee, Insider Dealing* (1976), para.32.

12. Even when there is no breach of fiduciary duty to that company, it may have an action for breach of confidence, see post III. Breach of confidence

13. Under the rule in *Trevor v Whitworth* (1887) 12 AppCas 409 a company was prohibited from purchasing its own shares. This rule was embodied in statutory form by CA 1980, s35(1). But this position was reversed by CA 1981, ss46-52, now CA 1985, ss162-169. Hence, it is now not necessarily the case that the company cannot exploit the information for its own benefit.

14. (1969) 248 N.E.2d 910 (N.Y.C.A.).

on several grounds. First, on general agency principles, an agent is liable when he converts to his own use something of value, such as confidential information which belongs to his company. Secondly, the company has a better claim to insider profits than insiders. Corporate recovery operated as a deterrent and the threat of double liability[15] should not be a bar to corporate recovery. Thirdly, though it was not necessary to establish that the company had been harmed, the company had an interest in the public acceptance and marketability of its securities. The effect of insider dealing could be to cast a cloud on the company's name, injure relations with shareholders and undermine public regard for its securities. However, this attempt to show corporate loss is not convincing. The public acceptance and marketability of a company's securities are more a function of a company's profitability than whether its management deal on inside information[16].

Two sets of proposals for legislative intervention could have impinged on the accountability of fiduciaries for insider profits, but neither was enacted. First, the Jenkins Committee[17] recommended a statutory provision that a director or officer of the company who acquired any information by virtue of his position should not be able to gain directly or indirectly an improper advantage for himself at the expense of the company. But the phrase 'at the expense of' was unsatisfactory, particularly in view of the then prohibition on a company purchasing it own shares[18].

Secondly, the Companies Bill 1978[19] contained sub-clauses that generally embodied the principles extracted from the cases discussed:

'(2) A director of a company shall not do anything or omit to do anything if the doing of that thing or the omission to do it, as the case may be, gives rise to a conflict, or might reasonably be expected to give rise to a conflict, between the duties of his office and his private interests, or without prejudice to the foregoing, between those duties and any duties he owes to any other person.

(3) Without prejudice to subsections (1) and (2) above, a director of a company or a person who has been a director of a company shall not, for the purpose of gaining, whether directly or indirectly, an advantage for himself –

(a) make use of any money or other property of the company; or

(b) make use of any relevant information[20] or of a relevant opportunity[21]–

15. See post, II. Liability to shareholders and others.
16. Prentice, op cit n11, p143, supra, at 90-91.
17. *Report of the Company Law Committee* (Chairman, Lord Justice Jenkins) Cmnd.1749 (1962), para.99(a).
18. *Trevor v Whitworth* (1887) 12 App Cas.409. This was reversed by CA 1981, ss46-52 (now CA 1985, ss162-169).
19. Clause 44.
Whereas the Jenkins Committee recommendation was stated to be in addition to and not in derogation of any other enactment or rule of law relating to directors' duties or liabilities, clause 44 of the 1978 Bill was expressed to have the effect of such derogation.
20. The Companies Bill 1978, cl 44(4), provided that in relation to a director of a company 'relevant information' meant 'any information which he obtained while a director or other officer of the company and which it was reasonable to expect him to disclose to the company or not to disclose to persons unconnected with the company'.
21. The Companies Bill 1978, cl 44(4) provided that in relation to a director of a company 'relevant opportunity' meant 'an opportunity which he had while a director or other officer of the company and which he had (a) by virtue of his position as a director or other officer of the company; or (b) in circumstances in which it was reasonable to expect him to disclose the fact that he had that opportunity to the company'.

    (i) if he does so while a director of the company in circumstances which give rise or might reasonably be expected to give rise to such a conflict; or

    (ii) if while a director of the company he had that use in contemplation in circumstances which gave rise or might reasonably have been expected to give rise to such a conflict'.

Liability arose when the information or opportunity was obtained while a director or other officer of the company, but was not limited to information obtained in that capacity. The information had to be 'confidential' or 'special' only to the extent that it was reasonable to expect him to disclose it to the company or not to disclose it to persons unconnected with the company. Whereas the information had to be obtained while a director or officer, liability extended to its use after he had ceased to hold such position provided that while a director he had that use in contemplation in circumstances liable to give rise to a conflict of duty and interest. However, the phrase 'advantage for himself' was open to criticism on the ground that it was just as objectionable when a director intended to benefit a third party.

    As there are uncertainties in important areas, legislation additional to existing common law rules would have the advantage, apart from being tailored to the specific issues raised by insider dealing, of clarifying several matters. These include whether liability extends to the avoidance of losses, the definition of insider in equity, enforcement problems and the quantum of recovery. It would also be necessary to deal with the application of the provision to take-over bids.

B. Definition of insider in equity

The courts have 'refrained judiciously'[1] from attempting a general definition of fiduciary. But an accurate and workable one for the purpose of the no-conflict rule has been proposed as:

> 'someone who undertakes to act for or on behalf of another in some particular matter or matters. That undertaking may be of a general character. It may be specific and limited. It is immaterial whether the undertaking is or is not in the form of a contract. It is immaterial that the undertaking is gratuitous. And the undertaking may be officiously assumed without request'[2].

Traditionally, certain legal relationships have been regarded as fiduciary in character. Examples are director-company, stockbroker-client, solicitor-client, principal-agent and trustee-beneficiary. However, the no-conflict rule applies not to a fixed class of legal relationship, but because a person has undertaken to act for or on behalf of another in some matter.

    The finding of such an undertaking is a question of fact in each case[3]. Where two people have dealt with each other only as principals, neither will be the other's fiduciary. Rather, the supervision of Equity begins when there is positive proof that a person has undertaken to act in a particular matter not as his own

---

1. P.D. Finn, *Fiduciary Obligations* (1977), para.467.
2. Ibid. This definition is expressed to be an elaboration upon that suggested in A. Scott, 'The Fiduciary Principle' (1949) 37 Calif.L.R.539 at 540.
3. Finn, op cit n1, supra, para.468.

principal, but in another's interests. The distinction is illustrated by two Australian cases. In a 1973 decision[4], it was held that in assuming a very loose agency for W in a company take-over, B was disabled from purchasing shares in the offeree company to the exclusion of W. In contrast, it was found in a 1969 decision[5] that an 'inchoate bargain' between three television companies to secure joint coverage of football matches did not preclude one company from obtaining certain exclusive rights of coverage for itself.

As to the range of persons who have in practice been found to have assumed fiduciary duties, the most frequent example within a company is a director. The readiness of the courts to find that the director-company relationship is fiduciary in character reflects the power and influence which directors, by virtue of their position, enjoy over the company.

Consistent with the finding of an undertaking, the relationship between officials[6] other than directors and the company can also be a fiduciary one. In the Canaero case[7], M and Z argued that, though they were directors, they did not owe fiduciary duties to Canaero because its parent company had deprived them of all significant decision-making powers and autonomy. This dubious argument was accepted by the Ontario Court of Appeal, but rejected by the Supreme Court of Canada. In holding that M and Z were 'top management', whose positions 'charged them with initiatives and responsibilities far removed from the obedient role of servants'[8], the Supreme Court approved the statement on fiduciary duties in Gower[9] that:

> 'these duties, except insofar as they depend on statutory provisions expressly limited to directors, are not so restricted but apply equally to any officials of the company who are authorised to act on its behalf and in particular to those acting in a managerial capacity'[10].

This statement assumes increased significance in view of the frequent practice in public companies for the board of directors to delegate management to a small body[11]. Most such managers are usually also directors, but the recent tendency to distinguish more clearly between (a) management which runs the business and (b) the board of directors which supervises management and outlines policy, may result in a practice of delegating managerial powers to professional managers who do not sit on the board. Whereas some statutory provisions would require amendment, equitable principles cover most potential developments.

It is thought that the position of an employee varies according to the nature of his duties. In accordance with the Canaero decision, an employee performing managerial functions would, subject to the finding of the requisite undertaking, be in a fiduciary relationship with the company. Conversely, the relation-

---

4. *Walden Properties Ltd. v Beaver Properties Pty. Ltd.* [1973] 2 N.S.W.L.R.815 cited by Finn op cit n1, p146, supra, para.468.
5. *Amalgamated Television Services Pty. Ltd. v Television Corpn Ltd.* [1969] 2 N.S.W.L.R.257 cited by Finn, op cit n1, p146, supra, para.468.
6. This term is used in preference to the technical one of 'officer' which is defined by CA 1985, s744 as, unless a contrary intention appears, 'a director, manager or secretary'. Though they will mainly be such 'officers', the term 'officials' includes others who also act on the company's behalf.
7. *Canadian Aero Service v O'Malley* (1973) 40 D.L.R.(3d) 371.
8. Ibid at 381.
9. L.C.B. Gower, *The Principles of Modern Company Law* (3rd ed.1969), p.518
10. *Canadian Aero Services v O'Malley* (1973) 40 D.L.R.(3d) 371 at 381.
11. *Gower*, pp574-575.

ship between the company and servants who work for but who do not undertake to act for it, is not fiduciary in character for the purpose of the no-conflict rule.

However, the courts have often remarked that, during the period of his employment, an employee is under a general duty 'to serve his master with good faith and fidelity'[12], though have not elaborated greatly on this 'rather vague duty'[13]. An employee's duties of good faith are apparently less extensive than those of a fiduciary[14]. But their duties of fidelity, which depend on the law of master and servant, amount to much the same. In *Reading v Attorney-General*,[15] a British army sergeant, who rode on the lorry carrying the goods, received large sums of money for help in smuggling liquor in and through Cairo. His uniform and rank of sergeant enabled it to avoid police inspection. After the military authorities had seized the money paid for his services, he petitioned the Crown for its return. Unanimously rejecting his petition, the House of Lords held that the Crown was entitled to retain the sergeant's receipts from his smuggling activities because he had used his uniform and the opportunities and facilities attached to it. Like the Court of Appeal[16], the House of Lords[17] approved the statement of Denning J. at first instance that liability to account arises:

> 'if a servant, in violation of his duty of honesty and good faith, takes advantage of his service to make a profit for himself, in this sense, that the assets of which he has control, or the facilities which he enjoys or the position which he occupies are the real cause of his obtaining the money as distinct from being the mere opportunity for getting it . . . '[18]

Whilst the action was not in form one for account of profits, it would clearly have succeeded as such. It thus seems that an action to account for profits to the company will be against an employee even when there is no fiduciary relationship and, as in the case of a fiduciary, irrespective of whether the company has been harmed[19].

Majority shareholders who are not directors or officials have not figured among those found by British courts to have assumed fiduciary duties. The courts have often stated that members must exercise their votes 'bona fide for the benefit of the company as a whole'[20] thereby implying that members are subject to the same duties as directors. These statements are misleading because the courts have repeatedly adopted the approach that, unlike directors or officials, members owe their position solely to their investment and held that members' votes are proprietary rights exerciseable in members' own interests, even when in conflict with the interests of the company[1]. However, the courts have intervened to restrain a fraud on the minority and it is now considered that:

12. *Robb v Green* [1895] 2 Q.B.315 at 320 per Smith L.J.
13. *Hivac v Park Royal Scientific Instruments* [1946] Ch169 at 174.
14. *Bell v Lever Bros.* [1932] A.C.161, H.L.
15. [1951] A.C.507. This decision is commented upon by G.Jones, 'Unjust enrichment and the fiduciary's duty of loyalty' (1968) 84 L.Q.R.472 at 476-477; H. Rajak, 'Fiduciary Duty of a Managing Director' (1972) 35 M.L.R. 655 at 659
16. [1949] 2 K.B.232 at 235.
17. [1951] A.C.507 at 514.
18. [1948] 2 K.B.268 at 275.
19. [1951] A.C.507 at 516.
20. Eg *Allen v Gold Reefs of West Africa* [1900] 1 Ch 656 at 671.
1. Eg *Burland v Earle* [1902] A.C.83, P.C.

'although members, unlike directors, are not required to act bona fide in the interests of others, they, like directors, must exercise their powers for a proper corporate purpose. The purpose is proper if it is to benefit the company or the generality of the members or class concerned. It is improper if it is primarily to injure other members, or, perhaps, to benefit extraneous interests whether of the persons voting for the resolution or of third parties. Where the effect of a resolution is to deprive the company of its property, or to enable the shares of a minority to be expropriated or to release the directors from their duties of good faith, the resolution will be ineffective unless it is shown positively that the purpose was proper. In other cases the resolution will be upheld unless it is shown that the purpose of those voting for it was improper or that reasonable men could not have regarded it as calculated to fulfil a proper purpose'[2].

Whilst the duties of members[3] may be owed to the company[4] or to the minority directly[5], these duties[6] are less onerous than those of a fiduciary. This background suggests that, though the finding of an undertaking is a question of fact, the courts will be slow to find that a majority shareholder owes fiduciary duties to the company or minority shareholders.

In contrast, the fiduciary duties owed by directors and officers have been extended by some US courts to controlling shareholders. In *Pearlman v Feldmann*[7], it was held that F, who had the triple role of dominant shareholder, chairman and president of a company, was accountable to minority shareholders for a premium on the sale of his holding, a consequence of which was to sacrifice some of the company's goodwill. But referring to the unusual nature of the profit, the court emphasised that the decision should not be taken to establish that a majority shareholder cannot sell his controlling holding without having to account to the company for his profits.

However, other courts have taken the view that a majority shareholder who sells his holding and obtains a higher price because of the control element must share the control premium with other shareholders on the ground either that control is a corporate asset which the majority cannot appropriate to themselves to the exclusion of the minority or that majority shareholders owe fiduciary duties to minority shareholders. In *Jones v Ahmanson & Co*[8]., minority shareholders succeeded in an action against the former holding company which had sold control. Traynor C.J. remarked that in California, the courts

2. *Gower*, p.629; on members' duties, see *Gower*, pp614-630.
3. In contrast, the duties of directors as such are owed only to the company, see post.
4. Eg in cases of expropriation of the company's property or of release of directors from their duties of good faith.
5. Eg in cases of expropriation of the shares of the minority.
6. However, the view that responsibility should be placed on those who direct received statutory recognition in certain provisions of companies legislation, such as the provisions now contained in CA 1985, s323 (see, ante, Chapter 3. Criminal Liability) and CA 1985, ss324-326, 732, Sch13, pts. II, III and IV (see, post, Chapter 5. Disclosure III. Insider reporting). For this purpose, 'director' includes any person occupying the position of director, by whatever name called and in relation to a company 'shadow director' means a person in accordance with whose directions or instructions the directors of the company are accustomed to act: CA 1985, s741(1) and (2).
Like other third parties, members will be liable if they knowingly participate in a breach of 'trust' by directors or officers, see post.
7. (1955) 219 F.2d.173, cert. denied 349 U.S.952; see ante A. Fiduciary duties
8. (1969) 460 P.2d.464 (Cal.S.C.). This decision is noted: '*Jones v Ahmanson*; The Fiduciary Obligations of Majority Shareholders' (1970) 70 Col.L.R.1088

'have often recognised that majority shareholders, either singly or acting in concert to accomplish a joint purpose, have a fiduciary responsibility to the minority and to the corporation to use their ability to control the corporation in a fair, just and equitable manner. Majority shareholders may not use their power to control corporate activities to benefit themselves alone or in a manner detrimental to the minority. Any use to which they put the corporation or their power to control the corporation must benefit all shareholders proportionately. . .'

Detailed consideration of the control premium is beyond the scope of this book. But an approach, which imposes fiduciary duties on those with the power and influence to run the company irrespective of whether they have been appointed directors or officers or their nominees have been so appointed, reflects the reality of corporate control.

The circumstances in which a third party involved in a breach of duty by a director or other fiduciary may be liable to account for profits are important in relation to tippee liability to the company. The cases suggest that a third party will be liable to the company if he either (a) induces a director to breach his fiduciary duties to the company[9] or (b) agrees with a director to engage in a course of conduct involving a breach of duty by the director[10]. These two causes of action are personal claims.

But in certain circumstances, a third party may be compelled to account as a constructive trustee for the company. First, a third party can be liable when he knowingly assists in a dishonest and fraudulent design on the part of the directors[11]. For the third party to have the requisite knowledge, he must know of (a) the existence of a trust (or a fiduciary relationship), (b) the existence of a dishonest or fraudulent design on the part of the trustee or fiduciary and (c) his own assistance in the dishonest design. The knowledge must be of facts, not of mere claims or allegations. The requirement of knowledge is satisfied by (i) actual knowledge, (ii) wilfully shutting one's eyes to the obvious, (iii) a wilful and reckless failure to make enquiries that an honest and reasonable man would have made, (iv) knowledge of circumstances which would indicate the facts to an honest and reasonable man and (v) knowledge of circumstances which would put an honest and reasonable man on inquiry[12]. It seems that a court should not be astute to impute knowledge where no actual knowledge exists. It is not necessary for the third party to receive trust property and hence the issue of whether information can be regarded as trust property is not relevant to such liability.

Secondly, a third party is a constructive trustee if he receives corporate property with actual or constructive knowledge of a breach of trust[13]. The extent to which information can be regarded as property is thus relevant in this context. It seems that the company may trace the property into the hands of the third party or a volunteer, but not a bona fide purchaser for value without notice

9. *Boulting v ACTAT* [1963] 2 Q.B.606; *Prudential Assurance v Lorenz* (1971) 11 K.I.R.78.
10. *Belmont Finance Corpn Ltd. v Williams Furniture Ltd. (No.2)* [1980] 1 All E.R.394. Liability arises under the tort of conspiracy.
11. *Baden, Delvaux and Lecuit v Société General pour Favoriser le Développement du Commerce et de l'Industrie en France SA* [1983] BCLC 325; *Belmont Finance Corpn Ltd. v. Williams Furniture Ltd. (No.2)* [1980] 1 All E.R.393, especially at 405 per Buckley L.J.
12. *Baden, Delvaux and Lecuit v Société General pour Favoriser le Développement du Commerce et de l'Industrie en France SA* [1983] BCLC 325
13. *Belmont Finance Corporation Ltd. v Williams Furniture Ltd. (No.2)* [1980] 1 All E.R.393.

of the breach[14].

It is unfortunate that the *Regal* case, in holding that the chairman of the directors was not liable to repay the profit made by those who took the shares in the subsidiary from him, provided an opportunity to infer an absence of third party liability in general. However, such inference should be treated with great caution since the House of Lords found as a fact that all transactions were bona fide. As the directors did not knowingly act in breach of trust, there must have been a similar lack of knowledge by the third parties. For the purpose of a constructive trust, it seems that, in the absence of actual knowledge, a court will not be astute to impute knowledge when the third party has merely assisted in the breach of trust without receiving trust property. But the view that the *Regal* decision is not conclusive against third party liability[15] is to be preferred.

In the US, the issue of third party liability to the company on the basis of equitable principles arose in *Schein v Chasen*[16]. Suing derivately on behalf of L Ltd., the plaintiff shareholders alleged that the defendants were jointly and severally liable to the company for actionable wrongs against the company. The action followed the disclosure of inside information about the company by its president to a stockbroker who, in turn, disclosed the information to a portfolio manager. The manager passed the information to a colleague and on receiving the information, the two portfolio managers each directed a different mutual fund to sell its holdings in L Ltd. After the president and two portfolio managers had been dismissed as defendants by the District Court for lack of personal jurisdiction, the action proceeded against the stockbroker, his firm and the two mutual funds. The plaintiffs did not allege a breach of the federal securities laws, but sought recovery on the grounds that the participants in the chain of wrong-doing were jointly and severally liable to the company under Florida law for misusing corporate information to their own advantage in breach of their duty to the company and that they must account to the company for the profits realised by the two mutual funds. The plaintiffs argued that inasmuch as there were no Florida cases directly in point, a Florida court would look to other jurisdictions and take a special interest in the decision in *Diamond v Oreamuno*[17]. But the defendants contended that under Florida case law, a complaint in a shareholders' derivative action which failed to allege both wrongful acts and damage to the company must be dismissed.

The US District Court dismissed the complaints, holding that they failed to state a claim under Florida law. In considering the possibility that Florida courts might follow the rationale of the New York decision in *Diamond v Oreamuno* and hence whether defendants would be liable under the rationale of *Diamond*, the District Court concluded that the complaints went far beyond the narrow holding of *Diamond*. By a majority, the Circuit Court of Appeals reversed the decision and found that though Florida law was controlling, it could find none that was decisive and so turned to the law of New York, notably *Diamond*. It was of opinion that preservation of corporate prestige and goodwill, which the *Diamond* rationale was designed to protect, meant that it was immaterial whether the director traded on his own account or passed on the information to outsiders who then dealt. The Circuit Court added that it would be self-defeating to restrict *Diamond* to directors and officers of the company, whilst

14. *Re Diplock* [1948] Ch465 regarding the nature and scope of the doctrine of tracing; *Baker v Medway Building and Supplies Ltd.* [1958] 1 W.L.R.1216
15. D.D. Prentice, 'Insider Trading' [1975] C.L.P.83 at 88-89.
16. Fla., 313 So.2d 739.
17. (1969) 248 N.E.2d 910 (N.Y.C.A.).

allowing their third party co-venturers to escape liability to the company. The defendants' lack of knowledge of the breach of a fiduciary obligation was thus not in issue.

However, the Supreme Court of Florida declined not only to give an expansive reading to *Diamond*, but also to adopt the ruling in *Diamond*. Adhering to the precedent established by Florida courts that actual damage to the company must be alleged in the complaint to substantiate a shareholder's derivative action, the Supreme Court held that under Florida law the investors were not liable to the company in such an action for profits realised on the sale of their holdings and that the stockbroker would not be jointly and severally liable with the investors for the profits realised on the sale[18]. It is also noted that in proceedings under the federal securities laws, the president had been found liable as a non-trading tipper and his act imputed to the company[19]. The Supreme Court thus preferred a method of analysis which, in relation to derivative suits, focussed not on the unfairness of profits from transactions based on inside information, but on the duty owed to the company by the various individuals involved.

C. Enforcement difficulties

The dearth of any reported decision on accountability to the company by an insider for insider dealing profits suggests that various factors militate against such an action. These will be dealt with from the standpoint of an action by the company and an action by a shareholder. Reference will then be made to the alternative remedy.

1. Action by the company

Enforcement of duties owed to the company is subject to the vagaries of the rule in *Foss v Harbottle*. Its generally accepted formulation is in two parts:

> 'the court will not interfere with the internal management of companies acting within their powers, and in fact it has no jurisdiction to do so. Again, it is clear law that in order to redress a wrong done to the company, or to recover moneys or damages alleged to be due to the company, the action should prima facie be brought by the company itself'[20].

The rule has been stated to derive from partnership principles as to the first part

---

18. The Florida Supreme Court quoted (Fla., 313 So 2d.739 at 743-746) with approval the minority opinion (which endorsed the objective of discouraging insider dealing but questioned the means) in the Circuit Court in terms that:
'the complaints here are barren of any allegation that the appellees . . . occupied any position, such as officer, director, employee, or agent which would create fiduciary obligations to [the company] . . . Liability in *Diamond* was predicated entirely on such a relationship, and in its absence, the *Diamond* rationale for liability ceases to exist.
. . . a view that a tippee is cloaked with state law fiduciary obligations to the corporation whose shares he trades is an unknown and untenable legal concept. Neither *Diamond* – itself a significant alteration of the common law principles applicable to an officer's or director's trading in his corporation's shares – nor the law of agency support such a holding'.
19. In relation to the liability of the company and the grant of an injunction against it, the lack of in-house rules had been an important factor.
20. *Burland v Earle* [1902] A.C.83 at 93 per Lord Davey.

and to depend on the corporation principle as to the second part[1]. Under partnership principles prevailing in 1843 when the rule was stated, the courts were averse to interfering in matters of internal management. Initially 'extended to companies', this approach came to apply primarily to companies as partnership law moved on. The corporation principle proceeds from the treatment of the company as a legal person separate from its members. Hence, wrongs to the company, including by directors when their duties are owed to the company alone and not to its members, must be remedied by an action by the company not by its members.

The rule bears the name of the first case in which it was clearly expressed. In *Foss v Harbottle*[2], two shareholders brought an action against five directors and others alleging various fraudulent and illegal transactions whereby the company's property had been misapplied and wasted. The action was dismissed on the ground that as the possibility of convening a general meeting of shareholders capable of controlling the acts of the existing board was not excluded by the allegations, there was nothing to prevent the company from obtaining redress in its corporate character in respect of those matters and hence the plaintiffs could not sue in a form of pleading which assumed the practical dissolution of the corporation.

In subsequent cases, the rule was extended to internal irregularities in the operation of the company. An early example was *Mozley v Alston*[3] in which two shareholders had sought a declaration that the persons purporting to act as directors had not been validly appointed. In *Macdougall v Gardiner*[4] the chairman had ruled that there could be no poll on a motion for the adjournment of a general meeting. When a single shareholder suing on behalf of himself and all other shareholders (except the directors) complained of breach of the articles, the court held that the proceedings should have been in the name of the company because it was for the majority to decide whether they wished to complain. Mellish L.J. was of opinion that:

> 'if the thing complained of is a thing which in substance the majority of the company are entitled to do, or if something has been done irregularly which the majority of the company are entitled to do regularly, or if something has been done illegally which the majority . . . are entitled to do legally, there can be no use in having litigation about it, the ultimate end of which is only that a meeting has to be called, and then ultimately the majority gets its wishes'[5].

Having long recognised the principle of majority rule in corporations, the courts had no difficulty in expressing this principle as the justification for the refusal to interfere with management. An act capable of ratification by ordinary resolution fell outside the purview of the court. Internal affairs were decided by the majority. The partnership principle could thus be merged into the corporation rule[6].

The principle of majority rule applied to decisions about legal proceedings. When the majority decided not to take proceedings against a director for breach

1. K.W. Wedderburn, 'Shareholders' Rights and the Rule in *Foss v Harbottle*' [1957] C.L.J.194 at 196-198 and [1958] C.L.J.93.
2. (1843) 2 Hare 461.
3. (1847) 1 Ph.790; 41 E.R.833.
4. (1875) 1 ChD.13, C.A.
5. Ibid at 25.
6. Wedderburn, op cit supra, at 198.

of duty, the minority had no locus standi as plaintiff. Hence, a potential plaintiff was in the dilemma either of enjoying majority support in which event the company is the proper plaintiff or of lacking such support so that no action lies[7].

Normally, the decision is taken by the board of directors[8] as a business judgment incidental to their management of the company. However, it is well settled that if the directors do not commence proceedings, (as will be the case if they are the potential defendants), the power to bring an action reverts to the general meeting[9]. Hence, in practice an individual shareholder is allowed to bring proceedings in the company's name. But if the defendants challenge his right to do so, the proceedings are stayed until a general meeting is held to decide whether the company should sue[10]. If the general meeting decides not to adopt the suit, the action is dismissed[11] and the shareholder and his solicitors on the record are liable for costs[12].

The effect is that proceedings are unlikely to be taken against directors or other controllers whilst they retain de facto control, especially as it seems that the courts have no power to prevent defendants who are shareholders from voting at the general meeting[13]. The likelihood of proceedings by the company is further reduced in that directors will be reluctant to take proceedings against another director or officer of the company. Thus, a characteristic of the leading cases for an account of profits has been that proceedings have been taken after either (i) a change in control, as in the *Regal* case, when a decision against the directors provides the new controllers with an unexpected windfall or (ii) a quarrel between directors, as in *Cooley* and *Canaero*, when the action may be prompted by vindictiveness rather than a concern for ethical standards or (iii) both, as in *Peso*. Hence, the comment that fact patterns in actions against directors for breach of their fiduciary duties are reminiscent of stories about the "falling out of thieves"[14].

Although the courts have often termed internal irregularities as wrongs against the company, it is unclear why those acts should not rather be viewed as infringements of the personal rights of each member under the statutory contract[15] constituted by the memorandum and articles[16]. The decision in *Salmon*[17] has been advanced[18] as authority for this latter proposition. Suing as a member, the plaintiff obtained an injunction to restrain a company from completing transactions entered into in breach of an article which required the consent of both managing directors of whom he was one. By indirectly enforcing a veto vested in him by the articles in his capacity as managing director, he ensured that the company's affairs were conducted in accordance with its articles. Though supported by subsequent authorities[19], this view involves

7. *Cotter v National Union of Seamen* [1929] 2 Ch58 at 111 per Russell L.J.
8. *Shaw & Sons (Salford) Ltd. v Shaw* [1935] 2 K.B.113, C.A.
9. *Pender v Lushington* (1877) 6 ChD.70.
10. *Danish Mercantile Co. Ltd. v Beaumont* [1951] Ch680, C.A.
11. *East Pant Du Mining Co. v. Merryweather* (1864) 2 Hem. & M. 254.
12. *Newbiggin Gas Co. v Armstrong* (1879) 13 ChD.310, C.A.
13. *Mason v Harris* (1879) 11 ChD.97, C.A.
14. D.D. Prentice, '*Regal (Hastings) Ltd. v Gulliver* – The Canadian Experience' (1967) 30 M.L.R.450.
15. CA 1985, s14(1).
16. *Gower*, p.642.
17. [1909] 1 Ch311, C.A.
18. Wedderburn, op cit n1, p153, supra [1957] C.L.J. 193 at 212.
19. Eg *Hogg v Cramphorn* [1967] Ch254; *Bamford v Bamford* [1970] Ch212, C.A.

disregarding innumerable weighty dicta and overruling several leading cases[20]. Paradoxically, it is well settled that a breach which could not be remedied by an ordinary resolution, constitutes an infringement of an individual membership right in respect of which a member has a right of action[1].

There is much to be said for the view that the courts have ceased to be moved by pure questions of principle, but have instead emphasised the practical advantages of the rule in *Foss v Harbottle*[2]. In addition to futile litigation[3], reasons for the rule cited by the courts include the need both to prevent a company from tearing itself to pieces[4] and to avoid a multiplicity of suits[5] so that the company is spared the harassment of "strike suits" started by innumerable plaintiffs. As to the latter, the courts seem to have paid less attention to the role of shareholder litigation in enforcing the duties of directors and controllers than to the example of some shareholders in the US who have threatened or started litigation with an eye on a quick settlement on the advice of lawyers rewarded under the contingency fee system. This is unfortunate because, apart from the distinction that unwarranted litigation in Britain is deterred by the practice whereby the unsuccessful litigant normally pays his own costs and the other side's taxed costs, the unjust consequences which flow from 'strike suits' can be curbed by procedural rules. Indeed, the courts of equity have long had powers to stay and consolidate actions[6] and to dismiss actions instigated for a collateral purpose amounting to an abuse of process[7]. Apart from requiring a member to sue in a representative capacity, further protection could be afforded both by giving the court a discretion to refuse to allow a particular member to control the litigation and by providing that an action could only be discontinued or settled with the court's approval[8].

2. Action by a shareholder

There have been two main obstacles to an action by a shareholder. These are the scope of the exceptions to the rule in *Foss v Harbottle* and the problem of costs. Both have been affected by recent developments.

(a) EXCEPTIONS TO THE RULE IN *FOSS V HARBOTTLE*

An inflexible application of the right of the majority of members to bar a minority action would have had two undesirable consequences[9]. First, even the limitations on the majority's powers imposed by the substantive law would have been stultified as long as the company remained a going concern, no action could effectively be brought to enforce them. Secondly, the fiduciary and other duties of directors could have been disregarded with impunity when the

20. *Gower*, p.319; G.D. Goldberg, 'The Enforcement of Outsider Rights under Section 20(1) of The Companies Act 1948' (1972) 35 M.L.R.362.
1. *Pender v Lushington* (1877) 6 ChD.70; *Edwards v Halliwell* [1950] 2 All E.R.1064, C.A.
2. *Gower*, p.642.
3. Eg *Macdougall v Gardiner* (1875) 1 ChD.13, C.A., see ante; *Cotter v National Union of Seamen* [1929] 2 Ch58.
4. *La Compagnie de Mayville v Whitley* [1896] 1 Ch788 at 807.
5. *Gray v Lewis* (1873) 8Ch App1035.
6. A.J. Boyle, 'The Minority Shareholder in the Nineteenth Century: A study in Anglo-American Legal History' (1965) 28 M.L.R.317 at 327, n.44.
7. Eg *Re Bellador Silk Ltd.* [1965] 1 All E.R.667.
8. See, post, 2. Action by a shareholder.
9. *Gower*, p.644.

directors had voting control.

Accordingly, exceptions to the rule in *Foss v Harbottle* have been recognised[10]. It is long settled that an action by a shareholder instead of the company is allowed[11] when (a) it is alleged that the company is acting or proposing to act ultra vires or (b) the act complained of could be effective only if resolved upon by more than a simple majority vote, as when a special or extraordinary resolution is required, but has not been validly passed or (c) it is alleged that the personal rights of the plaintiff shareholder have been or are about to be infringed or (d) those in control are perpetrating a fraud on the minority. But the Court of Appeal[12] has rejected the suggestion[13] that a further exception should be admitted in any other case where the interests of justice require that an exception be made to the rule in *Foss v Harbottle*. However, following the CA 1980[14], the pressure on a shareholder to establish one of these long-settled exceptions is reduced by the revised scope of the alternative remedy.

Nevertheless, the courts have come to recognise that it is misguided to prevent a minority shareholder commencing proceedings to attack an irregularity which could be rectified when the company has not in fact had the opportunity of deciding whether to rectify it. In *Hogg v Cramphorn*[15], the directors had issued shares to fend off a take-over bid. An individual shareholder alleged that in issuing the shares, the directors had exercised their powers for an improper purpose. Whilst holding that the shareholder could institute proceedings, Buckley J. also held that the issue of shares could be ratified by the general meeting and gave the company an opportunity to do so on the directors' undertaking not to exercise the votes attached to the newly issued shares. The directors were not thereby precluded from exercising the votes in respect of their initial holdings when voting on the resolution. At the general meeting, the majority ratified the issue. The *Hogg* decision was followed

---

10. This discussion of the exceptions to the rule in *Foss v Harbottle* draws on: *Gower*, Chapter 26, *Palmer*, Chapter 58 and K.W. Wedderburn, Shareholders' Rights and the Rule in *Foss v Harbottle*' [1957] C.L.J.194 at 204-215 and [1958] 93-103.

11. This statement of the exceptions is based on that of *Gower*, pp644-645.

12. *Prudential Assurance Co. Ltd. v Newman Industries Ltd. (No.2)* [1982] Ch 204.

13. *Eg Baillie v Oriental Telephone and Electric Co. Ltd.* [1915] 1 Ch503 at 518; *Cotter v National Union of Seamen* [1929] 2 Ch58 at 69; *Edwards v Halliwell* [1950] 2 All E.R.1064 at 1067.
This suggestion was considered in *Pavlides v Jensen* [1956] Ch565. A minority shareholder alleged that the directors had negligently sold a corporate asset at a gross undervaluation. After reviewing earlier cases, Danckwerts L.J. rejected the contention of a further exception as not supported by the authorities. However, the view that it was only intended to state that on the facts of that case a further exception would not be admitted was apparently supported by observations on this case by the Court of Appeal in *Heyting v Dupont* [1964] 1 W.L.R.843. In the latter, a minority shareholder alleged misfeasance against a majority shareholder in his capacity as director. Harman L.J. observed (at 854):
'there are cases which suggest that the rule [in *Foss v Harbottle*] is not a rigid one and that exception will be made where the justice of the case demands it. I am content . . . to assume that there may be misfeasance in respect of which the exception should be allowed, but I also agree . . . that this is emphatically not a case where the rule should be further stretched'.
Referring to the judgment of Harman L.J. and his own judgment, Buckley L.J. subsequently criticised the view that *Heyting v Dupont* was authority for a further exception and stated that the court had not found it necessary to reach a decision on the question (Palmer, para.58-22).
The controversy was renewed by *Prudential Assurance Co. Ltd. v Newman Industries Ltd. (No.2)* when the judgment of Vinelott J. [1981] Ch 257 was viewed as an affirmation of the principle that a minority action should be permitted in the interests of justice. However, the Court of Appeal restored the schematic range of exceptions, remarking that the 'interests of justice' exception was not a convincing practical test, 'particularly if it involves a full-dress trial before the test is applied'. [1982] 1 All E.R.354 at 366.

14. CA 1980, s75, now CA 1985, ss459-461.

15. [1967] Ch254.

and approved in *Bamford v Bamford*[16], which also involved the issue of shares to thwart an unwanted bid. In that case, the issue of shares to another company had been ratified by the general meeting though the other company had not voted. A minority shareholder brought proceedings to avoid the issue. The Court of Appeal held that the issue of shares, though in its inception a voidable transaction, had been validly ratified and approved. The action was then stayed. It is thought[17] that recent cases[18] establish that merely because an act could be ratified by the general meeting, a minority shareholder is not precluded from commencing proceedings. But these will be stayed upon ratification as the plaintiff's cause of action is thereby destroyed.

The form of action has long given rise to confusion. But in a recent case[19], consideration was given to the distinction between personal and derivative causes of action and the relationship of the representative form of action to each. In a personal action, a shareholder seeks to enforce duties owed to him, not the company, and to seek recovery for himself. The duty may be owed to him by the company, (as under the statutory contract)[20], or by the directors. Though it need not be, an action to enforce a personal right can be brought in a representative form. If so, it will be on behalf of himself and all other shareholders whose rights are the same as his own (the class being identified at the date of the wrong).

On the other hand, where an action is brought to enforce the company's rights, the action is a derivative one[1], so-called because the cause of action is derived from the company and, if successful, recovery is by the company and not by shareholders. Hence, it is irrelevant that the class of plaintiffs includes some who sue in respect of a wrong to the company before they became members. In an action within the exceptions to the rule in *Foss v Harbottle*, recovery of money due to or property belonging to the company cannot be ordered unless there is a derivative claim and hence such an action by minority shareholders to recover insiders' dealing profits on behalf of the company would be a derivative one. Since it is an equitable invention, the right to bring a derivative action will not be granted to someone who participated in the wrong.

As to the procedure in a derivative action[2], the minority shareholders sue on behalf of themselves and the other shareholders of the company at the date of the action, (except the alleged wrongdoers), against the alleged wrongdoers and the company. Despite the fact that the action is brought on the company's behalf, the company is made a defendant because neither the board nor the general meeting will authorise proceedings by the company in its own name. For the company to be bound by the litigation and judgment to be given in its favour, it must be joined as a party and so it appears as nominal defendant. To ensure that all other shareholders are bound by the result of the action, the minority shareholders should sue in a representative capacity on behalf of themselves and all other members other than the real defendants, (ie the alleged wrongdoers).

However, the obligations of the plaintiff in a derivative action have not been

---

16. [1970] Ch212.
17. *Gower*, p.646.
18. In addition to the *Hogg* and *Bamford* decisions, the decision in *Hodgson v Nalgo* [1972] 1 W.L.R.130 is cited as authority for this proposition.
19. *Prudential Assurance Co. Ltd. v Newman Industries Ltd. (No.2)* [1980] J.B.L.416 P.L.D.
20. CA 1985, s14.
1. This US term adopted by the Court of Appeal in *Wallersteiner v Moir* [1975] Q.B.373 was confirmed in *Prudential Assurance Co. Ltd. v Newman Industries Ltd. (No.2)* [1981] Ch 257.
2. R.S.C., Order 15, rule 12.

fully considered. It is apparently assumed that the plaintiff has complete control over the litigation until judgment so can discontinue or settle at will. Yet this leaves scope for abuse. In the event of a plaintiff dropping out in consideration of a payment to him, (probably by the company), it is thought[3] that he cannot retain the payment, but must account to the company as whose agent he was acting. But the position is not clear. It is also suggested[4] that a plaintiff's ability to discontinue or settle at will should be made subject to a rule that this will only be permitted with the court's consent after notice to all members.

Further confusion has surrounded the extent to which personal and derivative claims could be joined in the same action. The recent case of *Prudential Assurance Co. Ltd. v Newman Industries Ltd.*[5] provides a warning against expressing what is in reality a corporate matter as an individual wrong on the sole ground that the member is indirectly prejudiced by a fall in the company's profits. But when justified by reality, a derivative action can be combined with a personal action.

Three 'exceptions' to the rule in *Foss v Harbottle* will now be considered separately. These are: personal rights, fraud on the minority where the wrongdoers have control and the interests of justice.

(i) PERSONAL RIGHTS.   Personal rights spring either from the statutory contract[6] constituted by the memorandum and articles or another source, such as statute or a non-statutory contract as when a contract of service between the directors and company incorporates the articles as terms of agreement. In the event of an article forbidding the use of inside information in transactions between a member and another member or any other person being recognised as personal right, an individual member could sue in his own name and his right of action could not be barred by the majority. But it seems that remedies for such breach may be limited to a declaration or injunction[7]. In practice, other forms of contractual stipulation are preferred.

(ii) FRAUD ON THE MINORITY WHERE THE WRONGDOERS HAVE CONTROL.   This exception has two constituent parts. The act must constitute a fraud on the minority and the company must be prevented from taking proceedings against the wrongdoers by the votes which they control.

Fraud on the minority.   It is not easy to determine when an act constitutes a fraud on the minority. But both fraud and minority are used loosely[8]. Not confined to common law fraud in the sense of deceit, fraud in this context has a wider equitable meaning involving an abuse of power analogous to a breach of fiduciary duty. Moreover, the wrong need not be to the minority. Normally, the wrong will be to the company, though sometimes its harsh consequences will fall on those outvoted by the controllers.

However, the courts have readily accepted that a fraud on the minority includes a wrongful expropriation of corporate property for the controllers'

3. *Gower*, p.653
4. Ibid.
5. [1982] Ch 204.
6. CA 1985, s14.
7. Wedderburn, op cit n10, p156, supra [1957] C.L.J.194 at 211.
8. *Gower*, p.616.

benefit. A classic example is *Cook v Deeks*[9]. Hence, the significance of the debate on whether information constitutes property; in the event of inside information being considered as corporate property, a minority action could not be barred by the majority. Further uncertainty surrounds the issue of whether a matter is ratifiable[10].

Another category of conduct covered by the term fraud on the minority is voting for company resolutions not bona fide in the interests of the company as a whole[11]. Whilst not expected to divorce themselves completely from their own personal interests, shareholders must consider whether the proposal is beneficial not only to the members, but to a hypothetical member with, presumably, no personal interest other than as members. However, even when controllers do not consider this question, it will usually be impossible to prove it.

Releasing directors from their subjective duties of good faith also qualifies as a fraud on the minority. Directors' action in expropriating the company's property can apparently be authorised by a resolution of the company provided it is established that this was passed bona fide in the interests of the company[12]. But when directors do not act bona fide in the interests of the company it seems to be impossible to ratify. A resolution authorising directors not to act bona fide in the interests of the company cannot be in the interests of the company. Whilst it may be established that a resolution not to sue for a past breach of duty was bona fide in the interests of the company, (eg when it is not in its interests to spend money on litigation), it is difficult to see how its interests are served by releasing directors from liability so as to protect them from proceedings by an individual member on behalf of the company (eg for insider dealing). Hence, it is thought[13] that, though a resolution not to sue a fraudulent director may be valid if it is clearly shown to have been passed bona fide in the interest of the company, such a resolution will not validate the fraudulent act so that the directors will be liable at the suit of the individual shareholder.

Control.   The clearest way of proving the wrongdoers control the company is to show that both the directors and a general meeting have been invited but have refused to bring an action in the name of the company and that the refusal is attributable to the votes cast by the wrongdoers. But it is not necessary either to make a formal request to the directors or to convene a general meeting, provided the court can be satisfied that the wrongdoers are in effective control.

There is no difficulty when the wrongdoers hold a majority of voting shares. But a more problematic case is where persons with comparatively small shareholdings in a company in which shareholding is diffused, are able to control the company as a result of their control over proxies and the failure of many other shareholders to attend general meetings. A restricted view of control is unrealistic in modern company practice.

When the phenomenon of de facto control fell to be considered in *Pruden-*

9. [1916] 1 A.C.554, P.C.
10. See ante A. Fiduciary duties.
11. Such conduct falls within what now seems to be established as a general principle that the majority must always exercise their powers bona fide for the benefit of the company as a whole, subject to the exception laid down by CA 1985, s719, when the resolution makes provision for employees or former employees on the cessation or transfer of the whole or part of the undertaking of the company or any subsidiary; *Gower*, p.623 and Supplements.
12. *Regal (Hastings) Ltd. v Gulliver* [1942] 1 All E.R.378 H.L. cf *Cook v Deeks* [1916] 1 A.C.554, P.C.; see ante A. Fiduciary duties.
13. *Gower*, p.619.

tial Assurance Co. Ltd. v Newman Industries Ltd. (No. 2), it was the subject of judicial controversy. B and L, who were respectively chairman and chief executive of N, proposed a transaction whereby N would acquire various assets from TPG which had a 25.6% holding in N and faced a severe financial crisis. B and L were respectively non-executive chairman and vice-chairman/chief executive of TPG and had a 35% holding in TPG through their wholly-owned company, S. The TPG assets to be acquired by N had been grossly overvalued and N's shareholders approved the transaction after being sent a circular by the board of N containing statements which were tricky and misleading and known to be so by B and L. Neither B and L nor the board of N as a whole had voting control. P, a minority shareholder in N, sought, inter alia, compensation for N from B, L and TPG. At first instance[14], Vinelott J. took a broad view of control when he held that P was allowed to bring an action on behalf of the company on the basis that, given the board of N had been deceived by B and L and the members would look to the board for guidance, there was no real possibility of either the board or the members exercising a proper judgment on whether the company should commence litigation and P had shown that, in the special circumstances of the case, the interests of justice would otherwise be defeated in that an action which should have been pursued on behalf of the company would not be pursued. Disapproving of this approach which blurred the concepts of wrongdoer control and the interests of justice, the Court of Appeal[15] isolated the wrongdoer requirement and stated that 'control'.

> 'embraces a broad spectrum extending from an overall absolute majority of votes at one end to a majority of votes at the other end made up of those likely to be cast by the delinquent himself plus those voting with him as a result of influence or apathy'[16].

But the criteria to be applied await clarification.

Despite the broad language used by courts, it has been notoriously difficult for a minority shareholder to establish the exception of a fraud on the minority where the wrongdoers have control. The availability of a minority action on behalf of the company against an insider under this exception exists mainly at the level of theory.

(b) Costs

The other main obstacle to a minority shareholder's action is the cost of litigation. In the absence of a contingency fee system, a plaintiff is at risk as to costs. When, after a preliminary investigation, a potential plaintiff finds that he has no cause of action, he forfeits his investigation costs. If unsuccessful, the plaintiff bears his own costs and is usually also liable for the taxed costs of all the defendants, including the company. If successful, he recovers only his own taxed costs, not all his legal expenses. The outlay of such costs for a dubious return explains why few plaintiffs have had an investment substantial enough even to contemplate bringing proceedings. It may be that the only potential plaintiffs with a significant enough stake may be shareholders with sufficient

14. [1980] 2 All E.R.841 at 869.
15. [1982] 1 All E.R.354.
16. Ibid at 364.

influence to obtain confidential information on their own.

However, the size of this obstacle was reduced by the 1975 decision in *Wallersteiner v Moir (No. 2)*[17]. M was a shareholder in two companies of which W had been a director. The company, other shareholders and the DTI were not interested in investigating allegations that W had defrauded the company. W claimed damages for libel against M in respect of a circular letter sent to shareholders. M served a defence and counterclaim and claimed declarations that W had been guilty of fraud, misfeasance and breach of trust and orders that W should pay sums totalling about £½ million to the two companies. W did not deliver a reply or a defence to the counterclaim. The Court of Appeal (a) dismissed W's appeal against the striking out of his libel action, (b) gave judgment against W in default of defence for £234,773 with interest to be paid to the companies and interlocutory judgment for damages to be assessed on a loan transaction and (c) gave W leave to defend on the remaining issues, including the claim to declarations of fraud, misfeasance and breach of trust, provided that a satisfactory defence to the counterclaim was submitted for the court's approval within 28 days. Having spent his financial resources and been refused legal aid, M applied to the Court of Appeal for safeguards, including the approval of a contingency fee arrangement, for his costs in the action the benefit of which would go to the companies.

The Court of Appeal held that, since M was a minority shareholder suing on behalf of the companies, by reason of the Legal Aid Act 1974[18], he was not a 'person' who was eligible for legal aid. However, it held that in a minority shareholder's action it was open to the court to order that the company should indemnify the plaintiff against the costs incurred in the action. Arising on equitable principles, such indemnity was viewed as analogous to that which a trustee is entitled from his cestui que trust[19]. The test was whether it was reasonable and prudent in the interests of the company for the plaintiff to bring the action and he did so in good faith. The costs should be taxed on a common fund basis. As a general rule, the plaintiff should apply at the commencement of the action for authority to proceed with it. In this case, M was given an indemnity for the costs incurred by him on behalf of the companies up to and including discovery when he should obtain further directions from the court.

However, in *Smith v Croft*[20] a narrow interpretation was given to *Wallersteiner v Moir (No. 2)*. The plaintiff brought a minority shareholders' action alleging that the directors of a company had paid themselves excessive remuneration. The master made an order, ex parte, requiring the company to indemnify the plaintiffs against their costs in the action until the conclusion of discovery and the inspection of documents. A subsequent order by the master granted the plaintiffs liberty to have their costs taxed at three monthly intervals, but limited to 60%. On the company's application to set aside the first order and on appeal by the company and cross-appeal by the plaintiffs against the second order, the company's application and appeal were allowed.

Walton J. held that the plaintiffs in a minority shareholder's action should not be granted an order indemnifying them in costs before discovery where such an order could cause injustice. The application before the master should normally be heard inter partes, with affidavits being disclosed. Although it was

---

17. [1975] Q.B.373.
18. Legal Aid Act 1974, s25.
19. *Re Beddoe* [1893] 1 Ch547.
20. [1986] 1 W.I..R.580.

not appropriate to conduct an interim trial, the court should have regard to both the agreed and disputed facts to assess whether, applying the test of the standard of care which the prudent businessman would exercise in the conduct of his affairs, the action should be allowed to continue at the company's expense. Since it was clear from the undisputed facts that the plaintiffs' action had little chance of success and was being prosecuted against the wishes of the holders of the majority of independently held shares, it would be unjust to grant an indemnity. Walton J. added that an interim order for costs could be granted when plaintiffs established a genuine need, but even then it was appropriate to leave some proportion of the costs to be borne by them since otherwise there was no spur on them to proceed with the action which might ultimately be dismissed for want of prosecution.

The more radical suggestion of a contingency fee arrangement was rejected in *Wallersteiner v Moir (No. 2)*[1]. The Court of Appeal held that it would be unlawful as being contrary to public policy for a solicitor to accept a retainer from M to conduct the action on a contingency fee basis. But Lord Denning considered that, subject to the approval of the Law Society and the courts, public policy should favour contingency fees in derivative actions.

The introduction of the contingency fee raises the key policy issue of the role of the plaintiff's legal representative, particularly with regard to his role in enforcement and the amount of entrepreneurial scope allowed. Pointing to the mixed experience of the US, the attitude of the legal profession has traditionally been conservative. Yet the development of the contingency fee could have a dramatic impact on the enforcement of substantive insider provisions.

3. The alternative remedy

The rule in *Foss v Harbottle* was further eroded by the enactment in 1980 of the provision, now contained in the CA 1985, enabling a member to apply to the court by petition for an order on the ground that the affairs of the company are being or have been conducted in a manner which is unfairly prejudicial to the interests of some part of the members, (including at least himself), or that any actual or proposed act or omission of the company, (including any act or omission on its behalf), is or would be so prejudicial[2]. Following an inspector's report[3] or after exercising his powers either to require production of documents[4] or of entry and search of premises[5], the Secretary of State may also petition if it appears to him that some part of the members have been unfairly prejudiced[6]. The order may, inter alia, authorise civil proceedings to be brought in the name and on behalf of the company by such person or persons and on such terms as the court may direct[7]. An effect is thus to confer a discretion on the courts to waive the rule in *Foss v Harbottle* when unfair prejudice is established.

A matter for judicial interpretation, the scope of unfair prejudice remains a

1. [1975] Q.B.373.
2. CA 1985, s459(1).
3. Ibid, s437.
4. Ibid, s447.
5. Ibid, s448.
6. Ibid, s460(1).
7. Ibid, s461.

'rather elusive concept'[8]. In general terms, however, the test of unfairly prejudicial conduct is an objective, not a subjective one[9]. It is not necessary for the
petitioner to show that the persons with de facto control of the company have
acted deliberately in bad faith or with conscious intent to be unfair to him.

On the issue of how far a breach of directors' fiduciary duties may assist in
establishing unfair prejudice, judicial guidance is provided by three cases[10]
involving applications to strike out petitions (on the basis that in law there was
no case for the respondents to answer). In rejecting the applications, Hoffman
J. regarded allegations of breach of fiduciary duty as capable of establishing
unfair prejudice to minority shareholders in a private company or a small public
company[11]. By way of example[12], a breach of directors' duties not to mislead
shareholders (when making statements supporting one of two rival take-over
bids) was considered capable, at a subsequent hearing of the petition, of
establishing unfair prejudice.

Moreover, the court's unfettered discretion with regard to the terms of the
order enables it to place the person charged with the conduct of the action in
a more advantageous position as to costs than a plaintiff in a minority shareholder's action. The order may also deal with the obligations of the former in
relation to discontinuing or settling the action.

However, an important problem concerns the incentive to shareholders.
Unfairly prejudiced shareholders may lack the incentive to take one set of
proceedings merely to obtain authority to commence subsequent proceedings
on behalf of the company.

D. Legislative intervention

From the foregoing it is apparent that though a fiduciary's liability to account
for insider profits to his company may technically be very broad, enforcement
difficulties have discouraged proceedings to the extent that the risk of an action
against an insider for an account of profits to the company has been minimal.
Apart from reflecting the general policy of institutional investors in Britain, the
adage that a shareholder who disagrees with management should sell his
holding rather than litigate has particular relevance to insider dealing. For
corporate recovery to become an effective remedy, legislative intervention is
required.

However, accountability of insiders to the company has been criticised. According to the Justice Report[13], the drawbacks to this remedy are

'(i) the company will not normally itself have suffered any loss, and there
seems no reason in equity why it should benefit from the punishment of
the insider's misconduct
(ii) if the insider is a substantial shareholder, the damages paid by him will,
in part, indirectly return to him and he will still be left with a net profit on

8. A.J. Boyle, 'The Judicial Interpretation of Part XVII of the Companies Act 1985', in (ed.) B.G.
Pettet, *Company Law in Change* (Current Legal Problems) (1987), p.23.
9. *Re R.A. Noble & Sons (Clothing) Ltd.* [1983] BCLC 273.
10. Boyle, op cit 8, supra, pp25-26. The cases discussed are: *Re A Company (No.005287 of 1985)*,
[1986] 1 W.L.R.281; *Re a Company (No.008699 of 1985)*, (1986) 2 B.C.C.99,024, and *Re A Company
(No.00477 of 1986)* 2 B.C.C.99, 171
11. Boyle, op cit 8, supra, p.26.
12. *Re A Company (No.008699 of 1985)*, (1986) 2 B.C.C.99,024.
13. Justice, *Insider Trading* (1972).

the transaction
(iii) even if the rule in *Foss v Harbottle* were allowed, the practical
difficulties of ensuring that proceedings are taken by a shareholder on
behalf of the company would be very considerable'[14].

But its recommendations were anomalous. Stating that corporate recovery was
inappropriate as the 'primary remedy', it recommended that the fiduciary rules
governing the company's rights of action to recover insider profits should
neither be extended nor restricted[15].

These objections are not persuasive[16]. When applying strict fiduciary standards, the courts have not regarded the first objection as valid and the liability
of fiduciaries has not depended on whether there was a loss to the beneficiary[17].
As to the second objection, only a small proportion of insiders are substantial
shareholders. A 1969 survey of boardrooms found that directors of the top 100
industrial companies controlled (in aggregate) 7.5% of the equity votes of those
organisations[18]. In companies not admitted to the Official List, the percentage
is probably higher because ownership is often less diffuse. Yet even when a
proportion of the benefits ultimately revert to a substantial shareholder,
recovery by the company comes closer to achieving the aim of depriving the
insider of his profits, and thereby reducing the benefit of the transaction to the
insider, than allowing the insider to retain his entire profit. Like the first one,
this objection emphasises the demerits of the company's claim whilst disregarding the insider's unmeritorious conduct. The third objection underlined the
need for reform in relation to the derivative action rather than acceptance of
the obstacles to enforcement.

Though fiduciary principles are adequate to establish accountability to their
company by insiders, legislation would have the advantage of clarifying liability[19]. But its main impact would be on enforcement.

At the level of private enforcement[20], legislation could provide that when
there are reasonable grounds for supposing that the company has a cause of
action for recovery of insider profits and it has been invited to institute
proceedings and refused to do so or it has failed to prosecute proceedings
diligently, a shareholder may apply to the court for an order that he or another
person be authorised to commence or continue proceedings on behalf of the
company. The company could be ordered to bear the risk as to costs. In
determining whether to grant leave for the proceedings, the court should have
regard to the potential benefits to be derived from recovery to the company and
its shareholders and the costs of proceedings.

However, it is unlikely that private enforcement would be effective. In
deciding whether to petition to obtain authority to commence proceedings on

14. Ibid, para.32.
15. Ibid.
16. D.D. Prentice, 'Insider Trading' [1975] C.L.P.83 at 102: City Company Law Committee, *Insider
Dealing* (1976), para.32; D.D. Prentice, *The Companies Act 1980* (1980), para.334.
17. Eg *Industrial Development Consultants Ltd. v Cooley* [1972] 2 All E.R.162; *Reading v A-G* [1951]
A.C.507, see ante.
18. *The Times*, 9th September, 1969.
19. Eg as to the avoidance of a loss and the liability of tippees, see ante.
As to clarification of liability in relation to take-over bids, see J.A.C. Suter,' The Regulation of Insider
Dealing in Britain and France' (Doctoral thesis, E.U.I., Florence (1985)).
20. Canadian examples are discussed by: D.L. Johnston, *Canadian Securities Regulation* (1977),
pp308-309; M. Yontef, *Insider Trading*, p.629 at pp708-711 and L.H. Leigh, *Securities Regulation:
Problems in relation to sanctions*, p.513 at pp581-583, all in Consumer and Corporate Affairs Canada,
Proposals for a Securities Market Law for Canada, Vol.3 Background papers (1979).

behalf of the company, a shareholder's incentive is limited to the possibility of recovering his legal costs and of the eventual reversion to him of a proportion of the profits in his capacity as shareholder. An effect of prohibiting the contingency fee is to preclude an entrepreneurial role for legal representatives in this context.

Shortcomings in private enforcement raise the issue of whether a power to bring civil proceedings to recover insider dealing profits on behalf of the company should be vested in a regulatory agency. In addition to the Secretary of State's power to petition (following an inspector's report or after exercising his powers either to require production of documents or of entry and search of premises) in connection with unfairly prejudicial treatment under the CA 1985[1], a precedent for the involvement of a regulatory agency is found in the statutory power to bring civil proceedings on the company's behalf. This latter authorises the Secretary of State (following an inspector's report or after exercising his powers either to require production of documents or of entry and search of premises) to bring proceedings for and on behalf of the company when it appears to the Secretary of State that any such proceedings ought to be brought in the public interest[2]. The Secretary of State can thus overrule a refusal by controllers to take proceedings, though the infrequency of inspections[3] limits the occasions on which this power is even exerciseable.

Various factors support the involvement of a regulatory agency in enforcement[4]. The considerations of the private plaintiff with regard to cost compared to his proportionate share of recovery, the risks both from uncertainty in the law and of meeting the burden of proof and the difficulties of litigation when information is scarce are less relevant to the regulatory agency. With its relatively greater access to information and stronger investigative powers, a regulatory agency can conduct litigation more effectively.

With these advantages, a power vested in a regulatory agency to apply to the court for an order that it be authorised to commence or continue proceedings to recover insider dealing profits on behalf of the company, irrespective of whether there had been an inspector's report or an inspection of the company's books and papers under statutory powers, would be an important enforcement mechanism. But when cost-benefits point to proceedings, a more rigorous approach to enforcement is required than that adopted in relation to the powers of the Secretary of State to sue on behalf of a company and to petition in connection with unfairly prejudicial treatment.

Nevertheless, corporate recovery is subject to limitations. As to compensatory considerations, shareholders obtain no immediate benefit and sellers to insiders receive none. It is also doubtful whether a remedy restricted to accountability for profits constitutes a significant deterrent to those who might otherwise deal on inside information.

1. CA 1985, s460.
2. Ibid, n.438.
3. See, post, Chapter 7. Investigation, I. The Department of Trade and Industry
4. Yontef, op cit n20, p164, supra, at pp709-710.

II. LIABILITY TO SHAREHOLDERS AND OTHERS

A. The common law

Under the law of contract it is well settled that, in the absence of a specific duty of disclosure, silence does not amount to a misrepresentation. In *Bell v Lever Bros. Ltd.*[5], it was established that "failure to disclose a material fact which might influence the mind of a prudent contractor does not give the right to avoid the contract"[6]. But liability will be incurred when the non-disclosure is accompanied by some form of misrepresentation[7]. Though there are cases[8] indicating that placing an article on a public market is evidence of a representation, implied by conduct, that the goods are marketable and free from hidden defects, the principle applies only to selling transactions and is probably confined to latent defects and disease. However, under the terms of an express contract for the sale of securities, it is open to the parties to include a term that all material information has been fully disclosed.

Consequent upon the absence of a general duty to disclose material facts, the law of tort does not afford any significant protection against insider dealing. As a general rule, a mere non-disclosure is insufficient unless the defendant fails to correct a statement which, though true when made, has later become false to his knowledge[9]. A statement which is partially true may misrepresent the whole truth[10]. But the effect of the requirements for the plaintiff to prove further that the statement was made fraudulently and that the plaintiff was intended to act upon the statement, acted upon the statement and suffered damage by so doing, is that liability for deceit is difficult to establish[11].

An action for negligent misstatement, which is more readily available, may cover some insider transactions. In *Hedley Byrne & Co. v Heller and Partners*[12], the House of Lords indicated that when there is a special relationship between the person making the statement and the plaintiff relying on it, a negligent misstatement giving rise to economic loss permits recovery. In *Esso Petroleum v Mardon*[13], the rule in *Hedley Byrne* was stated as follows[14]:

'If a man, who has or professes to have special knowledge or skill, makes a representation by virtue thereof to another – be it advice, information or opinion – with the intention of inducing him to enter into a contract

5. [1932] A.C.161.
6. Ibid at 227 per Atkin L.J.
7. *Walters v Morgan* (1861) 3 De G.F. & J. 718, eg a word or gesture intended to induce a vendor to believe in the existence of a non-existing fact, which might influence the price of the subject to be sold.
8. *Bodger v Nichols* (1873) 28 L.T.441; *Ward v. Hobbs* (1878) 4 AppCas.13.
9. *Brownlie v Campbell* (1880) 5 AppCas.925.
10. *Arkwright v Newbold* [1881] 17 ChD.301.
11. *Winfield and Jolowicz on Tort*, Twelfth edition by W.V.H. Rogers (1984), Chapter 11.
12. [1964] A.C.465 H.L.
13. [1976] QB 801 C.A.
14. There are various formulations. A more restrictive one is that of the majority in *Mutual Life and Citizens' Assurance Co. Ltd. v Evatt* [1971] A.C.793, P.C., when it was stated (per Lord Diplock at 805) that there is no duty of care unless the defendant:
'lets it be known to the recipient of the advice that he claims to possess that degree of skill and competence and is willing to exercise that degree of diligence which is generally possessed and exercised by persons who carry on the business or profession of giving advice of the kind sought'. As this was a Privy Council decision, it is not binding on English judges and in *Esso Petroleum v Mardon* [1976] QB 801, the Court of Appeal preferred the less restrictive minority view.

with him, he is under a duty to use reasonable care to see that the representation is correct and that the advice, information or opinion is reliable. If he negligently gives unsound advice or misleading information or expresses an erroneous opinion and thereby induces the other side to enter into a contract with him, he is liable in damages'[15].

But the requirements of economic loss, reliance and a special relationship, whose nature is in turn surrounded by uncertainty, mean that such an action has no application to most forms of insider dealing.

In certain circumstances, the courts have held that directors are under a duty to act in good faith when advising shareholders. In *Gething v Kilner*, Brightman J. considered that in a take-over, directors of an offeree company would owe 'a duty to be honest and . . . not to mislead'[16] if they distributed circulars to shareholders. But doubts[17] whether this duty amounted to anything more than that imposed on everyone not to made deceitful or negligent misstatements were confirmed in *Prudential Assurance Co. Ltd. v Newman Industries Ltd. (No.2)*, which concerned the approval of the acquisition of a large block of assets from another company[18]. At first instance, this duty was classified as arising in tort and as being 'no more than a particular application, to directors who assume responsibility for giving advice to shareholders, of the general duty to act honestly and with due care'[19]. The Court of Appeal emphasised that in such an action the amount of damages awarded to a shareholder must be limited to loss suffered personally by the shareholder and that he cannot 'recover damages merely because the company in which he is interested has suffered damage'[20]. A broader basis of assessment could permit double recovery and would overturn the rule in *Foss v Harbottle*[1] and the principle of corporate personality.

At common law the issue of an insider's liability to shareholders was long considered to be governed by the leading case of *Percival v Wright*[2]. Unaware that directors were negotiating the sale of the company's undertaking on favourable terms, certain minority shareholders approached the company's secretary about finding a purchaser for their shares. In subsequent correspondence they named their price, which was initially based on an appraisal by an independent valuer and then amended to a higher price on the basis of a fresh appraisal in offering their holding to the chairman of the board. The shares were transferred to the chairman and two other directors. When the vendor shareholders later learnt of the negotiations for the sale of the company's undertaking, they brought an action for rescission on the ground that the directors ought to have disclosed those negotiations when treating for the purchase of the shares.

The plaintiffs' counsel argued that the directors were in a fiduciary position towards the shareholders and so should have disclosed the negotiations 'in which case the plaintiffs would have retained their shares, on the chance of the

---

15. *Esso Petroleum v Mardon* [1976] 2 W.L.R.583 at 595 per Lord Denning M.R.
16. [1972] 1 W.L.R.337 at 341.
17. D.D. Prentice, 'Insider Trading' [1975] C.L.P.83 at 85.
18. See, ante, I. Liability to the company, C. Enforcement difficulties.
19. [1980] 2 All E.R.841 at 858.
20. [1982] 1 All E.R.354 at 356.
1. See, ante, I. Liability to the company, C. Enforcement difficulties.
2. [1902] 2 Ch421.

sale going through'[3]. He accepted that there was no suggestion of unfair dealing or purchase at an undervalue. It was also conceded that the directors had no duty to disclose information acquired in the ordinary course of management, such as a large unexpected profit or the discovery of a new mine. But he tried to distinguish negotiations for the sale of the undertaking by arguing that in negotiating such a sale, the directors became trustees for sale 'for the benefit of the company and the shareholders, and could not purchase the interest of an ultimate beneficiary without disclosing those negotiations'[4]. Although at law the corporate undertaking belonged to the company, in equity it belonged to the shareholders and as trustees for sale of the undertaking, it was contended that the directors could not purchase the interest of a beneficiary without full disclosure:

> 'In this respect the shareholders inter se are in the same position as partners . . . If managing partners employ an agent to sell their business, he cannot purchase the share of a sleeping partner without disclosing the fact of his employment. It does not alter the rights of the shareholders inter se, though it affects their relations to the external world'[5].

In this case, the directors' non-disclosure of the negotiations for the sale of the company's undertaking entitled the plaintiffs to set aside the sale of their shares. In contrast, the defendants argued that even if the directors were trustees for sale of the undertaking, they were not trustees for sale of the plaintiff's shares and that the principle of corporate personality was inconsistent with the plaintiffs' contention.

Swinfen Eady J. held that the purchasing directors were under no obligation to disclose to the vendor shareholders the negotiations which ultimately proved abortive. The decision was based on two grounds. First, the contrary view would place directors in the 'most invidious position'[6] of not being able to buy or sell shares without disclosing negotiations when premature disclosure could well be against the company's best interests. Secondly, there was 'no question of unfair dealing in this case'[7]. The shareholders had taken the initiative by approaching the directors and by naming their price.

It was generally accepted that the decision provided authority for the proposition[8] that no fiduciary duty is owed by a director to individual members of his company, but only to the company itself. By implication, none is owed to a person who is not a member, such as a prospective purchaser of shares in the company. Hence, on the basis of insider dealing only, a director would not be liable to the other party if he dealt without disclosing the inside information. Though a decision of first instance only, its authority has not been doubted in a reported English case[9].

The decision in *Percival v Wright* has been much criticised. The emphasis on

3. Ibid at 423.
4. Ibid.
5. Ibid at 424.
6. Ibid at 426.
7. Ibid.
8. *Report of the Company Law Committee* (Chairman Lord Justice Jenkins), Cmnd.1749 (1962), para.89 (hereinafter the '*Jenkins Report*').
9. Its correctness was assumed in *Lynall v IRC* [1968] 3 All E.R.322 at 329 and *Crabtree v Hinchcliffe* [1971] 3 All E.R.967. But see post the New Zealand case of *Coleman v Myers* in which at first instance Mahon J. held that *Percival v Wright* was wrongly decided, but the New Zealand Court of Appeal distinguished it.

the principle of corporate personality, with its 'elevation of the corporate ghost (the persona ficta) over the flesh-and-blood owners of the company'[10], has been described as 'a monument to the ability of lawyers to hypnotise themselves with their own creations'[11]. The traditional interpretation of this 'calamitous'[12] decision is also regarded as 'mystifying'[13] having regard to the statutory contract[14] whereby the company and its shareholders normally agree that designated powers are to be conferred on the board alone. Whereas it is accepted that a legal, though not contractual, relationship is in consequence created between the board and the company and is designated by equity as a fiduciary one, no corresponding legal or fiduciary relationship appears to be created between the board and shareholders[15].

However, several factors support a more restrictive interpretation than the traditional one[16]. Not only did the negotiations prove abortive, but on the question of materiality the court was 'not in fact satisfied on the evidence that the board ever intended to sell'[17] the company's undertaking. In addition, it was the shareholders who took the initiative by seeking a buyer and naming a price and there was no suggestion of unfair dealing. There were also no immediate profits for which the directors could be asked to account. Hence, a preferable interpretation is to restrict the decision in *Percival v Wright* to actions for rescission for non-disclosure, thereby leaving open the question of liability to account for insider dealing profits.

Even under its traditional interpretation, *Percival v Wright* has been distinguished where directors have, by special arrangement, assumed obligations to act for and on behalf of shareholders. In *Allen v Hyatt*[18], the Privy Council imposed a fiduciary duty on directors in favour of shareholders on the ground that the directors in question had been appointed agents of the shareholders. The directors of a company who held less than one-third of its issued capital, negotiated the sale of the company with a third party who was trying to amalgamate several companies. Representing that majority consent was necessary to effect the amalgamation and before the price was settled, the directors induced individual shareholders to give them options to purchase. After the directors had exercised these options and paid the shareholders $22,883, the company was sold for $42,156 and a substantial holding for the directors in the new company. A group of shareholders sought a declaration that the directors were trustees for all the shareholders of the profits and for an account. Approving the decisions of the Canadian courts, the Judicial Committee held that the directors were trustees of the profit for the benefit of the shareholders. Viscount Haldane L.C. stated:

> 'The appellants appeared to have been under the impression that the directors of a company were entitled in all circumstances to act as though

10. L. Loss, 'The Fiduciary Concept as Applied to Trading by Corporate "Insiders" in the United States' (1970) 33 M.L.R. 34 at 40.
11. Ibid at 40-41.
12. L.C.B. Gower, 'Investor Protection in the U.S.A.' (1952) 15 M.L.R.446 at 452
13. P.D. Finn, *Fiduciary Obligations* (1977), para.20.
14. CA 1985, s14.
15. Finn. op cit n13, supra, paras.20 and 136-142. But the courts have imposed some equitable duties on directors when they make decisions which affect the rights of shareholders inter se, Finn, op cit n13, supra, paras.118 and 144.
16. D.D. Prentice, op cit n17, p167, supra, at 84-85; T. Hadden, *Company Law and Captialism* (2nd. ed.1977) at p.255.
17. [1902] 2 Ch421 at 422.
18. (1914) 30 T.L.R.444.

they owed no duty to individual shareholders. No doubt the duty of the directors was primarily one to the company itself. It might be that in circumstances such as those of *Percival v Wright*... they could deal at arm's length with a shareholder. But the facts in the present case were widely different from those in *Percival v Wright* and their Lordships thought that the directors must here be taken to have held themselves out to the individual shareholders as acting for them on the same footing as they were acting for the company itself, that was, as agents'[19].

As the Canadian courts also found the directors were guilty of fraud, the case was not regarded as significantly qualifying *Percival v Wright*, but limited to direct dealings in which a director is placed in a fiduciary relationship by the conduct of the parties.

Another reported instance of an agency relationship is *Breiss v. Woolley*[20]. R was managing director of Company X which was licensed to manufacture and sell synthetic cream in accordance with an approved formula. Unknown to other directors and shareholders, R disregarded this formula. Having started unauthorised negotiations for the sale of the shares of X to Company Y, he was subsequently authorised by the general meeting to take the matter further with a view to completing the transaction on stated terms. Throughout the negotiations, he did not disclose that the accounts were based on dishonest trading. On discovering the fraud after completion, the purchasers brought an action for damages against a shareholder of X who had no knowledge of R's fraudulent concealment. The House of Lords held that the general meeting had appointed R as agent for the shareholders to negotiate the sale of the shares with the result that the shareholders could not disclaim responsibility for any fraudulent misrepresentation in subsequent negotiations and were liable in damages.

Hence, in circumstances where he has by his actions placed himself in a fiduciary relationship with shareholders, a director who purchased shares in his company knowing that the offeror intended to increase his offer, but without disclosing the information to shareholders, would be accountable to selling shareholders[1]. A director would be regarded as having placed himself in such a fiduciary relationship when authorised by shareholders to negotiate with the offeror on their behalf.

However, until recently, the fact that directors negotiate with a prospective bidder and recommend the terms to shareholders was regarded as insufficient to raise the implication that they have placed themselves in a fiduciary relationship with shareholders[2]. But recent developments in City practice may lead to the conclusion that in a bid situation the conduct of offeree directors is such as normally to give rise to a fiduciary duty to shareholders[3]. Under the Code, an offer should first be put to the offeree board or its advisers rather than direct to shareholders[4]. The offeree board must circulate its views on the offer to shareholders[5], be satisfied that the offeror has adequate resources to implement

19. Ibid at 445.
20. [1954] A.C.333.
1. *Weinberg and Blank on Take-overs and Mergers*, Fourth edition by M.A. Weinberg, M.V. Blank and A.L. Greystoke (1979), para.2349 (hereinafter referred to as '*Weinberg and Blank*').
2. L.C.B. Gower, *The Principles of Modern Company Law* (3rd ed.1969), pp544-545; M.A. Weinberg, *Take-overs and Amalgamations* (2nd ed.1967), p.259.
3. *Weinberg and Blank*, para.2350.
4. Code, Rule 1.
5. Ibid, Rule 25.

the bid in full[6] and obtain competent independent advice[7]. Disclosure obligations concerning the document include a requirement that shareholders must be given all the facts in ample time to make an informed judgment on the merits or demerits of the offer[8]. Whilst lacking the force of law[9], the Code can be regarded as reflecting commercial practice and the factual relationship between directors and shareholders[10].

In the event of an action for an account of insider dealing profits being brought, two other developments suggest that the courts would now take the opportunity to distinguish *Percival v Wright* on its facts or to confine the decision to its restrictive interpretation and that even if the traditional interpretation was accepted at first instance, the decision would not be followed by a higher court. In consequence, there is good reason to believe that a director or other fiduciary could be held accountable to shareholders for insider dealing profits.

First, the 'quasi-partnership' nature of some companies has been judicially recognised[11]. The leading case is *Ebrahimi v. Westbourne Galleries Ltd*[12]. Having traded as partners, N and E incorporated their carpet business and became its directors. N's son was later made a director. N and E then held 400 shares each and N's son held 200. All profits were paid as directors' fees, not dividends. Relations deteriorated, with E alleging that N and his son were in effect milking the company for their own benefit. After his removal from office by the votes of N and his son, E ceased to participate in the management or profits of the company. He presented a petition both for the alternative remedy to winding-up in cases of oppression[13] and for a winding up order on the just and equitable ground[14]. At first instance, Plowman J. held that there were not sufficient grounds for the alternative remedy, but that E was entitled to a winding-up order. This order was reversed by the Court of Appeal, but restored by a unanimous House of Lords. It held that whilst a director must normally accept his lawful exclusion from office, an order under the just and equitable ground was available when there was some 'special underlying obligation' of his fellow members in good faith or confidence that he should participate in management as long as the business continued. In this case, it could be inferred that, after their long period in partnership, the formation of the company was agreed on the basis that the character of the association would, as a matter of personal relation and good faith, remain the same. Lord Wilberforce stated that the just and equitable provision enabled the court:

> 'to subject the exercise of legal rights to equitable considerations; considerations, that is, of a personal character arising between one individual and another, which may make it unjust, or inequitable, to insist on legal rights, or to exercise them in a particular way.
>
> It would be impossible, and wholly undesirable, to define the circumstances in which these considerations may arise. Certainly the fact that a company is a small one, or a private company, is not enough. There are

---

6. Ibid, Rule 1.
7. Ibid, Rule 3.
8. Ibid, Rule 23.
9. See, ante, Chapter 2. The Regulatory Framework.
10. *Weinberg and Blank*, para.2350.
11. B.A.K. Rider, 'Partnership law and its impact on "domestic companies"' (1979) 38 C.L.J.148.
12. [1973] A.C.360; [1972] 2 All E.R.492.
13. CA 1948, s210. This section was repealed by CA 1980, s88 and Sch4.
14. CA 1985, s517(g).

very many of these where the association is a purely commercial one, of which it can safely be said that the basis of association is adequately and exhaustively laid down in the articles. The super-imposition of equitable considerations requires something more, which typically may include one, or probably more, of the following elements:
(i) an association formed or continued on the basis of a personal relationship, involving mutual confidence – this element will often be found where a pre-existing partnership has been converted into a limited company;
(ii) an agreement, or understanding, that all, or some (for there may be "sleeping members") of the shareholders shall participate in the conduct of the business;
(iii) restriction upon the transfer of the members' interest in the company – so that if confidence is lost, or one member is removed from management, he cannot take out his stake and go elsewhere'[15].

It is not clear whether the principles laid down in *Ebrahimi* are of wider application than to winding-up on the just and equitable ground. But they are open to the interpretation that in their dealings with shareholders, directors will be expected to observe standards of good faith characteristic of a fiduciary's[16].

The second development was that in *Coleman v. Myers*[17] the New Zealand Court of Appeal declined to follow *Percival v Wright*. The plaintiffs, who had been minority shareholders in a small private company, had reluctantly sold their holdings to A, the company's managing director. Having acquired complete control, A liquidated some of the company's assets and distributed the proceeds as a dividend which more than reimbursed his acquisition expenses. The plaintiffs alleged that A and his father, who was company chairman, had obtained control by exploiting inside information about the true value of the company's assets and making fraudulent and careless misrepresentations about their intentions once they had acquired control. Their counsel argued that *Percival v Wright* was distinguishable on the facts, did not reflect current standards of directors' duties and, moreover, was wrongly decided. It had not been expressly approved in any Commonwealth decision and American developments were contrasted. The defence emphasised that *Percival v Wright* had not been questioned in any decided case. Whilst accepting that a director was under a fiduciary duty to the company not to use inside information improperly, it was contended that no such duty was owed to each shareholder individually.

At first instance, Mahon J. found for the defendants on all grounds because he considered the information was immaterial. Hence, his views were obiter. But he was of opinion that *Percival v Wright* was 'incorrectly decided'[18] since

'it was not necessary for the plaintiffs in *Percival v Wright* to assert that the fiduciary position brought into operation by the negotiations for purchase of the shareholders' shares was in any specific category. The judge seems to me to have not considered the further question whether the approach by the plaintiff shareholders to sell their shares to the directors did not create a fiduciary position of a more general kind in that the

15. [1972] 2 All E.R.492 at 500.
16. D.D. Prentice, *The Companies Act 1980* (1980), para.294.
17. [1977] 2 N.Z.L.R.225 and 298; B.A.K. Rider, '*Percival v Wright – Per Incuriam*' (1977) 40 M.L.R.471, and 'A Special Relationship on the Special Facts' (1978) 41 M.L.R.585.
18. [1977] 2 N.Z.L.R.225 at 274 and 278.

shareholders were now dealing with potential purchasers who alone had access to the knowledge of a material fact which, unknown to the shareholders, controlled the value of the shares which they desired to sell'[19].

The fiduciary duty owed by the directors to the plaintiff shareholders was thus based on the latter's lack of access to material information. But this wide view was rejected on appeal.

Allowing the appeal and awarding damages, the New Zealand Court of Appeal held that the respondent directors owed fiduciary duties to the shareholders. Referring to the special facts of the case, these duties were found to arise from the family character of the company, the position of father and son in the family and in the company, their high degree of inside knowledge and the way in which they went about the take-over and persuasion of shareholders. Accordingly, the directors were obliged (a) not to make deliberately or carelessly misleading statements to shareholders on matters material to the proposed dealing and (b) to disclose material matters as to which they knew or had reason to believe that the shareholder whom they were trying to persuade to sell was inadequately informed. In a take-over, asset-backing was a material factor. On the facts, breach of fiduciary duty and causation were established. The court also held that the respondent directors were in breach of their duty to exercise reasonable care when recommending their acceptance of the offer and that fraudulent misrepresentations of A had been established.

Although prepared to accept that *Percival v Wright* was correctly decided on its facts, the Court of Appeal restricted its application, stating that 'the view of some textbook writers . . . that a company director, while owing a fiduciary duty to his company will never have such a duty in respect of the shareholders'[20] was misconceived. Rather, Woodhouse J. commented:

> 'The standard of conduct required from a director in relation to dealings with a shareholder will differ depending upon all the surrounding circumstances and the nature of the responsibility which in a real and practical sense the director has assumed towards the shareholder. In the one case there may be a need to provide an explicit warning and a great deal of information concerning the proposed transaction. In another, there may be no need to speak at all. There will be intermediate situations. It is, however, an area of the law where the Courts can and should find some practical means of giving effect to sensible and fair principles of commercial morality in the cases that come before them; and while it may not be possible to lay down any general test as to when the fiduciary duty will arise for a company director or to prescribe the exact conduct which will always discharge it when it does, there are nevertheless some factors that will usually have an influence upon a decision one way or another. They include . . . dependence upon information and advice, the existence of a relationship of confidence, the significance of some particular transaction for the parties, and . . . the extent of any positive action taken by or on behalf of the director or directors to promote it'[1].

19. Ibid at 275.
20. [1977] 2 N.Z.L.R.225 at 323-324 per Woodhouse J.
1. Ibid at 326.

Even when a fiduciary relationship is found, it is by no means clear whether damages can be awarded when rescission is not possible. The majority view[2] was that damages could be awarded for breach of fiduciary duty. Cooke J. remarked that 'since the fusion of common law and equity and the twentieth century developments in the law of negligence any argument to the contrary would be of unattractive technicality'[3]. But in a subsequent English decision[4], the authorities on which he based his remark were dismissed as inconclusive on this matter. Moreover, compensation in equity is essentially of a restitutionary nature and 'considerations of causation, foreseeability and remoteness do not readily enter into the matter'[5]. In *Coleman v Myers*, the claim for compensation for breach of fiduciary duty was in the alternative to one based on the tort of negligence.

The view that directors may owe fiduciary duties to shareholders even in the absence of an agency relationship also seems to be supported by inspectors appointed by the Department to investigate the affairs of the First National Re-Investment Trust Ltd. In their 1974 interim report[6], the inspectors considered it was implicit in the disclosure obligations imposed on companies by the CA 1948 and the CA 1967 that 'the directors should supply to shareholders all the information concerning the company's affairs which the shareholders might reasonably expect to receive'[7]. *Percival v Wright* was expressly distinguished. They also criticised a director for sending to shareholders circulars about a rights issue which did not disclose all the facts.

As fiduciary duties are not confined to directors, it would also be open to the courts to impose liability on other fiduciaries. Hence, when the relevant factors were found to exist, a substantial shareholder could be held liable to another shareholder.

The failure of British courts to establish an insider's liability to shareholders contrasted with the position in the US[8]. Under the so-called 'majority' or 'strict' rule, a position similar to the rule laid down by the traditional interpretation of *Percival v Wright* was applied in most jurisdictions. Rejecting this approach, some courts followed a 'minority' or 'fiduciary' rule which held insiders to fiduciary standards in their dealings with shareholders and thus required full disclosure of all material facts. In what became the most widely followed rule, the remainder achieved a similar result by finding 'special circumstances' and applying the 'special facts' doctrine outlined by the Supreme Court in *Strong v Repide*[9]. However, these common law developments were overtaken by legislation.

Even if the British courts were to follow the preferable approach adopted by the New Zealand Court of Appeal, the protection afforded by the application of equitable principles is subject to limitations. It appears to be restricted to transactions in which the parties are in direct personal contact, termed 'face-to-face' transactions. It is also difficult to see how a relationship of confidence or dependence could arise between an insider and a third party who is not a member. Hence, the protection of equity would not extend to a third party who

2. This view was supported by Cooke and Casey JJ.
3. [1977] 2 N.Z.L.R.298 at 359.
4. *English v Dedham Vale Properties Ltd.* [1978] 1 W.L.R.93.
5. Ibid at 111 per Slade J.
6. *First Re-Investment Trust Ltd., Nelson Financial Trust Ltd., English and Scottish Unit Trust Holdings Ltd.,* Interim Report by D.C.H. Hirst, Q.C. and R.N.D. Langdon, FCA (1974).
7. Ibid at p.75.
8. L. Loss, *Securities Regulation* (2nd ed.1961; Supp.1969), Vol.III at pp.1446-1448.
9. 213 U.S.419 (1909).

·purchases shares from a selling insider[10]. Accordingly, legislation is required to lay down the principles of liability and the relief to be granted.

When measured against the standards set by the traditional view of the law on insider liability, a radical approach was proposed by the Jenkins Committee. It recommended[11] that a director of a company who, in any transaction relating to the securities of his company or any other company in the same group, makes improper use of a particular piece of confidential information which might be expected materially to affect the value of those securities, should be liable to compensate a person (whether or not he is a shareholder) who suffers from his action in so doing unless that information was known to that person. The Committee acknowledged[12] that it might well be very difficult for the other party to establish that he was dealing with a director (especially because of the method of settling transactions through the Stock Exchange). It could also be difficult for the other party to establish that the director dealt on the basis of inside information. Nevertheless, it considered a remedy should be provided.

This recommendation underlined the difficulties associated with fashioning a civil remedy for insider dealing. Until October 1986, transactions on the Stock Exchange were made through the agency of brokers with a jobber[13]. Jobbers acted as principals. Even when bargains were matched, there was not contractual nexus between the parties. If recovery were based on privity with an insider, it would thus have been to the benefit of jobbers. Yet such recovery would normally have conferred an arbitrary windfall on jobbers since in actively traded shares orders were merely channeled through them.

However, the difficulties were not confined to the consequences of the single capacity system and others arise with its replacement by the competing market maker system. Under the latter, any member of the Stock Exchange can act as jobber and broker and become a registered market maker. As a result, a member firm can now deal as a principal, as an agent or, subject to the client's agreement in accordance with Rule 312, as both.

On exchanges which permit dual capacity[14], transactions in actively traded shares can be very difficult to match. When the matching of transactions enables a person to show privity with the insider, recovery on that basis means that he receives an arbitrary windfall as a result of an entirely fortuitous event and others dealing at the same time with non-insiders receive nothing. On the other hand, recovery in favour of all those dealing during a specified period could result in astronomical awards against an insider.

Another difficulty is that of establishing loss or damage from insider dealing[15]. A common characteristic of both face-to-face transactions and open market transactions involving insiders is the superior information held by the insider. Though there is some scope for investigation and bargaining, a further feature of most face-to-face transactions is the dependence of one party on the other for information[16]. Notions of value will mainly be based on knowledge of

10. Prentice, op cit n17, p167, supra, at 85.
11. *Jenkins Report*, Cmnd.1749 (1962), para.99(b).
12. Ibid, para.89.
13. The implications of the jobbing system are discussed by (a) Justice, *Insider Trading* (1972), para.34; (b) Prentice, op cit n17, p167, supra, at 100 and (c) City Company Law Committee, *Insider Dealing* (1976), para.30.
14. W.H. Painter, *The Federal Securities Code and Corporate Disclosure* (1979), pp.183, 193-194.
15. See ante, Chapter 1. Introduction, III. Theoretical considerations, A. Efficiency issues, 2. Effects of insider dealing.
16. A. Bromberg and L. Lowenfels, *Securities Fraud and Commodities Fraud* (1979), 4.1.

the company's financial results or condition and of any market in its securities. Where one party is closer to the company or the market, the other depends on him for the information. The other may thus be able to prove reliance in the sense of a causal link between his conduct and that of the insider, though an alternative approach is to waive or presume such a requirement when the materiality of information is satisfied. However, a non-insider dealing on the open market will not normally be able to show a causal connection, as distinct from a temporal one, between his decision to deal and the presence of the insider in the market. The prospects of his being able to prove that his transactions were induced by the insider are minimal. Nevertheless, it is misconceived to conclude that an insider should be entitled to retain his profit.

B. Legislative proposals

Rather than attempting to develop a more flexible basis of recovery than privity, subsequent legislative proposals have marked a gradual retreat from providing a civil remedy to non-insiders in open-market transactions. The Companies Bill 1973[17] would have provided a civil remedy where a person in possession of inside information deals or procures another person to deal in the securities to which the inside information relates. In that event, the insider would have been liable to compensate any other party to the transaction who was not in possession of the information for any loss sustained by that party by reason of any difference between the price at which the securities were dealt with and the likely price if that information had been generally available. In market transactions a preferable way of expressing the value of securities would have been by reference to the price set by the market when it had absorbed the inside information. However, the 1973 Bill appears to have been restricted to transactions in which the parties were in privity. As no reference was made to jobbers, it was open to interpretation as enabling jobbers to recover in respect of stock kept on their books. Situations in which the parties were not in privity were left to the criminal law.

A more restrictive approach was proposed by the Companies Bill 1978. Apart from criminal liability in the case of Stock Exchange transactions, the 1978 Bill would have provided for criminal and civil liability, including rescission and damages, in respect of its requirement for disclosure of insider status in private deals[18]. In the event of an insider's failure to make such disclosure, the other party would have been given the same rights as to the rescission of the transaction as he would have had if he had entered into the transaction in reliance on a fraudulent representation made by the dealer[19]. For a person entitled to rescission or who, apart from any rule of law preventing rescission from being available in particular circumstances, would have been so entitled, the alternative of damages was also proposed[20]. Whilst the ability to rescind arose from non-disclosure of insider status, the measure of damages was calculated in terms of any loss sustained by reason of any difference between the

---

17. Companies Bill 1973, cl 15(3).
This provision is discussed by: The Law Society's Standing Committee on Company Law, *Memorandum on Clauses 1 to 19 of the Companies Bill* (1974), pp10-11 and Prentice, op cit n17, p167, supra at 101. Civil liability to the other party to the transaction is also discussed by the City Company Law Committee, op cit n13(c), p175, supra, paras.30-31.
18. See, ante, Chapter 3. Criminal Liability.
19. Companies Bill 1978, cl 61(1).
20. Ibid, cl 61(2).

transaction price and the price which the parties might have been expected to agree if any information available to the insider and likely materially to affect their price had been available to the other party[1]. These civil remedies were further stated not to deprive a person of a remedy for misrepresentation or breach of contract otherwise available to him[2]. The unsatisfactory nature of this proposal has already been discussed[3].

The CA 1980 marked the abandonment of any attempt to provide a civil remedy[4]. The reasons stated were the impossibility of linking buyers and sellers in a meaningful way and that insider dealing constitutes a wrong against the public rather than the individual. The imposition of a substantial fine, which was paid to the Exchequer for the benefit of the public, was seen as consistent with the public nature of the wrong[5]. However, exclusive reliance on criminal enforcement for the benefit of the public overlooks the consideration that an action for recovery for the private benefit of investors can also serve an important public purpose. Indeed, the government indicated that it was not opposed to sensible, workable civil remedies[6].

C. Comparative note on the US

The American Law Institute's Federal Securities Code[7] makes extensive provision for civil liability. A right of action for insider dealing arises where the defendant sells or buys a security for the issuer, if he knows a fact of special significance with respect to the issuer or the security that is not generally available unless (a) he reasonably believes that the fact is generally available or (b) if the other party to the transaction or his agent is identified that (i) he reasonably believes that that person knows it or (ii) that person in fact knows it from the insider or otherwise[8]. 'Insider' is broadly defined to mean (a) issuer, (b) a director or officer, or a person controlling, controlled by or under common control with the issuer, (c) a person whose relationship or former relationship to the issuer gives or gave him access to a fact of special significance about the issuer or the security that is not generally available[9] and (d) a person who learns such a fact from a person specified in this definition of insider, including a person specified in (d), unless it is found that that treatment would be inequitable on consideration of the circumstances and purposes of the Code[10]. Not confined to situations in which the parties are in privity, civil liability applies whether or not transactions are effected in the market.

Various defences are specified. A defence of correction is available when the defendant proves that the misrepresentation or omission was corrected in a

1. Ibid.
2. Ibid, cl61(3).
3. See, ante, Chapter 3. Criminal Liability.
4. IDA 1985, s8 expressly states that no transaction is void or voidable by reason only that it was entered into in breach of the insider dealing prohibitions.
5. Parliamentary Debates, Vol.979, No.125 (26th February, 1980), col.1276
6. Ibid, col.1275.
7. American Law Institute, Federal Securities Code (1980). This was drafted in the form of a Bill.
8. Federal Securities Code, s1703 (a) and (b). This provision is drafted by reference to ss1602(a)(1), 1602(b)(1) (1) (A) and 1613. S1603 deals with insider trading and a counterpart provision, s1703, imposes civil liability. The comment to s1603 describes it as 'the substantive codification of Rule 10b-5 as applicable to insider trading'.
9. By the Federal Securities Code, s1603(c). S1603 applies to an insider specified in part (c) of the definition of insider only to the extent that he knows a fact of special significance by virtue of his occupying that status.
10. American Law Institute, Federal Securities Code, s1603(b).

manner reasonably designed to bring the correction to the attention of the investing public[11]. But this defence is not available against a plaintiff who bought or sold (a) before the facts as corrected became generally available or (b) in justifiable reliance on the misrepresentation or omission. With regard to the plaintiff's knowledge, a defendant also has a defence if he proves that (a) the plaintiff bought or sold with knowledge of the relevant facts or documents or (b) the alleged falsity was obvious[12]. With regard to the defendant's conduct, a person also has a defence when he proves that at the time of the transaction he reasonably did not believe that there was a misrepresentation or violation[13]. The standard of reasonableness specified is that required of a prudent man under the circumstances in the conduct of his own affairs[14]. Placing the onus of proof on defendants operates as harshly on them as the contrary would on plaintiffs. But it can be supported by the consideration that the Code thereby reduced the risk of proof to those whom it seeks to protect.

However, in terms of the measure of damages, an important distinction is drawn according to whether or not transactions are effected in the market. In a transaction not effected in the market, the defendant is liable for rescission or damages[15]. Where the plaintiff is a buyer, the measure of damages is the amount that he paid (with interest) less (1) the value of the security as of the end of a reasonable period after (a) the time when all facts of special significance became generally available or (b) with respect to a plaintiff who proves that he did not know those facts until a later time or a plaintiff who the defendant proves knew those facts at an earlier time, that time and less (2) any return (with interest) that he received on the security[16]. An analogous provision applies when the plaintiff is a seller[17]. Special provision is made in respect of subsequent transactions by the plaintiff or defendant in the securities in question[18]. The rescission and damages formulae are designed to produce the mathematical equivalent[19] in order to minimise troublesome questions with respect to election and waiver of remedies and hence reduce any 'gamesmanship' factor which might be involved where the plaintiff fails to resell or purchase after learning all facts of special significance, thereby getting a 'free ride' at the defendant's expense[20]. In some circumstances, a defendant may be relieved of liability if he can prove that an increase or decrease in price would have

---

11. Ibid, s1703(d).
12. Ibid, s1703(e).
13. Ibid, s1703(f).
14. Ibid, s1703(g).
15. Ibid, s1703(a).
16. Ibid, s1708(a)(1).
17. Ibid, s1708(a)(2).
18. Ibid, s1708.
19. An illustration is given in American Law Institute, Federal Securities Code, Tentative Draft No.2 (1973), Comment 5(b) to Code Section 1402:
'S fraudulently sells to B at 100 and does not later replace his position by a purchase. B still holds the security. When the facts become known, the market falls to 40. B may seek either rescission . . . or damages . . . or he may plead in the alternative. Just before entry of decision, the market is 20. If B opts for damages, he gets 60 (100 minus 40). If he opts for rescission on tender of the security, he gets (interest and income aside) 100 minus the post-discovery market drop of 20 (40 minus 20), which is 80 but, since he gives up a security then worth 20, he gets 60 net, which is precisely what he would have received in damages; it makes no difference if he resold the security (at whatever price) after the facts became known and tendered an identical security that he repurchased in the market (at whatever price) since he gets the same credit of 20, which is the security's market value on the date of decision'.
20. American Law Institute, Federal Securities Code, Tentative Draft No.2 (1973), Comment 5(b) to Code Section 1402.

occurred in any event and so was not attributable to his conduct. Thus, where the plaintiff is a buyer, he can recover, on tender of the security, his purchase price, less any decrease that the defendant proves to have occurred in the market or other available price of a security since a reasonable period after (a) the time when all facts of special significance became generally available or (b) with respect to a plaintiff who proves that he did not know those facts until a later time or a plaintiff who the defendant proves knew those facts at an earlier time, that time[1]. A similar approach is adopted when the plaintiff is a seller[2].

Unlike transactions not effected in the market, the compensatory function of a civil remedy is rejected as inappropriate in respect of market transactions. In a market transaction, which is defined as a transaction 'effected in a manner which would make the matching of buyers and sellers substantially fortuitous'[3], the defendant is liable for damages to all persons who buy or sell securities of the same class between (a) the day when he first unlawfully sells or buys and (b) the day when all facts of special significance became generally available[4]. But an upper limit on the award of damages is imposed[5]. Provision is also made for a proration of damages procedure[6].

The creation of a wide right of action in market transactions raises complex problems relating to damages[7]. In contrast to criminal penalties which can be tailored to an offender's circumstances, the principles governing damages have traditionally required that quantum be computed arithmetically. Yet a right of recovery in favour of all those dealing during a specified period could result in astronomical liability and have disruptive economic consequences, particularly when awarded against a large entity. Though the award of large damages is desirable from a deterrent point of view, the creation of a right of action would nevertheless appear to be subject to the need to overcome the problem of astronomical recovery.

There are various alternatives[8]. One is not to permit rights of action outside privity in the contractual sense. On the Stock Exchange prior to October 1986, this would have been a device to protect jobbers rather than create a remedy in favour of investors who turned out to have dealt with insiders. Even where dual capacity is allowed, this requires 'tracing' and results in a random selection of plaintiffs. A second alternative is to permit wide rights of action, but limit the extent to which they can be vindicated by representative actions. Whilst designed to enable those who had sustained large damages to sue and thus permit recovery of substantial losses, such a limitation would probably have the effect of severely restricting the occasions when such actions would be brought. A third alternative is to permit wide rights of action with representative actions in aid, but to place arbitrary limits on the amount of total recovery. Though minimising the risk of disruptive economic consequences, this can reduce the amount recoverable by each individual plaintiff below that recoverable under accepted principles of private law. A fourth alternative is to permit wide rights

1. American Law Institute, Federal Securities Code, s1703(h)(1).
2. Ibid, s1703(h)(2).
3. Ibid, s1703(b).
4. Ibid.
5. Ibid. The assessment of damages is discussed post.
6. Ibid, s1711.
7. In the Canadian context these are discussed by L.H. Leigh, 'Securities Regulation: Problems in Relation to Sanctions', p.513 at pp561-563 in Consumer and Corporate Affairs Canada, *Proposals for a Securities Market Law for Canada*, Vol.3 Background papers (1979).
8. Leigh, op cit n7, supra, at p.562; W.H. Painter, *The Federal Securities Code and Corporate Disclosure* (1974) pp183, 193-194.

of action with representative actions in aid and without limits on recovery. But this runs the risk of astronomical liability.

The choice of alternatives depends on the emphasis to be placed on the public aspects of an action for damages, namely, its deterrent purpose. As the US experience indicates that agency enforcement is inadequate to enforce observance of the securities laws, any preference for leaving a matter such as insider dealing in the market to criminal and administrative proceedings is outweighed by the consideration that this can be unwise from the enforcement point of view[9]. This is borne out by the US experience which suggests that civil actions are required as a deterrent measure. In Britain, the creation of an extensive civil action with regard to insider dealing is justified by the factor that this is an area where the problems are great. Wide rights of action in other fields, such as manipulation in general, are thus a separate issue.

After eliminating the first and fourth alternatives due to the disadvantages attached, the choice can be reduced to the second and third alternatives. Though the second permits an action by those who have suffered large losses and wish to bring an action, it is likely that few will individually sustain losses large enough to justify complex and lengthy proceedings. Hence, an emphasis on deterrence points to the choice of the third alternative, subject to provision against astronomical recovery. Nevertheless, in the absence of the contingency fee and entrepreneurial attitudes in the legal profession, it is unrealistic to imagine that civil actions would be brought as frequently as in the US[10]. The greater the resistance to the provision of incentives to make proceedings rewarding to investors and their legal advisers, the heavier will be the reliance on the involvement of the regulatory agency in enforcement.

The approach of the Federal Securities Code to the problem of astronomical recovery in transactions effected in the market is to impose an upper limit to damages. First, the Code limits damages by providing that the measure of damages is reduced to the extent that the defendant proves that his violation did not 'cause' the loss[11]. Cause is defined in the following terms:

> 'A loss is "caused" by specified conduct to the extent that the conduct (a) was a substantial factor in producing the loss and (b) might reasonably have been expected to result in loss of the kind suffered'[12].

Secondly, the defendant's liability is further limited to the extent of his own trading. Thus, where he is a buyer, he is liable for the difference between the amount that he paid and the value of the securities purchased determined when all the facts of special significance become generally available[13]. An analogous provision applies when the defendant is a seller.

However, it has been doubted[14] whether these limitations, when combined with the proration of damages procedure, provide adequate incentives for plaintiffs to bring actions to recover damages. Under the proration machinery[15], the defendant notifies the court when there are multiple claims against him so that these can be stayed and consolidated. When the aggregate damages

9. Leigh, op cit n7, p179, supra, at pp562-563.
10. The US class rule is extensively discussed by Leigh, op cit n7, p179, supra, at pp564-581.
11. American Law Institute, Federal Securities Code, s1708(b)(2).
12. Ibid, s220.
13. Ibid, s1708(b)(3).
14. Painter, op cit n8, p179, supra, at p.215.
15. American Law Institute, Federal Securities Code, s1711

awarded exceed the upper limits, the damages may then be awarded pro rata among members of the plaintiff class. For the plaintiff who sustains large losses, proration has the disadvantage of requiring him to share the benefit of recovery with other plaintiffs whose claims are small and who are plaintiffs solely due to extensive class action procedures. It is unclear how often this result is likely to occur. But recognising that recovery by an individual plaintiff may be relatively small where the class is very large, the Code provides that proration among plaintiffs is required 'to the extent that the trial court determines that the expense of making the proration is warranted in relation to the amount that would be awarded to individual plaintiffs (or members of the class or sub-class)'[16]. When the expense is great and proration is not warranted, the Code permits the damages to be paid to the issuer if the issuer is not a defendant and where the trial court determines that under the circumstances, including the degree of ownership of the issuer by the defendants, that an award to the issuer would not be inequitable[17]. This provision bears some resemblance to the relief granted by the district court on remand in *Texas Gulf Sulphur* where the damages were required to be placed in an interest bearing account for three or more years for disposal on the court's directions upon application by the SEC or other interested person or on the court's own motion[18]. Any balance was to become the property of Texas Gulf Sulphur. The Code also empowers a court to distribute the fund to the Securities Investor Protection Corporation[19]. This alternative could prove useful where proration is not warranted and payment to the issuer is undesirable.

Although the Code's aim is to deprive insiders of their profits and to deter them from further insider dealing, it is doubted[20] whether its provisions are a substantial deterrent to those who might otherwise deal on inside information. The insider's liability is limited to the extent of his own dealing and in transactions effected in the market, proration will reduce recovery by an individual plaintiff where the class is large and may result in payment of the fund to the issuer or SIPC. In that event, the plaintiff's incentive for bringing proceedings is restricted to possible recovery of his legal fees[1]. Insofar as the incentives of potential plaintiffs are reduced, the provisions lose their deterrent effect because enforcement then depends upon actions by the SEC or criminal proceedings, which require reference to the Justice Department[2] and are subject to resource constraints.

On the basis of the Code's deterrent function in relation to market transactions, a suggested alternative[3], which also takes account of the need to avoid astronomical awards, is to strengthen the deterrent effect by providing for treble damages in the court's discretion. For this a precedent exists in US anti-trust laws. Except when the plaintiff class is small, this will not significantly increase an individual plaintiff's incentive to bring proceedings. But the possibility of treble damages being awarded may deter those who might otherwise deal on inside information. It is doubted whether the variation

16. Ibid, s1711(j)(1).
17. Ibid, s1711(j)(2).
18. *SEC v Texas Gulf Sulphur Co.*, 312 F.Supp77, 93 (S.D.N.Y.1970), aff'd in part and remanded in part 446 F.2d.1301 (2d.Cir.), cert. denied, 404 U.S.1005 (1971).
19. American Law Institute, Federal Securities Code, s1711(j)(3).
20. Painter, op cit n8, p179, supra, at pp216-217.
1. American Law Institute, Federal Securities Code, s1723(d).
2. Ibid, s1821(h).
3. Painter, op cit n8, p179, supra, at p.217.

permitted by the Code in the defined measure of damages[4] would extend to treble damages, particularly given the express prohibition on punitive damages[5].

Although the problem of astronomical recovery can be overcome by placing an upper limit on damages and the US experience suggests that civil actions are required as a deterrent measure, the creation of wide rights of action will not in itself constitute a deterrent to persons who would otherwise deal on inside information. The efficacy of such substantive provisions is dependent upon effective enforcement. An unfortunate consequence of the imposition of an upper limit to damages, when combined with the proration machinery, can be to diminish the incentives of potential plaintiffs. When aggregate losses are large but the loss to each individual is small, enforcement is discouraged. Hence, there is a need to devise methods of aggregating claims and to make it rewarding for potential plaintiffs and their legal advisers to bring proceedings. Other alternatives are to confer a statutory right of action by regulatory agency or to facilitate both private actions and actions by a regulatory agency.

In considering means of aggregating claims, the US experience is again instructive because the device of the US class action[6] is the most advanced technique in this context. But its application to claims for damages has been particularly controversial[7]. Though regarded in some quarters as the only

4. American Law Institute, Federal Securities Code, s1723(e).
5. Ibid, s1723(b).
6. The basic scheme of the rule was followed in the proposed Uniform Class Actions Rule adopted by the National Conference of Commissioners on Uniform State Laws in 1976 and is cited in part and outlined by Leigh, op cit n7, p179, supra, at pp565-566. Rule 23 provides in part:
'(a) Prerequisites to a Class Action. One or more members of a class may sue or be sued as representative parties on behalf of all only if (1) the class is so numerous that joinder of all members is impracticable, (2) there are questions of law or fact common to the class, (3) the claims or defences of the representative parties are typical of the claims or defences of the class, and (4) the representative parties will fairly and adequately protect the interests of the class.
(b) Class Actions Maintainable. An action may be maintained as a class action if the prerequisites of subdivision (a) are satisfied; and in addition (1) the prosecution of separate actions by or against individual members of the class would create a risk of (A) inconsistent or varying adjudications with respect to individual members of the class which would establish incompatible standards of conduct for the party opposing the class, or
(B) adjudications with respect to individual members of the class which would as a practical matter be dispositive of the interests of the other members not parties to the adjudications, or substantially impair or impede their ability to protect their interests; or
(2) the party opposing the class has acted or refused on grounds generally applicable to the class, thereby making appropriate final injunctive relief or corresponding declaratory relief with respect to the class as a whole;
or
(3) the court finds that the questions of law or fact common to the members of the class predominate over any questions affecting only individual members, and that a class action is superior to other available methods for the fair and efficient adjudication of the controversy. The matters pertinent to the findings include: (A) the interest of members of the class in individually controlling the prosecution or defence of separate actions; (B) the extent and nature of any litigation concerning the controversy already commenced by or against members of the class; (C) the desirability or undesirability of concentrating the litigation of the claims as the particular forum; (D) the difficulties likely to be encountered in the management of a class action'.
The rule also provides for a determination by the court, conditional or final, whether the action is to be maintained as a class action. The court is to direct to the members of the class the best notice practicable under the circumstances, including individual notice to all members who can be identified through reasonable effort. Subsection (c)(2) provides:
'The notice shall advise each member that (A) the court will exclude them from the class if he so requests by a specified date; (B) the judgment, whether favourable or not, will include all members who do not request exclusion and (C) any member who does not request exclusion may, if he so desires, enter an appearance through his Counsel'.
7. This discussion of the US class action draws on Leigh, op cit n7, p179 supra, at pp564-581.

means of redressing breaches of securities legislation, critics argue that the economic disruption consequent upon astronomical recovery indicates the folly of allowing huge actions by plaintiffs whose individual claims are small and who would never have sued but for extensive class action procedures. The class action is also seen as lending itself to blackmailing settlements. In addition, it is argued that if the function of the class action is deterrent, the appropriate response is either (a) to increase the criminal penalties and not rely on the class action or (b) to abandon the class action in favour of governmental action.

There are several issues. One is whether the class action should be viewed primarily as an instrument of public redress or one of private redress. There is no absolute exclusivity because an action essentially for the benefit of private plaintiffs can also serve an important public purpose. Though originating as an instrument of private redress, the US class action attained its real significance as a regulatory device in the public interest. If public redress is the desired result, there are further issues of what are the lessons of the US experience and of whether, in the light of that experience, another mode of public redress should be sought leaving the class action as a procedure in aid of private right. If the class action is viewed as an instrument of private redress, there remains the issue of its drafting.

These issues have been extensively discussed. Whilst there have been some notable exceptions, a US Senate report[8] found that most class actions involved classes small enough to render actions manageable and to make individual notice to class members possible. In those cases, the procedure was effective. But it considered that an emphasis on the protection of the interests of individual class members hindered class actions on behalf of large numbers of consumers with meritorious claims too small to support individual suits. Hence, other valid ends of consumer class actions, such as the prevention of unjust enrichment and deterrence, were frustrated. It concluded that legislation was needed to facilitate the use of the class action as an instrument to deprive defendants of unjust enrichment. There is also judicial recognition[9] that there are problems where wrongs have given rise to large numbers of individual losses, yet few such losses render individual actions for redress practicable. But this led the court to recommend consideration of the creation of an agency to vindicate consumer rights and express a preference for the injunction rather than damages as a remedy. As the Senate report did not consider in detail the consequences of its recommendation, a preferable approach is that deterrence can be provided for in the normal class action or by criminal injunctive or other proceedings.

As a mechanism for enforcing private rights, the US rule as drawn has numerous advantages. In combining claims, it results in a saving of judicial time. Whilst persons sharing some elements of common interest can finance expensive litigation, others who do not want to come into the class can opt out if they wish. The opting-out device means that persons who are ill-informed or ignorant of the ways in which their rights may be vindicated may be joined in the action. Yet the action can only be certified when the class action is a manageable and practical device.

The US class action thus provides a useful precedent for the development of a representative action against insiders in respect of transactions effected in the market. Yet as with liability to the company, the incentives of potential plaintiffs

8. Staff of U.S. Senate Commerce Committee, 93d Cong., 2d Sess; Class Action Study (1974), cited by Leigh, op cit n7, p179, supra, at pp567-576.
9. *Eisen v Carlisle and Jacquelin* 94 S.Ct.2140 (1973), aff'g 479 F.2d.1005 (2d.Cir.1970).

and their legal advisers are restricted by the system of costs[10]. It would thus be necessary to supplement the representative action with one brought by a regulatory agency to vindicate private rights. It has been seen that various factors support the involvement of a regulatory agency in enforcement[11]. A representative action by a regulatory agency could be made subject to the agency satisfying the court that it has been requested to take proceedings by the persons whose rights it vindicates and that such proceedings are in the public interest. Relevant heads of public interest could include the nature and extent of the insider dealing, the amount recoverable by individual plaintiffs, the requirements of deterrence and the availability of alternative machinery. But a rule would be needed to deal with the problem of overlap in the event of actions being brought both privately and by a regulatory agency.

As the same conduct could attract an action by other investors and an action by the insider's company, it is also necessary to consider the problem of double recovery. Express provisions are required as otherwise recovery could turn on who sued first. Thus, where a seller had successfully brought an action against an insider, it could be open to an insider to defend a subsequent action by the company on the ground that his profit has been extinguished. Though double recovery operates harshly against an insider, it strengthens the deterrent effect of the law. The Federal Securities Code contains a safeguard against double recovery by providing[12] that the profit recoverable under the short-swing profits rule is reduced by damages, interest or costs paid by the defendant to sellers or buyers pursuant to (1) a judgment in a claim under the Code provision[13] imposing civil liability or a comparable claim under state or foreign law or (2) settlement of such a claim if the defendant proves that the settlement was not collusive. But this safeguard can be distinguished on the basis that the short-swing profits rule imposes liability irrespective of whether inside information has in fact been used in trading. The problem of double recovery thus reinforces the importance of imposing upper limits on recovery and points to the need to devise a procedure for determining the proportions in which the company and other investors should share in recovery.

III. BREACH OF CONFIDENCE

Restrictions on the use of information divulged in confidence may afford a basis for protecting inside information[14]. Apart from cases where a contract expressly stipulates a confidential relationship, an obligation of confidence may be implied or imposed in certain circumstances by the courts[15]. Various statutes

10. See ante A. Liability to the company, 3. Enforcement difficulties.
11. Ibid.
12. American Law Institute, Federal Securities Code, s1714(1).
13. Ibid, s1703(a).
14. This discussion draws on: (a) G. Jones, 'Restitution of benefits obtained in breach of another's confidence' (1970) 86 L.Q.R.463; (b) The Law Commission, Working Paper No.58, *Breach of Confidence* (1974); (c) P.D. Finn, *Fiduciary Obligations* (1977), Chapter 19; (d) R. Goff and G. Jones, *Law of Restitution* (2nd ed.1978), Chapter 35 and (e) The Law Commission, *Breach of Confidentiality*, Cmnd.8388 (1981). The main headings are those of Finn.
15. The situation in which a person imparts information in confidence can be distinguished from that of the fiduciary who receives information in his capacity as fiduciary and exploits it for his own benefit (see ante I. Liability to the company). First, there may be no pre-existing fiduciary relationship before the information is imparted. Secondly, the source of the information is the confider, not a third party who passes the information to the fiduciary. Nevertheless, the two situations overlap.

also impinge on the use and misuse of information, but these have not been regarded as significant for the purpose of insider dealing regulation.

A. Duties of confidence imposed by express contractual stipulation

When a person, under the terms of an express contract, agrees to communicate specific information to another and/or permits that other to have access to material which may be a source of information, that person can stipulate in the contract that the information communicated or acquired shall be kept secret and confidential, that it can only be used by the recipient for the purposes designated in the agreement and that it can be further communicated only to the extent provided for in the agreement[16]. A confidential relationship may thus be fully constituted by express contractual stipulation.

Capable of covering a wide range of inside information, such stipulations are common in contracts of employment[17], consultancy agreements, licences for the exploitation of industrial information and agreements giving access to financial information for the purposes of raising finance or obtaining credit. Provision may also be made for the steps to be taken by the recipient to ensure that secrecy is maintained and for the duration of the secrecy obligation.

To the extent that empirical evidence appears to point to professional advisers using information received in that capacity[18], it would be open to corporate clients to require stipulations in contracts with their advisers which could form the basis of legal action in the event of breach. Whereas the prohibition on dealing in the IDA 1985 is confined to individuals, such express contractual stipulations could apply to persons, thereby affording a wider scope of application. Moreover, the risk of financial penalties would reinforce the need for employers to be alert to the possibility of employees being involved in insider dealing[19].

When the confidential relationship is defined by express contractual stipulation, the parties may state what matters will be treated as confidential as between themselves, even though a court would not necessarily so treat them in the absence of an express term[20]. Conversely, the contract may merely impose an obligation to maintain the secrecy of 'confidential information'. For convenience, the meaning of these words will be considered in the context of the implied or imposed duty of confidence.

B. The implied or imposed duty of confidence

In concluding that a duty of confidence exists outside an express contract, the courts have adopted differing approaches. In some cases[1], judicial intervention has been based on a readiness to imply a contractual obligation of confidence when information is communicated between parties in a contractual relationship. In other cases[2], a general equitable duty of confidence has been imposed

16. Finn, op cit n14(c), p184, supra, para.303.
17. A standard form is contained in the Encyclopaedia of Forms and Precedents (4th ed.1971), Vol.20 at 79, cl 9.
18. See, ante, Chapter 1. Introduction, II. Empirical assessment.
19. *Financial Times*, 21st February, 1987.
20. But it is thought that a court would only issue an injunction to protect information which is 'confidential information', Finn, op cit n14(c), p184, supra, para.304
1. Eg, *Robb v Green* [1895] 2 Q.B.315.
2. Eg, *A-G v Jonathan Cape* [1976] QB 752.

independently of contract. However, it has been suggested[3] that the implied contractual obligation does not differ from the equitable obligation, either in its content or the circumstances necessary to bring it into existence, though an equitable obligation can arise when no contractual relationship exists.

Although developments have been haphazard and the cases reflect conflicting judicial opinions, it is possible to identify two factors to which the courts attach importance in determining whether to impose or imply a duty of confidence. These are: (1) the nature of the relationship between the parties to the disclosure and (2) the nature of the information and the circumstances of the disclosure.

1. The nature of the relationship

Without extensively discussing the policy considerations, the courts have held that a duty of confidence arises in certain types of legal relationship. Recognition of the confidential character of these relationships is based on the types of communication associated with them.

The clearest example is provided by the relationship between the professional man and his client. In *Parry-Jones v Law Society*[4], Lord Denning commented:

'The law implies a term into the contract whereby a professional man is to keep his client's affairs secret and not to disclose them to anyone without just cause'[5].

It is long settled that the ranks of 'professional men' include solicitors[6], counsel[7], bankers[8] and accountants[9]. But whether other practitioners in the securities industry may be so categorised in law is unclear.

However, there is no generally accepted formulation of the scope of a professional man's duty of secrecy. In a banker-customer case, *Tournier v National Provincial and Union Bank of England*[10], Bankes L.J. observed:

'The privilege of non-disclosure to which a client or customer is entitled may vary according to the exact nature of the relationship between the client or the customer and the person on whom the duty rests. It need not be the same in the case of the counsel, the solicitor, the doctor, and the banker, though the underlying principle may be the same'[11].

Nevertheless, the duty appears to be widely drawn. In the *Tournier* case, the plaintiff was a customer of the defendant bank. A cheque was drawn by another customer of the defendants in favour of the plaintiff, who instead of paying it into his own account endorsed it to a third person with an account at another bank. When the cheque was returned to the defendants, their manager asked

3. Finn, op cit n14(c), p174, supra, paras.293, 299-300 and 306.
4. [1969] 1 Ch1.
5. Ibid at 7.
6. *Parry-Jones v Law Society* [1969] 1 Ch1.
7. *Carter v Palmer* (1839) 8 Cl. & Fin. 657 at 707.
8. *Tournier v National Provincial & Union Bank of England* [1924] 1 K.B.461
9. *Evitt v Price* (1827) 1 Sim. 483.
10. [1924] 1 K.B.461.
11. Ibid at 474.

that other bank the name of the person to whom it had been paid and was told it was a bookmaker. The defendants disclosed that information to third persons. By a majority, the Court of Appeal held that such disclosure constituted a breach of the defendants' duty to the plaintiff. Though the information was acquired not through the plaintiff's account, but through that of a drawer of the cheque, it was acquired by the defendants during the currency of the plaintiff's account and in their character as bankers[12].

The phrase 'in his character as' raises problems with regard to information derived from other sources during the confidential relationship. Dissenting, Scrutton L.J. pointed to the example of whether when:

> 'the banker hears from an entirely independent source that one of its customers has speculative dealings in oil, may it disclose that fact to another of its customers also interested in oil'[13].

The *Tournier* decision suggests that the duty of secrecy attaches when the bank seeks the information to help it make a decision on its treatment of the customer as it would be acting in its character as banker[14]. The position would be otherwise when information is obtained fortuitously and not in that character.

The employer-employee relationship is the one most frequently involved in an action under the law of confidence. Reflecting the view that the relationship 'between master and servant is always confidential, though in differing degrees'[15], a duty of confidence is readily implied. But the duty of confidence on an employee is limited to protecting confidential information from misuse[16].

Apart from these two classes of relationship, there are few reported decisions which indicate when the courts will imply that a duty of confidence arises out of the type of relationship itself. An exception is the fiduciary relationship when a duty of confidence will be implied to prevent a fiduciary improperly using confidential information obtained by virtue of his position[17].

2. The circumstances of the communication and the nature of the information

Outside these familiar types of legal relationship, greater uncertainty surrounds ad hoc relationships where the duty of confidence is founded solely on the fact of the communication of information to another in confidence. The uncertainty is attributed[18] less to difficulties over the general principles involved than to a dearth of case law on their application to particular cases.

In these situations, it seems that there are two prerequisites for the protection of information. First, the information must be communicated in circumstances importing an obligation of confidence. Secondly, the information itself must be

12. Ibid at 474 per Bankes L.J. and at 485 per Atkin L.J.
13. Ibid at 481.
14. Finn, op cit n14(c), p184, supra, para.311.
15. *Putsman v Taylor* [1927] 1 K.B.637 at 641 per Salter J. Whilst this quotation might unfortunately be taken to suggest that there are degrees within duties of confidence on employees, Salter J. seems to have intended to indicate that some employees are more likely to have access to confidential information than others. Finn, op cit n14(c), p184, supra, para.314 note 72.
16. See post, (b) The nature of the information.
17. Finn, op cit n14(c), p184, supra, para.321. Another exception concerns relationships of mutual trust and understanding, though there is only one reported case, namely, *Duchess of Argyll v Duke of Argyll* [1967] Ch302.
18. Finn, op cit n14(c), p184, supra, para.324.

confidential[19].

(a) COMMUNICATION IN CONFIDENCE

On the first prerequisite, two tests have mainly been used. Adopting the stance of the reasonable man, the courts have sometimes asked whether a reasonable man standing in the shoes of the recipient of the information would have realised upon reasonable grounds that the information was being given to him in confidence[20]. Whilst useful in assisting the court in its attempt to ascertain the understanding of the parties to the disclosure, a possible result is that a reasonable man may conclude he has received information in confidence, even though no confidential information was communicated to him and he will thus not be restrained from using the information.

In other cases, the courts have considered whether the information is confidential in character and then whether its disclosure was made solely for a particular purpose. This test has been applied in several industrial information cases[1], but could also be useful in relation to the unsolicited disclosure of information in circumstances that the discloser regarded the information as confidential and intends the information to be used only for a particular purpose[2], such as a joint undertaking by the parties to the disclosure.

Cases in which the existence of a duty of confidence is questioned mainly concern situations where protection is sought for information disclosed during negotiations for a contract which does not eventuate or where information is disclosed to contractors or sub-contractors for a particular purpose. In both types of situation, a duty of confidence is readily found to exist when the information disclosed is shown to be of a confidential nature.

(b) THE NATURE OF THE INFORMATION

As distinct from extending to all information communicated to the recipient, the duty of confidence imposed or implied by the courts in ad hoc relationships is limited to information which has 'the necessary quality of confidence about it'[3]. Information lacks this quality when it is 'something which is public property and knowledge'[4] and thus in the public domain. Some degree of secrecy is essential for information to be confidential.

However, the terms 'public' and 'secret' give rise to problems[5]. Certain information, particularly technical information, may be public knowledge even when disclosed to only a small section of the public. Other information may still not be public knowledge after disclosure to relatively large numbers. As was said by Cross J., whether an item of information is confidential 'must be a question

---

19. These two requirements, together with a third one of the unauthorised use of the information in question to the detriment of the discloser, were expressly referred to by Megarry J. in *Coco v A.N. Clark (Engineers)* [1969] R.P.C.41 at 47. The requirement of detriment to the discloser is discussed post, c. Breach of confidence.
20. Eg, *Coco v A.N. Clark (Engineers)* [1969] R.P.C.41 at 48.
1. Eg, *Saltman Engineering Co. v Campbell Engineering Co.* (1948) 65 R.P.C.203 at 213.
2. Finn, op cit n14(c), p184, supra, para.327.
3. *Saltman Engineering Co. v Campbell Engineering Co.* (1948) 65 R.P.C. 203 at 215.
4. Ibid.
5. Finn, op cit n14(c), p184, supra, paras.333-340; Jones, op cit n14(c), p184, supra, at 466-471

of degree depending on the particular case, but if relative secrecy remains, the plaintiff can still succeed'[6].

3. The defence of just cause or excuse

Despite the existence of a duty of confidence, the courts have not enforced the duty against those who break it when they have 'just cause or excuse for doing so'[7]. It is long settled that 'there is no confidence as to the disclosure of iniquity'[8] and that in enforcing duties of confidence, the court will not 'lend itself to the commission of fraud'[9]. It was thought that this defence was confined to cases where the confidential information related to the commission of a crime or civil wrong.

Recent authority regards this view as too limited. In *Initial Services Ltd. v Putterill*[10], a former employee disclosed information obtained from his employment to a newspaper and suggested the information showed that his employers should have registered an agreement under the Restrictive Trade Practices Act 1956 and had issued misleading circulars blaming increased charges on selective employment tax. The Court of Appeal refused to strike out a defence claim that the exception of iniquity was wide enough to justify the disclosure and it rejected a submission that the exception was restricted to cases where the confidential information related to crime or fraud. Lord Denning M.R. stated:

'It extends to any misconduct of such a nature that it ought in the public interest to be disclosed to others . . . The exception should extend to crimes, frauds and misdeeds, both those actually committed as well as those in contemplation provided always – and this is essential – that the disclosure is justified in the public interest'[11].

Reference was made to both the public interest and just cause or excuse in a 1973 case[12] in which the plaintiffs sought to restrain publication of a book alleged to contain extracts from confidential portions of their courses. A defence of disclosure in the public interest succeeded. Goff J. stated that confidential information was not a proper subject for protection when there is a public interest in its disclosure and there is 'just cause or excuse for breaking confidence'[13].

A restrictive view of the scope of this defence was apparently taken by the House of Lords in *British Steel Corporation v Granada Television Ltd*[14]. In a programme, Granada quoted from confidential BSC documents, which showed possible mismanagement and were unsolicited from a person inside BSC with access to them. BSC sought an order requiring Granada to disclose names of those who supplied the documents. At first instance, the judge ordered Granada to disclose the informant's identity and that order was upheld by the Court of

6. *Franchi v Franchi* [1967] R.P.C.149 at 153 per Cross J.
7. *Fraser v Evans* [1969] 1 Q.B.349 at 361 per Lord Denning M.R.
8. *Gartside v Outram* (1856) 26 L.J.Ch113 at 114 per Wood V.C.
9. Ibid at 116.
10. [1968] 1 Q.B.396.
11. Ibid at 405.
12. *Church of Scientology of California v Kaufman* [1973] R.P.C.635
13. Ibid at 649 per Goff J., who reached this conclusion after considering Lord Denning's judgments in *Fraser v Evans* [1969] 1 Q.B.349 and *Hubbard v. Vosper* [1972] 2 Q.B.84.
14. [1981] A.C.1096. The position of Granada would now be subject to the Contempt of Court Act 1981, s10.

Appeal. Granada's appeal to the House of Lords was dismissed. Though Granada did not allege that disclosure was in the public interest, consideration was given to the issue. In this connection, Lord Fraser stated:

> 'There is a public interest in maintaining the free flow of information to the press and therefore against obstructing informers. But there is also I think a very strong public interest in preserving confidentiality within any organisation, in order that it can operate efficiently, and also be free from suspicion that it is harbouring disloyal employees. There is no difference in this respect between a public corporation like BSC and an ordinary company . . . Unauthorised disclosure of confidential information about either is equally liable to damage efficiency and morale. In the present case, I am of opinion that the public interest in preserving confidentiality should prevail'[15].

Dissenting, Lord Salmon took a broader view, having regard to the parlous state of the BSC and the lack of safeguards for the public who bore the loss.

The admissibility of disclosure in the public interest as a defence was sanctioned by the House of Lords in *Attorney-General v Guardian Newspapers (No.2)*[16]. W, an ex-officer of the British security service, who had had access to highly classified information, proposed to publish his memoirs in Australia describing his experiences in the security service. The Attorney-General instituted proceedings in New South Wales to restrain publication and obtained interlocutory relief. Two British newspapers published reports on the forthcoming trial, including some of the allegations. On the day before the book's publication in the US, a third British newspaper published a serialised extract. The Attorney-General applied, inter alia, for injunctions to restrain the three newspapers from publishing information obtained from W and obtained interlocutory relief. At the trial, Scott J. discharged the interlocutory injunctions and dismissed the Attorney-General's claims for injunctions, though ordered an account of profits in respect of first publication of the serialised extract. The Court of Appeal dismissed the Attorney-General's appeal and the newspaper's cross-appeal against the order for account of profits. Dismissing the appeal and cross-appeal, the House of Lords held that the court would not grant an injunction restraining the publication of confidential information acquired by a Crown servant in the course of his employment by the Crown if it could be shown that publication of the information would not be contrary to the public interest. It was incumbent on the Crown to show not only that the information was confidential, but also that it was in the public interest that it should not be published if it wished to restrain the disclosure of government secrets. An injunction would not be granted if all possible damage to the Crown's interest had already been done by publication of the information abroad. An unresolved question was whether a person who, in breach of his duty of confidence, places information in the public domain remains under a duty thereafter not to exploit for his own benefit the information so disclosed, or whether he is released from his duty of confidence because the confidentiality no longer exists, notwithstanding that it was his own wrongful act that destroyed the confidentiality.

15. [1981] A.C.1096 at 1202.
16. [1988] 3 All E.R.545.

C. Breach of confidence

1. General

Considerable confusion surrounds the question of the nature of the obligation confidence imposes on a recipient and when such an obligation is breached. In the *Saltman* case[17], which concerned the protection of 'know-how', the duty of confidence was seen as one not to use the information without the discloser's consent. Lord Greene accepted that the law was correctly stated in the formula:

> 'If a defendant is proved to have used confidential information, directly or indirectly, from a plaintiff, without the consent, express or implied, of the plaintiff, he will be guilty of an infringement of the plaintiff's right'[18].

A new twist was given in *Seager v Copydex*[19], where information about a carpet grip was unconsciously plagiarised. Adding a requirement of prejudice to the discloser, Lord Denning stated:

> 'he who has received information shall not take advantage of it. He must not use it to the prejudice of him who gave it without obtaining his consent'[20].

These two statements have been regarded[1] as reconcilable on the ground that an infringement of the discloser's right is itself a prejudice to him. A requirement of actual prejudice to the discloser would, however, raise the problem of whether a breach of duty could be avoided by an offer to pay a reasonable sum for use of the information.

An alternative approach was floated in *Coco v A.N. Clark (Engineers) Ltd.*[2], which was a case involving unsuccessful negotiations for the manufacture of a moped engine. After questioning whether the duty is one not to use the information without consent or one not to use the information without paying for it and referring to the difficulties of an injunction in commercial cases, Megarry J. suggested a two-tier duty of confidence to avoid those difficulties in some cases:

> 'the essence of the duty seems more likely to be that of not using without paying, rather than of not using at all. It may be that in fields other than industry or commerce . . . the duty may exist in a more stringent form; but in the circumstances present in this case I think that the less stringent form is the more reasonable'[3].

The formulations of Lord Denning and Megarry J. have both attracted criticism[4]. An instance of the tail wagging the dog, the suggestion of Megarry J. is seen as a reason for remoulding the remedy, not the duty. But there is reason

---

17. *Saltman Engineering Co. v Campbell Engineering Co.* (1948) 65 R.P.C.203
18. Ibid at 213
19. [1967] 1 W.L.R.923.
20. Ibid at 931.
1. Finn, op cit n14(c), p184, supra, para.365.
2. [1969] R.P.C.41.
3. Ibid at 50.
4. Finn, op cit n14(c), p184, supra, para.367.

to support his questioning of the requirement of detriment to the discloser. A recipient can use confidential information for his own benefit without inflicting any damage or harm on the discloser. An example is the insider who deals on inside information. As a fiduciary misusing property, opportunity or information is liable to account for his profits, it would be anomalous, especially when the equitable foundation of the court's jurisdiction on matters of confidence is expressly invoked as in the *Seager* case[5], for there to be no account of profits under the law of confidence unless a loss is caused to the discloser in the making of profits. The formulation of Lord Greene is thus to be preferred.

The view that misuse of inside information could be a breach of confidence is supported by the 1977 decision of *Dunford & Elliott Ltd. v Johnson & Firth Brown Ltd*[6]. Having sustained severe losses, D & E decided to make a rights issue of £3 million to raise new capital. At a meeting on 25th October, 1976, between its financial advisers and its institutional shareholders, who held 43% of the issued shares, it was suggested that the institutional shareholders (the consortium) should underwrite the issue. The financial advisers produced a report on D & E's financial prospects and gave it to the consortium under a stipulation that the information was confidential and not to be used in any way to influence investment decisions. Considering that at least another £1 million was needed, the consortium on its own initiative invited two other companies, including a rival JFB, to underwrite £½ million each. As the consortium thought JFB should be placed in the same position as itself, JFB was shown the confidential information. It took detailed notes. D & E directors opposed JFB's participation and the consortium's proposal did not proceed. On 8th November, 1976, JFB made a press announcement that they were making an offer to D & E shareholders. After learning that the confidential information had been passed to JFB, D & E issued a writ claiming an injunction to forbid the use of the confidential information and to restrain the take-over bid due to be announced on 6th December, 1976.

At first instance, Mocatta J. granted the injunction. However, allowing the appeal by JFB, the Court of Appeal held that (1) the information in the report had the necessary quality of confidence and had been given in circumstances importing an obligation of confidence, (2) but it would not be reasonable for the court to enforce the stipulation as to confidence because the information having gone to the consortium and to the directors (some of whom had perfectly properly and with that knowledge made purchases of shares in October, 1976, which they fully disclosed), a number of shareholders were already in a preferential position. In addition, Roskill J. suggested that in order to avoid any possible future conflict of interest, the Panel should consider the problem of disclosure of information to selected shareholders in such circumstances.

The confusion surrounding an action for breach of confidence was highlighted in the Court of Appeal. In his judgment, Lord Denning quoted his statement in the *Seager* case[7] that a recipient must not take unfair advantage of information to the prejudice of the discloser without obtaining the latter's consent and referred to the three requisites of a communication in confidence, the confidential nature of the information and its unauthorised use to the

5. [1969] R.P.C.41.
6. [1977] I Lloyd's Rep.505 C.A.; B.A.K. Rider, 'Abuse of Inside Information' (1977) 127 N.L.J.830. This matter was also considered by the Panel: The Panel on Take-overs and Mergers, *Statements on Johnson & Firth Brown Limited/Dunford & Elliott Ltd.*, 6th and 23rd December, 1976.
7. [1967] 1 W.L.R.923 at 931.

detriment of the discloser mentioned by Megarry J. in the *Coco* case[8]. Doubting whether the three requisites covered 'the whole ground'[9], he considered there was a further principle that, by analogy to a covenant in restraint of trade[10], the court will not enforce a stipulation for confidence if it was not reasonable when made, nor if afterwards, owing to subsequent happenings, it became unreasonable to do so. He added:

> 'It seems to me that that principle applies to this case. Although Dunford & Elliott stipulated that this report was confidential, it seems to me that, as events turned out, it would be quite unreasonable that the Courts should enforce it. For one thing, it has since been discovered that Dunford & Elliott – or at any rate, their directors – have made considerable use themselves of the forecasts contained in the report . . . three of their directors, on Oct.7 and 8, bought 55,000 of the shares of Dunford & Elliott at a price of 14p – very nearly the lowest price they ever reached. I would imagine that they had some at least of the favourable forecasts – the confidential forecasts – before them at the time, and were better placed to buy the shares than outsiders. In addition, we know that Dunford & Elliott disclosed this confidential information to 43 per cent of the shareholders in the company . . . and to none of the others. This widespread use of the information drives a hole into the blanket of confidence; especially when that information is being used – or, shall I say misused – for the benefit of some potential shareholders and not for the benefit of the others'[11].

In support, he invoked the Code principle[12] that shareholders are entitled to adequate information and time to decide and its rule[13] that shareholders must be given all the facts in ample time to make an informed judgment on the merits. Even if the consortium had broken D & E's confidence, the breach did not necessarily 'spill over on to JFB'[14]. Whilst there was some evidence that JFB knew the information was confidential, they might have thought that its communication to them was permissible as potential underwriters and they had not promised not to use it. There was sufficient doubt that an injunction should not be granted. Though sceptical about JFB's claim that the information was not material to or used by them as it at least served to confirm their views, he considered the use of the information by the directors and its disclosure to 43% of shareholders meant there was no justification for withholding it from other potential subscribers or underwriters, including JFB. Detriment to D & E or their shareholders could be avoided by D & E sending out their own circulars, containing their own forecasts, to the whole body of shareholders. Moreover, an injunction would frustrate the bid forever.

Roskill J. emphasised the dilemma of D & E's financial advisers. Though worried about their position, their view was that the communication of the information to the institutional shareholders in their capacity as prospective underwriters would overcome the difficulties that would otherwise arise if the

8. [1969] R.P.C.41 at 47.
9. [1977] 1 Lloyd's Rep.505 at 509.
10. In support, he referred to *Shell U.K. Ltd. v Lostock Garage Ltd.* [1976] 1 W.L.R.1187.
11. [1977] 1 Lloyd's Rep.505 at 509-510.
12. Code, General Principle 3 (now General Principle 4).
13. Code, Rule 15 (now Rules 23, 24 and 25).
14. [1977] 1 Lloyd's Rep.505 at 510.

information were made available to them wearing their shareholders' hats. But he thought the analogy with a merchant bank, with two departments where it was desirable that one should not know what the other was doing, was mistaken. In this case, the approach was made to the institutional shareholders because they were shareholders. He accepted it was clear that most, if not all, of the shares in the rights issue would have been left with the underwriters and to that extent the institutional investors were going to receive the information as prospective underwriters not as present shareholders. Yet in substance and in form they would receive allotment letters which they would take up and it would be immaterial whether they did so as allottees of the allotments or as underwriters of the issue. The difficulty was that institutional shareholders had received in confidence information which was not available to and was never intended should be made available to the private shareholders, though D & E directors had it in the ordinary course of events. However, an injunction would not preserve the status quo, but would destroy the proposed bid. Apart from urging consideration of the problem by the Panel, his analysis led him to conclude:

> 'I do not see why this information which 43 per cent of the shareholders and the directors have already had should not, if the plaintiffs so wish, be made available to the others. The rules [of the City Code] so far from preventing this would seem to encourage it. If that is done, any possible damage to the shareholders resulting from any breach (if such there were) of confidentiality, will disappear'[15].

In its actual application, the further principle invoked by Lord Denning does not seem likely to produce a different result from his formulation in the *Seager* case[16] or that of Lord Greene in the *Saltman* case[17]. However, the suggestion that the information should lose protection because of the directors' dealings is open to question. In an action for breach of confidence, it is submitted that the better approach is to consider whether the information still has the necessary quality of confidence. Hence, the emphasis on the disclosure by D & E is a preferable basis for the decision. In disclosing the information to 43% of shareholders, D & E deprived it of a confidential quality which it would otherwise have possessed. Though the court declined to grant the relief sought, it seems that, on a different set of facts and subject to the observations above on detriment, misuse of inside information could be a breach of confidence.

The finding that the directors' share purchases were made 'perfectly properly' was prompted by their disclosure in accordance with statutory provisions. But in view of the assumptions made about the information available to the directors, this finding was apparently generous to the directors when considered by reference to prevailing commercial ethics.

2. Remedies

The main remedies[18] are an injunction, damages or an account of profits. Whereas the last two are alternative remedies, an injunction may be coupled with either. But it remains unclear when a court will grant one form of relief as

15. Ibid at 515.
16. *Seager v Copydex Ltd.* [1967] 1 W.L.R.923 at 931
17. *Saltman Engineering Co. v Campbell Engineering Co.* (1948) 65 R.P.C. 203 at 213.
18. Jones, op cit n14(a), p184, supra, at 488 also refers to quantum meruit claims, namely, a claim for recompense for work done or services rendered by the plaintiff to the defendant.

distinct from another. Further uncertainty surrounds the jurisdictional basis of some remedies, particularly damages.

(a) AN INJUNCTION

When granting an injunction for breach of confidence, the courts do not appear to have drawn any operative distinction between the common law contractual obligation and the equitable obligation[19]. It seems, though the point is still undecided, that in both instances the remedy is discretionary and not regarded as appropriate in every case, in which event the breach will sound only in damages.

An important consideration is the nature of the information[20]. Whereas information of a personal nature is readily afforded injunctive protection, an injunction may not be granted in respect of industrial or commercial information that is nothing very special, as when it could be obtained from a competent consultant.

Another consideration appears to be the recipient's good faith. An injunction will normally lie when an employee uses improper means to obtain confidential information or, having been given confidential information during the course of and for the purposes of his employment, subsequently uses the information after termination of his employment. It is thought[1] unlikely that a recipient, who has actually used the information for one purpose or on certain conditions would be heard to say that he acted in good faith in its subsequent use for a different purpose or outside those conditions. In the *Coco* case[2], Megarry J. stressed the injustice of an injunction against a defendant who had vainly and in good faith negotiated with the plaintiff on the basis that the benefits of any confidential information were to 'sound in monetary compensation to the communicator'[3]. An injunction would place him under 'a unique disability. He alone of all men must for a certain time abjure this field of endeavour however great his interest'[4]. Together with the *Seager* case[5], this decision suggests that when the recipient, though breaching his duty, has acted in good faith, only damages will be awarded against him.

Even when the court is willing to grant an injunction, difficulties arise regarding its terms or duration, particularly in industrial information cases when the information in question may already have become public knowledge or be soon likely to do so. In the former case, it is open to question whether an injunction should be granted since it would prevent a defendant from using information available for use by everyone else. In the latter case, the problem is one of duration. These difficulties would also be relevant to the grant of an injunction against an insider. The case law awaits clarification. A House of Lords decision, *O. Mustad & Son v Dosen*[6], suggests that the defendant's duty of confidence is discharged by publication of a secret. This statement is not easily

19. Finn, op cit n14(c), p184, supra, para.376.
20. Ibid, para.377.
1. Ibid, para.378.
2. *Coco v A.N. Clark (Engineers) Ltd.* [1969] R.P.C.41.
3. Ibid at 50.
4. Ibid at 49.
5. [1967] 1 W.L.R.923.
6. [1963] (1928) R.P.C.41.

reconciled with the dictum of Roxburgh J., accepted in *Seager v Copydex Ltd.*[7], that even then the defendant must not be allowed to abuse confidence and, because he has received the information in a form which lends itself to ready exploitation, get a 'headstart' over the plaintiff and the rest of the public[8]. It has been suggested[9] that these statements can be reconciled in that it was the plaintiff in the *Mustad* case who published the information. But when someone other than the plaintiff publishes the information, the court could grant an injunction for such period as is required to prevent the defendant obtaining an undue advantage from his breach.

(b) AN ACCOUNT OF PROFITS

In contrast to a fiduciary who misuses trust property, it seems that a defendant who misuses confidential information will not be required to account for his profits to his discloser unless the court is satisfied that the only liability stemming from the breach is not simply a liability to pay reasonable compensation for misuse of the information[10]. When there is nothing very special about the information, as when it could be obtained from a competent consultant, it may be unrealistic to claim that any of the profit is attributable to the information misused or that it should be the subject of an account. The defendant may merely have achieved a saving by not asking the consultant, for which he must pay but in damages. Conversely, an account is appropriate when the information itself is of a profit earning nature. In practice, the distinction may be difficult to draw.

There are few cases in which the plaintiff has elected for an account of profits. In the *Peter Pan* case[11], the defendants manufactured particular styles of goods from designs shown to them in confidence. Adopting a net profits approach, Pennycuick J. held that the amount of profit was the difference between the amount spent on manufacturing the articles and the price received on sale of the goods. He rejected a contention that the defendants' liability was limited to the differences between the profits actually made by use of the confidential information and those which would have been made if the goods had been manufactured without the use thereof, because 'the defendants could not have manufactured [the goods] at all without the use of confidential information'[12]. However, other than in the simplest cases, accounts are difficult and expensive to work out with the result that plaintiffs generally prefer to claim damages.

(c) DAMAGES

The basis on which the courts exercise jurisdiction to award damages raises the issue of the proper foundation of an action for breach of confidence. Damages are a common law remedy and as such can be awarded for breach of contract when the duty of confidence is imposed by the express or implied terms of a contract. The availability of damages was an important consideration which induced the courts to imply a contractual duty of confidence. However, the modern tendency is to imply a purely equitable duty. In that event, the court's

7. [1967] 1 W.L.R.923.
8. In *Terrapin Ltd. v Builders' Supply Co. (Hayes) Ltd.* [1960] R.P.C.128 at 130.
9. Jones, op cit n14(a), p184, supra, at 486.
10. Finn, op cit n14(c), p184, supra, para.383.
11. *Peter Pan Manufacturing Corpn v Corsets Silhouette Ltd.* [1963] R.P.C.45.
12. Ibid at 60.

jurisdiction to award damages is prima facie derived from Lord Cairns Act[13] which provides for the award of damages either in addition to or in substitution for an injunction. In a 1957 decision[14], the Court of Appeal left open the question of whether a court of equity could award damages for a breach of confidence under its inherent jurisdiction and apart from Lord Cairns Act. The question has not been specifically referred to in subsequent cases involving the award of damages, but it seems to follow from the decision in *Seager (No.2)*[15] where the basis for assessment of damages was expressed to be tortious on the analogy of the law of conversion of goods, that a claim for damages may now succeed independently of any prayer for equitable relief[16].

There has been little discussion of the principles governing the award of damages. In *Seager (No.2)*, the Court of Appeal directed that damages be assessed on the basis of the market value of the information in question as between a willing buyer and a willing seller[17]. Whilst this formula met the circumstances of the case, the case law provides no direct guidance as to the principles governing damages where the information is of a commercial nature.

In the Law Commission's view[18], the uncertainty in the basis of an action for breach of confidence which, in turn, generates uncertainty as to future developments, requires legislative intervention. To remove this uncertainty it has proposed that the existing action, insofar as it exists independently of a right of action for breach of contract, be abolished and the creation of a new tort of breach of statutory duty of confidence.

IV. BREACH OF STATUTORY DUTY

A. The Company Securities (Insider Dealing) Act 1985

In the absence of express provision in the IDA 1985 for civil liability, a further issue is whether the courts would imply civil liability on the basis of breach of statutory duty. In the US the readiness of the courts to imply private causes of action for damages arising out of breach of the anti-fraud provisions of the securities laws, notably s10(b) of the Securities Exchange Act 1934 and Rule 10b-5 made thereunder, has played a key role in developing civil liability for insider dealing[19].

In contrast, British courts have not been confronted with this issue. However, breaches of the Companies Acts have not given rise to the implication of private causes of action for damages and it is unlikely that the courts would imply such causes of action under the IDA 1985.

---

13. Chancery Amendment Act 1858, s2.
14. *Nichrotherm Electrical Co. Ltd. v Percy* [1957] R.P.C.207 at 213-214.
15. [1969] 1 W.L.R.809 at 813 and 815.
16. The Law Commission, op cit n14(b), p184, supra, para.34.
17. [1969] 1 W.L.R.809 at 814.
18. The Law Commission, op cit n14(b) and (e), p184, supra.
19. L. Loss, *Fundamentals of Securities Regulation* (1988), Chapters 9 and 10; D.M. Branson, 'Insider Trading' [1982] JBL 342, 413, 536 and J. Cottrell, 'Insider Dealing in the US' (1986) 136 N.L.J.88, 112, 150.

B. The Financial Services Act 1986

Under the FSA 1986, a right of action for damages is conferred, inter alia, on a person who suffers loss as a result of contravention of the SIB's conduct of business or other rules[20] (except the financial resources rules)[1]. The action is subject to the defences and other incidents applying to actions for breach of statutory duty[2]. Contraventions by a member of a recognised SRO or professional body of corresponding rules, are also actionable[3]. The remedy is limited to civil law only: a person is not guilty of an offence by reason of any relevant contravention and no such contravention invalidates a transaction[4].

The right of action for damages conferred by this provision was the focus of widespread opposition in the City. However, its relevance to insider dealing seems limited. It has been seen[5] that whilst in face-to-face transactions a non-insider may be able to prove reliance in the sense of a causal link between his conduct and that of the insider, a non-insider dealing on the open market will not normally be able to show a causal connection between his decision to deal and the presence of the insider in the market.

V. CONFLICTS OF INTEREST

Despite the frequency with which professional fiduciaries are faced with conflicts of interest, the courts have rarely been confronted with such situations. But in this area, other measures apply. Hence, for convenience, consideration of the general law regarding conflicts of interest is postponed to a subsequent chapter[6]. Instead, it will be dealt with as a preliminary to discussion of those other measures, notably the rules regulating the conduct of investment business made under the FSA 1986 and the City Code.

The absence of extensive provision for civil liability constitutes an important gap in insider dealing regulation since civil liability constitutes a necessary supplement to the criminal sanction and has the advantage of providing an enforcement technique with a lesser burden of proof. However, like the criminal sanction, enforcement is costly, particularly when there are investigation difficulties, and this consideration enhances the importance of preventive measures.

---

20. FSA 1986, s62(1).
1. Ibid, s62(3).
2. Ibid, s62(1).
3. Ibid, s62(2).
4. Ibid, s62(4).
5. See ante II. Liability to shareholders, A. The common law.
6. See, post, Chapter 6. Administrative regulation.

Chapter 5

Disclosure

As the primary protection against misuse of inside information is immediate and full disclosure of information by companies and insiders[1], such disclosure is implicit in insider dealing regulation. To the extent that misuse may thereby be reduced, so the need for direct regulation of insider transactions by the courts or administrative agencies is obviated. Yet when direct regulation is effected, insider reporting provisions may also facilitate enforcement.

Assessing disclosure from the point of view of insider dealing is complicated in that the extent of disclosure is considerably broader than if its focus was solely on the issue of insider dealing. The problem is accentuated by the recent trend to increased disclosure obligations[2]. From an initial concern with shareholder and creditor protection, disclosure has now evolved to include information responsive to the needs of employees, consumers and the public. In turn, this has prompted reconsideration of the rationale of disclosure.

In evaluating the role of disclosure in insider dealing regulation, consideration will initially be given to the rationale of corporate disclosure requirements and the current economic controversy over their effectiveness. The substantive provisions will then be examined by reference to timely disclosure and insider reporting.

I. THE RATIONALE OF DISCLOSURE REGULATION

There are several conceptions of disclosure regulation. These include market failure, market efficiency, the prevention of fraud and other improper conduct, and equality of access to information. Though not mutually exclusive, the emphasis to be attached to each reflects differing policy goals.

A. Market failure and the availability of information

The underlying rationale of disclosure is based on the externality or public good aspect of market failure. This aspect has already been considered[3].

B. Market efficiency and resource allocation

On the basis of the market failure rationale, the recent expansion in disclosure requirements has been concerned with creating a better informed investing

---

1. The Panel on Take-overs and Mergers, Report on the Year ended 31st March, 1977, Foreword by Lord Shawcross, p.4. 'the important thing is the disclosure of full and accurate information at the earliest possible moment'.
2. Whilst the main expansion has occurred in the US, to a lesser degree the development has been paralleled in Britain.
3. See, ante, Chapter 1, Introduction, III Theoretical considerations.

public. In 1973, the Department acknowledged the 'need for fuller disclosure ... as a spur to efficiency'[4]. Similarly, the Panel has stressed 'shareholders should be given sufficient evidence, facts and opinions on which an adequate judgment and decision can be reached'[5].

By enhancing the flow of information to the market, disclosure provides investors with fuller information on which to base investment decisions. In turn, this results in increased efficiency in the pricing mechanism and in the allocation of capital resources. in this connection, empirical studies of market efficiency lend support to the view that in Britain prices reflect the information available through the disclosure system[6].

The argument that increased disclosure results in better investment decisions and improved pricing efficiency appears logically sound. Nevertheless, doubts about existing systems of mandatory disclosure have been raised by a growing body of economic literature which questions whether pricing efficiency has improved as a result of disclosure regulation and, if so, whether the improvement is sufficient to justify the costs of the disclosure system. The discussion centres on empirical studies in the US which attempt to measure the effect of disclosure on the pricing of securities on both the new issue and the secondary markets.

1. New issues

The effectiveness of disclosure requirements was first challenged by Stigler[7]. His assertion that they 'had no important effect on the quality of new securities sold to the public'[8] was based on tests relating to the price performance of securities, correlation of security prices at various dates and the variance of price performance.

The price performance of large new issues for the five years subsequent to flotation was examined for both the 1923-28 and 1949-55 periods[9]. Adjustments were made for the effects of general market conditions. Stigler found the comparisons suggested 'investors in common stocks in the 1950s did little better than in the 1920s, indeed clearly no better if they held the securities only one or two years'[10].

However, the validity of this finding was undermined by numerous errors in data that biased the results in its favour. After correcting these errors, Friend and Herman[11] showed Stigler's and their evidence was consistent with improved performance in the post-SEC period as compared with the earlier years.

The comparison was supplemented by the inclusion in the post-SEC period of flotations in 1958 and the first half of 1959. Small issues were also added for 1923 and the first halves of 1928 and 1958. Again, they found evidence of superior relative price performance in the post-SEC period.

In response, Stigler[12] argued that further evidence showed the inclusion of data for 1928 was an inappropriately severe test of an unregulated new issue

4. The Department of Trade and Industry, *Company Law Reform*, Cmnd.5391 (1973), para5.
5. The Panel on Take-overs and Mergers, Report on the Year ended 31st March, 1978, p.15.
6. See, ante, Chapter 1, Introduction, III Theoretical considerations.
7. G.J. Stigler, 'Public Regulation of the Securities Markets' (1964) 37 J. Bus.117. This was reprinted in G.J. Stigler, *The Citizen and the State: Essays on Regulation* (1975).
8. Stigler op cit n7, supra, at 124.
9. New issues exceeding 2.5 million dollars in 1923-28 and 5 million dollars in 1949-55.
10. Stigler, op cit n7, supra, at 121.
11. I. Friend and E.S. Herman, 'The SEC through a Glass Darkly' (1964) 37 J. Bus.382.
12. G.J. Stigler, 'Comment' (1964) 37 J. Bus.414.

market since new companies are particularly vulnerable to a major depression. He also reclassified some stock and reduced the time span for assessing the performance of new issues. On the basis of revised data and after correcting previous errors, he asserted that the superior performance of the post-SEC period disappeared substantially: 'the differences are not statistically significant in any year'[13].

Again, Friend and Herman[14] questioned his interpretation of the evidence. Apart from finding his changes 'dubious'[15], they argued the evidence still strongly favoured superior new issue performance in the post-SEC period. The argument that 1929 was an inappropriate terminal date has also been criticised as having 'no merit'[16] since the tests basically compared new issue performance with the contemporaneous performance of the market.

Another test by Friend and Herman involved a comparison of the price performance of small issues just above and below the threshold for full disclosure in 1958. They found the price performance of small registered issues was superior to that of the unregistered issues.

As another measure of performance, Stigler[17] examined the correlation of security prices. This involved comparison of the correlation between the issue price and the price in the following year with the average correlation between prices in adjacent pairs of years after issue for both the pre- and post-SEC periods. In each case, prices were adjusted by a market index. The comparison is based on the presumption[18] that, after adjustment for market movement, prices reflect the productivity of underlying assets. As productivity in any year is correlated with productivity in adjacent years, adjusted stock prices in adjacent years should also be correlated. If new issue prices do not reflect the productivity of the underlying assets, the correlations of adjacent year prices involving new issue prices will be lower than other adjacent year correlations. On finding that the correlation involving the issue price rose from the pre- to the post-SEC period as compared with other adjacent year correlations, Stigler acknowledged 'an improvement in the structure of issue prices may be due to the SEC'[19]. But he added the analysis was incomplete.

An indication of whether the stock market is effecting the efficient allocation of resources should be provided by evidence that the performance of new issues is equal or superior to the market. Whilst not unanimous, the balance of evidence indicates registered issues generally earned higher returns compared to the market than issues that were unregistered because they were either offered in the pre-SEC period or below the full disclosure threshold in the post-SEC period. This would suggest improved allocational efficiency[20].

Further debate concerned Stigler's observation[1] that the variance of price performance for new issues was larger in the pre-SEC period. Whilst the greater variability of the stock market in the 1920s than in the 1950s meant the

13. Ibid, at 418.
14. I. Friend and E.S. Herman, 'Professor Stigler on Securities Regulation: A Further Comment' (1965) 38 J. Bus.106.
15. Ibid, at 107.
16. M. Mendelson, 'Economics and the assessment of disclosure requirements' (1978) 1 J.C.C.L.S.R. 49 at 57.
17. Stigler, op cit n12, p200, supra, at 419.
18. Mendelson, op cit n16, supra, at 52-58.
19. Stigler, op cit n12, p200, supra, at 419.
20. Mendelson, op cit n16, supra, at 58.
1. Stigler, op cit n7, p200, supra, at 122.

difference was exaggerated, the difference nonetheless remains even after making this adjustment[2].

The post-SEC reduction in variance was interpreted by Friend and Herman[3] as a reduction of risk attributable to disclosure. Stigler objected that a zero variance would mean investors in new issues would fare the same, but they could fare very badly or very well[4]. In reply, Friend and Herman assert his argument implies either that investors have no risk aversion or that the variance measure used has no relevance to risk, but he makes no attempt to justify these seemingly implausible positions[5].

2. The secondary market

The debate on the effect of disclosure on prices in the secondary market is primarily a debate between Benston and Friend. Whilst it centres around the same body of evidence, the differences stem from conflicting interpretations of this evidence.

In his initial challenge to disclosure requirements, Benston[6] examined the relationship between price changes and unexpected changes in financial variables such as net sales, cash flow, net operating income and adjusted net income. Though he concluded the evidence was not consistent with the assumption that published information was timely or relevant on average, his findings suggested statistically significant relations between price changes and the unexpected changes in each of the financial variables.

These findings were consistent with a subsequent report by Martin[7] that his own empirical evidence showed annual accounting information was relevant to investor decision-making. As well as complementing other evidence, he asserted his 'study uniquely provides an explicit test of the usefulness of a series of accounting variables taken together'[8].

Benston's findings also accorded with those of Gonedes. Gonedes reported:

> 'the results of our tests . . . are consistent with the statement that special accounting items convey information pertinent to establishing firms' equilibrium values. Also, our results are not consistent with the statement that no effect is associated with the disaggregation represented by the separate disclosure treatment accorded to special accounting items'[9].

Friend and Westerfield[10] objected to Benston's out of hand dismissal of the economic importance of his statistically significant results. In particular, he:

---

2. L. Fisher and J.H. Lorie, 'Some Studies of the Variability of Returns on Investments in Common Stock' (1970) 43 J.Bus.99..
3. Friend and Herman, op cit n11, p200, supra, at 392-393.
4. Stigler, op cit n12, p200, supra, at 419.
5. Friend and Herman, op cit n14, p201, supra, at 109.
6. G.J. Benston, 'The Effectiveness and Effects of the SEC's Accounting and Disclosure Requirements,' p.23, in (ed) H.G. Manne, *Economic Policy and the Regulation of Corporate Securities (1969)*.
7. A. 'Martin, 'An Empirical Test of the Relevance of Accounting Information for Investment Decisions' (1971) 23 J. Accoun.Research, Empirical Research in Accounting: Selected Studies, 1.
8. Ibid, at 31.
9. N. Gonedes, 'Risk Information and the Effects of Special Accounting Items in Capital Market Equilibrium' (1975) 3 J.Accoun.Research 220.
10. I. Friend and R. Westerfield, 'Required Disclosure and the Stock Market: Comment' (1975) 65 Amer. Econ.Rev.467.

'considers not too relevant for stock prices knowledge about changes in financial variables, in spite of the fact that he finds an increase of 100 per cent in the annual rate of net sales is associated with an increase in price of 10.4 per cent in the month of the announcement, and that changes in other variables are also associated with significant though proportionally smaller changes in price'[11].

They also criticised Benston for not allowing for the joint effects of unexpected changes in the different financial variables.

In a second set of tests, Benston[12] considered the effect of the required disclosure of sales on the securities of companies that were affected and those that were not affected by legislation. He found tests of changes in riskiness indicated the disclosure requirements had less effect on the securities of the 193 companies that did not previously disclose sales than on the 314 that did. Together with his findings that statistics on changes in the value of companies showed little difference between companies which did and did not disclose sales voluntarily and that disclosure requirements had not apparently contributed to a reduction in the volatility of returns from the two groups of securities, he concluded the disclosure requirements were of no apparent value to investors.

However, Friend and Westerfield questioned the use of sales information to distinguish between companies:

'net income would seem to be the more theoretically relevant variable and in fact is the more consistently significant in its effect on price according to his earlier test . . . It is interesting therefore that (with one possible exception) all of the 193 stocks which did not disclose sales did disclose net income as well as balance sheet and other financial data, so that Benston's second set of tests does not distinguish between non-disclosure and disclosure firms but between less and more disclosure firms'[13].

It was also asserted[14] that, on closer examination, his findings failed to support his conclusion that disclosure requirements had no effect on market prices.

The issue of whether disclosure requirements have improved efficiency is thus controversial. But in the US, the balance of evidence suggests the provisions have contributed to increased efficiency in pricing and thereby improved investors' assessments as to the potential productivity of alternative uses of capital resources.

Yet despite the belief of proponents of regulation that the improvements have been substantial, there is no measure of the extent. Issues of cost also need to be considered to compare against the benefits. Though methods of assessing costs are being developed[15], the inability to measure the benefits prevents economists from carrying out cost-benefit analysis of the regulation.

Similarly, economists cannot assess whether a particular form of disclosure regulation is desirable since effective disclosure results in a redistribution of wealth. As this latter is a political question, the issue of the desirability of the

11. Ibid, at 468.
12. G.J. Benston, 'Required Disclosure and the Stock Market: An Evaluation of the Securities Exchange Act of 1934' (1973) 63 Amer. Econ. Rev.132; G.J. Benston, 'Evaluation of the Securities Exchange Act of 1934', Financial Executive, May 1974, 28.
13. Friend and Westerfield, op cit n10, p202, supra, at 470.
14. Ibid; Mendelson, op cit n16, p201, supra, at 61.
15. A.A. Sommer, Jr., 'The U.S. Securities and Exchange Commission Disclosure Study' (1978) 1 J.C.C.L.S.R.145 at 152.

wealth redistribution falls outside the scope of economic analysis alone.

C. Prevention of fraud and improper conduct

As a method of preventing fraud and improper conduct, disclosure has gained widespread acceptance. In this context it performs a regulatory function by enhancing standards of behaviour and reducing the opportunities for fraudulent or improper activities[16]. Hence, it acts as an alternative form of regulation to the direct regulation of transactions.

Initial disclosure requirements were directed at both fraudulent practices and other abuses which, though not fraudulent, pointed to incompetent management. Further periodic extensions of disclosure requirements in response to abuses[17] underlined the commitment to disclosure as a means to reduce abuse and raise standards of behaviour.

The assumption is that disclosure inhibits conduct which causes embarrassment when made public. Public awareness and disapproval of certain practices are regarded as having a moralising effect by deterring unacceptable behaviour and thereby establishing the boundaries of acceptable conduct. Referring to the 'need for fuller disclosure . . . as a safeguard against malpractice'[18], the Department considers 'openness in company affairs is the first principle in securing responsible behaviour'[19].

However, further considerations preclude reliance on disclosure alone. The effectiveness of any group pressure effect is dependent on compliance with disclosure requirements. Hence, unless they concern information ascertainable independently of the particulars to be disclosed, requirements risk proving difficult to enforce. Yet as an arbiter of conduct, public opinion can be unpredictable and difficult to control. When in conflict with regulatory goals, it can inhibit legitimate transactions. Moreover, to the extent that the group pressure effect relies on the reaction of a large or influential number, it will not protect an oppressed minority with conflicting interests.

Yet the extension of criminal and civil liability in company law and securities regulation also enhanced the role of disclosure since, by facilitating detection, it served as a preliminary to enforcement. Compliance with disclosure provisions is encouraged by the suspicion of irregularities aroused following discovery of failure to disclose. As between public and private enforcement, disclosure can alleviate the difficulties of private enforcement, particularly by shareholders of their contractual and statutory rights and so reduce the need for public enforcement.

Nevertheless, the use of disclosure for enforcement needs to take account of other factors. For those intent on fraud or other improper conduct, infringement of disclosure requirements may be a prerequisite to concealment of the

---

16. This aspect is considered in: V. Brudney, 'Insiders, Outsiders and Informational Advantages under the Federal Securities Laws' (1979) Harv. L. Rev. 322; A.G. Anderson, 'The Disclosure Process in Federal Securities Regulation; A Brief Review' (1974) 25 Hastings L. Rev.311; R.L. Knauss, 'A Reappraisal of the Role of Disclosure' (1964) 62 Mich.L.Rev.614; Comment, 'Disclosure as a Legislative Device' (1962) 76 Harv.L.Rev.1272; L. Sealy, 'The "Disclosure" Philosophy and Company Law Reform' (1981) 2 Co. Law 51; W.M.H. Grover and J.C. Baillie, 'Disclosure Requirements,' p.353 at p.384 in Consumer and Corporate Affairs Canada, *Proposals for a Securities Market Law for Canada,* Vol.3 Background Papers (1979); B. Mercadal, 'Some Thoughts on the Disclosure Approach to Securities Regulation' (1978) 1 J.C.C.L.S.R.139.
17. H. Rose, *Disclosure in Company Accounts* (2nd ed. 1965).
18. The Department of Trade and Industry, op cit n4, p200, supra, para5.
19. Ibid, para10.

conduct giving rise to liability and when the stakes are high, sanctions for non-disclosure constitute less of a deterrent. Even when disclosure requirements are respected, financial and procedural considerations may limit shareholders' ability to enforce their rights. Indeed, shareholder control over management is generally regarded as ineffective. Given the costs of disclosure on those whose activities do not give rise to further liability, consideration must also be given to minimising this burden.

Although the emphasis on the protective role of disclosure predates the concern with the flow of information to the market, the two are intertwined. Informed investors and accurately priced securities make it more difficult to manipulate securities from their efficiently priced level. In turn, by eliminating the need for enforcement, disclosure results in the saving of costs. But there remains a conflict over the extent to which the efficiency and protective features should be allowed to interfere with each other.

Insider reporting requirements in Britain have reflected the evolution of disclosure as a regulatory technique. Initially imposed to raise standards of conduct, reliance on the deterrent effect of disclosure alone proved inadequate. With the introduction of criminal liability for insider dealing, reporting requirements may also serve an enforcement role. But a major purpose of the extension of statutory reporting requirements and their reinforcement by administrative measures has been to improve the flow of information to the market.

However, the role of disclosure in preventing fraud and manipulation has been challenged by Benston[20]. As well as pointing to scandals since the introduction of disclosure regulation, he relied on an empirical study of the financial statements of the 100 companies whose securities were subject to pools in 1929-33. The proportion of such companies revealing sales and cost of goods sold was almost the same as for companies whose securities were not included in the pools. He concluded that whilst the pools may or may not have been unfair to investors, their operations owed little to non-disclosure of accounting information.

But his arguments are unconvincing[1]. No assessment can be made of the fraud which would otherwise have occurred in the absence of disclosure regulation. It is also acknowledged that disclosure cannot deal with many forms of manipulation. Moreover, Benston confines his arguments to fraud. He does not deal with the issue of the role of disclosure regulation in relation to improper conduct, not involving fraud, and raising standards of behaviour in such areas as conflicts of interest.

D. Equality of access

Disclosure requirements are also regarded as a means of facilitating equal access to information. In attempting to make information available to all investors at more or less the same time so that the benefits of new information are not confined to insiders and market professionals, disclosure requirements seek to protect less informed investors from the more informed. Thus the Department endorses 'the general desirability of ensuring equality of information to all potential or actual investors' and the need 'to ensure, so far as is practically

---

20. Benston, op cit n12, p203, supra.
1. A.A. Sommer, Jr., 'The other side', Financial Executive, May 1974, 36.

possible, that the market operates freely on the basis of equality between buyer and seller'[2].

However, several factors may frustrate achievement of the objective of equality of access. First, there are timelag problems which are both practical and substantive. In practice, information will be available to someone before others. Substantively, disclosure is usually imposed well after the event so that most of the information will already have been disclosed and disseminated. Though timely disclosure provisions attempt to minimise the delay, they face a dilemma between speed and accuracy.

Secondly, empirical research[3] suggests that many investors do not use the information disclosed, but rely on other sources of information, such as stockbrokers. Studies have also shown that company reports are beyond the comprehension of some investors. Hence, any expansion of disclosure requirements needs to consider the extent to which regulation assumes investors are actively involved in interpreting the information or rely on intermediaries. This raises the issue of differential disclosure.

Differential disclosure involves the question of whether disclosure requirements should recognise the differing degrees of comprehension and technical competence among investors by requiring disclosure at more than one level. This could involve a concise statement of basic information, supplemented by more detailed disclosure for assessment either by investors or intermediaries whose assessments are then made available.

A third consideration concerns selective disclosure to intermediaries. The uneven possession of information among investors is often regarded as unfair. But the efficient market hypothesis implies that investors' interests may be protected by disclosure of information to a number of intermediaries who can compete with each other for the implications and interpretations of the information. The issue of selective disclosure should thus also take account of efficiency considerations.

Moreover, economic analysis suggests there are considerable incentives to search for non-publicly available information for trading purposes, though the process tends towards excessive information.[4] But as this is the converse of the public good argument which implies inadequate information, it would seem that opposing forces operate[5]. Some private search may be desirable to compensate for otherwise inadequate incentives to make public disclosure. Conversely, permitting too much can lead to inefficiencies.

Whilst the foregoing sets out the rationale for disclosure regulation, both its desirability and scope will continue to be matters of debate. But the trend towards the expansion of substantive disclosure requirements underlines the importance of disclosure regulation as an element of insider dealing regulation. The role of disclosure in this context will now be considered as regards substantive timely disclosure requirements.

II. TIMELY DISCLOSURE

A consequence of the difficulties associated with enforcement of insider

2. The Department of Trade and Industry, op cit n4, p200, supra, para15.
3. Eg, (ed) J.K. Courtis, *Communication via Annual Reports* (1981).
4. J. Hirschleiffer, 'The Private and Social Value of Information and the Reward to Inventive Activity' (1971) 61 Amer. Econ. Rev.561.
5. W.H. Beaver, *Financial Reporting: An Accounting Revolution* (1981), p.194.

prohibitions[6] is to enhance the importance of timely disclosure as an instrument of insider dealing regulation. More specifically, such disclosure contributes to the prompt and efficient performance by the market of its pricing and evaluation function and prevents insiders trading on advance knowledge of company developments.

Supported by statute[7] timely disclosure is imposed by Stock Exchange requirements[8]. In the context of take-overs and mergers, further provisions are contained in the Code.

In accordance with the object of securing the 'immediate release of information which might reasonably be expected to have a material effect on market activity in, and prices of, listed securities'[9], a general duty of timely disclosure is imposed by the Stock Exchange on listed companies (and an analogous provision extends this duty to USM companies[10]). In this respect, companies must notify the Quotations Department of:

'any information necessary to enable the holders of the company's listed securities and the public to appraise the position of the company and to avoid the establishment of a false market in its listed securities'[11].

This requirement is expressed to operate according to the 'guiding principle' that:

'information which is expected to be price-sensitive should be released immediately it is the subject of a decision. Until that point is reached, it is imperative that the strictest security within the issuer is observed'[12].

Expanding on this guiding principle, two principles are emphasised. Information should not be:

(1) 'released in such a way that Stock Exchange transactions may be entered into at prices which do not reflect the latest available information' nor

(2) 'divulged outside the company and its advisers in such a way as to place in a privileged dealing position any person or class or category of persons'[13].

6. See, ante, Chapter 3, Criminal Liability and, post, Chapter 6, Administrative Regulation.
7. Among the requirements for recognition of an investment exchange imposed by Sch4, FSA 1986, para2(2)(b) provides that the exchange must, where relevant, require issuers of investments dealt in on the exchange to comply with such obligations as will, so far as possible, afford to persons dealing in the investments proper information for determining their current value. By para2(3), in the case of securities to which Part IV of the Financial Services Act 1986 (Official Listing of Securities) applies, compliance by the Stock Exchange with the provisions of Part IV is treated as compliance by it with para2(2), Sch4, FSA 1986.
8. For listed companies, the timely disclosure provisions are contained in the Admission of Securities to Listing, Section 5 Continuing Obligations. For USM companies, the General Undertaking imposes similar requirements, though contains fewer explanatory notes. Whilst not considered further in this section, timely disclosure requirements are also imposed on companies whose securities are traded on the third market: *The Stock Exchange, The 3rd Market* (1987), Model terms for an undertaking to be given by a company to their sponsoring Member Firm.
9. Admission of Securities to Listing, Section 5, Chapter 1.
10. USM, General Undertaking, para1.
11. Admission of Securities to Listing, Section 5, Chapter 2, para1.
12. Ibid, Chapter 1.
13. Ibid, Chapter 2, Note 1.1.

Without derogating from these principles, companies may, in appropriate circumstances, give advance information in strict confidence to persons with whom negotiations are taking place with a view to making a contract or raising finance, such as prospective underwriters of a securities issue or providers of funds on loan. Persons receiving such information would be expected not to deal in the company's securities until its release[14].

In addition, an obligation to publish equivalent information is imposed on companies whose securities are also listed on other stock exchanges. Such companies must ensure that equivalent information is made available to the market at the Stock Exchange and each of such other exchanges[15].

With its ramifications of publicity and confidentiality, timely disclosure raises important issues. These include material information, the timing of disclosure and dissemination.

A. Material information

Determining material information poses difficulties not only in formulating possible tests or guidelines, but in differences in their application to particular companies. What may be material information in one company need not be in another.

1. Stock Exchange requirements

Whilst the Stock Exchange timely disclosure requirement is expressed to apply 'generally and apart from compliance with all specific requirements which follow'[16], specific provision is made for the disclosure of information (a) relating to major new developments, (b) immediately after approval by or on behalf of the board or (c) after the occurrence of other particular events. Not being exhaustive, these specific requirements can be viewed as a helpful checklist, with such itemisation providing a yardstick against which to measure materiality[17].

(a) MAJOR NEW DEVELOPMENTS

The company must notify any major new developments in its sphere of activity which are not public knowledge and which (a) in the case of a company having listed shares in issue may, by virtue of their effect on its assets and liabilities or financial position or on the general course of its business, lead to substantial movements in the price of its shares or (b) in the case of a company having listed debt securities in issue may significantly affect its ability to meet its commitments[18].

However, the Quotations Committee may dispense with publication of such information if publication might prejudice the company's business interests. Nevertheless, the Quotations Department must be informed in any event[19].

14. Ibid.
15. Ibid, Chapter 2, para3.
16. Ibid, para1.
17. A.R. Bromberg, 'Disclosure Programs for Publicly Held Companies – A Practical Guide' (1970) Duke L.J. 1139 at 1150-51.
18. Admission of Securities to Listing, Section 5, Chapter 2, para5.
19. Ibid, Chapter 2, Note 5.1.

(b) APPROVAL BY OR ON BEHALF OF THE BOARD

As a preliminary to disclosure immediately after approval by or on behalf of the board, a company must give the Quotations Department advance notification of the date for any board meeting at which the declaration or recommendation or payment of a dividend on listed shares is expected to be decided, or at which any announcement of the profits or losses in respect of any year, half-year or other period is to be approved for publication[20]. To facilitate publication by the Companies Announcements Office, ten days advance notification is recommended[1].

Immediately after approval by or on behalf of the board, particulars of these and other specified matters must then be notified[2]. The emphasis on disclosure is underlined by recommendations that the date of the board meeting should be fixed according to when such information needs to be made available outside the directors, employees and advisers necessarily concerned and that when a suitable date cannot be arranged, the board should delegate its power of approval to a committee so that the appropriate announcement can be made at the proper time[3].

Immediately after approval, a company must notify any decision to pay or make any dividend or other distribution on listed securities or to pass any such dividend or interest payment[4]. A schedule of suitable dates for companies to adopt when arranging dividend programmes is issued annually[5].

Similar notification of a preliminary announcement of profits or losses for any year, half-year or other period is required[6]. The recommended procedure for a preliminary profits statement for a full year is that as soon as possible after draft accounts, even though subject to final audit, have been agreed with auditors as the basis for completing the annual report, those accounts, adjusted to reflect any dividend decision, should be approved, in view of the price-sensitive nature as the basis of a preliminary profits statement. Completion of the annual report and accounts, involving a wider circle of persons than the directors, employees and advisers necessarily concerned would then proceed after the announcement[7].

In addition, any proposed change in capital structure (including that of the company's listed debt securities) must be so notified[8]. Following a decision to submit such a proposal to the board, no dealings (including option business) in any of the relevant securities should be effected by or on behalf of the company or any of its subsidiaries until the proposal has been announced or abandoned. Thus, care must be taken that any such proposal is capable of being finalised or made the subject of an interim announcement before any occasion arises to effect a purchase of any such securities for sinking fund purposes[9].

20. Ibid, Chapter 2, para.6; the analogous USM provision is General Undertaking, para2.
1. Ibid, Chapter 2, Note 6.1.
2. Ibid, Chapter 2, paras7-13; USM requirements are set out in General Undertaking, para3.
3. Ibid, Chapter 2, Note 1.13.
4. Ibid, Chapter 2, Para.7; the analogous USM provision is General Undertaking, para 3(a).
5. Ibid, Chapter 2, Note 7.1.
6. Ibid, Chapter 2, para8; the analogous USM provision is General Undertaking, para3 (b). Further requirements as to the publication and contents of half yearly reports and preliminary profits statements are contained in the Admission of Securities to Listing, Section 5, Chapter 2, paras 24 and 25.
7. Admission of Securities to Listing, Section 5, Chapter 2, Note 8.1.
8. Ibid, Chapter 2, para10; the analogous USM provision is para3(c).
9. Ibid, Chapter 2, Note 10.1.

However, an announcement of a new issue may be delayed while a marketing or underwriting is in progress[10]. Where the issue of further securities will result in a change in the terms of the exercise of options or warrants or of conversion of convertible debt securities or securities convertible or exchangeable into another class of securities, a simultaneous announcement of the effect of this change should be made[11].

Notification immediately after board approval is also required of any drawing or redemption of listed securities[12]. With regard to redeemable securities, the particulars to be given prior to any drawing should include the amount and date of the drawing and, in the case of a registered security, the period of the closing of the transfer books (or the date of the striking of the balance) for the drawing. After any drawing has been made, particulars of the amount of the security outstanding should be supplied. But purchases to meet the sinking fund requirements of the current year need not be notified[13].

(c) OCCURRENCE OF OTHER PARTICULAR EVENTS

Other disclosure requirements operate immediately after particular events. As major transactions affect a company's share price, the acquisition and realisation of assets must be notified[14] in accordance with provisions which divide such transactions into five classes for the purposes of disclosure[15]. Four categories of transactions, namely Classes 1-4, are classified by reference to percentage ratios in relation to (a) the value of the assets acquired or disposed of, compared with the assets of the acquiring or disposing company, (b) net profits attributable to the assets acquired or disposed of, compared with the assets of the acquiring or disposing company, (c) the aggregate value of the consideration given or received, compared with the assets of the acquiring or disposing company and (d) equity capital issued as consideration by the average of the published audited net profits of the company for the latest three years. The fifth class relates to very substantial acquisitions or reverse take-overs.

The most extensive disclosure provisions relate to Class 1 transactions (where any of the relevant percentage ratios is 15% or more) when, apart from an announcement to the Companies Announcements Office and the press, the company must either publish listing particulars or send a circular to shareholders[16]. As soon as possible after the terms of a Class 1 transaction have been agreed, the company must send six copies of an announcement to the Companies Announcements Office containing information in respect of (a) particulars of the assets being acquired or disposed of, including the name of any company or business where this is relevant, (b) a description of the trade carried on, (c) the aggregate value of the consideration, explaining how this is being satisfied, including the terms of any arrangements for payment on a deferred basis, (d) the value of the assets being acquired or disposed of, (e) the net profits attributable to the assets being acquired or disposed of, (f) the benefits expected to accrue to the company as a result of the transaction, (g) details of

10. Ibid, Chapter 2, Note 10.2.
11. Ibid, Chapter 2, Note 10.3.
12. Ibid, Chapter 2, para11; the analogous USM provision is para3(d).
13. Ibid, Chapter 2, Note 11.1.
14. Ibid, Chapter 2, para14; the analogous USM provision is para5(a), Note 1.
15. Ibid, Section 6, Chapter 1.
16. Ibid, Section 6, Chapter 1, para2. The provisions for transactions in Classes 2-4 and for very substantial acquisitions or reverse take-overs are also set out in Section 6, Chapter 1.

any service contracts of proposed directors of the company and (h) the application of the sale proceeds[17].

Any information to be disclosed to the Stock Exchange under the City Code must also be notified[18]. In particular, where an offer is due to expire, or becomes or is declared unconditional as to acceptances or is revised or extended, an announcement must be made to the Company Announcements Office by 9.00 a.m. at the latest on the dealing day next following[19]. Dealings of all parties and their associates in the shares of any offeror or offeree company on any day during the offer period, whether in the market or otherwise, must be disclosed to the Company Announcements Office not later than 12 noon on the dealing day following the date of the relevant transaction[20]. In addition, companies are reminded that disclosure obligations may arise in the course of a bid situation even though the listed company authorising dealing instructions in the relevant securities is not a party to the take-over.[1]

Similar disclosure is required in respect of other reporting requirements for securities transactions. In the case of a UK company, any information notified to the company under the provisions of the CA 1985 relating to disclosure of interests in voting shares in public companies, must be notified immediately[2]. However, the requirement to make an announcement will be deemed to have been discharged when notified as information to be disclosed under the City Code. It is in the company's interests to ensure that there is no duplication of announcement[3].

As regards directors' interests, immediate notification is required[4] of any matter which relates to securities which are or will be listed and which is either notified to the company pursuant to the statutory requirement for disclosure of directors' interests in securities[5] or required to be entered in the register of directors' interests[6]. Whereas statutory provisions require notification by a company to the Stock Exchange before the end of the day next following that on which the company received notification from the director[7], the Stock Exchange requires immediate notification[8]. The notification to the Companies Announcements Office must include the date on which the transaction was effected in addition to the details of the price and of the number, or amount, and class of securities concerned.[9]

In addition, in the case of companies not subject to the Companies Acts, notification must be made of equivalent information[10] in respect of the interests, including options, whether or not held through another party (corporate or otherwise), of each director, including his spouse and children under the age

17. Ibid, Section 6, Chapter 1, para4.2.
18. Ibid, Section 5, Chapter 2, para15; the analogous USM provision is para5(b).
19. Ibid, Chapter 2, Note 15.1.
20. Ibid.
1. Ibid.
2. Ibid, Chapter 2, para16(a) and Note 16.1; the analogous USM provision is para5(c); see post III. Insider reporting.
3. Ibid, Chapter 2, Note 16.2.
4. Ibid, Chapter 2, para16(b); the analogous USM provision is para5(g).
5. C.A.1985, ss324 and 328; see post III. Insider reporting.
6. Ibid, s325(3) and (4).
7. Ibid, s329.
8. Admission of Securities to Listing, Section 5, Chapter 2, Note 16.3.
9. Ibid, Note 16.4.
10. Ie, to that required under paras16(a) and (b).

of 18 years in, and, so far as is known to the company, of each holder of 5% or more of, the share capital of the company[11].

Notification is also required in relation to the purchases by the company of its own shares. As a preliminary, any decision by the board to submit to the company's shareholders a proposal for the company to be authorised to purchase its own shares must be notified immediately. An indication must be given as to whether the proposal relates to specific purchases, or to a general authorisation to make purchases. The outcome of the shareholders' meeting must also be notified immediately and four copies of the relevant resolutions forwarded to the Stock Exchange as soon as possible[12].

Subsequently, any purchase by the company, or the group of which the company is part, of its listed securities must be notified[13]. Purchases by a company of its own shares should be notified by 12 noon on the business day following dealing. The notification should include the number of shares purchased and the purchase price per share or the highest and lowest prices paid, where relevant[14]. Purchases of debt securities or convertible debt securities may be aggregated and an announcement should be made when 5% of the outstanding amount of a security has been acquired. If the company purchases further amounts of its securities, an announcement should be made whenever an additional 1% has been acquired[15].

Further notification requirements apply to any board decision to change the general character or nature of the business of the company or of the group[16] and to a change in the company's status for taxation purposes under the statutory provisions relating to close companies or approved investment trusts[17].

In regard to a company's capital, notification of various matters is required. A company having listed debt securities in issue must notify any new issues of debt securities and, in particular, any guarantee or security in respect thereof[18]. Any change in the rights attaching to any class of listed securities (including any change in the rate of interest carried by a debt security) and any change in the rights attaching to any shares into which any listed debt securities are convertible or exchangeable must also be notified[19]. In addition, the basis of allotment of securities offered generally to the public for cash, other than by a selective marketing, and of open offers to shareholders must be notified and appear in the press before dealings commence[20].

Despite the general wording of the Stock Exchange requirement, the scope of material information is narrower than on the New York Stock Exchange[1]. Indeed, a US company has cited the undemanding requirements for disclosure of sensitive trading information as a reason for seeking a listing in London[2]

.

---

11. Admission of Securities to Listing, Section 5, Chapter 2, para16(c).
12. Ibid, Chapter 2, Para.16(d); the analogous USM provision is para5(c).
13. Ibid, Chapter 2, para17.
14. Ibid, Chapter 2, Note 17.1.
15. Ibid, Chapter 2, Note 17.2.
16. Ibid, Chapter 2, para18; the analogous USM provision is para5(f).
17. Ibid, Chapter 2, para19.
18. Ibid, Chapter 2, para9.
19. Ibid, Chapter 2, para12.
20. Ibid, Chapter 2, para13.
1. New York Stock Exchange Company Manual, Agreement of Issuers in Listing Stock on Exchange.
2. *The Times*, 24th September, 1982.

2. The Code

Apart from provisions relating to the announcement of amended offers[3] and of acceptance levels[4] and to public disclosure of dealings by parties to a take-over and their associates, by significant shareholders and by connected exempt market makers in the course of a take-over[5], the Code imposes timely disclosure of bids.

In regard to the announcement of a possible offer, the Code provides that, except in the case of a mandatory offer under Rule 9 or until a firm intention to make an offer has been notified, a brief announcement that talks are taking place (there is no requirement to name the potential offeror in such an announcement) or that a potential offeror is considering making an offer will normally satisfy the obligations relating to the announcement of a possible offer[6].

The announcement of a firm intention to make an offer[7] must contain the terms of the offer, the identity of the offeror and all conditions (including normal conditions relating to acceptances, listing and increase of capital) to which the offer or its posting is subject[8]. The announcement must also state details of any existing holding in the offeree company: (a) which is owned or controlled by the offeror, or by any person acting in concert with the offeror, or (b) in respect of which the offeror either holds an option to purchase or has received an irrevocable commitment to accept the offer or (c) in respect of which any person acting in concert with the offeror holds an option to purchase. In addition, the announcement must give details of any indemnity or other arrangement with any offeror, with the offeree company or with an associate of any offeror or of the offeree company in relation to the relevant securities[9].

In the case of the announcement of an offer under Rule 9, a duty is placed on financial advisers. In particular, such announcement should include confirmation by the financial adviser or by another appropriate independent party that resources are available to the offeror sufficient to satisfy full acceptance of the offer.[10]

Further provisions relating to unambiguous language are set out in an accompanying note[11]. Thus, the language used in announcements should clearly and concisely reflect the position being described. In particular, the word 'agreement' should be used with the greatest care. Statements should be avoided which may give the impression that persons have committed themselves to certain courses of action (eg accepting in respect of their own shares) when they have not in fact done so.

Reference is also made in the Note to holdings by a group of which an adviser

---

3. Code, Rule 7.
4. Ibid, Rule 17.
5. See post, III. Insider reporting.
6. Code, Rule 2.4.
7. The Code, Rule 2.5(a) provides that the announcement of a firm intention to make an offer should be made only when an offeror has every reason to believe that it can and will continue to be able to implement the offer. Responsibility in this connection also rests on the financial adviser to the offeror.
8. Code, Rule 2.5(b).
9. Ie, of the kind referred to in Note 6(b) of Rule 8.
10. Ibid, Rule 2.5(c). However, the party confirming that resources are available will not be expected to produce the cash itself if, in giving the confirmation, it acted responsibly and took all reasonable steps to assure itself that the cash was available.
11. Code, Rule 2.5, Note 1.

is a member,[12] irrevocable commitments,[13] subjective conditions[14] and new conditions for increased or improved offers.[15] In particular, references to commitments to accept an offer must specify in what circumstances, if any, they will cease to be binding; for example, if a higher offer is made. As to subjective conditions, companies and their advisers should consult the Panel prior to the issue of any announcement containing conditions which are not entirely objective. In regard to holdings by a group of which an adviser is a member, disclosure requirements are relaxed for multi-service financial organisations in circumstances when secrecy might otherwise be breached. In particular, the Note states that it is accepted that, for reasons of secrecy, it would not be prudent to make enquires so as to include in an announcement details of offeree company shares held by other parts of an adviser's group; in such circumstances, details should be obtained as soon as possible after the announcement has been made and the Panel consulted. If the holdings are significant, a further announcement may be required.

B. Timing of disclosure

The timing of disclosure is crucial. Premature disclosure, especially before materiality, may upset transactions, cause competitive harm, encourage speculation and be misleading when developments do not occur as expected. But delayed disclosure deprives the market of mature information and encourages leaks, rumours and insider transactions[16].

1. Stock Exchange requirements

The 'guiding principle' is that 'information which is expected to be price-sensitive should be released immediately it is the subject of a decision'[17]. Until then, strict security within the company must be observed. In view of an announcement's possible effect on the market price of the company's listed securities, 'speed is of the essence'[18].

A further consideration is the range of persons to whom the relevant information is known. In this connection, it is provided that information should be released before the stage when it needs to be made available outside the directors, employees and advisers necessarily concerned[19]. The date of the requisite board meeting should be fixed with this consideration in mind; if a suitable date cannot be fixed, it may be necessary for the board to delegate its power of approval to a committee so that the appropriate announcement can be made at the proper time. Whilst a different criterion from materiality, reference to the range of persons is designed to prevent confidential information being known to large numbers with the consequent risk of leaks which could place persons in privileged dealing positions.

In regard to developing information, the importance of strict security is

12. Ibid, Note 2.
13. Ibid, Note 3.
14. Ibid, Note 4.
15. Ibid, Note 5.
16. A.R. Bromberg and L.D. Lowenfels, *Securities Fraud and Commodities Fraud* (1979), Vol.2, 7.4(6) (c).
17. Admission of Securities to Listing, Section 5, Chapter 1.
18. Ibid, Chapter 2, Note 1.7.
19. Ibid, Chapter 2, Note 1.13.

again emphasised[20]. The corollary is that a warning announcement should be made if at any time it is felt that the necessary degree of security cannot be maintained or that security may have been breached. In some situations the lack of a warning announcement may lead to the establishment of a false market. In particular, in merger and take-over transactions, a warning announcement or a temporary suspension of listing will normally be required where negotiations have reached a point at which an offeree company is reasonably confident that an offer will be made for its shares or where negotiations or discussions are extended to embrace more than a small group of people.

The timing of board meetings is expressed to be a matter for the convenience and judgment of individual boards[1]. However, as regards dividends, profits and other matters requiring announcement, it is recommended that decisions should, if possible, be taken and notified to the Company Announcements Office (CAO) before 5.30 p.m. to ensure release before the close of the Company News Service (CNS) at 6 p.m.

When a company is required by statute or otherwise to impart price sensitive information to a third party, the information should be notified to the CAO well before release to the third party so that it can be simultaneously released to the Stock Exchange[2]. Where the information relates to a proposal by the company which is subject to negotiation with employees or trade union representatives and which, if implemented, would be price sensitive, the company may defer the release of the information until such time as agreement has been reached as to the implementation of the proposal. Information provided to, and for the purpose only of, a government department or the Bank of England is excepted.

A similar procedure applies to proposed price sensitive announcements at shareholders' meetings. Where it is proposed to announce at any meeting of holders of listed securities information which might affect the market price of the company's securities, arrangements should be made for notification of that information to the CAO so that it can be released simultaneously through CNS[3].

Special provision is made for when directors consider that disclosure of information to the public might prejudice the company's business interests[4]. In that event, the Quotations Department must be consulted as soon as possible.

A particular area of security risk is identified as the release of an announcement subject to an embargo. All announcements should be free from embargo, except by special arrangement with the Department, for example, where there is to be a simultaneous release in other centres outside the UK or where release is to coincide with a press conference or similar event[5]. In such cases, any release requirements must be stated at the head of the announcement.

An important reservation is expressed regarding the practice of issuing announcements carrying a rider that further information is obtainable by telephoning a given number[6]. Such practice is acceptable only so long as on enquiry no important supplementary details are released to the caller which may result in dealings taking place with only one party to a bargain being in possession of such information.

20. Ibid, Chapter 2, Note 1.2.
1. Ibid, Chapter 2, Note 6.2.
2. Ibid, Chapter 2, Note 1.3.
3. Ibid, Chapter 2, Note 1.11.
4. Ibid, Chapter 2, Note 1.12.
5. Ibid, Chapter 2, Note 1.8.
6. Ibid, Chapter 2, Note 1.9.

2. *The Code*

In the context of take-overs and mergers, more detailed requirements for the timing of announcements are imposed by the Code. The emphasis on early announcements, coupled with secrecy requirements[7], has become progressively more marked since the 1977 Joint Statement by the Stock Exchange and Panel on the Announcement of Price-Sensitive Matters[8] and is in response to the pattern of price rises before a bid announcement[9].

(a) EARLY ANNOUNCEMENTS

The Code identifies five situations when an announcement is required[10]. The first is when a firm intention to make an offer (the making of which is not, or has ceased to be, subject to any pre-condition) is notified to the board of the offeree company from a serious source, irrespective of the attitude of the board to the offer.

Secondly, an announcement is required immediately upon an acquisition of shares which gives rise to an obligation to make an offer under Rule 9. The Code expressly provides that the announcement that an obligation has been incurred should not be delayed while full information is being obtained and that additional information can be the subject of a later supplementary announcement.

Thirdly, an announcement must be made when, following an approach to the offeree company, the offeree company is the subject of rumour and speculation, or there is an untoward movement in its share price. For this purpose, a movement of approximately 10% should be regarded as untoward[11].

In its 1984 Report[12], the Panel emphasised that it had always attached great importance to an immediate announcement in the event of an untoward movement in share price. It recognised that there could be an understandable conflict of objectives between the Panel, which requires that the market is properly informed, and companies and their advisers who would prefer to say nothing publicly until the transaction is fully agreed. Whilst acknowledging the arguments against making announcements too early, the Panel considered it was of paramount importance that where talks are in progress and there has been an untoward movement in the offeree company's share price an immediate announcement should be made, since the price movement demonstrates that shareholders have been exposed to the risk of being taken advantage of in the market. It emphasised that a statement that talks which may or may not lead to an offer are taking place will normally satisfy the Code's requirements.

---

7. Code, Rule 2. This rule is complemented by Rule 1 which requires that in the first instance the offer must be put forward to the board of the offeree company or to its advisers. If the offer, or an approach with a view to an offer being made, is not made by the ultimate offeror or potential offeror, the identity of that person must be disclosed at the outset. A board so approached is entitled to be satisfied that the offeror is, or will be, in a position to implement the offer in full.
8. Joint Statement issued by the Stock Exchange and the Panel on Take-overs and Mergers on 14th April, 1977, 'Announcement of Price-Sensitive Matters'. This is published as an Appendix to the Panel's Report on the Year ended 31st March, 1977, p.13.
9. See, ante, Chapter 1. Introduction, II. Empirical Assessment.
10. Code, Rule 2.2.
11. Ibid, Note on Rule 2.2. This Note imposes a requirement of consultation with the Panel when (a) there is such a movement or the offeree company is the subject of rumour and speculation and (b) it is not proposed to make an immediate announcement.
12. The Panel on Take-overs and Mergers, Report on the Year ended 31st March. 1984, pp8-9.

Fourthly, an announcement is required when, before an approach has been made, the offeree company is the subject of rumour and speculation or an untoward price movement and there are reasonable grounds for concluding that it is the potential offeror's actions (whether through inadequate security, purchasing of offeree company shares or otherwise) which have led to the situation. Again, a movement of approximately 10% should be regarded as untoward[13].

Fifthly, an announcement must be made when negotiations or discussions are about to be extended to include more than a very restricted number of people (outside those who need to know in the companies concerned and their immediate advisers). The Code adds that an offeror wishing to approach a wider group, for example, where a consortium to make an offer is being organised or where irrevocable commitments are being sought, should consult the Panel[14]. In its 1984 Report, the Panel expressed the view that the incidence of price rises before offer announcements would be reduced by a reduction in the number of people made aware of a potential offer and an increased willingness to make talks announcements at an earlier stage[15].

Responsibilities in regard to the making of an announcement are placed on both the offeror and the offeree company. Responsibility is placed on the offeror alone in two circumstances[16]. Before the board of an offeree company is approached, the responsibility for making an announcement can lie only with the offeror; the offeror should, therefore, keep a close watch on the potential offeree company's share price for signs of any untoward movement. The offeror is also responsible for making the announcement once a Rule 9 obligation has been incurred.

Thereafter, the primary responsibility is placed on the offeree. In this connection, the Code provides that following an approach to the board of the offeree company which may or may not lead to an offer, the primary responsibility for making an announcement will normally rest with the board of the offeree company, which must, therefore, keep a close watch on its share price[17]. It adds that where the offer is to be recommended and the Stock Exchange is likely to grant a temporary suspension, a possible alternative to an immediate announcement may be to obtain a suspension to be followed shortly by an announcement.

However, as to suspensions, it is emphasised in a Note[18] that a suspension will only be granted by the Stock Exchange at the request of the company whose

---

13. Code, Note on Rule 2.2. Again, this provision imposes a requirement of consultation with the Panel when (a) there is such a movement or the offeree company is the subject of rumour and speculation and (b) it is not proposed to make an immediate announcement.
14. In a Statement on Teacher (Distillers) Ltd., 7th July, 1977, the Panel were critical of a situation where about fifty shareholders and trustees were consulted about their willingness to give powers of attorney to directors to accept an offer. In its 1979 Report, the Panel emphasised the importance of the number of persons being consulted about a proposed offer and indicated that it would normally be critical of a failure to make an announcement when more than a very limited number of people have knowledge of the possibility of a bid. In particular, it regarded as unacceptable for a potential offeror to indicate to the offeree board that no offer would be made unless a stated percentage of share capital was first committed and then to attempt (often at a weekend) to gather commitments from a wide range of people, followed by a price rise on Monday morning and an announcement on Tuesday. In such circumstances, the offeree board should insist on a warning announcement or ask for a suspension of dealings before the gathering of commitments begins: The Panel on Take-overs and Mergers, Report on the Year ended 31st March, 1979, p.6.
15. The Panel on Take-overs and Mergers, Report on the Year ended 31st March, 1984, p.9.
16. Code, Rule 2.3.
17. Ibid.
18. Code, Rule 2.3, Note 1.

shares are to be suspended. Such suspension will not generally be granted for more than 48 hours. Rather, the primary obligation is to make the appropriate announcement as quickly as possible and the Panel will not be sympathetic to delay which is occasioned by an unsuccessful application for suspension.

Complementing its own duty of disclosure, a potential offeror is prohibited by the Code from attempting to prevent the board of an offeree company from making an announcement[19]. This provision was introduced to counter the practice of offerors insisting as a condition of negotiations that no announcement be made before a particular stage[20]. A potential offeror must also not attempt to prevent a request by the offeree board to the Stock Exchange to grant a temporary suspension of listing at any time the board thinks appropriate[1].

In its 1983 Report[2], the Panel again identified the making of announcements as an area of the Code which had given rise to difficulties[3]. After a number of untoward price movements in offeree shares shortly before the announcement of an offer or possible offer, the Panel emphasised Code requirements as to the making of announcements, with particular reference to two aspects. First, tactical considerations were stated not to be an acceptable reason for any delay in the fulfilment of announcement obligations. Secondly, far from an offeror ceasing to have any duties regarding the making of announcements after approaching the offeree, the offeror had a continuing obligation to make an announcement if the circumstances demanded it.

Its concern about offer announcements has since been emphasised by the Panel in a 1987 statement[4] and reiterated in its 1988 Annual Report.[5] In the 1987 Panel statement, reference was made to the reluctance of some offerors, when proposals are still tentative, to make an announcement on the grounds that, rumour and speculative activity notwithstanding, an announcement, in the absence of firm plans, may itself mislead the market. The Panel commented that, rather than being a justification for allowing uncertainty to continue, this problem could be avoided by a proper explanation; shareholders could then assess the probability of a bid emerging on the basis of the best information available, rather than on speculation. In particular, advisers should not delay an announcement simply because financing arrangements are not yet in place. Another important reason for compliance with Code early announcement requirements was that holdings are frequently acquired in companies which are the subject of take-over speculation, by investors who are not intending to make an offer. Though not obliged to do so, such investors sometimes state specifically that they do not intend to make an offer, thereby keeping the market informed. The effect of Code provisions indicating when an announcement was required[6] was, however, that in the absence of a statement that the investor is a possible offeror, the market is entitled to infer that there is no such intention. The Panel added this inference could only safely be drawn if all potential

---

19. Ibid, Rule 2.3.
20. An example of an offeror requiring no announcement as a term of the negotiations was provided in the Panel on Take-overs and Mergers, Statement on the Dickinson Robinson Group Limited/Royal Sovereign Group Limited, 20th June, 1977.
1. Code, Rule 2.3.
2. The Panel on Take-overs and Mergers, Report on the Year ended 31st March, 1983, p.10.
3. The making of announcements had previously been the subject of comment in The Panel on Take-overs and Mergers, Report on the Year ended 31st March, 1978, pp10-11 and Report on the Year ended 31st March, 1979, p.6.
4. The Panel on Take-overs and Mergers, Offer Announcements, 10th September, 1987.
5. The Panel on Take-overs and Mergers, Report on the Year ended 31st March, 1988, pp7-8.
6. Rule 2.2.

offerors comply promptly with their Code obligations. In addition to emphasising the importance of consulting it, the Panel concluded by stating that, in all cases, the fact that tactical considerations may make an announcement undesirable must not be allowed to influence the decision as to whether an announcement is necessary.

(b) SECRECY AND SECURITY

Complementing its emphasis on early announcements, the Code regulates the treatment of confidential information by imposing requirements of secrecy and security. These requirements are directed at both financial advisers and their clients.

At the very beginning of discussions, it is emphasised in a Note[7] that it should be an invariable routine for advisers to warn clients of the importance of secrecy and security. Attention should be drawn to the Code, in particular to the requirement of secrecy before announcements and to restrictions on dealings.[8]

As to secrecy, Rule 2.1 states that the vital importance of absolute secrecy before an announcement must be emphasised. All persons privy to confidential information, and particularly price sensitive information, concerning an offer or contemplated offer must treat that information as secret and may only pass it to another person if it is necessary to do so and if that person is made aware of the need for secrecy. All such persons must conduct themselves so as to minimise the chances of an accidental leak of information.

Two further aspects are spelt out in Notes. First, proof printing documents before a public announcement has been made is identified as carrying a particular risk of leaks of price sensitive information[9]. In cases where it is regarded as appropriate to undertake such printing, every possible precaution must be taken to ensure confidentiality.

The second concerns the special position of underwriters in the case of an underwritten cash alternative[10]. Because of the chances of a leak of price-sensitive information, the Note states that where a proposed offer is to be recommended and it is intended to provide a cash alternative by way of underwriting, the offeree company should, assuming no announcement has been made, request the Stock Exchange to grant a temporary suspension before the proposed offer is disclosed to any sub-underwriters. Where an offer is not recommended and hence a suspension is impracticable, a restricted number of sub-underwriters may be informed of the offer immediately before the announcement, provided that they are expressly warned of the confidential nature of the information.

Breach of the secrecy requirements has been a cause of concern to the Panel, voiced in its statements on individual bids and in annual reports. Its statements on individual bids[11] have revealed that leaks were due primarily to carelessness

7. Code, Rule 2.1, Note 1.
8. See Chapter 6, Administrative Regulation, I. Restrictions on dealings.
9. Code, Rule 2.1, Note 2.
10. Ibid, Rule 2.3, Note 2. When a share-for-share or loan stock-for-share offer is 'underwritten for cash', a merchant bank undertakes to purchase from accepting shareholders for cash at a stated price the shares and/or loan stock in the offeror company received by them upon acceptance of the offer, *Weinberg and Blank on Take-overs and Mergers*, Fourth Edition by M.A. Weinberg, M.V. Blank and A.L. Greystoke (1979), para609.
11. The Panel on Take-overs and Mergers, Statement on United Drapery Stores Limited/William Timpson Limited, 14th March, 1973; Statement on the Boots Company Limited/House of Fraser

and inadequate security precautions in offeree companies. However, the inconclusiveness of Panel investigations also emphasised the difficulties of discovering the source of the leak and of detecting instances of insider dealing.

The recurring nature of the secrecy problem was underlined by the Panel in its 1983 Report[12] when it again drew attention to the vital importance of absolute secrecy during the time when an offer is being planned. In a number of cases there had been an untoward price movement in offeree shares shortly before the announcement of an offer or possible offer. In this connection, the Panel referred to the Code provisions as to the timing of announcements.

C. Dissemination

1. Stock Exchange requirements

References to notification of information means delivery to the CAO in London for release through the CNS[13]. This is an electronic information dissemination service operated by CAO which provides access to the full text of announcements released. The text may be viewed on screen; if required, a print out may be obtained. Apart from full text announcements, the service publishes board meeting dates, 'ex benefit' details and other items of information relating to new listings, suspensions and restorations of listings or dealings.

The service transmits information from 8 a.m. to 6 p.m. on each business day[14]. Indices guide subscribers to the required information. The size and complexity of certain documents, such as reports and accounts or lengthy circulars, may render such documents unsuitable for processing through the system. In such cases, a reference is made to those items on the CNS indices and the documents are available for inspection at the CAO.

Announcements must be notified in a form that permits their rapid capture and processing by CNS[15]. A preference for electronic methods of delivery is stressed. Apart from telex, these include various electronic mail box services and direct communication links via telephone lines from the issuer's computer or word-processing equipment. Detailed guidelines contain information on the methods of communication between companies and the CAO, and the forms of presentation of announcements which should be used[16]. The importance of adherence to Stock Exchange recommendations is emphasised in the context of assisting in the rapid release of information, particularly announcements which cannot be transmitted in electronic form to the system.

Announcements may be sent to the CNS electronically at any time[17]. Information received overnight is released the following morning. Announcements notified up to 5.30 p.m. are released on the day of receipt. Announcements received after 5.30 p.m. are held over until the commencement of the service on the following morning. If not subject to a specific release requirement, news

Limited, 23rd July, 1974; Statement on Tootal Limited/Trutex Limited, 2nd October, 1975; Statement on Hewden-Stuart Plant Limited/A. Gunn (Holdings) Limited, 11th February, 1976, and Statement on the Dickinson Robinson Group Limited/Royal Sovereign Group Limited, 20th June, 1977.
12. The Panel on Take-overs and Mergers, Report on the Year ended 31st March, 1983, p.10.
13. Admission of Securities to Listing, Section 5, Chapter 1.
14. Ibid, Chapter 2, Note 1.4.
15. Ibid, Chapter 1.
16. Ibid, Chapter 2, Note 1.5.
17. Ibid, Chapter 2, Note 1.6.

may be transmitted by CNS from 7.30 a.m. to ensure that as much information as possible is available to the market by the time it opens.

Announcements are transmitted to the principal Unit Offices of the Stock Exchange and copies posted on all trading floors[18]. The CNS is available to subscribers countrywide, including subscription by press services. The salient points of selected price sensitive announcements may also be referred to on the Stock Exchange's edited news service[19].

However, when the press is unwilling to publish the information or merely reports a small part of it, dissemination can only be adequately ensured by a company sending a report to its shareholders. But this is more time-consuming and expensive[20].

If they are not to exploit their trading advantages, insiders may not deal on communication of the information to the CAO, but only on publication and an additional period for its absorption and evaluation. The effective waiting period will vary with the type of information and effectiveness of dissemination. Where a warning announcement is made, insiders would need to delay trading until matters are clarified by public disclosure of subsequent events.

2. The Code

An obligation to circulate announcements is imposed by the Code. Promptly after the first announcement of an offer or possible offer, a copy of the press notice or a circular summarising the terms and conditions of the offer must be sent by the offeree company to its shareholders and to the Panel[1].

III. INSIDER REPORTING

Insider reporting requirements may be imposed for several reasons. First, disclosure and resulting publicity are considered to have a deterrent effect. Secondly, they can facilitate enforcement of insider liabilities since the reports provide material evidence. Thirdly, the reports contain information about an insider's assessment of his company's securities[2] which may in turn affect the market's evaluation. Fourthly, reporting requirements which include substantial shareholders inform investors of a new influence on management and may thereby affect investment decisions.

Such considerations have received varying emphasis. Initially imposed in 1948[3] for its deterrent effect, in 1967 legislation requiring disclosure to the company of directors' interests in shares or debentures was repealed and replaced by more stringent requirements[4] and analogous provisions relating to substantial shareholders were also enacted[5]. The result was two separate sets of provisions with different bases for reporting:

18. Ibid, Chapter 2, Note 1.10.
19. Ibid, Chapter 2, Note 1.4.
20. W.H. Painter, *The Federal Securities Code and Corporate Disclosure* (1979), pp352-353.
1. Code, Rule 2.6.
2. As to empirical evidence in the US in support of the informational value of reporting by corporate insiders, see, ante, Chapter 1. Introduction.
3. C.A. 1948, ss195 and 198.
4. C.A. 1967, ss27-32.
5. Ibid, ss33-34.

'The provisions relating to directors were designed to prevent dealings by them with undisclosed insider information, whereas those relating to shareholders were primarily intended to protect directors against a secret build-up of a substantial shareholding with a view to a take-over. Anyone, however, with a substantial holding is likely to be in a position to acquire inside information and may, indeed, be a true controller of the company. Hence, in the second case also, disclosure of dealings helps to achieve the aim of discouraging insider trading'[6].

Both sets of provisions were subsequently modified and with the imposition of criminal liability in 1980, they could also serve an enforcement role[7]. The 1967 requirements for directors were amended in 1976 and 1981[8]. After amendment in 1976[9] those concerning substantial shareholders were repealed and replaced by the CA 1985[10]. This provided for the disclosure of interests in voting shares in public companies after the issue had gained prominence following the dawn raid on Consolidated Gold Fields shares in 1980. Large blocks of shares and ultimate ownership changed hands after rapid Stock Exchange purchases of which many shareholders were unaware and many bidders had mounted up interests unknown to the company. Such transactions gave rise to suspicion that there could have been exchange of inside information and that transactions had been organised in advance[11]. Both sets of provisions are now contained in the CA 1985[12], though further legislative change is anticipated.[13]

Further disclosure to the market is imposed by other provisions. Both sets of provisions in the Companies Act 1985 are reinforced by the Stock Exchange: for listed securities, by reason of the Admission of Securities to Listing and for USM securities, under the General Undertaking. The legislative provisions for disclosure of interests in voting shares in public companies are also supplemented by the 'Rules Governing Substantial Acquisitions of Shares', issued on the authority of the Panel[14]. In addition, the Code contains reporting obligations in connection with take-overs and mergers; apart from disclosure of dealings during the offer period[15], since 1982 it has further required the disclosure of an acquisition from a single shareholder prior to the announcement of a firm intention to make an offer[16] and in 1986, disclosure of dealings by connected exempt market-makers was imposed[17].

Before considering these reporting requirements in detail, the methods of representing shares should be noted. Insofar as they allow concealment of the

6. Gower, pp632-633.
7. In the absence of general provision for civil liability, the potential of reporting as a basis for enforcement is limited. For detection in respect of criminal liability introduced by the CA 1980, in practice reliance is placed on market surveillance.
8. C.A. 1976, ss24-25 and C.A. 1981, Sch3, para29.
9. C.A. 1976, ss26-27.
10. C.A. 1981, ss63-83.
11. The Panel on Take-overs and Mergers, Report on the Year ended 31st March, 1980, Foreword by Lord Shawcross, p.5
12. C.A. 1985, ss198-220, 324-326 and 328-329.
13. *Financial Times*, 8th December, 1988. This follows the publication of: Department of Trade and Industry, A Consultative Document (1988). The main proposals are to reduce the notifiable percentage from 5% to 3% and the time limit for notifications from 5 to 2 days.
14. These were initially issued by the CSI. They are administered by the Panel executive and known as the 'Substantial Acquisitions Rules' (the SARs).
15. Code, Rule 8.
16. Ibid, Rule 5.
17. Ibid, Rule 38.

true owners, methods of representing shares are inconsistent with reporting requirements. But difficulties arise in that the methods of representing shares are also influenced by considerations other than reporting requirements.

Whilst the power has not been exercised on a significant scale, the issue of bearer shares is permitted: a company may, if authorised by its articles, issue a share warrant to bearer with respect to any fully paid-up shares[18]. In such circumstances, the scope for evasion of reporting requirements is increased since the ownership of bearer shares is not registered and investigations into interests in voting shares are thus obstructed.

In regard to alternative approaches[19], prohibition of bearer shares would be draconian and might deprive companies of the commercial advantages of a wider market for their securities. Yet the intermediate solutions are also unsatisfactory. As directors can take into account the risk of bearer shares being used to evade reporting requirements when their issue is considered, it seems inappropriate on this ground alone to introduce a limitation on the proportion of a company's voting share capital in the form of bearer shares. The scope for abuse could be reduced by clarifying the legal position regarding the membership status of holders of bearer shares. Apart from stating that a holder of bearer shares is to be regarded as a member for all purposes, to prevent evasion of reporting requirements the law would need to require a holder of bearer shares to notify the company of his identity. But the purpose of bearer shares is thereby removed.

Rather than use bearer shares, the general practice is to issue shares registered in the name of the holder. The Cohen Report recognised the risk of a director acting on inside knowledge was 'increased by the practice of registering shares in the names of nominees'[20].

However, the prohibition of nominee registration has been consistently rejected. The 1973 White Paper argued:

> 'There is nothing inherently wrong in the practice of holding shares through nominees; and indeed there are many circumstances in which the practice is both normal and convenient on commercial or personal grounds. Furthermore, there is a large and complex area of common law and the law of trusts which would be involved in any attempt to forbid the practice even if it were thought desirable'[1].

Particular difficulties would arise from the statutory provision that no notice of any trust shall be entered on the register of members maintained by the company or be receivable by the registrar[2] and the principle that a company is not bound to recognise any equitable interest or any other right in a share except an absolute right in the registered holder[3].

Instead, the approach has been to identify circumstances in which concealment of a beneficial interest in a holding can be undesirable. The result has been statutory requirements for companies to maintain a register of directors' interests in securities and a register of interests in voting shares.

18. C.A. 1985, s188.
19. These are discussed in: The Department of Trade *Disclosure of Interests in Shares* (1980), paras.29-32; The Law Society, *Disclosure of Interests in Shares* Department of Trade Consultative Document, Memorandum by the Society's Standing Committee on Company Law (1980), para7.
20. Cohen Report, Cmd.6659 (1945), para86.
1. Department of Trade, *Company Law Reform*, Cmnd.5391 (1973), para21.
2. C.A. 1985, s360.
3. *Re Perkins, ex parte Mexican Santa Barbara Mining Co.* (1980) 24 Q.B.D. 613.

Apart from the methods of representing shares, further issues are raised by the substantive reporting requirements themselves. These mainly concern (a) the securities affected, (b) the definition of insider, (c) the operation of reporting, (d) exemptions and (e) sanctions and enforcement.

A. Securities to which the requirements relate

1. Companies Act 1985

(a) DIRECTORS' INTERESTS IN SHARES OR DEBENTURES

The securities affected vary according to the basis of reporting. The disclosure of directors' interests applies to shares in or debentures of the company or any other body corporate[4], being the company's subsidiary or holding company or a subsidiary of the company's holding company[5]. However, shares in a body corporate which is a wholly-owned subsidiary of another body corporate are excluded[6], since the director could only hold such shares as a nominee for another body corporate in the group.

(b) INTERESTS IN VOTING SHARES IN PUBLIC COMPANIES

In contrast, reflecting concern with disclosure of actual or potential controllers, other statutory provisions relating to the disclosure of interests in shares are limited to an interest in shares comprised in a public company's relevant share capital[7]. In this context, 'relevant share capital' means the company's issued share capital of a class carrying rights to vote in all circumstances at general meetings of the company[8]. Any temporary suspension of voting rights is declared irrelevant for this purpose[9]. The scope of these provisions is wider than the substantial shareholding requirements of the CA 1967 which applied only to voting shares in quoted companies[10]. Private companies are not included, though a degree of disclosure can be provided by controls imposed on the transfer of their shares.

2. Stock Exchange

Additional Stock Exchange obligations are drafted by reference to the legislation for disclosure of both (a) directors' interests in shares or debentures and (b) interests in voting shares in public companies. However, they are not confined to companies subject to the Companies Acts; but rather they are expressly stated to apply to companies not subject to the Companies Acts, but in respect of which equivalent information is required[11]. Nevertheless, the basis of Stock Exchange regulation means that their application is limited to companies

4. As defined in C.A.1985, s740.
5. C.A. 1985, s324(1).
6. Ibid, s324 (6).
7. Ibid, s198(1).
8. Ibid, s198(2).
9. Ibid, s198(2) (b).
10. C.A.1967, s33(10).
11. Admission of Securities to Listing, Section 5, Chapter 2, para16.

whose securities are or will be admitted to official listing or traded on the USM[12].

3. The SARs

Consistent with the aim of supplementing legislation for the disclosure of voting interests in shares and the scope of responsibilities of the former CSI, the disclosure imposed by the Substantial Acquisition Rules[13] (the SARs), applies to shares carrying voting rights or any rights over such shares in companies resident[14] in the UK, Channel Islands, Isle of Man or Irish Republic and listed on the Stock Exchange or traded under Rule 535.3[15]. Voting rights means all the voting rights attributable to the share capital of a company which are currently exerciseable at a general meeting[16].

4. The Code

The Code's scope of application to listed and unlisted public companies and relevant private companies, (ie those with some kind of public involvement in the previous ten years or the occurrence of another event relating to the company which is relevant under the Code)[17], within its residence criteria[18] imposes a wider reporting obligation. However, like the SARs, the Code requirement[19] for a person to disclose an acquisition from a single shareholder in the intended offeree company prior to the acquirer's announcement of a firm intention to make an offer, applies to shares carrying voting rights or any rights over such shares. Voting rights are likewise defined[20] as all the voting rights attributable to the share capital of a company which are currently exerciseable at a general meeting.

In regard to the Code's Rules for announcement of dealings during the offer period[1], the securities involved are those which would have a bearing on the offer. The Rule requiring disclosure of dealings by connected exempt market-makers[2] incorporates the same definition. Thus, for the purposes of these Rules, 'relevant securities' are defined[3] to include:

> (i) securities of the offeree company which are being offered for or which carry voting rights;

12. Under the Admission of Securities to Listing and the General Undertaking respectively. Though not considered further in this section, reporting requirements are also imposed on companies whose securities are traded on the third market: The Stock Exchange, The 3rd Market (1987), Model terms for an undertaking to be given by a company to their sponsoring Member Firm.
13. The Substantial Acquisition Rules, Rule 3.
14. A company is normally considered to be 'resident' only if it is incorporated in the UK, the Channel Islands, the Isle of Man or the Irish Republic and has its head office and place of central management in one of those jurisdictions, SARs, Introduction, 2. Scope.
15. Rule 535.3 contains special provisions relating to mineral exploration companies.
16. The SARs, Definitions.
17. Code, Introduction, para4(a); see, ante, Chapter 2. The Regulatory Framework..
18. Ibid.
19. Code, Rule 5.
20. Ibid, Definitions.
1. Code, Rules 8.1, 8.2 and 8.3.
2. Ibid, Rule 38.
3. Ibid, Notes on Rule 8, Note 2.

(ii) equity share capital of the offeree company and an offeror;
(iii) securities of an offeror which carry substantially the same rights as any to be issued as consideration for the offer;
(iv) securities of the offeree company and an offeror carrying conversion or subscription rights into any of the foregoing.

However, disclosure of dealings in relevant securities of an offeror is only required in the case of a securities exchange offer[4].

Further differences in disclosure requirements arise out of the definition of terms such as 'interests in shares or debentures' and 'interest in voting shares' under statutory requirements and 'rights over shares' under the SARs and the Code. Similarly, the Code requirement for disclosure of dealings in the offer period includes certain option transactions. But these differences will be considered subsequently[5].

B. The definition of insider

1. Companies Act 1985

(a) DIRECTORS' INTERESTS IN SHARES OR DEBENTURES

Statutory reporting requirements concerning directors' interests in securities apply to shadow directors as to directors[6] and involve a relatively straightforward determination of a small class. 'Director' is defined to include any person occupying the position of director, by whatever name called[7]. 'Shadow director' means a person in accordance with whose directions or instructions the directors of the company are accustomed to act[8]. However, professional advisers are excluded by the proviso that a person is not deemed a shadow director by reason only that the directors act on advice given by him in a professional capacity[9].

The interests of the director are extended to the interests of a spouse and infant children (including step-children)[10]. Nevertheless, this extension is narrower than the Code definition of 'associate', which includes close relatives and related trusts[11].

(b) INTERESTS IN VOTING SHARES IN PUBLIC COMPANIES

The scope of initial statutory provisions for the disclosure of substantial shareholdings was wider in that they applied to any person, whether a director

---

4. Ibid, Note 2 and Rule 38.5, Note 2. In Note 11 on Rule 8, it is emphasised that the requirements to disclose dealings apply also to dealings in the shares of unlisted public companies and of relevant private companies.
5. See post C. The operation of reporting.
6. C.A. 1985, s324(6).
7. Ibid, s741(1).
8. Ibid, s742(2).
9. Ibid.
10. Ibid, s328.
11. Code, Definitions.

or not, who became interested in 10% or more in nominal value of quoted share capital carrying unrestricted voting rights[12]. Their scope was further extended in 1976 when the threshold was reduced to 5% of any class of such shares, with provision for alteration by statutory instrument[13].

This wider approach was also adopted when the provisions for disclosure of voting interests in shares in public companies were enacted in 1981. These statutory provisions, now consolidated in the Companies Act 1985, require any person to inform the company when he (a) to his knowledge acquires any notifiable interest in the voting capital of the company or ceases to be interested in such shares, or (b) becomes aware that he has acquired any notifiable interest in such shares in which he was previously interested[14]. In addition, a person may be deemed to acquire a notifiable interest (otherwise than by such acquisition or disposal) when he is, or otherwise becomes, aware of any change of circumstances affecting facts relevant to the obligation to disclose a notifiable interest in respect of an existing interest in shares[15].

A notifiable interest is defined in the Act as an interest in voting shares of an aggregate nominal value of the share capital equal to 5% or more of the nominal value of the voting capital[16]. But the 5% threshold can be altered by statutory instrument, which may prescribe different percentages for different classes or descriptions of companies[17].

In addition, a person must notify the company of any significant change in his interest in shares above the 5% threshold[18]. A reportable change in a notifiable interest is 1% after rounding down[19].

However, a significant extension of reporting requirements was introduced in 1981 by the requirement for a person to whom family or corporate interests are attributed[20] and concert parties[1] similarly to notify the company as soon as his interest exceeds 5% of the issued voting share capital or passes one of the 1% thresholds. The obligation to notify also arises when a person ceases to be so interested in such shares.

These provisions introduced in 1981 reinforce the emphasis on disclosure by persons with privileged market information. Unlike many substantial shareholders over the initial 10% threshold, most 5% shareholders do not have privileged access to corporate information, particularly when the latter threshold is attained by virtue of a concert party agreement or understanding.

The aim of extending statutory provisions to concert parties[2] was to give companies early warning of combinations to acquire shares which could be as significant as acquisitions by a person and to prevent avoidance of disclosure provisions by the use of nominee companies, which are not technically within the other disclosure provisions, to amass significant holdings without falling under any obligation to notify the company involved[3]. But the inclusion of concert parties is also important to insider dealing regulation since the fact that

12. C.A. 1967, ss33-34.
13. C.A. 1976, s26.
14. C.A. 1985, s198(1).
15. Ibid, s198(3).
16. Ibid, ss199(1), (2) and (3) and 201(1). This is computed by the arithmetical formula.
17. C.A. 1985; s201(2).
18. Ibid, s199(4) and (5).
19. Ibid, s200.
20. Ibid, s203.
1. Ibid, s204.
2. These are agreements, whether legally binding or not, whose purpose is to acquire interests in shares.
3. The Companies Bill 1981, Standing Committee A, cols.457-458.

persons are acting in concert may not be known to shareholders, other investors or the company. Yet such information could affect the value of securities, particularly when the acquisition is to be used to influence policy or is made with a view to subsequent acquisition of a controlling interest.

Prior to the CA 1981, combinations of individuals or companies were not required by law to aggregate acquisitions for disclosure purposes merely because they were acting in concert. However, in its report on the Consolidated Gold Fields matter[4], the Stock Exchange recommended amendment of the law to require disclosure of interests held by persons acting in concert. It acknowledged such a requirement would:

> 'introduce an element of uncertainty into an area of law which is otherwise carefully drafted to allow certainty of interpretation'[5].

But it considered that supplementary guidance by self-regulatory bodies could achieve observance of the 'spirit' of the law. Likewise, the Panel Chairman advocated legislation should 'make it clear beyond doubt, as it is in the USA, that where persons acting in concert' acquire a substantial interest, details must be disclosed[6].

However, the Department considered legislation requiring the aggregation of acquisitions for disclosure purposes would cause great difficulties:

> 'The principle one, acknowledged by the Stock Exchange, is that the test of the existence of a 'concert party' must be one of intention. Proof of the existence of an arrangement to act in concert, which might be on a wholly informal basis, would be very difficult to establish. This is confirmed by the experience of the Takeover Panel, which, except in those cases covered by the presumptions stated in the Code, appears to have been able to determine the existence of such a concert party only ex post facto and largely on the basis of inferences from circumstantial evidence'[7].

The Department was also concerned[8] both about providing the degree of certainty appropriate in a statute creating a criminal offence and about the application of such a provision to many arrangements between investors and their agents which were not contrary to the spirit of the law. Such considerations led it to propose an extension of the existing law to include persons acting in concert when there was a common directing interest acting through third parties, particularly by elaborating the statutory definition of interest in shares. It further hinted that the Stock Exchange and CSI should strengthen their rules[9].

Despite the difficulties of formulating a satisfactory definition of 'concert party' the decision to legislate for disclosure by concert parties was preferable to the approach advocated by the Department. The latter would have required disclosure of numerous connections that were not concerned with transactions

4. The Stock Exchange, Report by a Special Committee of the Stock Exchange on dealings in the shares of Consolidated Gold Fields Ltd. (1980).
5. Ibid, para7.7.
6. The Panel on Take-overs and Mergers, op cit n11, p222, supra, p.3
7. The Department of Trade, *Disclosure of Interests in Shares* (1980), para10.
8. Ibid, paras 11 and 12.
9. Ibid, para14.

against which it was sought to strengthen the law[10] and also caused problems as difficult as those raised by the concert party concept. In addition, whilst self-regulation may assist in the observance of the spirit of legislation, it is inappropriate when the problem is not confined to the system of self-regulation since the effectiveness of self-regulation depends on a nexus between regulators and regulated.

Moreover, as regards the definition of concert party, the fact that the 'intention' requisite to the establishment of a concert party can only be ascertained ex post facto is not in itself a critical drawback. Although a person may wish to keep his acquisitions secret at the time of making them, other than in exceptional circumstances, their existence will become apparent when he attempts to take advantage of his holding and realise their full benefit. With hindsight, it should be possible to ascertain whether steps taken in accumulating the holding arose from the existence of a concert party. Furthermore, as a principal in a concert party will be aware of his membership of it and disclosure by any member will reveal its existence, other members may be reluctant to break the law when their failure to disclose could be established by the actions of any of their associates[11].

2. The Stock Exchange

Stock Exchange requirements are drafted by reference to statutory provisions. In respect of the relevant securities, the definition of insider thus draws on each set of statutory provisions, though the extension of Stock Exchange requirements to companies not subject to the Companies Acts[12] widens the category of persons on whom a reporting obligation is imposed.

3. The SARs

The SARs, which supplement the statutory provisions for disclosure of interests in voting shares in public companies, apply to a person if (a) as a result of the acquisition he comes to hold, with any shares or rights over shares already held by him, shares or rights over shares representing 15% or more of the voting rights in a company or (b) his holding of shares or rights over shares already represents 15% or more of the voting rights and as a result of the acquisition is increased to or beyond any whole percentage figure[13].

Associated persons are included: where two or more persons act by agreement or understanding in the acquisition by one or more of them of shares carrying voting rights, or rights over such shares, their holdings and acquisitions must be aggregated and treated as a holding or acquisition by one person for the purpose of the SARs. Each person acting in such manner must ensure that

10. An extension of disclosure requirements to persons and companies with a degree of common or mutual control or interest could in some cases indicate the existence of a combination for the purpose of control. But in many others, as with the directors of insurance companies or banks who are also directors of other listed companies, the circumstances giving rise to the disclosure obligation would not have such an underlying motive.
11. The Law Society, *Disclosure of Interests in Shares* Department of Trade Consultative Document, Memorandum by the Society's Standing Committee on Company Law (1980), paras1 and 2.
12. Admission of Securities to Listing, Section 5, Chapter 2, Para.16.
13. The SARs, Rule 3.

the obligations arising under the SARs are fulfilled[14].

With a view to keeping the market informed of acquisitions capable of sub-sequent exploitation, the definition of persons acting by agreement or under-standing extends to an investment manager in relation to the collective holdings of himself and of his discretionary clients. Thus, investments managed by a fund manager on a discretionary basis, and, unless the fund manager is an exempt fund manager for the purposes of the Code, shares owned by the fund manager or by any company (other than an exempt market-maker) control-ling[15], controlled by, or under the same control as the fund manager, are normally regarded as being the holding of one person for the purposes of the rule on persons acting by agreement or understanding[16]. In addition, if a person manages investment accounts on a discretionary basis, shares so managed will be treated, for the purpose of the rule on persons acting by agreement or understanding, as held by that person and not by the person on whose behalf the shares are managed. Except with the Panel's consent, where more than one discretionary investment management operation is conducted in the same group, shares held by all such operations will be treated, for the purpose of the rule on persons acting by agreement or understanding, as those of a single person and must be aggregated. In cases of doubt, the Panel should be consulted.[17]

To avoid overlap with other requirements of the SARs and the Code, the disclosure obligation does not apply in certain circumstances. Thus, the SARs specifically exclude the application of the disclosure obligation in respect of an acquisition either (a) pursuant to a tender offer[18] or (b) immediately before the person announces a firm intention to make an offer (whether or not the posting of the offer is to be subject to a pre-condition) provided that the offer will be publicly recommended by, or the acquisition is made with the agreement of, the board of the offeree company, and the acquisition is conditional upon the announcement of the offer.[19] In addition, the SARs themselves do not apply to an acquisition by a person (a) who has announced a firm intention to make an offer for the company, to which the Code applies, the posting of which is not, or has ceased to be, subject to a pre-condition (a person who makes such an announcement is subject to the Code in respect of acquisitions during the course of the offer), or (b) which results in his holding shares or rights over shares carrying in the aggregate 30% or more of the voting rights of the company (such a person becomes subject to the Code provisions relating to restrictions on acquisitions[20] and, if appropriate, the mandatory offer[1] and its terms[2]).

---

14. Ibid, Rule 5.
15. Note 1 at the end of the Definitions Section of the Code states that the normal test for whether a person is controlled by, controls or is under the same control as another person will be by reference to the definition of control. There may be other circumstances which the Panel will regard as giving rise to such a relationship (eg where a majority of the equity is owned by another person who does not have a majority of the voting rights); in cases of doubt, the Panel should be consulted.
16. The SARs, Rule 5, Note 2.
17. Ibid.
18. In accordance with Rule 4.
19. The SARs, Rules 2(b), (c) and 3.
20. Code, Rule 5.
1. Ibid, Rule 9.
2. The SARs, Introduction.

4. The Code

Additional disclosure obligations are imposed by the Code. Its requirement for disclosure of an acquisition from a single shareholder arises out of an exception to two restrictions on acquisitions.[3] First, a person[4] (including any person acting in concert with him) who holds shares or rights over shares which in the aggregate carry less than 30% of the voting rights of a company, may not acquire any shares carrying voting rights in that company or any rights over such shares which, when aggregated with the shares or rights over shares which he already holds, would carry 30% or more of the voting rights.[5] Secondly, a person, who already holds shares or rights over shares which in the aggregate carry 30% or more of the voting rights of a company but does not hold shares which carry more than 50% of the voting rights, may not acquire any shares carrying voting rights in that company or any rights over such shares which, when aggregated with the shares or rights over shares acquired by him in the previous twelve months, would carry more than 2% of the voting rights.[6]

However, these restrictions do not apply to an acquisition of shares carrying voting rights in a company, or rights over such shares, by a person at any time from a single shareholder if it is the only such acquisition within any period of seven days (unless the person has announced a firm intention to make an offer and the posting of the offer is not subject to a pre-condition).[7] For this purpose, a number of shareholders wishing to dispose of their shares or rights over their shares are treated as a single shareholder when they are all members of the same family or of a group of companies which is regarded as one for the purposes of notification of family and corporate interests under the statutory provisions for the disclosure of interests in voting shares in public companies.[8] Except with the Panel's consent, a market-maker will not be considered to be a single shareholder for the purpose of this exception.[9] But a person within this exception must disclose his acquisitions.[10]

In terms of the range of persons required to disclose their dealings, the most significant Code extension concerns the disclosure of dealings during the offer period. Disclosure must be made by an offeror, the offeree company and any associates of dealings for their own account or for the account of discretionary clients.[11] Except with the consent of the Panel, disclosure must be made by an exempt fund manager[12] connected with the offeror or offeree company in regard to dealings for the account of discretionary investment clients.[13] In addition, when a potential offeror has been the subject of an announcement that talks are taking place (whether or not the potential offeror has been named) or has announced that he is considering making an offer, disclosure

---

3. Code, Rule 5.
4. For the purposes of Rule 5, a person includes any person acting in concert with him.
5. Code, Rule 5.1(a).
6. Ibid, Rule 5.1(b).
7. Ibid, Rule 5.2(a).
8. Ibid, Rule 5.2, Note 1.
9. Ibid.
10. Ibid, Rule 5.4.
11. Ibid, Rule 8.1.
12. In the Definitions Section of the Code, an exempt fund manager is a person who manages investment accounts on a discretionary basis and is recognised by the Panel as an exempt fund manager for the purposes of the Code. Further clarification is contained in Notes to the Definition.
13. Code, Rule 8.1(b)(ii).

must be made by the potential offeror and persons acting in concert with it.[14] Dealings by an offeror, the offeree company and any associates for the account of non-discretionary investment clients (other than an offeror, the offeree company and any associates) must also be reported.[15] A recognised market-maker which is an associate by virtue only of paragraph (b) of the definition of associate[16] is not required to make disclosure in accordance with the Code requirements relating to dealings by parties and by associates for themselves or for discretionary clients during the offer period,[17] provided that the market-maker acts in a market-making capacity.[18] However, if he is an associate for any other reason but is not an exempt market-maker, he has an obligation to disclose under these requirements.

In addition, disclosure is required of 1% shareholders. Such a shareholder is a person who, whether or not an associate, owns or controls (directly or indirectly) 1% or more of any class of relevant securities of an offeror or of the offeree company, or as a result of any transaction will so own or control 1% or more.[19] For this purpose, two or more persons who act pursuant to an agreement or understanding, whether formal or informal, to acquire or control relevant securities, will be deemed to be a single person.[20] In regard to discretionary fund managers, the general principle is that if a person manages investment accounts on a discretionary basis, the relevant securities so managed will be treated, for the purpose of the rule requiring disclosure by 1% shareholders, as controlled by that person and not by the person on whose behalf the relevant securities are managed; hence, except with the consent of the Panel, where more than one discretionary investment management operation is conducted in the same group, relevant securities controlled by all such operations will be treated for the purpose of this rule as those of a single person and must be aggregated.[1] However, the rule requiring disclosure by 1% shareholders does not apply to recognised market-makers acting in that capacity.[2] Whilst reference is made in a Note[3] to the statutory provisions for disclosure of interests in voting shares in public companies, it is considered likely that a person within those statutory provisions will also be required to disclose under the rule applicable to 1% shareholders.

The definition of associate[4] is wide enough to include people not directly involved in a take-over bid. In this connection:

> 'It is not practicable to define associate in terms which would cover all the different relationships which may exist in an offer. The term associate is intended to cover all persons (whether or not acting in concert) who

14. Ibid, Notes on Rule 8, Note 12.
15. Code, Rule 8.2.
16. See post.
17. Ie, under Rule 8.1.
18. Code, Notes on Rule 8, Note 9.
19. Ibid, Rule 8.3(a).
20. Ibid, Rule 8.3(b).
1. Ibid, Rule 8.3(c). The Panel's approach to funds under discretionary management is also explained in Note 8, which adds that the beneficial owner would not normally, therefore, be concerned with disclosure to the extent that his investment is managed on a discretionary basis. This approach is stated, in Note 8, to assume that the discretionary fund manager does not take instructions from the beneficial owner on the dealings in question and that fund management arrangements are not established or used to avoid disclosure.
2. Code, Rule 8.3(d) and Note 9.
3. Ibid, Notes on Rule 8, Note 13.
4. Ibid, Definitions.

directly or indirectly own or deal in the shares of an offeror or the offeree company in an offer and who have (in addition to their normal interests as shareholders) an interest or potential interest, whether commercial, financial or personal, in the outcome of the offer.

Without prejudice to the generality of the foregoing, the term associate will normally include the following:

(1) an offeror's or the offeree company's parent, subsidiaries and fellow subsidiaries, and their associated companies, and companies of which such companies are associated companies (for this purpose ownership or control of 20% or more of the equity share capital of a company is regarded as the test of associated company status);

(2) banks[5] and financial and other professional advisers (including stock-brokers) to an offeror, the offeree company or any company covered in (1), including persons controlling,[6] controlled by or under the same control as such banks, financial and other professional advisers;

(3) the directors (together with their close relatives and related trusts) of an offeror, the offeree company or any company covered in (1);

(4) the pension funds of an offeror, the offeree company or any company covered in (1);

(5) any investment company, unit trust or other person whose investments an associate manages on a discretionary basis, in respect of the relevant investment accounts;

(6) a person who owns or controls 5% or more of any class of relevant securities (as defined in Rule 8) of an offeror or of the offeree company, including a person who as a result of any transaction owns or controls 5% or more. When two or more persons act pursuant to an agreement or understanding (formal or informal) to acquire or control such securities, they will be deemed to be a single person for the purpose of this paragraph. Relevant securities managed on a discretionary basis by an investment management group will, unless otherwise agreed by the Panel, also be deemed to be those of a single person (see Note 8 on Rule 8); and

(7) a company having a material trading arrangement with an offeror or offeree company.'

As many associates and other persons may not be fully aware of the provisions for disclosure of dealings, a general duty is imposed on stockbrokers, banks and others who deal in relevant securities on behalf of clients to ensure, so far as they are able, that those clients are aware of the disclosure obligations attaching to associates and other persons and that those clients are willing to comply with them.[7] Market-makers and dealers who deal directly with investors should, in appropriate cases, likewise draw attention to the relevant provisions. By way of dispensation, there is no requirement to establish whether a client is aware of such obligations when the total value of the dealings (excluding stamp duty and

5. References to a 'bank' are expressly stated not to apply to a bank whose sole relationship with a party to an offer is the provision of normal commercial banking services or such activities in connection with the offer as confirming that cash is available, handling acceptances and other registration work: Code, Definitions, Notes on Definitions, Note 2.

6. The normal test for whether a person is controlled by, controls or is under the same control as another person will be by reference to the definition of control. There may be other circumstances which the Panel will regard as giving rise to such a relationship (eg where a majority of the equity share capital is owned by another person who does not have a majority of the voting rights); in cases of doubt, the Panel should be consulted: Code, Definitions, Notes on Definitions, Note 1.

7. Code, Notes on Rule 8, Note 10.

commission) in any relevant security undertaken for a client during the same Stock Exchange account period is less than £25,000. However, this dispensation does not alter the obligation of principals, associates and other persons themselves to initiate disclosure of their own dealings, whatever total value is involved.

The scope of the responsibility for establishing whether a client is an associate was considered in a 1982 Panel statement on dealings in ACC[8] when a company associated with an offeror was found to have failed to disclose purchases of non-voting shares in the offeree during the offer period. London stockbrokers twice asked the Australian stockbroking firm, which was acting as adviser to the offeror and placed the order, as to whom the purchases should be booked and gained the understanding that the purchases were being made by the Australian firm for its own account. They argued that they were entitled to rely upon and acted reasonably in relying upon the answer given by the branch of a responsible Australian firm. But the Panel considered that the London stockbrokers could not 'escape some responsibility' for failure to prevent breaches of the Code: given the widely publicised circumstances of the bid, the scale of the operations and their Australian source, merely to enquire twice as to the name of the principal or in whose name the deal should be booked did not match up to the responsibility imposed by the Code.

A further category of persons on whom disclosure of dealings is imposed is an exempt market-maker connected with an offeror or the offeree company[9]. An exempt market-maker is a person who is registered as a market-maker with the Stock Exchange in relation to the relevant securities, or is accepted by the Panel as a market-maker in those securities, and, in either case, is recognised by the Panel as an exempt market-maker for the purposes of the Code[10]. A market-maker is connected with an offeror or the offeree company, as the case may be, if the market-maker is controlled by, controls or is under the same control as an offeror, the offeree, company or any bank or financial or other professional advisers (including stockbrokers) to an offeror or the offeree company[11].

Except in take-overs, there is thus a wide divergence between the definition of insider for disclosure purposes and for criminal liability. The application of disclosure requirements to 'persons' means that, in contrast to the restriction to individuals under the IDA 1985, companies are among those subject to disclosure of their holdings and dealings. Conversely, a significant omission from the disclosure requirements, yet within the definition for criminal liability, relates to many employees with access to inside information who are not required to disclose their holdings and dealings, except insofar as they also either (a) have notifiable interests in voting shares in public companies under the Companies Act 1985, or (b) in the case of listed and USM companies, fall within the notification requirements of the Model Code, or (c) fall within the disclosure requirements administered by the Panel. Whilst the benefits of reporting support a wide definition of insider as with take-overs, considerations of manageability make it otherwise impractical to extend the definition beyond those most likely to have inside information, namely, directors, senior officers and substantial shareholders.

---

8. Panel Statement on Associated Communications Corporation Plc, 23rd March, 1982; confirmed by the Appeal Committee, 26th March, 1982.
9. Code, Rule 38.
10. Code, Definitions. Further clarification is contained in Notes to this definition.
11. Ibid. A fund manager is connected in analogous circumstances.

C. The operation of reporting

1. General

(a) COMPANIES ACT 1985

i. Directors' interests in shares or debentures.   In respect of directors' interests, initial disclosure is imposed by statute on becoming a director, when a person must notify the company of his interests in shares or debentures[12]. Further notification is required, whilst a director, of the following occurrences regarding his interests: (a) becoming or ceasing to be interested in shares or debentures; (b) entering into a contract to sell shares or debentures; (c) assigning any right to subscribe for shares or debentures in the company granted to him by the company and (d) the granting by the company's holding company, subsidiary or fellow subsidiary of a right to subscribe for shares or debentures of that company, or the exercise or assignment of such a right[13].

Notification must be in writing and expressed to be in fulfilment of the disclosure obligation[14]. The report must give detailed particulars, including the number or amount and class of shares or debentures and also in respect of occurrences, the price or consideration and relevant dates[15].

The meaning of 'interest in shares and debentures' is defined in a broadly drafted Schedule which sets out the interests to be included[16]. An interest includes any kind of interest whatsoever in shares or debentures, irrespective of any restraints or restrictions to which the exercise of any rights attached to the interest is or may be subject. Hence, the imposition or removal of any such restraints or restrictions is not regarded as a creation or disposal of an interest and is not notifiable. A beneficiary of a trust, the property of which includes shares or debentures, is also taken to have an interest.

Likewise, a person is treated as having an interest in shares or debentures if (a) he enters into a contract for their purchase by him (whether for cash or other consideration) or (b) not being the registered holder, he is entitled to exercise any right conferred by the holding or to control the exercise of any such right. For this purpose, a person is treated as entitled to exercise or control the exercise of a right conferred by the holding of shares or debentures if he (a) has a right (whether subject to conditions or not) the exercise of which would make him so entitled or (b) is under an obligation (whether or not so subject) the fulfilment of which would make him so entitled. But a person is not treated as having an interest in shares or debentures by reason only of his having been appointed either (a) a proxy to vote at a specified meeting of a company or of any class of its members and at any adjournment of that meeting or (b) by a corporation to act as its representative at any meeting of a company or of any class of its members.

A person is also treated as having an interest in shares or debentures when a body corporate has an interest in them and (a) that body corporate or its directors are accustomed to act in accordance with his directions or instruc-

---

12. C.A. 1985, s324(1).
13. Ibid, s324(2).
14. Ibid, s324(1), (2) and (5).
15. Full details are set out in C.A. 1985, Sch13, Part III.
16. C.A. 1985, Sch13, Part I.

tions, or (b) he is entitled to exercise or control the exercise of one-third or more of the voting power at general meetings of that body corporate. For this latter purpose (and in order to include contingent arrangements), when a person is entitled to exercise or control the exercise of one-third or more of the voting power at general meetings of a body corporate and that body corporate is entitled to exercise or control the exercise of any of the voting power at general meetings of another body corporate ('the effective voting power'), then the effective voting power is taken to be exerciseable by that person.

In addition, options are included under the provisions whereby, otherwise than by virtue of having an interest under a trust, a person is treated as having an interest when either (a) he has a right to call for delivery of the shares or debentures to himself or to his order or (b) he has a right to acquire an interest in shares or debentures or is obliged to take an interest therein, whether or not the right or obligation is conditional.

Joint interests are included. Moreover, it is immaterial that shares in which a person has an interest are unidentifiable.

Conversely, the Schedule excludes other interests in shares and debentures. These concern interests arising under an authorised unit trust scheme and certain interests in trusts, such as an interest in reversion or remainder or of a bare or custodian trustee.

In addition, certain interests may be disregarded under regulations made by statutory instrument[17]. The disclosure requirements do not apply to interests of any person in his capacity as trustee or personal representative of any trust or estate of which the Public Trustee is also a trustee (otherwise than as custodian trustee) or personal representative. Also excepted are interests in a society registered under the Industrial and Provident Societies Act 1965, interests arising solely out of any limitation on the transferability of shares imposed by the memorandum or articles of the company which issued them and the interests of a person as trustee or beneficiary of a trust relating to certain retirement benefit schemes and superannuation funds approved for tax purposes. In addition, notification is not required to a company which is the wholly owned subsidiary of a body corporate incorporated outside Great Britain or by a director who is also the director of a body corporate of which the company is the wholly owned subsidiary.

In turn, a notification requirement is placed on a company whose shares or debentures are listed on a recognised stock exchange. Upon receipt of notification in respect of shares or debentures so listed, the company must notify that stock exchange[18].

Other reporting requirements are imposed on the company independently of notification. Whenever a company grants a director a right to subscribe for its shares or debentures, it must record in the register of directors' interests: the date when the right is granted, the period during which or time at which it is exerciseable, the consideration for the grant or appropriate negative statement, particulars of shares or debentures involved and the price to be paid (or the consideration, if otherwise than in money)[19]. Subsequently, on exercise of the right, the company must record: the fact of the exercise, the number or amount of shares or debentures in respect of which the interest is exercised, whether or not they were registered in the director's name and, if not, the names of the

---

17. C.A. 1985, s24(3). Companies (Disclosure of Directors' Interests) (Exceptions) Regulations 1985 (S.I. 1985/802).
18. Ibid, s329.
19. Ibid, s325(3).

persons registered and the amounts taken by each of them[20].

Further disclosure by the directors is required in certain documents. Statutory prospectus requirements provide for disclosure of any qualification shares of directors and options to subscribe[1]. More detailed disclosure is made in the directors' report, which must contain particulars of each director's holding at the beginning and end of the financial year[2].

ii. Interests in voting shares in public companies. As regards the statutory requirements relating to the disclosure of interests in voting shares in public companies, the obligation to notify known interests to the company arises where a person either (a) becomes aware that he has a notifiable interest in the voting capital which he did not previously have or (b) had such an interest but becomes aware that he no longer has such an interest or (c) both before and after the event, had such an interest but becomes aware that the percentage levels of his interest immediately before and after the event are not the same[3]. Whether a person has a notifiable interest depends on his knowledge of facts which would render his interest notifiable[4], not the occurrence of an event of which he may be unaware. This latter may arise when a person has an interest under a trust or by way of concert party.

Notification must be in writing, specify the share capital to which it relates and either (a) state the number of shares in which the person knows he was interested immediately after the relevant time or (b) where he no longer has a relevant interest, state that fact[5]. But the obligation is not treated as fulfilled unless the notice identifies the person and gives his address and when he is a director of the company, is expressed to be given in fulfilment of that obligation[6]. The different basis of reporting is thus underlined by the absence, in contrast to legislation for the disclosure of directors' interests, of a requirement to state the price or consideration. This absence also contrasts with Code requirements[7] for the disclosure of dealings in the offer period which, subject to one exception, impose disclosure of both the price of a purchase or sale as well as the number of shares involved.

When interests in shares arise otherwise than through holding them as registered holder, the reporting shareholder must disclose the identity of each registered holder to which the notification relates and the number of shares held by each registered holder so far as known to the person making the notification[8]. Further notification obligations are imposed when any details or changes in the particulars of which he was not aware at the time of initial notification subsequently come to his knowledge[9]. As an anti-avoidance provision, once a notifiable interest arises it continues until it is countered by an obligation to notify a cessation of interest in the relevant share capital[10].

A supplementary provision[11] counters avoidance of the notification require-

20. Ibid, s325(4).
1. Ibid, Sch3.
2. Ibid, s235 and Sch7.
3. Ibid, s199(4) and (5).
4. Ibid, s199(3).
5. Ibid, s202(1) and (2).
6. Ibid, s210(2).
7. Code, Rule 8, see post.
8. C.A. 1985, s202(3).
9. Ibid, s202(4).
10. Ibid, s202(6).
11. Ibid, s210(1).

ment by a person employing an agent to deal in interests in voting shares of a public company without informing him. Instead, when a person authorises an agent to deal in such interests, he must secure that the agent notifies him immediately of acquisitions or disposals of such interests which will or may place him under a notification obligation.

Interests in shares other than those held directly as a registered holder are defined in a broadly-drafted section[12] which sets out the interests to be included. An interest in shares includes any kind of interest whatsoever in the shares, with any restraints or restrictions on the exercise of any rights attaching to the interest to be disregarded. A beneficiary of a trust the property of which includes shares is taken to have an interest. An interest also comprises all forms of contract and option to acquire an interest in shares exerciseable at present or in the future and any form of agreement which may confer a present or future right to exercise or control the exercise of voting power or any right conferred by the holder of shares. A person is deemed entitled to exercise or control the rights conferred by shares if he has a right or obligation that would make him so entitled, thereby including a contingent arrangement which might otherwise have been used to hide an interest requiring disclosure until it suited the holder of such a right to make disclosure. Joint interests are included and it is immaterial that shares in which a person has an interest are unidentifiable.

Conversely, certain interests may be disregarded[13]. These include certain interests in trusts (such as an interest in reversion or remainder or of a bare or custodian trustee and any discretionary interest), interests arising under an authorised unit trust scheme, certain interests in settlements, exempt interests of jobbers, or market-makers, exempt security interests, interests of the President of the Family Division of the High Court in shares comprised in the estate of a deceased person and interests in shares held by the Accountant General of the Supreme Court. A proxy holder's interest is disregarded only when it is to vote at a specified meeting of the company or of any class of its members and at any adjournment of that meeting, or he has been appointed by a corporation to act at any meeting of a company or of any class of its members. Compared to the CA 1967, the notion of an interest held as security, whilst still exempted, is narrowed to a more limited number of bodies which lend money in the course of business, namely, recognised banks and licensed institutions, insurance companies, trustee savings banks and broker members of the Stock Exchange.

Other interests to be disregarded have been provided by statutory instruments. These interests concern the interests of beneficiaries under a retirement benefits scheme approved by the Inland Revenue or established by or under statutory provision, interests of the Public Trustee or of a bank or insurance company which is a trust corporation and has a place of business in the UK where it holds the interest in its capacity as trustee or personal representative and interests in an offeror under a bid to acquire all the shares of a company or all the shares of a particular class in shares whose holders have accepted the bid but where the total number of acceptances has not attained the percentage at which the bid becomes or may be declared unconditional[14]. In addition, an interest in shares listed or dealt in on the Stock Exchange need not be disclosed if the interest is held by a person who is authorised to deal under the FSA 1986 and if it arises only as a result of disposal powers conferred on him by an

---

12. C.A. 1985, s208.
13. Ibid, s209.
14. The Public Companies (Disclosure of Interests in Shares) (Exclusions) Regulations 1982, S.I.1982, No.677.

investment management agreement[15].

In relation to the obligation to notify the company of certain family and corporate interests and concert parties, the circumstances in which a person becomes or ceases to be interested in shares by virtue of another's interest are where the relationship comes into being or ceases, or where the relationship exists when such a related person acquires or disposes of an interest, or because the person in question joins a concert party or leaves one[16]. A person is deemed to have knowledge if he knows both that the related person has or had the interest and the relevant facts which make that interest attributable or no longer attributable, to him[17].

In the case of concert parties, additional notification provisions apply. These require a statement that a concert party is involved, together with particulars of the names and addresses of other parties to the agreement[18].

As regards the obligation to notify certain family and corporate interests, certain interests are attributed to a person as if they are his own[19], thereby complementing the provisions for interests in shares other than those held directly as a registered holder. As with directors' interests in shares or debentures, a person is taken to be interested in shares in which his spouse or any infant child or step-child is interested. A person is also deemed to be interested in shares if a body corporate is interested in them and either (a) that body corporate or its directors are accustomed to act in accordance with his directions or instructions, or (b) he is entitled to exercise or control the exercise of one-third or more of the voting power at general meetings of that body corporate. For the purposes of attribution of interest, a person who is entitled to exercise or control one-third[20] or more of the voting power at general meetings of a body corporate is treated to be entitled to control the exercise of any of the voting power at general meetings of any other corporation which the first corporation is entitled to exercise. A person is entitled to exercise control if he has a right the exercise of which would make him so entitled, or is under an obligation, the fulfilment of which would make him so entitled.

The approach adopted concerning concert parties involves identification of a relationship between different persons and provision for the mutual attribution of interests. Subject to two exceptions, a reporting requirement applies to agreements between two or more persons for the acquisition of shares in a target company, provided: (a) provisions exist in the agreement imposing obligations or restrictions on any one or more of the parties with respect to their use, retention or disposal of interests in that company's shares, whether or not together with any other interests of theirs in the target company's shares, and (b) an interest in the target company's shares is in fact acquired by any of the parties pursuant to the agreement[1]. Once such an interest has been acquired, the concert party rules will continue to apply irrespective of further acquisitions, changes in the parties or attempts to vary or discharge it[2]. Agreement is defined[3]

15. The Public Companies (Disclosure of Interests in Shares) (Investments Management Exclusion) Regulations 1988, S.I. 1988, No.706.
16. C.A. 1985, s207(2).
17. Ibid, s207(3).
18. Ibid, s205(4).
19. Ibid, s203. This section should be read subject to ss208 and 209 ante.
20. The one-third level slightly exceeds that which triggers the mandatory bid requirements for the City Code.
1. C.A. 1985, s204(1) and (2).
2. Ibid, s204(4).
3. Ibid, s204(5).

to include any meeting of minds, mutual understandings, expectations or undertakings express or implied and whether absolute or not. The two exceptions from the reporting requirement relate to (a) underwriting agreements confined to that purpose and matters incidental to it and (b) arrangements involving a meeting of minds, but no mutual reliance[4].

With a view to ensuring each member of a concert party is aware of the interests attributable to him so that he knows whether the notification requirement applies to his interest in shares, members of a concert party must keep each other informed of all relevant facts, such as existing interests, acquisitions and disposals of shares in the company concerned[5]. Notification must be in writing and is required as from the first acquisition in pursuance of the agreement.

(b) THE STOCK EXCHANGE

In the case of securities listed on the Stock Exchange or admitted to dealing on the USM, both sets of legislative provisions are supplemented by further requirements. On application for admission to listing on the Stock Exchange, the listing particulars must disclose the interests (distinguishing between beneficial and non-beneficial interests) of each director relating to securities which are or will be listed and which have been notified to the issuer under the Companies Act 1985[6] or are required to be entered in the register kept[7] under that Act[8]. In the case of companies not subject to that Act, disclosure must be made of the interests of each director, including his spouse and children under 18, whether or not held through another party, in the share capital of the company, together with any options in respect of such capital[9]. The listing particulars must also name any person other than a director, so far as is known to the issuer, who, directly or indirectly, is interested in 5% or more of the issuer's capital, together with the amount of each such person's interest[10]. On application for admission to dealing in the USM, similar information is required in the prospectus[11].

Under continuous disclosure requirements, the company must report to the Stock Exchange: (a) in the case of a UK company, information notified under the provisions of the Companies Act 1985[12] for disclosure of interests in voting shares[13], (b) as regards directors' interests, any matter notified to the company under the Companies Act 1985[14] or required to be entered in the register kept[15] under that Act[16] and (c) in the case of companies not subject to the Companies Acts, equivalent information to that required under (a) and (b) in respect of the interests, including options, whether or not held through another party (corporate or otherwise), of each director, including his spouse and children

4. Ibid, s204(6).
5. Ibid, s206.
6. C.A. 1985, ss324 or 328.
7. Ibid, s325.
8. Admission of Securities to Listing, Section 3, Chapter 2, para6.6.
9. Ibid.
10. Ibid, para3.9.
11. Green Book, Section C, para27.
12. C.A. 1985, ss198 and 212.
13. Admission of Securities to Listing, Section 5, Chapter 2, para16(a).
14. C.A. 1985, ss324 or 328.
15. Ibid, s325.
16. Admission of Securities to Listing, Section 5, Chapter 2, para16(b).

under the age of 18 years in, and, so far as is known to the company, of each holder of 5% or more of, the share capital[17]. A UK company must also make detailed disclosure in its annual report of directors' interests in securities and of substantial interests in voting shares in public companies[18]. In addition, the Model Code imposes disclosure by insiders to board meetings[19].

Like these requirements for securities listed on the Stock Exchange or admitted to dealing on the USM, the SARs and Code provisions emphasise disclosure to the market. In some circumstances, disclosure to the company and in documents for shareholders is also imposed.

(c) THE SARS

The disclosure requirement of the SARs[20] provides that after an acquisition of shares or rights over shares, a person must notify that acquisition and his total holding to the company and the Stock Exchange. The notification must distinguish between acquisitions and holdings of shares and rights over shares, specifying the nature of any rights concerned and giving the relevant number of shares in each case. A specimen disclosure form may be obtained from the Panel[1] and disclosures under this requirement should follow that format.

However, this disclosure requirement is wider than the statutory provision in that it requires a person to disclose any rights over shares. These are defined[2] to include any rights acquired by a person by virtue of an agreement to purchase shares or an option to acquire shares or an irrevocable commitment to accept an offer to be made by him.

(d) THE CODE

In connection with the Code requirement for disclosure of an acquisition from a single shareholder prior to the announcement of a firm intention to make an offer, a person must notify that acquisition and his consequent total holding of shares and rights over shares to the company, the Stock Exchange (Company Announcements Office) and the Panel.[3] The notification must distinguish between shares and rights over shares, specifying the nature of any rights concerned and giving the relevant numbers and the resultant holding in each case. To prevent avoidance by persons obtaining potential control, rights over shares similarly include any rights acquired by a person by virtue of an agreement to purchase shares or an option to acquire shares or an irrevocable commitment to accept an offer to be made by him.[4]

During the offer period, the Code provides for two main methods of disclosure. First, public disclosure is to the Stock Exchange, Panel and the press.[5] This method applies to dealings by an offeror or the offeree company

---

17. Ibid, para16(c).
18. Ibid, para20 (h) and (i); Green Book, General Undertaking, para10(h) and (i).
19. Model Code, Rules 2 and 5. The Model Code is discussed in Chapter 6, Administrative Regulation.
20. SARs, Rule 3.
1. Disclosure forms, Form SAR 3.
2. SARs, Definitions.
3. Code, Rule 5.4.
4. Ibid, Definitions.
5. Ibid, Notes on Rule 8, Note 4(a).

and by any associates for their own account[6] or (unless the associate is an exempt fund manager connected with an offeror or the offeree company) for the account of discretionary investment clients.[7] In addition, dealings by 1% shareholders must be reported in this manner[8]. Where an exempt fund manager is an associate by virtue of para(6) of the definition of associate or if the requirement for disclosure by 1% shareholders applies, public disclosure by an exempt fund manager is also required.[9]

The second method is private disclosure which, in turn, takes two forms. One requires disclosure to the Panel only;[10] except with the consent of the Panel, this form of private disclosure applies to dealings in relevant securities made for the account of discretionary investment clients by an associate which is an exempt fund manager connected with the offeror or offeree company.[11]

The other form of private disclosure requires disclosure to the Stock Exchange and Panel only.[12] This form applies to dealings in relevant securities by an offeror or the offeree company, and by any associates, for the account of non-discretionary investment clients (other than an offeror, the offeree company and any associates).[13]

Notes to these provisions make it clear that disclosure bears on a wider range of transactions than simply purchases and sales.[14] In an express reference to option transactions, disclosure is extended by Note to the taking, granting or exercising of an option (including a traded option contract) in respect of any relevant securities.[15] The exercise period (or in the case of exercise, the exercise date), the exercise price and any option money paid or received must be stated. In regard to option dealings and disclosure by 1% shareholders, a further Note states that in determining whether a disclosure obligation arises by reference to the 1% test, the Panel has regard to the percentage of relevant securities owned or controlled and no account is taken of the relevant securities which are the subject of an option.[16]

Dealings subject to the public disclosure method should be disclosed in writing (or by telex) to the Stock Exchange (Company Announcements Office) and are published on the Company News Service of the Stock Exchange.[17] Copies of such disclosures are sent by the Stock Exchange to the Panel. Hence, separate disclosure to the Panel and the press is unnecessary. In contrast, dealings subject to the second form of private disclosure, namely dealings by the parties and by associates for non-discretionary clients, are not published.[18] Such dealings should also be disclosed in writing (or by telex) to the Stock Exchange (Company Announcements Office). Copies of these disclosures are similarly sent to the Panel, to whom separate disclosure is, therefore, unnecessary.

---

6. Ibid, Rule 8.1(a).
7. Ibid, Rule 8.1(b)(i).
8. Ibid, Rule 8.3.
9. Ibid, Rule 8.1(b)(ii) under which this requirement is expressed to be in addition to private disclosure.
10. Ibid, Notes on Rule 8, Note 4(b).
11. Ibid, Rule 8.1(b)(ii).
12. Ibid, Notes on Rule 8, Note 4(b).
13. Ibid, Rule 8.2.
14. This aspect is emphasised in The Panel on Take-overs and Mergers, Statement on Turner and Newall Plc/AE Plc., 17th October, 1986; confirmed in the Statement by the Appeal Committee of the Panel on Take-overs and Mergers, 27th October, 1986.
15. Code, Notes on Rule 8, Note 2.
16. Ibid, Note 7.
17. Ibid, Note 4(a).
18. Ibid, Note 4(b).

Public disclosure may be made by the party concerned or by an agent acting on its behalf.[19] However, where there is more than one agent (eg a merchant bank and a stockbroker), particular care should be taken to ensure that the responsibility for disclosure is agreed between the parties and that it is neither overlooked nor duplicated.

A further warning concerns press announcements. Parties and their associates, who choose to make press announcements regarding dealings in addition to making formal disclosures, must ensure that no confusion results.[20]

In order to clarify which party is involved, details must be included in disclosures (public or private). For public disclosure,[1] a specimen disclosure form[2] may be obtained from the Panel; public disclosures should follow that format. A public disclosure of dealings must include the following information: (i) the total of the relevant securities in question of an offeror or of the offeree company purchased or sold; (ii) the prices paid or received; (iii) the identity of the associate or other person dealing and, if different, the owner or controller; (iv) if the dealing is by an associate, an explanation of how that status arises; (v) if the disclosure is made under the rule for disclosure by 1% shareholders,[3] a statement to that effect; (vi) the resultant total amount of relevant securities owned or controlled by the associate or other person in question (including those of any person with whom there is an agreement or understanding) and the percentage which it represents; and (vii) if relevant, details of any indemnity and other arrangements.[4] If an associate is an associate for more than one reason,[5] all the reasons must be specified.[6]

For the purpose of disclosing identity, the owner or controller must be specified, in addition to the person dealing.[7] Hence, the naming of nominees or vehicle companies is insufficient. The Panel may require additional information to be disclosed when it appears to be appropriate, for example, to identify other persons who have an interest in the securities in question. However, in the case of disclosure of dealings by fund managers on behalf of discretionary clients, the clients need not be named.

When a potential offeror has been the subject of an announcement that talks are taking place (whether or not the potential offeror has been named) or has announced that he is considering making an offer, the potential offeror and persons acting in concert with it must disclose dealings in accordance with the rule[8] for disclosure by parties and by associates for themselves or for discretionary clients.[9] Such disclosures must include the identity of the potential offeror as required by the above provision concerning disclosure of identity.[10]

In regard to private disclosure, the details required vary according to each of the two forms of private disclosure. For private disclosure in respect of dealings in relevant securities, made for the account of discretionary investment clients, by an associate which is an exempt fund manager connected with the offeror or

19. Ibid, Note 4(a).
20. Ibid.
1. Ibid, Note 5(a).
2. Code, Disclosure Forms, Form 8.1/8.3.
3. Code, Rule 8.3.
4. Ie. as required by Code, Notes on Rule 8, Note 6.
5. Eg. because he falls within paras(6) and (7) of the definition of associate.
6. Code, Notes on Rule 8, Note 5(a).
7. Ibid.
8. Ie. Rule 8.3.
9. Code, Notes on Rule 8, Note 12.
10. Ie. as required by Code, Notes on Rule 8, Note 5(a).

offeree company,[11] disclosure must be in the form required by the Panel.[12] As to private disclosure concerning dealings by parties and by associates for non-discretionary clients,[13] disclosure must include the identity of the associate dealing, the total of relevant securities purchased or sold and the prices paid or received.[14] A specimen disclosure form may be obtained from the Panel and disclosures under this requirement should follow that format.

Detailed provisions apply to an arrangement; this is defined to include, in addition to indemnity or option arrangements, any agreement or understanding, formal or informal, of whatever nature relating to relevant securities which may be an inducement to deal or refrain from dealing.[15] When an arrangement exists with any offeror, with the offeree company or with an associate of any offeror or of the offeree company in relation to relevant securities, details of such arrangement must immediately be disclosed whether or not any dealing takes place.[16]

Moreover, if any person is party to such an arrangement with any offeror or an associate of any offeror,[17] whether in respect of relevant securities of that offeror or the offeree company, not only will that render such person an associate of that offeror, but it is also likely to mean that such person is acting in concert with that offeror.[18] If any person is party to such an arrangement with an offeree company or an associate of the offeree company, not only will that render such person an associate of the offeree company, but other specified Code provisions[19] may be relevant.

Details of shareholdings and dealings must also be disclosed in the relevant documents. In addition to disclosing the shareholding of the offeror in the offeree, the offer document must state[20] the shareholdings in the offeror (in the case of a securities exchange offer only) and in the offeree company (i) in which the offeror directors are interested, (ii) which any persons acting in concert with the offeror own or control (with the names of such persons acting in concert), (iii) owned or controlled by any persons who, prior to the posting of the offer document, have irrevocably committed themselves to accept the offer, together with the names of such persons and (iv) owned or controlled by a person with whom the offeror or any person acting in concert with the offeror has any arrangement of the kind referred to in the Code provisions on disclosure of dealings during the offer period.[1] In addition, details of dealings (including dates and prices) within the last twelve months must be given.[2] Where there are no such shareholdings or dealings, an appropriate negative statement is required.[3] The offer document must disclose any arrangements, in relation to

11. Ie, as required by Code, Rule 8.1(b)(ii).
12. Code, Notes on Rule 8, Note 5(b).
13. Ie, as required by Code, Rule 8.2.
14. Code, Notes on Rule 8, Note 5(b).
15. Ibid, Note 6(a). This aspect is also emphasised in the Panel on Take-overs and Mergers, Statement on Turner and Newall Plc./AE Plc., 17th October, 1986; confirmed in the Statement by the Appeal Committee of the Panel on Take-overs and Mergers, 27th October, 1986.
16. Code, Notes on Rule 8, Note 6(b).
17. Ibid, Note 6(a).
18. In that case, Rules 4, 5, 6, 7, 9, 11 and 24 will be relevant.
19. Namely, Note 3 on Rule 9.1 and Rule 25.3.
20. Code, Rule 24.3(c).
1. Namely, Note 6(b) on Rule 8.
2. Code, Rule 24.3(c).
3. Ibid, Rule 24.3(b) and (c). In regard to disclosure of shareholdings, the requirement of an appropriate negative statement does not apply to categories (iii) and (iv) in the paragraph of the text accompanying this footnote (Rule 24(a)(iv) or (v)) if there are no such irrevocable commitments or arrangements: Rule 24.3(b)).

dealings in relevant securities, of the kind envisaged for the purpose of the Code provisions on disclosure of dealings during the offer period.[4] If there are no such arrangements, this should be stated.

In turn, the first major circular from the offeree to its shareholders (whether recommending acceptance or rejection of the offer) must state (i) the shareholdings of the offeree company in the offeror, (ii) those in the offeree company and in the offeror in which offeree directors are interested, (iii) those in the offeree company and (in the case of a securities exchange offer only) in the offeror owned or controlled by a subsidiary of the offeree company, by a pension fund of the offeree company or of a subsidiary of the offeree company, or by an adviser to the offeree company as specified in para.(2) of the definition of associate, but excluding exempt market-makers, (iv) the shareholdings in the offeree company and (in the case of a securities exchange offer only) in the offeror owned or controlled by a person who has an arrangement of the kind referred to in the Code provisions on disclosure of dealings during the offer period,[5] with the offeree company or with any person who is an associate of the offeree company by virtue of paras (1), (2), (3) or (4) of the definition of associate, (v) except with the consent of the Panel, the shareholdings in the offeree company and (in the case of a securities exchange offer only) in the offeror owned or controlled by persons whose investments are managed on a discretionary basis by fund managers (other than exempt fund managers) connected with the offeree company (the persons need not be named) and (vi) whether the directors of the offeree company intend, in respect of their own beneficial shareholdings, to accept or reject the offer.[6] Where, with the exception of (v), there are no such shareholdings, then an appropriate negative statement is required; this will not apply to category (iv) if there are no such arrangements.[7] In addition, particulars of dealings within the last twelve months must be given.[8] Where no such dealings have taken place, this fact should be stated.[9] As in the offer document, disclosure of certain arrangements in relation to dealings is required; if there are no such arrangements, a negative statement must be made.[10]

Documents subsequently sent to shareholders of the offeree company by either party must contain details of any material changes in information previously published by or on behalf of the relevant party during the offer period.[11] The matters to be updated include (a) shareholdings and dealings[12] and (b) arrangements in relation to dealings.[13]

In addition, dealings in relevant securities by an exempt market-maker connected with an offeror or the offeree company, whether in or outside the UK, should be aggregated and disclosed by the Stock Exchange, the Panel and the press.[14] The details to be disclosed are (i) total purchases and sales, (ii) the highest and lowest prices paid and received, (iii) whether the connection is with an offeror or the offeree company and (iv) in respect of dealings which take place outside the UK, the relevant overseas location. However, if the offer is not

4. Code, Rule 24.12.
5. Namely, Note 6(b) on Rule 8.
6. Code, Rule 25.3(a).
7. Ibid, Rule 25.3(b).
8. Ibid, Rule 25.3(c) (i) and (ii).
9. Ibid, Rule 25.3(c) (iii).
10. Ibid, Rule 25.5.
11. Ibid, Rule 27.1.
12. Ibid, Rules 24.3 and 25.3.
13. Ibid, Rules 24.12 and 25.5.
14. Ibid, Rule 38.5.

a securities exchange offer, there is no requirement to disclose dealings in securities of the offeror.[15]

Such announcements which are disclosed in writing (or by telex) to the Stock Exchange (Company Announcement Office) may be inspected there, so that disclosure to the press is unnecessary.[16] However, separate disclosure to the Panel is required.

2. Timing

(a) COMPANIES ACT 1985

When reporting is imposed for its deterrent effect on insiders and to create evidence for subsequent proceedings, the issue of timing is incidental to the requirement to report and immediate reporting of all transactions would impose an onerous burden, but, as underlined by empirical evidence,[17] timing becomes crucial when reporting is required for the benefit of the market. When large holdings are involved, the wider considerations of timely disclosure requirements apply.

Taking account of these factors, statutory provisions for disclosure of a director's interests require notification within five business days after the director becomes aware.[18] The company must enter the information in the register within three business days[19]. On receipt of notification in respect of listed securities, it must notify the Stock Exchange before the end of the next working day[20].

Similarly, the statutory obligation for disclosure of interests in voting shares of public companies must be fulfilled within five business days next following the day upon which the obligation arises[1]. The notification period regarding the obligation of each member of a concert party to notify the others of his interests is the same[2].

(b) STOCK EXCHANGE REQUIREMENTS, THE SARS AND THE CODE

Reflecting its market orientation, accelerated reporting is imposed by these provisions. In respect of listed and USM securities, the Stock Exchange requires immediate disclosure by the company upon receipt of notification under both sets of statutory provisions[3]. But such notification is subject to the statutory reporting periods. Though the Model Code requires prior notification of directors' dealing intentions to the board[4], it does not impose accelerated reporting of transactions.

15. Ibid, Rule 38.5, Note 2.
16. Ibid, Rule 38.5, Note 1.
17. J.H. Lorie and V. Niederhoffer, 'Predictive and Statistical Properties of Insider Trading' (1968) 11 J. Law and Economics 35. This study is dealt with in Chapter 1, Introduction, F. Empirical Studies 1 (b).
18. C.A. 1985, Sch13, Part II.
19. Ibid, Part IV.
20. Ibid, s329.
1. Ibid, ss202(1) and 220(2).
2. Ibid, s206(8).
3. Admission of Securities to Listing, Section 5, Chapter 2, para16; Green Book, General Undertaking, para5(c) and (g)
4. Model Code, Rule 2.

Speedier disclosure is imposed by the Code which requires disclosure not later than 12 noon on the business day following the date of the transaction[5]. Even if a transaction on one day is treated by the Stock Exchange as an early bargain for the next day the date of the transaction will, for this purpose, be the former day[6]. Similarly, the SARs provide for notification by 12 noon on the next business day[7].

3. Publicity

(a) COMPANIES ACT 1985

Disclosure under statutory provisions provides limited publicity. The register must be open to inspection by members and the public during business hours[8]. Copies may be obtained[9]. In addition, the register of directors' interests must be accessible at the A.G.M.[10] and details of their holdings are required in the directors' report[11]. Moreover, as the information is recorded separately by individual companies, details of transactions are not conveniently available.

Upon receipt of notification from a company regarding a director's interests in listed securities, the Stock Exchange is also empowered to publish the information in such manner as it thinks fit[12].

(b) STOCK EXCHANGE REQUIREMENTS, THE SARS AND THE CODE

Information disclosed under these provisions is more widely disseminated. Announcements under Stock Exchange requirements in respect of both sets of statutory provisions are released through the Company News Service and transmitted to the principal Unit Offices of the Stock Exchange, with copies posted on all trading floors[13]. Under the Code, public disclosure in respect of dealings by parties and by associates for themselves or for discretionary clients is to the Stock Exchange, the Panel and the press.[14] Dealings by 1% shareholders are similarly reported.[15] Private disclosure, involving dealings by parties and by associates for non-discretionary clients, is to the Stock Exchange and Panel; these disclosures are not published.[16] Private disclosure of dealings in relevant securities for the account of discretionary investment clients by an associate which is an exempt fund manager connected with the offeror or offeree company is to the Panel only.[17]

As details of directors' dealings are now disclosed to the Stock Exchange and generally published by it, the former requirement for companies to have

5. Code, Rules 5(4), 8 and 38.5, and Notes on Rule 8, Note 3.
6. Ibid, Notes on Rule 8, Note 3.
7. SARs, Rule 3.
8. C.A. 1985, s219(1) and Sch13, Part IV.
9. Ibid, s219(2) and Sch13, Part IV.
10. Ibid, Sch13, Part IV.
11 Ibid, s235(3) and Sch7, Part I.
12. C.A. 1985, s329(1).
13. Admission of Securities to Listing, Section 5, Chapter 2, Note 1.10.
14. Code, Notes on Rule 8, Note 4(a).
15. Ibid.
16. Code, Notes on Rule 8, Note 4(b).
17. Ibid; this requirement to disclose is subject to an exception where the Panel so consents: Rule 8.1 (b)(ii).

available for inspection before and during the AGM a statement of particulars of each director's dealings since the previous statement was available for exhibition, is no longer considered necessary. Nevertheless, it is regarded as helpful for all information of directors' dealings to be readily available to shareholders around the A.G.M. as such information is usually regarded as important by shareholders[18].

In addition, the Model Code[19] provides that a list of directors' dealings in the company's securities since the date of the previous list should be circulated to board members with board papers. Alternatively, the register should be available for inspection at every board meeting.

D. Exemptions

1. Companies Act 1985

Other than excluding certain interests in relation to reporting requirements[20], no provision is made by the CA 1985 for exemptions. In restricting disclosure to directors, the narrow range of corporate insiders required to report under the provisions for disclosure of directors' interests precludes provision for exemption on the basis of remoteness from access to inside information. Likewise, the aim of legislation for disclosure of interests in voting shares in public companies militates against provision for exemption.

2. Stock Exchange requirements, the SARs and the Code

Similarly, Stock Exchange requirements, the SARs and the Code do not provide for exemptions. Though covering a wide range of persons, the broad definition of insider by the Code is limited to the offer period.

However, extension of general reporting requirements to a wide range of persons would raise the issue of exemption. Rather than being advanced by a large number of reports by persons whose access to inside information is remote, the aims of insider reporting are better served by focusing on those with greatest scope for abuse of inside information. Even when certain persons are not within the reporting requirements, criminal liability may now arise under the IDA 1985 when inside information is misused.

E. Sanctions and enforcement

1. Penalties

(a) COMPANIES ACT 1985

Both sets of reporting requirements in the Companies Act 1985 give rise to criminal liability.

---

18. *Weinberg and Blank on Take-overs and Mergers,* Fourth Edition by M.A. Weinberg, M.V. Blank and A.L. Greystoke (1979), para2324.
19. Model Code, Rule 5.
20. See ante, C. The operation of reporting.

(i) Directors' interests in shares or debentures. As regards directors' interests, a person who fails to discharge, within the proper period, an obligation to notify the company of his interests or in purported fulfilment of such an obligation, knowingly or recklessly makes a false statement to the company is liable to a fine, imprisonment or both[1]. Failure to notify the Stock Exchange of a director's interests in listed securities renders the company and every officer in default liable to a fine and on continued contravention, a daily default fine[2]. But a restriction on prosecution is imposed by the provision that proceedings may only be instituted by or with the consent of the Department or the DPP[3].

In relation to the register of directors' interests, the company and every officer in default is liable to a fine or on continued contravention, to a daily default fine for several offences. These are: (a) failure to keep the register or to keep it in the manner prescribed; (b) refusal to allow inspection of the register; (c) failure to send a copy as required; (d) failure to notify the registrar of where the register is kept and (e) failure to make the register accessible at the A.G.M[4]. The court may also by order compel inspection of the register or direct that a copy be sent to the person requiring it[5].

(ii) Interests in voting shares in public companies. Similar penalties of a fine, imprisonment, or both, may be imposed on a person in breach of requirements to disclose interests in voting shares in public companies[6]. In this connection, it is an offence: (a) to fail to fulfil an obligation to notify known interests[7]; (b) in purported fulfilment of such an obligation, knowingly or recklessly to make to the company a statement which is false; (c) to fail to fulfil, within the proper period, an obligation to give another person information under the concert party requirements[8] (but it is a defence[9] for the accused to prove that it was not possible for him to give the notice to that other person within the proper period and that either (i) it has not since become possible for him to give the notice so required or (ii) he gave that notice as soon after the end of that period as it became possible for him to do so); and (d) to fail without reasonable excuse to secure notification by an agent. A restriction on prosecution is also imposed by the provision that proceedings may be instituted only by or with the consent of the Department or the DPP[10].

Liability for non-compliance by a company with this set of disclosure requirements is not limited to the company, but extends to persons who run the company. When a company is guilty of such offences and it is proved that the offence occurred with the consent or connivance of, or was attributable to any neglect on the part of any director, manager, secretary or other officer of the company or any person purporting to act as such (or in the case of a company managed by members, a member), that person shall also be deemed guilty[11].

Likewise, in relation to the register of interests in shares, the company and every officer in default is liable to a fine or on continued contravention, a default

1. C.A. 1985, ss324(7) and 328(6).
2. Ibid, s329(3).
3. Ibid, ss324(8), 328(7), 329(3) and 732.
4. Ibid, s326(1)-(4).
5. Ibid, s326(3).
6. Ibid, s210(3).
7. The obligation referred to is one imposed by Part VI of the Act.
8. The obligation referred to is one imposed by C.A. 1985, s206.
9. C.A. 1985, s210(4).
10. Ibid, ss210(6) and 732.
11. Ibid, ss210(6) and 733(2) and (3).

fine for several offences. These are: (a) failure to keep the register or to keep it in the manner prescribed[12]; (b) failure to notify a person of his inclusion in the register as a result of information furnished by another or to rectify the index where the register has been rectified[13]; (c) deletion of an entry in the register of interests, except when expressly authorised, and when an entry is wrongly deleted, failure to restore that entry to the register as soon as it is reasonably practicable[14]; (d) refusal to allow inspection of the register[15] and (e) failure to send a copy as required[16]. When a person's application (i) to have his name removed from the register as having been wrongly named as a member or as having an interest or (ii) to have his cesser of interest in a concert party recorded is refused by the company, he may apply to the court for an order to remove or include the information accordingly[17]. The court may also by order compel inspection of the register or direct that a copy be sent to the person requiring it[18].

Apart from criminal sanctions, administrative remedies are available. Since evasion of reporting requirements is facilitated by the use of nominees, special investigation powers are a prerequisite to enforcement. In addition to general powers of investigation, the Department has special powers to investigate directors' shareholdings and dealings and company ownership. When it encounters difficulties in ascertaining the facts in investigations into company ownership, the Department may impose restrictions on shares or debentures. But in 1981, increased powers were conferred on public companies to obtain disclosure of interests in their voting shares, thereby relegating the Department's powers to use as a last resort. Irrespective of any power in their articles to restrict shares, public companies may apply to the court for restrictions to be imposed on the shares in question when a person fails to provide the information required. These investigative powers and related restrictions will be considered subsequently[19].

(b) STOCK EXCHANGE REQUIREMENTS, THE SARS AND THE CODE

In regard to the additional reporting requirements relating to listed and USM securities, suspected breaches are investigated by the Stock Exchange. Likewise, suspected breaches of the SARs and Code are investigated by the Panel. In this connection, an expansion of the responsibilities of intermediaries in the 1988 Code sought to strengthen Panel investigations. In addition to intermediaries' general duty to ensure, so far as they are able, that their clients are willing to comply with the disclosure obligations, the Code states that intermediaries are expected to co-operate with the Panel in its dealings enquiries[20]. This requirement is expressed in terms that those who deal in relevant securities should appreciate that stockbrokers and other intermediaries will supply the Panel with relevant information as to those dealings, including identities of clients, as part of that co-operation. In cases of breach, the Stock Exchange and Panel can

12. Ibid, s211(10).
13. Ibid, s217(7).
14. Ibid, s218.
15. Ibid, s219(1).
16. Ibid, s219(2).
17. Ibid, s217(5).
18. Ibid, s219(4).
19. See, post, Chapter 7, Investigation.
20. Code, Notes on Rule 8, Note 10.

impose their own sanctions. But in the event of overlap with the CA 1985, enforcement is left to the Department[1].

2. Enforcement

In conjunction with an insider prosecution under the statutory prohibition on dealing, two prosecutions were initiated in 1982 for failure to disclose an interest in shares, but were not proceeded with[2]. A prosecution in 1985 for failure by a director to notify the company of an interest in shares of debentures resulted in a conviction[3]. Otherwise, there has been a dearth of prosecutions.

However, evidence of prima facie breaches has been found in investigations by inspectors appointed by the Department[4]. In a 1980 report, inspectors considered that three individuals had breached the statutory requirements for disclosure of directors' interests. In a 1982 report, inspectors recommended the prosecution of two directors for 'deliberate' breaches of statutory requirements relating to both directors' interests and substantial shareholders. But the Department took no further action on these reports.

A reluctance to prosecute is understandable in cases of genuine oversight or misunderstood obligations since the impact of a criminal prosecution may be out of proportion to the impropriety. But, apart from raising questions about the value of their appointment when inspectors' recommendations are rejected, failure to prosecute deliberate breaches suggests the Department attaches little importance to insider reporting.

Given the infrequency of investigations by inspectors appointed by the Department, examples of non-compliance found by inspectors probably reflect a tendency among many insiders to ignore statutory reporting requirements. Yet insofar as compliance is encouraged by fear of prosecution, the Department's record reinforces the tendency to disregard reporting requirements.

Similarly, the Stock Exchange has found instances of prima facie breaches of statutory requirements and reported their findings to the Department[5]. Public statements recording these prima facie breaches and their referral to the Department have been issued.

Likewise, the Panel has found breaches of the Code requirements[6]. Sanctions have been imposed.

However, the dearth of prosecution also underlines the problem of reliance on criminal liability. In order to widen the scope of liability, inspectors ap-

---

1. See, post, Chapter 6, Administrative Regulation and Chapter 7, Investigation.
2. The Department of Trade and Industry, Companies in 1982 (1983), p.15, Table 11.
3. Ibid, Companies in 1985 (1986), p.17, Table 11.
4. These include: (a) Kwik Save Discount Group, Report by D.S. Mangat and J.H. Dickman (1974); (b) Ozalid Group Holdings Ltd., Report by N. Butter, Q.C., and B.A. Kemp, F.C.A. (1980) and (c) Norwest Holst Ltd., Report by J. Davies, Q.C. and T. Harding, F.C.A. (1982).
5. Statement by the Special Committee of the Stock Exchange on Scottish and Universal Investments Ltd., 30th November, 1976; Stock Exchange Notice 115/74, Coley Rotolin Group Ltd., 4th November, 1974; Stock Exchange, News Release, Elliot Group of Peterborough Ltd., 16th February, 1978.
6. The Panel on Take-overs and Mergers, Statement by the City Panel on Stock Exchange dealings in the course of a take-over situation, 2nd April, 1971; Statement on Seafield Amalgamated Rubber Co. Ltd., 27th July, 1976 [1976] J.B.L.351; Statement on Turner and Newall Plc/AE Plc., 17th October, 1986; confirmed in the Statement by the Appeal Committee of the Panel on Take-overs and Mergers, 27th October, 1986; Statement on Hepworth Holdings Plc./Birmid Qualcast, 3rd March, 1987; Statement on Benlox Holdings Plc/Storehouse Group Plc., 6th November, 1987 and Statement on East Worcestershire Water Company, 22nd April, 1988.

pointed by the Department recommended in their report[7] on a company in 1982 that: (a) statutory reporting requirements be expressed to be duties to the shareholders as well; (b) a right of action be expressly given to shareholders affected by their breach and (c) those requirements be made to provide that in considering both the scope of the duty and its breach, courts be entitled to take into account City usage as expressed in the Code. They viewed these as providing: (a) a valuable reinforcement of Panel sanctions; (b) a much needed financial protection for shareholders whose interest may be adversely affected by a breach and (c) a measure of legal recognition for the Code which would be beneficial in bridging the gap between regulation by a business code and regulation by legislation. Whilst its effectiveness would currently be hindered by the problems of costs and enforcement associated with shareholder actions, a civil remedy of this nature potentially constitutes a more effective deterrent to insider dealing than criminal liability attaching to non-disclosure of interests in securities.

This proposal draws on the important US provision for the recapture of 'short swing' profits realised by listed insiders when attributable to a purchase and sale of an equity security within a six-month period. Based on the requirement for a director or officer of an issuer of a registered equity security or a beneficial owner of more than 10% of such a security to report to the SEC his beneficial ownership of the issuer's equity securities and changes in ownership[8], the 'short-swing' profits rule[9] provides:

> 'For the purpose of preventing the unfair use of information which may have been obtained by such beneficial owner, director or officer by reason of his relationship to the issuer, any profit realised by him from any purchase and sale, or any sale and purchase, of any equity security of such issuer (other than an exempted security) within any period of less than six months, unless such security was acquired in good faith in connection with a debt previously contracted, shall inure to and be recoverable by the issuer, irrespective of any intention on the part of such beneficial owner, director, or officer in entering into such transaction of holding the security purchased or of not re-purchasing the security sold for a period exceeding six months. Suit to recover such profit may be instituted at law or in equity in any court of competent jurisdiction by the issuer, or by the owner of any security of the issuer in the name and on behalf of the issuer if the issuer shall fail or refuse to bring such suit within sixty days after request or shall fail diligently to prosecute the same thereafter; but no such suit shall be brought more than two years after such profit was realised. This sub-section shall not be construed to cover any transaction where such beneficial owner was not such both at the time of the purchase and sale, or the sale and purchase, of the security involved, or any transactions which the Commission by rules and regulations may exempt as not comprehended within the purpose of this sub-section'.

However, the short-swing profits rule has attracted criticism[10]. The rule has operated in an arbitrary manner; whereas an insider is liable to repay profits

---

7. Norwest Holst Ltd., op cit n4(c), p251, supra, para321.
8. Securities Exchange Act 1934 s16(a).
9. Ibid, s16(b).
10. The effectiveness and criticisms of the short-swing profits rule are discussed more fully by: (a) L. Loss, *Securities Regulation* (2nd.ed., 1961) p.561 and (1969 Supp), p.1087; (b) L. Loss, 'The

when the transaction occurs within six months, even though he can show there was no unfair use of information, a transaction spread over six months and a day is not caught even when abuse of information is established. The interpretation of 'profit realised', 'purchase' and 'sale', the scope of exemptions and the problem of double liability have given rise to controversy. In addition, private enforcement by investors who, due to the derivative remedy need not have been security holders during the six-month period, coupled with their recovery of legal fees, has led to apparent champerty and maintenance. There is no guarantee against evasion by 'mutual back-scratching' by insiders in different companies or by trading through relatives and friends.

Moreover, the expansion of case law under Rule 10b-5 has challenged the assumption underlying the short-swing profits rule. Initially, it was thought that provision for an automatic remedy determined by objective criteria for short-swing profits was necessitated by the difficulties of proving that an insider knowingly used inside information to trade[11]. To the extent that these expectations have not been realised, the foundation of the short-swing profits rule has been undermined.

Despite these criticisms, the general view is that the short-swing profits rule has been very effective. Attributable to the simplicity of the elements of the cause of action, its effectiveness is regarded as such that:

> 'one may infer (1) that the section, now that a number of corporate insiders have felt its bite has been a considerable deterrent and (2) that an insider who does find himself a potential defendant is apt to conclude that he has no practicable alternative but to pay up'[12].

Far from removing the moral stigma attached to abuse of inside information, the short-swing profits rule appears to have underlined it. The rule is also regarded as operating on the whole against those whom it is intended to protect and overcoming the difficulties of proving an insider's state of mind when effecting a transaction. The fact that when a bona fide transaction is caught, the trader only loses his profit, counters the objection that directors who purchase shares to resist an unfavourable bid may be penalised. Where their objective is to protect shareholders as a whole, they should not object to disgorging profits and in buying shares to contest the bid, they purchase the shares from those whom they claim to protect below the price of the proposed bid which, in turn, they regard as too low. Nevertheless, the application of the 'lowest price in, the highest price out' principle has a penal element.

However, the short-swing profits rule is a deterrent rather than an adjuster of economic positions. Disgorgement of profits benefits the company, which is composed of the non-selling and the buying shareholders, as distinct from the selling shareholders who suffered the loss.

Although acknowledging some of the criticisms, the American Law Institute retained a short-swing profits rule in its Federal Securities Code[13] on the basis that the rule had acquired a 'symbolic significance' that deserved recognition[14].

Fiduciary Concept as Applied to Trading by Corporate "Insiders" in the United States' (1970) 33 M.L.R.34; (c) W. Painter, *The Federal Securities Code and Corporate Disclosure* (1979), Chapter 4 and (d) *Weinberg and Blank*, para2353.
11. Painter, op cit n10(c), p252, supra, p.79.
12. Loss, op cit n10(b), p252, at 40.
13. Section 1714.

The proposed Code rule contains amendments to the existing provision to codify exemptions established by rule and case law and to clarify the expectation that the SEC use its expanded rule-making authority 'so as to play a greater quasi-legislative role in this area than it has in the past'[15]. But it has been commented that retention should be determined by reference to deterrent grounds rather than mere symbolism[16].

Limited to listed insiders and 10% shareholders, the US short-swing profits rule does not extend to separate reporting requirements in connection with take-over bids. But British reporting requirements do not make the same distinction. The introduction of a short-swing profits rule to all persons required to disclose their interests in securities, especially in respect of interests in voting shares in public companies, would conflict with other regulatory goals. In particular, it would hinder market efficiency by discouraging bids through its impact on the profits of potential bidders. A distinction on the lines drawn in the US would thus seem necessary.

However, the problems associated with criminal liability for insider dealing under the IDA 1985 owe little to defective reporting requirements. Rather, they are attributable to substantive and enforcement difficulties.

Disclosure regulation thus constitutes a key element in insider dealing regulation, but further evaluation is postponed to the concluding chapter.

---

14. A.L.I. Federal Securities Code, Tentative Draft No.2 (1973) comments (1) and (2).
15. Ibid.
16. L.H. Leigh, 'Securities Regulation: Problems in Relation to Sanctions', p.513 at p.552 in Consumer and Corporate Affairs Canada, *Proposals for a Securities Market Law for Canada,* Vol.3 Background Papers (1979).

Chapter 6

Administrative Regulation

Apart from those discussed in preceding chapters, other measures make a significant contribution to insider dealing regulation. This chapter discusses the additional provisions which impinge on such regulation under the headings of restrictions on dealings, standards of conduct for investment business, conflicts of interest and enforcement.

I. RESTRICTIONS ON DEALINGS

A consequence of heavy reliance on self-regulation and Government reluctance to intervene in securities regulation has been a proliferation of measures, in the form of rules and regulations, codes of conduct and guidelines, setting standards of conduct for participants in the securities markets. These measures have been formulated by professional organisations, whose members have, in turn, devised in-house rules for employees.

A. The Stock Exchange Model Code

Partly as an example of its ability to regulate market conduct and partly to protect the company and individual directors against uninformed criticism, the Stock Exchange published in 1977 a Model Code for securities transactions by directors of listed companies.[1] Now appended to the continuing obligations of issuers whose securities have been admitted to listing (and formerly to the Listing Agreement) and to the General Undertaking, the Model Code has been revised to take account of the statutory provisions on insider dealing contained initially in the CA 1980 and subsequently in the IDA 1985. The Model Code is designed to set a minimum standard of good practice against which companies should measure their own internal codes.

Unlike the City Code, the Model Code is of general application and not confined to take-overs and mergers. Nevertheless, a limitation in its scope is that it is not applicable to foreign companies.[2]

After an introductory outline as to the scope of the Model Code and its relationship with statutory provisions, the Model Code is divided into Basic Principles and Model Rules. It thus follows the drafting style of the City Code.

At the outset, the Model Code reiterates the Stock Exchange's view that it is 'highly desirable' for directors of listed companies to hold securities in their own companies. It then seeks to reconcile the need for directors to be able to deal in such securities with protection against insider dealing allegations

---

1. The Stock Exchange, Model code for securities transactions by directors of listed companies, 25th October, 1977. The Model Code was the subject of a note in [1978] J.B.L. 63.
2. Admission of Securities to Listing, Section 5, Chapter 2, Note 45.1.

prompted by dealings before and during periods when price sensitive information is disclosed.

Whilst compliance with statutory prohibitions on insider dealing[3] is regarded
as 'axiomatic', the Stock Exchange states that special considerations apply to
directors of listed companies and hence wider restrictions are placed on their
freedom to deal. Even when not expressly prohibited by statute, it is regarded
as undesirable for a director to buy or sell his company's securities either (i)
where a director is himself unaware of a price sensitive matter under discussion,
(as when it has not yet been made known to the board), which is likely ultimately
to call for an exceptional announcement, and where for his own protection he
should be told not to deal or (ii) in the periods prior to the regular announcements of results and dividends. The Model Code also has broader application
in that the statutory prohibitions on dealing do not specifically relate to a
director's other interests or to the position of spouses or infant children.

The purpose of the Model Code is 'primarily to give guidance' on the two
occasions when it is regarded as undesirable for a director to deal, even though
he is not expressly prohibited by statute. Since it sees the Model Code as setting
a minimum standard, the Stock Exchange emphasises that the Model Code
should be regarded as setting guidelines rather than rigid rules to be followed
in every detail.

As regards the relationship between the IDA 1985 and the Model Code, it is
first necessary to be satisfied that a proposed dealing is not in breach of the
statutory prohibitions since compliance with the Model Code is not a defence.
By way of example, breach of the statutory prohibitions is not necessarily
precluded either (i) by compliance with the procedure set out in Basic Principle
5 (to establish the time at which an intended acquisition by a company shall be
deemed price sensitive information) or (ii) by dealing under the extenuating
circumstances indicated in Rule 3.1 (when a pressing financial commitment
must be met). Rather, subject to there being no breach of statutory prohibitions, Basic Principle 5 and Rule 3.1 are intended as guidance for the chairman
(or whoever is nominated to receive notification of dealing intentions) as to
circumstances where exceptions to the Model Code may be considered.

Unlike Panel statements on the City Code, interpretations of the Model Code
have not been provided on a case-by-case basis by the Stock Exchange, even
prior to the CA 1980. But reference to the Model Code was made in three Panel
statements in 1978-79.

To facilitate comparison with legislative prohibitions, the Model Code will be
considered under the same headings. These are the definition of insider, the
meaning of inside information, restrictions placed on insiders and sanctions.

1. The definition of insider

The approach adopted by the Model Code is mainly based on the concept of
listed insiders. Of these, the most important are directors. But the Model Code
applies to a wider category of persons even though its restrictions and procedures are defined by reference to directors.

Apart from directors, the category of listed insiders is wide enough to include
individuals who, under the IDA 1985 in the absence of the requisite connection
with a company, would usually fall within the definition of tippees. Thus, the
restrictions are regarded as equally applicable to dealings by a director's spouse

---

3. IDA 1985; see, ante, Chapter 3. Criminal Liability.

and by or on behalf of any infant child.[4]

In addition, when a director places investment funds under professional management, even where discretion is given, the Model Code states managers should nonetheless be made subject to the same restrictions and procedures as the director himself in respect of proposed dealings in the company's securities.[5] As a precaution, a director having funds under management should ensure that the investment manager is aware of the identity of any company of which he is a director.[6]

By combining the concept of listed insiders with an access test, certain employees are also included. Both individually and as a board, directors should ensure that any employee of the company or any director or employee of a subsidiary company, who acquires unpublished price sensitive information in relation to the market price of any listed company through his office or employment in the company or a subsidiary, deals in those securities in accordance with the Model Code.[7] In comparison to legislative provisions[8], this access test is a narrow one in that it is limited to certain employees and does not include other persons with a professional or business relationship with the company, such as financial advisers or important customers.

However, as responsibility for enforcement lies with the board, the Model Code definition of insider is largely explicable in terms of enforcement. With the exception of professional fund managers and members of a director's family, the insiders are subject to company codes of conduct.

Of the Panel statements which referred to the Model Code, one concerned dealings by a director[9], another by a director in his wife's name[10] and a third by an employee.[11] In this third statement, the Panel commented on the company's lapse in that though it had adopted the Model Code, it had not drawn the employee's attention to it.

2. The meaning of inside information

The Model Code expressly rejects an exhaustive definition of price sensitive information.[12] Nevertheless, it places a presumption on various matters required to be disclosed by listed companies under the'Continuing Obligations' provisions in the Admission of Securities to Listing being so regarded[13], namely: (a) any proposed change in capital structure (including that of the company's listed debt securities); (b) the acquisition and realisation of assets as from time to time required to be notified by Section 6, Chapter 1. 'Acquisitions and Realisations' in 'Admission of Securities to Listing'; (c) any information to be disclosed to the Stock Exchange under the City Code; (d) information notified to the company under insider reporting requirements;[14] (e) any decision by the Board to submit to the company's shareholders a proposal for the company to

4. Model Code, Model Rule 4.1.
5. Ibid, General Principle 7.
6. Ibid, Model Rule 4.2.
7. Ibid, Model Rule 6.
8. See, ante, Chapter 3. Criminal Liability.
9. The Panel on Take-overs and Mergers, Statement on W.H. Henshall (Addlestone) Ltd., 3rd July, 1978 [1979] J.B.L.46.
10. Ibid, Statement on J.B. Eastwood Ltd., 20th July, 1978 [1979] J.B.L.47.
11. Ibid, Statement on Chaddesley Investments Ltd., 7th February, 1979 [1979] J.B.L.273.
12. Model Code, Basic Principle 5.
13. Admission of Securities to Listing, Section 5, Chapter 2, paras 10 and 14-19.
14. See, ante, Chapter 5. Disclosure, III. Insider reporting requirements.

be authorised to purchase its own shares and the outcome of the shareholders' meeting; (f) any purchase by the company, or the group of which the company is part, of its listed securities; (g) any board decision to change the general character or nature of the business of the company or of the group or (h) a change in the company's status for taxation purposes under statutory provisions relating to close companies or approved investment trusts. Hence, the approach of the Model Code is that in laying down the disclosure required by the company, disclosure requirements not only settle the disclosure required of a company but by implication they also set the standards for dealing by insiders.

Apart from these matters of an exceptional nature, restrictions are placed on insiders in connection with regularly recurring information.[15] Profits, dividends and other distributions are so categorised. The restrictions apply whether or not such information is price-sensitive.

Responsibility for the publication of price sensitive information is placed on the company under Stock Exchange timely disclosure requirements.[16] The procedure for timing on notification of decisions on dividends, profit and other matters requiring announcement recognises the need for a period to elapse between the time of notification and the information becoming generally available.[17] But neither the Stock Exchange timely disclosure requirements nor the Model Code indicate a period for insiders to wait before trading.

However, if insiders are not to exploit their trading advantages, they should be required to refrain from dealing until the information has been disseminated to the investing public. In this connection, it is arguable that communication of the information to the Company Announcements Office under the Stock Exchange timely disclosure requirements and its release through the Company News Service constitute the first steps in a dissemination process which is completed after an additional period, following publication, that permits absorption and evaluation of the information.

Nevertheless, the US experience[18] illustrates that there can be no absolute criteria as to the length of the waiting period. This will usually depend upon the type of information involved, whether it is relatively complex or simple and the period of time necessary for it to be fully evaluated by investors. The American Stock Exchange has taken the view that at least twenty-four to forty-eight hours after general publication of the news in a national medium is required.[19]

The courts have also implied that news such as a mining discovery or the announcement of a new product may be more difficult to evaluate than an increase in earnings and that it may be reasonable to require a waiting period for the former, though possibly not for the latter. In *Texas Gulf Sulphur*, some insiders argued that the news of the significant mineral discovery had already been made public when they purchased their shares. The district court[20] held that a purchase after release of the information to the press, but before it had appeared on the Dow-Jones ticker had not violated Rule 10b.5 because the news had already become public. But this part of the district court's decision was reversed and a majority of the circuit court[1] emphasised the importance of

15. Model Code, Basic Principle 3(i).
16. See, ante, Chapter 5. Disclosure, II. Timely disclosure.
17. Admission of Securities to Listing, Section 5, Chapter 2, Note 6.2.
18. W.H. Painter, *The Federal Securities Code and Corporate Disclosure* (1979) at pp165-168.
19. Amex Disclosure Policies, American Stock Exchange Company Guide 401-406, reprinted in 2 Fed.Sec.L. Rep (CCH) 23, 124.
20. *SEC v Texas Gulf Sulphur Co.*, 258 F.Supp262, 288 (S.D.N.Y.1966) rev'd and remanded 401 F 2d.833 (2d.Cir.1968), cert. denied sub.nom. *Coates v SEC* 394 U.S.976 (1969).
1. *SEC v Texas Gulf Sulphur Co.*, 401 F.2d.833, 854 (2d.Cir.1968).

adequate dissemination to the investing public. Though the circuit court did not pass on the question of a reasonable waiting period, the majority noted:

> 'where the news is of a sort which is not readily translatable into investment action, insiders may not take advantage of their advance opportunity to evaluate the information by acting immediately upon dissemination.'[2]

Since the *Texas Gulf Sulphur* case, the waiting period required in court decisions has varied from one[3] to ten days following disclosure of the facts.[4] In a leading case, the court required a waiting period of nine trading days after public release of the information, reversing a district court opinion which had required a waiting period of twenty trading days.[5]

The Federal Securities Code deals with the issue by way of the 'safe harbour' rule. It provides:

> 'a fact is "generally available" one week (or any other period prescribed by Commission rule) after it is disclosed by means of a filing or press release or in any other manner reasonably designed to bring it to the attention of the investing public. Otherwise, the burden of proving that a fact is "generally available" is on the person who so asserts.'[6]

The difficulty is thus one of striking a balance between preventing insiders taking advantage of their advance knowledge to evaluate the information and penalising them by a waiting period unduly longer than the time required for the market to discount the news. But this may be before publication in the press the following morning or some other arbitrary period.

3. Restrictions placed on insiders

As with legislative provisions, the main restriction imposed on insiders by the Model Code is a prohibition on dealings. Insiders may also be restricted by other provisions on tipping. In addition, insiders are required to give prior notification of their intention to deal in any securities of their own company. Special provisions apply to directors involved in trusts.

(a) PROHIBITIONS ON DEALINGS

By way of general constraint, directors are informed that as they will always be thought to be in possession of more information than can at any particular time be published, they must accept that they cannot at all times feel free to deal in their companies' securities even when the statutory provisions would not prohibit them from doing so.[7] The Model Code prohibits dealings in three circumstances.

2. Ibid, 842.
3. *SEC v Texas Gulf Sulphur Co.*, 312 F.Supp77, 93 (S.D.N.Y.1970) aff'd in part and remanded in part 446 F.2d.1301 (2d.Cir.), cert. denied 404 U.S.1005 (1971).
4. *Fridrich v Bradford* [1974-1975 Transfer Binder] Fed.Sec.L.Rep.(CCH) 94, 723 (M.D.Tenn.1974), rev'd on other grounds, 542 F.2d.307 (6th Cir.1976).
5. *Mitchell v Texas Gulf Sulphur Co.*, 446 F.2d.90 (10th Cir.) cert. denied, 404 U.S.1004 (1971), rev'g in part *Reynolds v Texas Gulf Sulphur Co.*, 309 F.supp548 (D.Utah 1970).
6. American Law Institute, Federal Securities Code, s265.
7. Model Code, Basic Principle 2.

First, in an allusion to the US 'short-swing' profits rule,[8] directors must not deal in their companies' securities on considerations of a short-term nature.[9] But no provision is made for disgorgement and the imprecision of certain non-statutory provisions is here illustrated by the failure to define 'short-term'.

Secondly, directors must not deal when in possession of unpublished price sensitive information. Apart from the securities of the company of which he is a director,[10] the prohibition extends to dealings in securities of any other listed company when, by virtue of his position as a director of his own company, he is in possession of unpublished price sensitive information in relation to those securities.[11]

As with the legislative provisions, there are difficulties of proof in relation to breaches of prohibitions on dealing. However, an instance of a director dealing in securities of his own company was found in the 1978 Panel statement on J.B. Eastwood Ltd.,[12] which concerned the purchase of its shares by a director privy to preliminary take-over discussions.

The term 'securities' is not restricted to listed securities. Instead, references in the Model Code to 'securities' have the meanings ascribed to the term by the IDA 1985.[13]

Special provisions clarify the position in relation to options.[14] For the purpose of the Model Code, the grant to a director of an option to subscribe or purchase his company's securities is regarded as a dealing by him, if the price at which such option may be exercised is fixed at the time of such grant. If, however, an option is granted to a director on terms whereby the price at which such option may be exercised is to be fixed at the time of exercise, the dealing is to be regarded as taking place at the time of exercise.

Thirdly, with an emphasis on equity rather than efficiency considerations, other prohibitions apply even when a director is not necessarily in possession of unpublished price sensitive information. Whilst acknowledging that there must be periods when directors are in principle to be regarded as free to deal in their companies' securities, the Model Rules are formulated on the basis that dealings should not take place prior to the announcement of either (i) regularly recurring information, particularly profits, dividends and other distributions, or (ii) matters of an exceptional nature involving unpublished price sensitive information in relation to the market price of the securities of the company (or where relevant any other listed company).[15]

In regard to regularly recurring information, the prohibition on dealing for a minimum period prior to the announcement of such information, applies whether or not the information is price sensitive.[16] Lasting at least four months in the year, the prohibited period covers the two months immediately preceding both the preliminary announcement of the company's annual results and of the half-yearly results, together with dividends and distributions to be paid or passed.[17] The 1978 Panel statement on J.B. Eastwood Ltd., which involved

8. See, ante, Chapter 5. Disclosure, III. Insider Reporting.
9. Model Code, Basic Principle 1.
10. Model Code, Model Rule 1.1.
11. Ibid, Model Rule 1.2.
12. The Panel on Take-overs and Mergers, Statement on J.B. Eastwood Ltd., 20th July, 1978.
13. Model Code, Model Rule 7; s12, IDA 1985.
14. Model Code, Basic Principle 4.
15. Ibid, Basic Principle 3.
16. Ibid, Basic Principle 3(i).
17. Ibid, Model Rule 3.1.

purchases in the prohibited period, also revealed a breach of this prohibition.[18] Where companies produce quarterly results, modified dealing procedures appropriate to their case should be formulated in consultation with the Quotations Department.[19]

However, the prohibition is qualified, being inapplicable to sales in exceptional circumstances, such as to meet a pressing financial commitment.[20] But the prior notification procedure still applies.[1]

As to matters of an exceptional nature involving unpublished price sensitive information, the prohibition on dealing runs from the time when the likelihood of an announcement ultimately being necessary has become a reasonable probability.[2] As an example, the 1977 Model Code suggested that in the case of a material acquisition, this could be the signing of the heads of agreement.[3]

When a director has inside information on matters of an exceptional nature, he will normally be prohibited from dealing by the statutory provisions. Even if not, the Model Code prohibition applies.[4] Problems arise where the director has no such information personally. Based on the prior notification procedure within the company,[5] the proposed solution relies on the chairman or other director notified advising him that it would be inappropriate to deal. But this assumes that the chairman or other director notified is aware of the matter.

The wider scope of this third prohibition overcomes the difficulties of proof associated with a prohibition on dealing by insiders when in possession of inside information. But in so doing, it increases the equity constraints on insiders to the point where the freedom of insiders to deal when not in possession of inside information is restricted. The second and third prohibitions of the Model Code thus illustrate in contrasting ways the difficulties of using a prohibition on dealings as a regulatory device against insider dealing.

(b) RESTRICTIONS ON TIPPING

Consistent with the emphasis on the prevalence of tippee rather than insider dealing in the 1977 Joint Statement by the Stock Exchange and Panel,[6] the Model Code contains a prohibition against tipping by reference to an 'overriding principle' that 'under no circumstances should a director... make any unauthorised disclosure of any confidential information, whether to co-trustees or any other person'[7] This prohibition is, however, linked to confidential information as distinct from unpublished price-sensitive information and, in contrast to the City Code,[8] does not extend to circumstances where, as distinct from communicating confidential information, a director makes a recommendation as to dealing in the relevant securities.

Other Model Code provisions which impinge upon tipping are the restric-

---

18. The Panel on Take-overs and Mergers, Statement on J.B. Eastwood Ltd., 20th July, 1978.
19. Model Code, Model Rule 3.2.
20. Ibid, Model Rule 3.1.
1. Ibid, Model Rule 2; see post (iii) Prior notification procedure.
2. Ibid, Basic Principle 5.
3. Model Code (1977 edition), Basic Principle 5.
4. Model Code, Model Rule 1.
5. Ibid, Model Rule 2; see post (iii) Prior notification procedure.
6. Joint Statement issued by the Stock Exchange and the Panel on Take-overs and Mergers on 14th April, 1977, 'Announcement of Price-Sensitive Matters', see, ante, Chapter 1. Introduction, II. Empirical Assessment.
7. Model Code, Basic Principle 6.
8. City Code, Rule 4.1(b).

tions on dealings which are regarded as equally applicable to any dealings by the director's spouse or by or on behalf of any infant child and any other dealings in which, for the purposes of the Companies Act 1985,[9] he is or is to be treated as interested.[10]

Moreover, the communication of inside information may fall within other Stock Exchange provisions regulating the treatment of inside information, namely, the secrecy and security requirements contained in the Admission of Securities to Listing.[11] Though directed at companies, their effect is to require companies to impose restrictions on insiders requiring the maintenance of secrecy as regards inside information in their possession. Whilst unpublished price-sensitive information may be passed to third parties where necessary for professional reasons, such third parties are expected not to deal in a company's securities until the information has been published.

(c) PRIOR NOTIFICATION PROCEDURE

Supplementing insider reporting requirements which impose disclosure of transactions already effected, the Model Code requires a director to give prior notification of his intention to deal in any securities of his own company.[12] Under the prior notification procedure, the director should first notify the chairman (or other director(s) appointed for the specific purpose) and receive acknowledgment. For his own dealings, the chairman should notify the board at a board meeting or, alternatively, the other director(s) appointed for the purpose and receive acknowledgment. In his own case, the procedure to be followed by the other director appointed for the purpose is not specified.

In turn, the company should maintain a written record that the appropriate notification was given and acknowledged.[13] The procedure should also provide for the director concerned to have written confirmation to that effect. In addition, a list of directors' dealings in the company's securities since the date of the previous list should be circulated to members of the board with board papers.[14] Alternatively, the statutory register of directors' interests in shares or debentures[15] may be made available for inspection at each board meeting.

Reference to the prior notification procedure was made in both the 1978 Panel statement on W. H. Henshall (Addlestone) Ltd.[16] and the 1978 Panel statement on J. B. Eastwood Ltd.[17] But in neither case did the Panel comment on whether the Model Code had been breached.

(d) TRUSTS

The scope of the Model Code also extends to conflicts of interest facing directors involved in trusts. In principle, a director should seek to ensure that all dealings in which he is or is deemed to be interested should be conducted

---

9. See, ante, Chapter 5. Disclosure, III. Insider Reporting.
10. Model Code, Model Rule 4.1.
11. Admission of Securities to Listing, Section 5, Chapter 2, para1.1.
12. Model Code, Model Rule 2.1.
13. Ibid, Model Rule 2.2.
14. Ibid, Model Rule 5.
15. CA 1985, s325.
16. The Panel on Take-overs and Mergers, Statement on W.H. Henshall (Addlestone) Ltd., 3rd July, 1978.
17. Ibid, Statement on J.B. Eastwood Ltd., 20th July, 1978.

in accordance with the Model Code.[18] But it is recognised that a director's duty in this respect will depend on the particular circumstances.

A director who is sole trustee should follow the same procedure as for any dealings on his own account. The higher standards set by the Model Code are reiterated in its provision that, even if excepted from the general prohibitions imposed by statute under the special defences for trustees[19], he should deal only if he would be personally allowed to deal under the Model Code.

Where a director has co-trustees who are not directors of the company, he may not be able to ensure that the procedure applicable to his personal dealings is followed in respect of dealings on behalf of the trust. On the basis that the director/trustee has to avoid acting in breach of trust and, at the same time, to refrain from divulging or abusing confidential information, the Model Code acknowledges that it may not always be practicable to expect that trustees will refrain from dealing at a time when one of their number is not personally free to deal.

On the other hand, if a director, whether or not himself a trustee, has, as settlor or otherwise, an important influence over the decision of the trustees, the procedure applicable to his personal dealings ought to be followed and the trustees should not deal when he personally is not free to deal. Though prior to the Model Code, a situation of the kind envisaged by this requirement is provided by the Norbury Insulation/Hayeshaw bid.[20] However, the remoteness of interests may again render impracticable or inappropriate the imposition of a duty[1] on the director to seek to ensure that all dealings in which he is or is deemed to be interested should be conducted in accordance with the Model Code.

In this connection, certain precautions are to be taken. So that his co-trustees have notice of his competing fiduciary duties, a director who acts as trustee of a trust should ensure that his co-trustees are aware of the identity of any company of which he is a director so as to enable them to anticipate 'possible difficulties'[2]. When a director is a beneficiary, but not a trustee of a trust which deals in securities of the company, he should endeavour to ensure that the trustees notify him after they have dealt in such securities on behalf of the trust, in order that he in turn may notify the company.[3] For this purpose, he should ensure that the trustees are aware of the companies of which he is a director. Notification to the company appears to relate only to notification after dealing, not before. Notification of a dealing by the trustees to the beneficiary may also give rise to a duty of notification under the CA 1985[4] which requires a director to notify the company of his interests in shares in or debentures of the company or associated companies within five business days of the occurrence of the event giving rise to the obligation coming to his knowledge.

It is an overriding principle that under no circumstances should a director (i) deal where prohibited from doing so by the statutory provisions or (ii) make any unauthorised disclosure of any confidential information, whether to co-trustees or any other person or (iii) make any use of such information whether

---

18. Model Code, Basic Principle 6.
19. See, ante, Chapter 3. Criminal Liability.
20. The Panel on Take-overs and Mergers, Statement by the City Panel on Stock Exchange dealings in the course of a take-over situation, 2nd April, 1971; see post 2. The Panel on Take-overs and Mergers.
1. Under Model Code, Model Rule 4.1.
2. Model Code, Model Rule 4.2.
3. Ibid, Model Rule 4.3.
4. CA 1985, s325.

for the advantage of himself or others.[5] Though expressly stated to apply even in respect of those to whom he owes a fiduciary duty, it is unlikely that this provision would be upheld by the courts in those circumstances[6].

4. Sanctions

The Model Code makes no provision for sanctions. Its enforcement is an internal company matter. The enforcement role conferred on the board marked an important development in internal self-regulation. However, the Model Code will be ineffective where the board is dominated by one director who, in effect, can either dictate to or disregard the board.

Nevertheless, the main emphasis of the Model Code is preventive. The requirement of disclosure may discourage insider dealing in some instances and the development of internal company codes can have an educational effect. Above all, the threat of dismissal constitutes a significant deterrent for most directors and employees.

B. The Panel on Take-overs and Mergers

Apart from insider reporting and other disclosure requirements in relation to take-over and merger proposals, the Code deals with the problem of insider transactions by imposing restrictions on dealings by persons possessing confidential price sensitive information. In this connection, Rule 4, which is supplemented by Notes, imposes prohibitions against dealings before and during the offer in the following terms:

> '4.1 BY PERSONS OTHER THAN THE OFFEROR
> (a) No dealings of any kind (including option business) in the securities of the offeree company by any person, not being the offeror, who is privy to confidential price-sensitive information concerning an offer or contemplated offer may take place between the time when there is reason to suppose that an approach or an offer is contemplated and the announcement of the approach or offer or of the termination of the discussions.
> (b) No person who is privy to such information may make any recommendation to any other person as to dealing in the relevant securities.
> (c) No such dealings may take place in the securities of the offeror except where the proposed offer is not price-sensitive in relation to such securities.

> 4.2 BY THE OFFEROR AND CONCERT PARTIES
> During an offer period, the offeror and persons acting in concert with it must not sell any securities in the offeree company except with the prior consent of the Panel and following 24 hours public notice that such sales might be made. The Panel will not give consent for sales where a mandatory offer under Rule 9 is being made. Sales below the value of the offer will not be permitted. After there has been an announcement that sales may be made, neither the offeror nor persons acting in concert with

5. Model Code, Basic Principle 5.
6. See post B. II. Students of conduct for investment business, Conflicts of interest.

it may make further purchases and only in exceptional circumstances will the Panel permit the offer to be revised.'

The Code provisions were of particular significance in that they represented the main attempt by the industry to police insider dealing by means of administrative measures. In this connection, a number of insider dealing cases have been the subject of statements issued by the Panel, though these are not precedents.

However, with the passage of the CA 1980, the Code provisions fall within a broader framework of control and are to be read subject to the insider dealing provisions now contained in the IDA 1985.[7] All dealings are also subject to (a) Code restrictions on acquisitions from a single shareholder prior to the announcement of a firm intention to make an offer, (b) Code provisions relating to connected exempt market-makers and (c) the Substantial Acquisition Rules (SARs) issued on the authority of the Panel.

For the purpose of comparison with legislative and Model Code requirements, the Code provisions will also be analysed under the headings of the definition of insider, the meaning of inside information, restrictions placed on insiders and sanctions. But for convenience, consideration of provisions applicable to insiders faced with a conflict of interest is postponed to another section.

1. The definition of an insider

Rejecting the device of listed insiders, Rule 4.1 adopts a functional approach based on access to confidential price-sensitive information. Thus, it applies to 'any person, not being the offeror, who is privy to confidential price-sensitive information concerning an offer or contemplated offer'.

In the 1976 revised edition of the Code, which was in force when several Panel statements on insider dealing cases were issued, the access test applied to 'any person, not being the offeror, who is privy to the preliminary take-over or merger discussions or to an intention to make an offer'[8]. In that edition, it was stated that without prejudice to the generality of the Rule, a person would be so regarded if, on the assumption that he had received relevant information either: (1) he is a director or employee of one of the companies involved in the proposed offer; or (2) he is a professional adviser either to one of the companies involved in the proposed offer or to any director or employee of such a company; or (3) that information was received in the context of a confidential relationship and it was necessary that he received such information[9]. In addition, the spouse and close relatives and related trusts of such a person would be deemed to be in the same position as such a person.

The exemption of the offeror from the Rule 4.1 access test is made so that the offeror, despite its knowledge of the pending offer[10], may warehouse (though subject to reporting requirements)[11] and in consequence strengthen its position in making the offer. However, this exemption is narrowly construed. In general, it is not available either to individual members of a consortium[12] or to a person acting in concert with a potential offeror under an arrangement which

---

7. For detailed consideration of these statements, see J.A.C. Suter, *The Regulation of Insider Dealing in Britain and France* (Doctoral thesis 1985).
8. Code (1976 revised edition), Rule 30.
9. Ibid, Rule 30.
10. See, ante, Chapter 1. Introduction, III. Theoretical considerations, B. Equity issues, 3. Fairness.
11. See, ante, Chapter 5. Disclosure, III. Insider reporting.
12. Code, Notes on Rules 4.1 and 4.2, Note 2.

contains a benefit or potential benefit to the person acting in concert (beyond normal expenses and carrying costs).[13] The access test of Rule 4.1 thus includes insiders of the offeror and, in general, any person whom the offeror informs of the offer or contemplated offer and who could use advance information about the bid for their own benefit.

The warehousing purpose of the exemption of the offeror from Rule 4.1 is underlined by (a) the restrictions on dealing imposed on the offeror and concert parties by Rule 4.2 during the offer period and (b) the inclusion of the offeror in the access test when, after an announcement that offer discussions are taking place or that an approach or offer is contemplated, discussions are terminated or the offeror decides not to proceed with the offer. In that event, the offeror and 'any person privy to this information' are prohibited from dealing in the securities of the offeree (or, where relevant, the offeror) prior to an announcement of the position.[14]

Moreover, the exemption of the offeror from Rule 4.1 does not extend to certain other circumstances in which dealings may not take place. By way of example, a Note to Rules 4.1 and 4.2 specifies that an offeror or other persons may be restricted from dealing or procuring others to deal in circumstances where, before the announcement of the offer, the offeror has been supplied by the offeree company with confidential price sensitive information in the course of offer discussions.[15] In practice, the confidentiality of such information may be the subject of an express contractual stipulation.[16]

Two other categories of person connected with the offeror receive special mention. These are (a) fund managers connected with the offeror, unless they are exempt fund managers[17] and (b) connected exempt market-makers.[18]

Panel statements have covered a variety of insiders, though primarily those identified as such in the 1976 revised edition. Prominent among their number have been directors of the companies involved in the proposed offer. Breaches of the insider dealing provisions by directors of the offeror who were privy to the preliminary take-over or merger discussions or to an intention to make an offer, were found in (a) the 1971 Panel statement on the Norbury Insulation/ Hayeshaw Ltd. bid,[19] (b) the 1973 Panel statement on P.R. Grimshawe & Co., Grimshawe-Windsor merger[20] and (c) the 1976 Panel statement on Seafield Amalgamated Rubber Co. Ltd.[1] In other statements, there were instances of breaches by offeree directors privy to preliminary take-over or merger discussions between offeror and offeree, namely, (d) the 1978 Panel statement on J.B. Eastwood Ltd.[2] and (e) the 1979 Panel statements on IPH Ltd.[3] It is also arguable that on the facts of (f) the 1973 Panel Statement on CST/Grendon,[4] breaches were apparently committed by two directors of the offeree company.

13. Ibid, Note 3.
14. Ibid, Note 4.
15. Ibid, Note 1.
16. See, ante, Chapter 4. Civil Liability, III. Breach of confidence.
17. Code, Notes on Rules 4.1 and 4.2, Note 6.
18. Ibid, Note 7.
19. The Panel on Take-overs and Mergers, Statement by the City Panel on Stock Exchange dealings in the course of a take-over situation, 2nd April, 1971.
20. Ibid, Statement on P.R. Grimshawe & Co., Grimshawe-Windsor Merger [1973], J.B.L.43 G.K. Morse.
1. Ibid, Statement on Seafield Amalgamated Rubber Company Limited, 27th July 1976.
2. Ibid, Statement on J.B. Eastwood Limited, 20th July, 1978.
3. Ibid, Statement on Intereuropean Property Holdings Limited, 12th September, 1979 and Statement on Intereuropean Property Holdings Limited, 10th October, 1979.
4. Ibid, Statement on C.S.T. Investments Limited/Grendon Trust Limited, 20th December, 1973.

To a lesser extent, employees of the companies involved in the proposed offer have been found to have infringed the insider dealing prohibition of the Code. Examples of insider dealing by such employees are set out in (a) the 1973 Panel statement on P.R. Grimshawe & Co., Grimshawe-Windsor merger[5] and (b) the 1979 Panel statement on Chaddesley Investments (No.2).[6] In the latter, the insider was employed as the company's accountant.

Among professional advisers, financial advisers to the companies involved in the proposed offer have also been found in breach. Instances are contained in (a) the 1977 Panel statement on C.H. Johnson & Sons Ltd.[7] and (b) the 1979 Panel statement on Chaddesley Investments Ltd. (No.1).[8]

The inclusion of spouses, close relatives and related trusts of insiders within the access test also proved of assistance. This is evidenced by (a) the 1971 Panel statement on the Norbury Insulation/Hayeshaw Ltd. bid[9] and (b) the 1973 Panel statement on P.R. Grimshawe & Co., Grimshawe-Windsor merger.[10]

However, the importance of a functional approach based on access to confidential price sensitive information rather than reliance on an exhaustive list of specified insiders is underlined by other Panel statements. These statements also provide some guidance on the nature of the relationship required between the insider and the inside information.

The position of individuals who receive inside information in the course of their work was considered in the 1977 Panel statement on Ultra Electronic Holdings Ltd.,[11] in which financial advisers to shareholders in a potential offeree company were found to be in breach. On that occasion, the Panel took the opportunity to reiterate that:

> 'all who receive price-sensitive information in the course of their work must treat it as confidential and on no account endeavour to use the information for private purposes.'

Another individual who received inside information in discussions about his proposed appointment as a director was held to fall within the definition of insider. In its 1975 statement on Dexion-Comino International Ltd.,[12] the Panel emphasised that the Code prohibition on dealing by anyone 'who is privy to an intention to make an offer' forbade dealing in the shares in question by anyone who received information about an intended bid in circumstances which imposed on him a duty of confidentiality.

However, an instance of a tippee falling outside the definition of insider was provided by the 1976 Panel statement on Hewden-Stuart Plant Ltd./A. Gunn

5. Ibid, Statement on P.R. Grimshawe & Co., Grimshawe-Windsor Merger [1973] J.B.L.43 G.K Morse.
6. Ibid, Statement on Chaddesley Investments Limited, 7th February, 1979..
7. Ibid, Statement by the City Panel on Stock Exchange dealings in the course of a take-over situation, 2nd April, 1971.
8. Ibid, Statement on Chaddesley Investments Limited, 19th December, 1978, as amended 31st January, 1979.
9. Ibid, Statement by the City Panel on Stock Exchange dealings in the course of a take-over situation, 2nd April, 1971.
10. Ibid, Statement on P.R. Grimshawe & Co., Grimshawe-Windsor Merger [1973] J.B.L. 43 G.K. Morse.
11. Ibid, Statement on Ultra Electronic Holdings Limited, 22nd September, 1977.
12. Ibid, Statement on Dealings in Shares in Dexion-Comino International Limited, 25th April, 1975 .

(Holdings) Ltd.[13] On informing B, his host, that he would be unable to attend a wedding, the joint managing director of the intended offeree stated by way of explanation that he was involved in merger discussions. Before the offer was announced, B instructed his stockbroker to purchase shares in the offeree. On the basis that B was not connected with the offeree or the proposed offer, the Panel found that he could not be said to fall within the prohibition on dealing, then contained in Rule 30. On this occasion, it thus drew a distinction between information obtained in the course of a professional or business relationship and information obtained on a friendly basis. But stating that B knew or ought to have known that he received the information in confidence and that it was not to be acted upon, it recorded its disapproval of B's conduct.

The scope of the exemption of the offeror from the definition of insider was considered in the 1972 Panel statement on D.F. Lyons & Co. Ltd./Rowan and Boden Ltd.[14] This involved offers for Y Ltd., first by X Ltd. and subsequently by Z Ltd. Referring to A, who was chairman and managing director of X Ltd., the Panel stated:

> 'So far as his offer was concerned, there was no ban on market dealings. The offer, to the preliminary discussions or intention of which he was privy, was an offer by a third party, which offer, although at the same figure as his own, might in the event be preferred by the market - as indeed it was.'

Notwithstanding this, X Ltd. went into the market to purchase further Y Ltd. shares. It was then announced that Z Ltd., having purchased 60% of the issued shares from X Ltd. and its associates, would make a general offer. This led to an immediate rise in the share price. The Panel found that the conduct of X Ltd., under A's direction, constituted a breach of the prohibition on dealing, then imposed by Rule 30.

In several instances, the difficulty of detecting these insiders was increased by nominee dealings. Purchases of shares in Seafield Amalgamated Rubber at the instance of an offeror director were made in the name of his secretary 'to avoid embarrassment'.[15] In the Racal/Ultra bid, the investment manager employed in a small merchant bank bought shares for a close relative.[16] As well as giving instructions for the purchase of 20,000 IPH shares for himself, an offeror director stated that he had arranged for a US bank to purchase 5,000 IPH shares for an individual he named for whom he held an effective power of attorney.[17] In the bid by JWI for Johnson, the assistant manager of a bank involved in the negotiations placed an order to purchase 2,000 Johnson shares in the name of a friend who was out of the country at the time and had no knowledge of the purchase.[18] After accepting the JWI offer in respect of the 2,000 shares, the friend paid over the profit on the transaction to the assistant manager.

Another example of a nominee dealing was provided in the Cargill bid for Eastwood when an offeree director bought shares in his wife's name and later volunteered to pay the profit to charity.[19] But the difficulty of detection was

13. Ibid, Statement on Hewden-Stuart Plant Limited/A. Gunn (Holdings) Limited, llth February, 1976 .

14. lbid, Statement on D.F. Lyons & Co. Limited/Rowan and Boden Limited, 2nd October, 1972.

15. Ibid, Statement on Seafield Amalgamated Rubber Company Limited, 27th July, 1976.

16. Ibid, Statement on Ultra Electronic Holdings Limited, 22nd September, 1977.

17. Ibid, Statement on Intereuropean Property Holdings Limited, l0th October, 1979.

18. Ibid, Statement on C.H. Johnson & Sons Limited, 28th November, 1977.

19. Ibid, Statement on J.B. Eastwood Limited, 20th July, 1978; see ante A. The Stock Exchange Model Code.

minimised in that the nominee was his wife and by his subsequent notification of the purchase to the company.

2. *The meaning of inside information*

A take-over bid provides an example of market information, namely, information which is external to the company, but which will have an impact on the market price of a company's securities independently of any expected changes in the company's earnings or assets.[20] Corporate information emanates from within the company and directly relates to expected earnings or assets. It includes knowledge of a potential merger. The policy of the American Law Institute in its Federal Securities Code is that:

> 'So far as an "insider's" use of market information is concerned, there is no reason in... principle... to distinguish between material information that is intrinsic to the company... and market information that will not affect the company's assets or earning power'.[1]

The approach of Rule 4.1 accords with ALI policy. Between (a) the time when there is reason to suppose that an approach or an offer is contemplated and (b) the announcement of the approach or offer or of the termination of the discussions, the inside information is confidential price-sensitive information concerning an offer or contemplated offer.[2] After (a) an announcement that offer discussions are taking place or that an approach or offer is contemplated but before (b) an announcement that discussions are terminated or that the offeror has decided not to proceed with an offer, the inside information is the termination of discussions or the offeror's decision not to proceed with the offer.[3]

However, the application of these formulations to particular facts can be very difficult. In take-over or merger negotiations, the point at which there develops a degree of precision sufficient to constitute 'confidential price-sensitive information concerning an offer or contemplated offer' will depend both on the type of negotiations and the understanding of the parties. The spectrum may range from preliminary and tentative negotiations to a phase where there exists a more definite understanding of negotiations yet without agreement as to how differences will be resolved to a more or less final stage when all but relatively unimportant details have been agreed.[4]

The difficulty was acknowledged by the Panel in an early statement.[5] Referring to A Ltd.'s decision to make a bid for B Ltd. 'sometime in the autumn of 1970', the Panel stated:

> 'It is difficult to pinpoint the exact date at which the intention to make such a bid was first formed or at which, in the language of Rule 30,[6] there were preliminary discussions or reasons to suppose that an approach would be made. We are satisfied that by the 9th November the intention

20. See, ante, Chapter 1. Introduction.
1. American Law Institute, Federal Securities Code, s1603, Comment 2(j).
2. Code, Rule 4.1.
3. Ibid, Notes on Rules 4.1 and 4.2, Note 4.
4. W.H. Painter, *The Federal Securities Code and Corporate Disclosure* (1979) p.174.
5. The Panel on Take-overs and Mergers, Statement by the City Panel on Stock Exchange dealings in the course of a take-over situation, 2nd April, 1971.
6. The provision of the Code then in force which contained the prohibition on dealing.

was sufficiently crystallised to result in [financial advisers] being instructed.'

A public offer was announced on 19th November. Regular purchases of B Ltd. shares were made from end-October to mid-December on the orders of A Ltd.'s managing director. Those during 9-19th November were found to have infringed the insider dealing prohibitions of the Code.

The Panel gave more detailed consideration to this difficulty in its two statements on Chaddesley Investments in 1979. In the first,[7] the Panel acknowledged that Rule 30 did not refer specifically to a sale of shares which might lead to a mandatory offer, that it forbade the release of information relating to the potential offer (rather than specifically forbidding the giving of advice based on that information) and that it contemplated the insider himself dealing in the shares. It added:

'The Rule, like the rest of the Code is not expressed in precise and detailed language: it is expressly stated and has been repeatedly emphasised that the spirit of the Code must be observed, as indeed [A] has acknowledged. In the view of the Panel [A] must have been aware at the time when he advised the purchase of the shares that the probable result of B's desire to sell its holding would be a chain of events that would have a favourable impact on the share price. Rule 30 is specifically concerned with an insider dealing in shares but it cannot be accepted (and nor did [A] represent) that an insider escapes criticism if he advises someone else to deal.'

On this basis, the Panel considered that A's action in advising an investment client to purchase shares in X Ltd., when he was privy to B's wishes to dispose of its shares (a 38% stake), was contrary to the 'spirit' of Rule 30.

In the second Chaddesley statement,[8] the Panel considered whether the company's accountant had infringed the Code. It stated:

'The fact was that [C] knew that things were in train which were liable to be beneficial to shareholders and the Panel considers it is irrelevant that the exact shape of the deal which finally emerged may not have been within the scope of [C's] knowledge at the time he dealt.'

The two Panel statements on Chaddesley Investments thus point to the difficulty of applying formulations of inside information to particular facts. At most, it can be concluded that the degree of precision required will emerge between the extremes of preliminary and tentative negotiations and of the final stage when all but relatively unimportant details have been agreed.

This conclusion is supported by the 1979 Panel statement on IPH Ltd. (No.1).[9] Disregarding a purchase of shares by an offeree director in December, the Panel found that only a January purchase of shares in a company, for which an offer was announced in February, infringed the Rule 30 prohibition on dealing. In so doing, the Panel by implication reiterated its stance as to the emergence of the degree of precision required. Likewise, in a second Panel

7. The Panel on Take-overs and Mergers, Statement on Chaddesley Investments Limited, 19th December, 1978, as amended 31st January, 1979.
8. Ibid, Statement on Chaddesley Investments Limited, 7th February, 1979.
9. Ibid, Statement on Intereuropean Property Holdings Limited, 12th September, 1979.

statement on IPH Ltd.[10] in 1979, the Panel considered that another offeree director had acted in clear breach of Rule 30 in making a purchase of shares on 16th January.

In its 1975 statement on Dexion-Comino[11], the Panel made it clear that inside knowledge of the accuracy of a rumour constituted inside information. It found, and A did not dispute, that he was privy to the intention to make an offer. The Panel added:

> 'even if there were rumours that a bid was to be made, [A] knew that the rumours were in fact true. He was thus an insider in a better position than other investors who had at most merely heard a rumour.'

3. Restrictions on insiders

As with legislative and Model Code provisions, the central provision is a prohibition on dealings by insiders. This is supplemented by a prohibition on tipping. The additional provisions applicable to insiders faced with a conflict of interest will be considered in the next section.

(a) PROHIBITION ON DEALINGS

The prohibition on dealings applies in five circumstances. First, any person (not being the offeror) who is privy to confidential price sensitive information concerning an offer or contemplated offer, is prohibited from dealing in the securities of the offeree between the time when there is reason to suppose that an approach or an offer is contemplated and the announcement of the approach or offer or of the termination of the discussions.[12] No dealings of any kind (including option business) may take place.

The second prohibition relates to a prohibition on such dealings in the securities of the offeror. But this prohibition is qualified. Unlike the Model Code prohibition on dealings by insiders prior to the announcement of regularly recurring information whether or not the information is price sensitive, this second Code prohibition does not apply where the proposed offer is not price sensitive in relation to the securities of the offeror.[13]

The third prohibition applies when, after an announcement that offer discussions are taking place or that an approach or offer is contemplated, discussions are terminated or the offeror decides not to proceed with an offer. In those circumstances, the offeror and any person privy to this information are prohibited from dealing in the securities of the offeree (or, where relevant, the offeror) prior to an announcement of the position.[14]

A fourth prohibition is one on dealing contrary to published advice. In particular, directors and financial advisers to a company who own shares in that company must not deal in such shares contrary to any advice they have given to shareholders, or to any advice with which it can be reasonably assumed that they

---

10. Ibid, Statement on Intereuropean Property Holdings Limited, 10th October, 1979.
11. Ibid, Statement on Dealings in Shares in Dexion-Comino International Limited, 25th April, 1975.
12. Code, Rule 4.1(a).
13. Ibid, Rule 4.1(c).
14. Ibid, Notes on Rules 4.1 and 4.2, Note 4.

were associated, without giving sufficient public notice of their intentions.[15]

A fifth prohibition concerns transactions in the offer period by the offeror and concert parties in offeree securities. During an offer period, the offeror and persons acting in concert with it must not sell any securities in the offeree company except with the Panel's prior consent and following 24 hours public notice that such sales might be made.[16] Panel consent will not be given for sales either (a) where a mandatory offer under Rule 9 is being made, or (b) below the value of the offer. After an announcement that sales may be made, neither the offeror nor persons acting in concert with it may make further purchases and only in exceptional circumstances will the Panel permit the offer to be revised.

The nature of the first prohibition was spelt out by the Panel in its statement on D. F. Lyons & Co./Rowan and Boden Ltd.[17] Having found that the conduct of X Ltd., under A's direction, constituted a breach of Rule 30, the Panel added:

> 'It is unnecessary to consider to what extent, had the market been aware of the impending offer by [Z Ltd.], the price of the [Y Ltd.], shares would have hardened (as indeed it did when the facts were known) or whether those who sold their shares to [X Ltd.], and associates during those days in the middle of August were damnified in the sense that had the facts been known they would have secured a higher price. Rule 30 contains an absolute prohibition. As the Panel again emphasised, this Rule is directed against 'insider' dealings and in so far as such dealings come within their jurisdiction (which is only the case in mergers or take-overs) the City Panel is determined to apply it.'

In regard to the qualified prohibition on dealings in the securities of the offeror, it has been suggested[18] that a proposed offer will not be price sensitive in relation to such securities when the offer is a cash offer and the offeree company is significantly smaller than the offeror. But a proposed offer will nearly always be price sensitive when the consideration offered is shares in the offeror company. An example of dealings in the securities of the offeror infringing the prohibition on dealing was contained in the 1973 Panel statement on P. R. Grimshawe & Co., Grimshawe-Windsor merger.[19]

On various occasions, it has been asserted that individuals in breach of the Code were unaware of its provisions.[20] However, the closely-knit nature of the community to which securities regulation applies, has made pleas of ignorance of the Code implausible.

At the Panel hearing relating to the Norbury Insulation/Hayeshaw bid, it was contended on behalf of X, the managing director of the offeror, and Y, a stockbroker, that they were unfamiliar with the requirements of the Code. In a 1971 statement[1], the Panel indicated that it was not and was 'unlikely to be

15. Ibid, Note 5.
16. Ibid, Rule 4.2.
17. The Panel on Take-overs and Mergers, Statement on D.F. Lyons & Co. Limited/Rowan and Boden Limited, 2nd October, 1972.
18. *Weinberg and Blank on Take-overs and Mergers*, Fourth Edition by M.A. Weinberg, M.V. Blank and A.L. Greystoke (1979), para2329.
19. The Panel on Take-overs and Mergers, Statement on P.R. Grimshawe & Co., Grimshawe-Windsor Merger [1973] J.B.L.43 G.K. Morse.
20. See also the Panel statement on Associated Communications Corporation PLC, 23rd March, 1982, discussed in Chapter 5. Disclosure, III. Insider Reporting.
1. The Panel on Take-overs and Mergers, Statement by the City Panel on Stock Exchange dealings in the course of a take-over situation, 2nd April, 1971.

impressed by pleas of ignorance of the Code'.

Further references to ignorance of the Code were made in both 1979 statements on IPH Ltd. In the first[2], the claim of B, who was chairman and chief executive of the offeree and had infringed Rule 30, that he had been unaware of the terms of the Code was dismissed with the comment that a company chairman should know the terms of the Code. In the second[3] concerning a breach of Rule 30 by C, who was an offeree director and declined to attend the Panel hearing, the Panel remarked that as a chartered accountant and a director of a public company, C could hardly plead ignorance of the terms of the Code.

(b) PROHIBITION ON TIPPING

To counter avoidance of the prohibition on dealing by an insider making a recommendation as to dealing, no person who is privy to confidential price sensitive information concerning an offer or contemplated offer may make any recommendation to any other person as to dealing in the relevant securities.[4] The treatment of inside information is further regulated by secrecy and security requirements.[5]

4. Sanctions

In the current edition of the Code, the sanctions now available are set out in the Introduction.[6] In the event of the Panel finding in disciplinary proceedings that there has been a breach of the Code, it may have recourse to private reprimand, to public censure, to reporting the offender's conduct to another regulatory authority (eg the Department of Trade and Industry, the Stock Exchange, SIB or the relevant SRO) and/or to requiring further action to be taken, as it thinks fit. In addition, for those who do not conduct themselves in accordance with best business standards and so according to the Code, reference is made to the facilities of the UK securities markets being withheld.

In insider dealing cases, the Panel has frequently had recourse to public censure. An example was the offeree director who made the purchases of shares in his wife's name referred to in the Panel statement on J.B. Eastwood Ltd.[7] In the Norbury Insulation/Hayeshaw Ltd. bid,[8] the offeror director, X, was regarded as deserving the most severe censure, both for his breaches of the insider dealing and reporting requirements of the Code and for his subsequent lack of frankness with the Panel. Others regarded as deserving severe censure included: (a) the two offeree directors in IPH Ltd.[9]; (b) the offeror director at

2. Ibid, Statement on Intereuropean Property Holdings Limited, 12th September, 1979.
3. Ibid, Statement on Intereuropean Property Holdings Limited, 10th October, 1979.
4. Code, Rule 4.1(b).
5. See, ante, Chapter 5. Disclosure, II. Timely disclosure.
6. Paras.1(c) and 3(d). In a Policy Statement dated 28th April, 1969 issued with the first edition of the Code, the Panel indicated that, in the event of a breach of the Code, the Panel would have recourse to (a) private or public censure or (b) in a more flagrant case, to further action designed to deprive the offender temporarily or permanently of his ability to practise in the field of take-overs and mergers.
7. The Panel on Take-overs and Mergers, Statement on J.B. Eastwood Limited, 20th July, 1978.
8. Ibid, Statement by the City Panel on Stock Exchange dealings in the course of a take-over situation, 2nd April, 1971.
9. Ibid, Statement on Intereuropean Property Holdings Limited, 12th September, 1979, and Statement on Intereuropean Property Holdings Limited, 10th October, 1979.

whose instance purchases of shares in Seafield Amalgamated Rubber were made in the name of his secretary;[10] (c) in the Panel statement on Ultra Electronic Holdings Ltd., the financial adviser who had built up a substantial holding for clients in a potential offeree;[11] (d) in the Panel statement on D. F. Lyons & Co. Ltd./Rowan and Boden Ltd.,[12] A who was chairman and managing director of Lyons Ltd. and privy to preliminary discussions or an intention of an offer by a third party for a company in respect of which his own company had already made an offer and (e) the company accountant in Chaddesley (No.2).[13] In addition, the financial adviser, C, referred to in the Panel statement on Mount Charlotte Investments Ltd./Gale Lister & Co. Ltd.[14] was found to be deserving of grave censure for dealing in his company's own shareholding in the offeree in a manner inconsistent with its advice to other shareholders and after it had informed shareholders of its intention to accept an agreed offer.

Other insiders were reprimanded. Among those reprimanded for breach of Rule 30 were: (a) in the Panel statement on Dexion-Comino International Ltd.[15], C who received inside information in discussions about his proposed appointment as a director and (b) in the JWI/Johnson bid,[16] the assistant manager at a major branch of a bank which had taken part in the preliminary negotiations. In the Panel statement on Hewden-Stuart Plant Ltd./A. Gunn (Holdings) Ltd.[17],the joint managing director of Gunn, A, was reprimanded for not observing the strict secrecy requirements of Rule 7 after he had told B, his host, that because he was involved in merger discussions, he would be unable to go to a wedding ceremony, but would be able to go to the reception. Those individuals were named.

In other cases, the Panel expressed its disapproval of conduct. Its statement on Chaddesley Investments (No.1)[18] concerned a breach of the 'spirit of Rule 30' by A regarding his advice to an investment client to buy Chaddesley shares at a time when, as CAPI's agent in connection with a possible sale, he was privy to CAPI's wish to dispose of its holding in Chaddesley. After stating that the transaction was not one for personal gain and that Schlesingers had since altered their arrangements so as to prevent a repetition, the Panel recorded its 'strong disapproval' of A's conduct. In the Sime Darby/Seafield Amalgamated Rubber bid,[19] the Panel criticised C, who was in a subordinate role under B's influence, for his part in collaborating with A and B in the presentation of false information to the Panel. Though finding in the Hewden-Stuart/Gunn merger that B was not an insider within Rule 30, the Panel recorded its disapproval of B's conduct.[20] Like all those who were publicly censured or reprimanded, the

10. Ibid, Statement on Seafield Amalgamated Rubber Company Limited, 27th July, 1976.
11. Ibid, Statement on Ultra Electronic Holdings Limited, 22nd September, 1977.
12. Ibid, Statement on D.F. Lyons & Co. Limited/Rowan and Boden Limited, 2nd October, 1972.
13. Ibid, Statement on Chaddesley Investments Limited, 7th February, 1979.
14. Ibid, Statement on Mount Charlotte Investments Ltd./Gale Lister & Co. Ltd., 16th January, 1974; Appeal Committee, Statement on Mount Charlotte Investments Ltd./Gale Lister & Co. Ltd., 21st January, 1974.
15. Ibid, Statement on Dealings in Shares in Dexion-Comino International Limited, 25th April, 1975.
16. Ibid, Statement on C.H. Johnson & Sons Limited, 28th November, 1977.
17. Ibid, Statement on Hewden-Stuart Plant Limited/A. Gunn (Holdings) Limited, 11th February, 1976.
18. Ibid, Statement on Chaddesley Investments Limited, 19th December, 1978, as amended 31st January, 1979.
19. Ibid, Statement on Seafield Amalgamated Rubber Company Limited, 27th July, 1976.
20. The Panel on Take-overs and Mergers, Statement on Hewden-Stuart Plant Limited/A. Gunn (Holdings) Limited, 11th February, 1976.

names of these individuals were published.

However, resort to publicity was not systematic. In its statement on Ultra Electronic Holdings[1], the Panel also considered a purchase of Ultra shares by an investment manager employed in a small merchant bank who bought shares for a close relative after being informed by the stockbroker of the offer to buy the holdings held by clients. Stating that the manager was entirely frank at all stages of the investigation and had admitted the purchase was an error of judgment, the Panel decided that in the circumstances as disclosed the case could be adequately dealt with by a severe caution as to future conduct. Neither the manager nor the merchant bank were named. But by failing to give a more detailed account of those circumstances, the Panel was not seen to be consistent in its use of public criticism.

In assessing the effectiveness of public criticism, whether expressed in terms of public censure, reprimand or 'disapproval', there are several considerations to be taken into account. Even if many investors are either not interested in or unaware of public criticism contained in the Panel statement, the person so named may well be affected by it. On the basis that it threatens to harm a person's reputation and hence diminish respect from his peers, the usefulness of public criticism as a sanction has been emphasised by the Panel. After referring to public criticism as its main sanction, in 1978 the Panel stated:

> 'The publication of a critical statement by the Panel has proved to be a powerful weapon particularly in the case of someone professionally engaged in an activity where a reputation for strictly ethical behaviour remains a paramount asset and mention of a name alone can lead to some loss of reputation, irrespective of what may be said by way of mitigation. In recognition of this, rather than out of any desire to shrink from naming names, the Panel has sometimes expressed its criticism in private.'[2]

The Panel's view is supported by evidence that insiders feared and resented their names being made public. With regard to the statement on dealings in Dexion-Comino,[3] C appealed to the Appeal Committee against publication of the Panel statement, (the facts were not in dispute), on the ground that publication was too severe a penalty on the facts of the case. The appeal was dismissed. In relation to the Panel statement on Ultra Electronic Holdings Ltd.,[4] the financial adviser who had built up a substantial holding for clients in a potential offeree, unsuccessfully appealed to the Appeal Committee against the findings of the Panel and against publication. Similar appeals were made by the company accountant in Chaddesley (No.2)[5] and by the merchant bank and its director named in Chaddesley (No.l),[6] though in the latter the Appeal Committee made some alterations to wording which the appellants had argued carried inferences which it felt sure were not intended. Regarding the Panel

1. Ibid, Statement on Ultra Electronic Holdings Limited, 22nd September, 1977.
2. Committee to Review the Functioning of Financial Institutions, Second Stage Evidence, Vol.l. The Panel on Take-overs and Mergers (1979), para88.
3. The Panel on Take-overs and Mergers, Statement on Dealings in Shares in Dexion-Comino International Limited, 25th April, 1975.
4. Ibid, Statement on Ultra Electronic Holdings Limited, 22nd September, 1977.
5. Ibid, Statement on Chaddesley Investments Limited, 7th February, 1979; Statement of the Appeal Committee of the Panel on Take-overs and Mergers, 16th March, 1979.
6. The Panel on Take-overs and Mergers, Statement on Chaddesley Investments Limited, 19th December, 1978, as amended 31st January, 1979; Statement of Appeals Committee of the Panel on Take-overs and Mergers, 31st January, 1979.

statement on D. F. Lyons & Co. Ltd./Rowan & Boden Ltd.,[7] the chairman and managing director of Lyons Ltd., A, did not dispute the finding of a breach of Rule 30, but contended before the Appeal Committee that it was an innocent breach and did not warrant public censure of such severity. Concluding that there was no justification for altering the Panel's findings and conclusions, the Appeal Committee dismissed the appeal. But it made minor alterations to the wording of the Panel statement which A had argued carried inferences which it felt sure were not intended.

In a small closely-knit community, it is also possible to underestimate the impact of private as well as public censure. With regard to such sanctions, the City Capital Markets Committee argued in 1974:

> 'The effectiveness of the Panel's moral sanctions (public and private reprimand) has sometimes been discounted by persons not familiar with the tensions and pressures of a securities market. Professional reputation and goodwill are usually the most valuable assets of those who draw their livelihood from the securities market. Although intangible these assets have real value and have a direct and material effect on the earning power of companies and firms. Integrity and ability are the chief constituents of these intangible assets but neither has value without the other. Business inevitably tends to flow to those who have both integrity and ability. While it may take decades to build up a professional reputation in the capital market, it can be destroyed in an instant. For this reason a reprimand from the Panel can seriously damage a market practitioner.'[8]

However, it is also easy to exaggerate the extent of shared values in the City. In relation to a 1957 bid, it was observed:

> 'The bitterness and the division ran deep. The network of gentility and politeness broke down completely; far from keeping in touch with each other, the opposing merchant banks indulged in personal animosity and their partners literally crossed the road to avoid each other. The worst aspect of the matter of course was that the public had had a ringside seat to observe that, when it came down to ethics and propriety, the top figures of the City, far from being in agreement, were at each other's throats.'[9]

Subsequently, the Notes on Amalgamations and then the Code were introduced after other well-publicised bids had raised important questions of City practice. Further threats are posed by the internationalisation of the securities markets and with the abolition of fixed commissions, greater competition between financial institutions.

Moreover, the Panel has acknowledged that the effects of criticism are felt more keenly by established individuals. Thus, it commented that some of the most difficult cases concerned 'individuals in a relatively small way of business for whom the penalties available to the Panel did not have the same terrors'.[10]

7. The Panel on Take-overs and Mergers, Statement on D.F. Lyons & Co. Limited/Rowan and Boden Limited, 2nd October, 1972; Statement of the Appeals Committee of the Panel on Take-overs and Mergers, 27th October, 1972.
8. City Capital Markets Committee, Supervision of the Securities Market (1974), para35.
9. E. Stamp and C. Marley, Accounting Principles and the City Code: the case for reform (1970), p.8.
10. The Panel on Take-overs and Mergers, op cit n2, p275, supra, para90.

There is also a danger of public criticism degenerating into public argument, particularly when the standards themselves are the subject of controversy. This was illustrated by the Sime Darby/Seafield Amalgamated Rubber bid when the Panel considered the position of Z, a director of the merchant bank which acted for Sime Darby, in relation to the duty of financial advisers to assist Panel investigations. The Panel concluded that Z 'showed not simply a serious error of judgment, but a failure to observe the standard of conduct' required and asserted that advisers' duty to the Panel should override any duty to a client.[11] The merchant bank retorted that the Panel's formulation was capable of giving rise to practical difficulties and that after an internal investigation into Z's position by a committee which included three independent members, the board affirmed its 'complete confidence in the integrity and professional competence' of Z.[12] Challenged by the reference to an internal investigation with an independent element, the Panel subsequently retreated from its initial assertion.[13]

In another case, public criticism prompted further argument about the individual concerned. Following the statement on Mount Charlotte Investments Ltd./Gale Lister Ltd. by the Panel and its Appeal Committee,[14] the financial adviser in the statements, C, issued a public statement in terms that damaging and misleading statements had been made about him to which he took strong exception. Asserting that the Appeal Committee had not considered his personal position and that he had been censured for breach of the General Principles of the Code, he stated that he felt the personal nature of the sentence had been unduly severe and he was taking such action as was available to him to clear his name.[15] Having indicated that it was seriously considering refusing to renew C's licence to deal in securities, the DTI subsequently renewed his licence after a reference to the independent Tribunal which recommended renewal.[16] Another public statement was issued by a Gale Lister director who stated that he had suggested to C that the shares be sold and that the Panel's decision was unjustified and unfair.[17] In a further public statement, C added that he was satisfied he had cleared his name and that so far as he was concerned, the matter was closed and he could get on with the new businesses in which he was interested.[18]

Taking these various considerations into account, there is reason to suppose that public criticism can be a useful sanction when the conduct falls short of generally accepted standards. Hence, it would be mistaken to discount the deterrent effect of public criticism, particularly when used consistently. But the effectiveness of public criticism is subject to limitations and a penalty so restricted is also inappropriate to insider dealing since it enables insiders to retain their profits.

The mixed impact of public criticism is underlined when its use as a sanction is considered in conjunction with ancillary devices which the Panel attempted

11. Ibid, Statement on Seafield Amalgamated Rubber Company Limited, 27th July, 1976.
12. *The Times*, 31st July, 1976.
13. The Panel on Take-overs and Mergers, Report on the Year ended 31st March, 1977, p.10.
14. The Panel on Take-overs and Mergers, Statement on Mount Charlotte Investments Ltd./Gale Lister & Co. Ltd., 16th January, 1974; Appeal Committee, Statement on Mount Charlotte Investments Ltd./Gale Lister & Co. Ltd., 31st January, 1974.
15. *The Times*, 1st February, 1974; *The Financial Times*, 1st February, 1974.
16. *The Times*, 23rd November, 1974; *The Financial Times*, 23rd November, 1974; *The Guardian*, 23rd November, 1974.
17. Ibid.
18. *The Financial Times*, 23rd November, 1974.

to evolve. These mainly concern preventing directors from continuing to hold office and monetary payments.

Where the Panel sought to prevent directors from continuing to hold office, it encountered difficulties of enforcement. In its statement on the Norbury Insulation/Hayeshaw bid, the Panel doubted A's fitness to remain managing director.[19] Though he subsequently resigned, A was reappointed to the board one year later.[20] In the Sime Darby/Seafield Amalgamated Rubber bid,[1] the Panel's view that A had 'shown himself unfitted to be a director of public companies' was also not capable of enforcement.

Yet there have been instances of people losing their positions. In the JWI/Johnson bid, the assistant manager left his employment with the bank.[2] In its statement on J. B. Eastwood Ltd,[3] the Panel reported that, after an internal company inquiry, the director had resigned and later left the employment of the company. Following the statements on Mount Charlotte Investments Ltd./Gale Lister Ltd.,[4] the financial adviser, C, was dismissed as chairman and resigned under pressure from several other companies. But within thirteen months he had become chairman of another group.[5]

With regard to monetary payments, fines were rejected as outside the powers of the professional associations involved.[6] Nevertheless, in several cases insiders were deprived of their profits, payment being made either to a company or to charity. In the Norbury Insulation/Hayeshaw bid[7], the Panel was assured that after its enquiry began, the profits made by A Ltd. were paid over to Norbury Insulation on the instructions of the company's finance director in his capacity as protector of the family trusts. In P.R. Grimshawe & Co., Grimshawe-Windsor merger[8], the directors, employees and their families in breach of Rule 30 were 'ordered' to pay their profits of £47,000 to the company, the amount being calculated as the difference between the placing price and the average market price in the first four days of dealings after the end of suspension by the Stock Exchange less the cost which would have been incurred in selling the shares. In the event, the insiders retained their profits because the financial advisers to PRG at the time of the bid, at risk as to an action for negligence, repaid this amount to the company since they considered that the breach had been inadvertent.

In other cases, profits were paid to charity. With regard to the dealings in IPH Ltd., the chairman and chief executive of IPH Ltd. was required and agreed to

19. The Panel on Take-overs and Mergers, Statement by the City Panel on Stock Exchange dealings in the course of a take-over situation, 2nd April, 1971.
20. B.A.K. Rider, 'Self-Regulation: The British approach to policing conduct in the securities business, with particular reference to the role of the City Panel on Take-overs and Mergers in the regulation of insider trading' (1978) 1 JCCLSR 319 at 328.
1. The Panel on Take-overs and Mergers, Statement on Seafield Amalgamated Rubber Company Ltd., 27th July, 1976.
2. Ibid, Statement on C.H. Johnson & Sons Limited, 28th November, 1977.
3. Ibid, Statement on J.B. Eastwood, 20th July, 1978.
4. Ibid, Statement on Mount Charlotte Investments Ltd./Gale Lister & Co. Ltd., 16th January, 1974; Appeal Committee, Statement on Mount Charlotte Investments Ltd./Gale Lister & Co. Ltd., 31st January, 1974.
5. Rider, op cit n9, p276, supra, at 330.
6. Stamp and Marley, op cit n9, p276, supra, p.43; P.L. Davies, *The Regulation of Take-overs and Mergers* (1976), p.42.
7. The Panel on Take-overs and Mergers, Statement by the City Panel on Stock Exchange dealings in the course of a take-over situation, 2nd April, 1971.
8. Ibid, Statement on P.R. Grimshawe & Co., Grimshawe-Windsor Merger [1973] J.B.L.43 G.K. Morse.

pay over his profit to a charity nominated by the Panel[9] and the other IPH director, C, was ordered and agreed to pay over the profit on the 20,000 shares purchased for himself but not in respect of nominee dealing.[10] In its statement on J.B. Eastwood Ltd.[11], the Panel reported that the director who purchased shares in his wife's name had already volunteered to pay over his profit to charity. Similarly, in the JWI/Johnson bid[12], the assistant manager agreed to pay over the profit to a charity approved by the Panel. In the Panel statement on Ultra Electronic Holdings Ltd.[13], the financial adviser who had built up a substantial holding for clients in a potential offeree and realised a profit of about £7,000 on his own purchase and subsequent sale, was recommended and agreed to pay his net gain to charity. In relation to C in the Dexion-Comino statement[14] who received inside information in discussions about his proposed appointment as a director, the Panel recorded its agreement that it would be appropriate for him to donate the gross profit on the transaction of some £2,000 to a charity approved by it. In Chaddesley (No.2)[15], the company accountant agreed to pay to a charity approved by the Panel more than 80% of the net gain arising out of the two purchases of options in Chaddesley shares. The accountant told the Panel that whilst the original purchase of options was his alone, he borrowed from relations so that the options could be exercised on the understanding that his relatives would participate in the profit arising from the two transactions. Before the Panel meeting, he had remitted the amount they had advanced, together with some of their share of the profit. He agreed to pay to charity the net gain attributable to his own portion of the total profit and that retained on his relatives' behalf which accounted for most of their profit. Whilst regretting the refusal of his relatives to surrender the element of profit already received, the Panel indicated that it was not contemplating any further action in that respect.

Where the effects of publicity were keenly felt, the Panel was thus able to combine public criticism with securing disgorgement in a high proportion of cases. In developing this remedial device, the Panel was thereby able to fill a gap in the range of sanctions available to it in circumstances where the conduct deserved more than censure. Disgorgement of profits had the advantage of being better tailored to insider dealing, though in the form made by insiders in breach of Rule 30 it was subject to the limitation that payment to a company or to charity was of no assistance to other investors. Indeed, an effect of disgorgement to charity was to present insiders in a more favourable light than if disgorgement had been in favour of a company or other investors.

Yet ultimately, despite the use of such mandatory expressions as 'ordered' or 'required', these payments to the company or to charity stemmed from insiders' willingness to pay. This was evidenced both by the part payment of profits in cases such as the company accountant in Chaddesley (No.2)[16] and C, the other IPH director,[17] and by the absence of reference to disgorgement in other

9. Ibid, Statement on Intereuropean Property Holdings Limited, 12th September, 1979.
10 Ibid, Statement on Intereuropean Property Holdings Limited, 10th October, 1979.
11. Ibid, Statement on J.B. Eastwood Limited, 20th July, 1978.
12. Ibid, Statement on C.H. Johnson & Sons Limited, 28th November, 1977.
13. Ibid, Statement on Ultra Electronic Holdings Limited, 22nd September, 1977.
14. Ibid, Statement on Dealings in Shares in Dexion-Comino International Limited, 25th April, 1975.
15. Ibid, Statement on Chaddesley Investments Limited, 7th February, 1979.
16. Ibid.
17. Ibid, Statement on Intereuropean Property Holdings Limited, 10th October, 1979.

statements.[18]

C. The conduct of business rules

For authorised persons under the FSA 1986, additional restrictions on dealings by their officers and employees are imposed by conduct of business rules; these impose duties on the firm as well as specify the requirements to be made of officers and employees. The restrictions on dealing are supplemented by compliance procedures and reviews. Because of their extended influence and for simplicity, references are to the SIB rules.[19]

1. Duties of the firm

As to the duties of the firm, these relate not only to its own officers and employees, but also to certain customers. Concerning the former, a firm is required to take all reasonable steps to procure that each officer and each employee of the firm observe these requirements as to dealings.[20] In this connection, the firm must ensure that (a) those requirements are set out in a written notice given to each officer and each employee of the firm, (b) each officer and each employee signs an undertaking that he will observe those requirements and (c) in the case of an employee, it is a term of his contract of employment with the firm that he shall observe the requirements.

In regard to certain customers, a firm which effects a transaction in an investment of any description with or on behalf of a customer whom it knows to be an officer or employee of a person who carries on investment business in relation to investments of that description must inform that person of the effecting of the transaction, its terms and the identity of the parties to it, unless it has good reason to believe that that person has consented to the transaction being effected.[1]

2. Requirements to be made of officers and employees

An extended application is given to these requirements in that they are drawn by reference not only to officers and employees, but also to persons connected with them. For these purposes, a person is connected with an officer or employee of a firm if he is so connected with that officer or employee, by reason of any domestic or business relationship (other than that arising solely because he is a customer of the firm), that that officer or employee can reasonably be expected (a) to have influence over that person's judgment as to how his property is to be invested and how he is to exercise any rights attaching to his investment, or (b) to be consulted before any such judgment is made.[2]

---

18. Eg, The Panel on Take-overs and Mergers, Statement on D.F. Lyons & Co. Limited/Rowan and Boden Limited, 2nd October, 1972; Statement on Hewden-Stuart Plant Limited/A. Gunn (Holdings) Limited, llth February, 1976; Statement on Seafield Amalgamated Rubber Company Limited, 27th July, 1976 and Statement on Ultra Electronic Holdings Limited, 22nd September, 1977, (regarding the unnamed investment manager employed in a small merchant bank).
19. See post II. Standards of Conduct for Investment Business.
20. Rule 14.02(1). The duties of the firm are expressed to be on the basis that the requirements do not apply to an investment which is a life policy: Rule 14.02(1) and (2).
1. Rule 14.02(2).
2. Rule 14.01.

Directed largely against conflicts of duty and interest, the requirements impose a general obligation of prior consent and of disclosure. In particular, an officer or employee of a firm should not, on his own account or on that of a person connected with him, effect any transaction relating to an investment of a description in relation to which the firm carries on investment business unless he does so with the consent of the firm given in accordance with these provisions and he should, forthwith upon the effecting of such a transaction, inform the firm that it has been effected.[3] For this purpose, the firm's consent may be a general consent relating to all transactions except where the transaction is with a customer of the firm (other than a market counterparty) in which case the consent must be specific to the transaction in question.[4]

Whilst such consent is often conditional on the transaction being effected in-house, a further disclosure requirement is imposed in circumstances where an officer or employee of a firm effects a transaction relating to an investment of a description in which the firm carries on investment business, either on his own account or that of a person connected with him, with or through the agency of another firm.[5] In that event, the officer or employee should inform that other firm, in relation to that transaction, that he is an officer or employee of the first-mentioned firm. In addition, he should not request or accept from that other firm any credit or special dealings facilities in connection with the transaction unless the first-mentioned firm has consented to his doing so specifically in relation to that transaction.

In two circumstances, a prohibition is imposed on dealing. First, an officer or employee of a firm should not, on his own account or on that of a person connected with him, effect any transaction relating to an investment at any time if he knows that the firm is forbidden by rules 5.15, 5.20 or 5.21 (limitation of trading because of customers' orders, recommendations based on research and analysis and insider dealing respectively) to effect that transaction at that time on the firm's own account or, in the case of rules 5.15 and 5.20, would be so forbidden but for the provisions of paragraph (3) and (4) respectively of those rules.[6] Secondly, an officer or employee of a firm should not, on his own account or on that of a person connected with him, acquire or dispose of any investment if to do so would to his knowledge involve him in a conflict of his own interest or of an interest of a person connected with him with that of any customer or with his duty to any customer.[7]

Concerning the observance of these requirements, an officer or employee of a firm should take all reasonable steps within his power to ensure that any person connected with him, when that person is acting on his own account, observes these requirements as though they applied to that person.[8] But this provision does not apply where the person connected with the officer or employee of the firm is an officer or employee of another authorised person and the person so connected acts on his own account in connection with a transaction relating to an investment of a description in relation to which that other authorised person carries on investment business.

3. Rule 14.03(3). In addition, a firm must make a written record of each consent given and transaction notified under this provision; each such record shall be kept for a period of three years from the time when the consent ceases to be relevant or the transaction is notified, as the case may be: Rule 16.13.
4. Rule 14.03(4).
5. Rule 14.03(5).
6. Rule 14.03(1).
7. Rule 14.03(2).
8. Rule 14.03(6).

3. Compliance procedures and reviews

In regard to compliance procedures, a firm must establish and maintain rules and procedures by reference to which each officer, employee and appointed representative can ensure that he complies with the requirements of the FSA 1986 and SIB rules and regulations thereunder in his dealings with or on behalf of customers of the firm.[9] The compliance procedures must be in writing, except in the case of very small firms.[10] These procedures must be reviewed every twelve months to ensure that they are effective.[11]

D. Other professional organisations

1. The Institute of Directors

Having published Guidelines for Directors on insider dealing in 1973 and reformulated its guidance following the CA 1980, the Institute of Directors published further guidance for members on insider dealing in 1985.[12] This centres on a Code of Conduct whose initial provision sets out the Institute's view that whilst it is in the interests of a company for directors to hold shares in it, this is subject to the proviso that directors should regard any shares they so hold as a long-term investment and not deal in them with a view to making profits or avoiding losses in the short-term.

Drawing on the prohibitions of the IDA 1985, the Code of Conduct contains four elementary rules forbidding a member of the Institute: (a) with inside information about a company (whether or not his own) from dealing in the securities of the company concerned; (b) who knowingly receives inside information from an insider whether directly or indirectly, from dealing in the securities of a company to which it relates; (c) with inside information, from passing it to another person if that person (or someone else) is likely to use that information to deal in the securities to which it relates and (d) with inside information, from encouraging another person to deal in the securities to which it relates. After reminding members that in respect of dealings to which the IDA 1985 applies, such conduct could result in criminal liability, the Institute comments that it expects members to observe the rules in regard to any dealings and any securities about which they hold or obtain inside information. A duty is also imposed on members who are directors of companies quoted on the Stock Exchange, including the USM, to ensure that their company adopts and enforces the Stock Exchange Model Code. The Institute's Code of Conduct adds that members who are directors of unquoted companies should endeavour to ensure that their company adopts a code similar to the Stock Exchange Model Code, with particular reference to prior notification of potential dealings.

The Code of Conduct is supplemented by an outline of the insider dealing

---

9. Rule 15.01.
10. Rules 15.01(2) and 16.15. The exception applies where the number of persons who are employees or officers of the firm, of any appointed representative of the firm, of any connected company of the firm which is itself a firm or of any appointed representative or connected company of the firm which is itself a firm does not in the aggregate exceed ten.
11. Rules 15.01(3) and 15.02.
12. Institute of Directors, *Insider Dealing* (1985).

provisions of the 1985 Act and the scope of civil liability. The Stock Exchange Model Code and Rules 2.1 (secrecy) and 4.1 (prohibited dealings by persons other than the offeror) of the Code are endorsed and reproduced. As well as setting out the criminal and civil liabilities, the Institute reiterates its assessment of the 'moral and economic sanctions' in the following terms:

'News travels fast on the Stock Exchange, and a company can quickly get the label 'a director's company' - meaning that directors of that company are in the habit of making deals in their own companies' shares. Few things can more rapidly impair a company's investment status. And few things, let it be said, can do more damage to the reputation of directors as a whole in the eyes of the public. A director who flouts this elementary rule is plainly unfit for office.'[13]

2. *The Society of Investment Analysts*

On the basis that, as a professional body, it should take the initiative in issuing detailed guidelines as to the professional conduct of members in specific areas of professional concern, the SIA issued its first set of such guidelines in 1981 covering various aspects of professional activity that could potentially involve insider dealings.[14] As distinct from a compliance programme[15], the SIA Guidelines to Insider Dealing give guidance on the insider dealing legislation introduced by the CA 1980 in relation to professional situations likely to be encountered by investment analysts.

At the outset, the Guidelines emphasise that the legislation does not and should not be used to prevent communication between investors or analysts and companies.[16] Referring to its concern that companies might use the legislation as an excuse to reduce their contact with analysts and impede the dissemination of corporate information, the SIA argues that meetings between company officers and investment groups improve the general level of information and reduce the potential for insider dealing. But it adds that the information should not be price-sensitive and company officers should be encouraged to make a general release of the content of remarks made at such meetings. In the US, the SEC's view was summarised by a former chairman in terms that:

'the process of private meetings and discussions between corporate officers and analysts is substantially risk free as long as it consists of providing links in a chain of analytical information, and public disclosure is made of anything of sharp and immediate significance which is communicated.'[17]

Nevertheless, it is doubtful whether many investment analysts could in practice forego seeking to elicit inside information before its public disclosure and it

13. Ibid, p.14.
14. The Society of Investment Analysts, Guidelines to Insider Dealing (May, 1981). These Guidelines have been the subject of comment by: B.A.K. Rider, 'Guidelines interpret problem areas of insider dealing law for analysts' (1981) 2 Co.Law 182 and A.W. Henfrey, 'Professional Conduct for Investment Analysts' (1982) 3 Co.Law 11.
15. Eg, CSI, Guidelines for Personal Dealings by Fund Managers, CSI No.4 (October, 1982).
16. SIA Guidelines, Guideline 1.
17. Cited by Rider, op cit n14, supra, at 183.

may also be that some would regard meetings between company officers and investment groups as a waste of time if they merely elicit publicly available information.[18]

On the question of what constitutes inside information under the legislation, a second Guideline states that price sensitive information only falls within the scope of the legislation if it is specific unpublished information which, if generally known, would materially affect the price of the securities.[19] Subject to judicial interpretation of the wording of the legislation, specific matters are taken to include, by way of example, those items of company information required to be notified to the Quotations Department by the Stock Exchange listing requirements[20] or treated as price sensitive in the Stock Exchange Model Code.[1] With regard to the notification of the acquisition and realisation of assets under the listing requirements[2], it suggests as indicative that whereas larger transactions categorised as Class 1[3] and Class 2[4] must be notified, a Class 3 transaction is generally not required to be notified[5], even though specific.

As to mosaic information, Guideline 3 provides that the analyst who employs the 'mosaic' method, collecting and evaluating information, some part of which may be non-public, but no individual element of which contravenes the legislation[6] is not acting illegally, even if the conclusion which he reaches had it been communicated as information by an insider[7] would have constituted inside information under the legislation.[8] As an example, if an investment analyst is able to construct from a number of pieces of non-material information a model and the conclusion which he reaches, having fitted the pieces together himself, amounts to price sensitive information, then he has not contravened the law. A contrary interpretation would seriously inhibit investment analysts.

A reminder is contained in Guideline 4 that an individual is defined by the legislation[9] as being connected with the company and therefore an insider[10] not only if he is a director, but also if he occupies a position either within the company or through a professional relationship which would be expected to give him access to unpublished price sensitive information. In consequence, it adds that when an investor involves himself directly in management decisions

18. W.H. Painter, *The Federal Securities Code and Corporate Disclosure* (1979), p.355.
19. SIA Guidelines, Guideline 2.
20. See, ante, Chapter 5. Disclosure, III. Timely disclosure.
1. See, ante, 1. The Stock Exchange Model Code.
2. The Admission of Securities to Listing, Section 5, Chapter 2, para14 and Section 6, Chapter 1.
3. A Class 1 transaction is one where a comparison on any one of the following bases amounts to 15% or more: (i) the value of the assets acquired or disposed of, compared with the assets of the acquiring or disposing company; (ii) net profits (after deducting all charges except taxation and excluding extraordinary items) attributable to the assets acquired or disposed of, compared with those of the acquiring or disposing company; (iii) the aggregate value of the consideration given or received compared with the assets of the acquiring or disposing company; (iv) equity capital issued as consideration by the acquiring company compared with the equity capital previously in issue, The Admission of Securities to Listing, Section 6, Chapter 1, para3.1.
4. A Class 2 transaction is one where the relevant figures amount to 5% or more, but do not fall within Class 1: The Admission of Securities to Listing, Section 6, Chapter 1, para4.1.
5. A Class 3 transaction is one where the relevant figures are less than 5%. In these cases an announcement is only required where the consideration includes securities for which listing will be sought and should include the amount of the securities being issued and brief details of the assets being acquired: The Admission of Securities to Listing, Section 6, Chapter 1, paras5.1 and 5.2.
6. IDA 1985, s10.
7. Within IDA 1985, s1.
8. IDA 1985, s10.
9. Ibid, s9.
10. Within IDA 1985, s1.

of a company, for example to help in the solution of a particular problem, he will have placed himself in a professional relationship, be connected personally and be prohibited from dealing in the shares for a period of six months following the ending of his special relationship.

With regard to the risk of becoming a tippee, Guideline 5 adds that an analyst who finds himself in possession of price-sensitive information should recognise that the transmission both to him and by him of that information may itself constitute contravention of the legislation. If information falling within the legislation is communicated to anyone who might be expected to deal on it (such as a client) or to persuade someone else to deal on it, then the communication itself is illegal. Attention is drawn to the fact that this provision is stricter than in the US where liability arises only when dealing takes place. The SIA emphasises that there is thus a critical distinction to be made between the principle of Guideline 3 and that of Guideline 5. It adds that analysts should recognise that they may be better judges of the price-sensitivity of information than informants.

A sixth Guideline records the SIA's view that information which does not fall within the legislation[11] when received cannot do so retrospectively. This view is stated to be based both on current US practice and general legal principle, not derived from the wording of the legislation. Under this Guideline, information which becomes price sensitive after a period when it was not so at the time of the original publication cannot lay the analyst open to retroactive penalty in respect of actions he has taken while the information was not price sensitive. If it has not been published and becomes price sensitive, then the investment analyst is bound for the future by the provisions of the legislation.

As to publication, Guideline 7 states that information falling within the legislation[12] is removed from that category immediately it has appeared in any generally available published form. The purpose of this Guideline is to put into the context of the analytical profession the wording of the legislation which defines 'unpublished' as 'not generally known to those persons ... likely to deal in those securities'.[13] This Guideline is based on the belief that information published in, for instance, a trade journal, a local newspaper or the Stock Exchange notice board, would not normally be found to have fallen within such wording if tested at law.

The SIA concludes by stating that, though it expects prosecutions under the legislation to prove rare in practice, it intends to monitor developments closely. In addition, it asserts that far from constituting a serious problem for members of the public and companies who deal with investment analysts, insider dealing by members is 'at most, restricted to isolated occurrences.'

E. In-house rules

The requirements of the Stock Exchange Model Code and the conduct of business rules have contributed to the growth of in-house rules. The incorporation of security and compliance requirements into contracts of employment, whose breach can be sanctioned by dismissal[14], has constituted an important

---

11. IDA 1985, sl0.
12. Ibid.
13. Ibid, sl0(b).
14. Subject to an employee's right not to be unfairly dismissed under the Employment Protection (Consolidation) Act 1978, Part V.

development both within listed and USM companies and with regard to others professionally involved in the securities industry.

Traditionally there has been a marked reluctance by employers to make public any information about action taken under in-house rules. There were also gaps in the comprehensiveness of in-house rules, with particular concern about the control of financial journalists.[15]

Recently, however, action taken under in-house rules has received publicity. A well-publicised example occurred in 1988 when three merchant banks each dismissed a member of staff for what appeared to be possible breaches of insider dealing rules.[16] In another case in 1988, the securities subsidiary of a banking group dismissed two market-makers for allegedly dealing on its behalf in shares in a client immediately before the client announced an important planned sale.[17]

F. EEC developments

In the attempt to harmonise the capital market laws of the Member States[18], various measures have been adopted or proposed and others are being prepared.[19] Of those impinging upon aspects of insider dealing regulation[20], two have particular significance in regard to the prohibition on dealing.

1. Commission Recommendation of 25 July 1977

In its 1977 Recommendation concerning a European code of conduct relating to transactions in transferable securities[1], the EEC Commission included a general prohibition on dealing by insiders in the following terms:

> 'Any person who comes into possession of information, in exercising his profession or carrying out his duties, which is not public and which relates to a company or to the market in its securities or to any event of general interest to the market, which is price-sensitive, should refrain from carrying out, directly or indirectly, any transaction in which such information is used, and should refrain from giving the information to another person so that he may profit from it before the information becomes public.'[2]

Though this Recommendation, which does not bind Member States as to the

15. J.A.C. Suter, *The Regulation of Insider Dealing in Britain and France* (1985), Chapter 6. Administrative Regulation, III. Restrictions on dealings, B. Britain, 5. In-house rules.
16. *The Observer*, 14th August, 1988.
17. *The Sunday Telegraph*, 14th August, 1988. One of the market-makers claimed damages, alleging wrongful dismissal.
18. For a discussion of this subject, see R.M. Buxbaum and K.J. Hopt, *Legal Harmonisation and the Business Enterprise* (1988), p.167 et seq.
19. Ibid, pp255-256.
20. Eg, a Draft Directive on information to be published when major holdings in the capital of a listed company are acquired or disposed of; this Draft Directive was submitted by the Commission to the Council on 23 December 1987 [1986] 2 C.M.L.R.241.
1. Commission Recommendation of 25 July 1977 concerning a European code of conduct relating to transactions in transferable securities 77/534/EEC, O.J., 1977, L212/37 (20 August 1977) and textual corrections in O.J., 1977, L244/28 (18 November 1977).
2. Ibid, Supplementary principle 9. To implement this provision, the CSI issued a Code of Conduct for Dealers in Securities, CSI, Code of Conduct for Dealers in Securities, CSI No.1 (May 1980).

results to be achieved, appears to have had little impact on the development of regulation or on those who operate on or are in a position to influence the working of the securities markets, it has provided a basis for co-operation within the EEC, both through meetings of the representatives of the regulatory authorities[3] and between those authorities in the conduct of investigations which have assumed an international dimension.

2. Draft Insider Trading Directive

Submitted by the Commission to the Council in 1987[4] and approved by the Parliament (subject to amendment) in 1988[5], this draft Directive seeks to co-ordinate regulations on insider dealing. In an amendment by the Parliament, the legal basis of the draft was changed from co-ordination of safeguards required of companies and firms under Article 54(3)(g) to the establishment and functioning of the internal market under Article 100A. The recitals acknowledge that most Member States have no rules and regulations prohibiting insider dealing and those that do exist differ appreciably.

Subject to the need to comply with the Directive, the stringency of regulation may continue to differ. Under Article 4, Member States may lay down more stringent rules than those contained in the Directive, provided they are non-discriminatory.

A dual approach to regulation is adopted. Apart from restrictions on dealings, the Draft Directive acknowledges the preventive role of disclosure, with Article 7 imposing a timely disclosure requirement.

With a view to better regulation, responsibility for overseeing implementation is conferred on the Contact Committee established by the 1979 Admissions Directive.[6] The Committee's additional functions are defined in Article 10 as: (a) to facilitate the harmonised implementation of the Insider Trading Directive especially as regards penalties, through regular consultations on any practical problems arising from its application on which exchanges of view are deemed useful and (b) to advise the Commission on any amendment to be made to that Directive.

In regard to restrictions on dealings, the Draft Directive contains five main features: the definition of insider, the meaning of inside information, the restrictions placed on insiders, penalties and enforcement authorities.

(a) THE DEFINITION OF INSIDER

A functional approach based on an access test is adopted by Article 1, which refers to 'any person who, in the exercise of his employment, profession or duties, acquires inside information'. An access test also applies to a tippee, who is defined by Article 3 as 'any person who has knowingly obtained inside

---

3. T.P. Lee, M.C. Robert, A. Hirsch and I.M. Pollack, 'Secrecy laws and other obstacles to international co-operation' (1982) 4 JCCLSR 287 at 296.
4. Proposal for a Council Directive co-ordinating regulations on insider trading, O.J., 1987, C.153/8 (11 June 1987). Article 12 envisages Member States being required to take the measures necessary to comply with the Directive by 31 December 1990.
5. O.J., 1988, C. 187/91, (18 July 1988). This section is based on this draft which incorporates the Parliament's proposed amendments.
6. Conditions for Admission of Securities to Official Listing at Stock Exchanges, March 5, 1979 (Dir.79/279/EEC, O.J., 1979, L66/21), art.20.

information from a person who has acquired that information in the exercise of his profession or duties.'

(b) THE MEANING OF INSIDE INFORMATION

The term 'inside information' is defined by Article 6 so as to exclude information of a general nature. Rather inside information is information inaccessible or not available to the public of a specific nature and relating to one or more issuers of transferable securities or to one or more transferable securities which, if it were published, would have a material effect on the price of the transferable security or transferable securities in question. The importance of dissemination is acknowledged by the definition of 'publication' for these purposes as 'the effective disclosure of inside information in such a manner sufficient to ensure its availability to the investing public'.

(c) RESTRICTIONS PLACED ON INSIDERS

The basic restriction is a prohibition on dealing, imposed by Article 1. Member States are required to prohibit an insider from taking advantage of inside information to buy or sell on their territory, either directly or indirectly, transferable securities admitted to trading on their stock exchange markets. Where the transaction is effected on a stock exchange market, it is deemed to be carried out in the Member State where that market is situated or operates. Where the transaction is effected outside a stock exchange market, it is deemed to be carried out in the Member State in which the other party to the transaction is resident.

In regard to certain private deals, Member States are given an option. Framed in terms of a presumption that such deals are to be regulated, Article 1 provides that unless Member States specifically waive the prohibition, it shall apply to transferable securities bought or sold outside a stock exchange market without the involvement of a professional intermediary.

A further restriction is a prohibition on tipping, contained in Article 2. This requires Member States to prohibit any person who is resident in their territory and acquires inside information in the exercise of his employment, profession or duties from either (a) disclosing that inside information to a third party unless such disclosure is authorised as part of the normal course of exercising his employment profession or duties, or (b) using that inside information to recommend a third party to buy or sell transferable securities admitted to trading on their stock exchange markets.

In regard to tippees, the prohibition on dealing imposed on an insider within Article 1 is extended, by reference, to tippees by Article 3. Similarly, tippees are prohibited from either disclosing the inside information to a third party, or using that inside information to recommend a third party to buy or sell transferable securities admitted to trading on their stock exchange markets.

The term 'transferable securities' is given an extended meaning by Article 5. Thus, transferable securities include not only securities usually traded on the stock exchange market, such as shares and debt securities, but also traded options relating to such securities.

(d) PENALTIES

A wide discretion is afforded by Article 11, which provides that Member States shall determine the penalties to be applied for infringement of the measures taken pursuant to the Directive. However, the objective of the eventual harmonisation of penalties is suggested by the provision for the Commission to put forward proposals for harmonising the penalties imposed in each Member State. The development of civil remedies is likewise encouraged by the provision that, for the purpose of Article 11, appropriate civil remedies shall involve the payment of an indemnity by those profiting by the use of inside information to those who can show that they have thereby suffered a loss.

(e) ENFORCEMENT AUTHORITIES

With a view to ensuring the application of provisions adopted pursuant to the Directive, Member States are required by Article 8 to designate one or more competent authorities; the Commission must be informed accordingly, with details (if appropriate) as to how duties have been allocated. The competent authorities must be given all such supervisory and investigatory powers as may be necessary for the exercise of their duties. Giving impetus to developments in international co-operation, the competent authorities in the Member States must co-operate wherever necessary for the purpose of carrying out their duties and exchange any information for that purpose.

II. STANDARDS OF CONDUCT FOR INVESTMENT BUSINESS

The rules regulating the conduct of investment business by persons authorised under the FSA 1986, complement the criteria for obtaining authorisation, notably the 'fit and proper person' test.[7] These rules seek to ensure, on a continuing basis, the observance of standards of conduct by persons authorised to carry on investment business.

In regard to these continuing requirements, statutory rule-making powers are conferred on the SIB by Chapter V of Part I, FSA 1986. In particular, it has power to make rules regulating the conduct of business by authorised persons.[8] This power is subject to the proviso that such rules do not apply to members of a recognised SRO or persons certified by an RPB in respect of investment business in the carrying on of which they are subject to the rules of the organisation or body.[9] In thus limiting the persons to whom the SIB rules apply,[10] this proviso emphasises the important role of recognised SROs and RPBs in relation to continuing requirements for authorised persons.

However, the SIB conduct of business rules have an extended influence on the standards of conduct laid down by a recognised SRO or an RPB. This is due, first, to the requirement that, as a condition of recognition, the rules of the SRO governing the carrying on of investment business of any kind by its members must afford investors protection at least equivalent to that afforded in respect

7. FSA 1986, s27(3) and Sch2, para 1(1).
8. Ibid, s48(1).
9. Ibid.
10. The SIB conduct of business rules apply mainly to persons directly authorised under ss25-30 and to persons authorised in other Member States (ss31-34).

of investment business of that kind by the rules and regulations in force under
Chapter V of Part I, FSA 1986.[11] Secondly, this extended SIB influence is due to
the similar safeguards for investors which are required of an RPB. Such a body
must have rules regulating the carrying on of investment business by persons
certified by it and those rules must, in respect of investment business of any kind
regulated by them, afford to investors the same equivalent protection.[12]

In considering the substantive requirements in regard to the standards of
conduct applicable to authorised persons, the emphasis in this section will, in
view of this SIB influence and for simplicity, be on the SIB rules rather than on
the various rules made by recognised SROs and RPBs. However, the role of these
organisations and bodies, especially the SROs, in regard to enforcement should
not thereby be underestimated. In addition, in the context of take-overs and
mergers, reference will be made to the requirements of the Panel on Take-overs
and Mergers.

Important amendments to these SIB rules are due in 1989. The focus of
intense criticism, the present rules have been criticised for being drafted in
technical language. Their replacement by a new rule book, with a set of clearly
worded principles as the foundation for regulation, has been announced.[13]

A. Standards of conduct applicable to authorised persons

1. The conduct of business rules (the 'CBRs')

The SIB's statutory power to make CBRs[14] is elaborated upon in both general
and specific terms. As to specific matters, SIB rules may make provision:[15] (a)
prohibiting a person from carrying on, or holding himself out as carrying on,
investment business of any specified kind; (b) prohibiting a person from
carrying on or holding himself out as carrying on investment business of a kind
or on a scale other than that notified; (c) prohibiting a person from carrying on
investment business in relation to persons other than those of a specified class
or description; (d) regulating the manner in which a person may hold himself
out as carrying on investment business; (e) regulating the manner in which a
person makes a market in any investments; (f) as to the form and content of
advertisements in respect of investment business;[16] (g) requiring the principals
of appointed representatives to impose restrictions on the investment business
carried out by them; (h) requiring the disclosure of the amount or value of
commission or other inducements; (i) enabling or requiring information
obtained by an authorised person in the course of carrying on one part of his
business to be withheld by him from persons with whom he deals in the course
of carrying on another part ('Chinese Walls'); (j) as to the circumstances and
manner in which and the time when or the period during which action may be
taken for the purpose of stabilising the price of investments of any specified
description; (k) for arrangements for the settlement of disputes; (l) requiring

11. FSA 1986, Sch2, para3(1).
12. Ibid, Sch3, para3(1).
13. *The Financial Times*, 19th November, 1988.
14. FSA 1986, s48(1).
15. Ibid, s48(2).
16. By s48(5), FSA 1986; advertisements in connection with listing arrangements are excluded and
the CBRs on advertisements have effect subject to Part V, FSA 1986 (Offers of Unlisted Securities).

the keeping of accounts and other records, as to their form and content and for their inspection, and (m) requiring a person to whom the rules apply to make provision for the protection of investors in the event of the cessation of his investment business in consequence of his death, incapacity or otherwise.

This list is not exhaustive. It is without prejudice to the generality of the SIB's statutory power to make CBRs. Hence, such rules may make either provision for matters other than those listed or, with one exception, further provision for the matters there mentioned.[17] The CBRs may also regulate the carrying on in connection with investment business of any business which is held out as being for the purposes of investment.[18]

There is also a power of modification for particular cases. On application by a person subject to the CBRs, the SIB may alter the requirements of the rules to adapt them to particular circumstances.[19] The power is not to be exercised unless compliance with the requirements in question would be unduly burdensome for the applicant having regard to the benefit which compliance would confer on investors and the alteration would not result in any undue risk to investors.

The objectives of the CBRs are expressed in terms of a variety of values. Like other rules and regulations made under Part I, FSA 1986, the CBRs must: (a) promote high standards of integrity and fair dealing in the conduct of investment business; (b) make proper provision for requiring an authorised person to act with due skill, care and diligence in providing any service which he provides or holds himself out as willing to provide; (c) make proper provision for requiring an authorised person to subordinate his own interests to those of his clients and to act fairly between his clients and (d) make proper provision for requiring an authorised person to ensure that, in anything done by him for the persons with whom he deals, due regard is had to their circumstances.[20]

However, this variety of values complicates consideration of the CBRs from the point of view of insider dealing regulation. As with disclosure requirements, the scope of the CBRs is considerably broader than if the focus was solely on the issue of insider dealing.

Conflicts of interest are a particularly important area for insider dealing regulation and most of the CBRs relevant to insider dealing will be considered in that context. As the position is further complicated by the general law on conflicts of interest, consideration of conflicts of interest is reserved to a separate part of this section.

In addition, with a view to bolstering the authority of the Panel on Takeovers and Mergers, obligations are imposed on authorised persons by rule 2.12.[1] These are based on a prohibition on acting for certain persons and a duty to co-operate with the Panel, with non-compliance rendering an authorised person liable to administrative sanctions.

In regard to the prohibition on acting for certain persons, a firm must not act for any person in connection with a take-over of a company, a merger of one company with another or such an acquisition by a person of shares in a company as will result in him holding a large number of those shares if the firm has reason

---

17. FSA 1986, s48(3). As to the exception, the CBRs must not impose limits on the amount or value of commission or other inducements paid or provided in connection with investment business.
18. FSA 1986, s48(4).
19. Ibid, s50(1) and (2).
20. Ibid, Sch8, paras1-4.
1. This followed a review of the Panel's role by the Department of Trade and Industry, the Bank of England, the Treasury, the Stock Exchange, SIB and the Panel: The Panel on Take-overs and Mergers, Report on the Year ended 31st March, 1987, p.6.

to believe that the person for whom the firm so acts is not likely to comply with standards of conduct for the time being expected in the UK concerning the practices of those involved in take-overs, mergers or acquisitions such as the one in question.[2] The circumstances in which a firm might have 'reason to believe' that a person is not likely to comply with these standards remain to be clarified. Having regard to previous Panel statements, it seems that the Panel itself would be unlikely to suggest this course of action unless there was repeated defiance of the Code and of Panel rulings (as in the St. Piran case).[3] Rather, this provision seems more likely to operate as a preventive measure, prompting firms to check that customers will observe Code requirements.

As to the duty to co-operate with the Panel, a firm which is acting or has acted for any person in connection with any such take-over, merger or acquisition must (a) co-operate with the Panel in providing all information, books and documents concerning that take-over, merger or acquisition requested by the Panel which is or are in the possession or under the control of the firm, and (b) otherwise render all such assistance as the firm is reasonably able to do to enable the Panel fully to investigate any matter relating thereto.[4] This duty is imposed in the light of the Panel's past investigative difficulties, underlined in the case of insider dealing.[5]

2. The Panel on Take-overs and Mergers

As the Panel requirements relevant to insider dealing regulation concern conflicts of interest, consideration of these requirements is likewise postponed to a separate part of this section. Like the CBRs, the scope of Panel requirements is broader than if the focus was solely on insider dealing.

B. Conflicts of interest

Conflicts of interest abound in the securities industry as a result of the many functions performed by financial conglomerates and individuals in them for a wide range of clients. In this connection, a single institution may be involved in several of the following functions: underwriting of corporate issues, private placings of securities, advising corporate and investment clients; investment management, unit trust and pension fund management, stockbroking, market-making and banking. Individuals within those institutions may also act as company directors, whether or not the particular company is also a client.

There is thus scope for conflicts of interest in many situations. By way of example,[6] the underwriting arm may be tempted to pressure the investment management arm to subscribe, in respect of discretionary accounts, to corpo-

---

2. Rule 2.12(1).
3. The Panel on Take-overs and Mergers, Statement on St. Piran Ltd., 1st April, 1980; Statement on St. Piran Ltd., 23rd May, 1980; Statement of the Appeal Committee of the Panel on Take-overs and Mergers, St. Piran, 11th June, 1980; The Panel on Take-overs and Mergers, Statement, 10th September, 1983.
4. Rule 2.12(2).
5. J.A.C. Suter, *The Regulation of Insider Dealing in Britain and France* (1985), pp7.95-7.110.
6. Further examples are set out in: R. Pennington, *How Conflicts of interest may arise*, p.1 at p.5, J. Gower, *Conflicts of Interest and the City Revolution*, p.7 at pp8-9, and P.R. Wood, 'Financial Conglomerates and Conflicts of Interest', p.59 at pp60-61 in (ed.) R.M. Goode, *Conflicts of interest in the changing financial world* (1986); N.S. Poser, 'Chinese Wall or Emperor's New Clothes?' (1) (1988) 9 Co. Law 119 at 121 and *Financial Times*, 17th August, 1988.

rate issues underwritten by the institution. In regard to the fund management arm, the corporate finance arm may be tempted to pressure fund managers to support its clients by purchasing securities in those clients. The broking arm may be tempted to prefer a particularly valuable client over other clients, by giving it first access to information or recommendation or by executing its order at better prices. As to banking, the banking arm could be embarrassed by being banker to an offeree in a contested take-over in which the offeror was being advised by the corporate finance arm.

For the purposes of this section, the term 'conflict of interest' covers situations giving rise to an actual or potential breach of obligation. The term describes 'a temptation not necessarily a yielding'.[7] A conflict of interest may arise because the party owing the duty either has inconsistent interests of his own to protect or owes an inconsistent duty to a third party.

The main measures relating to conflicts of interest in situations relevant to insider dealing regulation[8] have been administrative, notably the Conduct of Business Rules made under the FSA 1986 and the City Code. But as a preliminary, consideration will be given to the general law.

1. The general law

The fundamental principle that fiduciaries must not place themselves in a position where their interest and duty conflict has been discussed in a previous chapter.[9] The considerations there discussed are also important in the context of a conflict between the firm's own interest and its duty to a client.

However, there is another important type of conflict of interest, namely, that arising from the principle that a fiduciary must not place himself in a position where his duty to one client conflicts with his duty to another. An example of this type of conflict is that between the duty of a firm's corporate finance department to an issuer and the duty of its investment management department to a client.

The general principle with regard to double commission was stated in *Fulwood v Hurley*.[10] In reply to the defendant's inquiry, the plaintiff, who was a hotel broker, sent him a list of hotels, together with orders to view and a letter which concluded 'if business is done we shall act for you at the usual brokerage'. After viewing one of the hotels and conducting direct negotiations with the owner, the defendant purchased it. The owner paid commission to the plaintiff, who subsequently sued the defendant for an additional commission, alleging a commission on the terms of the letter. Affirming the decision of the Divisional Court, the Court of Appeal held that the terms of the letter were not sufficient to establish a contract by the defendant, as purchaser, to pay a double commission to the plaintiff and that the plaintiff, who was plainly acting as agent to the vendor, was not entitled to enter into such a contract with the defendant without

---

7. M.Q. Connelly, 'The Licensing of Securities Market Actors', p.1269 at p.1352 in Consumer and Corporate Affairs Canada, *Proposals for a Securities Market Law for Canada*, Vol.3 Background papers (1974).
8. This section does not deal with conflicts of interest in the securities industry generally; these are discussed by Pennington, Gower and Wood in (ed.) Goode, op cit n6, p292, supra. In addition, conflicts of interest in banking and in the accquntancy profession are discussed respectively by T. Prime, 'Conflicts of Interest: Legal Rules and Equitable Principles', p.ll and M. Fowle, 'Conflicts of Interest and the Accountancy Profession', p.33 in (ed.) Goode, op cit n6, p292, supra.
9. See, ante, Chapter 4. Civil Liability.
10. [1928] 1 KB 498, CA.

the fullest disclosure to both vendor and purchaser, which he had failed to make or show. Lord Hanworth, M.R., stated the principle as follows:

> 'if and so long as the agent is the agent of one party, he cannot engage to become the agent of another principal without the leave of the first principal with whom he has originally established his agency.'[11]

Similarly, Scrutton L.J. expressed the principle in terms that:

> 'No agent who has accepted an employment from one principal can in law accept an engagement inconsistent with his duty to the first principal from a second principal, unless he makes the fullest disclosure to each principal of his interest, and obtains the consent of each principal to the double employment.'[12]

However, in the absence of such disclosure and consent, there has been scant judicial consideration of the position of professional fiduciaries who have conflicts of interest. Guidance is limited to two recent cases involving insurance brokers. In both cases, Lloyds underwriters instructed the brokers who placed the insurance to obtain an assessor's report in respect of claims made under the policies. A consequence of this practice was that when a claim arose under a policy, the broker might then become an agent of both the underwriter and the assured in certain respects.

The practice was condemned in 1969 by Megaw J. in *Anglo-African Merchants Ltd. v Bayley.*[13] The plaintiffs wished to obtain insurance cover against all risks for army surplus clothing about twenty-three years old. In response to a query whether the goods were secondhand, the plaintiffs told brokers that the goods were new and the slip for the insurable interest described the clothing as 'new men's clothes'. When a portion of the clothing was stolen from the warehouse, the plaintiffs claimed on the policy. The defendant underwriter repudiated liability. It was held that the plaintiff's claim failed for non-disclosure of material facts. When the practice came to his attention, Megaw J. remarked:

> 'The broker is, apparently, entitled to accept these instructions without a by-your-leave from his principal, the assured, and without the principal being told by the agent that he is accepting instructions from the adverse, or potentially adverse party.
>
> If an insurance broker, before he accepts instructions to place an insurance, discloses to his client that he wishes to be free to act in the way suggested, and if the would-be assured, fully informed as to the broker's intention to accept such instructions from the insurers and as to the possible implications of such collaboration between his agent and the opposite party, is prepared to agree that the broker may so act, good and well. In the absence of such express and fully informed consent, in my opinion, it would be a breach of duty on the part of the insurance broker so to act.'[14]

These remarks were obiter dicta.

11. Ibid at 502.
12. Ibid.
13. [1969] 2 All E.R. 421.
14. Ibid at 428-429.

However, the propriety of the practice was fundamental to the 1970 decision of Donaldson J. on the issues raised in *North and South Trust Co. v Berkeley*.[15] The plaintiffs claimed on a policy of insurance for goods in transit and through their brokers, asked for an early settlement of the claim. On the underwriters' instructions, the brokers informed the plaintiffs that there was no evidence to show that the underwriters were entirely liable for the losses. The plaintiffs did not accept this rejection. At the underwriters' request, the brokers obtained an assessor's report. This was shown to the underwriters who reiterated their rejection of the plaintiffs' claim. When the plaintiffs commenced an action against the defendant under the policy, the defendant put the plaintiffs to proof of their claim and alleged fraud and non-disclosure. Lists of documents were exchanged, but the defendants claimed that the assessor's report was privileged from disclosure. The plaintiffs then claimed declarations against the brokers that they were entitled to possession and delivery up or inspection of any documents then or previously in the possession of the brokers relating to or in any way connected with the insurances effected by the brokers on the plaintiffs' behalf. The defendant claimed an injunction against the brokers restraining them from complying with this claim. In interpleader proceedings by the brokers, the issue was ordered to be tried whether the plaintiffs were, or the defendant was, entitled to delivery up or inspection of, inter alia, the assessors' report or the copies thereof.

Donaldson J. held that as Lloyd's brokers, the brokers were acting as the plaintiffs' agents in effecting the policy and in everything done in consequence thereof. As agents, it was inconsistent with their duty to the plaintiffs to act as agents of the defendant without the plaintiffs' leave. Accordingly, the brokers were in breach of their duty to the plaintiffs in acting on the defendant's behalf in procuring the assessors' report on the claim, even though in doing so they were acting in accordance with a long standing practice of Lloyd's underwriters to use the Lloyd's brokers who placed the insurance as their channel of communication with the assessors, for that practice was wholly unreasonable and therefore incapable of being a legal usage. However, it was also held that it did not follow that because the brokers acted in breach of their duty to the plaintiffs, they were bound to disclose any information obtained whilst so acting, including information which they would not have obtained except on the terms that it would be kept confidential from the plaintiffs. The reason given was that the information so obtained was not a benefit to brokers, as agents, for which they were accountable to the plaintiffs, nor was it acquired in the service of the plaintiffs or in the discharge of any duty to them. Accordingly, the plaintiffs were not entitled to delivery up or inspection of the assessors' report or the copies thereof.

The plaintiffs did not contend that any of the documents were their property or even that they had a direct right to possession of them. Instead, their claim to the information was based on the proposition that without his principal's fully informed consent, an agent cannot in law place himself in a position where he owes a duty to another which is inconsistent with his duty to his principal. This proposition was accepted by Donaldson J., subject to slight amplification:

'Fully informed consent apart, an agent cannot lawfully place himself in a position in which he owes a duty to another which is inconsistent with his duty to his principal, but if, nevertheless, he does so, his action is not a

15. [1971] 1 All E.R. 980. This decision was noted by M. Kay and D. Yates, 'An Unremedied Breach of a Fiduciary Duty' (1972) 35 M.L.R. 78.

nullity. It is to be accepted as a fact, with all the special consequences flowing from its unlawful nature. Thus ... his unlawful act provides him with no defence to a claim by his true principal for compensation for loss resulting from the agent's inability, due to the conflict of duties, fully to discharge his duty to that principal. Further, it may provide the true principal with a cause of action against the agent for an account and payment over of any benefit which the agent has received in the course of the unlawful agency.'[16]

In this connection, Donaldson J. added that where an agent was employed to make a contract between his true principal and another for whom he was also acting as agent, the true principal could avoid the resulting contract. It was also well established that where the other principal knew of the agency and the transaction resulted in a sale, the court would, as between the two principals, presume that the other principal would have bought at a higher price or would have sold at a lower price to the extent of the payment which he unlawfully made to the agent.

At the heart of the submission of the plaintiffs' counsel was the proposition:

'If X, a third party, knowing that A is the agent of P, the principal, enters into an agreement with A involving duties which are inconsistent with those owed by A to P, then, in the absence of the fully informed consent of P, X acts at his own peril, and where there is any resulting conflict between X's interests and P's interests the law will prefer the interests of P.'[17]

Though no authority was cited for it, Donaldson J. thought this contained 'much that is sound'[18] and considered that 'the law prefers P's interests to the extent of avoiding any resulting contracts and calling X to account in relation to any commission paid to A.'[19] However, he criticised as unsupported 'either by principle or authority'[20], counsel's application of the general to the particular in this form:

'If, knowing of A's agency for P, X passed information or documents to A relevant to matters which are the subject of that agency, X cannot complain if A complies with his duty to P to pass on that information or to show those documents to P, however confidential that information or those documents might otherwise be, unless X has first obtained the fully informed consent of P to A receiving that information or those documents exclusively on behalf of X.'[1]

His criticism was that it assumed the agent was under a duty to pass on to his principal information which he could not have obtained save on terms that it would be kept confidential from his principal. Despite his remark that an agent would be accountable to his true principal for any benefit received in the course of the unlawful agency[2] and subsequent comment that an agent is liable to

16. [1971] 1 All E.R.980 at 992.
17. Ibid at 992-993.
18. Ibid at 993.
19. Ibid.
20. Ibid.
1. Ibid.
2. Ibid at 992.

compensate his true principal in respect of loss caused by his breach of duty[3], he considered that information was 'not a benefit to the agent for which he would be accountable.'[4] But this view is open to objection[5] on the ground that the information could only be acquired by the agent in the course of his breach of duty. The effect of upholding the confidential character of the second agency is seemingly to permit the interests of the second principal to prevail over those of the true principal in circumstances within the general proposition already apparently accepted.

An admitted difficulty with this objection is that the information was not a benefit to the agent himself in the way that commission would have been.[6] But it is contended that the real problem stems from the fact that most claims by a first principal against his agent who has acted for a third party are claims based on unjust enrichment.[7] Hence, the question is whether the principal's remedy is (a) proprietary, enabling him to claim anything received by the agent or (b) personal so that he is confined to the agent's profits.

An alternative approach is contained in the American Restatements of Agency. This imposes a duty of disclosure on the agent subject to the proviso that such disclosure must not be in breach of a duty to a third person.[8] Where this involves a conflict of duties and in spite of this the agent proceeds to act for the second principal, if the second principal has knowledge of the first agency, then the second agreement is illegal and unenforceable.[9] Thus, the effect of rendering the second agency illegal and unenforceable is to relieve the agent of his duty of confidentiality to the second principal. Whilst admitting that the second agency is unlawful[10], Donaldson J. did not seem to hold it unenforceable. A consequence is that the duty of confidentiality imposed by the second agency is upheld at the expense of the duty of disclosure imposed by the first.[11]

As to the plaintiffs' submission that the information was property which the brokers had wrongfully acquired in the plaintiffs' service, Donaldson J. was of opinion that there were 'at least three answers to this'[12]. First, he observed that it was by no means clear that information was property in this context. It is thought[13] that this observation was prompted by comments on *Boardman v Phipps*[14] which, it has been seen[15], concerned an agent's use of information belonging to the principal to acquire a benefit for the agent. Yet this case can be distinguished in that the information did not originally belong to the plaintiffs and it was not alleged that the brokers profited from its use. The issue of whether information should be classified as property has already been discussed.[16] Secondly, even if the information was property, the property was never acquired by the brokers, but was merely in their custody. But it is difficult to see how a person who has custody of documents and knows their contents can be regarded as not having acquired the information. Thirdly, he stated that,

3. Ibid at 993.
4. Ibid.
5. Kay and Yates, op cit n15, p295, supra, at 80-81.
6. Ibid at 80.
7. G. Jones, 'Unjust Enrichment and the Fiduciary's Duty of Loyalty' (1968) L.Q.R.472 at 498.
8. Para.381.
9. Para.391.
10. [1971] 1 All E.R.980 at 992.
11. Kay and Yates, op cit n15, p295, supra, at 80.
12. [1971] 1 All E.R.980 at 993.
13. Kay and Yates, op cit n15, p295, supra.
14. [1967] 2 A.C.46.
15. See, ante, Chapter 4. Civil Liability, I. Liability to the company.
16. Ibid.

though wrongfully acquired, the information was not acquired in the service of the plaintiffs. Since the information had been wrongfully acquired and the rights of the true principal are supposed to be preferred to those of the second principal, it is not clear why the fact that the information was not acquired in the plaintiffs' service should be conclusive.[17] Donaldson J. suggested that the only way in which counsel's proposition might be made good was by treating the common knowledge of the underwriter and brokers as constituting an implied waiver of the implied seal of confidentiality with which the information was impressed. In this case, he stated that such an argument could not succeed unless knowledge was to be imputed of the impropriety of the agency to the defendant and to the brokers as a matter of law because neither in fact knew that they were acting in a wrongful manner.[18] But he added that this approach would not apply in future cases.

The fallacy underlying the plaintiffs' claim was stated as being that in acting for the underwriters, the brokers:

> 'were undertaking duties which inhibited the proper performance of their duties towards the plaintiffs, but insofar as they acted for the defendant they were not acting in discharge of any duty towards the plaintiffs.'[19]

Though acknowledged to be undeniable, this statement has been criticised as irrelevant in that the plaintiffs' claim arose 'not from the discharging of a duty owed to them but from the breach of such a duty - a breach of which the defendants had knowledge at the time when the information was procured for them by the brokers'.[20]

However, Donaldson J. considered that the plaintiffs had a legitimate complaint in that the brokers 'wore the plaintiffs' hat and the underwriters' hat side by side, and in consequence, as was only to be expected neither hat fitted properly'.[1] They could claim damages 'if and to the extent that the partial dislodgment of their hat has caused them loss or damage'.[2] But they were asking to see what the brokers were 'keeping under the underwriters' hat and for that there is no warrant'.[3]

A further problem concerns the remedy available to the plaintiffs. The acknowledgment of Donaldson J. that his approach in this case would not apply in future cases prompted the comment:

> 'Presumably future plaintiffs should at least obtain their declarations on the basis of the agent as a constructive trustee of the information. Even if the information is not regarded as property there seems no reason to suppose that the equity which restrains the transmission of confidential information in breach of some confidential relationship[4], will not equally

17. Kay and Yates, op cit n15, p295, supra, at 82.
18. [1971] 1 All E.R.980 at 993.
19. Ibid.
20. Kay and Yates, op cit n15, p295, supra, at 82.
1. [1971] 1 All E.R.980 at 993.
2. Ibid.
3. Ibid .
4. See ante: *Boardman v Phipps* [1967] 2 A.C.46 especially per Lord Upjohn at 127-128 (Chapter 4. Civil Liability, I. Liability to the company); and Chapter 4. Civil Liability, III. Breach of confidence.

compel disclosure where the information has been obtained in breach of the duty arising from such a relationship.'[5]

Despite his encouragement[6], the plaintiffs did not appeal against the decision of Donaldson J.

In the absence of full disclosure to and consent by their clients, there remained uncertainties in the law relating to fiduciaries faced with conflicts of interest. Legislative protection for fiduciaries in the securities industry was limited to two situations.

First, with the passage of the CA 1980, it has been seen[7] that limited protection was afforded to trustees and personal representatives. However, no provision was thereby made for others acting in a fiduciary capacity who had conflicts of interest.

Secondly, provisions in the Licensed Dealers (Conduct of Business) Rules 1983 requiring the disclosure of material interests expressly recognised the concept of the Chinese Wall. When a licensed dealer had or was deemed to have a material interest in a proposed transaction relating to investments, he was required (a) before effecting the transaction for or with a client, to notify the client of the nature and extent of that material interest and (b) forthwith thereafter, to give the client written confirmation of that notification.[8] But the disclosure obligation did not apply where part of the business dealing with the client was divided by a Chinese Wall from part of the business in which the interest arose and it was reasonable to assume that no individual who was involved in the transaction on behalf of the licensed dealer, whether directly or indirectly, was aware of the interest in question.[9] The term 'Chinese Wall' was defined as:

'an established arrangement whereby information known to persons in one part of a business is not available (directly or indirectly) to those involved in another part of the business and it is accepted that in each of the parts of the business so divided decisions will be taken without reference to any interest which any other such part or any person in any such part of the business may have in the matter.'[10]

The provisions of the 1983 Rules, however, likewise did not extend beyond licensed dealers to other fiduciaries faced with conflicts of interest.

For other multiple fiduciaries in the securities industry, provisions relating to conflicts of interest were contained in self-regulatory measures, notably those of the Stock Exchange and the Panel. In consequence, those fiduciaries remained at risk of challenge, in the courts, as to the propriety of their practices.

Mindful of this risk, banking interests sought exemption, under the FSA 1986, from the general law relating to conflicts of interest. Apart from the need for rules for the conduct of investment business to be 'certain and practicable', it was argued that:

5. Kay and Yates, op cit n15, p295, supra, at 83.
6. [1971] 1 All E.R.980 at 990.
7. See, ante, Chapter 3. Criminal Liability, II. Statutory provisions, C. Restrictions placed on insiders, 2. Defences and exclusions, (e) Trustees and personal representatives
8. The Licensed Dealers (Conduct of Business) Rules 1983, S.I.1983 No.585, r.8(1) (now repealed).
9. Ibid, r.8(2)(a). There was also an underwriting exception, r.8(2)(b).
10. Ibid, r.2.

'If the conduct of business rules made in or under the Financial Services Act are comprehensive then the continued application to "investment business" of the general equitable rules regarding conflicts of interest and duty would be unnecessary.'[11]

However, this approach differed from that advocated by Professor Gower. In his 1984 report[12], he considered that the conduct of business rules should have as their object to provide the essential minimum protection to investors in regard to such matters as conflicts of interest. Pre-eminent among these rules were those providing for 'full and frank disclosure in circumstances where there is a conflict of interests or of interest and duty'.[13] In regard to Chinese Walls, he added:

'Such conflicts ... are aggravated by the increasing tendency for a wide range of ... services to be provided by a single firm or group. The wider the range the greater the risk of conflicts which cannot be wholly avoided by erecting Chinese Walls.'[14]

Professor Gower concluded that any rules of conduct should be subject to 'basic principles of law', including the rule that 'an agent cannot act as a principal unless there is full disclosure to, and informed consent by, the client'.[15]

This reluctance to endorse Chinese Walls was followed in the 1985 White Paper on Financial Services.[16] In particular, the Department of Trade and Industry stated that the Government was not convinced that 'total reliance can be placed on Chinese Walls because they restrict flows of information and not the conflicts of interest themselves'.[17]

In turn, the FSA 1986 did not contain an exemption from the general law on conflicts of interest. However, the Chinese Wall was expressly recognised in the Conduct of Business Rules made under that legislation.[18] The result was that whilst the existence of a Chinese Wall would not relieve an institution of liability under the general law, the Chinese Wall could constitute a defence under specific conduct of business rules made under the FSA 1986.

The effect of compliance with the conduct of business rules under the general law relating to conflicts of interest has not been judicially considered. If the application of the general law is not pre-empted in these circumstances, any protection from civil liability afforded by the existence of a Chinese Wall may prove illusory.[19] Nevertheless, the courts may be reluctant to hold that there has been a breach of the general law relating to conflicts of interest in circumstances where the existence of a Chinese Wall prevents a breach of the conduct of business rules. Hence, developments in the general law may be influenced by the conduct of business rules.

11. Barclays de Zoete Wedd, *Problems of the Existing Law of Fiduciary Duties under Dual Capacity* (1985), p.7.
12. *Review of Investor Protection*, Report: Part I by L.C.B. Gower, Cmnd.9125 (1984).
13. Ibid, para 6.30.
14. Ibid.
15. Ibid.
16. Department of Trade and Industry, *Financial Services in the United Kingdom*, Cmnd. 9432 (1985).
17. Ibid, para7.4.
18. See post 2. The conduct of business rules.
19. Poser, op cit n6, p292, supra, at 168.

2. The conduct of business rules

The CBRs do not readily lend themselves to mutually exclusive categories. However, by way of broad division, in this part they are separated into (a) insider dealing and (b) advice and transactions which are not fully disinterested.

(a) INSIDER DEALING

A prohibition on dealing on its own account by the firm is imposed, subject to two exceptions. Drafted by reference to the criminal liability under the IDA 1985, the prohibition in r.5.21[20] states that if an officer or employee of a firm is prohibited by the IDA 1985 from effecting a transaction, then the firm shall not effect such a transaction as a principal on its own account. However, the prohibition does not apply where (a) the only reason why that officer or employee was so prohibited was because of his knowledge of the firm's intentions or (b) none of the officers or employees of the firm involved in effecting or arranging for the effecting, of the transaction on behalf of the firm knew or ought to have known of the circumstances giving rise to that prohibition. Embodying a 'Chinese Wall' provision, r.5.21 adds that none of the officers or employees shall be regarded as having a duty to know of those circumstances if (i) arrangements exist within the firm, or within a group which includes the firm, for securing that information obtained by individuals employed in one part of the firm's business or of the group's business, as the case may be, will be withheld from individuals employed in another part of it, and (ii) those officers or employees are individuals from whom information about those circumstances is intended to be withheld under those arrangements.

In terms of enforcement, the effect of this prohibition is to extend liability for insider dealing from officers and employees to the firm itself in circumstances that, in the case of breach, give rise to a different category of sanctions, namely, those available under the FSA 1986. Moreover, the shift from the criminal law to administrative regulation means that the heavy burden of proof under criminal law is not required.

Both exceptions to the prohibition of r.5.21 run parallel with the approach in the IDA 1985. In regard to knowledge of intentions, the IDA 1985 contains a defence for the completion of transactions.[1] Concerning the second, it has been seen that liability under the IDA 1985 largely depends on an individual's knowledge that he is dealing on the basis of unpublished price sensitive information and that an extension of liability to companies would involve provision for a Chinese Wall defence where barriers to internal communication had been erected.[2]

In addition to regulating dealings by the firm and by its officers and employees[3], further provision is made with a view to protecting persons dealing with the firm. In particular, a firm must use its best endeavours that no officer or employee of the firm effects a transaction on behalf of the firm with or for any person if that officer or employee has reason to believe that the effecting of that transaction by that person is prohibited by the IDA 1985.[4]

---

20. AFBD, r.5.17.7; FIMBRA, r.4.24; IMRO, ChIV, r.11.06; TSA, r.570.
1. See, ante, Chapter 3. Criminal Liability.
2. Ibid.
3. See ante I. Restrictions on dealings, C. The Conduct of business rules.
4. Rule 5.21(2); AFBD, r.15.17.1; FIMBRA, r.4.24(2); IMRO, ChIV, r.11.07; TSA, r.570.

(b) ADVICE AND TRANSACTIONS WHICH ARE NOT FULLY DISINTERESTED

An authorised person who undertakes to give investment advice relating to particular securities thereby assumes fiduciary obligations. Yet because authorised persons are generally free to invest in securities on their own account, including those in which their clients are interested, authorised persons may often find themselves in situations of conflict of interest. An example[5] would be where a customer asked his broker to sell his holding of a particular security, but the broker had an interest in persuading the customer not to sell because the broker had a very large position in the securities of the same issuer.

Another example of conflict of interest would arise in the event of an adviser purchasing shares for his own account, then recommending the security to customers and subsequently selling the shares at a profit upon the market price rise following the recommendation. Such an adviser with a large number of clients could be in a position to create his own inside information.

Conflicts of interest arising from an authorised person's advisory functions are accentuated in the case of discretionary fund management. For in performing his discretionary management role, he is making the investment decisions on behalf of the managed funds.

Many situations of conflicts of interest fall outside the scope of insider dealing legislation. However, they can involve advice or transactions by a person with informational advantages, notably as regards either market information or information which is not unpublished price-sensitive information, yet is material to a particular transaction, which are as unerodable as those which fuel calls for insider dealing regulation.

In this context, reference will be made to five main CBRs. These concern: self-dealing and dual agency; disclosure of a firm's material interests in transactions; disclosure of material interests in regard to published recommendations; limitations on a firm's trading because of customers' orders and recommendations based on research and analysis.

(i) *Self dealing and dual agency* . The introduction of dual capacity sharply increased the scope for conflicts of interest for securities firms, notably when itself dealing as principal with a customer or when acting as agent for both counterparties. The regulation of self-dealing and dual agency operates by way of a prohibition on dealing except in certain circumstances where full disclosure is made by the firm and the customer consents to the transaction.

The rule on self-dealing and dual agency[6] prohibits a firm from either (a) buying an investment from, or selling an investment to, a customer as a principal on its own account or as an agent for an associate of the firm, or (b) acting as an agent for a customer in relation to a transaction in which the firm is also acting as an agent for the counterparty, save in certain limited circumstances. These main exceptions[7] are where: (i) the customer has, with full knowledge of

---

5. Cited in a discussion of conflicts of interest by M.Q. Connelly, 'The Licensing of Securities Market Actors', p.1269 at pp1365-1374 in Consumer and Corporate Affairs Canada, *Proposals for a Securities Market Law for Canada*, Vol.3 Background papers (1979).
6. Rule 5.07. This rule enables a firm to comply with the best execution rule (Rule 5.04) when required to do so. Within its scope of application, the best execution rule requires a firm to ensure that a transaction is effected on the best terms available with reliable counterparties. The SRO provisions equivalent to Rule 5.07 are: AFBD, r.5.10; FIMBRA, r.4.14; IMRO, ChIV, r.l0; TSA, r.760.
7. Rule 5.07(i), (ii), (iii) and (v).

the circumstances, given his express agreement to the firms effecting that particular transaction in that particular way, or (ii) in a case within (a) the firm is a market maker in the investment the subject of the transaction or the transaction is entered into for the purpose of enabling the firm or the associate, as the case may be, on the instructions of the customer, to effect a contemporaneous matching transaction with another person, or (iii) the transaction relates to a readily realisable investment and the customer agreement authorises the firm to effect transactions in such investments in that particular way generally and without particular reference to the customer, or (iv) the transaction is effected for a discretionary managed portfolio which is managed by the firm and the authority conferred on the firm by the customer agreement to effect transactions without reference to the customer extends to effecting transactions in that particular way. This rule does not apply where no duty of best execution is owed to a customer under rule 5.04.

(ii) *Disclosure of firm's material interest in transactions.* This rule[8] applies where a firm has directly or indirectly a material interest of any description in a transaction or in the fact of its being effected (other than the interest arising solely from the firm's participation therein), or has a relationship of any description with another person such as to place the firm in a position where its duty to or its interest in relation to that other person conflicts with its duty to the customer. In such circumstances, a firm must neither effect a transaction with or for a customer who is not a market counterparty or an execution-only customer nor recommend the effecting of a transaction with or for a customer who is not a market counterparty save in two situations.[9] These are that either (a) the firm has disclosed to the customer the nature of the firm's interest in the transaction or the nature of the conflict with its duty to the customer and, in the case of the effecting of a transaction, the customer has consented to the transaction's being effected on his behalf, or (b) in the case of the effecting of a transaction on behalf of a customer but without prior reference to him, the firm is authorised by the customer agreement to effect transactions in which the firm has an interest of that description or, as the case may be, a relationship of that description without prior reference to the customer.

Examples of interests requiring disclosure by the firm are set out in a Practice Note. Thus, a material interest in a transaction could arise when either (a) the firm recommends to or effects for a customer a purchase of an investment the issue of which is being underwritten by the firm or (b) the transaction relates to an issue of shares in or debentures of a company and the firm or an associate of the firm is a substantial creditor of the company. A firm has an interest in the fact of a transaction's being effected when the transaction (a) relates to an investment in which the firm is a market maker or (b) concerns a future or an option relating to property of any description and the firm is a dealer in property of that description. For this purpose, the SIB considers disclosure of the fact of being such a market maker or dealer as adequate disclosure of such interests. In addition, a firm is in a position of conflict of duty where the transaction relates to shares in or debentures of a company and the firm is (a) a financial adviser to the company or (b) advising someone who is contemplating a substantial acquisition of shares in the company.

8. Rule 5.08. Equivalent SRO provisions are AFBD, r.5.8; FIMBRA, r.4.7.1; IMRO, ChIV, r.9; TSA, r.570.
9. Rule 5.08(1).

There is a Chinese Wall exception.[10] In particular, the prohibition does not apply when, by reference to the standard Chinese Wall provision, none of the individuals involved in effecting or arranging for the effecting of that transaction or making the recommendation knew or ought to have known of the interest or conflict.

(iii) Disclosure of material interests in regard to published recommendations.   Specific provision for disclosure of material interests is made in regard to published recommendations.[11] This rule applies to any journal, tip-sheet, broker's circular or other publication (including sound broadcasting or television) which is issued at regular intervals from time to time and will or may contain recommendations as to the acquisition, retention or disposal of investments of any description.[12]

The disclosure obligation arises when a relevant publication includes a recommendation concerning an investment of any description and the firm which issues the publication would directly or indirectly have any material interest in any transaction in investments of that description likely to be effected as a result of that recommendation.[13] In such circumstances, the recommendation must be accompanied by a statement disclosing the nature and extent of that interest. To illustrate the circumstances requiring disclosure, a Practice Note cites as examples the situations where (a) the firm recommends the effecting of transactions and will receive commission in respect of such transactions and (b) the firm recommends subscription to the securities of a company and an associate of the firm has a contract to supply raw materials to the company. By way of exception, this rule does not require disclosure when, by reference to the standard Chinese Wall provision, none of the individuals involved in the making of the recommendation knew or ought to have known of that interest.[14]

(iv) limitations on firm's trading because of customers' orders.   Limitations are placed on the freedom of a firm which executes customers' orders[15] to trade on its own account ahead of customers' orders, thereby regulating the conflict between the firm's duty to customers and its own interests and the informational advantage enjoyed by the firm. In particular, where a firm has an instruction from a customer or it has made a decision on behalf of a customer to effect a transaction of sale (or purchase) of an investment of any description and that instruction or decision has not been executed, the firm shall not effect a transaction of sale (or purchase) of an investment of that description as a principal on its own account.[16]

Conflicts between customers are also regulated. In this connection, in the

---

10. Rule 5.08(2).
11. Rule 8.08.
12. Rule 8.01.
13. Rule 8.08(1); but in relation to such interest as arises solely because the firm or an associate carries on investment business which includes effecting transactions for the firm's or the associate's own account in investments of that description or in interests in such investments, it shall, subject to r.8.07 (disclosure of long or short position), be sufficient for the statement to disclose that fact.
14. Rule 8.08(2). In addition, by r.8.08(3), this rule does not require disclosure of the fact that a long or short position exists to be accompanied by disclosure of the extent of that position.
15. Rule 5.15. Equivalent SRO provisions are: AFBD, r.5.9; FIMBRA, r.4.13.4; IMRO, ChIV, r.11.01-11.03; TSA r.410.
16. Rule 5.15(1). Analogous provisions relating to connected customers are contained in Rule 15(2).

above cicumstances, the firm must not effect such a transaction either (a) on behalf of a customer whose instructions to effect the transaction were received at a time later than the time when the unexecuted transactions were received or the unexecuted decision was made or (b) in pursuance of a decision to effect the transaction on behalf of a customer which was taken at a time later than the time when the unexecuted instructions were received or the unexecuted decision was made.[17]

There are various exceptions.[18] With a view to promoting market liquidity, this rule does not prohibit a firm from effecting a transaction because of the existence of an unexecuted instruction or decision if the firm in a recognised market maker in the investment the subject of the transaction and it effects that transaction in accordance with the rules of the relevant recognised or designated investment exchange.[19] The firm may also deal when, by reference to the standard Chinese Wall provision, none of the individuals involved in effecting the transaction knew or ought to have known of the unexecuted instruction or decision.[20] Adding that it is a question of fact in each case whether an individual had a duty to know of an unexecuted transaction, a Practice Note states that it is unlikely that individuals in one branch of a firm would have a duty to know about unexecuted instructions in other branches.

(v) *Recommendations based on research and analysis.* Restrictions are also placed, by r.5.20[1], on the firm's freedom to trade in advance of releasing recommendations based on research and analysis. Prima facie this rule applies in relation to any firm which regularly publishes to its customers or to any class of customers the results of research into or analysis of the factors likely to influence the future performance of investments of any description or recommendations to acquire, hold or dispose of such investments based on such results.[2] However, the breadth of the rule is limited by the proviso that the rule does not apply when what is published is accompanied by a statement that the research and analysis has been procured by the firm for its own purposes and the results of it are being made available to the firm's customers only incidentally.

Subject to two exceptions, the general rule contained in r.5.20(3) is based on a prohibition on certain transactions when a firm, to which r.5.20 applies, has in its possession the results of any such research or analysis as referred to above and has reason to believe that it will or may publish to any of its customers those results or a recommendation based on them to acquire or to dispose of amounts of an investment of any description. In such circumstances, the firm shall not effect or initiate a transaction of purchase (where the recommendation is to acquire or the results would suggest acquisition) or sale (where the recommendation is to dispose of or the results would suggest disposal) in any amount of that investment, either as a principal on its own account or on behalf of a customer whom the firm knows or ought reasonably to know to be a connected customer[3], until the results or recommendations have been published in

17. Rule 5.15(1).
18. Rule 5.15(3).
19. Rule 5.15(3)(c).
20. Rule 5.15(3)(d).
1. Equivalent SRO provisions are: AFBD, r.6.5; FIMBRA, r.4.12.3; IMRO, ChIV, r.11.04-11.05; TSA, r.380.
2. Rule 5.20(1).
3. The term 'connected customer', in relation to a firm, is defined by r.1.04 as meaning any customer of the firm who is (a) a partner of the firm, or (b) an employee of the firm, or (c) an

accordance with r.5.20(2). In general[4], this latter requires publication of the results or recommendations to all customers to whom the firm regularly publishes those results or recommendations.

Not limited to the firm's own results and recommendations, the prohibition on the firm also extends to those of an associate.[5] In particular, when a firm has an associate which is prohibited by r.5.20(3) (or a corresponding rule of a recognised SRO) from purchasing or selling any investment and knows that that associate has in its possession the results of the relevant research or analysis, the firm shall not purchase or sell, as the case may be, any amount of that investment as a principal on its own account or on behalf of any of its customers whom the firm knows or ought reasonably to know to be connected customers.[6]

The two exceptions are very broad. First, the prohibition does not apply in the case of an investment if, by reference to the standard Chinese Wall provision, none of the individuals involved in the sale or purchase of that investment knew or ought to have known of the results of the research and analysis in question.[7] Based on anticipated customer demand, a second exception[8] arises when the firm has reason to believe that publication of a recommendation to acquire an investment of any description, or the results of research and analysis which would suggest such acquisition, would result in customers wishing to purchase amounts of that investment from the firm in such quantities that the firm would be unable to satisfy that demand without itself first purchasing amounts of that investment in the market. In such circumstances, notwithstanding the prohibition in r.5.20(3), the firm may, before it publishes that recommendation or those results, make such purchases of that investment as it reasonably believes (a) to be necessary to enable it to satisfy the expected demand, and (b) will not in themselves significantly increase the prevailing market price of that investment. A disclosure requirement applies to purchases in pursuance of this second exception, with the firm being required to disclose to its customers the fact of having made such purchases when it publishes to them any recommendation to acquire amounts of that investment or the results of research or analysis which would suggest such acquisition.[9]

appointed representative of the firm, or (d) an employee of an appointed representative of the firm, or (e) where the firm is a company, a controller or officer of the firm, or (f) the spouse or infant child or step-child of any individual described above or of a sole trader, or (g) a person in his capacity as trustee of a trust (other than an occupational pension scheme) the beneficiaries of which he knows or ought reasonably to know include any person described above, or (h) a company (other than a regulated insurance company) which is a connected company of the firm.

4. However, there is a broadly drawn exception. For this purpose, a firm need not take the same steps in relation to all such customers so long as (a) it takes such steps in relation to any such customer as the firm has agreed with that customer it will take to communicate such results or recommendations to him, and (b) where the medium of communication is such that it is not possible to publish all such customers simultaneously, those to whom prior publication is made are not selected so as regularly to favour particular customers.

5. The term 'associate', in relation to a firm, is defined by r.1.04 as meaning (a) where the firm is a partnership, a partner in or a manager of the firm, or (b) an appointed representative of the firm, or (c) a connected company of the firm, or (d) where the firm is a company, a controller or officer of the firm.

6. Rule 5.20(5).
7. Rule 5.20(4).
8. Rule 5.20(6).
9. Rule 5.20(7).

(c) THE OPERATION OF CHINESE WALLS

The regularity of references to Chinese Walls in the CBRs is indicative of the reliance placed on Chinese Walls to act as a barrier to information passing between the various parts of multi-service financial organisations, faced with the increased scope for conflicts of interest following Big Bang. The operation of Chinese Walls has, however, given rise to difficulties in practice.[10]

Critics of such multi-service financial organisations now argue that the policing of Chinese Walls has become unduly complex and costly.[11] Coupled with the risk of losing clients when breaches are publicised, these costs outweigh any synergies or returns of scale derived from the establishment of such organisations. Lending some credence to this view, most firms have acknowledged that the synergies have not lived up to initial expectations. Indeed, firms which stayed loyal to their original niches or made limited diversifications have retained or increased their market shares.

The most difficult problems[12] have occurred in relation to departments whose operations cannot be completely segregated, save by undermining the rationale for establishing multi-service financial organisations. For example, stockbroking analysts have been encouraged to supply corporate finance departments with ideas on the possible restructuring of their sectors.

Other weaknesses in Chinese Wall arrangements were highlighted in a 1988 case.[13] A corporate client, A, informed[14] a managing director responsible for corporate finance stockbroking in X, which was a securities subsidiary of a banking group, that it was about to announce the sale of a hotel chain. This was likely to prompt a share price rise. The managing director passed the information to an equity saleswoman, specialising in the sector. To make maximum use of the advance information, she telephoned the analyst for advice on how the sale would affect A's share price. Her telephone conversation was overheard by two market-makers in the sector, who had agreed to sell about £1 million of A's shares, which they had not then bought. This would cost the securities subsidiary about £50,000 when the share price rose. At the end of her telephone conversation, the saleswoman told them that anything they had heard was privileged information and they could not use it to deal before the announcement. Faced with a large potential loss, the market-makers bought £2 million of A's shares from other market-makers, who subsequently complained. The incident, which cost the two market-makers their jobs, was attributable to two factors: the unnecessary passing of information along a line and the design and layout of the securities operation in the temporary building of the securities subsidiary.

The practice of restricted lists[15], adopted by some US investment banks, appears not to have been taken up in the City. This practice consists of publishing a list of restricted securities in which no-one (including market-makers) is allowed to take a position. Some UK firms consider these lists encourage private insider dealing by alerting employees to possible activity in

10. See also 3. The Panel on Take-overs and Mergers.
11. *The Financial Times*, 17th August, 1988; *The Times*, 13th August, 1988 and 16th August, 1988.
12. *The Financial Times*, 17th August, 1988.
13. Ibid.
14. Companies and securities firms claim that such advance calls are made as a courtesy and to prime analysts and market-makers so that they can give considered advice to clients and deal as soon as the announcement is made. However, Stock Exchange regulators consider the practice should end.
15. *The Financial Times*, 17th August, 1988.

the securities. However, US firms often add innocuous securities to the list to reduce this danger.

3. The Panel on Take-overs and Mergers

The Panel has encountered problems in various areas. On occasions, cases before the Panel have led to provisions relating to a problem encountered in practice being incorporated in Notes to the Code. Examples are underwriting immediately before a bid announcement[16] and dealings by financial advisers and published advice.[17] In addition, the Panel issued a statement in 1970[18] relating to the possession of confidential price sensitive information about companies to which an institution acts as corporate advisers or on whose boards members of the firm sit, whilst the institution is also engaged as investment adviser to funds or individual clients whose investment portfolio it manages.

However, the changes in the securities industry, particularly the introduction of dual capacity on the Stock Exchange, entailed fundamental revision of measures relating to conflict of interest.[19] Now contained in an Appendix[20] to the Code, a Guidance Note on conflicts of interest faced by financial advisers identifies two areas where such conflicts may arise, namely, those resulting from the possession of material confidential information or where the adviser is part of a multi-service financial institution.

(a) MATERIAL CONFIDENTIAL INFORMATION

This guidance is concerned with the situation where the adviser is in possession of material confidential information relating to the other party, for example, because it was a previous client or because of involvement in an earlier transaction. The Note states that, in certain circumstances, this may necessitate the financial adviser declining to act, for example, because the information is such that a conflict of interest is likely to arise. In particular, such a conflict may be incapable of resolution simply by isolating information within the relevant organisation or by assigning different personnel to the transaction.[1]

(b) SEGREGATION OF BUSINESS

With the establishment of multi-service financial organisations as a result of

16. Code, Rule 2.3, Note 2; see, ante, Chapter 5. Disclosure, II. Timely disclosure, B. Timing of disclosure, 2. The Code, (b) Secrecy and security. This followed the Panel on Take-overs and Mergers, Statements on Johnson and Firth Brown Limited/Dunford and Elliott Ltd., 6th December, 1976 and 23rd December, 1976.
17. Code, Rule 4, Note 5; see ante I. Restrictions on dealings, B. The Panel on Take-overs and Mergers, 3. Restrictions on insiders. This followed the Panel on Take-overs and Mergers, Statement on Mount Charlotte Investments Ltd./Gale Lister & Co. Ltd., 16th January, 1974; Appeal Committee of the Panel on Take-overs and Mergers, Statement on Mount Charlotte Investments Ltd./Gale Lister & Co. Ltd., 30th January, 1974.
18. The Panel on Take-overs and Mergers, Report on the Year ended 31st March, 1970, pp10-14: Appendix 1, The Use of Confidential Price-Sensitive Information. Non-compliance with these principles was found in the Panel on Take-overs and Mergers, Statement on Chaddesley Investments Limited, 19th December, 1978, as amended 31st January, 1979.
19. The Panel on Take-overs and Mergers, Multi-Service Financial Organisations and the Take-over Code, 6 October 1986.
20. Appendix 3.
1. The problem was considered in the Panel Statement on Tozer, Kemsley & Millbourn (Holdings) Plc./Molins Plc., 30 June 1987.

Big Bang, the Panel had to consider two main issues.[2] One was the extent to which part of such an organisation could deal as principal, whether as market maker or otherwise, in securities of companies involved in a take-over, when another part of the organisation was acting as financial adviser to one of the companies. When part of an organisation was managing funds on a discretionary basis, another issue was the extent to which dealings in securities relevant to a takeover effected by the fund manager on behalf of its clients should have Code consequences.

The Panel's general approach was to allow exempt market-makers and fund managers to continue their operations during the course of an offer, broadly without Code consequences, provided it could be established that those operations were being run wholly independently and, in particular, without regard to the interests of clients of the corporate finance arm.[3] A corollary was that dealings by those persons should be subject to disclosure so that the Panel and others interested in the take-over could be satisfied that those operations were, in practice, being conducted independently. To meet these requirements, important amendments were made to the Code in October 1986.

Without expressly using the term 'Chinese Wall', the Guidance Note states the concepts of 'exempt fund managers'[4] and 'exempt market makers'[5] in the Code are in recognition of the fact that fund management and market making may be conducted on a day-to-day basis quite separately within the same organisation. However, placing the onus on the organisation itself, it adds that it is necessary for such organisations to satisfy the Panel that this is the case. To this end, such organisations are required to arrange their affairs to ensure not only total segregation of those operations, but also that those operations are conducted without regard for the interests of other parts of the same organisation or of their clients. The role of compliance departments of such organisations is emphasised.

In a clear rebuke to a stockbroking and market-making firm for a breach of Chinese Walls, in 1988 the Panel imposed its first suspension of exempt market-making status after investigations disclosed two breaches of Rule 38.1.[6] This states that an exempt market maker connected with an offeror or the offeree company must not carry out any dealings with the purpose of assisting the offeror or the offeree company, as the case may be. In this case, A was a corporate broker to X. The latter faced a contested offer from Y and a recommended offer from Z. In its offer announcement on 8th September, Z stated that it owned 1.45 million shares in X. These were purchased on 6th September. On learning that the purchases were from A, the Panel commenced an investigation. This established no impropriety in the sale of 0.45 million of the shares, sold on behalf of an independent institutional client in the ordinary course of business.

The position concerning the remaining one million shares was different. First, in early September, A's market maker in X contemplated selling half his long position in X's shares of about one million. He identified a securities firm,

2. The Panel on Take-overs and Mergers, Report on the Year ended 31st March, 1987, p.7.
3. Ibid.
4. An exempt fund manager is a person who manages investment accounts on a discretionary basis and is recognised by the Panel as an exempt fund manager for the purposes of the Code: Code, Definitions.
5. An exempt market-maker is a person who is registered as a market maker with the Stock Exchange in relation to the relevant securities, or is accepted by the Panel as a market maker in those securities, and, in either case, is recognised by the Panel as an exempt market maker for the purposes of the Code: Code, Definitions.
6. The Take-over Panel, Raine Industries Plc/Tarmac Plc/Ruberoid Plc., 19th October, 1988.

acting for Y, as probable purchasers. However, a senior director responsible for A's equity market making advised him not to sell to Y because this could reflect on A's position since it acted as corporate broker to X. In the light of Rule 38.1, the Panel found this was clearly a consideration which should not have been taken into account and thus amounted to a breach. Secondly, a few days later, a member of the agency broking team was informed of the market maker's wish to reduce his holding. The broker warned X that a block of its shares was being offered for sale. As a result, it was eventually arranged that the shares were purchased by a broker who it later transpired was acting for Z. A was unaware of the purchaser's identity and Z was not aware of the source of the shares. The Panel considered that in such a situation the corporate finance arm became party to the market-maker's activities and that the activities of all those in the organisation could be taken into account in deciding whether a breach had occurred. Interpreting Rule 38.1 in accordance with the principle of separation it was designed to secure, the Panel found a second breach of the rule.

After emphasising A's full co-operation with the investigation, the Panel concluded that the case 'demonstrated inexperience and incompetence on the part of a number of people within [A] in an area which is of utmost importance to the integrity of the market'. Referring to the serious nature of the breaches, the Panel imposed a three-month suspension of exempt market maker status. During this period, A would be required to satisfy the Panel executive that it had put in place, and was successfully operating, a system which would ensure that there would be no repetition of the breach. The loss of exempt status meant that if during the period of suspension A's broking arm gave financial advice to a company involved in a bid, its market making arm would not be able to deal in those shares. In addition, the Panel had required A to make available to an associate of Y, and provide an underwriting facility in respect of, one million shares on the terms of Y's cash alternative offer.

In this case, it was considered in the financial press[7] that the loss of exempt status, for a firm with less than 30 clients, was not a great hardship. However, in trying to attract new corporate clients, the publicity could prove a hindrance. More generally, the view was expressed:

> 'Times are hard in the broking business, and it cannot be hoped that rule-breaking will be stopped entirely. Reversion to a single capacity jobbing system, for instance, would only solve part of the problem. Corporate advisers will always be tempted to help their clients ... when they command blocks of stock in either bidder or target. Well before Big Bang, it was not unknown for merchant banks to call on funds under management to swing a bid either way, and it will doubtless happen again.'[8]

In dealing with breaches of other parts of Rule 38, the Panel had previously limited itself to criticism of those involved and to requiring them to restore the status quo. A 1988 Panel statement[9] concerned dealings in a cash offer made by A for B. In the weeks following the announcement, X, who were A's brokers, purchased shares on behalf of A amounting to 0.8% of B's issued share capital. The purchases were from Y, the exempt market making subsidiary in a financial services group. A fellow subsidiary of Y was financial adviser to A. The purchases

---

7. *The Financial Times*, 20th October, 1988.
8. Ibid.
9. The Panel on Take-overs and Mergers, Peachey Property Corporation plc./Estates Property Investment Company plc., 17th March, 1988.

breached Rule 38.2, which provides that an offeror and persons acting in concert with it must not deal as principals with an exempt market maker connected with the offeror in relevant securities of the offeree company during the offer period. Its purpose is to ensure that an exempt market maker connected with an offeror does not use its exempt status, under which only limited disclosure of dealings is required, to acquire covertly offeree shares thus benefiting or assisting the offeror. Y was an exempt market-maker connected with A for the purpose of the Code.

The breaches were attributed by the Panel to ineffective communication within X and Y as to their relationships with A and to individuals within X and Y who transacted the bargains not being sufficiently aware of Rule 38.2. Following the Panel's involvement, the shares purchased in breach of Rule 38.2 were sold to investment institutions unconnected with A. The Panel agreed that, notwithstanding Rule 4.2[10], the sale would not prevent A from making any further purchases of B's shares and/or revising the offer. The Panel added that whilst satisfied that the breaches were inadvertent, Rule 38.2 also states that it is generally for the advisers to the offeror to ensure compliance with this Rule rather than the market maker. As the adviser to A which directly initiated the series of purchases in breach of Rule 38.2, the Panel considered that X had primary responsibility and was to be criticised. However, since Y were specifically notified by X of the relevant relationships at the time of the first bargain, Y also had to accept a degree of criticism.

III. ENFORCEMENT

Just as the administrative measures outlined supplement this area of regulation, so their enforcement gives rise to additional sanctions. To assist this enforcement activity, investigative powers are conferred on those responsible for this area of regulation.[11]

A. The Department of Trade and Industry

1. Investment business

In regard to statutory control over investment business, the Department's enforcement role has diminished. Whereas it was responsible for enforcing the narrower licensing requirements of the PFIA 1958 relating to the business of dealing in securities, its delegation to the SIB of responsibility for authorisation to carry on investment business relieves it of the immediate responsibility for this area of enforcement under the FSA 1986.

2. Directors

However, the Department retains enforcement responsibility under the Company Directors Disqualification Act 1986. In particular, the Secretary of State may apply to the High Court for a disqualification order against any person who

10. See, ante, I. Restrictions on dealings, B. The Panel on Take-overs and Mergers.
11. See, post, Chapter 7. Investigation. As consideration of these investigative powers is postponed to that chapter, the emphasis in this section will be on administrative sanctions.

is or has been a director or shadow director of any company when, on the basis of certain reports or information, it appears to the Secretary of State that it is expedient in the public interest that such an order should be made.[12] As to the relevant reports or information, these are either a report by inspectors appointed to investigate, inter alia, a company's affairs or suspected contravention of the insider dealing leglislation, or information obtained under the powers of preliminary investigation into companies or the powers to investigate the affairs of a person carrying on investment business.[13] The court may make a disqualification order when it is satisfied that his conduct in relation to the company makes him unfit to be concerned in its management.[14] The maximum period of disqualification is fifteen years.[15]

B. The Securities and Investments Board

1. Disqualification directions

Where the SIB considers that an individual is not a fit and proper person to be employed in connection with investment business, it may give a direction (a 'disqualification direction') prohibiting that person from employment in investment business, either generally or of a specified kind, without its written consent.[16] The term 'employment' is widely defined to include employment otherwise than under a contract of service[17], thereby extending to those working as 'freelances'. Any consent given by the SIB may be subject to conditions and restrictions and these may be varied.[18]

The expression 'fit and proper' is not defined in the FSA 1986. However, the rule books of individual SROs indicate the type of factors taken into account. In this connection, the TSA considers financial integrity, good reputation and character, absence of convictions, efficiency and honesty, and suitable experience and/or qualifications.[19] In view of these factors, a conviction for insider dealing suggests that a person would not be a 'fit and proper' person for this purpose.

Non-compliance with a disqualification direction is an offence. A person who accepts or continues in employment in contravention of a disqualification direction is liable to a fine not exceeding the fifth level on the standard scale.[20]

Authorised persons have a duty to take reasonable care not to employ or to continue to employ a person in contravention of a disqualification direction. This would be likely to require checking the register of individuals subject to a disqualification direction.[1] Whilst no penalty is specified for breach, the author-

12. Company Directors Disqualification Act 1986, s8(1) and (3).
13. Ie, under: CA 1985, s437; FSA 1986, s177; CA 1985, ss447-448 and FSA 1986, s105 respectively; see, post, Chapter 7. Investigation.
14. Company Directors Disqualification Act 1986, s8(2) and Sch9.
15. Ibid, s8(4).
16. FSA 1986, s59(1). The disqualification direction must specify the date on which it is to take effect and a copy must be served on the person to whom it relates: s59(2).
17. FSA 1986, s59(8).
18. Ibid, s59(3). Where the SIB proposes to give a disqualification direction or to refuse an application for its consent or the variation of consent, it must give written notice of its intention, giving its reasons and particulars of the person's right to have the case referred to the Financial Services Tribunal: s59(4).
19 TSA, ChXI.
20. FSA 1986, s59(5).
1. Established under s102(1)(e), FSA 1986.

ised person could be liable to disciplinary measures by his professional body and to the sanctions contained in ss 60-62, FSA 1986.[2]

2. Public statement as to person's misconduct

The SIB has a power to publish a statement by a person holding an authorisation granted by it or an authorisation in another Member State.[3] However, as this power does not extend to members of an SRO or persons certified by an RPB (who are subject to the disciplinary rules of that organisation), it is of limited importance. Before publishing such a statement, the SIB must give the person concerned written notice of the proposed statement and of the reasons for which it proposes to act.[4] Where another person is identified in the notice in a way that might prejudice him in any office or employment, the SIB must also serve a notice on him unless it considers this impracticable.[5] There is a right of referral to the Financial Services Tribunal.[6]

3. Injunctions and restitution orders

Concerning injunctions, the SIB may apply to the High Court for an injunction to restrain the contravention of its conduct of business or other rules, the statutory provisions relating to misleading statements and practices, the unsolicited calls regulations, the restrictions on advertising or the prohibition on employment of individuals who are not a fit and proper person.[7] Alternatively, an order may be made requiring the person concerned to take steps to remedy the contravention.[8] An injunction may also be obtained in relation to a breach of the rules of a recognised SRO, professional body, investment exchange or clearing house, but only in circumstances where the relevant body is unable or unwilling to take appropriate steps to restrain or to remedy the contravention.[9] In the context of insider dealing regulation, the relevance of this remedy lies primarily in the field of preventive measures, such as disclosure. Thus, in the event of non-disclosure, an order could contribute to improved compliance procedures.

In regard to restriction orders, the High Court may, on an application by the SIB, require any authorised person who has contravened these provisions to pay into court, or appoint a receiver to recover from him, a prescribed sum for distribution to investors who have suffered loss as a consequence.[10] The prescribed sum is calculated by reference to the profits which have accrued to the authorised person as a result of the contravention and/or the loss or other adverse effect suffered by investors.[11] As to distribution, any amount paid into court by, or recovered from, a person in pursuance of a restitution order shall be paid out to such person or distributed among such persons as the court may

2. As to s62 (action for damage), see Chapter 4. Civil liability, IV. Breach of statutory duty. As to ss60 and 61, see below.
3. FSA 1986, s60(1).
4. Ibid, s60(2).
5. Ibid, s60(3).
6. Ibid, s60(4).
7. Ibid, s61(1)(a)(i)-(iii), (b) and (c).
8. Ibid, s61(1).
9. Ibid, s61(1)(a)(iv), (2).
10. Ibid, s61(4).
11. Ibid, s61(3).

direct, being a person or persons appearing to the court to have entered into transactions with that person as a result of which the profits concerned have accrued to him or the loss or adverse effect has been suffered.[12] For these purposes, the court may require the person concerned to furnish it with accounts and other information which may need to be verified.[13]

A restitution order offers limited scope for the recovery of insider dealing profits. In particular, it provides a mechanism for payment into court and resulting profits. It is, however, limited to a breach of rules by an authorised person and so would not extend to dealings by employees for their own account. Moreover, as distinct from involving the identification of those who deal contemporaneously with an insider, distribution cannot be made in circumstances where those who have suffered loss as a result of the contravention cannot be identified. Their identification is not, however, a prerequisite to payment of the prescribed sum into court.

C. The Self-Regulating Organisations

In accordance with the statutory requirement to have adequate arrangements and resources for monitoring and enforcement of compliance with its rules and any other relevant investment business rules[14], the rulebooks of individual SROs contain a variety of disciplinary sanctions and powers of intervention in a member's business. Provision is also made for an appeals procedure against the exercise of these powers.[15] In turn, the outcome of an SRO investigation may be notified to other regulatory authorities, notably the Department or the SIB.[16]

As to disciplinary sanctions, an SRO may, in order of severity, give recommendations or advice, issue written reprimands or censure (which may be made public) and suspend or expel members.[17] A fine may also be imposed.

In regard to powers of intervention[18], an SRO may prohibit member firms from entering into transactions of a specified kind, soliciting business from persons of a specified kind or carrying on business either in a specified manner or otherwise than in a specified manner. An SRO may also require a member to refrain from disposing of or otherwise dealing with any of its assets or any of its specified assets. In addition, it may require that assets of a particular value be maintained in the UK or that assets of a specified class or description be transferred to a trustee appointed by the SRO.

D. The Stock Exchange

1. Members

Of the penalties available[19], resort was had to expulsion in a case following

12. Ibid, s61(6).
13. Ibid, s61(7).
14. FSA 1986, Sch2. para4.
15. AFBD, r.9.1.6; FIMBRA, r.19, IMRO, ChVIII. r.7.09; TSA, ChV, r.70.
16. AFBD, r.9.2.6(f); FIMBRA, r.20.2; IMRO, ChVIII, r.3.03; TSA, ChV.r.30.01.
17. AFBD, r.9.4.6., r.9.9, r.9.10; FIMBRA, r.18.8; IMRO, ChVIII, r.7.07, r.13.07; ChV. r.40.14.
18. AFBD, r.9.7; FIMBRA, r.17.2; IMRO, ChVIII, r.4.5; TSA, r.60.01-60.11.
19. See, ante, Chapter 2. The Regulatory Framework, IX. Recognised investment exchanges and clearing houses, A. Recognised investment exchanges, 1. The International Stock Exchange.

conviction of a member under the IDA 1985.[20] This case concerned the joint managing director of the securities arm in a merchant banking group.[1]

2. *Listed companies*

Non-compliance with the continuing obligations of the listing requirements, notably in regard to disclosure, may lead to a suspension of listing.[2] Stock Exchange members are not permitted to deal in the suspended securities.[3]

However, the main impact of this sanction may not be felt by those responsible for the breach. Suspension deprives shareholders of the use of the market of the Stock Exchange and of the ready availability of an up-to-date price for their securities there. Accordingly, the sanction of suspension of listing is 'not lightly exercised'.[4]

E. The Panel on Take-overs and Mergers

Reference has been made to the sanctions available to the Panel and to their application in the context of the Code prohibition on dealings by insiders.[5] It has also been seen that sanctions may be imposed in the event of breach of Code insider reporting requirements[6] and conflict of interest provisions.[7]

---

20. (1987) 137 N.L.J. 1034.
1. See, ante, Chapter 3. Criminal Liability.
2. Admission of Securities to Listing, Section 5, Chapter 1.
3. The Rules of the International Stock Exchange, r.535.1.
4. The Stock Exchange Quotations Department, Review of the Year to 31st March, 1983, p.4.
5. See ante I. Restrictions on dealings, B. The Panel on Take-overs and Mergers.
6. See, ante, Chapter 5. Disclosure, III. Insider reporting, E. Sanctions and enforcement.
7. See ante II. Standards of conduct for investment business, B. Conflicts of interest, 3. The Panel on Take-overs and Mergers.

Chapter 7

Investigation

In view of the emphasis on collective enforcement, the investigative powers and activities of the regulatory authorities are central to the effectiveness of insider dealing requirements. Apart from discovering information that may be used in subsequent proceedings, their investigations provide information on which to base decisions about regulatory developments.

Even when rights of action are conferred on individuals, such investigative powers and activities retain their importance. In many cases, the complexity of transactions and use of nominees precludes investigation by individuals since the costs of investigation are disproportionate to the sums involved.

However, the optimal distribution of investigative resources requires a balance in the distribution of responsibilities. Due to their expertise and authority, there are often cost advantages in investigations by regulatory authorities. Moreover, the costs can be set against the wider public benefits sought. Nevertheless, limits are placed on their investigative activities by civil liberties considerations and by available resources. High costs thus impose selective investigation. Yet when supported by sufficient resources or authority, others may be as well placed to obtain information, thereby relieving the pressures on regulatory authorities and contributing to the more efficient and equitable use of the latter's investigative resources. Examples of the extension of investigative powers beyond those conferred on the regulatory authorities are those conferred on companies to investigate interests in shares and the stricter reporting requirements imposed on auditors.

This distribution of investigative responsibilities for insider dealing was significantly altered as a result of the general legislation, enacted in 1980, imposing a prohibition on insider dealing, enforceable by criminal penalties. Previously, the main investigative tasks were performed by the Stock Exchange and Panel for the purpose of administrative enforcement. The reports of inspectors appointed by the Department also contained details of insider transactions, but these findings were more a source of information about insider practices than a preliminary to enforcement.

Following the CA 1980, the Department became the main authority responsible for investigating suspected breaches of the legislation, though it is reliant on the Stock Exchange for key aspects of the investigation in the early stages, namely, market surveillance and collection of details of dealings. Subsequently, the Department's investigative role was strengthened by the FSA 1986 empowering it to appoint inspectors to investigate suspected insider dealing offences. Moreover, any findings of insider dealing in apparent breach of the legislation (now contained in the IDA 1985) set out in the reports of inspectors appointed by the Department under the CA 1985 have more significant enforcement implications. In addition, the increased powers conferred on companies to require information with respect to interests in its voting shares enhance the role of company investigations in the enforcement of reporting requirements. Apart from the Department, control over prosecutions is also conferred on the

DPP whose lack of investigative staff could result in police involvement in investigations. Moreover, with the establishment of the Serious Fraud Office by the Criminal Justice Act 1987, investigators acting under the powers conferred by that Act may in the course of investigations find circumstances suggesting insider dealing.

In contrast, the role of self-regulatory bodies in investigations was diminished due to the overlap of administrative prohibitions with the prohibitions, enforceable by criminal penalties, introduced by the CA 1980. In particular, the scope of Panel investigations was reduced to matters associated with the criminal prohibitions, such as leaks of information, the timing of bid announcements and reporting requirements under the Code.

Evaluation of investigative powers and activities thus requires consideration of the role of the Department, the Serious Fraud Office, the Police, the Securities and Investments Board, the Self-Regulating Organisations, the Stock Exchange, the Panel and companies. International aspects will also be considered.

I. THE DEPARTMENT OF TRADE AND INDUSTRY

As the Government department concerned with trade and commerce, the Department has a key role in the enforcement of legislation relating to companies and the securities markets. In investigating suspected non-compliance, the Department has statutory powers which (a) confer powers of preliminary investigation[1], enabling it to call for a company's books or papers and (b) authorise it to appoint an inspector to investigate the affairs[2] or ownership[3] of a company, certain dealings in securities by directors[4] and, since 1986, insider dealing[5].

As to the exercise of these powers, it has been Departmental practice to conduct a preliminary investigation into about 25% of applications[6]. However, appointments of inspectors to investigate the affairs or ownership of a company or certain dealings in securities by directors have traditionally been infrequent. In the period 1948-1986, 218 appointments were made with the annual average in the 1980s being four[7].

The issue of investigative powers aroused particular controversy in relation to enforcement of the insider dealing provisions introduced by the CA 1980. In contrast to the 1978 Bill, the CA 1980 did not contain power to appoint an inspector to investigate suspected breaches. However, in the FSA 1986, provision was made both for the Department to appoint inspectors to investigate cases of suspected insider dealing[8] and for the issue of search warrants[9].

After reviewing the Department's investigation powers and procedures, the Secretary of State announced four main conclusions in 1988[10]. First, the present

1. CA 1985, s447.
2. Ibid, ss431-432.
3. Ibid, s442.
4. Ibid, s446.
5. FSA 1986, s177.
6. Department of Trade and Industry, Handbook of the Companies Inspection System (1986), Appendix A.
7. Ibid; Department of Trade and Industry, Companies in 1986-87 (1987), p.19.
8. FSA 1986, s177.
9. Ibid, s199.
10. Department of Trade and Industry, Press Notice, Review of Investigation Powers under Companies and Financial Services Acts, 11 May, 1988.

range of investigation powers would be retained, though there was a need for more scope and flexibility in their use. Secondly, the powers of preliminary investigation should be extended and strengthened. Thirdly, the appointment of inspectors under the FSA 1986 to investigate suspected insider dealing would not normally be announced except when in the public interest; in contrast, major investigation under the CA 1985 into the affairs or ownership of a company would continue to be announced. Fourthly, increased resources would be devoted to investigation work and the Department's key enforcement activities would be reorganised. The proposals required some amendments to legislation and these would be introduced on the next convenient occasion.

A. Preliminary investigations

With a view to making better use of investigative resources, the power to inspect companies' books or papers introduced by the CA 1967 enables the Department to require production of documents without appointing an inspector. Under this power, the Department may at any time, if it thinks there is good reason to do so, give directions to a company[11] requiring it, at such time and place as may be specified in the directions, to produce such books or papers as may be so specified or authorise an officer of the Department to require the company, to produce to him forthwith any books or papers which he may specify[12]. Such directions may also be made to any person who appears to be in possession of the books or papers[13].

The power includes a power to take copies of or extracts from books or papers[14], to require the person in possession or a past or present officer or employee of the company to provide an explanation of any of them[15] and if the books or papers are not produced, to require the person who was required to produce them to state to the best of his knowledge and belief where they are[16]. A statement made by a person in compliance with any such requirement may be used in evidence against him[17].

In regard to the appointment of officers to exercise these powers, it seems that there is no need for the rules of natural justice to be observed. In particular, a company or other person is not entitled to advance warning[18]. But in the exercise of these powers, directions to produce documents must not be unreasonable or excessive and officers giving the notice must act fairly[19].

Non-compliance with the requirements to produce documents or to provide an explanation or to make a statement is an offence[20]; but it is a defence for a company or other person required to produce books or papers to prove that they were not in his possession or under his control and that it was not reasonably practicable for him to produce them[1]. In addition, it is an offence for a person knowingly or recklessly to make a false explanation or statement in

11. The bodies subject to such directions are set out in CA 1985, s447(1).
12. CA 1985, s447(2) and (3).
13. Ibid, s447(4).
14. Ibid, s447(5)(a)(i).
15. Ibid, s447(5)(a)(ii).
16. Ibid, s447(5)(b).
17. Ibid, s447(8).
18. *Norwest Holst Ltd. v Secretary of State for Trade* [1978] Ch 201.
19. *R v Secretary of State for Trade, ex p Perestrello* [1981] Q.B.19; [1980] 3 All E.R.28.
20. CA 1985, s447(6).
1. Ibid, s447(7).

purported compliance with these requirements[2]. Irrespective of whether a direction has been made by the Department, it is also an offence for an officer of a company (a) to destroy, mutilate or falsify a document affecting the company's property or affairs, or to be a party thereto, unless he proves that he had no intention to conceal the state of affairs of the company or to defeat the law or (b) fraudulently to part with, alter or make an omission from any such document or to be a party thereto[3].

The power to require production of documents is also supported by one for entry and search of premises[4]. When a Justice of the Peace (J.P.) is satisfied that there are reasonable grounds for suspecting that there are on any premises any books or papers of which production has been required by virtue of the CA 1985[5] and which have not been produced in connection therewith, he may issue a warrant for the entry and search of premises and for seizure of such documents. The documents may be retained for three months or until the conclusion of criminal proceedings commenced under specific statutes, including the IDA 1985[6].

A saving is made for privileged information. As to legal professional privilege, nothing in the provisions relating to seizure of books and papers compels the production by any person of a document which he would in High Court proceedings be entitled to refuse to produce on grounds of legal professional privilege or authorises the taking of possession of any such document which is in his possession[7]. Less extensive protection is afforded to bankers who are not required to produce a document relating to the affairs of a customer unless either (a) this appears necessary to the Department for the purpose of investigating the affairs of the banker or (b) the customer is a person on whom a requirement to produce documents, provide an explanation or make a statement has been imposed by specific statutory provisions[8]

Restrictions are imposed on the use of information obtained under these powers. Apart from when made to a competent authority or with the company's previous written consent, disclosure is not permitted unless required:[9] (a) with a view to the institution of or otherwise for the purposes of criminal proceedings, (b) with a view to the institution of, or otherwise for the purposes of, proceedings on an application under ss6-8, Company Directors Disqualification Act 1986; (c) for the purposes of the examination of any person by inspectors appointed to investigate the affairs[10] or ownership[11] of a company or certain dealings in securities by directors[12], in the course of their investigations; (d) for the purpose of enabling the Secretary of State to exercise in relation to that or any other body, any of his functions under the CA 1985, the IDA 1985, the Insurance Companies Act 1982, the Insolvency Act 1986, the Company Directors Disqualification Act 1986 or the FSA 1986[13]; (e) for the purposes of

2. Ibid, s451.
3. Ibid, s450.
4. Ibid, s448.
5. Ibid, s447.
6. Ibid, s448(4).
7. Ibid, s452(2).
8. Ibid, s452(3). The specific statutory provisions are CA 1985, s447 and the Insurance Companies Act 1982, s44(2)-(4).
9. CA 1985, s449 as amended by FSA 1986, Sch13, para9(1). In addition, publication or disclosure is not precluded in the circumstances specified in s449(1A) CA 1985, inserted by para9(2), Sch13 FSA 1986.
10. CA 1985, ss431 and 432.
11. Ibid, s442.
12. Ibid, s446.
13. An analogous provision in relation to Northern Ireland is contained in s449(1)(dd) CA 1985.

proceedings under the power to enter and search premises[14]; (f) for the purpose of enabling certain persons, including the Bank of England, the Deposit Protection Board, the Insurance Brokers Registration Council, an official receiver and a recognised professional body under the Insolvency Act 1986, to discharge various specified functions[15]; (g) for any purpose mentioned in s.180 (1)(b), (e), (h), (n) or (p), FSA 1986; (h) with a view to the institution of, or otherwise for the purposes of, any disciplinary proceedings relating to the exercise by a solicitor, auditor, accountant, valuer or actuary of his professional duties and (i) for the purpose of enabling or assisting an authority in a country or territory outside the UK to exercise corresponding supervisory functions[16]. Disclosure in breach of this provision is an offence[17]. A 'competent authority' includes the Secretary of State, an inspector appointed by the Department under the CA 1985[18], the Treasury or an officer of the Treasury, the Bank of England or an officer or servant of the Bank, the Lord Advocate, the DPP, the SIB or an officer or servant of the SIB, a person appointed or authorised to exercise specified investigative powers under ss.94, 106 or 177, FSA 1986 (ie including investigations into insider dealing) or any officer or servant of such a person, the body administering a compensation fund under the FSA 1986 or any officer or servant of such a body, the Chief Registrar of Friendly Societies and the Industrial Assurance Commissioner or any officer or servant of either of them, or any constable and procurator fiscal[19].

A discretionary power of disclosure is conferred on the Secretary of State[20]. Under this power, he may, if he thinks fit, disclose any information obtained under the provisions of the CA 1985 (ss431-453) for the investigation of companies and their affairs and for the requisition of documents to (a) any person who is a competent authority[1] or (b) in any circumstances in which or for any purpose for which the provisions imposing restrictions on the use of information obtained under the power of preliminary investigation do not preclude the disclosure of information.

Nevertheless, disclosure is not permitted for use in evidence in civil proceedings generally. Preliminary investigations are not a substitute for the absence of a simplified court procedure for the supply of information to, or access to records for, shareholders.

However, in other respects, the power of preliminary investigation is free of the restrictions and difficulties associated with a full investigation. First, there is no need to bring the case within the specific heads required for the appointment of an inspector[2]. Instead, the Department can give directions provided it thinks there is 'good reason' to do so. There is no statutory definition of 'good reason', though limits, albeit not exhaustive on its discretion were summarised in the *Perestrello* case[3]. In practice, 'good reason' is taken to include grounds for suspicion of fraud, misfeasance, misconduct, conduct unfairly

14. CA 1985, s448.
15. Namely, those specified in s449(1)(f), (g), (i), (j) and (k), CA 1985 (inserted by para9(1)(c), Sch13, FSA 1986).
16. For the definition of 'corresponding supervisory functions', see s449(1A) CA 1985 inserted by para9(2), Sch13 FSA 1986.
17. CA 1985, s449(2).
18. Under ss431-453, CA 1985.
19. CA 1985, s449(3), as substituted by para9(3), Sch13, FSA 1986.
20. CA 1985, s451A, inserted by para10, Sch13 FSA 1986.
1. For the purpose of s449, CA 1985.
2. As under CA 1985, s432; see post.
3. *R v Secretary of State for Trade, ex p Perestrello* [1981] Q.B.19; [1980] 3 All E.R.28.

prejudicial to shareholders or failure to provide shareholders with information they may reasonably expect[4].

Secondly, the exercise of this power does not strain administrative resources to the same extent as full investigations by outside inspectors. Whereas full investigations may last several years, preliminary investigations are usually completed within a few weeks[5].

Thirdly, the power of preliminary investigation enables the Department to make enquiries more discreetly than by appointing an inspector[6]. A public announcement is made when inspectors have been appointed to investigate a public limited company[7].

B. Investigations by inspectors

More extensive powers are conferred on the Department to investigate a company's affairs[8], the ownership of a company[9], certain dealings in securities by directors[10] and insider dealing[11]. Such investigations are carried out by one or more inspectors appointed by the Department, though investigations into company ownership may be carried out by the Department without appointing an inspector[12].

1. Investigation into the affairs of a company

(a) THE APPOINTMENT OF INSPECTORS

Whilst a distinction can be drawn between the mandatory duty to appoint inspectors and discretionary powers of appointment, the mandatory duty is of little practical significance and applicants are usually reliant on the Department's discretionary powers. Hence, the exercise of its discretion assumes particular importance.

(i) The mandatory duty of appointment. The Department's mandatory duty to appoint one or more competent inspectors arises only when the court by order declares that the company's affairs ought to be so investigated[13]. But this is a more expensive procedure than an application to the Department to exercise its discretionary powers. Moreover, for a court order to be made it seems that applicants must show a prima facie case for investigation[14]. In one case the declaration of a $7^{1}/_{2}\%$ dividend during a period when the company's losses amounted to nearly £1 million was held to be sufficient[15]. Little use is made of

---

4. Department of Trade and Industry, Handbook of the Companies Inspection System (1986), para10.
5. Ibid.
6. Ibid, para9.
7. Ibid, para18.
8. CA 1985, ss431-441.
9. Ibid, ss442-445.
10. Ibid, s446.
11. FSA 1986, ss177-178.
12. CA 1985, s444.
13. Ibid, s432(1)..
14. *Re Miles Aircraft Ltd. (No.2)* [1948] W.N.178
15. Ibid.

this provision.

(ii) Discretionary powers of appointment.   Discretionary powers of appointment are conferred on the Department both on an application by members or the company and on its own initiative. To a considerable extent, these powers overlap.

As to the former, the Department may appoint inspectors upon the application of 200 or more members, of members holding one-tenth of the issued shares[16], or of the company[17]. The application must be supported by such evidence as the Department may require for the purpose of showing that the applicants have good reason for requiring the investigation[18]. The Department can also require security for costs, to an amount not exceeding £5,000 or such other sum as the Secretary of State may by order specify[19]. However, this power has been little used because, on receipt of an application, the Department has normally proceeded to consider the matter under its other discretionary power of appointment[20].

Of greater practical importance, its other discretionary power enables the Department to appoint inspectors to investigate a company's affairs when there are circumstances suggesting that: (a) the company's affairs are being or have been conducted with intent to defraud its creditors or the creditors of any other person, or otherwise for a fraudulent or unlawful purpose, or in a manner that is unfairly prejudicial to some part of its members;[1] (b) any actual or proposed act or omission of the company, (including an act or omission on its behalf), is or would be so prejudicial, or the company was formed for any fraudulent or unlawful purpose[2]; (c) the persons concerned with the company's formation or the management of its affairs have in connection therewith been guilty of fraud, misfeasance or other misconduct towards it or its members[3] or (d) the company's members have not been given all the information with respect to its affairs which they might reasonably expect[4].

In regard to this last head, inspectors have referred in reports[5] to the obligation on directors to disclose all relevant information to shareholders which may be inferred from the power of appointment under this head. In turn, this points to the importance of investigation in improving disclosure[6] and thus

---

16. Where the company does not have a share capital, the application must be made by not less than one-fifth of registered members.
17. CA 1985, s431(2).
18. Ibid, s431(3).
19. Ibid, s431(4).
20. The Company Law Committee (Chairman: Lord Justice Jenkins), Minutes of Evidence (1962), para6946. At that time, such application could only be made by members, the provision for application by a company being subsequently introduced by s86(1), CA 1981.
1. CA 1985, s432(2)(a). By s432(4), this reference to 'members' includes any person who is not a member, but to whom shares in the company have been transferred or transmitted by operation of law.
2. CA 1985, s432(2)(b).
3. Ibid, s432(2)(c).
4. Ibid, s432(2)(d).
5. First Re-Investment Trust Ltd., Nelson Financial Trust Ltd., English and Scottish Unit Trust Holdings Ltd., Interim Report by D.C.H. Hirst, Q.C. and R.N.D. Langdon, F.C.A. (1974); Australian Estates Ltd., First Re-Investment Trust Ltd., Nelson Financial Trust Ltd., English and Scottish Unit Trust Holdings Ltd., Second and Final Report by D.C.H. Hirst, Q.C. and R.N.D. Langdon, F.C.A. (1975); Ferguson and General Investments Ltd., (formerly known as Dowgate and General Investments Ltd.); C.S.T. Investments Ltd., Report by J. Jackson, Q.C. and K.L. Young, T.D., FCA (1979).
6. T. Hadden, 'Fraud in the City: Enforcing the Rules' (1980) 1 Co. Law 9 at 12

contributing to the efficient and fair operation of the securities markets.

Inspectors' powers also extend to related companies. If inspectors appointed to investigate a company's affairs[7] think it necessary for the purposes of their investigation to investigate the affairs of any body corporate which is or at any relevant time has been the company's subsidiary or holding company, or a subsidiary of its holding company or a holding company of its subsidiary, they have power to do so[8]. Moreover, they must report on the affairs of the other body corporate so far as they think the results of their investigation of its affairs are relevant to the investigation of the affairs of the first-mentioned company[9].

(iii) Exercise of the discretion to investigate.   The Department's cautious approach to the exercise of its discretion is evidenced by the low numbers of appointments in relation to applications received. In 1986, it received 496 applications for an investigation, ordered a preliminary investigation in 133 cases and in five cases appointed inspectors to investigate[10].

In deciding whether to appoint inspectors, the Department's discretion is unqualified. The exercise of its discretion is ultimately determined by the circumstances of each case. Hence the decision is not readily susceptible to control by the courts.

Indeed, the principal challenge to the exercise of the Department's discretion arose following a decision to appoint inspectors, not a refusal to do so. In *Norwest Holst Ltd. v Secretary of State for Trade*[11], the company applied for a declaration that the inspectors' appointment was ultra vires and of no effect and for an injunction to restrain them from beginning their investigation. In the High Court, the action was struck out on the ground that it was frivolous, vexatious and an abuse of the process of the court. In contrast to the Department's view of the purpose of an investigation, Foster J. stated 'the words "circumstances suggesting" do not in my judgment amount to a prima facie case but something much less'[12].

Dismissing the company's appeal, the Court of Appeal held that the Department's decision was no more than an administrative decision, the effect of which was to set in train an investigation at which those involved would have an opportunity of stating their case. There was, therefore, nothing in the rules of natural justice which required the Department to give the company an opportunity of stating its case before deciding to set up the investigation. The only requirement was that the decision should be made in good faith and, in this case, there was no evidence to the contrary. On the question of judicial review of the exercise of the Secretary of State's discretion, Ormrod, L.J. stated:

'Once it is held that the Secretary of State is not obliged in accordance with the ordinary principles of justice to disclose the information on which he has exercised his discretion, it must follow that the company cannot establish a prima facie case for reviewing the discretion unless, of course, the Secretary of State has already disclosed all the material on which he has based his decision, which he clearly has not done'[13].

7. Ie, under ss431-432, CA 1985.
8. CA 1985, s433(1).
9. Ibid.
10. Department of Trade and Industry, Companies in 1986-87 (1987), p.19.
11. [1978] Ch 201.
12. Ibid at 289.
13. Ibid at 295.

Illustrative of the courts' conservative view of the jurisdiction to review discretionary powers[14], the case also emphasised the difficulties of challenging the Department's exercise of its discretion in the courts on the grounds of illegality.

However, the other form of control, namely, a political one by Parliament concerned with the merits of intra vires decisions, has proved illusory. Under the doctrine of ministerial responsibility, the Secretary of State is answerable to Parliament for decisions made under discretionary powers. As the policy content of a particular decision is usually insufficient to give rise to a debate, MPs have traditionally relied on two other methods. First, questions may be raised in the House of Commons. Ill-suited to modern administrative practice, their limited usefulness has been more apparent as a means of obtaining information about policy than of challenging particular decisions. Secondly, MPs may ask the Minister responsible for an explanation. Based on informal contacts between MPs and Departments, this procedure is more likely to result in clarification of the reasons for a particular decision than in its reversal.

Acknowledging the ineffectiveness of these methods, the office of Parliamentary Commissioner for Administration, (the 'Ombudsman'), was created by statute[15] in 1967 in an attempt to improve control of particular decisions. On occasions, the Ombudsman has considered the Department's discretionary powers to appoint an inspector[16]. His reports are instructive both for the way the discretion is exercised and his view of the relevant policies and procedures. But they have not resulted in more frequent appointments.

However, criticism of the Department's failure to exercise its discretion is merely one aspect of dissatisfaction with the inspection system. Even when inspectors are appointed, further criticisms concern the conduct of and the results of investigation.

(b) THE CONDUCT OF INVESTIGATIONS

The main criticisms of the conduct of investigations highlight conflicting considerations. On the one hand, the effectiveness of an investigation requires that extensive powers be conferred on inspectors. On the other hand, extensive powers and the potentially onerous consequences of an investigation have given rise to concern about safeguards for those under investigation.

(i) Production of documents and evidence.   Inspectors' powers to obtain evidence from officers or agents of the company, and of any other company whose affairs are investigated as a related company, derive from the duty of all such persons to produce all books and documents of or relating to the company, or the related company[17], which are in their custody or power, to attend before the inspector when required to do so and otherwise to give inspectors all assistance in connection with the investigation which they are reasonably able to give[18]. An inspector may also examine them on oath and administer an oath accordingly[19]. For this purpose, extended meanings are given to 'officers or agents' to include

14. *De Smith: Judicial Review of Administrative Action*, Fourth Edition by J.M. Evans (1980), p.297.
15. Parliamentary Commissioner Act 1967.
16. Case C.107/B, Fourth Report of the Parliamentary Commissioner (1971-72), H.C.490, p.209; First Report of the Parliamentary Commissioner (1972-73), H.C.1188, p.169.
17. As defined by s433(1), CA 1985.
18. CA 1985, s434(1).
19. Ibid, s434(3).

past, as well as present, officers[20] or agents and to 'agents' to include bankers, solicitors and auditors[1]. A receiver and manager may also be the agent of the company[2], but 'agent' does not include a company's counsel acting as such[3].

Following a 1981 amendment[4], the range of persons under a duty to assist inspectors was extended to persons other than officers and agents. In this regard, when inspectors consider a person other than an officer or agent of the company or other body corporate is or may be in possession of information concerning its affairs, they may require that person to produce to them any books or documents in his custody or power relating to the company or other body corporate, to attend before them and otherwise to give them all reasonable assistance with the investigation[5]. Such persons may likewise be examined on oath[6]. They can include stockbrokers, market-makers and other financial intermediaries.

As regards directors' bank accounts, inspectors are authorised to require a director or past director of a company or related company under investigation to produce all documents in his possession or control relating to a bank account of any description[7]. The account may be maintained alone or jointly with another person and in Britain or elsewhere. For the power to be exerciseable, an inspector must have reasonable grounds to believe that payments have been made in or out of a specific account in respect of any one or more of the following: (a) failure to disclose directors' emoluments[8]; (b) any money which has resulted from or been used in the financing of an undisclosed transaction, arrangement or agreement, or (c) any money which has been in any way connected with an act or omission, or series of acts or omissions, which on the part of that director constituted misconduct (whether fraudulent or not) towards the company or body corporate or its members. In this connection, an 'undisclosed' transaction, arrangement or agreement is one: (a) particulars of which should have been[9] but were not disclosed in the accounts, namely, in regard to substantial contracts between companies and their directors or persons connected with a director; (b) in respect of which an amount outstanding was not included in the aggregate amounts required to be disclosed in the accounts under statutory provisions relating to transactions between recognised banks and their directors[10], or (c) particulars of which were not included in the register of transactions[11]. These powers are wide enough to give inspectors access when there is prima facie evidence of imprudence or negligence.

However, they are also subject to several limitations[12]. First, the requirement of reasonable grounds renders the exercise of the powers susceptible to challenge by judicial review[13]. Secondly, inspectors must specify the account in

---

20. By CA 1985, s744 'officer' includes a director, manager or secretary.
1. CA 1985, s434(4).
2. Per Winn J. in *R. v Board of Trade, ex parte St. Martin's Preserving Co. Ltd.* [1965] 1 QB 603.
3. CA 1985, s744.
4. CA 1981, s87(1).
5. CA 1985, s434(2).
6. Ibid, s434(3).
7. Ibid, s435.
8. Ibid, Sch5, paras24-26.
9. Ibid, s232 and Sch6, Part I.
10. Ibid, s234 and Sch6, part III.
11. Ibid, s343.
12. D. Chaikin, 'The Companies Act 1981' (1982) 3 Co. Law 115 at 116-117.
13. *R. v IRC, ex p Rossminster Ltd.* [1980] AC 952, which overruled *Liversidge v Anderson* [1942] A.C.206.

question. But in the absence of a duty on directors to identify bank accounts in which they are interested, inspectors will often be unable to ascertain the point of deposit of an unaccounted flow of money. Thirdly, inspectors are likely to encounter insuperable difficulties in identifying accounts held by a director's nominee or situate overseas[14]. Fourthly, a saving for banks precludes inspectors obtaining information from banks about a director's own account, even when the director is in breach of these requirements.

Non-compliance with the provisions for the production of documents and evidence is not itself a criminal offence. Instead, if a person required to assist inspectors refuses (a) to produce any book or document, (including in relation to directors' bank accounts), which it is his duty[15] to produce, (b) to attend before inspectors when required to do so, or (c) to answer any question put to him by the inspectors, the inspectors may certify the refusal to the court[16].After enquiring into the case and after hearing any witnesses against or on behalf of the alleged offender or any statement which may be offered in defence, the court may punish the offender as if he had been guilty of contempt of court[17]. The penalty thus lies in the judge's discretion. The recommendation of the Dowgate inspectors that non-compliance be made an extradictable offence was not implemented[18].

Inspectors' powers to obtain evidence are subject to a saving for legal professional privilege and bankers. Legal professional privilege is available to lawyers who are required to disclose only a client's name and address[19]. The term 'lawyer' is not defined, but would include a solicitor and counsel. The privilege is that of the client. Less extensive protection is afforded to the company's bankers who are not required to disclose information as to the affairs of any customers other than the company[20].

(ii) Admissibility.   As to the admissibility of statements in evidence, an answer given by a person to a question put to him in exercise of powers conferred on inspectors[1] to require production of documents and evidence, may be used in evidence against him[2].

The scope of admissibility was considered in *London and County Securities Ltd. v Nicholson*[3]. In an investigation into the affairs of the company, evidence on oath was given by several parties, including its auditors, and was amplified by correspondence between the inspectors and auditors' solicitors. After publication of the inspectors' report, the company and its liquidators sued its auditors for negligence. When the Department passed to the liquidator documents containing sworn and unsworn statements by the auditors on the understanding that they were to be treated as confidential except in conducting litigation as liquidator, the auditors sought to exclude these documents from the proceedings.

14. E.J. Hew, 'Inspectors want access to directors' private accounts' (1980) 1 Co. Law 152.
15. Under CA 1985, ss434 or 435.
16. CA 1985, s436(1) and (2).
17. Ibid, s436(3).
18. Ferguson and General Investments Ltd. (formerly known as Dowgate and General Investments Ltd.); CST Investments Ltd., Report by J. Jackson, Q.C. and K.L. Young, T.D., FCA (1979).
19. CA 1985, s452(1) and (2).
20. Ibid, s452(1) and (3).
1. Ibid, s434.
2. Ibid, s434(5).
3. *London and County Securities Ltd. v Nicholson* [1980] 1 W.L.R.948; D.A. Chaikin, 'Dept. of Trade evidence held to be admissible in private civil litigation' (1980) 1 Co. Law 295.

The court held that both at common law and under statute[4], the sworn and unsworn evidence of the auditors was admissible in criminal and civil proceedings. On the issue of admissibility, the court considered there were two competing public interests. The general presumption supported placing all relevant evidence before the court. The countervailing public interest in excluding evidence that would cause a loss of confidence by potential witnesses would be difficult to establish, though the court would take note of the Department's views. In this case, the Department's willingness to pass the documents to the liquidator suggested that it did not see any public interest in preserving confidentiality. As evidence in investigations can be used in civil proceedings by the Department on behalf of a company, the court felt witnesses were unlikely to be any less candid if the same evidence was available in civil proceedings by the company and the liquidator.

Although the court refused to decide the issue of admissibility concerning an action by a private individual to right a wrong to him individually, its reasoning suggests that all evidence given to inspectors is admissible in private suits for fraud, negligence and defamation. Directors are thus put on notice that self-incriminating replies to inspectors may provide a basis for subsequent civil proceedings. But the extent to which the decision provides scope for private civil proceedings is subject to the Department's willingness to pass to private parties copies of evidence compiled by inspectors.

However, private parties are not entitled as of right to transcripts of evidence. In *R. v Cheltenham Justices, ex parte Secretary of State for Trade and another*[5], a director who was prosecuted following an investigation, requested, for the purposes of his defence, copies of the transcripts of evidence of all witnesses other than himself and copies of correspondence put before the inspectors. After the Department refused this request, a Justice of the Peace issued a witness summons for the inspector to attend with transcripts of evidence and the correspondence. The Secretary of State and the inspector applied for an order of certiorari to quash the witness summons.

A Divisional Court granted the application. It held that the evidence required to be produced by the witness summons on its face would not be admissible evidence at the respondent's trial since it was required only for use in cross-examination at the trial to contradict statements a witness might make by reference to what he had said previously at the investigation. Hence, the evidence could not be material evidence in the trial. Lord Widgery, C.J. added that even if the evidence was material, it should not be produced because the public interest in maintaining sources of information in respect of investigation into the affairs of a company would outweigh the private disadvantage of non-disclosure of the evidence.

The effect of the provisions as to admissibility on the privilege against self-incrimination is unclear[6]. It seems that refusal to answer a question on the ground that it might incriminate the maker will not be punished as contempt[7]. The position may be different if the question is put or allowed by the court, though support for this view is based on a decision[8] that a bankrupt must answer incriminating questions at his public examination. But in this case, the bank-

---

4. CA 1967, s50. This provision is now CA 1985, s434(5).
5. *R. v Cheltenham Justices, ex p Secretary of State* [1977] 1 All E.R.460.
6. R.D. Fraser, 'Administrative Powers of Investigation into Companies' (1971) 34 M.L.R. 260 at 266.
7. *McClelland, Pope and Langley Ltd. v Howard* [1968] 1 All E.R. 569n.
8. *Re Atherton* [1912] 2 K.B.251.

rupt was protected by the Bankruptcy Act[9] against the use of answers in subsequent criminal proceedings, whereas the Companies Acts contain no such provisions in respect of company investigations. This lack of protection suggests the privilege is not so qualified in company investigations.

(iii) Inspectors' reports.   On conclusion of an investigation, inspectors must make a final report to the Department[10]. In addition, they may make interim reports and may be so directed by the Department[11].

However, completion of a report is not a prerequisite to further action. Inspectors may inform the Department of matters tending to show an offence has been committed without the need for an interim report[12]

As to liability for defamation, it seems that the inspectors' report and any other communication by them to the Department are protected by absolute privilege. But as the investigation is not a judicial proceeding, witnesses are only protected by qualified privilege[13].

The dissemination of inspectors' reports lies with the Department, not with the inspectors themselves. When inspectors are appointed by order of the court, the Department must furnish a copy to the court[14]. Whilst not under a duty to send a copy to the company, the Department may do so in its discretion[15]. It may also in its discretion, on request and payment of a fee, furnish a copy to any member of the company or other body corporate which has been investigated, any person whose conduct is referred to in the report, the auditors of that company or body corporate, the applicants for the investigation and any other person whose financial interests appear to be affected by matters dealt with in the report, including as a creditor of the company or body corporate[16].

The decision whether to publish a report also rests with the Department, which may cause a report to be printed and published[17]. Whereas a report on a public company is usually published, reports on private companies are published only where there are issues of general public interest[18].

A copy of the report, certified by the Secretary of State as a true copy, is admissible in any legal proceedings as evidence of the inspectors' opinion in relation to any matter contained in the report[19]. But it is not a legal decision and the inspectors' opinions are not binding upon any person as is a judgment of the court[20]. Whilst this distinction reflects the inquisitorial, as opposed to judicial, character of an investigation, the usefulness of a report in subsequent proceedings is limited in that it is not evidence of findings of fact. Nevertheless, coupled with the provision for admissibility of statements in evidence, a report can facilitate proceedings against management.

---

9. Bankruptcy Act 1890, s27(2).
10. CA 1985, s437(1).
11. Ibid.
12. Ibid, s433(2).
13. *Re Pergamon Press Ltd.* [1970] 3 All E.R.535 at 539 per Lord Denning, M.R.
14. CA 1985, s437(2).
15. Ibid, s437(3)(a).
16. Ibid, s437(3)(b).
17. Ibid, s437(3)(c).
18. Department of Trade and Industry, op cit, n10, p323, supra, para23.
19. Ibid, s441.
20. *Re Grosvenor and West End Rly Terminus Hotel Co. Ltd.* (1897) 76 L.T.337; *Re S.B.A. Properties Ltd.* [1967] 1 W.L.R.799 at 806 per Pennycuick J.

(c) RESULTS OF INVESTIGATIONS

Consistent with the strength of evidence usually required before inspectors are appointed, inspectors' reports frequently contain particulars of matters which could give rise to criminal and civil liability. In view of the purpose of investigations and the expense of inspectors' reports, the issue of subsequent action raises questions as to the efficacy of reports.

When a report suggests that an offence has been committed, the Department may institute criminal proceedings. However, the Department may decline to follow inspectors' recommendations, as evidenced by the Norwest Holst report[1]. Criminal proceedings by the Department mainly relate to a company's failure to forward an annual return, to deliver accounts or to keep accounting records[2], for which neither a preliminary investigation nor a full investigation is a prerequisite.

The Department also has extensive powers to institute civil proceedings. First, if it appears to the Department from an inspectors' report that it is expedient in the public interest that the company should be wound up, the Department may petition for the company to be wound up on the just and equitable ground, unless the company is already being wound up by the court[3].

Secondly, the Department may commence civil proceedings in the name and on behalf of the company where it appears from an inspectors' report that such proceedings ought to be brought in the public interest[4]. The Department must indemnify the company against costs[5] which are recoverable in the same way as the costs of an inspection[6]. The significance of this power is increased by the difficulties encountered by shareholders in instituting proceedings on behalf of the company[7], but it has been used sparingly.

Thirdly, the Department may petition for the alternative remedy, under the CA 1985[8]. If it appears to the Department that the company's business is being conducted in a manner unfairly prejudicial to any part of the members, the Department may present a petition for the relief of members thereby prejudiced. The term 'unfairly prejudicial' supersedes 'oppressive'[9]. No order was made under this earlier provision[10].

Fourthly, the Department may, on the basis of a report by inspectors, apply to the court for a disqualification order to be made against any person who is or has been a director of any company[11].

The Department's decisions on subsequent proceedings are also important in determining the distribution of the expenses of investigations. Initially, these expenses are borne by the Department[12], though it can require security for costs on an application by the company or its members[13]. After an investigation, the expenses may be recovered: (a) from a person convicted on a prosecution

1. Norwest Holst Ltd., Report by J. Davies, Q.C. and T. Harding, FCA (1982).
2. Department of Trade and Industry, Companies in 1985 (1986), Table 11.
3. CA 1985, s440.
4. Ibid, s438(1).
5. Ibid, s438(2).
6. See post at text to footnote 15.
7. See, ante, Chapter 4. Civil Liability.
8. CA 1985, s460.
9. Under CA 1948, s210.
10. R. Instone, *Inspectors, Investigations and their Aftermath* [1978] J.B.L. 121.
11. Ie, J.B.L. 121 under Company Directors Disqualification Act 1986, s8.
12. CA 1985, s439(1).
13. Ibid, s431(4).

instituted as a result of the investigation, or ordered to pay all or part of the costs of civil proceedings brought by the Department on the company's behalf to the extent ordered by the court; (b) from a company in whose name such proceedings are brought by the Department to the extent of sums or property recovered; (c) when an inspector was not appointed upon the Department's own motion, from any company dealt with by the report except so far as the Department otherwise directs and (d) in the case of an inspector appointed on application by the company or its members[14], from the applicants to the extent directed by the company[15]. As most appointments have been made on the Department's own motion, its reluctance to institute further proceedings has increased the burden on public funds.

Many of the matters disclosed in inspectors' reports are indicative more of breaches of equitable duties by directors and of the provisions now consolidated in the CA 1985 in the context of general company fraud than misconduct in securities dealings. Nevertheless, in some investigations, cases of insider dealing and conduct approaching insider dealing have been discovered by inspectors[16].

A well-publicised instance concerned the sale in 1972 of approximately 80% of the issued ordinary share capital of the National Group of Unit Trusts by a group of companies to a controlling director, his family and associates, who resold the shares in 1973 for a profit of over £5 million. After the inspectors' reports[17] set out a complex series of transactions and revealed the purchases and sales were based on inside information, the director offered to make restitution of profit and subsequently his estate repaid profits and interest of over £7 million.

In the Dowgate investigation, inspectors reported, inter alia, on transactions that prepared the ground for a take-over of Grendon Trust Ltd. by X and his associates[18]. Two Grendon directors, A and B, allegedly tried to sell nearly 30% of its share capital to R Ltd. But the transaction did not proceed owing to disagreement between Grendon directors and the fact that a merchant bank went to the Panel. According to the inspectors, R Ltd., which had a 15% holding, was attempting to acquire control without making a take-over offer. Having allegedly kept in constant communication with A and B, X went to a merchant bank for finance, purchased the shares held by R Ltd. and as a result of

14. Under CA 1985, s431.
15. CA 1985, s439(2)-(5).
16. Eg, (a) First Re-Investment Trust Ltd., Nelson Financial Trust Ltd., English and Scottish Unit Trust Holdings Ltd., Interim Report by D.C.H. Hirst, Q.C. and R.N.D. Langdon, F.C.A. (1974); Australian Estates Ltd., First Re-Investment Trust Ltd., Nelson Financial Trust Ltd., English and Scottish Unit Trust Holdings Ltd., Second and Final Report by D.C.-H. Hirst, Q.C. and R.N.D. Langdon F.C.A. (1975) (b) John Willment Automobiles Ltd., Report by P.J. Millett, Q.C. and N.R. Harris, F.C.A. (1975); (c) London and County Securities Group Ltd., Capebourne Ltd., Standfield Properties Ltd., Hibernian Property Co. Ltd., Briman Properties Ltd., Avon Land Securities Ltd., Report by A.P. Leggatt, Q.C. and D.C. Hobson, F.C.A. (1976); (d) Edward Wood and Company Ltd., Skibben Winton Construction Ltd., Report by D.J. Clarkson, Q.C. and K.A. McKinley, C.A. (1977); (e) Ferguson and General Investments Ltd. (formerly known as Dowgate and General Investments Ltd.); CST Investments Ltd., Report by J. Jackson, Q.C. and K.L. Young, T.D., F.C.A. (1979); (f) Ozalid Group Holdings Ltd., Report by N. Butter, Q.C. and B.A. Kemp F.C.A. (1980); (g) The Central Provinces Manganese Ore Company Ltd., Data Investment Ltd., Report by P.J. Millett, Q.C. and I.M. Bowrie, C.A. (1980) and (h) Norwest Holst Ltd., Report by J. Davies, Q.C. and T. Harding, F.C.A. (1982)
Breaches of insider reporting requirements (CA 1967, s27) were found in: (i) Kwik Save Discount Group, Report by D.S. Mangat and J.H. Dickman (1974); (j) Ozalid Group Holdings Ltd., op.cit (f) supra and (k) Norwest Holst Ltd., op cit (h) supra.
17. First Re-Investment Trust Ltd., op cit n16, supra.
18. Ferguson and General Investments Ltd., op cit n16, supra.

warehousing shares with nominees and further market purchases, acquired a 35% holding which was not disclosed in accordance with the reporting requirements of the CA 1967[19], then in force.

In the course of an investigation into Darjeeling Holdings Ltd.[20], inspectors were appointed to investigate the affairs of other companies connected with Darjeeling. In their report on the connected companies[1], the inspectors set out a series of transactions whereby controlling interests in a number of public companies, in particular Central Provinces Manganese Ore Co. Ltd. and Darjeeling, were acquired by two business associates through their ownership of certain private companies. When the value of their acquisitions fell, they proceeded to 'shuffle the shares' so that losses were passed on to the outside shareholders in the public companies, an additional £750,000 was extracted from the companies and most of the assets involved ended up in the hands of the private companies. The inspectors concluded that no thought was ever given to the interests of the outside shareholders. They were also critical of the auditors and the weakness and inexperience of some of the directors of the public companies. In another investigation into other companies[2] involving the main participants and similar manipulative transactions, the inspectors concluded that outside shareholders did not suffer any great loss.

The Ozalid investigation[3] found circumstances suggesting insider dealing and breaches of the insider reporting requirements. Inspectors were appointed after the company had encountered a number of problems during 1970-77 culminating in its take-over by a Dutch group on terms which left shareholders dissatisfied. Apart from managerial problems, these problems included unauthorised and undisclosed overseas payments to directors and share transactions involving the board. The main focus of the investigation was on the overseas payments and difficulties in tracing these payments led inspectors to recommend statutory provision for access to directors' bank accounts[4].

As regards the share transactions, the inspectors found circumstances suggesting that the chairman and two directors were in breach of the statutory requirements to disclose their interests in shares[5]. In addition, they were critical of transactions which they considered to be based on inside information. On the recommendation of the Ozalid chairman, 2,000 shares in X were purchased on behalf of a trust involving his family at a time when he knew Ozalid were likely to acquire X. The shares were sold at a profit almost immediately after the announcement of the merger. The inspectors considered that 'a person in the position of [the chairman] and with inside information as to a likely acquisition should not use his knowledge in the way that he did'[6]. Another individual was regarded as having had sufficient information about the likelihood of the acquisition to render his purchases of shares in his own name, 'undesirable'[7]. Referring to the purchase of shares in Y by a director at a time when he and others were negotiating the possible acquisition of Y on Ozalid's behalf and the

19. CA 1967, s33.
20. Darjeeling Holdings Ltd., Interim and Final Reports by P.J. Millett, Q.C. and I.M. Bowie, CA (1980).
1. The Central Provinces Manganese Ore Company Ltd., op cit n16(g), p330, supra.
2. Bandara Investments Ltd.; Bandarapola Ceylon Company Ltd., Report by P.J. Millett, Q.C. and I.M. Bowie CA (1980).
3. Ozalid Group Holdings Ltd., op cit n16(f), p330, supra.
4. Ibid, paras 179 and 520.
5. Ibid, para 264.
6. Ibid, para 277.
7. Ibid.

subsequent sale of these shares at a profit, the inspectors also considered that 'the purchase and sale of these shares were influenced by inside information and [he] should not have used his knowledge in this way'[8]. However, in respect of other dealings which they regarded as 'unorthodox', the inspectors reported that they were unable to identify the person or persons responsible because the shares were purchased by nominees resident abroad using Swiss bank accounts[9].

Owing to the Department's reluctance to appoint inspectors, the terms of reference for investigations, the delays involved and the expense, the procedure for appointing inspectors to investigate a company's affairs is ill-suited to enforcement of the IDA 1985, where the need for swift investigation underlines the importance of devising arrangements to assist the enforcement of a criminal prohibition rather than the preparation of a report which serves other purposes. These considerations are reinforced by the provisions for investigation of company ownership and of certain dealings in securities by directors.

2. Investigation into the ownership of a company

On the few occasions that they have been invoked, the statutory powers of investigation into company ownership have been used with a view to enabling existing controllers to ascertain the identity of a potential take-over bidder[10]. In view of the prevalence of insider dealing in the context of take-overs and mergers, they may also assist the discovery of instances of insider dealing.

These broad powers authorise the Department to investigate and report on the membership of any company, and otherwise with respect to the company, for the purpose of determining the true persons who are or have been financially interested in the success or failure (real or apparent) of the company or able to control or materially to influence its policy[11]. Normally the Department exercises these powers by appointing one or more inspectors in accordance with its mandatory duty[12] or under its discretionary power[13], but an investigation may be conducted by the Department without appointing an inspector[14].

In contrast to the discretionary nature of the corresponding power to investigate the affairs of a company, the appointment of inspectors to investigate ownership is mandatory[15] when an application is made by 200 or more members or by members holding one-tenth of the issued shares[16] unless the Department is satisfied that the application is vexatious[17]. The Department may exclude from the investigation any matter which the application seeks to have included when it is satisfied that it is unreasonable for that matter to be investigated[18]. But it cannot ask for security as the costs of an investigation into company ownership

8. Ibid, para 293.
9. Ibid.
10. *Gower's Principles of Modern Company Law*, Fourth Edition by L.C.B. Gower, J.S. Cronin, A.J. Easson and Lord Wedderburn of Charlton (1979), p.675.
11. C A 1985, s442(1).
12. Ibid, s442(3).
13. Ibid, s442(1).
14. Ibid, s444.
15. Ibid, s442(3).
16. Namely, the number of applicants or the amount of shares required for the appointment of an inspector under C A 1985, s431. Where the company does not have a share capital, the application must be made by not less than one-fifth of registered members.
17. C A 1985, s442(3)(a).
18. Ibid, s442(3)(b).

must be borne by the Department[19]. The Department has taken a restrictive view of its mandatory duty[20].

The Department's discretionary power of appointment is very broad. It may appoint inspectors when it considers there is good reason to do so[1].

Both in accordance with its mandatory duty and under its discretionary power, appointments by the Department have been infrequent. In 1985 and 1986, three investigations were authorised each year[2].

The appointment of inspectors may define the scope of their investigation (whether as respects the matter or period to which it is to extend or otherwise) and in particular may limit the investigation to matters connected with particular shares or debentures[3]. Subject to the terms of their appointment, the inspectors' powers extend to the investigation of any circumstances suggesting the existence of an arrangement or understanding which, though not legally binding, is or was observed or likely to be observed in practice and which is relevant to the purposes of the investigation[4].

In conducting an investigation into company ownership, inspectors have generally the same powers as for the conduct of an investigation into the affairs of a company. Subject to certain variations, the powers regarding related companies[5], production of evidence[6] and inspectors' reports[7] are incorporated by reference[8]. The saving for legal professional privilege and bankers also applies[9].

There are three significant variations. First, the power to call for directors' bank accounts[10] is denied to inspectors investigating company ownership, even though the information may be relevant to the investigation.

Secondly, inspectors' powers extend to (a) all persons who are or have been, or whom the inspector has reasonable cause to believe to be or have been, financially interested in the success or failure or apparent success or failure of the company or persons able to control or materially influence its policy (including persons concerned only on behalf of others) and (b) any other person whom the inspector has reasonable cause to believe possesses information relevant to the investigation[11]. This latter can thus place stockbrokers and financial intermediaries under a duty to assist in investigations.

However, the term 'apparent' in relation to success or failure seems to mean that if a person was likely to benefit from the fact that a company appears to be either flourishing or failing so that the value of its securities would tend to rise or fall accordingly, the inspector would be entitled to investigate such matters. Hence, if an attempt is made to falsify the market value of shares in contrast to their true value, for example by concealing facts which should have been made

19. Ibid, s443(4).
20. J.A.C. Suter, *The Regulation of Insider Dealing in Britain and France* (Doctoral thesis 1985), Chapter 7. pp52-53.
1. C A 1985, s442(1).
2. Department of Trade and Industry, Companies in 1986-87 (1987), p.19.
3. CA 1985, s.442(2).
4. Ibid, s442(4).
5. Ibid, s433(1).
6. Ibid, ss434 and 436.
7. Ibid, s437.
8. Ibid, s443.
9. Ibid, s452.
10. Ibid, s435.
11. Ibid, s443(2).

available, an inspector may be appointed and directed to investigate the circumstances[12].

The third variation relates to reports. If the Secretary of State considers that there is good reason for not divulging part of a report, he may omit that part from disclosure[13]. He may also cause the Registrar to keep a copy of the report with that part omitted or, in the case of any other such report, a copy of the whole report[14].

The Department's discretionary powers are extended by provision for investigation by the Department without appointing an inspector. Where it appears to the Department that there is good reason to investigate the ownership of any shares in or debentures of a company and that it is unnecessary to appoint inspectors for the purpose, it may require any person whom it has reasonable cause to believe to have or to be able to obtain any information as to the present and past interests in those shares or debentures and the names and addresses of the persons interested and of any persons who act or have acted on their behalf in relation to the shares or debentures, to give it any such information[15]. This power thus enables the Department to require stockbrokers or financial intermediaries to give any relevant information which they have or are able to obtain. Non-compliance is an offence[16].

A distinguishing feature of investigations into company ownership is the Department's power by order to direct that shares and debentures be subject to the restrictions of Part XV, CA 1985[17] (ss454-457). These restrictions can be imposed when it appears that there is difficulty in finding out the relevant facts. An order may thus be made against securities whose holder claims that full disclosure is precluded by foreign secrecy laws.

Under a restriction order, any transfer of securities is void, voting rights are not exerciseable, no further issues may be made deriving from those securities and, except in a liquidation, no payment may be made of any sums due from the company on those securities[18]. Subject to an exception for agreements contingent upon an order of the court or the Secretary of State's approval of the sale[19], the CA 1985 also renders void (a) an agreement to transfer securities subject to a restriction order[20] and (b) an agreement to transfer any rights to be issued with other securities deriving from the ownership of restricted securities or to receive any payment on them (other than in a liquidation)[1]. Non-compliance with the restrictions[2] or the issue of shares in contravention of them is an offence[3], though a prosecution in England and Wales may only be instituted by, or with the consent of, the Department[4].

Provision is also made for relaxation and removal of restrictions. Where securities are by order subject to restrictions, application may be made to the

---

12. *Palmer's Company Law* (24th edn), under the general editorship of C.M. Schmitthoff with specialist editors, Vol.1 'The Treatise' (1987), para 7 1-21..
13. C A 1985, s443(3).
14. Ibid.
15. Ibid, s444(1). The definition of 'an interest in shares or debentures' in relation to s444(1) is contained in s444(2).
16. C A 1985, s444(3).
17. Ibid, s445.
18. Ibid, s454(1).
19. Ibid, s456(3).
20. Ibid, s454(2).
1. Ibid, s454(3).
2. Ibid, s455(1).
3. Ibid, s455(2).
4. Ibid, s455(3).

court for an order directing that the shares be no longer so subject[5]. Where the order applying the restrictions was made by the Secretary of State, or he has refused to make an order disapplying them, the application may be made by any person aggrieved[6]. However, the court or Secretary of State may make an order removing the restrictions only if (a) it or he is satisfied that the relevant facts have been disclosed to the company and no unfair advantage has accrued to any person as a result of the earlier failure to make that disclosure or (b) the securities are to be sold and it or he approves the sale[7]. An order directing that the securities shall cease to be the subject of restrictions, which is expressed to be made either to permit a transfer of shares or under an order for sale of securities made by the court, may continue the restrictions on the issue of further securities and on payments from the company[8].

An important power relating to securities subject to a restriction order, authorises the court, on the application of the company or the Secretary of State, to order the securities to be sold, subject to the court's approval of the terms of sale[9]. The court may also direct that the securities shall cease to be subject to restrictions[10]. If an order for sale is made, the Secretary of State, the company, the person appointed to effect the sale and any other person interested in the securities may apply to the court for such further order relating to the sale or transfer of the securities as the court thinks fit[11]. Hence, when an order has been made removing restrictions on transfers and on voting rights but continuing those on the issue of further securities and on payments from the company, it is not necessary to establish either of the grounds for removal of restrictions before a further order can be made, lifting the continuing restrictions. The proceeds of sale must be paid into court for the benefit of those beneficially interested in the shares and any such person may apply to the court for the whole or part of those proceeds to be paid to him[12].

3. Investigation of certain dealings in securities by directors

Prior to the FSA 1986[13], the Department's power to appoint inspectors to investigate suspected breaches of legislation relating to dealings by insiders was limited to a discretionary power, initially conferred by the CA 1967. Where it appears to the Department that there are circumstances suggesting that contraventions may have occurred, in relation to a company's shares or debentures, of the provisions of the CA 1985 (a) penalising certain option dealings[14] and (b) requiring disclosure of the interests of directors or their spouses or children in shares or debentures of the company[15], the Department may appoint one or more inspectors to carry out such investigations as are required to establish whether contraventions have occurred and to report their

5. Ibid, s456(1).
6. Ibid, s456(2). As to the position where the order was made by the court under C A 1985, s216, see post VIII. Companies.
7. Ibid, s456(3). As to the meaning of 'sold' under s456(3)(b), see *Re Westminster Property Group Plc* [1985] 2 All E.R. 426, C.A.
8. C A 1985, s456(6).
9. Ibid, s456(4).
10. Ibid.
11. Ibid, s456(5).
12. Ibid, s457.
13. See post, *4. Insider dealing investigations*.
14. CA 1985, s323; see, ante, Chapter 3. Criminal Liability.
15. Ibid, ss324 (taken with Sch13) and 328(3)-(5); see, ante, Chapter 5. Disclosure.

findings to the Department[16]. The appointment may be for a limited period and
the investigation may be confined to a particular class of shares or debentures[17].
The expenses of the investigation are borne by the Department[18].

In conducting such an investigation, inspectors have the powers[19] conferred
on inspectors appointed to investigate the affairs of the company[20]. But in
relation to any other body corporate, this investigative power extends to the
company's subsidiaries, holding company or subsidiaries of its holding company[1] (though not to a holding company of its subsidiary)[2]. The saving for legal
professional privilege also applies[3].

In addition, a duty to assist inspectors is imposed on: (a) an individual who
is an authorised person within the meaning of the FSA 1986; (b) an individual
who holds a permission granted under para23 of Sch1 to that Act; (c) an officer
(past or present) of a body corporate which is such an authorised person or
holds such a permission; (d) a partner (past or present) in a partnership which
is such an authorised person or holds such a permission and (e) a member of
the governing body or officer (in either case whether past or present) of an
unincorporated association which is such an authorised person or holds such
a permission[4].

Inspectors may make interim reports to the Department and must do so if
directed by the Department; on conclusion of their investigation, they must
make a final report to the Department[5]. The report may be written or printed
as the Department directs and the Department may cause it to be published[6].
There is no provision for supplying a copy of the report to any person.

This power of investigation has been exercised on only two occasions. An
investigation commenced in 1973 into Kwik Save Discount Ltd. and was
followed by a report in 1974[7]. Though inspectors found circumstances suggesting breach of the requirements for disclosure of the interests of directors or
their spouses or children in the shares of the company, no further action was
taken. The power was subsequently exercised in 1978 in relation to the Elliott
Group of Peterborough when inspectors were appointed on the basis of
evidence submitted by the Stock Exchange on the specific issue of directors'
share dealings[8], but no report has been published.

4. Insider dealing investigations

Whereas the insider dealing legislation, introduced in 1980, did not contain a
special investigative power, a power to appoint inspectors to investigate suspected insider dealing was introduced by the FSA 1986. In particular, when it
appears to the Department that there are circumstances suggesting contraven-

---

16. Ibid, s446(1).
17. Ibid, s446(2).
18. Ibid, s446(7).
19. Under CA 1985, ss434-436.
20. CA 1985, s446(3).
1. Ibid.
2. Cf. CA 1985, s433(1).
3. CA 1985, s452.
4. CA 1985, s446(4), FSA 1986, Sch16, para 21.
5. Ibid, s446(5).
6. Ibid.
7. Kwik Save Discount Group, Report by D.S. Mangat and J.H. Dickman (1974).
8. Department of Trade, Companies in 1978 (1979), p.4; Stock Exchange, News Release, Elliott
Group of Peterborough Ltd., 16th February, 1978.

tion of the IDA 1985, it may appoint one or more inspectors to carry out such investigations as are required to establish whether or not any such contravention has occurred and to report their findings to the Department[9]. The appointment may limit the period during which he is to continue his investigation or confine it to particular matters[10].

A duty to assist inspectors is imposed on a wide range of persons. This duty is expressed to apply to any person who is or may be able to give information concerning contravention of the IDA 1985[11].

However, the scope of these powers is limited by the reference to the IDA 1985 with the result that they do not extend back to the CA 1980, the legislation which created the criminal offence of insider dealing. Hence, transactions prior to the IDA 1985 fall outside the scope of these investigative powers, thereby thwarting the Department's plans to reopen old files on suspected insider dealing[12]. For such transactions investigation by inspectors would be dependent upon the existence of circumstances enabling the Department to appoint inspectors to investigate under the legislation now contained in the CA 1985.

When inspectors consider any person is or may be able to give information concerning contravention of the IDA 1985, they have power to require that person (a) to produce to them any document in his possession or under his control relating to the company in relation to whose securities the contravention is suspected to have occurred or to its securities; (b) to attend before them and (c) otherwise to give them all assistance in connection with the investigation which he is reasonably able to give[13]. A duty is expressly imposed on that person to comply with such requirement[14]. The term 'document' is defined to include information recorded in any form; in regard to information recorded otherwise than in legible form, references to its production include references to producing a copy of the information in legible form[15]. Though this investigative provision is not inserted in the IDA 1985, it is considered[16] that since the investigations relate to contraventions of that Act, 'securities' has the meaning given by that Act[17].

Inspectors are authorised to examine such persons on oath and to administer the oath accordingly[18]. A respondent's statement may be used in evidence against him[19].

Inspectors are required to make such interim reports to the Department as they think fit or it may direct[20]. On conclusion of their investigation, they must make a final report to the Department[1].

Inspectors' powers to obtain evidence are again subject to a saving for legal professional privilege and bankers. In regard to the former, a person is not required to disclose any information or produce any document which he would be entitled to refuse to disclose or produce on grounds of legal professional

9. FSA 1986, s177(1).
10. Ibid, s177(2).
11. Ibid, s177(3).
12. *The Times*, 1st August, 1988.
13. FSA 1986, s177(3).
14. Ibid.
15. Ibid, s177(10).
16. A. Page and R. Ferguson, *Financial Services Act 1986* (1987), p.192.
17. IDA 1985, s12.
18. FSA 1986, s177(4).
19. Ibid, s177(6).
20. Ibid, s177(5).
1. Ibid.

privilege in proceedings in the High Court or on grounds of confidentiality as between client and professional legal adviser in proceedings in the Court of Session[2].

As to the latter, the saving for banking confidentiality is narrowly drawn. A person carrying on the business of banking is not required by these investigative powers to disclose any information or produce any document relating to a customer's affairs unless the customer is a person who the inspectors have reason to believe may be able to give information concerning a suspected contravention and the Department is satisfied that the disclosure or production is necessary for the purposes of the investigation[3]. The first element of the power to require disclosure is thus based on the inspectors' reasonable belief in the customers' ability to provide information rather than being restricted to a customer suspected of an offence under the IDA 1985. However, the extent to which inspectors will seek to exercise this power and the Department's willingness to concur remain to be clarified[4].

Specific provision is made for liens. Thus, where a person claims a lien on a document, its production is without prejudice to his lien[5].

Significant powers of entry to search premises for evidence are also conferred. When a Justice of the Peace is satisfied on information on oath laid by or on behalf of the Secretary of State that there are reasonable grounds for believing that an offence has been committed under ss1, 2, 4 or 5 IDA 1985 and that there are on any premises documents relevant to the question whether that offence has been committed, he may issue a warrant[6]. Such warrant shall authorise a constable, together with any other person named in it and any other constable to enter and search the premises and to take possession (and copies) of documents appearing to be relevant to the question of whether an offence under those provisions has been committed[7]. In addition, any person named in the warrant may be required to provide an explanation of the documents or to state where they may be found[8]. The documents may be retained for three months or until the conclusion of the criminal proceedings specified in the IDA 1985[9]. Obstruction of the exercise of the warrant or failure without reasonable excuse to comply with a requirement to provide an explanation of documents or to state where they may be found, is an offence[10].

In addition, penalties can be imposed for failure to co-operate with inspectors. When a person refuses either (a) to comply with a request to produce documents, to attend before inspectors or to assist them as required[11] or (b) to answer a question put to him by inspectors in an insider dealing investigation, the inspectors have power to certify the failure to co-operate to the court, which may inquire into the case[12]. If satisfied that the failure to co-operate lacked reasonable excuse, the court may (a) punish the offender as if he had been guilty of contempt of court or (b) direct that the Department exercise its powers under

2. Ibid, s177(7).
3. Ibid, s177(8). The 'business of banking' is not defined.
4. B. Rider, D. Chaikin and C. Abrams, *Guide to the Financial Services Act* (1987), p.117.
5. FSA 1986, s177(3).
6. Ibid, s199(1).
7. Ibid, s199(3).
8. Ibid.
9. Ibid, s199(5). By s199(9), the term 'documents' is defined to include information recorded in any form; in regard to information recorded otherwise than in legible form, references to its production include references to producing a copy of the information in legible form.
10. FSA 1986, s199(6).
11. By FSA 1986, s177(3).
12. FSA 1986, s178(1).

this provision[13]. In the case of an offender not within the jurisdiction, the court may give such a direction when satisfied that he was notified of his rights to appear before the court and of the powers available under this provision[14].

The term 'reasonable excuse' is partially defined by the FSA 1986 where a person has been dealing for or on account of another. In particular, a person is not regarded as having a reasonable excuse for refusing to comply with a request or answer a question in a case where the contravention or suspected contravention being investigated relates to dealing by him on the instructions or for the account of another person, by reason that at the time of the refusal either (a) he did not know that other person's identity or (b) he was subject to the law of a country or territory outside the UK which prohibited him from disclosing information relating to the dealing without that other person's consent, if he might have obtained that consent or obtained exemption from that law[15]. This latter condition is based on the premise that 'if an overseas bank could know the identity of the principal behind a transaction on a UK market, who may have committed a criminal offence, but chooses not to find out, then it is reasonable for that bank to have restrictions imposed on its UK activities'[16].

In circumstances outside this partial definition, the meaning of 'reasonable excuse' has been judicially considered[17]. The business correspondent of a national newspaper published two articles in which he accurately forecast the result of inquiries made by the Monopolies and Mergers Commission and the Office of Fair Trading into two take-over bids. It was apparent from the articles that in writing them the journalist had used information leaked to him from an official source or given to him by a source close to the leak. Inspectors appointed by the Secretary of State to investigate suspected leaks from government departments of price sensitive information about take-over bids requested the journalist, pursuant to s177(9) FSA 1986, to reveal the sources of his information on which the articles were based. The journalist refused to divulge his sources and the inspectors certified the matter for an inquiry by the court into his refusal. The judge dismissed the inspectors' application on the ground that the journalist had a 'reasonable excuse' within s178(2) for refusing to comply with the inspectors' request. On appeal by the inspectors, the Court of Appeal held that, as was the case under s10 of the Contempt of Court Act 1981, what would otherwise be a reasonable excuse would not avail the journalist if it was established that disclosure of his sources was 'necessary . . . for the prevention of . . . crime'. The court further held that the inspectors had established the necessity of disclosure. The journalist appealed to the House of Lords, contending that the inspectors had not identified the particular crime which was sought to be prevented.

Dismissing the appeal, the House of Lords held that on the true construction of s10 of the 1981 Act a person could be in contempt for refusing to disclose his source of information if the disclosure was necessary for the prevention of crime generally rather than a particular identifiable future crime. Accordingly, since the purpose of the inspectors' inquiry was to expose the leaking of official information and criminal insider trading and to consider measures to prevent future leaks and insider trading and since, on the evidence, the journalist's

13. Ibid, s178(2).
14. Ibid.
15. Ibid, s178(6).
16. H.C. Deb., Vol. 99, col. 525 (1986).
17. Re an inquiry under the Company Securities (Insider Dealing) Act 1985 [1988] AC 660, [1988] 1 All E.R. 203.

information was necessary for that purpose, the journalist could not avail himself of the protection of s10, but was required to reveal his sources on pain of being committed for contempt under s178(2). However, the House of Lords added that in deciding whether a person has without reasonable excuse failed to comply with a request or to answer a question under s177 the court must satisfy itself on the evidence placed before it and must not merely act as a rubber stamp to support the inspectors' view.

On the case being remitted to the High Court to consider the question of punishment, the journalist was fined £20,000 for refusing to divulge his sources of information[18]. The Vice-Chancellor stated that there were special circumstances, notably the fact that the articles had been published before the FSA 1986 came into force and there had thus been no reason to expect that publication would lead to conflict with the law. The Vice-Chancellor also accepted that the journalist was acting from a true, genuine and conscientious objection. However, publication of the articles before the FSA 1986 came into force did not exempt him from punishment. That was because he had since had many opportunities to rethink his position and because of the importance of the inspectors' investigation and the possible stamping out of insider dealing. Nevertheless, it was not an appropriate case for a custodial sentence, partly because of the journalist's genuinely held ethical objection and partly because such a sentence would be 'more likely to lead to the creation of a martyr than to bring home to those breaking the law the wrongness of so doing'[19]. In fixing the size of the fine, the Vice-Chancellor indicated that he took into consideration the fact of having been told that it would be paid by the newspaper, not by the journalist personally.

In regard to a direction by the court that the Department exercise its powers under s178, the powers available vary according to whether or not the person is an authorised person in the jurisdiction. Where the offender is an authorised person, the Department may serve a notice[20] on him: (a) cancelling any authorisation of his to carry on investment business after the expiry of a specified period after service of the notice; (b) disqualifying him from becoming authorised to carry on investment business after the expiry of a specified period; (c) restricting any authorisation of his in respect of investment business during a specified period to the performance of contracts entered into before the notice comes into force; (d) prohibiting him from entering into transactions of a specified kind or entering into them except in specified circumstances or to a specified extent; (e) prohibiting him from soliciting business from persons of a specified kind or otherwise than from such persons, or (f) prohibiting him from carrying on business in a specified manner or otherwise than in a specified manner[1]. In regard to notices cancelling or restricting authorisation[2], the 'specified period' must be such period as appears to the Department reasonable to enable the person on whom notice is served to complete the performance of any contracts entered into before the notice comes into force and to terminate such of them as are of a continuing nature[3].

Such a notice[4] may be revoked at any time by the Department by serving a

---

18. *The Observer*, 17th January, 1988; *The Financial Times*, 27th January, 1988.
19. *The Financial Times*, 27th January, 1988.
20. As to the manner of serving a notice, see FSA 1986, s204.
1. FSA 1986, s178(3).
2. Ie, under FSA 1986, s178(3)(a) and (c).
3. FSA 1986, s178(4).
4. Ie, a notice served under FSA 1986, s178(3).

revocation notice[5]. Moreover, it must be revoked if it appears to the Department that he has agreed to comply with the relevant request or answer the relevant question[6].

As to the effect of revoking a notice cancelling authorisation, revocation shall not have the effect of reviving the authorisation cancelled by the notice except where the person would (apart from the notice) at the time of the revocation be an authorised person by virtue of his membership of a recognised self-regulating organisation or certification by a recognised professional body[7]. But this provision is not to be construed as preventing any person who has been subject to such a notice from again becoming authorised after a revocation of the notice[8].

Provision is also made for notification to regulators. Where the Department serves (a) a notice[9] on a person authorised by virtue of an authorisation granted by a designated agency, membership of a recognised self-regulating organisation or certification by a recognised professional body or (b) a revocation notice[10] on such an authorised person at the time of service of the notice being revoked, it must serve a copy of the notice on that agency, organisation or body[11].

In the case of an unauthorised person, the Department may prohibit an authorised person from knowingly transacting investment business of a specified kind, or in specified circumstances or to a specified extent, with or on behalf of an unauthorised person[12]. An authorised person in breach of such prohibition must be treated as having contravened the rules for the conduct of investment business made under the FSA 1986[13], or in the case of a person who is authorised by virtue of membership of a recognised SRO or certification by an RPB, the rules of that organisation or body[14].

These powers concerning penalties for failure to co-operate with inspectors[15], like the powers of entry to search premises for evidence of an insider dealing offence[16], can be transferred to the SIB. However, any such transfer is subject to the reservation that they are exerciseable concurrently with the Secretary of State and subject to such conditions or restrictions as the Secretary of State may from time to time impose.[17]

Following an investigation by inspectors into insider dealing, the Secretary of State may bring criminal proceedings under the IDA 1985[18]. He may also, where it appears to him from a report made by inspectors that it is expedient in the public interest that a disqualification order should be made against any person who is or has been a director or shadow director of any company, apply to the court for such an order to be made[19].

5. FSA 1986, s178(7).
6. Ibid.
7. Ibid, s178(8).
8. Ibid.
9. Ie, a notice under FSA 1986, s178(3).
10. Ie, a notice under FSA 1986, s178(7).
11. FSA 1986, s178(9).
12. Ibid, s178(5).
13. Ie, under Chapter V of Part I of FSA 1986.
14. FSA 1986, s178(5).
15. Ie, under FSA 1986, s178.
16. Ie, under FSA 1986, s199.
17. FSA 1986, ss178(10) and 199(7).
18. See, ante, Chapter 3. Criminal Liability.
19. Company Directors Disqualification Act 1986, s8.

II. THE SERIOUS FRAUD OFFICE

Extensive investigative powers are conferred by the Criminal Justice Act 1987 on the Director of the Serious Fraud Office to enable him to investigate any suspected offence which appears to him on reasonable grounds to involve serious or complex fraud[20]. The permissible scope of an investigation is thus subject to two important limitations. First, an investigation is contingent upon the existence of a suspected offence; it is insufficient that matters raise questions of general importance relating to serious or complex fraud. Secondly, the suspected offence must relate to serious or complex fraud. Neither the expression 'serious or complex fraud' nor the term 'fraud' is defined for the purposes of the 1987 Act. However, in the Roskill report, it was stated:

> 'Fraud' is not a defined term; there has never been any general offence of criminal fraud in English law. There are in fact several hundred criminal offences on the statute book, together with a few common law offences, which may form the basis of a charge of fraud, in that one of the main ingredients of what is generally understood to be fraud may be present, such as dishonest practice, deception, false disclosure, concealment of assets or other activities of that nature. The principal offences in the present armoury of the criminal law against fraud include obtaining property by deception, false accounting, fraudulent trading, theft and the common law offence of conspiracy to defraud'[1].

In a more detailed description of types of fraud, the Roskill report, whilst noting that insider dealing was a specific statutory offence, referred to insider dealing as one of several different kinds of Stock Exchange fraud[2]. Whilst insider dealing can sometimes be fraudulent, two considerations militate against a finding of fraud in many cases of insider dealing[3]. First, there is no intention to deprive another of an opportunity which is regarded in law as belonging to that other. Secondly, there is no general legal rule requiring full disclosure even in face to face transactions.

Within the permissible scope of an investigation, the power to commence an investigation is a broad one. The Director's powers are exerciseable, for the purposes of such an investigation, in any case where it appears to him that there is good reason to do so for the purpose of investigating the affairs, or any aspect of the affairs, of any person[4].

The Director has ample powers to require the attendance of witnesses and the production of documents. In particular, the Director may by notice in writing require the person under investigation, or any other person whom he has reason to believe has relevant information, to attend before the Director at a specified time and place and answer questions or otherwise furnish information with respect to any matter relevant to the investigation[5]. The Director may

---

20. Criminal Justice Act 1987, s1(3).
1. Report of the Fraud Trials Committee (Chairman: The Right Honourable the Lord Roskill, P.C.) (1980) para 3.2.
2. Ibid, Appendix F. Although not treated as applicable to insider dealing, the balance of opinion considered that s13, Prevention of Fraud (Investments) Act 1958 was capable of applying to insider dealing: J.A.C. Suter, *The Regulation of Insider Dealing in Britain and France* (Doctoral Thesis, 1985), pp3, 9-10.
3. L.H. Leigh, *The Control of Commercial Fraud* (1982), pp118-119.
4. Criminal Justice Act 1987, s2(1).
5. Ibid, s2(2).

also by notice in writing require the person under investigation or any other person to produce at a specified time and place any specified documents which appear to the Director to relate to any matter relevant to the investigation or any documents of a specified class which appear to him so to relate[6]. The power includes a power to take copies or extracts from the documents, to require the person producing them to provide an explanation of any of them and if the documents are not produced, to require the person who was required to produce them to state to the best of his knowledge and belief where they are[7]. The term 'documents' is defined to include information recorded in any form and, in relation to information recorded otherwise than in legible form, references to its production include references to producing a copy of the information in legible form[8].

The powers to require attendance of witnesses and production of documents are supported by powers of search and seizure, but these latter are subject to two checks. First, the authority of a Justice of the Peace is a prerequisite to their exercise. Where on information on oath laid by a member of the Serious Fraud Office, a J.P. is satisfied that there are reasonable grounds for suspecting that a person has failed to comply with an obligation to produce documents, that it is not practicable to serve a written notice for their production or the service of such a notice might seriously prejudice the investigation and that the documents are on the premises specified in the information, he may issue a warrant authorising a constable to enter and search the premises and to seize such documents[9]. Secondly, on the execution of a warrant, a constable must be accompanied by an appropriate person, unless it is not practicable in the circumstances[10]. For this purpose, 'appropriate person' means a member of the Serious Fraud Office or some other person whom the Director has authorised to accompany the constable[11].

As to the subsequent use of evidence, a statement by a person may be used in evidence against him on a prosecution either for an offence of knowingly or recklessly making a statement which is false or misleading in a material particular[12], or for some other offence where in giving evidence he makes a statement inconsistent with it[13].

The Director's powers of investigation are subject to a saving for legal professional privilege and bankers. Legal professional privilege is available to a lawyer except that he may be required to furnish the name and address of a client[14]. A person carrying on the business of banking is not required to disclose information or produce a document in respect of which he owes an obligation of confidence unless either the person to whom the obligation of confidence is owed consents to the disclosure or production, or the Director has authorised the making of the requirement (or, if it is impracticable for him to act personally, a member of the Serious Fraud Office designated by him for this purpose has done so)[15].

6. Ibid, s2(3).
7. Ibid.
8. Ibid, s2(18).
9. Ibid, s2(4) and (5).
10. Ibid, s2(6).
11. Ibid, s2(7).
12. Under the Criminal Justice Act 1987, s2(14).
13. Criminal Justice Act 1987, s2(8).
14. Ibid, s2(9).
15. Ibid, s2(10).

A limited power is conferred on the Director to authorise persons (other than members of the Serious Fraud Office to whom functions may be assigned) to exercise his investigative powers. In this connection, the Director may authorise any competent investigator (other than a constable) who is not a member of the Serious Fraud Office to exercise on his behalf the investigative powers conferred on him[16]. Such an authority may only be granted for the purpose of investigating the affairs, or any aspect of the affairs, of a person specified in the authority[17]. A person so authorised may be required to produce evidence of his authority[18].

Non-compliance is, in the absence of reasonable excuse, an offence[19]. In addition, it is an offence for a person knowingly or recklessly to make a false or misleading statement in purported compliance with these requirements[20]. It is also an offence for a person, who knows or suspects that an investigation by the police or the Serious Fraud Office into serious or complex fraud is being or is likely to be carried out, to falsify, conceal, destroy or otherwise dispose (or to cause or to permit the falsification, concealment, destruction or disposal) of documents which he knows or suspects are or would be relevant to such an investigation; but it is a defence to prove that there was no intent to conceal the facts disclosed by the documents from persons carrying out such an investigation[1]. These offences are punishable by a fine, imprisonment or both[2].

Special provision is made in relation to the disclosure of information. Where the Serious Fraud Office is conducting a prosecution not relating to inland revenue, the court may not include prosecution evidence under s78, Police and Criminal Evidence Act 1984 (discretion to exclude unfair evidence) by reason only of the fact that the information was disclosed by the Commissioners of Inland Revenue, or an officer of the Commissioners, for the purpose of a prosecution relating to inland revenue[3]. In the case of information subject to a statutory obligation of secrecy other than under the Taxes Management Act 1970[4], the obligation does not operate to prohibit disclosure of that information to any person in his capacity as a member of the Serious Fraud Office; but any information so disclosed may only be disclosed by a member of the Serious Fraud Office, designated for the purpose by the Director, and only for the purposes of a prosecution in England and Wales or elsewhere[5]. In addition, the Director may enter into a written agreement for the supply of information to or by him subject to an obligation not to disclose such information other than for a specified purpose[6].

Subject to these disclosure provisions[7], information obtained by any person in his capacity as a member of the Serious Fraud Office may be disclosed by a member of that Office, designated by the Director: (a) to any government department or other authority or body discharging its functions on behalf of the Crown; (b) to any competent authority; (c) for the purposes of any prosecution

16. Ibid, .2(11).
17. Ibid.
18. Ibid, s2(12).
19. Ibid, s2(13).
20. Ibid, s2(14).
1. Ibid, s2(16).
2. Ibid, s2(13), (15) and (17).
3. Ibid, s3(2).
4. The Criminal Justice Act 1987, s3(1) makes provision in relation to an obligation of secrecy under the Taxes Management Act 1970.
5. Criminal Justice Act 1987, s3(3).
6. Ibid, s3(4).
7. Namely, the Criminal Justice Act 1987, s3(1), (3) and (4).

in England and Wales or elsewhere and (d) for the purposes of assisting any public or other authority designated by an order made by the Secretary of State to discharge the functions specified in the order[8]. A 'competent authority' includes an inspector appointed under the CA 1985 or to investigate insider dealing under s177, FSA 1986, an Official Receiver, the Accountant in Bankruptcy, an Official Assignee, a person appointed to carry out an investigation under s55, Building Societies Act 1986, an inspector appointed under s94, FSA 1986 or s38, Banking Act 1987, a person exercising powers by virtue of s106, FSA or s44(2) Insurance Companies Act 1982, any body having supervisory, regulatory or disciplinary functions in relation to any profession or any area of commercial activity and any person or body having, under the law of any country or territory outside the UK, corresponding functions to those in this provision[9].

In view of the investigative powers conferred by the FSA 1986, suspected offences of insider dealing will normally be investigated by inspectors appointed under those powers. Nevertheless, investigators acting under the powers conferred by the 1987 Act may in the course of investigations find circumstances suggesting insider dealing.

III. THE POLICE

From the outset, the Department has assumed the main responsibility for enforcing the criminal prohibition on insider dealing, now contained in the IDA 1985. With the conferral on the Department, by s177 FSA 1986, of the power to appoint inspectors to investigate suspected offences of insider dealing, this practice is reinforced. However, in conducting investigations on behalf of the DPP, on whom a right of prosecution is conferred by the legislation[10], the police may be involved in investigating suspected breaches of the insider dealing prohibitions. Such involvement may also stem from police work in conjunction with the Serious Fraud Office[11]. Moreover, the powers of entry under warrant, introduced by s199 FSA 1986, to search premises for evidence relevant to the question of whether an offence has been committed, envisage police involvement. Whilst this provision substantially increases police powers, the additional powers conferred by s177 FSA, 1986 on inspectors[12] mean that unless full co-operation is forthcoming from persons able to assist an investigation[13], inspectors are better placed to pursue an investigation into a suspected offence of insider dealing.

IV. THE SECURITIES AND INVESTMENTS BOARD

Broad powers are conferred on the SIB by the FSA 1986[14] to investigate 'the affairs . . . of any person so far as is relevant to any investment business which he

---

8. Criminal Justice Act 1987, s3(5).
9. Ibid, s3(6).
10. IDA 1985, s8(2).
11. See ante II. The Serious Fraud Office.
12. Although every member of the public is under a moral or social duty to assist the police, a person is under no general legal duty to answer questions put to him. Instead, conduct which can adversely affect police efficiency is penalised: *Halsbury's Laws of England* (Fourth Edition), Vol. 36, paras 321 and 322.
13. See ante I. The Department of Trade and Industry, *4. Insider dealing investigations*.
14. These powers are also exerciseable by the Department of Trade and Industry: FSA 1986,

is or was carrying on or appears . . . to be or to have been carrying on'. The powers are exerciseable when it appears to the SIB that there is good reason to do so[15].

Under these powers, the person under investigation and any connected person[16] may be required to attend before the SIB at a specified time and place and answer questions or provide information with respect to any matter relevant to the investigation[17]. He may also be required to produce documents[18]; this power includes a power to take copies or extracts from documents, to require the person producing them or any connected person to provide an explanation of any of them and if such documents are not produced, to require the person who was required to produce them to state, to the best of his knowledge and belief, where they are. The term 'documents' includes information in any form and in relation to information recorded otherwise than in legible form, references to its production include references to producing a copy of the information in legible form[19]. A statement made by a person in compliance with these requirements may be used in evidence against him[20].

A saving is made for legal professional privilege and for bankers. In regard to the former, a person is not required to disclose any information or produce any document which he would be entitled to refuse to disclose or produce on grounds of legal professional privilege in proceedings in the High Court or on grounds of confidentiality as between client and professional legal adviser in proceedings in the Court of Session, except that a lawyer may be required to furnish the name and address of his client[1].

As to the latter, the saving for banking confidentiality is again narrowly drawn. An institution authorised under the Banking Act 1987 is not required by these powers to disclose any information or produce any document relating to a customer's affairs unless the SIB considers it necessary for the purpose of investigating any investment business carried on, or appearing to be carried on or to have been carried on, by the institution or customer, or if the customer is a related company of the person under investigation, by that person[2].

Specific provision is made for liens. Thus, where a person claims a lien on a document, its production is without prejudice to his lien[3].

Failure to comply, without reasonable excuse, with these provisions is an offence[4]. It is punishable on summary conviction by imprisonment for up to six months or by a fine up to the fifth level on the standard scale or both.

The SIB is also authorised to delegate these powers to an officer or other competent person[5]. However, that person's authority will be limited to investi-

---

ss105(1) and 114(8) and the Financial Services Act 1986 (Delegation) Order 1987, S.I.1987 No. 942.
15. FSA 1986, s105(1). However, an exempted person is not subject to these investigation powers unless he is an appointed representative or the investigation is in respect of investment business in respect of which he is not exempted: s105(2). In addition, a member of a recognised SRO or a person certified by an RPB may not be investigated unless that organisation or body has requested the SIB to investigate or it appears to the SIB that the organisation or body is unable or unwilling to investigate in a satisfactory manner: s105(2).
16. FSA 1986, s105(3).
17. The term 'connected person' is defined in s105(9), FSA 1986.
18. FSA 1986, s105(4).
19. Ibid, s105(9).
20. Ibid, s105(5).
1. Ibid, s105(6).
2. Ibid, s105(7).
3. Ibid, s105(8).
4. Ibid, s105(10).
5. Ibid, s106(1). This power is also exerciseable by the Department of Trade and Industry: FSA 1986,

gating the affairs, or any aspect of the affairs, of specified persons. An investigator who is not one of the Secretary of State's officers must make a report on his findings[6].

Following an investigation into an investment business, the Secretary of State may petition for the winding up of a company[7] or for the disqualification of a director under the Company Directors Disqualification Act 1986[8].

However, a High Court decision[9] has limited the scope of these powers. In this case, a businessman sought judicial review of a demand by the Secretary of State that he should disclose certain documents for the purposes of an investigation into his alleged investment business. In particular, he objected to the validity of the demand on the ground, inter alia, that no activities carried on before December 18, 1986 (the appointed day for s105 to come into force) were capable of amounting to investment business. A Divisional Court held that a person whose alleged investment business was under investigation could not be required to disclose documents relating to transactions which took place before December 18, 1986, in that activities conducted before that date were not 'investment business' for statutory purposes.

The SIB's powers of investigation are supplemented by a power to call for information[10]. In particular, the SIB has power to require, inter alia, a recognised SRO, RPB, recognised investment exchange or recognised clearing house to provide it with such information as it may reasonably require for the exercise of its functions under the FSA 1986.

V. THE SELF-REGULATING ORGANISATIONS

As a prerequisite to recognition under the FSA 1986, an SRO must have adequate arrangements and resources for the effective monitoring and enforcement of compliance with its rules and with any rules and regulations to which its members are subject under Chapter V (Conduct of Investment Business) of Part I, FSA 1986[11]. It must also have effective arrangements for the investigation of complaints against members[12].

Consistent with these requirements, SRO rule books provide for the conduct of an investigation when there appear to be circumstances suggesting that a member is not a fit and proper person, that there has been contravention of the rules by a member firm or that an investigation is desirable for the protection of investors[13]. In turn, member firms are required to produce documents and provide information, to permit officers and employees to answer questions and to co-operate generally with investigations[14].

ss106(1) and 114(8) and the Financial Services Act 1986 (Delegation) Order 1987, S.I.1987 No. 942.
6. FSA 1986, s106(3).
7. CA 1985, s440 as amended by FSA 1986, s198(1).
8. S8, as amended by FSA 1986, s198(2).
9. *R v Secretary of State for Trade and Industry, ex parte R* [1989] 1 All ER 647.
10. FSA 1986, s104.
11. FSA 1986, Sch2, para 4.
12. Ibid, para 6.
13. AFBD, r.9.2; FIMBRA, r.18.2; IMRO, ChVIII, r.l. and TSA, ChV, r.30.3.
14. AFBD, r.9.2.5; FIMBRA, r.18.2.4; IMRO, ChVIII, r.2.02 and TSA, ChV, r.30.3.

VI. THE STOCK EXCHANGE

Although the CA 1980 shifted the main responsibility for enforcement from the self-regulatory agencies to government, the Stock Exchange retains a significant role in enforcement, notably as an important source of information. Investigation with a view to resort to its own sanctions is now ancillary to its revised role in enforcement.

A. Market surveillance

Market surveillance changed significantly following the introduction, in October 1986, of the Stock Exchange Automated Quotations (SEAQ) system[15]. This is an electronic information system at the centre of the Stock Exchange's collection and display of equity market trading information for its U.K. Equity and International Equity Markets. Market makers are required not only to maintain on SEAQ the two-way (buy and sell) prices at which they are prepared to deal, but also to report deals promptly. In this way, Stock Exchange computers receive information on every deal made through the Stock Exchange.

A continuous general surveillance of share price movements is effected by staff in the Quotations Department using an on-line computer system[16]. This monitors the price movement of every listed equity security – on a transaction basis – throughout the time that SEAQ operates. When the price movement of a security exceeds predetermined limits, details are printed out. An attempt is made, by reference to articles in the financial press, market commentaries and company announcements, to establish the reason for the fluctuation. When the fluctuation cannot be explained by publicly available information, the company's brokers are contacted.

Where there are developments which have not been publicly announced, the company is normally asked to make such information public immediately. When untoward activity has apparently occurred prior to an announcement, the matter is referred to the Surveillance Division for further investigation.

An increase in activity due to changes in the structure of the market and the general market conditions was reported by the Quotations Department in its Review of the Year to 31st March, 1987[17]. In the period to 27th October, 1986, the average daily activity comprised 82 exceptional price movements, of which 78 could be explained on the basis of publicly available information, thus leaving 4 for the reasons to be established with brokers. In the period from 27th October, 1986, the average daily activity increased to 98 exceptional price movements of which 90 could be explained on the basis of publicly available information, thus leaving 8 for the reasons to be established with brokers.

B. Investigations into dealings

Responsibility for investigation into dealings lies with the Surveillance Division,

15. The International Stock Exchange, Report and Accounts 1988 (1988), p.22; Office of Fair Trading, *The International Stock Exchange*, A Report by the Director General of Fair Trading to the Secretary of State for Trade and Industry (1988), para 3.5 and the *Sunday Times*, 21st August, 1988.
16. Regulation of Issuers, International Stock Exchange Quotations Department, Review of the Year to 31st March, 1987 (1987), pp20-22.
17. Ibid, p.22.

which comprises 62 staff[18]. Within the Division there is an Insider Dealing Group of 12 staff. The Division maintains close liaison with both the Department and the Panel.

On average, the Surveillance Division looks at 40 potentially suspicious deals each week and follows up 20. The Insider Dealing Group is then usually involved on 10 of those[19].

Although Surveillance Division staff may be alerted as a result of price movements, most deals investigated register no significant price movements[20]. Rather staff tend to be alerted by a change in the typical deal size, an order from broking firms which do not normally deal in a specific stock or a repeat trade by one investor over a short period[1].

The investigative work centres on the interrogation of computerised databases of deals carried out[2]. The database covering all deals made through the Stock Exchange includes the name of the broking firm behind each bargain and its client reference number. Users of the database can obtain a print-out of all deals carried out under a particular client reference number. According to the head of the Surveillance Division, much of the work is 'unglamorous sifting, checking and matching trades. The art of the game is to build interrogation systems to ensure that bells ring and whistles blow when there's something fishy'[3].

In assembling evidence, Surveillance Division staff may be assisted by tape-recordings of conversations[4]. During the period since 1985, most large securities firms have introduced the practice of attaching tape recorders to the telephones of market makers and salesmen. Whilst the purpose was to resolve disputes over whether a deal had been agreed, the practice can prove vital for compliance or surveillance purposes. Moreover, audio-digited tape technology enables computers to pick up key words from tape-recordings. Such devices can greatly reduce the time spent on investigation, which would otherwise involve listening to, and transcribing, tapes over a longer period.

The usefulness of tape-recordings of conversations was underlined in 1988.[5] As employees of a securities firm were required by in-house rules to place all deals through the firm's broking arm, the firm would normally have been able to pick up a particular employee's dealings through its own database. However, the suspicion was that the employee had dealt through another broker. An examination of tape recordings of his conversations disclosed that he had received and passed on inside information about an impending bid to a friend who then dealt in shares.

VII. THE PANEL ON TAKE-OVERS AND MERGERS

Prior to the CA 1980 imposing criminal liability for insider dealing, the Panel was the most successful among the regulatory agencies in detecting cases of

---

18. *The Sunday Times*, 21st August, 1988.
19. *The Financial Times*, 17th August, 1988.
20. Ibid.
1. *The Sunday Times*, 21st August, 1988.
2. *The Financial Times*, 17th August, 1988.
3. Ibid.
4. Ibid.
5. Ibid.

insider dealing[6]. However, due to the overlap of the Code prohibition on dealing with the prohibitions now contained in the IDA 1985, its enforcement role now relates to compliance with other Code requirements associated with insider dealing regulation, such as the confidentiality of price sensitive information before disclosure, the timing of bid announcements[7], disclosure (including reporting requirements)[8] and the conflicts of interest in multi-service financial organisations[9].

As the Panel has no market surveillance, close co-operation between the Panel executive and the Stock Exchange is particularly important. With the more sophisticated equipment available since Big Bang to the Surveillance Division of the Stock Exchange, this co-operation has enabled the Panel to monitor dealings in relevant securities during an offer. In a recent development, the Panel's dealings monitoring unit has been assisted by staff seconded from the Stock Exchange[10]. As a result of such monitoring, the Panel is able to identify substantial dealing activity, or unusual price movements, with a view to detecting possible breaches of the Code and cases of market manipulation through lack of disclosure. The Panel has reported these arrangements as being a significant improvement in the means of monitoring transactions[11].

VIII. COMPANIES

Reflecting the government's view that investigative responsibilities in respect of interests in shares should, so far as possible, fall on the companies concerned rather than the Department[12], the powers conferred on public companies[13] were strengthened by the CA 1981[14] to require information relating to interests in their voting shares. These powers of investigation, which are exercisable either on a company's own initiative or on the requisition of members, have particular significance for enforcement of reporting requirements relating to interests in voting shares in public companies[15].

Acting on its own initiative, a public company may by notice in writing require any person whom it knows or has reasonable cause to believe to be or, at any time during the three years immediately preceding the date on which the notice is issued, to have been interested in shares comprised in the company's relevant share capital, to confirm that fact or not, and if it be confirmed, to give certain information about his interest[16]. An investigation can thus commence with persons other than members, thereby facilitating inquiries where a chain of nominees is involved. There is an exemption from disclosure by persons

6. J.A.C. Suter, *The Regulation of Insider Dealing in Britain and France* (Doctoral thesis 1985), Chapter 6, pp61-89..
7. The Panel on Take-overs and Mergers, Report on the Year ended 31st March, 1981, pp6-8.
8. See, ante, Chapter 5. Disclosure.
9. See, ante, Chapter 6. Administrative regulation.
10. The Panel on Take-overs and Mergers, Report on the Year ended 31st March, 1988, p.6.
11. Ibid, Report on the Year ended 31st March, 1987, p.6 and op cit n10, supra.
12. Parliamentary Debates, House of Commons Official Report,. Standing Committee A, Companies (No. 2) Bill, col.484 (1981).
13. These were previously contained in CA 1976, s27.
14. CA 1981, ss.74-77. These provisions are now contained in CA 1985, ss212-216, 455-457.
15. See, ante, Chapter 5. Disclosure, III. Insider Reporting.
16. CA 1985, s212(1).

exempted by the Secretary of State after consultation with the Bank of England[17].

The definition of interest in shares is wider than for notification purposes. As well as family and corporate interests, concert parties[18] and options to subscribe for shares[19], it extends to interests to be disregarded for notification purposes[20]. Apart from avoiding disputes over information that a company may require, this wider definition means that an investigation may assist in determining whether the exemptions from notification are being abused.

In regard to the information required, a notice may require the addressee: (a) to give particulars of his own past or present interest in shares comprised in the relevant share capital in the company held by him at any time during the previous three years; (b) to give, so far as he knows, particulars of the identity of the person who held that interest immediately upon the addressee ceasing to hold it[1]. To enable a company to identify interested persons and look for any links between them, particulars given as to (a) and (b) must include those as to the identity of persons interested in the shares and whether they are or were parties to an agreement to which the concert party provisions of the CA 1985[2] apply or relating to the exercise of any of the rights conferred by the shareholding[3]. The notice must state a reasonable time within which information must be given in writing[4]. However, the absence of a duty of inquiry was considered likely to render this investigative power ineffective in the case of professionals who act as nominees without knowing either the precise identity or intentions of their principals[5].

On receipt of information in response to a notice, the company must record against the name of the registered holder of those shares in a separate part of the register of share interests (a) the fact and date of a requirement to disclose information and (b) information relating to present interests held by any person[6]. The information is restricted to present interests, though the investigation may have covered past interests.

In addition, a duty to investigate on the requisition of members[7] is provided for to deal with situations where a significant minority of members suspect that a person or persons with undisclosed substantial interests control the company and so are reluctant to initiate an investigation by the company that would disclose their position. This provision requires a company to exercise its powers of investigation on the requisition of members holding, at the date of the requisition, not less than one-tenth of the paid-up capital of the company entitled to vote at a general meeting[8]. The requisition must state that the requisitionists are requiring the company to exercise its investigative powers, specify the manner in which they require those powers to be exercised and give reasonable grounds for requiring the company to exercise those powers in the

17. Ibid, s216(5).
18. Ibid, s212(5).
19. Ibid, s212(6).
20. Ibid, s212(5).
1. Ibid, s212(2).
2. Ibid, s204.
3. Ibid, s212(3).
4. Ibid, s212(4)
5. D. Chaikin, 'The Companies Act 1981' (1982) 3 Co. Law 115 at 120.
6. CA 1985, s213.
7. Ibid, s214.
8. Ibid, s214(1).

manner specified[9]. Upon deposit of a requisition that complies with these requirements, the company is under a duty to exercise its powers in the manner specified in the requisition[10].

Two provisions seek to counter delay. First, when a company has not concluded its investigation within three months of the date of deposit of the requisition, the company is placed under a duty to prepare an interim report in respect of that period and each succeeding period of three months[11]. Interim reports must be available at the company's registered office within a reasonable period (not exceeding fifteen days) after the end of the three month period to which it relates[12].

Secondly, an investigation is regarded as concluded when the company has made all such inquiries as are necessary or expedient for the purposes of the requisition and, in the case of each such inquiry, either a response has been received by the company or the time allowed for a response has elapsed[13]. On conclusion of the investigation, it is the company's duty to prepare and make available at its registered office a report of the investigation within a reasonable period, not exceeding fifteen days, after the conclusion of the investigation[14]. Provision is also made for the exclusion from reports of certain information concerning subsidiaries and substantial holdings in bodies incorporated or carrying on business outside the U.K. where the Secretary of State agrees that disclosure would be harmful[15].

Non-compliance with the duty to investigate, to notify requisitionists of a report's availability for inspection or to keep the report for the period specified is an offence[16]. The company and every officer in default is liable to a fine.

The duty to provide information in an investigation is supported by two sanctions. Any person who (a) fails to comply with a notice to give information or (b) in purported compliance with such a notice, makes any statement which he knows to be false in a material particular or recklessly makes any statement which is false in a material particular is guilty of an offence and liable to imprisonment or a fine, or both[17]. As a directors' liability clause applies to these offences, directors and other individuals who run the affairs of a company required to provide information, to whose consent or connivance or neglect the offence was due, are guilty of an offence[18]. However, no offence is committed when a person proves that the requirement to give the information was frivolous or vexatious[19].

In addition, the company may apply to the court for an order directing that shares be subject to the restrictions of Part XV, CA 1985[20].

Whereas the power to require information extends to any person who the company knows or has reasonable cause to believe to be interested in shares[1], an application to the court can only be made where the person is or was

9. Ibid, s214(2).
10. Ibid, s214(4).
11. Ibid, s215(2).
12. Ibid, s215(2) and (3).
13. Ibid, s215(6).
14. Ibid, s215(1) and (3).
15. Ibid, s215(4).
16. Ibid, s214(5) and s.215(8).
17. Ibid, s216(3).
18. Ibid, s733.
19. Ibid, s216(4).
20. Ie, CA 1985, ss454-457, see ante I. The Department of Trade and Industry, B. Investigations by inspectors, 2. Investigation into the ownership of a company.
1. CA 1985, s212(1).

interested in any shares of the company[2]. As it seems that no application can be made to the court when the company merely reasonably believes a person is or was so interested, restriction orders cannot be made in those unclear cases where an investigation by the company is most necessary[3].

When a restriction order is made, the company or any person aggrieved may apply to the court for an order removing the restrictions[4]. The statutory powers relating to the maintenance or removal of restrictions on shares and sales by order of the court imposed under Part XV, CA 1985[5] extend to investigations by companies, except that the powers exercisable by the court or by the Secretary of State or Department are exercisable only by the court in the context of company investigations[6].

By relating the restriction order sanction for failure to provide information to the provisions for investigation of company ownership, the government sought to achieve two effects[7]. First, a person should not be able to avoid the imposition of a restriction order on shares by pleading that he is a resident of a foreign country whose laws forbid disclosure. Secondly, a person aggrieved would not be entitled to have restrictions removed merely by establishing that he had not provided the requisite information. Hence, a person may be denied the benefit of an unfair advantage derived from earlier non-disclosure. In these circumstances, the court could require an applicant to establish that no unfair advantage had been gained from the failure to provide information or it could require the shares to be sold as a condition of removing restrictions. In the absence of further precision in the CA 1985, an important role is left to the court.

The power of the company to apply to the court for a restriction order is additional to any power in the company's memorandum or articles purporting to impose similar restrictions[8]. However, there are doubts about the validity of these latter powers insofar as they are regarded as infringing the right of a buyer of securities to expect registration and the right of the seller to have his name removed from the register[9].

An early case in which restrictions on shares were imposed, by the Court of Session, was *House of Fraser Plc, Petitioners*[10]. The company asked X to indicate the persons interested in the shares registered in X's name. X stated that the shares were held for German bankers who had acquired them for the account of an investment client. In reply to the company, the German bankers stated that, apart from some shares in which they had a beneficial interest, the shares were ultimately held to the order of an Eastern overseas investor, but failed to disclose the identity of the investor on the ground that the arrangement with the investor was subject to a confidentiality agreement. The Court of Session, without issuing opinions, granted an interim order subjecting the shares to the statutory restrictions, then specified in CA 1948, s174(2)(a) and (b).

In two subsequent cases, the courts have emphasised the unqualified nature of a public company's right to know who are the real owners of its voting shares. In *Re F.H. Lloyd Holdings Plc*[11], shares in the company were registered in the

2. Ibid, s216(1).
3. L.H. Leigh and H.C. Edey, *The Companies Act 1981* (1981), para 330.
4. CA 1985, s456(1) and (2).
5. Ie, CA 1985, ss456-457.
6. Ibid.
7. Leigh and Edey, op cit n3, supra, para 331.
8. CA 1985, s216(2).
9. Chaikin, op cit n5, p351, supra, at 120.
10. [1983] SLT 500.
11. [1985] BCLC 293.

name of an English nominee company for a Luxembourg company. The company served notice on the Luxembourg company requiring information as to the identity of the persons who had interests in the shares held on behalf of the Luxembourg company. The Luxembourg company did not provide the information required since, if it did so without its client's consent, it would be subject to sanctions under Luxembourg criminal law. The company sought an order that the shares held on behalf of the Luxemboug company be made subject to restrictions imposed in connection with investigations into company ownership. The Luxembourg company argued that, as it was a foreign company, the court lacked jurisdiction to make the order or, alternatively, that the court should exercise its discretion not to make the order sought.

Nourse J. granted the order. The English nominee company held the shares and its contractual right against the company in trust for the Luxembourg company, who thus held a beneficial interest in the shares. Since the trust property was situated in England and the trustee was resident in England, the Luxembourg company's beneficial interest was situated in England. Accordingly, the actual principle that U.K. legislation applied to a foreigner's interests in English property, whether or not he had an actual presence in England, meant that the legislative provisions concerned[12], namely, those relating to the power of a public company to require information with respect to interests in the voting shares and the penalties for failure to provide such information, were applicable to the Luxembourg company. Moreover, there was no justification for interpreting the term 'any person' in these provisions as not including foreigners who had not by coming into the UK made themselves subject to British jurisdiction. The court, therefore, had jurisdiction to grant the order sought. In this connection, Nourse J. stated that the clear purpose of the legislation 'is to give a public company, and ultimately the public at large, a prima facie unqualified right to know who are the real owners of its voting shares'[13]. Whilst the court would not exercise its discretion to impose penalties where the company's requirement for information was frivolous or vexatious, it was not necessary for the company to show that it had a real ground for believing that the person interested in the shares was seeking to build up a substantial holding in the company. This was a proper case in which the court should exercise its discretion to grant the order sought.

This decision was applied by the Court of Appeal in *Re Geers Gross Plc*[14]. E agreed with GG, a publicly quoted company, not to acquire more than 20% of its share capital. Suspecting a breach of this agreement by use of nominess, GG obtained an order imposing restrictions on the transfer of a block of 450,000 shares (approximately 3% of its share capital) which was held by a nominee company on behalf of a Swiss bank. The bank refused to disclose the names of its clients who had bought the shares. Subsequently, the nominee company and the bank applied for an order lifting the restriction on transfer in order to allow the sale of 410,000 shares in the stock market and the completion of the sale of 40,000 shares which had already been contracted to be sold. The applicants contended that the mere fact that the shares were to be sold was in itself sufficient reason for the court to approve the sale under CA 1985, s456(3)(b)[15].

12. CA 1981, ss74(1) and 77(1), now CA 1985, ss212(1) and 216(1).
13. [1985] BCLC 293 at 300.
14. [1988] 1 All ER 224; [1987] 1 WLR 1649.
15. This provision is outlined in I. The Department of Trade and Industry, B. Investigations by inspectors, 2. Investigation into the ownership of a company.

The judge refused to lift the restriction[16].

Dismissing the applicants' appeal, the Court of Appeal held that, since a public company had a prima facie unqualified right to know who were the real owners of its voting shares, the court could take into account, when deciding whether to give approval under s456(3)(b) to the sale of shares, whether there had been a failure to disclose relevant facts about the shares. Because GG would be less able to determine the beneficial ownership of the shares and whether E had breached the agreement once the shares were sold, the applicants' failure to disclose the identity of the owners of the shares was sufficient reason for the court to refuse to give approval to the sale of the shares, notwithstanding that innocent purchasers of the shares might be deprived of the benefit of ownership for an indefinite period.

These two decisions illustrate that a public company's unqualified right to know who were the real owners of its voting shares overrides not only a duty of confidence owed to clients, but also the interests of innocent third parties. The difficulty of overseas companies, notably banks, is particularly acute since disclosure of the information sought would give rise to criminal liability in some jurisdictions and, more generally, to a breach of the obligation of secrecy owed to clients. For such companies, initiatives in the sphere of international co-operation among investigators assume particular importance.

The enhanced investigative powers conferred on public companies have enabled them to conduct more extensive investigations, thereby facilitating improved use of the investigative resources of the regulatory authorities. However, difficulties may emerge; as the Department has acknowledged[17], there does not appear to have been a case where the registered owner of shares was a foreign resident.

IX. INTERNATIONAL ASPECTS

A. Internationalisation of the securities markets

The internationalisation of securities markets, with the multiple listing of securities, cross-frontier dealings in securities and the potential for 24-hour trading, also increases the potential for insider dealing. In particular, internationalisation affords greater scope for insiders either to use foreign financial institutions or to trade on extra-territorial securities markets.

Such increased potential for insider dealing raises difficulties for investigators. These difficulties stem from the fact that traditionally securities regulation, including insider dealing regulation, has been developed for a domestic securities market.

In domestic transactions, a considerable amount of information is available, even though its processing may be time-consuming and proof of an insider dealing offence may be complicated. The regulatory authorities also have broad powers of investigation. In addition, disclosure requirements ensure that the regulatory authorities collect a considerable amount of information on a regular basis for other purposes; in general, this is available to investigators.

Transactions with a foreign element raised difficulties for investigators. The

16. [1987] 1 WLR 837.
17. Department of Trade and Industry, *Disclosure of Interests in Shares, A. Consultative Document* (1988), para 2.9.

problem of foreign orders has long been recognised[18] and, in the 1980s, there has been growing concern about the difficulty of discovering the beneficial owners of shares in a company where the registered holder is a foreign entity[19].

However, internationalisation, with the introduction of overseas participants in the UK securities market and overseas transactions in UK securities, raises acute difficulties for investigators, notably in relation to insider dealing. Their ability to investigate suspected insider dealing involving other jurisdictions can be hampered by foreign non-disclosure laws, such as bank secrecy, and by the difficulty of obtaining information from abroad. Pending developments to enhance international regulation, they are left to apply an essentially domestic system of investigation to transactions for which it is not equipped.

In considering these investigative problems, reference will be made to aspects of US securities laws and their application abroad because the importance of these problems has been emphasised in the controversies between US authorities, particularly the SEC, and Swiss banks. The emergence of these problems and the attempt to mitigate the conflicts have underlined some specific problems arising from the internationalisation of securities trading.

B. Foreign non-disclosure laws

A recurring source of difficulty encountered in international investigations are foreign non-disclosure laws which, on their face, prohibit compliance with requests or orders to produce evidence. Such laws take the form of bank secrecy and blocking laws.

1. Bank secrecy laws

Bank secrecy laws primarily protect the personal right of clients to preserve the confidentiality of information entrusted to banks. These laws are common to many legal systems, though with considerable differences in scope and sanctions.

Such laws appear to serve three main purposes. First, they maintain the confidential relationship between bankers and their clients. Secondly, they afford protection to clients against governmental expropriation of their financial assets. Thirdly, they promote banking activity and the economy and when substantial foreign funds are attracted, contribute to the country's development as an international financial centre.

More specifically, bank secrecy laws prohibit the disclosure of confidential information entrusted to bankers by clients unless either the client consents to disclosure or the banker's duty of confidence is overridden by a duty imposed by law compelling disclosure. The extent to which the duty of confidence is overridden by such other duties varies considerably among legal systems. In this connection, the UK law on banking secrecy is regarded as relatively weak[20].

18. E.g. Committee to Review the Functioning of Financial Institutions, Second Stage Evidence, Vol. 4 The Stock Exchange (1979), para 59; The Panel on Take-overs and Mergers, Statement on Dunford and Elliott Ltd., 26th May, 1978 [1978] J.B.L. 367.
19. T.P. Lee, 'Current Changes in London Securities Markets: Some Domestic and International Regulatory Issues', p.132 at 143 in (eds) K.K. Lian, H.H.M. Chan, H.P. Kee and P.N. Pillai, *Current Development in International Securities Commodities and Financial Future Markets* (1986).
20. L. Collins, 'Banking Secrecy and the Enforcement of Securities Legislation', p.81 in (ed.) R.M. Goode, *Conflicts of interest in the changing financial world* (1986).

Other differences relate to sanctions. Countries such as the US, the UK and Canada restrict liability for breach of the banker's duty of confidence to civil sanctions. In contrast, countries such as Switzerland, Luxembourg and the Cayman Islands impose criminal penalties.

As it has been well-documented, Switzerland provides a convenient example of bank secrecy[1]. Responsive to a concern for the privacy of customers, Swiss bank secrecy is based on a 1934 Law which made it a criminal offence to divulge secrets entrusted to a bank. The 1934 Law reinforced established principles of banking secrecy, including personal financial privacy rights under the Civil Code, the contractual duty of confidentiality between banker and clients based on the Code of Obligations and the protection afforded to Swiss trade and industry against economic espionage by the Criminal Code. In turn, these stringent secrecy provisions helped attract substantial foreign funds with the result that the interests of a powerful banking community militated against measures that could significantly discourage foreign investment. Yet concern about Switzerland's reputation as a financial centre and the need to combat economic crime contributed to a recognition that certain interests should override secrecy. Thus, federal and cantonal law placed limits on bank secrecy. But the general effect was to permit disclosure to government authorities or other persons in Switzerland only under a specific court order or with the customer's express permission.

Further limitations have now been imposed not only by international agreement[2], but also by private agreement among Swiss banks. In regard to the latter, an important development was the 1977 Swiss Banking Agreement[3] signed by all Swiss banks. Its twin objects were (1) to ensure that the identity of clients was reliably ascertained and (2) to prevent improper use of banking secrecy in regard to (a) the opening and keeping of accounts and deposits of securities without ascertaining the owner's identity and (b) the acceptance of funds acquired, recognisable to the bank, by acts that, according to Swiss law, were punishable or called for extradition or (c) aiding and abetting capital flight and tax evasion. Subsequently, this Agreement was renewed in sharper form in 1982 as an Agreement between the Swiss National Bank and the Swiss Bankers' Association[4]. After the Swiss National Bank had indicated that it did not intend to renew the 1982 Agreement, the Swiss Bankers' Association drew up a new version of the Code in 1987 for signature by its members[5]. Due to run until 1992, the 1987 Agreement includes more stringent provisions to prevent clients concealing their identity behind lawyers or trustees.

2. Blocking laws

Whereas bank secrecy laws protect the private rights of clients, blocking laws assert a national interest in the confidentiality of certain categories of information. In consequence, they cannot be waived by private parties.

1. This account of Swiss bank secrecy draws on J.E. Siegel, 'United States Insider Trading Prohibition in Conflict with Swiss Bank Secrecy' (1983) 4 JCCLSR 353 at 357-358.
2. See post C. Obtaining information from abroad, 2. Bilateral and multilateral agreements.
3. Agreement on the observance of care in accepting funds and on the practising of bank secrecy (1977). This Agreement, the 'Swiss Banking Agreement', is set out as an annex to T.P. Lee, M-C. Robert, A. Hirsch and I.M. Pollack, 'Secrecy Laws and other obstacles to international co-operation' (1982) 4 JCCLSR 287 at 308.
4. *The Financial Times*, 24th March, 1987.
5. Ibid.

Adopted mainly in the last thirty years, most blocking statutes are a response to the extraterritorial application of US laws and discovery procedures, particularly in antitrust proceedings. They condition the disclosure, inspection, copying or removal of documents on the consent of governmental authorities.

In the UK, the Protection of Trading Interests Act 1980 was passed to provide protection from requirements, prohibitions and judgments imposed or given under the laws of other countries and affecting the trading or other interests of persons in the UK. This Act contains three main sets of measures[6]. First, the Secretary of State for Trade and Industry is authorised to forbid compliance by British citizens and businesses with the orders of foreign authorities, where those orders have extraterritorial effect and prejudice British trading interests. In particular, the Secretary of State may give directions prohibiting compliance with a requirement by overseas courts and authorities to produce documents or furnish information[7]. Secondly, a prohibition is imposed on the enforcement by UK courts of foreign judgments for multiple damages and certain other judgments relating to the control of competition. Thirdly, a right is conferred on British citizens or businesses against whom multiple damages have been awarded to recover the non-compensatory element from the original plaintiff by an action in the UK.

By the time of the FSA 1986, the growing importance of the exchange of information between regulatory authorities resulted in a difference in emphasis. In particular, provision was made for disclosure under statutory authority to various regulatory authorities[8]. However, the Secretary of State for Trade and Industry has control over the disclosure of information overseas. In this connection, he is authorised to give directions, in the public interest, prohibiting or otherwise restricting the disclosure of information overseas[9]. Breach of a direction is an offence.

C. Obtaining information from abroad

In the international sphere, one of the main concerns of the regulatory authorities has been the scope for the exchange of information and mutual assistance in order to enforce securities laws. In the UK, this is evidenced in the provision in the FSA 1986[10] for disclosure under statutory authority to various regulatory bodies. In particular, information may be disclosed for the purpose of enabling or assisting an authority in a country or a territory outside the UK to exercise, inter alia, functions corresponding to those of the Secretary of State under the FSA 1986, those of the Bank of England under the Banking Act 1987 or those of the competent authority for the purposes of Part IV[11] of the FSA 1986 or any other functions in connection with rules of law corresponding to the provisions of the IDA 1985 or Part VII[12] of the FSA 1986 relating to insider dealing.

Attempts to increase the information obtainable from abroad have taken four main forms. These are: informal co-operation between regulators; bilateral and multilateral agreements; litigation and the proposed 'waiver by conduct'

6. A.V. Lowe, 'Blocking Extraterritorial Jurisdiction: The British Protection of Trading Interests Act, 1980' (1981) 75 Am.J.Int'l L.257.
7. The Protection of Trading Interest Act 1980 s2.
8. FSA 1986, s180(6); see post C. Obtaining information from abroad.
9. Ibid, s181.
10. S180(6), as amended by Banking Act 1987, Sch6, para 27(3).
11. Official Listing of Securities, ss142-157.
12. Insider Dealing, ss173-178.

rule. To an important extent, developments in this field have been prompted by the strength of the US interest in enforcing its securities laws, with particular reference to the difficulty of foreign non-disclosure laws.

There is, however, a difference in emphasis between US and UK authorities. Whereas the US authorities primarily seek information for use in investigations or civil proceedings, the emphasis of the UK authorities is rather on investigations or criminal proceedings. This difference in emphasis can, therefore, affect the usefulness of particular agreements, though the main methods remain the same.

1. Informal co-operation between regulators

Although not formally recognised by law, informal co-operation occurs between regulators. By way of example, the Head of the Surveillance Division of the Stock Exchange makes weekly calls to his counterparts at the SEC, in Canada and in Australia[13]. Moreover, a striking illustration of the importance of informal co-operation occurred when the SEC alerted the UK authorities to the Guinness affair[14].

2. Bilateral and multilateral agreements

Apart from voluntary co-operation between regulatory authorities, the main methods for obtaining evidence abroad have traditionally been the Hague Convention and letters rogatory. These traditional methods have, however, proved inadequate for gathering information prior to litigation.

To assist regulatory authorities at the investigative stage before a decision is made as to the institution of proceedings, a significant development in regard to international aspects of securities regulation has been the conclusion of mutual assistance treaties and other agreements, mainly in the form of Memoranda of Understanding. The importance of these initiatives has been reinforced by the disadvantages associated with obtaining evidence through litigation[15] and the proposed 'waiver by conduct' rule[16].

(a) THE HAGUE CONVENTION

The main multilateral agreement for taking evidence abroad is the Hague Convention on the Taking of Evidence Abroad in Civil or Commercial Matters[17]. It provides two mechanisms, namely, letters of request and taking of evidence by diplomatic officers, consular agents and commissioners.

In the SEC's experience[18], the Hague Convention has provided a useful mechanism for obtaining evidence from neutral witnesses. It is, in general, available to the SEC only after proceedings have been commenced in a US District Court. However, in most instances, the SEC needs foreign co-operation

13. *The Financial Times*, 17th August, 1988.
14. L.C.B. Gower, 'Big Bang and City Regulation' (1988) 1 M.L.R. 1 at 21.
15. See post, 3. Litigation.
16. See post, 4. The proposed 'waiver by conduct' rule.
17. The Hague Conference on Private International Law, Convention on the Taking of Evidence Abroad in Civil or Commercial Matters, The Hague, October 7-26, 1968 (1969) 8 I.L.M.31.
18. C.C. Cox, 'Internationalisation of the capital markets: the experience of the Securities and Exchange Commission' (1987) 11 Md. Journal of International Law and Trade 201 at 217.

in obtaining evidence and completing an investigation before commencing such proceedings. In addition, in the SEC experience, it is often difficult to obtain evidence pursuant to this Convention when those in possession of evidence oppose its production.

In particular, the Convention does not remove the difficulties associated with foreign non-disclosure laws because it does not compel disclosure[19]. In regard to the taking of evidence by diplomatic officers, consular agents and commissioners, such persons are authorised to secure evidence without compulsion or if the foreign nation grants permission for disclosure[20]. Information may also be obtained when a foreign nation permits parties to proceed with discovery[1]. An important limitation in regard to letters of request is imposed by Article 23, which states that a Contracting State may at the time of signature, ratification or accession, declare that it will not execute letters of request issued for the purpose of obtaining pre-trial discovery of documents as known in Common Law countries. In this connection, the UK declared that it has the right to choose not to execute letters of request[2]. Indeed, many countries agreed to this Convention on condition that no pre-trial discovery may take place pursuant to Convention procedures[3].

Nevertheless, the usefulness of mechanisms for obtaining evidence from abroad was illustrated, in the UK, in the High Court judgment in 1984 concerning judicial assistance in the Sante Fe case[4]. The District Court for the Southern District of New York issued Letters Rogatory addressed to the High Court for the examination of witnesses in proceedings brought in that court by the SEC against purchasers of stock and options in Santa Fe, alleging insider dealing before the announcement of a merger with the Kuwait Petroleum Corporation. The High Court made an order, ex parte, requiring the examination of the witnesses. Two of the proposed witnesses had been employed in London by a Luxembourg bank through whose London branch purchases of stock and options in Santa Fe had occurred. The two employees sought to set aside the order requiring the examination on the grounds, inter alia, that (a) they were forbidden by Luxembourg law from revealing the identity of the bank's clients and (b) the Letters Rogatory did not require evidence but discovery and hence it was not possible to give effect to them, having regard to the UK's reservation about the use of the Hague Convention to obtain discovery and the guidance given by the House of Lords on the interpretation of the Evidence (Proceedings in Other Jurisdictions) Act 1975[5]. Drake J. dismissed the application to set aside the order and upheld the request for judicial assistance. He expressed doubt whether disclosure of confidential information by the applicants in legal proceedings in England would constitute an offence under Luxembourg law. In any event, he considered that there was no real or substantial risk of them being charged with any criminal offence in Luxem-

19. Comment, 'The Future of Global Securities Transactions: Blocking the Success of Market Links' (1987) 11 Md. Journal of International Law and Trade 283 at 304.
20. Comment, op cit n19, supra, at 303-304. In particular, reference is made to arts. 16 and 21 of the Convention.
1. Comment, op cit n19, supra, at 304. Reference is made to art.17 of the Convention.
2. Comment, op cit n19, supra, at 305.
3. Cox, op cit n18, supra, at 217.
4. United Kingdom: High Court of Justice (Queen's Bench Division) Judgment concerning Judicial Assistance in the Santa Fe Case (1984) 23 I.L.M.511; L. Collins, 'Banking Secrecy and the Enforcement of Securities Legislation', p.81 at 87 in (ed.) R.M. Goode, *Conflicts of interest in the changing financial world* (1986).
5. *In re Westinghouse Uranium Contract* [1978] A.C. 547.

bourg, even if one existed.

However, on the issue of bank secrecy, Drake J. considered that there could be circumstances in which disclosure was not in the public interest:

> 'There is . . . a public interest in maintaining the confidential relationship between banker and client, so that wherever a banker seeks to be excused from answering a question which would involve the breach of that confidentiality, it is proper . . . for the Court to consider such a request and to judge it in the context of the circumstances in which it is made. There is . . . also clearly a public interest, and a very strong one, in not permitting the confidential relationship between banker and client to be used as a cloak to conceal improper or fraudulent activities evidence of which would otherwise be available to be used in legal proceedings, whether here or abroad.
> Each case must depend . . . on its particular facts'[6].

(b) MUTUAL ASSISTANCE TREATIES

(i) European Convention on Mutual Assistance in Criminal Matters. An early Council of Europe convention designed to facilitate the obtaining of information and evidence was this 1959 Convention covering the general range of criminal offences. This Convention mainly provides for letters rogatory, the service of writs and records of judicial verdicts, the appearance of witnesses, experts and prosecuted persons, the laying of information in connection with proceedings and the exchange of information from judicial records. In particular, provision is made for direct communication between judicial authorities. This Convention has not, however, been ratified by all signatories and other signatories[7] have ratified it with reservations. The UK is not a signatory, but legislation to enable the UK to become a party to the Convention is anticipated[8].

(ii) European Convention for Mutual Assistance in Insider Dealing. A multilateral agreement on insider dealing is this convention being prepared by the Council of Europe[9]. Following a conference on insider dealing held in Milan in 1983 attended by Council of Europe delegates, the Council of Europe decided to work on a draft international convention for administrative, criminal and civil co-operation in the enforcement of insider dealing[10]. The draft was adopted by the Committee for Legal Co-operation (le Comité de Coopération juridique) in November 1987 and then submitted to the Steering Committee on Criminal Policy (le Comité directeur de politique criminelle) for consideration of the criminal aspects. It should then be placed before the Committee of Ministers. It is anticipated that this convention will quickly be ratified by the majority of Member States in the Council of Europe.

The purpose of the Convention is, in the first instance, to provide, as between

---

6. (1984) 23 I.L.M. 511 at 516.
7. Council of Europe Chart showing signatures and ratification of conversions and agreements concluded within the Council of Europe, 1st July 1987.
8. *The Times*, 25th February, 1988.
9. La Commission des opérations de bourse, Rapport annuel 1987 (1988), pp255-256.
10. Ibid, Rapport annuel 1985 (1986), p.132.

states who ratify the Convention, for international assistance in the exchange of information relating to insider dealing. To this end, the convention contains provisions relating to the definition of the offence and of an insider, the content of the assistance envisaged, the use of information obtained and professional secrecy. In addition, the Convention provides for mutual assistance in criminal matters, involving a specific procedure by reference to the 1959 European Convention on Mutual Assistance in Criminal Matters. States can decide either to apply the 1959 Convention or to withdraw their reservations in relation to insider dealing.

(iii) The Commonwealth Scheme on Mutual Assistance in Criminal Matters.   Agreed by Commonwealth Law Ministers in August 1986, this Scheme provides for wide-ranging assistance, including search and seizure, examination of witnesses, transfer of prisoners to give evidence, service of documents and freezing and forfeiture of illegal assets[11]. Legislation to enable the UK to join this Scheme is expected[12]. This Scheme will complement co-operation through the Commonwealth Secretariat's Commercial Crime Unit[13].

(iv) The United States-Switzerland: Treaty on Mutual Assistance in Criminal Matters.   Concluded in 1973, the US-Switzerland: Treaty on Mutual Assistance in Criminal Matters[14] came into force in 1977. This Treaty empowers Swiss judges to order a banker to give evidence on an application for assistance by the US. By November 1987 an application for assistance by the US. By November 1987 US requests to Switzerland totalled about 400, mainly involving fraud or narcotics cases; Swiss requests to the US totalled about 150[15]. However, an important limitation has been a requirement of dual criminality so that the information requested must relate to conduct punishable as a criminal offence in both countries. Due to insider dealing having been made a criminal offence in Switzerland only in 1988[16], insider dealing has not been a matter on which assistance could be given under the Treaty.

Since its entry into force, this Treaty has prompted two understandings. First, a Memorandum of Understanding on insider trading was concluded between the two countries in 1982[17]. Secondly, a Memorandum of Understanding concluded in 1987, commits both countries to use the Treaty as a first resort in gathering evidence, use their best efforts to achieve a mutual interpretation of the Treaty and streamline the process of giving assistance[18].

11. B.A.K. Rider, D.A. Chaikin, C. Abrams, *Guide to the Financial Services Act 1986* (1986), para1305.
12. *The Times*, 25th February, 1988.
13. Rider, op cit n11, supra.
14. United States – Switzerland: Treaty on Mutual Assistance in Criminal Matters, May 25th 1973 (1973) 12 I.L.M.916; Switzerland – United States: Understanding concerning Treaty on Mutual Assistance in Criminal Matters, December 23, 1975 (1975) 15 I.L.M.283. This Treaty is discussed by Siegel., op cit n1, p357, supra, at 360-361 and by J.M. Fedders, F.B. Wade, M.D. Mann and M. Beizer, 'Waiver by Conduct – A Possible Response to the Internationalisation of the Securities Markets' (1984) 6 JCCLSR 1 at 10-11.
15. Note (1988) 27 I.L.M.480.
16. *The Times*, 20th June, 1988; *The Financial Times*, 28th June, 1988 and (1988) Bulletin of Legal Developments, p.133.
17. See post, c. Memoranda of Understanding.
18. Switzerland-United States: Memorandum of Understanding on Mutual Assistance in Criminal Matters and Ancillary Administrative Proceedings (1988) 27 I.L.M.480.

(v) Other Mutual Assistance Treaties. Other treaties relating to mutual assistance in criminal matters have been concluded. In particular, the US signed such a treaty with Canada in 1985[19] and with the UK in 1986 concerning the Cayman Islands[20].

(C) MEMORANDA OF UNDERSTANDING

A number of Memoranda of Understanding have been concluded to facilitate the exchange of information in securities transactions, including insider dealing. These Memoranda lack the binding force of international treaties.

(i) the US-Swiss Memorandum of Understanding. In order to fill the gap relating to insider dealing in the 1977 Mutual Assistance Treaty, a Memorandum of Understanding concluded in 1982[1] resulted in Swiss banks being able to co-operate in SEC investigations into insider dealing. Apart from recording an exchange of opinions and related understandings reached in relation to the 1977 Treaty, the parties also entered into understandings in regard to the 1977 private Agreement among Members of the Swiss Bankers' Association[2]. The result was the establishment of a complex procedure for sharing information. Thus, a SEC request for information was passed by the Department of Justice to the Swiss Federal Office for Police Matters, which submitted the request to a Commission of Enquiry established by the Swiss Bankers' Association. When the transaction in question related either to a business merger or the acquisition of a substantial holding and met other requirements in the agreement, the Swiss bank involved could be asked to provide a detailed report of the transaction and to freeze the account of the customer under suspicion[3].

Known as Agreement XVI, this further Agreement of the Swiss Bankers' association[4] attached to the Memorandum of Understanding provides an alternative method for handling requests for information from the SEC on the subject of misuse of inside information. Agreement XVI, involving banks in Switzerland trading in US securities markets, applies to transactions relating to mergers and the acquisition of a 10% holding. Appointed by the Swiss Bankers' Association, a Commission of Inquiry considers SEC requests for information, which are forwarded to it by the Federal Office for Police Matters with a report, containing the evidence requested, to be forwarded to the SEC, unless the bank's report establishes to the Commission's reasonable satisfaction that a

19. Canada-United States: Treaty on Mutual Legal Assistance in Criminal Matters, March 18, 1985, (1985) 24 I.L.M.1092.
20. Treaty between the United States of America and the United Kingdom of Great Britain and Northern Ireland concerning the Cayman Islands relating to Mutual Legal Assistance in Criminal Matters, July 3, 1986. This Treaty is printed in the Appendix to Comment, 'A Comparative Analysis of Recent Accords which Facilitate Transnational SEC Investigations of Insider Trading' (1987) 11 Md. Journal of International Law and Trade 243 at 267.
1. Switzerland-United States: Memorandum of Understanding to Establish Mutually Acceptable Means for Improving International Law Enforcement Co-operation in the Field of Insider Trading, August 31, 1982 (1983) 22 I.L.M.I.
2. See ante B. Foreign non-disclosure laws, 1. Bank secrecy laws.
3. An example of the use of the U.S.-Swiss Memorandum of Understanding is contained in Comment, 'A Comparative Analysis of Recent Accords which Facilitate Transnational SEC Investigations of Insider Trading' (1987) 11 Md. Journal of International Law and Trade 243 at 252.
4. Agreement XVI of the Swiss Bankers' Association with regard to the handling of requests for information from the Securities and Exchange Commission of the US on the subject of misuse of inside information (1983) 22 I.L.M. 7.

customer did not order a purchase or sale subject to the SEC's request or is not an insider as defined by the Agreement. If the conditions for the supply of information to the SEC are not fulfilled, the Commission delivers to the Federal Office for Police Matters a report to be forwarded to the SEC, explaining the reasons. When the SEC's dispute with the customer is resolved and its investigation concluded, the frozen funds, together with accrued interest, are unfrozen and returned to the customer or remitted to the SEC under a court order. The banks must inform clients of the contents of the Agreement. When clients have not expressly agreed to waive the protection afforded by secrecy laws, they are thus on notice that orders for transactions to be effected in the US will be deemed to constitute such waiver.

(ii) The US-UK Memorandum of Understanding.   A broader agreement is the Memorandum of Understanding on the exchange of information in matters relating to securities and futures concluded in September 1986 between the Department of Trade and Industry and the Securities and Exchange Commission (SEC) and the Commodities Futures Trading Commission (CFTC)[5]. The Memorandum sets out the basis upon which these regulatory authorities reciprocally propose to exchange information to facilitate the performance of their functions regarding the legal rules or requirements of the US and the UK[6]. For securities matters, the Memorandum includes not only matters relating to investment business, but also:

> 'the statutes, rules and requirements of the United States and the United Kingdom . . . relating to the prevention of insider dealing in, misrepresentation in the course of dealing in, and market manipulation in, securities listed on an investment exchange or a national securities exchange, or quoted in an automated inter-dealer quotation system, or traded over-the-counter, where the exchange, system, or over-the-counter market is situated within, and a material part of any of the relevant transactions in securities are effected within, the territory of the requesting Authority'[7].

The Memorandum does not give rise to a right for a private party to obtain, suppress or exclude any evidence or to challenge execution of a request for assistance[8]. In response to requests made in accordance with the specified procedure and subject to the conditions imposed in the Memorandum, each signatory authority is required to assist the other by providing any information that is either already in its hands or that it can by its best efforts obtain in order to enable the other to secure compliance with the relevant legal rules and requirements[9]. Assistance may be denied on grounds of public interest[10]. Moreover, the Memorandum does not extend to information held by the

---

5. Memorandum of Understanding on Exchange of Information between the United States Securities and Exchange Commission and the United Kingdom Department of Trade and Industry in Matters relating to Securities and between the United States Commodity Futures Trading Commission and the United Kingdom Department of Trade and Industry in Matters relating to Futures, September 23, 1986 (1986) 25 I.L.M.1431; hereinafter the 'US-UK Memorandum of Understanding'.
6. The US-UK Memorandum of Understanding, para2.
7. Ibid, para1(h)(i).
8. Ibid, para 3.
9. Ibid, para 4.
10. Ibid, para 5.

Department solely by virtue of powers and functions relating to matters other than securities, investments, futures or company law[11].

In regard to procedure, a request for information is to be in writing, though in urgent cases, the request itself may be oral, with written confirmation following within ten days[12]. As to the main details, the request must specify the information required, the purpose for which the information is sought, the grounds on which breach of the legal rule or requirement is suspected and the identity of the person whose conduct causes concern[13]. In addition, the requested information must be reasonably relevant to securing compliance with the legal rule or requirement specified[14]. If the authority in receipt of the request is not satisfied that a request fully complies with these requirements, it may require the Director of the Division of Enforcement of the SEC or CFTC or the Under Secretary, Financial Services Division of the Department to certify that the request is cognizable under the terms of the Memorandum[15]. Such certification is not open to challenge, save on substantial grounds which are to be fully stated in writing.

As to the conditions imposed, information is to be used for three purposes[16]. First, it may be used to secure compliance with or enforcement of the legal rule or requirement specified in the request, and also other applicable legal rules or requirements in proceedings in which violation of the legal rule or requirement specified in the request is alleged. Secondly, the information may be used to secure compliance with or enforcement of a legal rule or requirement not specified in the request in proceedings in which a violation of the legal rule or requirement is not alleged, if before such use, the authority seeking the information notifies its intention to the other authority which, in turn, does not object. Thirdly, the information can be used for conducting a civil or administrative enforcement proceeding, assisting in a criminal prosecution, or conducting any investigation related thereto for any general charge applicable to the violation of the legal rule or requirement identified in the request. An obligation of confidentiality[17] attaches to any information furnished under the Memorandum in accordance with detailed provisions laid down, unless the information is disclosed in furtherance of the purpose for which it was requested[18]. When the costs of providing or obtaining the information are substantial, the authority in receipt of the request may require the requesting authority to undertake to pay those costs[19].

The Memorandum is expressed to be an 'interim understanding'. The regulatory authorities are to use their best efforts to ensure that treaty negotiations begin within one year[20].

(iii) Other Memoranda of Understanding.　A Memorandum of Understanding has also been negotiated between the Department of Trade and Industry and the Japanese Ministry of Finance. Signed in April 1987, this Memorandum seems

11. Ibid, para 6.
12. Ibid, para 7(a).
13. Ibid, para 7(b).
14. Ibid, para 7(d).
15. Ibid, para 7.
16. Ibid, para 8.
17. Ibid, para 9.
18. Ie, under para 8.
19. The US-UK Memorandum of Understanding, para 13.
20. Ibid, para 17.

less likely to develop into a full agreement[1].

Other Memoranda are being negotiated. These include regulatory authorities in France, Switzerland and Australia[2].

These developments mirror those in the US. Apart from the US-Swiss and the US-UK Memoranda of Understanding, US authorities have concluded Memoranda with Japan[3] and Canada[4].

3. Litigation

Notwithstanding informal co-operation between regulators and the conclusion of bilateral and multilateral agreements, evidence has also been obtained through litigation. In this connection, a significant development was the 1981 US decision in *SEC v Banca della Svizzera Italiana (BSI)*[5], with its rejection of a foreign intermediary's reliance on foreign non-disclosure laws to support refusal to disclose information to the SEC. Like the proposed 'waiver by conduct' rule, this decision should be set against the background of attempts, in the 1970s, to reach an international solution in regard to foreign non-disclosure laws having proved inconclusive.

The *BSI* case followed a SEC investigation into transactions in the common stock and call options for the common stock of St. Joe Mineral Corporation between 10th and 12th March; during this period, an offer for the company was announced. These transactions were carried out on BSI's instructions and realised a profit of $1.4 million for its principals. The SEC concluded that the transactions were probably based on inside information about the bid. After issuing a temporary restraining order to freeze the proceeds in BSI's New York bank account, the Federal District Court ordered BSI to disclose the identity of its principals insofar as permitted by law. Relying on this qualification, BSI argued that it could not comply with the order on the grounds that disclosure would subject the bank and its officers to the risk of imprisonment, fine, civil liability and administrative sanctions in Switzerland. The SEC then applied for an order compelling BSI to answer and imposing contempt sanctions for non-compliance. The sanctions requested included a fine for each day of non-compliance, a ban on trading in US securities markets, a total freeze on BSI assets in the US, divestiture of all properties owned by BSI within the US and an order for the arrest of any BSI officer, director or controller in the US.

At a hearing on the SEC's application, Judge Pollack indicated that he would sign the order for contempt sanctions the following week unless BSI had obtained waivers of confidentiality from clients. The sanctions would include fines and a ban on trading in US markets. These threats prompted BSI to disclose the names of four companies for whom the transactions had been carried out and of the individual who placed the orders on the companies' behalf. These disclosures were crucial. Although the individual, who was a close

1. City Brief (1988) N.L.J.106; P. Farmery,' Towards a Tougher Regime Against Insider Dealing - Part II' (1988) 9 B.L.R.3.
2. Farmery, op cit n1, supra, at 3.
3. Japan-United States: Memorandum of the U.S. Securities and Exchange Commission and the Securities Bureau of the Japanese Ministry of Finance on the Sharing of Information, May 23, 1986 (1986) 25 I.L.M.1429.
4. Canada-United States: Memorandum of Understanding on Administration and Enforcement of Securities Laws, January 7, 1988. (1988) 27 I.L.M.412.
5. Siegel, op cit n1, p357, supra, at 361-367; Fedders, op cit n14, p362, supra, at 8-9 and T.J. Andre, 'Disclosure ordered on Swiss bank accused of trading on inside information' (1982) 3 Co. Law 142.

friend and adviser of the head of the offeror, had come to the SEC's attention early in its investigation, he gave no formal reply when subpoenaed. Following the information from BSI, the SEC was able to proceed against him.

However, these disclosures were insufficient to prevent Judge Pollack issuing a written opinion to support his view that the order compelling disclosure was justified:

> 'It would be a travesty of justice to permit a foreign company to invade American markets, violate American laws if indeed they were violated, withdraw profits and resist accountability for itself and its principals by claiming their anonymity under foreign law'.

Referring to foreign law conflict cases which he regarded as having used a flexible approach to determine the appropriateness of a disclosure order, he considered the national interest at stake: whereas there was Congressional concern in the US about the use of foreign banks to evade its securities laws, the Swiss government had expressed no objection to the SEC investigation. He added that Swiss secrecy laws ought to protect the bank's customers, not the bank. In this case, he found that the bank had acted in bad faith by deliberately using the Swiss non-disclosure law to evade, in a commercial transaction for profit to it, the strictures of American securities laws against insider dealing.

Although the SEC obtained the information sought, the approach in the *BSI* case did not offer a general solution to investigative difficulties associated with secrecy laws. The procedure involved was slow and costly. Whilst effective against BSI with its substantial assets in the US, the threat of sanctions could prove counter-productive in other cases. Instead of placing orders on US markets, Swiss banks could deal in US securities on the London or Zurich exchanges. Alternatively, Swiss banks could withdraw their assets and activities from the US. Either response by Swiss banks risked harming the US economy.

Nevertheless, the effectiveness of the threat of sanctions against BSI served as a warning of the potential use of sanctions against financial institutions with substantial assets and activities in the US and for whom withdrawal from the US was unattractive. With incentives for both sides to compromise, a Memorandum of Understanding was concluded between the US and Switzerland in 1982[6].

4. The proposed 'waiver by conduct' rule

An attempt to develop a general approach to the problem of conflict between foreign non-disclosure laws and US securities laws was made by the SEC in its proposal for a 'waiver by conduct' rule[7]. Under this proposal, the act of engaging in a securities transaction in the US would constitute a waiver of any secrecy provision that a foreign financial institution, customer or agent might claim. Its rationale is based on a distinction between a foreign financial intermediary that accepts and holds deposits within a nation with bank secrecy or blocking statutes and an institution in the same jurisdiction that effects securities transactions outside its territory: whereas there is a reasonable expectation in the former case that the customer is entitled to the protection of secrecy laws, there should be no legitimate expectation of protection in the latter case since the financial institution and its customer act outside the

6. See ante 2. Bilateral and multilateral agreements, c. Memoranda of Understanding.
7. Fedders, op cit n14, p362, supra, at 25-28; *The Financial Times*, 22nd August, 1984.

territory and beyond its jurisdiction. In a securities transaction effected within the US through a foreign financial institution, the act of cloaking the transaction with a veil of secrecy is regarded as occurring within the US and as incompatible with US sovereignty. Whilst these principles could be developed on a case-by-case basis, legislation was seen as promoting their acceptance by placing investors on notice of the consequences of effecting transactions on US markets.

The importance of international recognition of the 'waiver by conduct' approach was acknowledged in the context of blocking statutes. A policy of restraint in applying blocking statutes to securities transactions in the US was urged on the basis of self-interest having regard to the common interests of nations in fair and honest securities markets and to the dangers that a country which applied blocking statutes would become a haven for international fraud, whose victims would include its own citizens.

However, there were two main difficulties in the 'waiver by conduct' approach. The first was the extraterritoriality of US securities laws[8]. The 'waiver by conduct' approach diminishes the importance of foreign non-disclosure laws, namely, bank secrecy and blocking laws. In particular, it envisages that the US would obtain evidence without the express consent of the foreign country or without regard to non-disclosure laws. Even if an individual could be considered as having waived his interest in a secrecy provision, the problem of blocking laws remained in that, since they protect a national interest, the privilege can therefore be considered as that of the state.

The second difficulty was the potential for ill-will among the US and other countries. Indeed, such ill-will risked being counterproductive to international co-operation in the exchange of information. Moreover, other countries could retaliate by passing more stringent non-disclosure laws, hindering US participation in their securities markets and channeling investment elsewhere than the US.

Following strong opposition to the 'waiver by conduct' approach, the SEC recognised that the proposal was poorly received and has indicated its commitment to exploring alternatives. This reconsideration calls for a constructive response. It is clear that the US will persist in its attempt to end the double standard of regulation between those trading within the US and those trading from outside the US. In that all countries with active securities markets are susceptible to fraud, insider dealing and other securities offences perpetrated behind non-disclosure laws, the problem is not confined to the US.

Moreover, the difficulties associated with the 'waiver by conduct' approach underline the importance of international co-operation in gathering evidence abroad, notwithstanding the time involved and conflicting interests to be resolved in negotiations. Progress seems dependent on achieving a balance between US initiatives and international co-operation in the exchange of information.

D. EEC developments

In the context of EEC measures to harmonise the capital market laws of the

---

8. Comment, op cit n19, p360, supra, at 317 and Cox, op cit n18, p359, supra, at 218.

Member States[9], the Draft Directive on Insider Trading contains provisions seeking to ensure the application of provisions adopted pursuant to the Directive. To this end, Member States are required by Article 8 to designate one or more competent authorities; the Commission must be informed accordingly, with details (if appropriate) as to how duties have been allocated. The competent authorities must be given all such supervisory powers as may be necessary for the exercise of their duties. Giving impetus to developments in international co-operation, the competent authorities in the Member States must co-operate wherever necessary for the purpose of carrying out their duties and exchange any information for that purpose.

To protect confidentiality, Member States are required by Article 9 to impose an obligation of professional secrecy on all current and former employees of the competent authorities. Information subject to this obligation may only be divulged under provisions laid down by law.

However, it is expressly stated in Article 9 that such professional secrecy must not preclude exchanges of information between Member States by the competent authorities designated under Article 8. In turn, where information is thus exchanged, it must be covered by the obligation of professional secrecy imposed on current and former employees of the competent authorities in receipt of that information.

In addition, restrictions are imposed on the use of information received by the authorities designated under Article 8. Without prejudice to cases falling under criminal law, such authorities may use that information only for the exercise of their duties and in connection with administrative or judicial proceedings specifically relating thereto.

The Draft Directive on Insider Trading also confers additional functions on the Contact Committee established by the 1979 Admissions Directive[10]. These are: (a) to facilitate the harmonised implementation of the Insider Trading Directive through regular consultations on any practical problems arising from its application on which exchanges of view are deemed useful and (b) to advise the Commission on any amendments to be made to that Directive.

9. See, ante, Chapter 6. Administrative Regulation, I. Restrictions on Dealing, D. EEC Developments.
10. Conditions for Admission of Securities to Official Listing at Stock Exchange, March 5, 1979 (Dir.79/279/EEC; O.J.1979, L66/21), art.20.

Chapter 8

Conclusion

In the introductory chapter to this book, three questions raised by the regulation of insider dealing were posed. In the light of the discussion in ensuing chapters, these will be considered in turn.

I. SHOULD INSIDER DEALING BE REGULATED?

Although this question raises important policy considerations, the imposition of criminal liability for insider dealing was not preceded by detailed analysis of the efficiency and equity issues involved. Rather, the decision to impose liability was taken on the basis of vague references to issues of equity, whether expressed in terms of ethical standards, public confidence and fairness, and with scant reference to issues of efficiency.

Accordingly, in this book, policy considerations have been discussed by reference to the US debate in which challenges on efficiency grounds to the orthodox view in support of insider dealing regulation prompted fresh analysis of efficiency and equity issues and of the tension between them. In view of the implications for the distribution of wealth between insiders and other investors, the prospects of consensus are remote.

In the search for a principle governing dealings based on inside information, policy considerations support the principle of the unerodable informational advantage. This principle would prohibit transactions where one party possesses an informational advantage that public investors may not lawfully overcome, regardless of their diligence or resources.

Apart from being controversial, the principle of the unerodable informational advantage may not prove satisfactory on closer scrutiny in that it can produce results that are unacceptable in practice. But subject to the proviso that it is merely a presumption which needs to be revised in the light of events, such a principle provides a basis for devising regulation that can be applied in a predictable manner.

However, the imposition of regulation is fraught with difficulties. These have been highlighted by the two main theories advanced by economists to explain the existence of economic regulation.

The public interest theory, which asserted that regulation was introduced for the protection and benefit of the public or large subsections thereof, has proved inadequate to describe the operation of regulation in practice. Hence, the view that the mere existence of a market failure provided the justification for regulation, with its assumption that regulation operated effectively and costlessly, has been discredited. The reformulation, which attributes regulatory failures to legal and procedural problems that can be remedied, considers that reforms based on improving performance by a clearer definition of regulatory goals would facilitate assessment of performance and accountability and ease the pressure from interest groups in the regulated industry. Yet it overlooks evidence that socially undesirable results of regulation may be sought by interest groups in the industry. When viewed as an honest but unsuccessful attempt to promote the public interest, the public interest theory is more plausible in the light of the intractable nature of many problems assigned to regulatory agencies and of the cost of effective legislative supervision. But this theory fails to explain how perception of the public interest is given legislative expression, particularly when in conflict with private interests.

Rejecting the correction of market imperfections as the goal of regulation, the capture theory, the economic version of which regards regulation as an attempt by competing interest groups to acquire economic privileges, fails to provide a basis for predicting which industries will be regulated. Instead, it provides a list of criteria to predict whether an industry will obtain favourable regulation. Other weaknesses of the capture theory are that it neglects the role of regulators, overlooks differences in the behaviour of regulators and of elected politicians, does not allow for competition between regulatory agencies and fails to explain the public interest rhetoric of regulatory discussion and policy.

Whilst open to criticism, both the public interest theory and the capture theory provide useful insights for analysis. Yet in so doing these two theories of economic regulation open up rather than resolve the difficulties associated with the imposition of regulation.

II. WHY DOES INSIDER DEALING REGULATION TAKE ITS PRESENT FORM?

As with nearly all legislative proposals, the decision to introduce legislation prohibiting insider dealing was presented by successive Conservative and Labour Governments as the policies of that particular Government. But in each instance, these policy decisions stemmed from the response of various interest groups to an issue on which action was regarded as necessary.

Consensus about the need for action was slow to emerge. Instead, the initial response of the self-regulatory agencies to calls for action was to play down the extent of insider dealing. Consistent with this approach, early attempts at regulation comprised insider reporting requirements, the administrative measures of the self-regulatory agencies, a criminal prohibition on various option dealings by directors and common law obligations. However, increasing public disquiet about the efficacy of these measures prompted a change of response, which was heralded by the Panel chairman's call[1] in 1972 for insider dealing to be made a criminal offence and set out in subsequent statements[2] by the Stock Exchange and Panel.

In terms of the economic version of the capture theory of regulation, these self-regulatory agencies were small well-organised groups with a substantial interest in regulation. Whereas the Stock Exchange was then a private association of brokers and jobbers, the Panel was established as a self-regulatory agency by professional associations with authority over their members, a striking feature of its composition being the dominance of producer groups. Their ability to organise an effective response to threats of legislation to regulate the

1. Statement by Lord Shawcross, Chairman of the City Panel on Take-overs and Mergers, 26th October, 1972.
2. Eg, The Panel on Take-overs and Mergers, Statement on Insider Dealing, 2nd February, 1973 and Supervision of the Securities Market (1975), p.5; Committee to Review the Functioning of Financial Institutions, Second Stage Evidence, Vol. 1 the Panel on Take-overs and Mergers (1975), para 104.

securities markets was evidenced by the development of the Stock Exchange's regulatory role and the establishment of the Panel to form a scheme of self-regulation administered by representatives of those professionally involved in the securities industry. In consequence, Governmental regulation was kept to a minimum and threatened legislation did not materialise. In relation to the main aspects of City practice for which they were responsible, the self-regulatory agencies were able to secure compliance with their own measures to an extent that satisfied Government, but they proved unable to overcome the problem of insider dealing.

By the early 1970s, further instances of insider dealing, together with evidence of unethical practices in company management, threatened the continuance of regulatory arrangements. Whilst critics of self-regulation seized upon such conduct to support the establishment of a companies commission, the Conservative Government was sensitive to the risk of being regarded by the electorate as protectors of 'speculators' and others whose conduct attracted public attention. Recognising that opposition to action on insider dealing was politically unacceptable, the representatives of the small well-organised groups that had established the self-regulatory scheme sought to organise a favourable response to the form of insider dealing regulation, having regard to the interests of those groups in the existing regulatory framework.

Consideration of the form of insider dealing regulation was obscured by two aspects of the debate on the regulation of the securities markets. First, this debate was mainly conducted in terms of the advantages and limitations of self-regulation (often used synonymously with non-statutory regulation) on the one hand and of statutory regulation on the other, rather than in terms of the balance to be achieved both between Governmental regulation and self-regulation and between statutory and non-statutory regulation.

Secondly, discussion of the alternatives to the existing regulatory framework was often confined to a simplistic comparison with the SEC and focused on its shortcomings. Yet the SEC was established after a cycle of speculative boom and collapse on the stock market, together with associated abuse, and before the development of self-regulatory bodies that could make a significant contribution to regulation. Far from the establishment of a commission being incompatible with the delegation of regulation to self-regulatory bodies under commission supervision, such delegation is permitted by legislation and following improvements in self-regulation, has increased. Examples of such delegation are also provided in Canada, Australia and New Zealand. In view of the role already played by the self-regulatory agencies in Britain, it would have been more realistic to consider, in the alternative, a smaller version of such a commission in a framework in which the balance between Governmental regulation and self-regulation took account of the contribution made by the self-regulatory agencies.

As between the choice of instruments to regulate insider dealing, Stock Exchange and Panel responses on the form of such regulation focused on a prohibition on dealing by insiders on the basis of inside information rather than mandated disclosure of information by companies and insiders and supported the enforcement of such a prohibition by criminal penalities. This can be attributed to considerations beyond those associated with the regulation of insider dealing.

In regard to the prohibition on dealing, resort to the criminal law provided a ready technique for responding to pressure to regulate insider dealing. In contrast, detailed consideration of other measures to enforce such a prohibition involved sensitive issues. An attempt to extend and strengthen the administrative prohibitions of the self-regulatory agencies would have involved, at least in relation to investigation and sanctions, conferring statutory powers to which those agencies were then opposed. Provision for a civil remedy, though having the advantage of providing an enforcement technique with a lesser burden of proof, raised difficult issues at the level of formulation, such as whether liability should be to the company and/or other investors, the problem in market transactions of linking buyers and sellers in any meaningful way and the quantum of damages. But the mere fact of raising difficult issues at the level of formulation ran the risk of prompting analysis of issues at the level of enforcement, with inadequacies in arrangements for enforcement lending support to the establishment of a Governmental commission.

In comparison with a prohibition on dealing, little consideration was given to the other instrument of insider dealing regulation, namely, mandated disclosure of information. In the general context of company law reform, the Department of Trade and Industry referred to a growing appreciation of the need for fuller corporate disclosure both as a spur to efficiency and as a safeguard against malpractice[3]. Whilst asserting that in many instances unusual activity before a bid announcement arose from a leak, the Stock Exchange and Panel stressed the need for absolute secrecy[4]. With its implied recognition of a public duty to disclose information, a significant increase in disclosure obligations ran counter to the City view that supervision of quoted companies was primarily a matter for self-regulatory agencies, with their private status and lack of public accountability. Reliance on disclosure also had political disadvantages. When further instances of insider dealing came to light, there would be renewed criticism of inadequate penalties to impose on insiders. It also failed to deflect criticism from self-regulatory agencies to Governmental agencies responsible for enforcement of a statutory prohibition.

As the insider dealing proposals in the 1973 Companies Bill were lost in the Parliamentary dissolution, the ability of producer-dominated small groups to obtain a favourable response to the form of insider dealing regulation was not ultimately tested. The clauses in the 1973 Bill did not reflect precisely the response of the Stock Exchange and Panel in that, though providing for criminal liability, they also contained a civil remedy. Yet the scope of this remedy appears to have been restricted to transactions in which the parties were in privity. Consumers would thus have derived only limited benefit from such a remedy, though failure to formulate a workable civil remedy in open market transactions was further due not only to the dearth of consumer groups, but also to the fact that some of those calling for a statutory prohibition on insider dealing were less interested in the precise form of insider dealing regulation than in the wider scheme of regulation of the securities markets. Without obtaining unqualified implementation of their proposals, the producer-dominated small groups would still have benefited from the 1973 Bill at the expense of consumers with diminished interest in regulation.

Faced with a Labour Government, the City had reason, on the basis of proposals made by a Labour Party Working Group in a 1974 'Green Paper'[5], to fear far-reaching reform. But this was to overlook other factors. One was a distaste in the Labour Party for reforms intended to improve capitalism. Thus,

3. Department of Trade and Industry, *Company Law Reform,* Cmnd.5391 (1973), para 5.
4. The Panel on Take-overs and Mergers, Statement on Insider Dealing, 2nd February, 1973.
5. *The Community and the Company,* Report of a Working Group of the Labour Party Industrial Policy Sub-Committee (1974), p.5.

its General Secretary acknowledged, in the Foreword to the Green Paper, that some socialists might wonder why the Labour Party should devote time to considering a major reform of company law. Another was the changed political context. As the Labour Party did not suffer the handicap of being associated, either in terms of ideology or resources, with City interests, a Labour Government was less vulnerable than a Conservative Government to charges of protecting unethical practices in the City. Hence, for the Conservative opposition, there was no political mileage in attacking the Labour Government for failing to implement ambitious proposals to reform the City, particularly when those reform proposals aroused such strong opposition from City interests with which the Conservative Party was identified.

However, in an attempt to enhance the appeal of the 1978 Companies Bill, introduced to implement the EEC Second Directive[6], insider dealing clauses were included. A variation on the 1973 Bill was that the 1978 Bill provided for criminal and civil liability, including rescission and damages, in respect of its requirement for disclosure of insider status in private deals. In market transactions, reliance was placed on criminal penalties.

In contrast to the reception accorded to the 1973 Bill, doubts about the 1978 Bill were widely voiced in the City[7]. On the basis that the proposed legislation would work effectively, there were fears that the wider definitions in the 1978 Bill would deter directors and employees from investing in their own companies and inhibit information searches by analysts and the dissemination of information by companies. Other doubts stemmed from the view that legislation, not merely in the form proposed by the 1978 Bill, would be ineffective. These were concerned with the effect of a possible prosecution on the investigative process. One view, shared by the Chairman of the Stock Exchange, was that professionals who had previously co-operated in Stock Exchange and Panel investigations could not be expected to do so when evidence might incriminate them and their principals. It was further considered that as people were likely to be unco-operative in investigations whose outcome could be a criminal prosecution and as problems of proof would make it difficult to secure a conviction, the result could be that people, such as those shunned in the City following administrative sanctions, could operate with impunity.

The doubts in the City about insider dealing legislation were also reflected in the Conservative Party. Signalling a change of policy, the Conservative spokesman for Trade questioned the desirability of making insider dealing on the Stock Exchange a criminal offence[8]. Whilst stating that insider dealing was an abuse of trust involving an act of dishonesty deserving of speedy and effective retribution, he argued that Parliament should be cautious about creating new crimes in response to political pressure, particularly when the forces of law were so fully stretched. Caution was also necessary if it was suspected that a criminal deterrent might be more rather than less difficult to enforce and if there was insufficient consensus on how the crime should be defined. He also voiced his scepticism about whether it would be possible to draft a criminal sanction without damaging legitimate business. But the Party's policy options were kept

6. EEC Second Directive on Company Law 77/91, O.J.1977 L 26/1. This set out certain minimum requirements regarding the formation of companies and the maintenance, increase and reduction of capital.
7. *The Times,* 28th September, 2nd, 12th and 26th October and 1st November, 1978; *Investors Chronicle,* 29th September, 13th October and 10th November, 1978.
8. *The Times,* 21st November, 1978.

open: though the Conservative spokesman on Trade stated he was 'prejudiced'[9] against the proposal in the Bill, the Party might be prepared to accept the insider dealing clauses if a more satisfactory form of words could be found.

Although in apparent contradiction to the public position previously adopted by the City, doubts about a legislative approach were not such that City interest groups changed their policy of supporting this course of action. Once a Bill had been introduced, a reversal of policy by Government would have been difficult to secure, particularly by a Labour Government sensitive to charges from its own supporters of surrendering to City lobbying. In view of the inability of self-regulation to tackle the problem, City opposition to a legislative approach had the political drawback of being misinterpreted by critics of self-regulation. Against the background of a continuing debate on the regulatory framework, such opposition could well have tipped the political balance in favour of those who supported the establishment of a Governmental commission. Wider political considerations relating to the preservation of the existing regulatory framework thus dictated that City policy should be to negotiate amendments to the form of the proposed insider dealing legislation rather than to oppose a legislative approach as such.

In the event, the hazards facing the passage of legislation were again underlined by the dissolution of Parliament and consequent loss of the 1978 Bill. Hence, the ability of City interests to benefit from the form of legislation remained untested.

As to company law reform, the legislative programme of the Conservative Government elected in 1979 was initially planned by reference to the need to implement EEC Directives[10]. With implementation of the Second Directive overdue, the Government introduced a Companies Bill in 1979 largely reproducing those parts of the 1978 Bill designed to implement that Directive. After rushing this Bill through Parliament, it intended to introduce another Companies Bill in 1980 implementing the Fourth Directive[11]. More controversial matters, such as insider dealing, would be reconsidered in a White Paper later in 1979. Renewed controversy on the scale that accompanied the proposals of the 1978 Bill would further postpone insider dealing legislation; otherwise it would be added to the 1980 Companies Bill. The Stock Exchange and CSI resubmitted their views, with the Chairman of the Stock Exchange expressing confidence that the Government would take account of their suggestions and consult them on issues such as the definition of insider[12].

However, when it became apparent that the decision to delay insider dealing legislation was a gift to the Opposition, the Minister of State announced[13] a change of plans on the Second Reading of the 1979 Bill to the effect that the Government would introduce amendments to make insider dealing a criminal offence. In the event, the 1979 Bill, apart from implementing the Second Directive, also provided for the duties of directors and conflicts of interests and the protection of minorities with the result that the CA 1980 made more extensive reforms than initially intended. Limited to criminal liability in respect of market transactions and more narrowly drawn than those of the 1978 Bill, its insider dealing provisions were more acceptable to City interests. But the wider

9. Ibid.
10. *The Daily Telegraph,* 22nd May, 26th June and 31st July, 1979.
11. EEC Fourth Directive on Company Law 78/660, O.J.1978 L. 222/11. This sets out requirements for the disclosure of financial information and the contents of annual accounts.
12. *The Daily Telegraph,* 31st July, 1979.
13. Ibid, 23rd October, 1979.

implications of such legislation for the functioning of the regulatory system, which provoked much of the controversy surrounding the 1978 Bill, were glossed over.

In the defensive struggle by the self-regulatory agencies against criticism of self-regulation, the criminal prohibition on dealing in the CA 1980 relieved them of an embarrassing problem by shifting primary responsibility for it into the Governmental sphere. Those agencies were left to redefine the scope of self-regulation so that in addition to disclosure requirements, it applied to unethical conduct which, though not illegal, fell short of generally accepted standards. In consequence, in the short term, their regulatory role in the securities market was in other respects preserved intact.

This approach was encouraged by Government policy that the existing regulatory framework should be retained. Like the Bank of England, the Department of Trade did not support the creation of any new institution to centralise supervision of the securities market on the lines of the SEC. On behalf of successive governments, it also did not seek statutory powers of intervention or supervision of self-regulation. Together with the Bank of England, the Department of Trade was self-regulation's most valuable ally.

Apart from a prohibition on dealing, there was increased recognition of the role of disclosure in insider dealing regulation. An example was the Panel chairman's emphasis in 1977 on the importance of full and accurate information at the earliest possible moment.[14] However, extension of disclosure has encountered strong resistance, underlining the conflicting interests of different groups and giving credence to the suggestion in the capture theory that regulation does not serve one economic interest exclusively. Proposals for increased disclosure on the lines drawn up by the accounting profession in 1975,[15] initially received Governmental support,[16] but renewed emphasis on the expense of compliance and the value of information led to a partial retreat from this position in 1979.[17] As to standard setting by the profession, doubts were expressed about the ability of the Accounting Standards Committee (ASC) to react to fast-changing financial conditions.[18] Thus, a first inadequate inflation accounting standard[19] was issued in 1980 as Government came close to reversing a fifteen-year period of inflation. As a result, the ASC was perceived as representing the interests of auditors and managers of large companies rather than users of accounts.

It is difficult to measure the impact of the CA 1980 or of any other measure relating to insider dealing. Such a measure forms only one element in a wider scheme of regulation. Moreover, the publicity accorded to instances of insider dealing and related unethical conduct and the discussion of insider dealing regulation throughout the 1970s make it difficult to separate implementation of a particular measure, such as the CA 1980, from the influence of the surrounding publicity and discussion. These difficulties are compounded by a lack of empirical evidence, which is not merely a deficiency of information that is likely to be remedied.

Despite its limitations, empirical evidence suggests that there has been a spreading out of the problem so that, though not so confined, the more prevalent aspect is tippee dealing. It thus seems that there has been a shift in

14. The Panel on Take-overs and Mergers, Report on the Year ended 31st March, 1977, p.4.
15. Accounting Standards Steering Committee, The Corporate Report (1975).
16. Department of Trade, *The Future of Company Reports*, Cmnd.6888 (1977).
17. Ibid, *Company Accounting and Disclosure*, Cmnd.7654 (1979).
18. *The Financial Times*, 23rd August, 1984.
19. SSAP 16 Current Cost Accounting (1980).

emphasis, though it is not possible to attribute such shift to any particular form of regulation. The influence of surrounding publicity and discussion has also been acknowledged. According to two views in 1976 and 1978 respectively:

'the publicity has resulted in a considerable tightening up on insider dealing and other abuses over the last decade on the traditional internal and informal basis'[20], and

'all the pressure to have insider dealing made a criminal offence has done the world of good. It has tightened people up.'[1]

Recent empirical evidence, albeit circumstantial, suggests that whilst the CA 1980 apparently had an initial deterrent effect, this soon diminished.

The ineffectiveness of insider dealing regulation following the CA 1980 invites comparison with the record of the Panel on Take-overs and Mergers in relation to the prohibition on insider dealing contained in the City Code. When measured against a platonic ideal, the Panel's record can readily be criticised. But when compared with the reality of experience of the enforcement of prohibitions on dealing by a regulatory agency, its record was a good one. It is a telling criticism of enforcement of the CA 1980 that in the four years prior to its enactment and in the limited sphere of take-overs and mergers, the Panel issued statements disclosing breaches of the Code prohibition on insider dealing on significantly more occasions than the Department of Trade and Industry brought successful prosecutions under the CA 1980 in the four years following its enactment. Yet the consensus is that, far from being restricted to the 'small fry' hitherto detected, insider dealing still occurs on a large scale.

Accordingly, there has been scant reason to suppose that in the sphere of take-overs and mergers the CA 1980 constitutes an advance over the Code prohibition that it replaced. Any advance seems dependent on a long-term educational effect. But the factors which point to caution in the use of criminal sanction are particularly relevant to insider dealing.

In reality, the CA 1980, though enabling formal equity considerations to be presented, was enacted on terms that precluded effective enforcement. Just as the self-regulatory agencies had been hindered by their lack of investigative powers, so responsibility for enforcement was conferred on the Department of Trade, whose investigative powers were ill-suited to enforcement even when foreign orders were not involved. The absence of a power to compel disclosure of financial records in the course of an investigation when an offence was reasonably suspected to have been committed meant that for enforcement of the 1980 Act, investigation officers of the Department of Trade and Industry were, except to the extent that assistance was afforded by Stock Exchange enquiries, reliant on the creation of an impression of authority and the willingness of people to produce documents and answer questions. For an offence such as insider dealing where the cost benefits of breaking the law are more likely to be evaluated rationally, the deterrent effect is reduced by the prospects of breach not being detected. Reliance was thus placed on a narrowly defined criminal measure to be enforced, with the attendant difficulty of the heavy burden of proof in relation to an offence which by its nature is difficult to prove, by a regulatory authority with defective investigative powers and whose lack of resources meant that enforcement of the insider dealing prohibitions

20. P. Milne, *The Stock Market and Company Finance* (1976), p.19.
1. Mr. David Hopkinson, investment manager, quoted in *The Times*, 1st November, 1978.

was not given a high priority.

The regulatory agencies were reticent about the impact of the 1980 Act. But reflecting the weakneses in its approach, the 1980 Act was criticised in the financial press in 1984 in the following terms:

> 'the treatment of insider dealing as a criminal offence has limited the effectiveness of the self-regulatory agencies . . . The result is the worst of both worlds. The legislation lacks real teeth and yet inhibits the free-wheeling approach of City watchdogs.'[2]

Nevertheless, proposals for reform continued the emphasis on a prohibition on dealing enforceable by criminal penalties. Apart from the transfer of the provisions of Part V, CA 1980 to an Investor Protection Act, the Gower Report recommended the removal of obvious anomalies.[3] In particular, statutory provisions should be extended to cover market dealings in any securities, or options or futures relating to securities (whether of a company or not), and all public servants (central or local). Major changes were rejected on the basis that the insider dealing provisions of Part V, CA 1980 had been enacted 'so recently - and not without trauma'.[4]

In the event, subsequent legislative development was a three-stage process, with attempts to defuse public disquiet about insider dealing maintaining the emphasis on the prohibition on dealing enforceable by criminal penalties. First, the provisions of Part V, CA 1980 were transferred to the IDA 1985. Secondly, the scope of this legislation was widened,[5] as a result of the FSA 1986 to extend to public servants and to include dealings in contracts for differences where the underlying investments are securities. In addition, the FSA 1986 empowered the Secretary of State to appoint inspectors to investigate suspected insider dealing offences, with significant additional powers being conferred in this connection.[6] Thirdly, the maximum penalties for breach of the prohibition on dealing of the IDA were increased by the Criminal Justice Act 1988.[7]

III. HOW SHOULD INSIDER DEALING BE REGULATED?

Whilst a uniform approach to an issue such as the regulation of insider dealing is attractive, difficulties stem from the different stages reached in the development of regulation and of policy formulation. The proposals discussed are therefore considered by reference to the British context. Nevertheless, they may have wider significance, just as the development of insider dealing regulation in Britain needs to benefit from experience elsewhere. With the internationalisation of the securities markets, the importance of an international approach is increased. But such an approach can best be achieved when individual countries have made further progress in co-operating in the implementation of measures which have previously been regarded as impractical.

The background against which proposals to regulate insider dealing fall to be discussed differs from that of the 1970s. First, the regulatory framework has

---

2. *The Financial Times,* 29th October, 1984.
3. *Review of Investor Protection, Report: Part I* by L.C.B. Gower, Cmnd.9125 (1984), para 9.36.
4. Ibid, para 9.34.
5. See, ante, Chapter 3. Criminal Liability.
6. See, ante, Chapter 7. Investigation.
7. See, ante, Chapter 3. Criminal Liability.

undergone far-reaching changes as a result of the FSA 1986. Secondly, important changes in market structure have flowed from 'Big Bang' in 1986. Thirdly, the internationalisation of the securities markets has raised difficulties for investigations, particularly in relation to insider dealing. Fourthly, the balance between statutory and non-statutory regulation has been altered not only by the provisions of the FSA 1986 relating to the regulatory framework but also by implementation of the EEC Directives on listed securities. Fifthly, assessments of the performance of regulators have been revised. In particular, the Stock Exchange's recent record is regarded as a marked improvement on its past performance.

Proposals to regulate insider dealing will be discussed by reference to the two instruments used to regulate insider dealing, namely, a prohibition on dealing by insiders on the basis of inside information and mandated disclosure of information by companies and individuals. These two instruments are considered in turn.

A. Prohibition on dealing

From the experience of the legislation introduced by the CA 1980 and now contained in the IDA 1985, it is apparent that a prohibition on dealing by insiders on the basis of inside information enforceable by criminal penalties, has only a limited role to play in insider dealing regulation. The heavy burden of proof in relation to an offence which, by its nature is difficult to prove, renders enforcement of such a prohibition by criminal penalties particularly costly. Few regulatory agencies will be willing to waste resources on efforts to enforce measures that it is impracticable to enforce.

In terms of enforcing a prohibition on dealing, the absence of comprehensive provision for civil liability, to other investors as well as to the company, is an important gap in regulation. A useful supplement to the criminal sanction, civil liability has the advantage of providing an enforcement technique with a lesser burden of proof. Such civil liability for insider dealing would also be consistent with expanded provision for civil remedies in the FSA 1986. Though there are difficult issues at the level of formulation, these are not insuperable.

Other consequences could flow from provision for civil liability. One could be the development of a practice in some cases whereby, without admitting liability, an insider agreed to disgorge his profits. In addition, the courts could make injunctive orders, enforceable by contempt sanctions.

However, enforcement is dependent on the involvement both of a regulatory agency and of private plaintiffs. In the case of agency enforcement, the costs of enforcement can be balanced against the wider public benefits sought. Yet it is clear from the US experience that agency enforcement is inadequate.

The involvement of private plaintiffs is dependent on the availability of incentives to bring proceedings. But, apart from increasing the costs of agency enforcement, the costs of litigation and its associated delays prohibit enforcement by most private plaintiffs. In an action by a company for recovery of profits, these considerations would normally preclude proceedings by a small or medium sized company. For a minority shareholder, the disincentives in terms of costs are even greater. The costs and delays of civil litigation also make it unrealistic to expect effective enforcement by means of class actions by other investors.

Receiving increasing professional support, public disquiet about the costs, delays, complexity and consequent inaccessibility of the courts resulted in the establishment by the Lord Chancellor of the Civil Justice Review, its report being published in June, 1988.[8] A significant feature was its recommendation that the prohibition on contingency fees and other forms of incentive schemes should be open to re-examination.[9] Whilst cautious in its comments, the Review recognised that the difficulties associated with contingency fees could be controlled by specific regulations rather than a general prohibition.[10] This recommendation for re-examination has found support elsewhere. Established by the Law Society and the Bar to report on the future of the legal profession, the Marre Committee subsequently concluded, in its report published in July 1988, that contingency fees should not be introduced at present, but should be the subject of further research and discussion.[11] In line with these recommendations, the Chairman of the Bar Council announced, in July, 1988, that the Bar had set up a working group of practising barristers to consider the implications of contingency fees.[12] In turn, the Law Society indicated, in August, 1988,[13] that it would consider approaching the Government with a view to removal of the prohibition on contingency fees in the Solicitors Act 1974[14] and then amending the Solicitors' Practice Rules.[15] The Society's decision to review contingency fees follows the widespread response to the 1987 Report of the Law Society's Working Party on the Funding of Litigation, entitled 'Access to Civil Justice'. In the event of these reviews leading to the introduction of contingency fees or other forms of incentive schemes, there could be important implications for facilitating the enforcement by private plaintiffs of a civil remedy for insider dealing. In this context, a related issue for consideration is the practice of awarding costs to a successful defendant.

As with a criminal prohibition, enforcement of a civil remedy will frequently be thwarted in the case of transactions with a foreign element, notably when insiders either use foreign financial institutions to trade in the British securities markets or trade in British securities overseas. With securities regulation having traditionally been developed for the domestic securities markets, internationalisation raises acute difficulties for regulators. For insider dealing regulation, these difficulties centre on the problem of obtaining information from abroad and, in particular, that of foreign non-disclosure laws. Far from being confined to British regulatory agencies, the difficulties are encountered by other regulatory agencies, including the SEC. Against the background of a common interest in developing procedures for the exchange of information and mutual assistance, regulators have sought to tackle the difficulties by way of informal co-operation, disclosure under statutory authority and multilateral and bilateral agreements. However, as long as significant obstacles to enforcement remain in regard to transactions with a foreign element, a double standard of regulation will continue to apply.

Administrative measures (apart from those relating to disclosure of information by companies and insider reporting requirements), are also essential.

8. The Report of the Review Body on Civil Justice, Cm.394 (1988).
9. Ibid, para 389 and Recommendation 58. The issues have received further consideration in the context of the Lord Chancellor's review of the legal profession: Contingency fees, Cmnd 571 (1989).
10. A recent review of the issues is contained in the Editorial (1988) 132 New Law Journal 413.
11. 'A Time for Change', The Report of the Committee on the Future of the Legal Profession (1988), Chapter 10; (1988) 132 New Law Journal 489 and 495.
12. (1988) 132 New Law Journal 491.
13. *The Times,* 8th August, 1988.
14. Section 59.
15. Solicitors' Practice Rules 1988, Rule 8.

Where conduct involves a fine distinction between permissible and impermissible conduct, reliance on criminal or civil liability can result in ineffective enforcement. In particular, in the case of market professionals it is misplaced to overlook the impact of administrative measures or automatically attribute their use to favouritism. Their use must, however, be sensitive to the danger of blatantly favourable practices for market professionals so that when conduct clearly falls within a criminal or civil prohibition, administrative enforcement is inappropriate.

Early attempts to devise administrative measures were beset by enforcement difficulties. Though not all attributable to non-statutory regulation by self-regulatory bodies as distinct from a statutory scheme of regulation involving enforcement by government department, these enforcement difficulties contributed to the introduction of the prohibition on dealing, enforceable by criminal penalties, in the CA 1980.

With the enactment of a criminal prohibition on dealing, the scope of self-regulation was redefined so that, apart from disclosure requirements, it applied to unethical conduct which though not illegal, fell short of generally accepted standards. Since the observance of high standards of conduct can be encouraged by education and discipline, codes and guidelines on insider dealing formulated by self-regulatory agencies and other professional associations, as supplemented by in-house rules, have an important role to play in developing high standards.

However, educational efforts are inadequate unless the measures in question are enforced against those who do not observe the standards set. The initial failure to enforce the redefined self-regulatory measures suggested that the standards set were not as generally accepted as claimed. The imprecision of some codes and guidelines also cast doubts on any expectation that they would be enforced.

Yet the far-reaching changes in the securities industry since Big Bang point to an enhanced role for administrative measures. Thus, the removal or modification of traditional lines of demarcation between different types of financial services has raised new problems of regulation and supervision as some conventional measures of providing protection became obsolete, eg the broker-jobber distinction, and others have had to be established, as exemplified in the SIB rulebook. Prior to Big Bang, market surveillance arrangements rendered enforcement of insider dealing requirements largely dependent on rumours and unusual price movements being picked up by the market. With the more sophisticated equipment available since Big Bang to the Surveillance Division of the Stock Exchange, its ability to monitor deals made through the Stock Exchange has been greatly enhanced. In investigating suspected insider dealing, co-operation with securities firms assumes increased importance, particularly in the light of the recent practice of tape-recording the telephone conversations of market-makers and salesmen.

These changes have entailed a significant revision of administrative measures. But unless they are vigorously monitored and enforced, the protection afforded to investors risks further erosion, so that only the law, with its attendant enforcement shortcomings, remains to restrict the conduct of insiders.

B. Mandated disclosure of information

The significance of disclosure is enhanced by the limitations associated with enforcement of a prohibition on dealing whether by criminal, civil or administrative penalties. By their preventive effect, disclosure requirements constitute a key instrument in insider dealing regulation.

The scope for expansion of disclosure requirements is apparent from the importance attached to contacts with companies by information intermediaries, complaints of inadequate disclosure in the financial press and empirical evidence relating to the efficient markets theory. In relation to insider dealing, such expansion concerns disclosure relevant to price appraisal.

On a cost-benefit basis, extended timely disclosure requirements are most efficient since they do not impose increased disclosure burdens on all companies irrespective of whether the information is relevant to price appraisal. Nevertheless, it would not be feasible to devise a disclosure system exclusively pertinent to price appraisal.

The choice of measures to enforce timely disclosure requirements is particularly difficult. Resort to a criminal penalty is attractive, but there is a risk of it inhibiting communication between companies and regulatory agencies. Introduction of a civil remedy in favour of investors following a company's non-compliance with timely disclosure requirements would be going far beyond anything devised to date. Under existing administrative measures, a decision to suspend the shares of a company can be devastating to the company, particularly one in financial difficulties, and also operate to the disadvantage of shareholders.

However, determining the optimal amount of disclosure is a question of balance. The costs of compliance with increased disclosure requirements may make it less worthwhile for companies to come to the market or make take-over bids. If so, this raises the issue of whether the benefits derived by investors are worth the price paid in lost or lesser opportunities. Whilst difficult to quantify such cost benefits, the costs involved may be questioned since many investors do not study disclosure documents before making investment decisions. This last consideration is dismissed by some on the basis that sophisticated investors act on disclosures so that the information is read by the market. Hence, increased disclosure results in greater efficiency. But this argument overlooks the costs of compliance which are paid by investors. When the costs of compliance prevent companies coming to the market or making take-overs, market efficiency loses its importance. This suggests that a balance is required between the amount of disclosure needed to achieve market efficiency so that investors can learn the basic facts about their investments yet not so much that the process of coming to the market or making take-over bids becomes unprofitable.

Even the recent increase in disclosure regulation highlights the issue of differential disclosure. When information is understood only by sophisticated investors, it adds to the advantage of sophisticated investors over other investors. But the simultaneous provision of information understandable to other investors does not reduce this advantage. Differences in user sophistication are of crucial competitive significance, especially in an efficient market in which prices rapidly reflect new information and only investors with private information can expect to outperform the market. As mandated disclosure is not a private source, it only benefits those who act fastest and make the most accurate predictions.

Yet these advantages for sophisticated investors do not constitute insider dealing. Rather, the increased sophistication of disclosure requirements reduces the opportunities for insider dealing since the information is made available to all sophisticated investors and none has prior access. Moreover, the divergent views of parties to a transaction are based on different interpretations of the same information rather than information known to one party, but undisclosed to the other.

Nevertheless, tensions remain in the flow of information between investors or analysts and companies. Notwithstanding the provisions applicable to meetings between company officers and investment groups, it is doubtful whether many analysts could in practice refrain from seeking to elicit inside information before its public disclosure. Control of abuse lies mainly with company officers.

In addition, insider reporting requirements have not been developed to their full potential. Though difficult to assess, they have probably had a deterrent and educational effect. But this has been limited by the failure to enforce the requirements which suggests that, even though enforcement is costly, the benefits have been regarded too narrowly. The effectiveness of insider reporting requirements would also be enhanced by a provision for the recovery of short-term profits from corporate insiders, enforceable by the issuer or by a shareholder in the event of an issuer failing to take steps to recover such profits. Nevertheless, a short swing profits rule is a deterrent rather than an adjuster of economic positions.

The recent concern to define insider liability has tended to imply that disclosure has been an ineffective form of regulation. Whilst acknowledging that disclosure alone is inadequate, the foregoing also suggests that disclosure has not been used enough.

The expansion of disclosure requirements is supported by further considerations. First, the usefulness of civil liability as an adjuster of economic positions is restricted. Corporate recovery of insider profits benefits the company, which is composed of the non-selling and the buying shareholders, not the selling shareholders. In the case of recovery by other investors in market transactions, the upper ceiling on damages limits adjustment of economic positions. Secondly, disclosure requirements for companies, particularly those for timely disclosure by listed companies, are directed at fewer persons than general prohibitions on insider dealing. Thirdly, to the extent that the problem is tippee dealing, the prospects of detecting breaches of prohibitions on dealing are reduced.

In developing measures to regulate insider dealing, a key element is the provision of adequate resources for regulation. Whilst the costs of policy and surveillance should fall on the taxpayer, the remaining costs could be met by those regulated and ultimately borne by their clients.

In determining the amount of resources to be spent on regulation of particular conduct, the costs of regulation should be balanced, so far as practicable, against the benefits of regulation. It seems that the costs of stringent regulation of insider dealing would far exceed the benefits obtainable. Having a more modest impact and subject to cost benefit considerations, the proposals in this section should nevertheless constitute an improvement on existing regulation. But it would be misguided to entertain exaggerated expectations of what regulation can achieve, particularly as the task of insider dealing regulation appears to remain the more difficult one of creating or changing values than of confirming them.

Appendix

In this rapidly-changing area of regulation, there have been several developments not mentioned in the main text. This Appendix seeks to provide a brief update.

A. THE 'COUNTY NATWEST REPORT'

The report on County NatWest Ltd, County NatWest Securities Ltd[1] ('CNW' and 'CNWS'), by inspectors appointed by the Department of Trade and Industry under CA 1985, s 432(2) concerns several areas of City practice mentioned in this book. The report was published in July 1989.

The investigation focused on one of the City's largest financing transactions in 1987. An offer by Blue Arrow Plc, the UK's largest employment services group, for Manpower, a US company, was announced in August 1987. It was to be financed by a £837 m rights issue. The bid was successful. However, the rights issue closed on 28 September with a take-up level of only 38%. The underwriters, CNW, announced publicly the following day that 48.9% of the issue had been taken up and that the balance had been sold in the market. CNW did not disclose that it had been left with a financial interest in 13.4% of Blue Arrow's enlarged share capital. As a result of the stock market crash in October 1987, the Blue Arrow share price dropped considerably. The NWIB Group sustained substantial losses resulting from its involvement with Blue Arrow, namely £47.4 m in 1987 and £17.7 m in 1988. During February–August 1988, internal enquiries into the circumstances of the Blue Arrow rights issue were carried out by employees of the NWB Group; reports were submitted to the Bank of England and the Department of Trade and Industry. In December 1988, the inspectors were appointed by the Secretary of State to investigate the affairs of CNW and CNWS. In particular, they were asked to investigate the role of these two companies in the offer by Blue Arrow for Manpower and their subsequent interests in the Blue Arrow shares.

An early part of the report contains a description of the parties relevant to the investigation. After referring to the National Westminster Bank Plc ('NWB') as a clearing bank, the inspectors outlined its position as the holding company of various specialist subsidiaries. Investment banking activities were identified as carried out by NWB's wholly-owned subsidiary NatWest Investment Bank Ltd ('NWIB'), itself the holding company of CNW and CNWS. Another NWB subsidiary concerned in the investigation was Handelsbank (86.8% owned). A further group of companies relevant to the investigation was that of the Union Bank of Switzerland ('UBS'), a major Swiss bank with a branch in London. Its UK subsidiary, Phillips and Drew Ltd, was the holding company of Phillips and Drew Securities Ltd ('P&D'), which acted as stockbroker to Blue Arrow until February 1989.

An important aspect of the report concerned the extent to which parties involved in the investigation were subject to disclose requirements. These were based on the CA 1985, notably ss 198–210, and Stock Exchange provisions.

The issue of disclosure first arose in connection with Blue Arrow's purchases of Manpower shares in July 1987 prior to the announcement of the offer. These were made principally to reduce the financial impact on Blue Arrow of the costs it would incur in the event of a rival, higher, offer causing Blue Arrow's offer to fail. Under Stock Exchange 'Class 2' requirements,[2] a listed company is required to make an immediate announcement to the market of certain specified transactions for a consideration representing between 5% and 15% of the listed company's consolidated net assets. Blue Arrow's purchases exceeded its Class 2 limit. However, attempts were made to avoid a Class 2 announcement. After an unsuccessful approach to the Stock Exchange for a waiver, P&D wrote to the Stock Exchange explaining 'the background to the muddle' and enclosed a letter from an Executive Director of CNW proffering an explanation of why no Class 2 announcement had been made. Subsequently, the announcement of the offer included a statement indicating Blue

---

1 *County NatWest Limited, County NatWest Securities Limited* Report by M. Crystal QC and D. L. Spence CA (1989).
2 *The Admission of Securities to Listing* Section 6, Chapter 1.

Arrow's holding in Manpower but the inspectors note that Blue Arrow did not make a Class 2 announcement. The inspectors were critical of the conduct of various named executives of CNW and P&D.

The disclosure issue again arose following the closure of the rights issue on 8 September with a take-up level of only 38%. That evening it was decided to 'add in' shares belonging to CNW, P&D and Blue Arrow's financial advisers in the US in relation to the bid. Acceptances were thereby raised to just over 48.8%. Regarding various named executives of CNW and P&D as responsible for the decision to 'add in' the shares, the inspectors criticised the conduct of those executives, stating that the executives knew that the decision to 'add in' was to enable public statements to be made the next day to prospective placees and to the market in terms that the take-up level was of the order of 50%. On 29 September P&D and CNW proceeded with the placing of the rump of Blue Arrow shares: 35.78% of the rights issue were placed with third parties, the remainder being retained by CNW and P&D. However, a CNW press release, issued to the market that morning by the Stock Exchange, stated that acceptance had been received for 48.9% of the shares and that all remaining new ordinary shares had been sold in the market at an average net price of approximately 166.25 p per share. The inspectors considered the press release was misleading in two material respects. First, the statement as to the level of acceptances was 'not the whole truth'; the figure of 48.9% was only achieved by the 'adding in' decision. Secondly, the claim that all the remaining shares had been sold in the market disguised the fact that a very substantial number of shares remained with CNW and P&D. The justifications offered for the press release were that the statements were literally true, that they legitimately helped to protect the Blue Arrow share price, that Blue Arrow authorised the statement concerning the level of acceptances and that the expression 'sold in the market' simply referred to the mechanics of sale. Rejecting these justifications, the inspectors concluded: 'This public announcement was the inevitable culmination of the decisions made on the evening of 28 September to attempt to save the rights issue. Those involved in making those decisions must have appreciated that the market was going to be misled.' Whilst finding that primary responsibility for the press release lay with CNW, the inspectors added that this did not absolve P&D from responsibility for the misleading information given to the market. Individual executives of CNW and P&D were again criticised.

Following the rights issue and the placing, CNW's financial interest in 13.4% of Blue Arrow's enlarged share capital raised the issue of disclosure under the CA 1985. To avoid disclosure, CNW split the holding into three tranches of less than 5% each. One of 4.99% was left with its Corporate Advisory Department, another of 4.43% was 'acquired' by CNWS and the third tranche of 3.99% was expected to be held by P&D under a profit and loss sharing arrangement.

In regard to the CNWS tranche, this was in three parts: a small position on its trading book, a small 'back book' under the control of the acting head of its UK Market Making Division and a large 'back back book' funded by CNW and for which CNWS would have no responsibility. The CNWS representatives were unhappy about the arrangements, particularly the legality of relying on the 'market maker's exemption' under CA 1985, s 209, in relation to the 'back back book'. Rejecting arguments in support of the legality of this exemption, the inspectors considered that 'the purported use of the market maker's exemption was both unacceptable and inappropriate'.

As to the 3.9% tranche expected to be held by P&D, this tranche was in fact taken by UBS. The UBS president's terms included what he viewed as an attractive rate of interest, the absence of any market risk (ie a risk on the share price) and confirmation that from a legal and regulatory point of view the transaction was in order. On reviewing the arrangement, P&D's solicitors considered the legal point involved: 'is finely balanced and in our view the weight of argument is just, but by no means conclusively, in your favour. We have also commented that, irrespective of a consideration of the legal issues, any publicity given to this arrangement would be adverse to UBS and Phillips & Drew since the arrangement consists of an endeavour to avoid a legal obligation to notify an interest in shares.' CNW's solicitors were of the opinion that the arrangement would not result in UBS having to make disclosure. Endorsing the view of P&D's solicitors, the inspectors considered that the arrangement consisted of an endeavour to avoid a legal obligation to notify an interest in shares. They were of the opinion that 'as the law now stands', the arrangement made succeeded in this but that this was unacceptable, as it was open to abuse, and the Secretary of State should consider amending the CA 1985 to prevent such abuse. The inspectors were also critical of inaccuracies, including the backdating of events, in the letters between CNW and UBS arranging the indemnity.

Another matter investigated by the inspectors was a full-page advertisement by P&D in the Financial Times on 2 October 1987. This claimed P&D 'have successfully placed at a premium the 258 m shares not taken up by existing shareholders'. The inspectors considered the claim to have been 'seriously misleading', given that CNW and P&D had had to retain over 77 m shares. Two P&D executives were criticised.

The problem of disclosure under the CA 1985 re-surfaced in November 1987 when it emerged that Handelsbank held over one million Blue Arrow shares. Aggregation of the Handelsbank and CNW holdings in Blue Arrow (excluding shares transferred to CNWS) resulted in a figure exceeding 5%. In the event, one million Blue Arrow shares were transferred from CNW to CNWS to be added to the holding in the 'back back book'. In its written submission to the inspectors, the NWB Group accepted, without making any admission as to the legal provision, that this transfer was not 'an appropriate use of the market-maker's exemption'. The inspectors add: 'We would go further. The matters . . . amounted to deliberate evasion of obligations of disclosure'. A CNW executive was singled out for criticism.

At the end of November 1987, senior executives of NWB became directly involved in attempts to resolve the disclosure and financial problems arising from CNW's financial interests in Blue Arrow shares. They had concluded that: 'due to the depressed state of the market in general and the [Blue Arrow] share price in particular', its stance in relation to disclosure was 'increasingly inappropriate'. A main NWB board director met two CNW executives and recorded: 'We need to continue our conversation with the Chairman and his Deputies to agree that the UBS holding can be placed, leaving us to consider a declaration of around an 8.5% interest . . . On the other hand, disclosing a 13.5% interest would be untenable regarding their [ie the two CNW executives'] own position and the reputation of the Bank and its Corporate Finance Division. They feel there would be severe repercussions from placees.' The CNW chief executive reported on the position to the NWB Board on 8 December and sought a capital injection of £80 m. In relation to the sequence of events resulting in CNW taking on to their book 9.5% of Blue Arrow shares, the minutes of that meeting recorded that: 'Considerable concern was expressed that this particular transaction should have been undertaken. Although some justification of the original decision was given, it was acknowledged that the sanctioning process had not been sufficiently sound, and this was being remedied.

It was accepted that when the position was announced, it was preferable that the full loss should be disclosed, rather than emerge as a series of unfortunate events'. In regard to the arrangements with UBS and resolving the problems, the NWB chairman later told inspectors that there was very considerable concern about the indemnity: 'Directors . . . found it difficult to understand how one could have a profit and loss sharing arrangement without having an interest in the shares. . . .' He added that the Board 'wanted the thing to be cleared up . . . in one go'. In December a settlement was negotiated whereby CNW was to be released from any liability to UBS under the UBS indemnities on the basis that UBS retained its holding; the settlement involved payment of £30 m to UBS.

Public disclosure was made on 17 December with the issue of two press releases. One announced an injection of £80 m by NWB into CNW. The other announced that: 'County NatWest has notified the Board of Blue Arrow that it has become interested in 9.5% of the issued share capital of Blue Arrow. This interest results from the acquisition today by County NatWest of 32.3 m shares previously held as trading stock by County NatWest Securities. These shares have been added to County NatWest's existing shareholding of 35.3 m Blue Arrow shares.' The inspectors' main comment on this public disclosure was in the following terms: 'We accept that there was no legal obligation to make public disclosure in the announcements either of NWB Group's total interest or of the UBS arrangements. Accordingly, the question whether disclosure of these matters should have been made in the announcements on 17 December 1987 was a matter for the commercial judgment of those concerned. With the benefit of hindsight we believe that it would have been better if reference had been made to both these matters in the announcements.'

In addition, the NWB Group system to enable it to comply with disclosure obligations was, in the inspectors' view, not satisfactory. In particular, they noted that the first time any single individual in NWB knew that NWB had a notifiable interest in 5% or more of Blue Arrow's issued share capital was in November 1987 when a Deputy Chairman of NWB attended an Executive committee meeting of Handelsbank. The inspectors concluded: 'The obligation to disclose can be postponed through inefficiency. We regard this as unacceptable as it is clearly open to abuse. We recommend that the Secretary of State for Trade and Industry should consider whether the Companies Act 1985 ought not to be suitably amended.'

Apart from disclosure of the transactions so far considered, the inspectors investigated other dealings. One set of dealings concerned the purchases by a CNW director and a number of other staff in the Corporate Advisory Division of between 500 and 1,000 shares each in Blue Arrow on 1 October. CNW house rules did not prohibit staff from purchasing shares in client companies provided prior written approval was given by an appropriate CNW director; such approval was given. The authorisation forms were sent to the director responsible for compliance. After raising no initial objection to these purchases, the latter subsequently had second thoughts on appreciating that some of the purchasers were aware of the proposed appointment of a new Blue Arrow chief executive. This had not yet been announced to the market. The Compliance Department then gave instructions to unwind the purchases. The CNW chief executive later told inspectors that in his view individuals in the Corporate Advisory Division should not have dealt in the shares of client companies; the inspectors record their agreement with this view.

In other purchases in early October, CNW raised its hedging cover by purchasing further FT–SE 100 Index put option contracts. At one stage, NWIB was thought to hold between 80% and 90% of all such contracts available in the market. The inspectors questioned the individual who executed the option hedge about the impact of the Blue Arrow share price on the FT–SE 100 Index. The inspectors' concern stemmed from the nondisclosure to the market of CNW's financial interest in Blue Arrow shares. The individual considered that: 'The overhang of a shareholding of that size would have undoubtedly reduced – could have reduced – the value of the Blue Arrow share price. That is, being a component in the FT–SE Index would have actually reduced the FT–SE Index.' In its written submission to the inspectors, the NWB Group is reported as having submitted that there could be no question of insider dealing because the IDA 1985 is inapplicable to an index, rather than to securities of a company. The inspectors record their disagreement on the basis that, with effect from 12 January 1987, s 176 of the FSA 1986 added a new s 13(1A) to the IDA 1985 and that one of the consequences was to bring FT–SE 100 Index put option contracts within the scope of the IDA 1985. The inspectors added that, in their view, it would not be fair to criticise the individual in question for executing and managing the option hedge.

The inspectors also considered the briefing by CNW of both NWB and the Bank of England. On 29 September there were meetings at NWB, involving Deputy Chairmen of NWB, three executive directors of NWB and two CNW executives. The CNW executives gave assurances to the NWB directors as to the legal position of the arrangements and as to Blue Arrow's knowledge of the position; they also indicated that the Bank of England was 'in the picture' (the inspectors note that in fact the Bank was approached the next day). The inspectors considered that due to insufficient experience, the three executive directors of NWB were unable to examine critically what they were being told by the CNW executives; in particular the NWB directors failed to ask about alternative courses of action. The inspectors criticised the conduct of the NWB directors. Subsequently, two of the NWB directors briefed three Deputy Chairmen. Having regard to what the latter were told about the extent to which legal advice had been taken and the assurance that the Bank of England had been informed, the inspectors were of the view that it would not be fair to criticise the three Deputy Chairmen.

At CNW's subsequent briefing of the Bank of England, the Bank's main concern was the extent of CNW's exposure in Blue Arrow. A query about the legality of the position met with the response that CNW had taken 'double', even 'treble', legal advice. The inspectors comment that there was no justification for this statement and that it left the Bank with a 'highly misleading impression'. They conclude: 'In its written submission the NWB Group stated that it accepted full responsibility for the way in which the Blue Arrow trans- action was dealt with and did not seek to share that responsibility in any way with the Bank of England. We agree with this approach. It is understandable that importance was attached to keeping the Bank of England informed. However, the provision of information (even if it had been accurate) would not have legitimised what had been done. Nor could anyone in CNW or the NWB Group have reasonably believed that it would have done.' The inspectors' final conclusion was in the following terms: 'The events referred to in this report give rise to concern. The market was misled. Provisions of the Companies Act 1985 were not complied with. There was no justification for what happened. The relevant law is in an unsatisfactory state . . . We have recommended to the Secretary of State for Trade and Industry that appropriate changes be made.' They also stressed the importance of steps to be taken by the NWB Group.

Publication of the report attracted wide publicity. It has also prompted several resig- nations[3], of which the most prominent have been those of the three NatWest directors criticised in the report and of the NWB Chairman. In addition, criticism has been made of the inspection procedure[4], notably on the ground that individuals criticised do not have a right of appeal.

Although the inspectors did not conclude by recommending the prosecution of parti- cular individuals or institutions, the report is being considered by the Serious Fraud Office. It is also being considered by the Bank of England, the Stock Exchange and the SROs involved[5]. Moreover the possibility of legal action by investors has been raised[6].

A broader issue is the extent to which matters of the kind described in the report occur. An early reaction to this issue in the financial press was: 'County . . . told the inspectors on several points that it was following common practice. In the curious half-world of the corporate deal-maker, it is not easy to be sure about that. In this case, the client, the parent board and even the in-house stockbroker were largely unaware of what was going on. The best defence, certainly, is the publication of cases like this one; no company wants an adviser which will land it in the headlines for the wrong reasons'.[7]

B. CONTINGENCY FEES

Contingency fees were the subject of a Green Paper[8], published by the Government in January 1989. Subsequently, in its White Paper on legal services published in July 1989[9], the Government indicated that the consultation was generally opposed to the introduction of a system of contingency fees which would permit clients to offer their lawyers a percen- tage of any damages if successful and that option had been rejected. However, there was little objection in principle or practice to clients being able to agree with their lawyers con- ditional fees on the speculative basis already permitted in Scotland, or to permitting a specified moderate percentage uplift on the normal bill which parties to such agreements could contract to pay. The Government therefore proposed to implement that proposal.

C. EEC DRAFT INSIDER TRADING DIRECTIVE

Modified proposals are expected to be adopted at the end of 1989[10].

3 *The Financial Times* 26 and 28 July 1989; *The Guardian* 25 and 28 July 1989.
4 *The Financial Times* 27 July 1989.
5 Ibid, 21 July 1989; *The Observer* 30 July 1989.
6 *The Independent* 29 July 1989.
7 *The Financial Times* 21 July 1989.
8 Lord Chancellor's Department, Contingency Fees, Cm 571 (1989).
9 Legal Services: A Framework for the Future, Cm 740 (1989), ch 14.
10 *The Financial Times* 16 June 1989; *The Times* 17 June 1989.

D. THE PANEL ON TAKEOVERS AND MERGERS

In an important development in relation to sanctions, the Panel announced in July 1989[11] that Guinness must make payments to some former Distillers shareholders to remedy certain breaches of the Takeover Code by Guinness during its 1986 bid for Distillers. Guinness has informed the Panel that the remedy is likely to cost it up to £85 m (including interest).

E. DISCLOSURE OF INTERESTS IN A COMPANY'S SHARES

In August 1989 two leading UK securities firms were each fined £10,000 for offences under CA 1985, s 212.[12]

Two High Court decisions have confirmed applications under CA 1985, s 216, for an order that shares be subject to the restriction of Part 15 of that Act.

In *Re Lonrho Plc*[13], Mr Justice Hoffmann held that restrictions on shares are not imposed as a penalty; and the court will not make an ex parte restriction order on the grounds of inaccuracies in shareholders' replies to company requests for particulars of interest if they may be adequately explained on investigation at a full hearing, and if undertakings given by the shareholders are sufficient to protect the company's interests pending that hearing.

In *Re Lonrho Plc*[14], Mr Justice Peter Gibson held that a share restriction order has to be made in full so that all the statutory restrictions are imposed, or not at all; and the court has no power to qualify the order to enable chargees of the shares to enjoy their full rights as secured creditors.

F. SIB PROPOSALS RELATING TO THE CONDUCT OF INVESTMENT BUSINESS

In August 1989 the SIB issued proposals for a new approach to regulating the conduct of investment business[15]. Whilst these would not alter the regulatory framework established by the FSA 1986, the proposals involve a different structure for the rules.

In the proposed three-tier structure, the top tier would consist of ten principles, outlining the basic requirements for investment firms. The next tier would comprise core rules (46 in the SIB draft). SROs could derogate from particular core rules, subject to satisfying the SIB that investors will not suffer. The third tier is of detailed guidance, comprising both legally-enforceable rules and codes of conduct which would not be so enforceable. The latter would be a guide to acceptable practice.

The SIB approach is being assisted by amendments to the FSA 1986 by a Companies Bill due to receive the Royal Assent in autumn 1989. As a result of one proposed amendment, the requirement for SRO rule books to provide an equivalent level of protection to that of SIB would be replaced by a subjective test of whether an SRO rule book is 'adequate'. In addition, investors would lose their right under FSA 1986, s 62 to bring actions for damages as a result of any breach of the rule books. Instead investors would only be able to take legal action for breach of the 'core rules'. However, the codes of conduct could be used as evidence in an action for breach of the 'core rules'. The regulatory agencies themselves could take action for breaches of the ten principles of the codes of conduct.

G. INTERNATIONAL ASPECTS

Proposals marking the first step in the creation of internationally agreed rules for the securities industry are due to be made at the annual conference of the International Organisation of Securities Commissions (IOCSO) in September 1989[16]. Details have not so far been publicly discussed.

The IOSCO is now the leading international body for securities regulators with 50 members, including the SEC and the SIB.

11 The Takeover Panel, Guinness Plc/The Distillers Company Plc, 14 July 1989.
12 *The Financial Times* 18 August 1989.
13 Ibid, 1 February 1989.
14 Ibid, 11 July 1989.
15 Ibid, 9 and 13 August 1989.
16 Ibid, 14 August 1989.

Index